Ford Escort & Mercury Lynx Automotive Repair Manual

by Alan Ahlstrand and John H Haynes
Member of the Guild of Motoring Writers

Models covered:
All Ford Escort and Mercury Lynx models
1981 through 1990
Does not include diesel engine information

(3X6 – 789)

ABCDE

Haynes Publishing Group
Sparkford Nr Yeovil
Somerset BA22 7JJ England

Haynes North America, Inc
861 Lawrence Drive
Newbury Park
California 91320 USA

Acknowledgements

We are grateful to the Ford Motor Company for assistance with technical information, certain illustrations and vehicle photos. The Champion Spark Plug Company supplied the illustrations of various spark plug conditions. Technical writers who contributed to this project include Ed Scott.

A book in the **Haynes Automotive Repair Manual Series**

Printed in the U.S.A.

ISBN 1 56392 004 2

Library of Congress Catalog Card Number 91-75875

Contents

1982 Ford Escort four-door hatchback

1981 Mercury Lynx three-door hatchback

About this manual

Its purpose

The purpose of this manual is to help you get the best value from your vehicle. It can do so in several ways. It can help you decide what work must be done, even if you choose to have it done by a dealer service department or a repair shop; it provides information and procedures for routine maintenance and servicing; and it offers diagnostic and repair procedures to follow when trouble occurs.

We hope you use the manual to tackle the work yourself. For many simpler jobs, doing it yourself may be quicker than arranging an appointment to get the vehicle into a shop and making the trips to leave it and pick it up. More importantly, a lot of money can be saved by avoiding the expense the shop must pass on to you to cover its labor and overhead costs. An added benefit is the sense of satisfaction and accomplishment that you feel after doing the job yourself.

Using the manual

The manual is divided into Chapters. Each Chapter is divided into numbered Sections, which are headed in bold type between horizontal lines. Each Section consists of consecutively numbered paragraphs.

At the beginning of each numbered Section you will be referred to any illustrations which apply to the procedures in that Section. The reference numbers used in illustration captions pinpoint the pertinent Section and the Step within that Section. That is, illustration 3.2 means the illustration refers to Section 3 and Step (or paragraph) 2 within that Section.

Procedures, once described in the text, are not normally repeated. When it's necessary to refer to another Chapter, the reference will be given as Chapter and Section number. Cross references given without use of the word "Chapter" apply to Sections and/or paragraphs in the same Chapter. For example, "see Section 8" means in the same Chapter.

References to the left or right side of the vehicle assume you are sitting in the driver's seat, facing forward.

Even though we have prepared this manual with extreme care, neither the publisher nor the author can accept responsibility for any errors in, or omissions from, the information given.

NOTE

A **Note** provides information necessary to properly complete a procedure or information which will make the procedure easier to understand.

CAUTION

A **Caution** provides a special procedure or special steps which must be taken while completing the procedure where the **Caution** is found. Not heeding a **Caution** can result in damage to the assembly being worked on.

WARNING

A **Warning** provides a special procedure or special steps which must be taken while completing the procedure where the **Warning** is found. Not heeding a **Warning** can result in personal injury.

Introduction to the Ford Escort and Mercury Lynx

These front-wheel drive models feature unitized construction and four-wheel independent suspension. Models are available in two-door, four-door and station wagon body styles.

The transversely mounted four-cylinder engine drives the front wheels through a four-speed or five-speed manual or three-speed automatic transaxle by way of unequal length driveaxles. The rack-and-pinion steering gear is mounted behind the engine and is available with power assist. Brakes are discs at the front and drum-type at the rear with vacuum assist optional.

Vehicle identification numbers

Modifications are a continuing and unpublicized process in vehicle manufacturing. Since spare parts lists and manuals are compiled on a numerical basis, the individual vehicle numbers are necessary to correctly identify the component required.

Vehicle Identification Number (VIN)

This very important identification number is stamped on a plate attached to the dashboard inside the windshield on the driver's side of the vehicle (see illustration). The VIN also appears on the Vehicle Certificate of Title and Registration. It contains information such as where and when the vehicle was manufactured, the model year and the body style.

Vehicle Certification Label

The Vehicle Certification Label is attached to the driver's side door pillar (see illustration). Information on this label includes the name of the manufacturer, the month and year of production, the Gross Vehicle Weight Rating (GVWR), the Gross Axle Weight Rating (GAWR) and the certification statement.

Engine Identification Label

You'll sometimes need to give the number on this label when ordering parts. The label is located on the timing belt cover (see illustration).

1FABP42D9BH100001
VEHICLE IDENTIFICATION NUMBER

The Vehicle Identification Number (VIN) is visible from outside the vehicle through the driver's side of the windshield

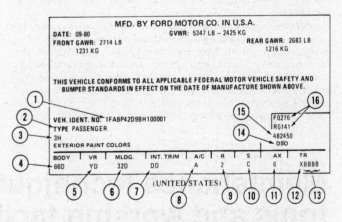

The Vehicle Certification Label is located on the left front door pillar

1	Vehicle identification number	9 Radio
2	Vehicle type	10 Sun/moon roof
3	Paint	11 Axle ratio
4	Body type code	12 Transmission
5	Vinyl roof	13 Springs – front left and right, rear left and right (4 codes)
6	Body side molding	14 District sales office
7	Trim code	15 Order number
8	Air conditioning	16 Accessories

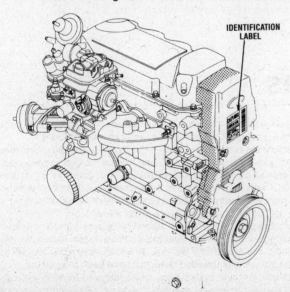

The engine identification label is located on the timing belt cover of the engine

Buying parts

Replacement parts are available from many sources, which generally fall into one of two categories – authorized dealer parts departments and independent retail auto parts stores. Our advice concerning these parts is as follows:

Retail auto parts stores: Good auto parts stores will stock frequently needed components which wear out relatively fast, such as clutch components, exhaust systems, brake parts, tune-up parts, etc. These stores often supply new or reconditioned parts on an exchange basis, which can save a considerable amount of money. Discount auto parts stores are often very good places to buy materials and parts needed for general vehicle maintenance such as oil, grease, filters, spark plugs, belts, touch-up paint, bulbs, etc. They also usually sell tools and general accessories, have con-

venient hours, charge lower prices and can often be found not far from home.

Authorized dealer parts department: This is the best source for parts which are unique to the vehicle and not generally available elsewhere (such as major engine parts, transmission parts, trim pieces, etc.).

Warranty information: If the vehicle is still covered under warranty, be sure that any replacement parts purchased – regardless of the source – do not invalidate the warranty!

To be sure of obtaining the correct parts, have engine and chassis numbers available and, if possible, take the old parts along for positive identification.

Maintenance techniques, tools and working facilities

Maintenance techniques

There are a number of techniques involved in maintenance and repair that will be referred to throughout this manual. Application of these techniques will enable the home mechanic to be more efficient, better organized and capable of performing the various tasks properly, which will ensure that the repair job is thorough and complete.

Fasteners

Fasteners are nuts, bolts, studs and screws used to hold two or more parts together. There are a few things to keep in mind when working with fasteners. Almost all of them use a locking device of some type, either a lockwasher, locknut, locking tab or thread adhesive. All threaded fasteners should be clean and straight, with undamaged threads and undamaged corners on the hex head where the wrench fits. Develop the habit of replacing all damaged nuts and bolts with new ones. Special locknuts

with nylon or fiber inserts can only be used once. If they are removed, they lose their locking ability and must be replaced with new ones.

Rusted nuts and bolts should be treated with a penetrating fluid to ease removal and prevent breakage. Some mechanics use turpentine in a spout-type oil can, which works quite well. After applying the rust penetrant, let it work for a few minutes before trying to loosen the nut or bolt. Badly rusted fasteners may have to be chiseled or sawed off or removed with a special nut breaker, available at tool stores.

If a bolt or stud breaks off in an assembly, it can be drilled and removed with a special tool commonly available for this purpose. Most automotive machine shops can perform this task, as well as other repair procedures, such as the repair of threaded holes that have been stripped out.

Flat washers and lockwashers, when removed from an assembly, should always be replaced exactly as removed. Replace any damaged washers with new ones. Never use a lockwasher on any soft metal surface (such as aluminum), thin sheet metal or plastic.

Fastener sizes

For a number of reasons, automobile manufacturers are making wider and wider use of metric fasteners. Therefore, it is important to be able to tell the difference between standard (sometimes called U.S. or SAE) and metric hardware, since they cannot be interchanged.

All bolts, whether standard or metric, are sized according to diameter, thread pitch and length. For example, a standard 1/2 – 13 x 1 bolt is 1/2 inch in diameter, has 13 threads per inch and is 1 inch long. An M12 – 1.75 x 25 metric bolt is 12 mm in diameter, has a thread pitch of 1.75 mm (the distance between threads) and is 25 mm long. The two bolts are nearly identical, and easily confused, but they are not interchangeable.

In addition to the differences in diameter, thread pitch and length, metric and standard bolts can also be distinguished by examining the bolt heads. To begin with, the distance across the flats on a standard bolt head is measured in inches, while the same dimension on a metric bolt is sized in millimeters (the same is true for nuts). As a result, a standard wrench should not be used on a metric bolt and a metric wrench should not be used on a standard bolt. Also, most standard bolts have slashes radiating out from the center of the head to denote the grade or strength of the bolt, which is an indication of the amount of torque that can be applied to it. The greater the number of slashes, the greater the strength of the bolt. Grades 0 through 5 are commonly used on automobiles. Metric bolts have a property class (grade) number, rather than a slash, molded into their heads to indicate bolt strength. In this case, the higher the number, the stronger the bolt. Property class numbers 8.8, 9.8 and 10.9 are commonly used on automobiles.

Strength markings can also be used to distinguish standard hex nuts from metric hex nuts. Many standard nuts have dots stamped into one side, while metric nuts are marked with a number. The greater the number of dots, or the higher the number, the greater the strength of the nut.

Metric studs are also marked on their ends according to property class (grade). Larger studs are numbered (the same as metric bolts), while smaller studs carry a geometric code to denote grade.

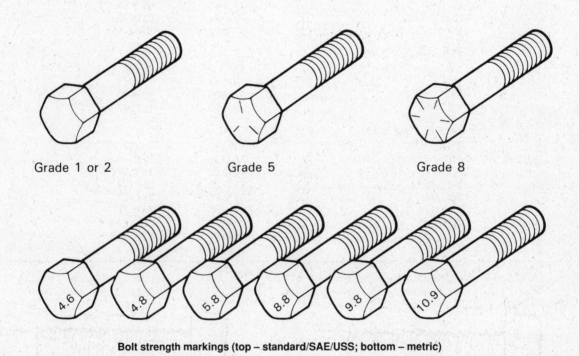

Grade 1 or 2　　　　　Grade 5　　　　　Grade 8

Bolt strength markings (top – standard/SAE/USS; bottom – metric)

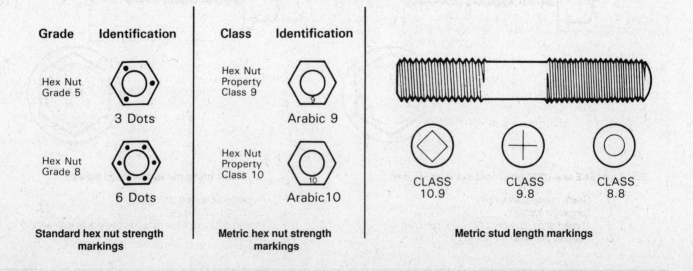

Standard hex nut strength markings

Metric hex nut strength markings

Metric stud length markings

It should be noted that many fasteners, especially Grades 0 through 2, have no distinguishing marks on them. When such is the case, the only way to determine whether it is standard or metric is to measure the thread pitch or compare it to a known fastener of the same size.

Standard fasteners are often referred to as SAE, as opposed to metric. However, it should be noted that SAE technically refers to a non-metric *fine thread* fastener only. Coarse thread non-metric fasteners are referred to as USS sizes.

Since fasteners of the same size (both standard and metric) may have different strength ratings, be sure to reinstall any bolts, studs or nuts removed from your vehicle in their original locations. Also, when replacing a fastener with a new one, make sure that the new one has a strength rating equal to or greater than the original.

Tightening sequences and procedures

Most threaded fasteners should be tightened to a specific torque value (torque is the twisting force applied to a threaded component such as a nut or bolt). Overtightening the fastener can weaken it and cause it to break, while undertightening can cause it to eventually come loose. Bolts, screws and studs, depending on the material they are made of and their thread diameters, have specific torque values, many of which are noted in the Specifications at the beginning of each Chapter. Be sure to follow the torque recommendations closely. For fasteners not assigned a specific torque, a general torque value chart is presented here as a guide. These torque values are for dry (unlubricated) fasteners threaded into steel or cast iron (not aluminum). As was previously mentioned, the size and grade of a fastener determine the amount of torque that can safely be

Metric thread sizes	Ft-lbs	Nm
M-6	6 to 9	9 to 12
M-8	14 to 21	19 to 28
M-10	28 to 40	38 to 54
M-12	50 to 71	68 to 96
M-14	80 to 140	109 to 154

Pipe thread sizes		
1/8	5 to 8	7 to 10
1/4	12 to 18	17 to 24
3/8	22 to 33	30 to 44
1/2	25 to 35	34 to 47

U.S. thread sizes		
1/4 – 20	6 to 9	9 to 12
5/16 – 18	12 to 18	17 to 24
5/16 – 24	14 to 20	19 to 27
3/8 – 16	22 to 32	30 to 43
3/8 – 24	27 to 38	37 to 51
7/16 – 14	40 to 55	55 to 74
7/16 – 20	40 to 60	55 to 81
1/2 – 13	55 to 80	75 to 108

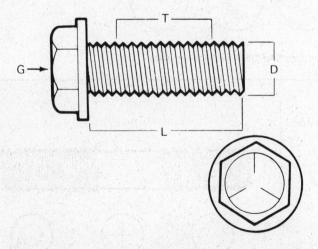

Standard (SAE and USS) bolt dimensions/grade marks

- G Grade marks (bolt length)
- L Length (in inches)
- T Thread pitch (number of threads per inch)
- D Nominal diameter (in inches)

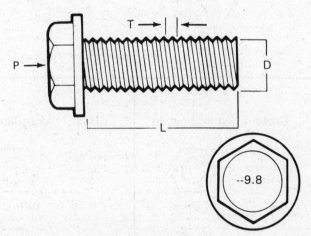

Metric bolt dimensions/grade marks

- P Property class (bolt strength)
- L Length (in millimeters)
- T Thread pitch (distance between threads in millimeters)
- D Diameter

applied to it. The figures listed here are approximate for Grade 2 and Grade 3 fasteners. Higher grades can tolerate higher torque values.

Fasteners laid out in a pattern, such as cylinder head bolts, oil pan bolts, differential cover bolts, etc., must be loosened or tightened in sequence to avoid warping the component. This sequence will normally be shown in the appropriate Chapter. If a specific pattern is not given, the following procedures can be used to prevent warping.

Initially, the bolts or nuts should be assembled finger-tight only. Next, they should be tightened one full turn each, in a criss-cross or diagonal pattern. After each one has been tightened one full turn, return to the first one and tighten them all one-half turn, following the same pattern. Finally, tighten each of them one-quarter turn at a time until each fastener has been tightened to the proper torque. To loosen and remove the fasteners, the procedure would be reversed.

Component disassembly

Component disassembly should be done with care and purpose to help ensure that the parts go back together properly. Always keep track of the sequence in which parts are removed. Make note of special characteristics or marks on parts that can be installed more than one way, such as a grooved thrust washer on a shaft. It is a good idea to lay the disassembled parts out on a clean surface in the order that they were removed. It may also be helpful to make sketches or take instant photos of components before removal.

When removing fasteners from a component, keep track of their locations. Sometimes threading a bolt back in a part, or putting the washers and nut back on a stud, can prevent mix-ups later. If nuts and bolts cannot be returned to their original locations, they should be kept in a compartmented box or a series of small boxes. A cupcake or muffin tin is ideal for this purpose, since each cavity can hold the bolts and nuts from a particular area (i.e. oil pan bolts, valve cover bolts, engine mount bolts, etc.). A pan of this type is especially helpful when working on assemblies with very small parts, such as the carburetor, alternator, valve train or interior dash and trim pieces. The cavities can be marked with paint or tape to identify the contents.

Whenever wiring looms, harnesses or connectors are separated, it is a good idea to identify the two halves with numbered pieces of masking tape so they can be easily reconnected.

Gasket sealing surfaces

Throughout any vehicle, gaskets are used to seal the mating surfaces between two parts and keep lubricants, fluids, vacuum or pressure contained in an assembly.

Many times these gaskets are coated with a liquid or paste-type gasket sealing compound before assembly. Age, heat and pressure can sometimes cause the two parts to stick together so tightly that they are very difficult to separate. Often, the assembly can be loosened by striking it with a soft-face hammer near the mating surfaces. A regular hammer can be used if a block of wood is placed between the hammer and the part. Do not hammer on cast parts or parts that could be easily damaged. With any particularly stubborn part, always recheck to make sure that every fastener has been removed.

Avoid using a screwdriver or bar to pry apart an assembly, as they can easily mar the gasket sealing surfaces of the parts, which must remain smooth. If prying is absolutely necessary, use an old broom handle, but keep in mind that extra clean up will be necessary if the wood splinters.

After the parts are separated, the old gasket must be carefully scraped off and the gasket surfaces cleaned. Stubborn gasket material can be soaked with rust penetrant or treated with a special chemical to soften it so it can be easily scraped off. A scraper can be fashioned from a piece of copper tubing by flattening and sharpening one end. Copper is recommended because it is usually softer than the surfaces to be scraped, which reduces the chance of gouging the part. Some gaskets can be removed with a wire brush, but regardless of the method used, the mating surfaces must be left clean and smooth. If for some reason the gasket surface is gouged, then a gasket sealer thick enough to fill scratches will have to be used during reassembly of the components. For most applications, a nondrying (or semi-drying) gasket sealer should be used.

Hose removal tips

Warning: *If the vehicle is equipped with air conditioning, do not disconnect any of the A/C hoses without first having the system depressurized by a dealer service department or a service station.*

Hose removal precautions closely parallel gasket removal precautions. Avoid scratching or gouging the surface that the hose mates against or the connection may leak. This is especially true for radiator hoses. Because of various chemical reactions, the rubber in hoses can bond itself to the metal spigot that the hose fits over. To remove a hose, first loosen the hose clamps that secure it to the spigot. Then, with slip-joint pliers, grab the hose at the clamp and rotate it around the spigot. Work it back and forth until it is completely free, then pull it off. Silicone or other lubricants will ease removal if they can be applied between the hose and the outside of the spigot. Apply the same lubricant to the inside of the hose and the outside of the spigot to simplify installation.

As a last resort (and if the hose is to be replaced with a new one anyway), the rubber can be slit with a knife and the hose peeled from the spigot. If this must be done, be careful that the metal connection is not damaged.

If a hose clamp is broken or damaged, do not reuse it. Wire-type clamps usually weaken with age, so it is a good idea to replace them with screw-type clamps whenever a hose is removed.

Tools

A selection of good tools is a basic requirement for anyone who plans to maintain and repair his or her own vehicle. For the owner who has few tools, the initial investment might seem high, but when compared to the spiraling costs of professional auto maintenance and repair, it is a wise one.

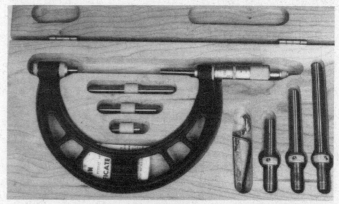

Micrometer set

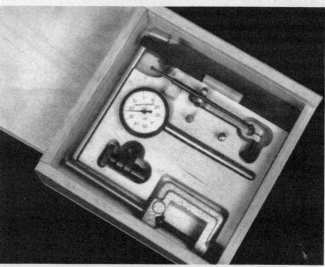

Dial indicator set

Dial Caliper

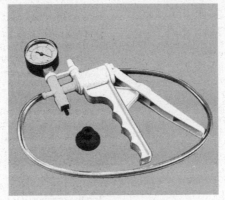

Hand-operated vacuum pump

Timing light

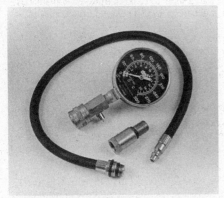

Compression gauge with spark plug hole adapter

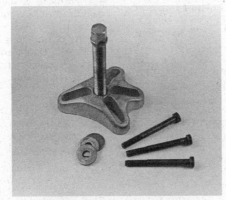

Damper/steering wheel puller

General purpose puller

Hydraulic lifter removal tool

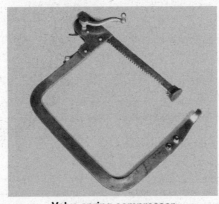

Valve spring compressor

Valve spring compressor

Ridge reamer

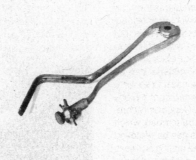

Piston ring groove cleaning tool

Ring removal/installation tool

Ring compressor

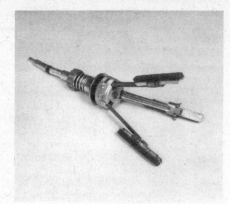

Cylinder hone

Brake hold-down tool

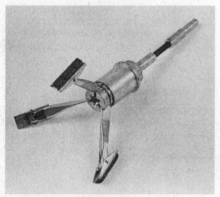

Brake cylinder hone

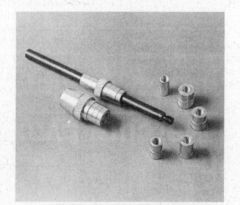

Clutch plate alignment tool

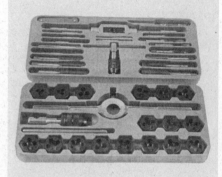

Tap and die set

To help the owner decide which tools are needed to perform the tasks detailed in this manual, the following tool lists are offered: *Maintenance and minor repair, Repair/overhaul* and *Special*.

The newcomer to practical mechanics should start off with the maintenance and minor repair tool kit, which is adequate for the simpler jobs performed on a vehicle. Then, as confidence and experience grow, the owner can tackle more difficult tasks, buying additional tools as they are needed. Eventually the basic kit will be expanded into the repair and overhaul tool set. Over a period of time, the experienced do-it-yourselfer will assemble a tool set complete enough for most repair and overhaul procedures and will add tools from the special category when it is felt that the expense is justified by the frequency of use.

Maintenance and minor repair tool kit

The tools in this list should be considered the minimum required for performance of routine maintenance, servicing and minor repair work. We recommend the purchase of combination wrenches (box-end and open-end combined in one wrench). While more expensive than open end wrenches, they offer the advantages of both types of wrench.

Combination wrench set (1/4-inch to 1 inch or 6 mm to 19 mm)
Adjustable wrench, 8 inch
Spark plug wrench with rubber insert
Spark plug gap adjusting tool
Feeler gauge set
Brake bleeder wrench
Standard screwdriver (5/16-inch x 6 inch)
Phillips screwdriver (No. 2 x 6 inch)
Combination pliers – 6 inch
Hacksaw and assortment of blades
Tire pressure gauge
Grease gun
Oil can
Fine emery cloth
Wire brush

Battery post and cable cleaning tool
Oil filter wrench
Funnel (medium size)
Safety goggles
Jackstands(2)
Drain pan

Note: *If basic tune-ups are going to be part of routine maintenance, it will be necessary to purchase a good quality stroboscopic timing light and combination tachometer/dwell meter. Although they are included in the list of special tools, it is mentioned here because they are absolutely necessary for tuning most vehicles properly.*

Repair and overhaul tool set

These tools are essential for anyone who plans to perform major repairs and are in addition to those in the maintenance and minor repair tool kit. Included is a comprehensive set of sockets which, though expensive, are invaluable because of their versatility, especially when various extensions and drives are available. We recommend the 1/2-inch drive over the 3/8-inch drive. Although the larger drive is bulky and more expensive, it has the capacity of accepting a very wide range of large sockets. Ideally, however, the mechanic should have a 3/8-inch drive set and a 1/2-inch drive set.

Socket set(s)
Reversible ratchet
Extension – 10 inch
Universal joint
Torque wrench (same size drive as sockets)
Ball peen hammer – 8 ounce
Soft-face hammer (plastic/rubber)
Standard screwdriver (1/4-inch x 6 inch)
Standard screwdriver (stubby – 5/16-inch)
Phillips screwdriver (No. 3 x 8 inch)
Phillips screwdriver (stubby – No. 2)

Pliers – vise grip
Pliers – lineman's
Pliers – needle nose
Pliers – snap-ring (internal and external)
Cold chisel – 1/2-inch
Scribe
Scraper (made from flattened copper tubing)
Centerpunch
Pin punches (1/16, 1/8, 3/16-inch)
Steel rule/straightedge – 12 inch
Allen wrench set (1/8 to 3/8-inch or 4 mm to 10 mm)
A selection of files
Wire brush (large)
Jackstands (second set)
Jack (scissor or hydraulic type)

Note: *Another tool which is often useful is an electric drill with a chuck capacity of 3/8-inch and a set of good quality drill bits.*

Special tools

The tools in this list include those which are not used regularly, are expensive to buy, or which need to be used in accordance with their manufacturer's instructions. Unless these tools will be used frequently, it is not very economical to purchase many of them. A consideration would be to split the cost and use between yourself and a friend or friends. In addition, most of these tools can be obtained from a tool rental shop on a temporary basis.

This list primarily contains only those tools and instruments widely available to the public, and not those special tools produced by the vehicle manufacturer for distribution to dealer service departments. Occasionally, references to the manufacturer's special tools are included in the text of this manual. Generally, an alternative method of doing the job without the special tool is offered. However, sometimes there is no alternative to their use. Where this is the case, and the tool cannot be purchased or borrowed, the work should be turned over to the dealer service department or an automotive repair shop.

Valve spring compressor
Piston ring groove cleaning tool
Piston ring compressor
Piston ring installation tool
Cylinder compression gauge
Cylinder ridge reamer
Cylinder surfacing hone
Cylinder bore gauge
Micrometers and/or dial calipers
Hydraulic lifter removal tool
Balljoint separator
Universal-type puller
Impact screwdriver
Dial indicator set
Stroboscopic timing light (inductive pick-up)
Hand operated vacuum/pressure pump
Tachometer/dwell meter
Universal electrical multimeter
Cable hoist
Brake spring removal and installation tools
Floor jack

Buying tools

For the do-it-yourselfer who is just starting to get involved in vehicle maintenance and repair, there are a number of options available when purchasing tools. If maintenance and minor repair is the extent of the work to be done, the purchase of individual tools is satisfactory. If, on the other hand, extensive work is planned, it would be a good idea to purchase a modest tool set from one of the large retail chain stores. A set can usually be bought at a substantial savings over the individual tool prices, and they often come with a tool box. As additional tools are needed, add–on sets, individual tools and a larger tool box can be purchased to expand the tool selection. Building a tool set gradually allows the cost of the tools to be spread over a longer period of time and gives the mechanic the freedom to choose only those tools that will actually be used.

Tool stores will often be the only source of some of the special tools that are needed, but regardless of where tools are bought, try to avoid cheap ones, especially when buying screwdrivers and sockets, because they won't last very long. The expense involved in replacing cheap tools will eventually be greater than the initial cost of quality tools.

Care and maintenance of tools

Good tools are expensive, so it makes sense to treat them with respect. Keep them clean and in usable condition and store them properly when not in use. Always wipe off any dirt, grease or metal chips before putting them away. Never leave tools lying around in the work area. Upon completion of a job, always check closely under the hood for tools that may have been left there so they won't get lost during a test drive.

Some tools, such as screwdrivers, pliers, wrenches and sockets, can be hung on a panel mounted on the garage or workshop wall, while others should be kept in a tool box or tray. Measuring instruments, gauges, meters, etc. must be carefully stored where they cannot be damaged by weather or impact from other tools.

When tools are used with care and stored properly, they will last a very long time. Even with the best of care, though, tools will wear out if used frequently. When a tool is damaged or worn out, replace it. Subsequent jobs will be safer and more enjoyable if you do.

Working facilities

Not to be overlooked when discussing tools is the workshop. If anything more than routine maintenance is to be carried out, some sort of suitable work area is essential.

It is understood, and appreciated, that many home mechanics do not have a good workshop or garage available, and end up removing an engine or doing major repairs outside. It is recommended, however, that the overhaul or repair be completed under the cover of a roof.

A clean, flat workbench or table of comfortable working height is an absolute necessity. The workbench should be equipped with a vise that has a jaw opening of at least four inches.

As mentioned previously, some clean, dry storage space is also required for tools, as well as the lubricants, fluids, cleaning solvents, etc. which soon become necessary.

Sometimes waste oil and fluids, drained from the engine or cooling system during normal maintenance or repairs, present a disposal problem. To avoid pouring them on the ground or into a sewage system, pour the used fluids into large containers, seal them with caps and take them to an authorized disposal site or recycling center. Plastic jugs, such as old antifreeze containers, are ideal for this purpose.

Always keep a supply of old newspapers and clean rags available. Old towels are excellent for mopping up spills. Many mechanics use rolls of paper towels for most work because they are readily available and disposable. To help keep the area under the vehicle clean, a large cardboard box can be cut open and flattened to protect the garage or shop floor.

Whenever working over a painted surface, such as when leaning over a fender to service something under the hood, always cover it with an old blanket or bedspread to protect the finish. Vinyl covered pads, made especially for this purpose, are available at auto parts stores.

Booster battery (jump) starting

Observe these precautions when using a booster battery to start a vehicle:

a) Before connecting the booster battery, make sure the ignition switch is in the Off position.

b) Turn off the lights, heater and other electrical loads.

c) Your eyes should be shielded. Safety goggles are a good idea.

d) Make sure the booster battery is the same voltage as the dead one in the vehicle.

e) The two vehicles MUST NOT TOUCH each other!

f) Make sure the transmission is in Neutral (manual) or Park (automatic).

g) If the booster battery is not a maintenance-free type, remove the vent caps and lay a cloth over the vent holes.

Connect the red jumper cable to the positive (+) terminals of each battery.

Connect one end of the black jumper cable to the negative (−) terminal of the booster battery. The other end of this cable should be connected to a good ground on the vehicle to be started, such as a bolt or bracket on the engine block **(see illustration)**. Make sure the cable will not come into contact with the fan, drivebelts or other moving parts of the engine.

Start the engine using the booster battery, then, with the engine running at idle speed, disconnect the jumper cables in the reverse order of connection.

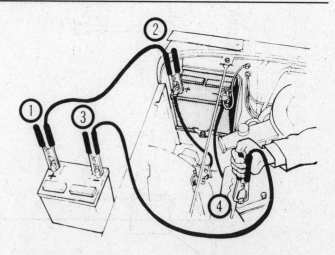

Make the booster battery cable connections in the numerical order shown (note that the negative cable of the booster battery is NOT attached to the negative terminal of the dead battery)

Jacking and towing

Jacking

The jack supplied with the vehicle should be used only for raising the vehicle when changing a tire or placing jackstands under the frame. **Warning:** *Never work under the vehicle or start the engine when this jack is being used as the only means of support.*

The vehicle should be on level ground with the wheels blocked and the transaxle in Park (automatic) or Neutral (manual). If a tire is being changed, loosen the lug nuts one-half turn and leave them in place until the wheel is raised off the ground. If the vehicle is equipped with plastic lug nut caps, they must first be removed by hand or pried off with the tapered end of the lug nut wrench. Make sure no one is in the vehicle as it's being raised off the ground.

Place the jack under the side of the vehicle and adjust the jack height until it fits into the notch in the vertical rocker panel flange nearest the wheel to be changed **(see illustration)**. If you're using a floorjack, use the frame lifting point nearest the wheel to be changed **(see illustration)**. Operate the jack with a slow, smooth motion until the wheel is raised off the ground. Remove the lug nuts, pull off the wheel, install the spare and thread the lug nuts back on with the bevelled sides facing in. Tighten them snugly, but wait until the vehicle is lowered to tighten them completely.

Lower the vehicle, remove the jack and tighten the lug nuts (if loosened or removed) in a criss-cross pattern. If possible, tighten them with a torque wrench (see Chapter 1 for the torque figures). If you don't have access to a torque wrench, have the nuts checked by a service station or repair shop as soon as possible. Retighten the lug nuts after 500 miles.

If the vehicle is equipped with a temporary spare tire, remember that it is intended only for temporary use until the regular tire can be repaired. Do not exceed the maximum speed that the tire is rated for.

Towing

The vehicle should be towed with the front (drive) wheels off the ground if possible. If the vehicle must be towed with the front wheels on the ground, observe the following conditions:

a) Clamp the steering wheel in the straight-ahead position with a towing clamp designed for the purpose. Do not use the vehicle's steering lock; the ignition key must be in the unlocked position.

b) If the vehicle has an automatic transaxle, do not tow faster than 35 mph or farther than 50 miles, or the transaxle may be damaged.

c) The transaxle and differential must be in working condition.

It any of the conditions can't be met, the vehicle must be towed with the front wheels on a dolly.

Equipment specifically designed for towing should be used. It should be attached to the main structural members of the vehicle, not the bumpers or brackets. Do not use J-hooks at either end of the car. They will damage steering and suspension components.

While towing, don't exceed 50 mph (35 mph on rough roads).

Safety is a major consideration while towing and all applicable state and local laws must be obeyed. A safety chain system must be used at all times. Remember that power steering and power brakes will not work with the engine off.

USE APPROPRIATE NOTCH
(FRONT OR REAR)

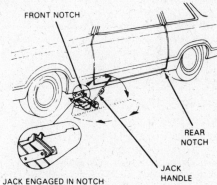

Chassis jacking points

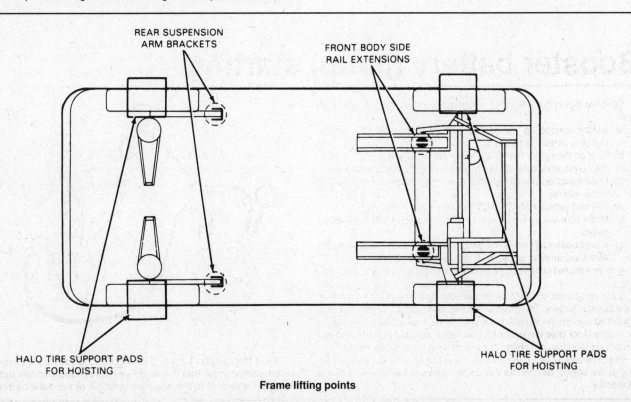

Frame lifting points

Automotive chemicals and lubricants

A number of automotive chemicals and lubricants are available for use during vehicle maintenance and repair. They include a wide variety of products ranging from cleaning solvents and degreasers to lubricants and protective sprays for rubber, plastic and vinyl.

Cleaners

Carburetor cleaner and choke cleaner is a strong solvent for gum, varnish and carbon. Most carburetor cleaners leave a dry-type lubricant film which will not harden or gum up. Because of this film it is not recommended for use on electrical components.

Brake system cleaner is used to remove grease and brake fluid from the brake system, where clean surfaces are absolutely necessary. It leaves no residue and often eliminates brake squeal caused by contaminants.

Electrical cleaner removes oxidation, corrosion and carbon deposits from electrical contacts, restoring full current flow. It can also be used to clean spark plugs, carburetor jets, voltage regulators and other parts where an oil-free surface is desired.

Demoisturants remove water and moisture from electrical components such as alternators, voltage regulators, electrical connectors and fuse blocks. They are non-conductive, non-corrosive and non-flammable.

Degreasers are heavy-duty solvents used to remove grease from the outside of the engine and from chassis components. They can be sprayed or brushed on and, depending on the type, are rinsed off either with water or solvent.

Lubricants

Motor oil is the lubricant formulated for use in engines. It normally contains a wide variety of additives to prevent corrosion and reduce foaming and wear. Motor oil comes in various weights (viscosity ratings) from 5 to 80. The recommended weight of the oil depends on the season, temperature and the demands on the engine. Light oil is used in cold climates and under light load conditions. Heavy oil is used in hot climates and where high loads are encountered. Multi-viscosity oils are designed to have characteristics of both light and heavy oils and are available in a number of weights from 5W-20 to 20W-50.

Gear oil is designed to be used in differentials, manual transmissions and other areas where high-temperature lubrication is required.

Chassis and wheel bearing grease is a heavy grease used where increased loads and friction are encountered, such as for wheel bearings, balljoints, tie-rod ends and universal joints.

High-temperature wheel bearing grease is designed to withstand the extreme temperatures encountered by wheel bearings in disc brake equipped vehicles. It usually contains molybdenum disulfide (moly), which is a dry-type lubricant.

White grease is a heavy grease for metal-to-metal applications where water is a problem. White grease stays soft under both low and high temperatures (usually from −100 to +190-degrees F), and will not wash off or dilute in the presence of water.

Assembly lube is a special extreme pressure lubricant, usually containing moly, used to lubricate high-load parts (such as main and rod bearings and cam lobes) for initial start-up of a new engine. The assembly lube lubricates the parts without being squeezed out or washed away until the engine oiling system begins to function.

Silicone lubricants are used to protect rubber, plastic, vinyl and nylon parts.

Graphite lubricants are used where oils cannot be used due to contamination problems, such as in locks. The dry graphite will lubricate metal parts while remaining uncontaminated by dirt, water, oil or acids. It is electrically conductive and will not foul electrical contacts in locks such as the ignition switch.

Moly penetrants loosen and lubricate frozen, rusted and corroded fasteners and prevent future rusting or freezing.

Heat-sink grease is a special electrically non-conductive grease that is used for mounting electronic ignition modules where it is essential that heat is transferred away from the module.

Sealants

RTV sealant is one of the most widely used gasket compounds. Made from silicone, RTV is air curing, it seals, bonds, waterproofs, fills surface irregularities, remains flexible, doesn't shrink, is relatively easy to remove, and is used as a supplementary sealer with almost all low and medium temperature gaskets.

Anaerobic sealant is much like RTV in that it can be used either to seal gaskets or to form gaskets by itself. It remains flexible, is solvent resistant and fills surface imperfections. The difference between an anaerobic sealant and an RTV-type sealant is in the curing. RTV cures when exposed to air, while an anaerobic sealant cures only in the absence of air. This means that an anaerobic sealant cures only after the assembly of parts, sealing them together.

Thread and pipe sealant is used for sealing hydraulic and pneumatic fittings and vacuum lines. It is usually made from a Teflon compound, and comes in a spray, a paint-on liquid and as a wrap-around tape.

Chemicals

Anti-seize compound prevents seizing, galling, cold welding, rust and corrosion in fasteners. High-temperature anti-seize, usually made with copper and graphite lubricants, is used for exhaust system and exhaust manifold bolts.

Anaerobic locking compounds are used to keep fasteners from vibrating or working loose and cure only after installation, in the absence of air. Medium strength locking compound is used for small nuts, bolts and screws that may be removed later. High-strength locking compound is for large nuts, bolts and studs which aren't removed on a regular basis.

Oil additives range from viscosity index improvers to chemical treatments that claim to reduce internal engine friction. It should be noted that most oil manufacturers caution against using additives with their oils.

Gas additives perform several functions, depending on their chemical makeup. They usually contain solvents that help dissolve gum and varnish that build up on carburetor, fuel injection and intake parts. They also serve to break down carbon deposits that form on the inside surfaces of the combustion chambers. Some additives contain upper cylinder lubricants for valves and piston rings, and others contain chemicals to remove condensation from the gas tank.

Miscellaneous

Brake fluid is specially formulated hydraulic fluid that can withstand the heat and pressure encountered in brake systems. Care must be taken so this fluid does not come in contact with painted surfaces or plastics. An opened container should always be resealed to prevent contamination by water or dirt.

Weatherstrip adhesive is used to bond weatherstripping around doors, windows and trunk lids. It is sometimes used to attach trim pieces.

Undercoating is a petroleum-based, tar-like substance that is designed to protect metal surfaces on the underside of the vehicle from corrosion. It also acts as a sound-deadening agent by insulating the bottom of the vehicle.

Waxes and polishes are used to help protect painted and plated surfaces from the weather. Different types of paint may require the use of different types of wax and polish. Some polishes utilize a chemical or abrasive cleaner to help remove the top layer of oxidized (dull) paint on older vehicles. In recent years many non-wax polishes that contain a wide variety of chemicals such as polymers and silicones have been introduced. These non-wax polishes are usually easier to apply and last longer than conventional waxes and polishes.

Safety first!

Regardless of how enthusiastic you may be about getting on with the job at hand, take the time to ensure that your safety is not jeopardized. A moment's lack of attention can result in an accident, as can failure to observe certain simple safety precautions. The possibility of an accident will always exist, and the following points should not be considered a comprehensive list of all dangers. Rather, they are intended to make you aware of the risks and to encourage a safety conscious approach to all work you carry out on your vehicle.

Essential DOs and DON'Ts

DON'T rely on a jack when working under the vehicle. Always use approved jackstands to support the weight of the vehicle and place them under the recommended lift or support points.

DON'T attempt to loosen extremely tight fasteners (i.e. wheel lug nuts) while the vehicle is on a jack – it may fall.

DON'T start the engine without first making sure that the transmission is in Neutral (or Park where applicable) and the parking brake is set.

DON'T remove the radiator cap from a hot cooling system – let it cool or cover it with a cloth and release the pressure gradually.

DON'T attempt to drain the engine oil until you are sure it has cooled to the point that it will not burn you.

DON'T touch any part of the engine or exhaust system until it has cooled sufficiently to avoid burns.

DON'T siphon toxic liquids such as gasoline, antifreeze and brake fluid by mouth, or allow them to remain on your skin.

DON'T inhale brake lining dust – it is potentially hazardous (see *Asbestos* below)

DON'T allow spilled oil or grease to remain on the floor – wipe it up before someone slips on it.

DON'T use loose fitting wrenches or other tools which may slip and cause injury.

DON'T push on wrenches when loosening or tightening nuts or bolts. Always try to pull the wrench toward you. If the situation calls for pushing the wrench away, push with an open hand to avoid scraped knuckles if the wrench should slip.

DON'T attempt to lift a heavy component alone – get someone to help you.

DON'T rush or take unsafe shortcuts to finish a job.

DON'T allow children or animals in or around the vehicle while you are working on it.

DO wear eye protection when using power tools such as a drill, sander, bench grinder, etc. and when working under a vehicle.

DO keep loose clothing and long hair well out of the way of moving parts.

DO make sure that any hoist used has a safe working load rating adequate for the job.

DO get someone to check on you periodically when working alone on a vehicle.

DO carry out work in a logical sequence and make sure that everything is correctly assembled and tightened.

DO keep chemicals and fluids tightly capped and out of the reach of children and pets.

DO remember that your vehicle's safety affects that of yourself and others. If in doubt on any point, get professional advice.

Asbestos

Certain friction, insulating, sealing, and other products – such as brake linings, brake bands, clutch linings, torque converters, gaskets, etc. – contain asbestos. *Extreme care must be taken to avoid inhalation of dust from such products, since it is hazardous to health*. If in doubt, assume that they *do* contain asbestos.

Fire

Remember at all times that gasoline is highly flammable. Never smoke or have any kind of open flame around when working on a vehicle. But the risk does not end there. A spark caused by an electrical short circuit, by two metal surfaces contacting each other, or even by static electricity built up in your body under certain conditions, can ignite gasoline vapors, which in a confined space are highly explosive. Do not, under any circumstances, use gasoline for cleaning parts. Use an approved safety solvent.

Always disconnect the battery ground (–) cable *at the battery* before working on any part of the fuel system or electrical system. Never risk spilling fuel on a hot engine or exhaust component.

It is strongly recommended that a fire extinguisher suitable for use on fuel and electrical fires be kept handy in the garage or workshop at all times. Never try to extinguish a fuel or electrical fire with water.

Fumes

Certain fumes are highly toxic and can quickly cause unconsciousness and even death if inhaled to any extent. Gasoline vapor falls into this category, as do the vapors from some cleaning solvents. Any draining or pouring of such volatile fluids should be done in a well ventilated area.

When using cleaning fluids and solvents, read the instructions on the container carefully. Never use materials from unmarked containers.

Never run the engine in an enclosed space, such as a garage. Exhaust fumes contain carbon monoxide, which is extremely poisonous. If you need to run the engine, always do so in the open air, or at least have the rear of the vehicle outside the work area.

If you are fortunate enough to have the use of an inspection pit, never drain or pour gasoline and never run the engine while the vehicle is over the pit. The fumes, being heavier than air, will concentrate in the pit with possibly lethal results.

The battery

Never create a spark or allow a bare light bulb near a battery. They normally give off a certain amount of hydrogen gas, which is highly explosive.

Always disconnect the battery ground (–) cable *at the battery* before working on the fuel or electrical systems.

If possible, loosen the filler caps or cover when charging the battery from an external source (this does not apply to sealed or maintenance-free batteries). Do not charge at an excessive rate or the battery may burst.

Take care when adding water to a non maintenance-free battery and when carrying a battery. The electrolyte, even when diluted, is very corrosive and should not be allowed to contact clothing or skin.

Always wear eye protection when cleaning the battery to prevent the caustic deposits from entering your eyes.

Household current

When using an electric power tool, inspection light, etc., which operates on household current, always make sure that the tool is correctly connected to its plug and that, where necessary, it is properly grounded. Do not use such items in damp conditions and, again, do not create a spark or apply excessive heat in the vicinity of fuel or fuel vapor.

Secondary ignition system voltage

A severe electric shock can result from touching certain parts of the ignition system (such as the spark plug wires) when the engine is running or being cranked, particularly if components are damp or the insulation is defective. In the case of an electronic ignition system, the secondary system voltage is much higher and could prove fatal.

Conversion factors

Length (distance)
Inches (in)	X	25.4	= Millimetres (mm)	X	0.0394	= Inches (in)
Feet (ft)	X	0.305	= Metres (m)	X	3.281	= Feet (ft)
Miles	X	1.609	= Kilometres (km)	X	0.621	= Miles

Volume (capacity)
Cubic inches (cu in; in³)	X	16.387	= Cubic centimetres (cc; cm³)	X	0.061	= Cubic inches (cu in; in³)
Imperial pints (Imp pt)	X	0.568	= Litres (l)	X	1.76	= Imperial pints (Imp pt)
Imperial quarts (Imp qt)	X	1.137	= Litres (l)	X	0.88	= Imperial quarts (Imp qt)
Imperial quarts (Imp qt)	X	1.201	= US quarts (US qt)	X	0.833	= Imperial quarts (Imp qt)
US quarts (US qt)	X	0.946	= Litres (l)	X	1.057	= US quarts (US qt)
Imperial gallons (Imp gal)	X	4.546	= Litres (l)	X	0.22	= Imperial gallons (Imp gal)
Imperial gallons (Imp gal)	X	1.201	= US gallons (US gal)	X	0.833	= Imperial gallons (Imp gal)
US gallons (US gal)	X	3.785	= Litres (l)	X	0.264	= US gallons (US gal)

Mass (weight)
Ounces (oz)	X	28.35	= Grams (g)	X	0.035	= Ounces (oz)
Pounds (lb)	X	0.454	= Kilograms (kg)	X	2.205	= Pounds (lb)

Force
Ounces-force (ozf; oz)	X	0.278	= Newtons (N)	X	3.6	= Ounces-force (ozf; oz)
Pounds-force (lbf; lb)	X	4.448	= Newtons (N)	X	0.225	= Pounds-force (lbf; lb)
Newtons (N)	X	0.1	= Kilograms-force (kgf; kg)	X	9.81	= Newtons (N)

Pressure
Pounds-force per square inch (psi; lbf/in²; lb/in²)	X	0.070	= Kilograms-force per square centimetre (kgf/cm²; kg/cm²)	X	14.223	= Pounds-force per square inch (psi; lbf/in²; lb/in²)
Pounds-force per square inch (psi; lbf/in²; lb/in²)	X	0.068	= Atmospheres (atm)	X	14.696	= Pounds-force per square inch (psi; lbf/in²; lb/in²)
Pounds-force per square inch (psi; lbf/in²; lb/in²)	X	0.069	= Bars	X	14.5	= Pounds-force per square inch (psi; lbf/in²; lb/in²)
Pounds-force per square inch (psi; lbf/in²; lb/in²)	X	6.895	= Kilopascals (kPa)	X	0.145	= Pounds-force per square inch (psi; lbf/in²; lb/in²)
Kilopascals (kPa)	X	0.01	= Kilograms-force per square centimetre (kgf/cm²; kg/cm²)	X	98.1	= Kilopascals (kPa)

Torque (moment of force)
Pounds-force inches (lbf in; lb in)	X	1.152	= Kilograms-force centimetre (kgf cm; kg cm)	X	0.868	= Pounds-force inches (lbf in; lb in)
Pounds-force inches (lbf in; lb in)	X	0.113	= Newton metres (Nm)	X	8.85	= Pounds-force inches (lbf in; lb in)
Pounds-force inches (lbf in; lb in)	X	0.083	= Pounds-force feet (lbf ft; lb ft)	X	12	= Pounds-force inches (lbf in; lb in)
Pounds-force feet (lbf ft; lb ft)	X	0.138	= Kilograms-force metres (kgf m; kg m)	X	7.233	= Pounds-force feet (lbf ft; lb ft)
Pounds-force feet (lbf ft; lb ft)	X	1.356	= Newton metres (Nm)	X	0.738	= Pounds-force feet (lbf ft; lb ft)
Newton metres (Nm)	X	0.102	= Kilograms-force metres (kgf m; kg m)	X	9.804	= Newton metres (Nm)

Power
Horsepower (hp)	X	745.7	= Watts (W)	X	0.0013	= Horsepower (hp)

Velocity (speed)
Miles per hour (miles/hr; mph)	X	1.609	= Kilometres per hour (km/hr; kph)	X	0.621	= Miles per hour (miles/hr; mph)

Fuel consumption*
Miles per gallon, Imperial (mpg)	X	0.354	= Kilometres per litre (km/l)	X	2.825	= Miles per gallon, Imperial (mpg)
Miles per gallon, US (mpg)	X	0.425	= Kilometres per litre (km/l)	X	2.352	= Miles per gallon, US (mpg)

Temperature
Degrees Fahrenheit = (°C x 1.8) + 32   Degrees Celsius (Degrees Centigrade; °C) = (°F - 32) x 0.56

*It is common practice to convert from miles per gallon (mpg) to litres/100 kilometres (l/100km),
where mpg (Imperial) x l/100 km = 282 and mpg (US) x l/100 km = 235

Troubleshooting

Contents

This section provides an easy reference guide to the more common problems which may occur during the operation of your vehicle. These problems and possible causes are grouped under various components or systems; i.e. Engine, Cooling System, etc., and also refer to the Chapter and/or Section which deals with the problem.

Remember that successful troubleshooting is not a mysterious black art practiced only by professional mechanics. It's simply the result of a bit of knowledge combined with an intelligent, systematic approach to the problem. Always work by a process of elimination, starting with the simplest solution and working through to the most complex – and never overlook the obvious. Anyone can forget to fill the gas tank or leave the lights on overnight, so don't assume that you are above such oversights.

Finally, always get clear in your mind why a problem has occurred and take steps to ensure that it doesn't happen again. If the electrical system fails because of a poor connection, check all other connections in the system to make sure that they don't fail as well. If a particular fuse continues to blow, find out why – don't just go on replacing fuses. Remember, failure of a small component can often be indicative of potential failure or incorrect functioning of a more important component or system.

Engine

1   Engine will not rotate when attempting to start

1   Battery terminal connections loose or corroded. Check the cable terminals at the battery. Tighten the cable or remove corrosion as necessary.
2   Battery discharged or faulty. If the cable connections are clean and tight on the battery posts, turn the key to the On position and switch on the headlights and/or windshield wipers. If they fail to function, the battery is discharged.
3   Automatic transaxle not completely engaged in Park or Neutral or clutch pedal not completely depressed.
4   Broken, loose or disconnected wiring in the starting circuit. Inspect all wiring and connectors at the battery, starter solenoid and ignition switch.
5   Starter motor pinion jammed in flywheel ring gear. If manual transaxle, place transaxle in gear and rock the vehicle to manually turn the engine. Remove starter (see Chapter 5) and inspect pinion and flywheel at earliest convenience.
6   Starter solenoid faulty (see Chapter 5).
7   Starter motor faulty (see Chapter 5).
8   Ignition switch faulty (see Chapter 12).

2   Engine rotates but will not start

1   Fuel tank empty.
2   Fault in the carburetor or fuel injection system (see Chapter 4).
3   Battery discharged (engine rotates slowly). Check the operation of electrical components as described in the previous Section.
4   Battery terminal connections loose or corroded (see previous Section).
5   Fuel pump faulty (see Chapter 4).
6   Excessive moisture on, or damage to, ignition components (see Chapter 5).
7   Worn, faulty or incorrectly gapped spark plugs (see Chapter 1).
8   Broken, loose or disconnected wiring in the starting circuit (see previous Section).
9   Distributor loose, causing ignition timing to change. Turn the distributor as necessary to start the engine, then set the ignition timing as soon as possible (see Chapter 5).
10   Broken, loose or disconnected wires at the ignition coil or faulty coil (see Chapter 5).

3   Starter motor operates without rotating engine

1   Starter pinion sticking. Remove the starter (see Chapter 5) and inspect.
2   Starter pinion or flywheel/driveplate teeth worn or broken. Remove the flywheel/driveplate access cover and inspect.

4   Engine hard to start when cold

1   Battery discharged or low. Check as described in Section 1.
2   Fault in the fuel or electrical systems (see Chapters 4 and 5).
3   Carburetor in need of overhaul (carbureted models) (see Chapter 4).
4   Distributor rotor carbon tracked and/or damaged (see Chapters 1 and 5).
5   Choke control stuck or inoperative (carbureted models) (see Chapters 1 and 4).

5   Engine hard to start when hot

1   Air filter clogged (see Chapter 1).
2   Fault in the fuel or electrical systems (see Chapters 4 and 5).
3   Fuel not reaching the carburetor (carburetor-equipped models).
4   Corroded battery connections, especially ground (see Chapter 1).

6   Starter motor noisy or excessively rough in engagement

1   Pinion or flywheel gear teeth worn or broken. Remove the cover at the left end of the engine (if so equipped) and inspect.
2   Starter motor mounting bolts loose or missing.

7   Engine starts but stops immediately

1   Loose or faulty electrical connections at distributor, coil or alternator.
2   Fault in the fuel or electrical systems (see Chapters 4 and 5).
3   Insufficient fuel reaching the carburetor or fuel injection system. Check the fuel pump (see Chapter 4).
4   Vacuum leak at the gasket surfaces of the intake manifold, or carburetor/throttle body. Make sure all mounting bolts/nuts are tightened securely and all vacuum hoses connected to the carburetor and manifold are positioned properly and in good condition.

8   Engine lopes while idling or idles erratically

1   Vacuum leakage. Check the mounting bolts/nuts at the carburetor/throttle body and intake manifold for tightness. Make sure all vacuum hoses are connected and in good condition. Use a stethoscope or a length of fuel hose held against your ear to listen for vacuum leaks while the engine is running. A hissing sound will be heard. A soapy water solution will also detect leaks. **Warning:** *Be careful of rotating engine components when probing with the fuel-hose stethoscope.*
2   Fault in the fuel or electrical systems (see Chapters 4 and 5).
3   Leaking EGR valve or plugged PCV valve (see Chapters 1 and 6).
4   Air filter clogged (see Chapter 1).
5   Fuel pump not delivering sufficient fuel to the carburetor or fuel injection system (see Chapter 4).
6   Carburetor out of adjustment (see Chapter 4).
7   Leaking head gasket. Perform a compression check (see Chapter 2).
8   Camshaft lobes worn (see Chapter 2).

9 Engine misses at idle speed

1   Spark plugs worn or not gapped properly (see Chapter 1).
2   Fault in the fuel or electrical systems (see Chapters 4 and 5).
3   Faulty spark plug wires (see Chapter 1).

10 Engine misses throughout driving speed range

1   Fuel filter clogged and/or impurities in the fuel system (see Chapter 1).
2   Faulty or incorrectly gapped spark plugs (see Chapter 1).
3   Fault in the fuel or electrical systems (see Chapters 4 and 5).
4   Incorrect ignition timing (see Chapter 5).
5   Cracked distributor cap, disconnected distributor wires and damaged distributor components (see Chapter 1).
6   Defective spark plug wires (see Chapter 1).
7   Faulty emissions system components (see Chapter 6).
8   Low or uneven cylinder compression pressures. Perform a compression test (see Chapter 2).
9   Weak or faulty ignition system (see Chapter 5).
10 Vacuum leaks at the carburetor/throttle body, intake manifold or vacuum hoses (see Section 8).

11 Engine stalls

1   Idle speed incorrect. Refer to the VECI label and Chapter 1.
2   Fuel filter clogged and/or water and impurities in the fuel system (see Chapter 1).
3   Distributor components damp or damaged (see Chapter 5).
4   Fault in the fuel system or sensors (see Chapters 4 and 6).
5   Faulty emissions system components (see Chapter 6).
6   Faulty or incorrectly gapped spark plugs (see Chapter 1). Also check the spark plug wires (see Chapter 1).
7   Vacuum leak at the carburetor/throttle body, intake manifold or vacuum hoses. Check as described in Section 8.

12 Engine lacks power

1   Incorrect ignition timing (see Chapter 5).
2   Fault in the fuel or electrical systems (see Chapters 4 and 5).
3   Excessive play in the distributor shaft. At the same time, check for a damaged rotor, faulty distributor cap, wires, etc. (see Chapters 1 and 5).
4   Faulty or incorrectly gapped spark plugs (see Chapter 1).
5   Carburetor not adjusted properly or excessively worn (carbureted models) (see Chapter 4).
6   Faulty coil (see Chapter 5).
7   Brakes binding (see Chapter 1 and Chapter 9).
8   Automatic transaxle fluid level incorrect (see Chapter 1).
9   Clutch slipping (see Chapter 8).
10 Fuel filter clogged and/or impurities in the fuel system (see Chapter 1).
11 Emissions control system not functioning properly (see Chapter 6).
12 Use of substandard fuel. Fill the tank with the proper octane fuel.
13 Low or uneven cylinder compression pressures. Perform a compression test (see Chapter 2).

13 Engine backfires

1   Emissions system not functioning properly (see Chapter 6).

2   Fault in the fuel or electrical systems (see Chapters 4 and 5).
3   Ignition timing incorrect (see Chapter 5).
4   Faulty secondary ignition system (cracked spark plug insulator, faulty plug wires, distributor cap and/or rotor) (see Chapters 1 and 5).
5   Carburetor or fuel injection system in need of adjustment or worn excessively (see Chapter 4).
6   Vacuum leak at the carburetor/throttle body, intake manifold or vacuum hoses. Check as described in Section 8.
7   Valves sticking (see Chapter 2).

14 Pinging or knocking engine sounds during acceleration or uphill

1   Incorrect grade of fuel. Fill the tank with fuel of the proper octane rating.
2   Fault in the fuel or electrical systems (see Chapters 4 and 5).
3   Ignition timing incorrect (see Chapter 5).
4   Carburetor in need of adjustment (carbureted models) (see Chapter 4).
5   Improper spark plugs. Check the plug type against the VECI label located in the engine compartment. Also check the plugs and wires for damage (see Chapter 1).
6   Worn or damaged distributor components (see Chapter 5).
7   Faulty emissions system (see Chapter 6).
8   Vacuum leak. Check as described in Section 8.

15 Engine diesels (continues to run) after switching off

1   Idle speed too high. Refer to Chapter 1.
2   Fault in the fuel or electrical systems (see Chapters 4 and 5).
3   Ignition timing incorrectly adjusted (see Chapter 5).
4   Thermo-controlled air cleaner heat valve not operating properly (see Chapters 1 and 6).
5   Excessive engine operating temperature. Probable causes of this are a malfunctioning thermostat, clogged radiator or faulty water pump (see Chapter 3).

Engine electrical system

16 Battery will not hold a charge

1   Alternator drivebelt defective or not adjusted properly (see Chapter 1).
2   Electrolyte level low or battery discharged (see Chapter 1).
3   Battery terminals loose or corroded (see Chapter 1).
4   Alternator not charging properly (see Chapter 5).
5   Loose, broken or faulty wiring in the charging circuit (see Chapter 5).
6   Short in the vehicle wiring causing a continuous drain on the battery (refer to Chapter 12 and the Wiring Diagrams).
7   Battery defective internally.

17 Alternator light fails to go out

1   Fault in the alternator or charging circuit (see Chapter 5).
2   Alternator drivebelt defective or not properly adjusted (see Chapter 1).

18   Alternator light fails to come on when key is turned on

1   Instrument cluster warning light bulb defective (see Chapter 12).
2   Alternator faulty (see Chapter 5).
3   Fault in the instrument cluster printed circuit, dashboard wiring or bulb holder (see Chapter 12).

Fuel system

19   Excessive fuel consumption

1   Dirty or clogged air filter element (see Chapter 1).
2   Incorrectly set ignition timing (see Chapter 5).
3   Choke sticking or improperly adjusted (carbureted models) (see Chapter 1).
4   Emissions system not functioning properly (see Chapter 6).
5   Fault in the fuel or electrical systems (see Chapters 4 and 5).
6   Carburetor or fuel injection system internal parts excessively worn or damaged (see Chapter 4).
7   Low tire pressure or incorrect tire size (see Chapter 1).

20   Fuel leakage and/or fuel odor

1   Leak in a fuel feed or vent line (see Chapter 4).
2   Tank overfilled. Fill only to automatic shut-off.
3   Evaporative emissions system canister clogged (see Chapter 6).
4   Vapor leaks from system lines (see Chapter 4).
5   Carburetor or fuel injection system internal parts excessively worn or out of adjustment (see Chapter 4).

Cooling system

21   Overheating

1   Insufficient coolant in the system (see Chapter 1).
2   Water pump drivebelt defective or not adjusted properly (see Chapter 1).
3   Radiator core blocked or radiator grille dirty and restricted (see Chapter 3).
4   Thermostat faulty (see Chapter 3).
5   Fan blades broken or cracked (see Chapter 3).
6   Fault in electric fan motor or wiring (see Chapter 3).
7   Radiator cap not maintaining proper pressure. Have the cap pressure tested by gas station or repair shop.
8   Ignition timing incorrect (see Chapter 5).

22   Overcooling

1   Thermostat faulty (see Chapter 3).
2   Inaccurate temperature gauge (see Chapter 12).

23   External coolant leakage

1   Deteriorated or damaged hoses or loose clamps. Replace hoses and/or tighten the clamps at the hose connections (see Chapter 1).
2   Water pump seals defective. If this is the case, water will drip from the weep hole in the water pump body (see Chapter 3).

3   Leakage from radiator core or header tank. This will require the radiator to be professionally repaired (see Chapter 3 for removal procedures).
4   Engine block drain plug leaking (see Chapter 1) or water jacket core plugs leaking (see Chapter 2).

24   Internal coolant leakage

Note: *Internal coolant leaks can usually be detected by examining the oil. Check the dipstick and inside of the cylinder head cover for water deposits and an oil consistency like that of a milkshake.*
1   Leaking cylinder head gasket. Have the cooling system pressure tested.
2   Cracked cylinder bore or cylinder head. Dismantle the engine and inspect (see Chapter 2).

25   Coolant loss

1   Too much coolant in the system (see Chapter 1).
2   Coolant boiling away due to overheating (see Section 15).
3   External or internal leakage (see Sections 23 and 24).
4   Faulty radiator cap. Have the cap pressure tested.

26   Poor coolant circulation

1   Inoperative water pump. A quick test is to pinch the top radiator hose closed with your hand while the engine is idling, then let it loose. You should feel the surge of coolant if the pump is working properly (see Chapter 1).
2   Restriction in the cooling system. Drain, flush and refill the system (see Chapter 1). If necessary, remove the radiator (see Chapter 3) and have it reverse flushed.
3   Water pump drivebelt defective or not adjusted properly (see Chapter 1).
4   Thermostat sticking (see Chapter 3).

Clutch

27   Fails to release (pedal pressed to the floor – shift lever does not move freely in and out of Reverse)

1   Improper linkage adjustment (see Chapter 8).
2   Linkage malfunction (see Chapter 8).
3   Clutch plate warped or damaged (see Chapter 8).

28   Clutch slips (engine speed increases with no increase in vehicle speed)

1   Linkage out of adjustment (see Chapter 8).
2   Clutch plate oil soaked or lining worn. Remove clutch (see Chapter 8) and inspect.
3   Clutch plate not seated. It may take 30 or 40 normal starts for a new one to seat.

29   Grabbing (chattering) as clutch is engaged

1   Oil on clutch plate lining. Remove (see Chapter 8) and inspect. Correct any leakage source.
2   Worn or loose engine or transaxle mounts. These units move slightly when the clutch is released. Inspect the mounts and bolts (see Chapter 2).

3   Worn splines on clutch plate hub. Remove the clutch components (see Chapter 8) and inspect.
4   Warped pressure plate or flywheel. Remove the clutch components and inspect.
5   Weak diaphragm spring, allowing pressure plate to bounce on engagement. Remove the clutch components and inspect.

30   Squeal or rumble with clutch fully disengaged (pedal depressed)

1   Worn, defective or broken release bearing (see Chapter 8).
2   Worn or broken pressure plate springs (or diaphragm fingers) (see Chapter 8).

31   Clutch pedal stays on floor

1   Linkage or release bearing binding. Inspect the linkage or remove the clutch components as necessary.
2   Linkage springs being over-traveled. Adjust linkage for proper lash. Make sure proper pedal stop (bumper) is installed.

Manual transaxle

Note: *All of the following Sections are covered in Chapter 7 unless otherwise noted.*

32   Knocking noise at low speeds

1   Worn driveaxle constant velocity (CV) joints (see Chapter 8).
2   Worn side gear shaft counterbore in differential case (see Chapter 7A).*

33   Noise most pronounced when turning

Differential gear noise (see Chapter 7A).*

34   Clunk on acceleration or deceleration

1   Loose engine or transaxle mounts (see Chapters 2 and 7A).
2   Worn differential pinion shaft in case.*
3   Worn side gear shaft counterbore in differential case (see Chapter 7A).*
4   Worn or damaged driveaxle inner CV joints (see Chapter 8).

35   Noisy in Neutral with engine running

1   Input shaft bearing worn.
2   Damaged main drive gear bearing.
3   Worn countershaft bearings.
4   Worn or damaged countershaft endplay shims.

36   Noisy in all gears

1   Any of the above causes, and/or:
2   Insufficient lubricant (see the checking procedures in Chapter 1).

37   Noisy in one particular gear

1   Worn, damaged or chipped gear teeth for that particular gear.
2   Worn or damaged synchronizer for that particular gear.

38   Slips out of gear

1   Damaged shift linkage.
2   Interference between the floor shift handle and console.
3   Broken or loose engine mounts.
4   Shift mechanism stabilizer bar loose.
5   Improperly installed shifter boot.
6   Damaged or worn transaxle internal components.

39   Difficulty in engaging gears

1   Clutch not releasing completely (see clutch adjustment in Chapter 1).
2   Loose, damaged or out-of-adjustment shift linkage. Make a thorough inspection, replacing parts as necessary (see Chapter 7).

40   Leaks lubricant

1   Excessive amount of lubricant in the transaxle (see Chapter 1 for correct checking procedures). Drain lubricant as required.
2   Side cover loose or gasket damaged.
3   Driveaxle oil seal or speedometer oil seal in need of replacement (see Chapter 7).
* These repairs are beyond the scope of the home mechanic, but are included here so you can more clearly communicate with the shop that does the work.

Automatic transaxle

Note: *Due to the complexity of the automatic transaxle, it's difficult for the home mechanic to properly diagnose and service this component. For problems other than the following, the vehicle should be taken to a dealer service department or a transmission shop.*

41   General shift mechanism problems

1   Chapter 7 deals with checking and adjusting the shift linkage on automatic transaxles. Common problems which may be attributed to poorly adjusted linkage are:
    Engine starting in gears other than Park or Neutral.
    Indicator on shifter pointing to a gear other than the one actually being selected.
    Vehicle moves when in Park.
2   Refer to Chapter 7 to adjust the linkage.

42   Transaxle will not downshift with accelerator pedal pressed to the floor

Chapter 7 deals with adjusting the TV linkage to enable the transaxle to downshift properly.

43   Transaxle slips, shifts roughly, is noisy or has no drive in forward or reverse gears

1   There are many probable causes for the above problems, but the home mechanic should be concerned with only one possibility – fluid level.
2   Before taking the vehicle to a repair shop, check the level and condition of the fluid as described in Chapter 1. Correct fluid level as necessary or change the fluid and filter if needed. If the problem persists, have a professional diagnose the probable cause.

44   Fluid leakage

1   Automatic transaxle fluid is a deep red color when new, but it can darken with age. Fluid leaks should not be confused with engine oil, which can easily be blown by air flow to the transaxle. A good way to tell the difference is to place a drop of transaxle fluid from the dipstick on a clean, lint-free paper towel, then do the same thing with a drop of engine oil. This will enable you to compare the two.
2   To pinpoint a leak, first remove all built-up dirt and grime from around the transaxle. Degreasing agents and/or steam cleaning will achieve this. With the underside clean, drive the vehicle at low speeds so air flow will not blow the leak far from its source. Raise the vehicle and determine where the leak is coming from. Common areas of leakage are:
   a) **Pan:** Tighten the mounting bolts and/or replace the pan gasket as necessary (see Chapter 1).
   b) **Filler pipe:** Replace the rubber seal where the pipe enters the transaxle case.
   c) **Transaxle lubricant lines:** Tighten the connectors where the lines enter the transaxle case and/or replace the lines.
   d) **Vent pipe:** Transaxle overfilled and/or water in lubricant (see checking procedures, Chapter 1).
   e) **Speedometer connector:** Replace the O-ring where the speedometer cable enters the transaxle case (see Chapter 7).

45   Transaxle lubricant brown or has a burned smell

Transaxle lubricant burned (see Chapter 1).

Driveaxles

46   Clicking noise in turns

Worn or damaged outer joint. Check for cut or damaged seals. Repair as necessary (see Chapter 8).

47   Knock or clunk when accelerating after coasting

Worn or damaged inner joint. Check for cut or damaged seals. Repair as necessary (see Chapter 8).

48   Shudder or vibration during acceleration

1   Excessive joint angle. Have checked and correct as necessary (see Chapter 8).
2   Worn or damaged CV joints. Repair or replace as necessary (see Chapter 8).
3   Sticking CV joint assembly. Correct or replace as necessary (see Chapter 8).

49   Vibration at highway speeds

1   Out-of-balance front wheels or tires (see Chapters 1 and 10).
2   Out-of-round front tires (see Chapters 1 and 10).
3   Worn CV joints (see Chapter 8).

Rear axle

50   Noise

1   Road noise. No corrective procedures available.
2   Tire noise. Inspect tires and check tire pressures (see Chapter 1).
3   Rear wheel bearings loose, worn or damaged (see Chapter 1).

Brakes

Note: *Before assuming that a brake problem exists, make sure that the tires are in good condition and inflated properly (see Chapter 1), that the front end alignment is correct and that the vehicle is not loaded with weight in an unequal manner.*

51   Vehicle pulls to one side during braking

1   Incorrect tire pressures (see Chapter 1).
2   Front end out of alignment (have the front end aligned).
3   Front or rear tires not matched to one another.
4   Restricted brake lines or hoses (see Chapter 9).
5   Defective, damaged or oil contaminated disc brake pads on one side. Inspect as described in Chapter 9.
6   Excessive wear of brake pad material or disc on one side. Inspect and correct as necessary.
7   Loose or disconnected front suspension components. Inspect and tighten all bolts to the specified torque (see Chapter 10).
8   Defective caliper assembly. Remove the caliper and inspect for a stuck piston or other damage (see Chapter 9).

52   Noise (high-pitched squeal with the brakes applied)

Disc brake pads worn out. The noise comes from the wear sensor rubbing against the disc (does not apply to all vehicles) or the actual pad backing plate itself if the material is completely worn away. Replace the pads with new ones immediately (see Chapter 9). If the pad material has worn completely away, the brake discs should be inspected for damage as described in Chapter 9.

53   Excessive brake pedal travel

1   Partial brake system failure. Inspect the entire system (see Chapter 9) and correct as required.
2   Insufficient fluid in the master cylinder. Check (see Chapter 1), add fluid and bleed the system if necessary (see Chapter 9).
3   Rear brakes not adjusting properly. Make a series of starts and stops while the vehicle is in Reverse. If this does not correct the situation, remove the drums and inspect the self-adjusters (see Chapter 9).

54   Brake pedal feels spongy when depressed

1   Air in the hydraulic lines. Bleed the brake system (see Chapter 9).

2   Faulty flexible hoses. Inspect all system hoses and lines. Replace parts as necessary.
3   Master cylinder mounting bolts/nuts loose.
4   Master cylinder defective (see Chapter 9).

55   Excessive effort required to stop vehicle

1   Power brake booster not operating properly (see Chapter 9).
2   Excessively worn linings or pads. Inspect and replace if necessary (see Chapter 9).
3   One or more caliper pistons or wheel cylinders seized or sticking. Inspect and rebuild as required (see Chapter 9).
4   Brake linings or pads contaminated with oil or grease. Inspect and replace as required (see Chapter 9).
5   New pads or shoes installed and not yet seated. It will take a while for the new material to seat against the drum (or rotor).

56   Pedal travels to the floor with little resistance

1   Little or no fluid in the master cylinder reservoir caused by leaking wheel cylinder(s), leaking caliper piston(s), loose, damaged or disconnected brake lines. Inspect the entire system and correct as necessary.
2   Worn master cylinder (see Chapter 9).
3   Loose, damaged or disconnected brake lines (see Chapter 9).

57   Brake pedal pulsates during brake application

1   Caliper improperly installed. Remove and inspect (see Chapter 9).
2   Disc or drum defective. Remove (see Chapter 9) and check for excessive lateral runout and parallelism. Have the disc or drum resurfaced or replace it with a new one.

58   Dragging brakes

1   Incorrect adjustment of brake light switch (see Chapter 9).
2   Master cylinder pistons not returning correctly (see Chapter 9).
3   Restricted brake lines or hoses (see Chapters 1 and 9).
4   Incorrect parking brake adjustment (see Chapter 9).

59   Grabbing or uneven braking action

1   Malfunctioning proportioning valve (see Chapter 9).
2   Malfunction of power brake booster unit (see Chapter 9).
3   Binding brake pedal mechanism (see Chapter 9).

60   Parking brake does not hold

    Parking brake linkage improperly adjusted (see Chapters 1 and 9).

Suspension and steering systems

61   Vehicle pulls to one side

1   Tire pressures uneven (see Chapter 1).
2   Defective tire (see Chapter 1).
3   Excessive wear in suspension or steering components (see Chapter 10).

4   Front end in need of alignment.
5   Front brakes dragging. Check the calipers for binding (see Chapter 9).

62   Shimmy, shake or vibration

1   Tire or wheel out-of-balance or out-of-round. Have professionally balanced.
2   Loose, worn or out-of-adjustment rear wheel bearings (see Chapter 1).
3   Shock absorbers and/or suspension components worn or damaged (see Chapter 10).
4   Excessive wheel runout.
5   Blister or bump on tire.

63   Excessive pitching and/or rolling around corners or during braking

1   Worn strut dampers (see Chapter 10).
2   Broken or weak springs and/or suspension components. Inspect as described in Chapter 10.
3   Loose stabilizer bar (see Chapter 10).

64   Excessively stiff steering

1   Lack of fluid in power steering fluid reservoir (see Chapter 1).
2   Incorrect tire pressures (see Chapter 1).
3   Front end out of alignment.

65   Excessive play in steering

1   Wheel bearing(s) worn (see Chapter 1).
2   Tie-rod end loose (see Chapter 10).
3   Steering gear loose (see Chapter 10).
4   Worn or loose steering intermediate shaft (see Chapter 10).

66   Lack of power assistance

1   Steering pump drivebelt faulty or not adjusted properly (see Chapter 1).
2   Fluid level low (see Chapter 1).
3   Hoses or lines restricted. Inspect and replace parts as necessary.
4   Air in power steering system. Bleed the system (see Chapter 10).

67   Excessive tire wear (not specific to one area)

1   Incorrect tire pressures (see Chapter 1).
2   Tires out-of-balance. Have professionally balanced.
3   Wheels damaged. Inspect and replace as necessary.
4   Suspension or steering components excessively worn (see Chapter 10).
5   Overloaded vehicle
6   Tires not rotated regularly.

68   Excessive tire wear on outside edge

1   Inflation pressures incorrect (see Chapter 1).

2 Excessive speed in turns.
3 Front end alignment incorrect (excessive toe-in). Have professionally aligned.
4 Suspension arm bent or twisted (see Chapter 10).

69 Excessive tire wear on inside edge

1 Inflation pressures incorrect (see Chapter 1).
2 Front end alignment incorrect. Have professionally aligned.
3 Loose or damaged steering components (see Chapter 10).

70 Tire tread worn in one place

1 Tires out-of-balance.
2 Damaged or buckled wheel. Inspect and replace if necessary.
3 Defective tire (see Chapter 1).

71 Wheel makes a thumping noise

1 Blister or bump on tire.
2 Improper strut damper action (see Chapter 10).

72 Poor returnability of steering to center

1 Lack of lubrication at balljoints and tie-rod ends (see Chapter 10).
2 Binding in balljoints (see Chapter 10).
3 Binding in steering column (see Chapter 10).
4 Lack of lubricant in steering gear assembly (see Chapter 10).
5 Front wheel alignment (see Chapter 10).

73 Abnormal noise at the front end

1 Loose wheel lug nuts (see Chapter 1 for torque specifications).
2 Lack of lubrication at balljoints and tie-rod ends (see Chapters 1 and 10).
3 Damaged strut mounting (see Chapter 10).
4 Worn control arm bushings or tie-rod ends (see Chapter 10).

5 Loose stabilizer bar (see Chapter 10).
6 Loose suspension bolts (see Chapter 10).

74 Wander or poor steering stability

1 Mismatched or uneven tires (see Chapter 10).
2 Wheel alignment (see Chapter 10).
3 Worn strut assemblies (see Chapter 10).
4 Loose stabilizer bar (see Chapter 10).
5 Broken or sagging springs (see Chapter 10).
6 Wheel alignment (see Chapter 10).

75 Erratic steering when braking

1 Wheel bearings worn (see Chapter 1).
2 Broken or sagging springs (see Chapter 10).
3 Leaking wheel cylinder or caliper (see Chapter 9).
4 Warped rotors or drums (see Chapter 9).

76 Suspension bottoms

1 Overloaded vehicle
2 Worn strut dampers (see Chapter 10).
3 Incorrect, broken or sagging springs (see Chapter 10).

77 Cupped tires

1 Front or rear wheel alignment (see Chapter 10).
2 Worn strut dampers (see Chapter 10).
3 Worn wheel bearings (see Chapter 1).
4 Excessive tire or wheel runout (see Chapter 10).
5 Worn balljoints (see Chapter 10).

78 Rattling or clicking noise in steering gear

1 Insufficient or improper lubricant in steering gear assembly.
2 Steering gear attachment loose (see Chapter 10).

Chapter 1 Tune-up and routine maintenance

Contents

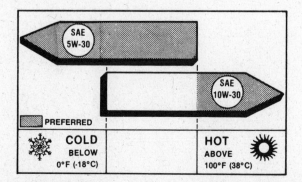

Specifications

Recommended lubricants and fluids

Engine oil
  Type . . . . API grade SG fuel-efficient oil
  Viscosity . . . . See accompanying chart
  Capacity (with filter change) . . . . 4.0 qts
Brake fluid type . . . . DOT 3 heavy-duty brake fluid
Power steering fluid type . . . . Motorcraft MERCON automatic transmission fluid (part no. XT-2-QDX)
Automatic transaxle fluid
  Type . . . . Motorcraft MERCON automatic transmission fluid (part no. XT-2-QDX)
  Capacity
    Drain and refill 3.0
    Total (including torque converter) 9.8

ENGINE OIL VISCOSITY CHART

For best fuel economy and cold starting, select the lowest SAE viscosity grade oil for the expected temperature range

Manual transaxle lubricant
  Type
    1981 through 1987 . . . .   Motorcraft MERCON automatic transmission fluid (part no. XT-2-QDX) or
            Type F automatic transmission fluid (part no. XT-1-QF)
    1988 on . . . .   Motorcraft MERCON automatic transmission fluid (part no. XT-2-QDX)
  Capacity (approximate)
    Four speed . . . .   5.2 pts*
    Five speed . . . .   6.2 pts*
Coolant type . . . .   A 50/50 mixture of ethylene glycol-based antifreeze and water
Cooling system capacity in quarts (approximate)
  1981 through 1984 . . . .   8.1
  1985
    Manual transaxle without air conditioning 6.5
    Manual transaxle with air conditioning 7.0
    Automatic transaxle without air conditioning 6.6
    Automatic transaxle with air conditioning 7.1
  1986 on
    Manual transaxle 7.5
    Automatic transaxle without air conditioning 6.4
    Automatic transaxle with air conditioning 6.9

Fill to bottom of filler hole.

Drivebelt tension (measured with special gauge)

1981
  1/4-inch V-belt
    New belt . . . .   50 to 80 lbs
    Used belt . . . .   30 lbs
  Ribbed belt
    4K
      New belt . . . .   90 to 120 lbs
      Used belt . . . .   60 lbs
    5K
      New belt . . . .   110 to 140 lbs
      Used belt . . . .   75 lbs
1982 and 1983
  1/4-inch V-belt
    New belt . . . .   50 to 80 lbs
    Used belt . . . .   40 to 60 lbs
    Allowable minimum . . . .   40 lbs
  4K ribbed belt (air pump)
    New belt . . . .   90 to 130 lbs
    Used belt . . . .   90 to 120 lbs
    Allowable minimum . . . .   55 lbs
  4K ribbed belt (except air pump)
    New belt . . . .   110 to 150 lbs
    Used belt . . . .   100 to 130 lbs
    Allowable minimum . . . .   65 lbs
  5K ribbed belt (fixed)
    New belt . . . .   130 to 170 lbs
    Used belt . . . .   120 to 150 lbs
    Allowable minimum . . . .   80 lbs
1984 and 1985
  Low-mount air pump (without power steering)
    New belt . . . .   90 to 130 lbs
    Used belt . . . .   80 to 100 lbs
    Allowable minimum . . . .   60 lbs
  High-mount air pump and power steering pump
    New belt . . . .   50 to 90 lbs
    Used belt . . . .   40 to 60 lbs
    Allowable minimum . . . .   40 lbs
  Alternator
    New belt . . . .   150 to 190 lbs
    Used belt . . . .   140 to 160 lbs
    Allowable minimum . . . .   90 lbs
1986
  Low-mount air pump (without power steering)
    New belt . . . .   90 to 130 lbs
    Used belt . . . .   40 to 60 lbs
    Allowable minimum . . . .   40 lbs

High-mount air pump and power steering pump
New belt .... 50 to 90 lbs
Used belt .... 40 to 60 lbs
Allowable minimum .... 40 lbs
Alternator
New belt .... 120 to 160 lbs
Used belt .... 110 to 130 lbs
Allowable minimum .... 70 lbs
1987 and 1988
Power steering pump
New belt .... 100 to 140 lbs
Used belt .... 80 to 100 lbs
Allowable minimum .... 40 lbs
Alternator
New belt .... 120 to 160 lbs
Used belt .... 110 to 130 lbs
Allowable minimum .... 70 lbs
1989 on
Power steering pump
New belt .... 140 ± 20 lbs
Used belt .... 110 ± 10 lbs
Allowable minimum .... 40 lbs
Alternator
New belt .... 160 ± 20 lbs
Used belt .... 130 ± 10 lbs
Allowable minimum .... 70 lbs

1.3L engine

1.6L engine

Brakes
Disc brake pad thickness (minimum) .... 1/8 inch
Drum brake shoe lining thickness (minimum) .... 1/16 inch

Ignition system
Spark plug type
1981 .... Champion RC12YC
1982 .... Champion RS12YC
1983
Carbureted .... Champion RS12YC
Fuel injected .... Champion RS10LC
1984 on
Turbo .... Champion RS9YC
Non-turbo .... Champion RS10LC
Spark plug gap
1984 Turbo .... 0.035 inch
All others .... 0.044 inch

1.9L engine

Cylinder location and distributor rotation

Torque specifications
Ft-lbs (unless otherwise indicated)
Wheel lug nuts .... 85 to 105
Spark plugs .... 96 to 180 in-lbs
Oil pan drain plug
1981 through 1984 16
1985 on .... 15 to 25
Automatic transaxle pan bolts .... 69 to 95 in-lbs

---

1   Introduction

Warning: *The electric cooling fan on these models can activate at any time, even when the ignition is in the Off position. Disconnect the fan motor or negative battery cable when working in the vicinity of the fan.*

This Chapter is designed to help the home mechanic maintain the Ford Escort with the goals of maximum performance, economy, safety and reliability in mind.

On the following pages is a master maintenance schedule, followed by procedures dealing specifically with each item on the schedule. Visual checks, adjustments, component replacement and other helpful items are included. Refer to the accompanying illustrations for the locations of various components.

Servicing your vehicle in accordance with the mileage/time maintenance schedule and the step-by-step procedures will result in a planned maintenance program that should produce a long and reliable service life. Keep in mind that it is a comprehensive plan, so maintaining some items but not others at the specified intervals will not produce the same results.

As you service your vehicle, you will discover that many of the procedures can – and should – be grouped together because of the nature of the particular procedure you're performing or because of the close proximity of two otherwise unrelated components to one another.

For example, if the vehicle is raised for chassis lubrication, you should inspect the exhaust, suspension, steering and fuel systems while you're under the vehicle. When you're rotating the tires, it makes good sense to check the brakes since the wheels are already removed. Finally, let's suppose you have to borrow or rent a torque wrench. Even if you only need it to tighten the spark plugs, you might as well check the torque of as many critical fasteners as time allows.

The first step in this maintenance program is to prepare yourself before the actual work begins. Read through all the procedures you're planning to do, then gather up all the parts and tools needed. If it looks as if you might run into problems during a particular job, seek advice from a mechanic or an experienced do-it-yourselfer.

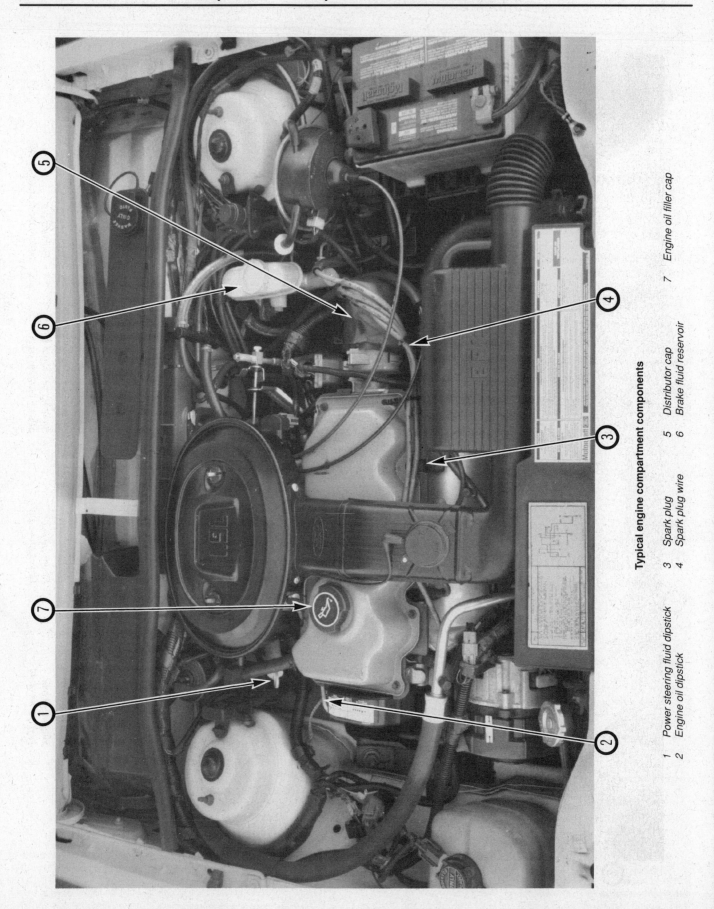

Typical engine compartment components

1 Power steering fluid dipstick	3 Distributor cap	5 Spark plug	7 Engine oil filler cap
2 Engine oil dipstick	4 Spark plug wire	6 Brake fluid reservoir	

Typical engine compartment underside components

1	Radiator hose	3	Brake caliper
2	Engine drivebelt	4	Driveaxle boot
		5	Steering gear boot
		6	Engine oil drain plug
		7	Exhaust pipe
		8	Automatic transaxle pan

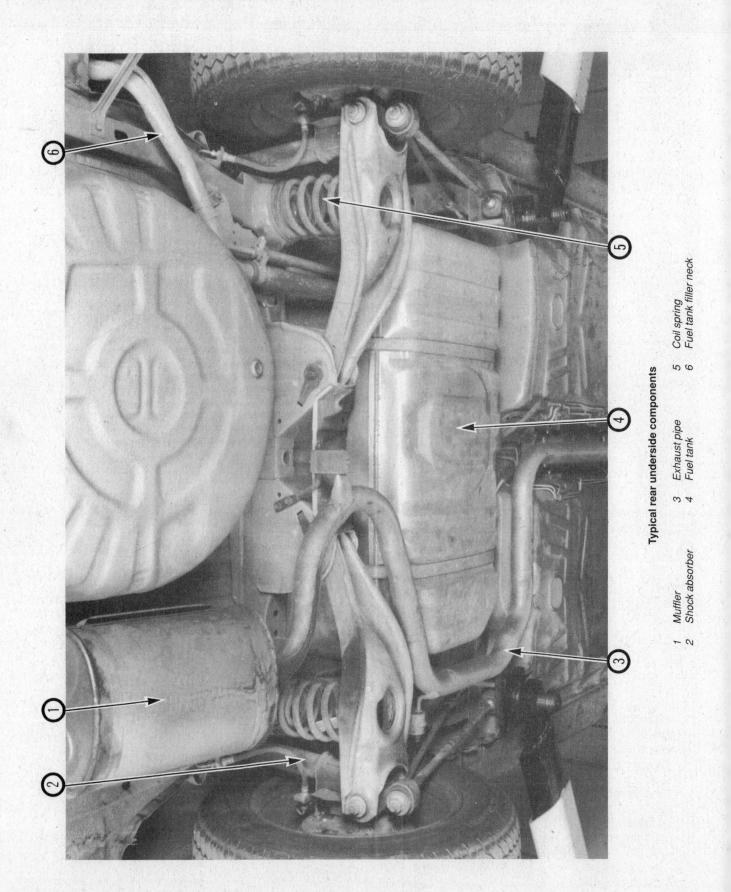

Typical rear underside components

1	Muffler	3	Exhaust pipe
2	Shock absorber.	4	Fuel tank
5	Coil spring		
6	Fuel tank filler neck		

2 Ford Escort/Mercury Lynx maintenance schedule

The following maintenance intervals are based on the assumption that the vehicle owner will be doing the maintenance or service work, as opposed to having a dealer service department do the work. Although the time/mileage intervals are loosely based on factory recommendations, most have been shortened to ensure, for example, that such items as lubricants and fluids are checked/changed at intervals that promote maximum engine/driveline service life. Also, subject to the preference of the individual owner interested in keeping his or her vehicle in peak condition at all times, and with the vehicle's ultimate resale in mind, many of the maintenance procedures may be performed more often than recommended in the following schedule. We encourage such owner initiative.

When the vehicle is new it should be serviced initially by a factory authorized dealer service department to protect the factory warranty. In many cases the initial maintenance check is done at no cost to the owner.

Every 250 miles or weekly, whichever comes first

Check the engine oil level (see Section 4)
Check the engine coolant level (see Section 4)
Check the windshield washer fluid level (see Section 4)
Check the brake fluid level (see Section 4)
Check the tires and tire pressures (see Section 5)

Every 3000 miles or 3 months, whichever comes first

All items listed above plus . . .
Check the power steering fluid level (see Section 6)
Check the automatic transaxle fluid level (see Section 7)
Change the engine oil and oil filter (see Section 8)

Every 6000 miles or 6 months, whichever comes first

All items listed above plus . . .
Adjust the clutch pedal (see Section 9)
Inspect/replace the underhood hoses (see Section 10)
Check/adjust the drivebelts (see Section 11)
Check/service the battery (see Section 12)

Every 12,000 miles or 12 months, whichever comes first

All items listed above plus . . .
Inspect/replace the windshield wiper blades (see Section 13)
Replace the air filter (see Section 14)
Replace the crankcase ventilation filter (models so equipped) (see Section 15)
Check/replace the PCV valve (models so equipped) (see Section 15)
Check the fuel system (see Section 16)
Replace the fuel filter (see Section 17)
Inspect the cooling system (see Section 18)
Inspect the exhaust system (see Section 19)
Rotate the tires (see Section 20)
Inspect the steering and suspension components (see Section 21)*

Inspect the brake system (see Section 22)
Lubricate the parking brake linkage (see Section 22)
Lubricate the automatic transaxle shift linkage (see Section 23)
Lubricate the clutch linkage (see Section 24)
Check/replenish the manual transaxle lubricant (see Section 25)

Every 30,000 miles or 30 months, whichever comes first

Replace the spark plugs (see Section 26)
Check/replace the spark plug wires, distributor cap and rotor (see Section 27)*
Service the cooling system (drain, flush and refill) (see Section 28)
Change the automatic transaxle fluid and filter (see Section 29)**

Every 60,000 miles or 60 months, whichever comes first

Replace the timing belt (some 1981 and 1982 models only)
Note: *to determine whether or not your engine needs the timing belt replaced at these intervals, check the timing belt cover on the engine. Models requiring regular belt replacement will have a sticker on the cover.*

* This item is affected by "severe" operating conditions as described below. If the vehicle in question is operated under "severe" conditions, perform all maintenance indicated with an asterisk (*) at 6000-mile/six-month intervals. Consider the conditions "severe" if most driving is done . . .
In dusty areas
When towing a trailer
At low speeds or with extended idling periods
When outside temperatures remain below freezing and most trips are less than four miles.
** If most driving is done under one or more of the following conditions, change the automatic transaxle fluid every 12,000 miles.
In heavy city traffic where the outside temperature regularly reaches 90-degrees F (32-degrees C) or higher
In hilly or mountainous terrain
Frequent trailer pulling

1

4.2   The engine oil dipstick is in one of several locations, depending on model (see text)

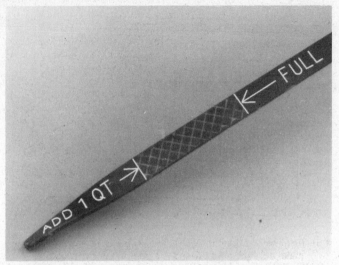

4.4   The oil level should be in the SAFE range – if it's below the L or ADD line, add enough oil to bring it up to or near the F or FULL line

3   Tune-up general information

The term tune-up is used in this manual to represent a combination of individual operations rather than one specific procedure.

If, from the time the vehicle is new, the routine maintenance schedule is followed closely and frequent checks are made of fluid levels and high wear items, as suggested throughout this manual, the engine will be kept in relatively good running condition and the need for additional work will be minimized.

More likely than not, however, there will be times when the engine is running poorly. This is even more likely if a used vehicle, which has not received regular and frequent maintenance checks, is purchased. In such cases, an engine tune-up will be needed outside of the regular routine maintenance intervals.

The first step in any tune-up or diagnostic procedure to help correct a poor-running engine is a cylinder compression check. A compression check (see Chapter 2 Part C) will help determine the condition of internal engine components and should be used as a guide for tune-up and repair procedures. If, for instance, a compression check indicates serious internal engine wear, a conventional tune-up will not improve the performance of the engine and would be a waste of time and money. Because of its importance, the compression check should be done by someone with the right equipment and the knowledge to use it properly.

The following procedures are those most often needed to bring a generally poor-running engine back into a proper state of tune.

Minor tune-up

Clean, inspect and test the battery (see Section 12)
Check all engine related fluids (see Section 4)
Check and adjust the drivebelts (see Section 11)
Replace the spark plugs (see Section 26)
Inspect the distributor cap and rotor (see Section 27)
Inspect the spark plug and coil wires (see Section 27)
Check/replace the PCV valve (models so equipped) (see Section 15)
Check the air filter (see Section 14)
Check the crankcase ventilation filter (models so equipped) (see Section 14)
Check the cooling system (see Section 18)
Check all underhood hoses (see Section 10)

Major tune-up

All items listed under Minor tune-up, plus . . .
Check the EGR system (see Chapter 6)
Check the ignition system (see Chapter 5)
Check the charging system (see Chapter 5)

Check the fuel system (see Chapter 4)
Replace the air and crankcase ventilation filters (see Sections 14 and 15)
Replace the distributor cap and rotor (see Section 27)
Replace the spark plug wires (see Section 27)

4   Fluid level checks

1   Fluids are an essential part of the lubrication, cooling, brake and windshield washer systems. Because the fluids gradually become depleted and/or contaminated during normal operation of the vehicle, they must be periodically replenished. See Recommended lubricants, fluids and capacities at the beginning of this Chapter before adding fluid to any of the following components. **Note:** *The vehicle must be on level ground when fluid levels are checked.*

Engine oil

Refer to illustrations 4.2, 4.4 and 4.6

2   The oil level is checked with a dipstick, which is located on the engine **(see illustration)**. The dipstick handle may be near the master cylinder, at the back of the engine or at the timing belt end of the engine. The dipstick extends through a metal tube down into the oil pan.

3   The oil level should be checked before the vehicle has been driven, or about 15 minutes after the engine has been shut off. If the oil is checked immediately after driving the vehicle, some of the oil will remain in the upper part of the engine, resulting in an inaccurate reading on the dipstick.

4   Pull the dipstick from the tube and wipe all the oil from the end with a clean rag or paper towel. Insert the clean dipstick all the way back into the tube and pull it out again. Note the oil at the end of the dipstick. At its highest point, the level should be above the L or ADD mark, in the SAFE range **(see illustration)**.

5   It takes one quart of oil to raise the level from the L or ADD mark to the F or FULL mark. Do not allow the level to drop below the L or ADD mark, or oil starvation may cause engine damage. Conversely, overfilling the engine (adding oil above the F or FULL mark) may cause oil fouled spark plugs, oil leaks or oil seal failures.

6   To add oil, remove the filler cap located on the valve cover **(see illustration)**. After adding oil, wait a few minutes to allow the level to stabilize, then pull out the dipstick and check the level again. Add more oil if required. Install the filler cap and tighten it by hand only.

7   Checking the oil level is an important preventive maintenance step. A consistently low oil level indicates oil leakage through damaged seals, defective gaskets or worn rings or valve guides. The condition of the oil

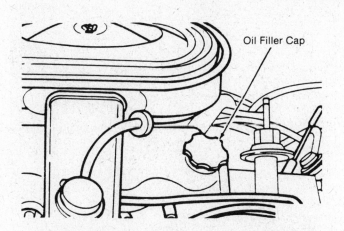

4.6 Turn the oil filler cap counterclockwise to remove it – always make sure the area around the opening is clean before unscrewing the cap (to prevent dirt from contaminating the engine)

4.8 The coolant reservoir is clearly marked with LOW and FULL marks – make sure the level is slightly above the LOW mark when the engine is cold and at or near the FULL mark when the engine is warmed up

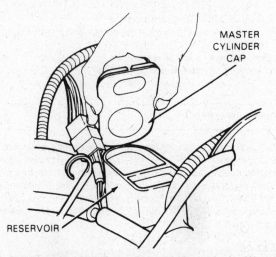

4.15 The brake fluid level should be within 1/4-inch of the top of the cast-iron reservoir – pry back the cover clip and lift off the cover and gasket to check the fluid level

should also be checked. If the oil looks milky in color or has water droplets in it, the cylinder head gasket may be blown or the head or block may be cracked. The engine should be checked immediately. Whenever you check the oil level, slide your thumb and index finger up the dipstick before wiping off the oil. If you see small dirt or metal particles clinging to the dipstick, the oil should be changed (see Section 8).

Engine coolant

Refer to illustration 4.8

Warning: *Do not allow antifreeze to come in contact with your skin or painted surfaces of the vehicle. Flush contaminated areas immediately with plenty of water. Do not store new coolant or leave old coolant lying around where it's accessible to children or pets – they are attracted by its sweet smell. Ingestion of even a small amount of coolant can be fatal! Wipe up garage floor and drip pan coolant spills immediately. Keep antifreeze containers covered and repair leaks in your cooling system immediately.*

8   All vehicles covered by this manual are equipped with a pressurized coolant recovery system. A white plastic coolant reservoir located in the right front corner of the engine compartment is connected by a hose to the radiator filler neck. The coolant and windshield washer reservoirs on some

models are very close to each other, so always be sure to add only the correct fluids to each; the filler caps are clearly marked **(see illustration)**. If the engine overheats, coolant escapes through a valve in the radiator cap and travels through the hose into the reservoir. As the engine cools, the coolant is automatically drawn back into the cooling system to maintain the correct level.

9   The coolant level in the reservoir should be checked regularly. **Warning:** *Do not remove the radiator cap to check the coolant level when the engine is warm.* The level in the reservoir varies with the temperature of the engine. When the engine is cold, the coolant level should be at or slightly above the LOW mark on the reservoir. Once the engine has warmed up, the level should be at or near the FULL mark. If it isn't, allow the engine to cool, then remove the cap from the reservoir and add a 50/50 mixture of ethylene glycol-based antifreeze and water.

10   Drive the vehicle and recheck the coolant level. Do not use rust inhibitors or additives. If only a small amount of coolant is required to bring the system up to the proper level, water can be used. However, repeated additions of water will dilute the antifreeze and water solution. In order to maintain the proper ratio of antifreeze and water, always top up the coolant level with the correct mixture. An empty plastic milk jug or bleach bottle makes an excellent container for mixing coolant.

11   If the coolant level drops consistently, there may be a leak in the system. Inspect the radiator, hoses, filler cap, drain plugs and water pump (see Section 18). If no leaks are noted, have the radiator cap pressure tested by a service station.

12   If you have to remove the radiator cap, wait until the engine has cooled completely, then wrap a thick cloth around the cap and turn it to the first stop. If coolant or steam escapes, let the engine cool down longer, then remove the cap.

13   Check the condition of the coolant as well. It should be relatively clear. If it is brown or rust colored, the system should be drained, flushed and refilled. Even if the coolant appears to be normal, the corrosion inhibitors wear out, so it must be replaced at the specified intervals.

Brake fluid

Refer to illustrations 4.15 and 4.16

14   The master cylinder is mounted in the left rear corner of the engine compartment.

15   If the master cylinder has a cast-iron reservoir, carefully clean all dirt from the outside of the master cylinder. Pull or pry the spring clip off the cover, then lift the cover and gasket off of the cylinder **(see illustration)**. Fluid level should be within 1/4-inch of the top of the reservoir.

4.16   The brake fluid level should be kept between the MIN and MAX marks on the translucent plastic reservoir – unscrew the cap to add fluid

4.22b   The front windshield washer fluid reservoir on later models is at the rear of the engine compartment

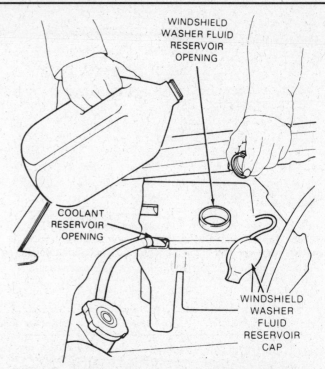

4.22a   The front windshield washer fluid reservoir on early models is at the right front corner of the engine compartment – be careful not to confuse it with the coolant reservoir

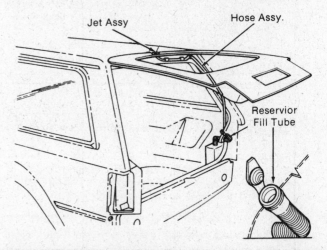

4.23a   The rear windshield washer reservoir on four-door station wagons is located on the right side of the luggage area – add fluid through the fill tube

16   If the master cylinder has a plastic reservoir, the fluid level should be between the MAX and MIN lines on the side of the reservoir **(see illustration)**. If the fluid level is low, wipe the top of the reservoir and the cap with a clean rag to prevent contamination of the system as the cap is unscrewed.

17   Add only the specified brake fluid to the reservoir (see Recommended lubricants and fluids at the front of this Chapter or your owner's manual). Mixing different types of brake fluid can damage the system. Fill the reservoir to the MAX line (plastic reservoir) or to 1/4-inch of the top of the reservoir (cast-iron reservoir). **Warning:** *Brake fluid can harm your eyes and damage painted surfaces, so use extreme caution when handling or pouring it. Do not use brake fluid that has been standing open or is more than one year old. Brake fluid absorbs moisture from the air. Excess moisture can cause damage to the braking system.*

18   While the reservoir cap or cap is off, check the master cylinder reservoir for contamination. If rust deposits, dirt particles or water droplets are present, the system should be drained and refilled by a dealer service department or repair shop.

19   After filling the reservoir to the proper level, make sure the cap or cover is seated to prevent fluid leakage and/or contamination.

20   The fluid level in the master cylinder will drop slightly as the brake shoes or pads at each wheel wear down during normal operation. If the brake fluid level drops significantly, check the entire system for leaks im-

mediately. Examine all brake lines, hoses and connections, along with the calipers, wheel cylinders and master cylinder (see Section 22).

21   When checking the fluid level, if you discover one or both reservoirs empty or nearly empty, the brake system should be bled (see Chapter 9).

Windshield washer fluid

Refer to illustrations 4.22a, 4.22b, 4.23a and 4.23b

22   The front windshield washer fluid reservoir is mounted in the engine compartment. On early models, it's next to the coolant reservoir; on later models, it's mounted on the firewall side of the engine compartment **(see illustrations)**.

23   The rear windshield washer on four-door station wagons is in the right rear corner of the luggage area **(see illustration)**. On hatchback models, the reservoir is in the left rear corner of the luggage area **(see illustration)**. Add fluid when necessary through the filler hose.

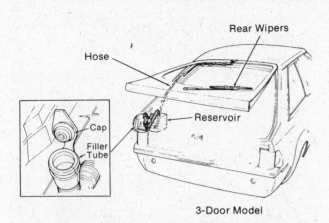

4.23b The rear windshield washer reservoir on hatchbacks is located on the left side of the luggage area – add fluid through the filler tube

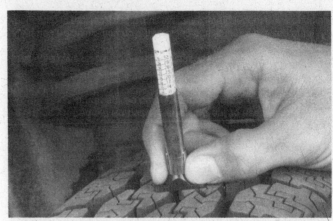

5.2 A tread depth indicator should be used to monitor tire wear – they are available at auto parts stores and service stations and cost very little

Condition	Probable cause	Corrective action	Condition	Probable cause	Corrective action
Shoulder wear	• Underinflation (both sides wear) • Incorrect wheel camber (one side wear) • Hard cornering • Lack of rotation	• Measure and adjust pressure. • Repair or replace axle and suspension parts. • Reduce speed. • Rotate tires.	Feathered edge Toe wear	• Incorrect toe	• Adjust toe-in.
Center wear	• Overinflation • Lack of rotation	• Measure and adjust pressure. • Rotate tires.	Uneven wear	• Incorrect camber or caster • Malfunctioning suspension • Unbalanced wheel • Out-of-round brake drum • Lack of rotation	• Repair or replace axle and suspension parts. • Repair or replace suspension parts. • Balance or replace. • Turn or replace. • Rotate tires.

5.3 This chart will help you determine the condition of your tires, the probable cause(s) of abnormal wear and the corrective action necessary

24 In milder climates, plain water can be used in the reservoir, but it should be kept no more than 2/3 full to allow for expansion if the water freezes. In colder climates, use windshield washer system antifreeze, available at any auto parts store, to lower the freezing point of the fluid. Mix the antifreeze with water in accordance with the manufacturer's directions on the container. **Caution:** *Do not use cooling system antifreeze – it will damage the vehicle's paint.*

5 Tire and tire pressure checks

Refer to illustrations 5.2, 5.3, 5.4a, 5.4b and 5.8

1   Periodic inspection of the tires may spare you the inconvenience of being stranded with a flat tire. It can also provide you with vital information regarding possible problems in the steering and suspension systems before major damage occurs.

2   The original tires on this vehicle are equipped with 1/2-inch side bands that will appear when tread depth reaches 1/16-inch, but they don't appear until the tires are worn out. Tread wear can be monitored with a simple, inexpensive device known as a tread depth indicator (**see illustration**).

3   Note any abnormal tread wear (**see illustration**). Tread pattern irregularities such as cupping, flat spots and more wear on one side than the other are indications of front end alignment and/or balance problems. If any of these conditions are noted, take the vehicle to a tire shop or service station to correct the problem.

4   Look closely for cuts, punctures and embedded nails or tacks. Sometimes a tire will hold air pressure for a short time or leak down very slowly after a nail has embedded itself in the tread. If a slow leak persists, check

5.4a   If a tire loses air on a steady basis, check the valve core first to make sure it's snug (special inexpensive wrenches are commonly available at auto parts stores)

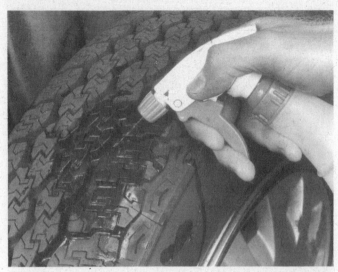

5.4b   If the valve core is tight, raise the corner of the vehicle with the low tire and spray a soapy water solution onto the tread as the tire is turned slowly – slow leaks will cause bubbles to appear

5.8   To extend the life of the tires, check the air pressure at least once a week with an accurate gauge (don't forget the spare!)

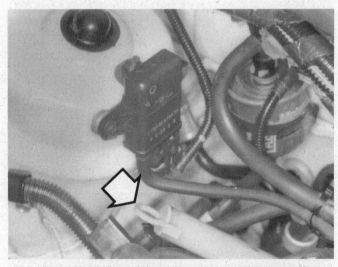

6.2   Remove the dipstick from the power steering reservoir to check the fluid level – add fluid through the same tube the dipstick was removed from

the valve stem core to make sure it is tight **(see illustration)**. Examine the tread for an object that may have embedded itself in the tire or for a "plug" that may have begun to leak (radial tire punctures are repaired with a plug that is installed in the puncture). If a puncture is suspected, it can be easily verified by spraying a solution of soapy water onto the puncture area **(see illustration)**. The soapy solution will bubble if there is a leak. Unless the puncture is unusually large, a tire shop or service station can normally repair the tire.

5   Carefully inspect the inner sidewall of each tire for evidence of brake fluid leakage. If you see any, inspect the brakes immediately.

6   Correct air pressure adds miles to the lifespan of the tires, improves mileage and enhances overall ride quality. Tire pressure cannot be accurately estimated by looking at a tire, especially if it's a radial. A tire pressure gauge is essential. Keep an accurate gauge in the glovebox. The pressure gauges attached to the nozzles of air hoses at gas stations are often inaccurate.

7   Always check tire pressure when the tires are cold. Cold, in this case, means the vehicle has not been driven over a mile in the three hours preceding a tire pressure check. A pressure rise of four to eight pounds is not uncommon once the tires are warm.

8   Unscrew the valve cap protruding from the wheel or hubcap and push the gauge firmly onto the valve stem **(see illustration)**. Note the reading on the gauge and compare the figure to the recommended tire pressure shown on the tire placard on the driver's side door. Be sure to reinstall the valve cap to keep dirt and moisture out of the valve stem mechanism. Check all four tires and, if necessary, add enough air to bring them up to the recommended pressure.

9   Don't forget to keep the spare tire inflated to the specified pressure (see your owner's manual or the tire sidewall). Note that the pressure recommended for the compact spare is higher than for the tires on the vehicle.

6   Power steering fluid level check

Refer to illustration 6.2

1   Check the power steering fluid level periodically to avoid steering system problems, such as damage to the pump. **Caution:** *DO NOT hold the steering wheel against either stop (extreme left or right turn) for more than five seconds. If you do, the power steering pump could be damaged.*

7.4   The automatic transaxle dipstick is located in a tube near the battery on some models

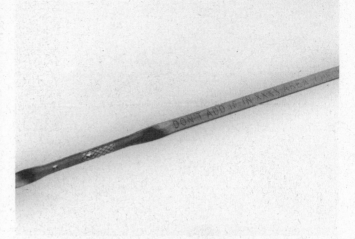

7.6   If the fluid in the transaxle is cold, the level should be between the two lower holes; if the fluid is hot, it should be between the two upper holes

2   The power steering reservoir, located at the right rear corner of the engine compartment, has a dipstick with separate scales for a hot or cold engine **(see illustration)**.
3   Park the vehicle on level ground and apply the parking brake.
4   Run the engine until it has reached normal operating temperature. With the engine at idle, turn the steering wheel back and forth about 10 times to get any air out of the steering system. Shut the engine off with the wheels in the straight ahead position.
5   Note the fluid level on the HOT side of the dipstick. It must be in the FULL HOT range.
6   Add small amounts of fluid until the level is correct. **Caution:** *Do not overfill the reservoir. If too much fluid is added, remove the excess with a clean syringe or suction pump.*
7   Check the power steering hoses and connections for leaks and wear (see Section 10).
8   Check the condition and tension of the power steering pump drivebelt (see Section 11).

7   Automatic transaxle fluid level check

Refer to illustrations 7.4 and 7.6

1   The automatic transaxle fluid level should be carefully maintained. Low fluid level can lead to slipping or loss of drive, while overfilling can cause foaming and loss of fluid. Either condition can cause transaxle damage.
2   Since transmission fluid expands as it heats up, the fluid level should only be checked when the transaxle is warm (at normal operating temperature). If the vehicle has just been driven over 20 miles (32 km), the transaxle can be considered warm. **Caution:** *If the vehicle has just been driven for a long time at high speed or in city traffic in hot weather, or if it has been pulling a trailer, an accurate fluid level reading cannot be obtained. Allow the transaxle to cool down for about 30 minutes.* You can also check the transaxle fluid level when the transaxle is cold. If the vehicle has not been driven for over five hours and the fluid is about room temperature (70 to 95-degrees F), the transaxle is cold. However, the fluid level is normally checked with the transaxle warm to ensure accurate results.
3   Immediately after driving the vehicle, park it on a level surface, set the parking brake and start the engine. While the engine is idling, depress the brake pedal and move the selector lever through all the gear ranges, beginning and ending in Park.
4   Locate the automatic transaxle dipstick in the engine compartment **(see illustration)**. On later 1.9L EFI HO models, the dipstick is under the air filter at the left front corner of the engine compartment.

5   With the engine still idling, pull the dipstick from the tube, wipe it off with a clean rag, push it all the way back into the tube and withdraw it again, then note the fluid level.
6   If the transaxle is cold, the indicated level should be between the two lower holes; if the transaxle is hot, the fluid level should be between the two upper holes or lines **(see illustration)**. If the level is low, add the specified automatic transmission fluid through the dipstick tube. Use a funnel to prevent spills.
7   Add just enough of the recommended fluid to fill the transaxle to the proper level. It takes about one pint to raise the level from the lower to the upper hole when the fluid is hot, so add the fluid a little at a time and keep checking the level until it's correct.
8   The condition of the fluid should also be checked along with the level. If the fluid is black or a dark reddish-brown color, or if it smells burned, it should be changed (see Section 29). If you are in doubt about its condition, purchase some new fluid and compare the two for color and smell.

18   Engine oil and filter change

Refer to illustrations 8.2, 8.7, 8.12 and 8.16

1   Frequent oil changes are among the most important preventive maintenance procedures that can be done by the home mechanic. As engine oil ages, it becomes diluted and contaminated, which leads to premature engine wear. Although some sources recommend oil filter changes every other oil change, a new filter should be installed every time the oil is changed.
2   Make sure that you have all the necessary tools before you begin this procedure **(see illustration)**. You should also have plenty of rags or newspapers handy for mopping up oil spills.
3   Access to the oil drain plug and filter will be improved if the vehicle can be lifted on a hoist, driven onto ramps or supported by jackstands. **Warning:** *Do not work under a vehicle supported only by a bumper, hydraulic or scissors-type jack – always use jackstands!*
4   If you haven't changed the oil on this vehicle before, get under it and locate the oil drain plug and the oil filter. The exhaust components will be hot as you work, so note how they are routed to avoid touching them when you are under the vehicle.
5   Start the engine and allow it to reach normal operating temperature – oil and sludge will flow out more easily when warm. Park on a level surface and shut off the engine when it's warmed up. Remove the oil filler cap.
6   Raise the vehicle and support it on jackstands. Make sure it is safely supported!

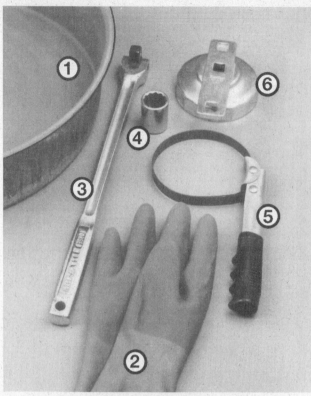

8.2   These tools are required when changing the engine oil and filter

1   *Drain pan* – *It should be fairly shallow in depth, but wide to prevent spills*
2   *Rubber gloves* – *When removing the drain plug and filter, you will get oil on your hands (the gloves will prevent burns)*
3   *Breaker bar* – *Sometimes the oil drain plug is tight and a long breaker bar is needed to loosen it*
4   *Socket* – *To be used with the breaker bar or a ratchet (must be the correct size to fit the drain plug – six-point preferred)*
5   *Filter wrench* – *This is a metal band-type wrench, which requires clearance around the filter to be effective*
6   *Filter wrench* – *This type fits on the bottom of the filter and can be turned with a ratchet or breaker bar (different size wrenches are available for different types of filters)*

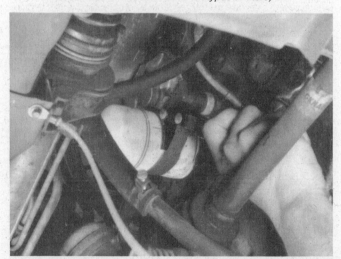

8.12   The oil filter is usually on very tight and will require a special wrench for removal – DO NOT use the wrench to tighten the new filter!

8.7   Use a box-end wrench or six-point socket to remove the oil drain plug without rounding it off

8.16   Lubricate the oil filter gasket with clean engine oil before installing the filter on the engine

7   Being careful not to touch the hot exhaust components, position a drain pan under the plug in the bottom of the engine oil pan **(see illustration)**, then remove the plug. It's a good idea to wear an old glove while unscrewing the plug the final few turns to avoid being scalded by hot oil.
8   It may be necessary to move the drain pan slightly as oil flow slows to a trickle. Inspect the old oil for the presence of metal particles.
9   After all the oil has drained, wipe off the drain plug with a clean rag. Any small metal particles clinging to the plug would immediately contaminate the new oil.
10   Clean the area around the drain plug opening, reinstall the plug and tighten it securely, being careful not to strip the threads.
11   Move the drain pan into position under the oil filter, located on the rear (firewall side) of the engine.
12   Loosen the oil filter by turning it counterclockwise with a filter wrench **(see illustration)**. Any standard filter wrench will work.
13   Sometimes the oil filter is screwed on so tightly that it cannot be loosened. If it is, punch a metal bar or long screwdriver directly through it, as close to the engine as possible, and use it as a lever to turn the filter. Be prepared for oil to spurt out of the canister as it is punctured.
14   Once the filter is loose, use your hands to unscrew it from the block. Just as the filter is detached from the block, immediately tilt the open end up to prevent the oil inside the filter from spilling out. **Warning:** *The engine exhaust manifold and exhaust system components may still be hot, so be careful.*

15   Using a clean rag, wipe off the mounting surface on the block. Make sure the old gasket does not remain stuck to the mounting surface.

16   Compare the old filter with the new one to make sure they are the same type. Smear some engine oil on the rubber gasket of the new filter and screw it into place **(see illustration)**. Overtightening the filter will damage the gasket, so don't use a filter wrench. Most filter manufacturers recommend tightening the filter by hand only. Normally they should be tightened 3/4-turn after the gasket contacts the block, but be sure to follow the directions on the filter or container.

17   Remove all tools and materials from under the vehicle, being careful not to spill the oil in the drain pan, then lower the vehicle.

18   Add 3-1/2 quarts of new oil to the engine (see Section 4 if necessary). Use a funnel to prevent oil from spilling onto the top of the engine. Wait a few minutes to allow the oil to drain into the pan, then check the level on the dipstick. If the oil level is in the SAFE range, install the filler cap.

19   Start the engine and run it for about a minute. While the engine is running, look under the vehicle and check for leaks at the oil pan drain plug and around the oil filter. If either one is leaking, stop the engine and tighten the plug or filter slightly.

20   Stop the engine, wait a few minutes, then recheck the level on the dipstick. Add oil as necessary to bring the level into the SAFE range.

21   During the first few trips after an oil change, make it a point to check frequently for leaks and proper oil level.

22   The old oil drained from the engine cannot be reused in its present state and should be discarded. Oil reclamation centers, auto repair shops and gas stations will normally accept the oil, which can be recycled. After the oil has cooled, it can be drained into a container (plastic jugs, bottles, milk cartons, etc.) for transport to a disposal site.

---

9   Clutch pedal adjustment

The clutch on these models is self-adjusting. There is no means of manual adjustment. Excessive clutch pedal effort, failure of the clutch to disengage or noise from the adjuster indicates worn or damaged parts. Refer to Chapter 8 for repair procedures.

---

10   Underhood hose check and replacement

Warning: *Replacement of air conditioning hoses must be left to a dealer service department or air conditioning shop that has the equipment to depressurize the system safely. Never remove air conditioning components or hoses until the system has been depressurized.*

General

1   High temperatures under the hood can cause the deterioration of the rubber and plastic hoses used for engine, accessory and emission systems operation. Inspect the hoses periodically for cracks, loose clamps, material hardening and leaks.

2   Information specific to the cooling system hoses can be found in Section 18.

3   Most (but not all) hoses are secured to the fittings with clamps. Where clamps are used, check to be sure they haven't lost their tension, allowing the hose to leak. If clamps aren't used, make sure the hose has not expanded and/or hardened where it slips over the fitting, allowing it to leak.

PCV system hose

4   To reduce hydrocarbon emissions, crankcase blow-by gas on most models is vented through the PCV valve in the valve cover to the intake manifold via a rubber hose. The blow-by gases mix with incoming air in the intake manifold before being burned in the combustion chambers.

5   Check the PCV hose for cracks, leaks and other damage. Disconnect it from the valve cover and the intake manifold and check the inside for obstructions. If it's clogged, clean it out with solvent.

Vacuum hoses

6   It is quite common for vacuum hoses, especially those in the emissions system, to be color coded or identified by colored stripes molded into each hose. Various systems require hoses with different wall thicknesses, collapse resistance and temperature resistance. When replacing hoses, be sure the new ones are made of the same material.

7   Often the only effective way to check a hose is to remove it completely from the vehicle. If more than one hose is removed, be sure to label the hoses and fittings to ensure correct installation.

8   When checking vacuum hoses, be sure to include any plastic T-fittings in the check. Inspect the fittings for cracks and the hose where it fits over each fitting for distortion, which could cause leakage.

9   A small piece of vacuum hose (1/4-inch inside diameter) can be used as a stethoscope to detect vacuum leaks. Hold one end of the hose to your ear and probe around vacuum hoses and fittings, listening for the "hissing" sound characteristic of a vacuum leak. **Warning:** *When probing with the vacuum hose stethoscope, be careful not to allow your body or the hose to come into contact with moving engine components such as drivebelts, the cooling fan, etc.*

Fuel hose

Warning: *Gasoline is extremely flammable, so take extra precautions when you work on any part of the fuel system. Don't smoke or allow open flames or bare light bulbs near the work area, and don't work in a garage where a natural gas-type appliance (such as a water heater or clothes dryer) with a pilot light is present. If you spill any fuel on your skin, rinse it off immediately with soap and water. When you perform any kind of work on the fuel system, wear safety glasses and have a Class B type fire extinguisher on hand. The fuel system on fuel-injected models is under pressure. You must relieve this pressure before servicing the fuel lines. Refer to Chapter 4 for the fuel pressure relief procedure.*

10   Check all rubber fuel lines for deterioration and chafing. Check especially for cracks in areas where the hose bends and just before fittings, such as where a hose attaches to the fuel tank, fuel filter or a fuel injection component.

11   If any fuel lines show damage, deterioration or wear, they should be replaced (see Chapter 4). Be sure to use fuel line that is designed for use in fuel injection systems and is an exact duplicate of the original.

12   Spring-type clamps are commonly used on fuel lines. These clamps often lose their tension over a period of time, and can be "sprung" during the removal process. As a result, it is recommended that all spring-type clamps be replaced with screw clamps whenever a hose is replaced.

Metal lines

13   Sections of metal line are often used for the fuel line between the fuel pump and fuel injection unit. Check carefully to be sure the line has not been bent and crimped and that cracks have not started in the line, particularly where bends occur.

14   If a section of metal fuel line must be replaced, use seamless steel tubing only, since copper and aluminum tubing do not have the strength necessary to withstand vibration caused by the engine.

Warning: *The fuel system pressure must be relieved before any fuel lines can be replaced* (see Chapter 4).

15   Check the metal brake lines where they enter the master cylinder and brake proportioning unit (if used) for cracks in the lines and loose fittings. Any sign of brake fluid leakage calls for an immediate thorough inspection of the brake system.

---

11   Drivebelt check, adjustment and replacement

---

1   The accessory drivebelts, also referred to as V-belts or simply fan belts, are located at the right end of the engine. The condition and tension of the drivebelts are critical to the operation of the engine and accessories. Excessive tension causes bearing wear, while insufficient tension produces slippage, noise, component vibration and belt failure. Because of their composition and the high stresses to which they are subjected, drivebelts stretch and deteriorate as they get older. As a result, they must be periodically checked and adjusted.

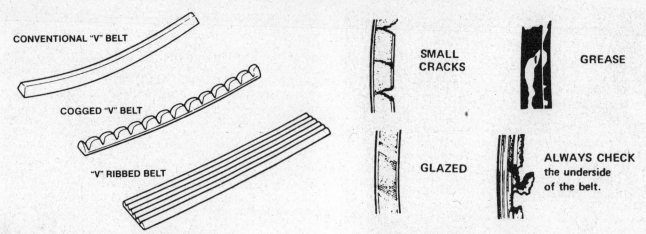

11.2   Different types of drivebelts are used to power the various accessories mounted on the engine

11.3   Here are some of the common problems associated with drivebelts (check the belts very carefully to prevent an untimely breakdown)

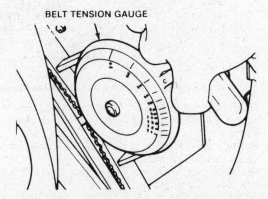

11.4   A drivebelt tension gauge is recommended for checking the belts (the unit illustrated is a Burroughs model – follow the tool manufacturer's instructions)

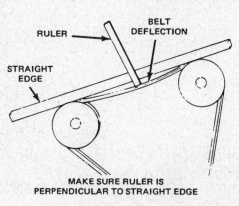

11.5   Measuring drivebelt deflection with a straightedge and ruler

Check

Refer to illustrations 11.2, 11.3, 11.4 and 11.5

2   The number and type of belts used on a particular vehicle depends on the accessories installed **(see illustration)**.

3   With the engine off, open the hood and locate the drivebelts at the right end of the engine. With a flashlight, check each belt for separation of the rubber plies from each side of the core, a severed core, separation of the ribs from the rubber, cracks, torn or worn ribs and cracks in the inner ridges of the ribs. Also check for fraying and glazing, which give belts a shiny appearance **(see illustration)**. Both sides of each belt should be inspected, which means you'll have to twist them to check the undersides. Use your fingers to feel a belt where you can't see it. If any of the above conditions are evident, replace the belt as described below.

4   To check the tension of each belt in accordance with factory recommendations, install a drivebelt tension gauge (special tool no. T63L-8620-A or equivalent) **(see illustration)**. Measure the tension in accordance with the tension gauge instructions and compare your measurement to the figure listed in this Chapter's Specifications for a used belt. **Note:** *A "new" belt is defined as any belt which has not been run; a "used" belt is one that has been run for more than ten minutes.*

5   The special gauge is the most accurate way to check belt tension. However, if you don't have a gauge, and cannot borrow one, the following "rule-of-thumb" method is recommended as an alternative for V-belts. Lay a straightedge across the longest free span (the distance between two pulleys) of the belt. Push down firmly on the belt at a point half way between the pulleys and see how much the belt moves (deflects). Measure the deflection with a ruler **(see illustration)**. The belt should deflect 1/8 to 1/4-inch if the distance from pulley center-to-pulley center is less than 12-inches; it should deflect from 1/8 to 3/8-inch if the distance from pulley center-to-pulley center is over 12-inches.

Adjustment

Refer to illustrations 11.8a and 11.8b

6   All drivebelts require periodic adjustment. To adjust, move the belt-driven accessory on the bracket.

7   For each accessory, there will be a locking bolt and a pivot bolt or nut. Both must be loosened slightly to enable you to move the component. **Note:** *On all air conditioned models, the alternator belt also drives the air conditioning compressor. This belt is adjusted by moving the alternator.*

8   After the two bolts have been loosened **(see illustrations)**, move the component as needed to tighten or loosen the bolt. Many accessories are equipped with a square hole designed to accept a 1/2-inch square drive breaker bar. The bar can be used to lever the component and tension the drivebelt. Others have a cast lug which is designed to accept an open-end wrench, which can be used to pry the accessory. **Caution:** *The high-mount air pump used on models equipped with a 1.6L engine and power steering is adjusted with hand pressure only. Do not pry against it.* Whenever it's necessary to pry against an accessory to tighten a drivebelt, be very careful not to damage the accessory or the point the prybar rests against.

9   Hold the accessory in position and check the belt tension. If it's correct, tighten the two bolts until snug, then recheck the tension. If it's alright, tighten the two bolts completely.

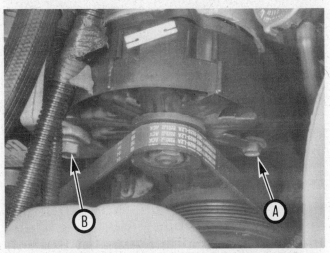

11.8a   Alternator adjustment (A) and pivot (B) bolts

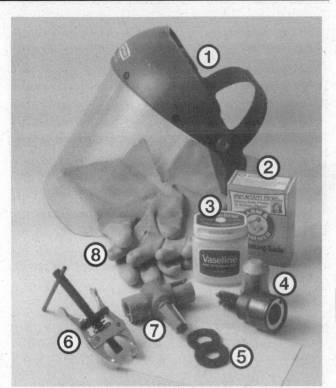

12.1   Tools and materials required for battery maintenance

1   *Face shield/safety goggles* – *When removing corrosion with a brush, the acidic particles can easily fly up into your eyes*
2   *Baking soda* – *A solution of baking soda and water can be used to neutralize corrosion*
3   *Petroleum jelly* – *A layer of this on the battery posts will help prevent corrosion*
4   *Battery post/cable cleaner* – *This wire brush cleaning tool will remove all traces of corrosion from the battery posts and cable clamps*
5   *Treated felt washers* – *Placing one of these on each post, directly under the cable clamps, will help prevent corrosion*
6   *Puller* – *Sometimes the cable clamps are very difficult to pull off the posts, even after the nut/bolt has been completely loosened. This tool pulls the clamp straight up and off the post without damage.*
7   *Battery post/cable cleaner* – *Here is another cleaning tool which is a slightly different version of number 4 above, but it does the same thing*
8   *Rubber gloves* – *Another safety item to consider when servicing the battery; remember that's acid inside the battery!*

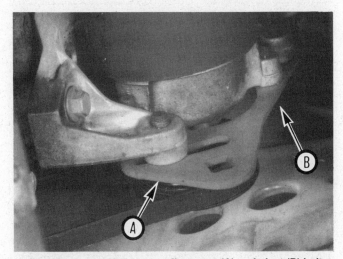

11.8b   Power steering pump adjustment (A) and pivot (B) bolts

Replacement

10   To replace a belt, follow the above procedures for drivebelt adjustment, but slip the belt off the pulleys and remove it. Since belts tend to wear out more or less at the same time, it's a good idea to replace all of them at the same time. Mark each belt and the corresponding pulley grooves so the replacement belts can be installed properly.

11   Take the old belts with you when purchasing new ones in order to make a direct comparison for length, width and design.

12   When replacing a V-ribbed drivebelt (the wide one used to drive the power steering pump and air conditioning compressor), make sure that it fits properly into the pulley grooves – it must be completely engaged and ride in the center of each pulley.

13   Adjust the belts as described earlier in this Section.

---

12   Battery check, maintenance and charging

Warning: *Certain precautions must be followed when checking and servicing the battery. Hydrogen gas, which is highly flammable, is always present in the battery cells, so keep lighted tobacco and all other open flames and sparks away from the battery. The electrolyte inside the battery is actually dilute sulfuric acid, which will cause injury if splashed on your skin or in your eyes. It will also ruin clothes and painted surfaces. When removing the battery cables, always detach the negative cable first and hook it up last!*

Check and maintenance

Refer to illustrations 12.1, 12.8a, 12.8b, 12.8c and 12.8d

1   Battery maintenance is an important procedure which will help ensure that you are not stranded because of a dead battery. Several tools are required for this procedure **(see illustration)**.

2   Before servicing the battery, always turn the engine and all accessories off and disconnect the cable from the negative terminal of the battery.

3   A sealed (sometimes called maintenance-free) battery is standard equipment on the these models. The cell caps cannot be removed, no electrolyte checks are required and water cannot be added to the cells. However, if an aftermarket battery has been installed and it is a type that requires regular maintenance, the following procedure can be used.

4   Check the electrolyte level in each of the battery cells. It must be above the plates. There's usually a split-ring indicator in each cell to indicate the correct level. If the level is low, add distilled water only, then install the cell caps. **Caution:** *Overfilling the cells may cause electrolyte to spill*

12.8a   Battery terminal corrosion usually appears as light, fluffy powder

12.8b   Removing the cable from a battery post with a wrench – sometimes a special battery pliers is required for this procedure if corrosion has caused deterioration of the nut hex (always remove the ground cable first and hook it up last!)

12.8c   Regardless of the type of tool used on the battery posts, a clean, shiny surface should be the result

12.8d   When cleaning the cable clamps, all corrosion must be removed (the inside of the clamp is tapered to match the taper on the post, so don't remove too much material)

over during periods of heavy charging, causing corrosion and damage to nearby components.

5   If the positive terminal and cable clamp on your vehicle's battery is equipped with a rubber protector, make sure that it's not torn or damaged. It should completely cover the terminal.

6   The external condition of the battery should be checked periodically. Look for damage such as a cracked case.

7   Check the tightness of the battery cable clamps to ensure good electrical connections and inspect the entire length of each cable, looking for cracked or abraded insulation and frayed conductors.

8   If corrosion (visible as white, fluffy deposits) is evident, remove the cables from the terminals, clean them with a battery brush and reinstall them **(see illustrations)**. Corrosion can be kept to a minimum by installing specially treated washers available at auto parts stores or by applying a layer of petroleum jelly or grease to the terminals and cable clamps after they are assembled.

9   Make sure that the battery carrier is in good condition and that the hold-down clamp bolt is tight. If the battery is removed (see Chapter 5 for the removal and installation procedure), make sure that no parts remain in the bottom of the carrier when it's reinstalled. When reinstalling the hold-down clamp, don't overtighten the bolt.

10   Corrosion on the carrier, battery case and surrounding areas can be removed with a solution of water and baking soda. Apply the mixture with a small brush, let it work, then rinse it off with plenty of clean water.

11   Any metal parts of the vehicle damaged by corrosion should be coated with a zinc-based primer, then painted.

Charging

12   Remove all of the cell caps (if equipped) and cover the holes with a clean cloth to prevent spattering electrolyte. Disconnect the negative battery cable and hook the battery charger leads to the battery posts (positive to positive, negative to negative), then plug in the charger. Make sure it is set at 12 volts if it has a selector switch.

13   If you're using a charger with a rate higher than two amps, check the battery regularly during charging to make sure it doesn't overheat. If you're using a trickle charger, you can safely let the battery charge overnight after you've checked it regularly for the first couple of hours.

14   If the battery has removeable cell caps, measure the specific gravity with a hydrometer every hour during the last few hours of the charging cycle. Hydrometers are available inexpensively from auto parts stores – follow the instructions that come with the hydrometer. Consider the battery charged when there's no change in the specific gravity reading for two hours and the electrolyte in the cells is gassing (bubbling) freely. The specific gravity reading from each cell should be very close to the others. If not, the battery probably has a bad cell(s).

15   Some batteries with sealed tops have built-in hydrometers on the top that indicate the state of charge by the color displayed in the hydrometer window. Normally, a bright-colored hydrometer indicates a full charge and a dark hydrometer indicates the battery still needs charging. Check the battery manufacturer's instructions to be sure you know what the colors mean.

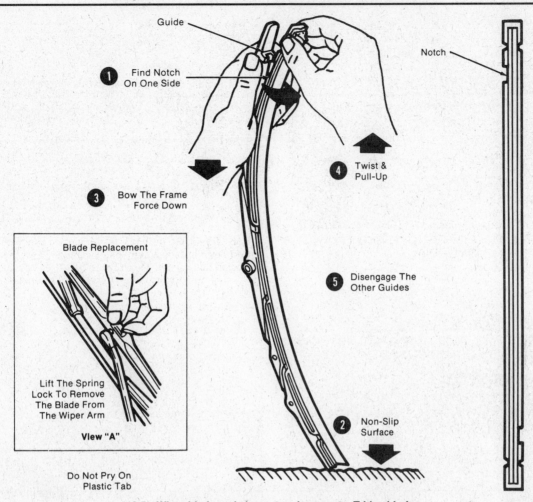

13.5   Wiper blade and element replacement – Tridon blades

16   If the battery has a sealed top and no built-in hydrometer, you can hook up a digital voltmeter across the battery terminals to check the charge. A fully charged battery should read 12.6 volts or higher.

17   Further information on the battery and jump starting can be found in Chapter 5 and at the front of this manual.

13   Windshield wiper blade check and replacement

1   Road film can build up on the wiper blades and affect their efficiency, so they should be washed regularly with a mild detergent solution.

Check

2   The windshield wiper and blade assembly should be inspected periodically for damage, loose components and cracked or worn blade elements. The action of the wiping mechanism can loosen bolts, nuts and fasteners, so they should be checked and tightened, as necessary, at the same time the wiper blades are checked.

3   If the wiper blade elements are cracked, worn or warped, or no longer clean adequately, they should be replaced with new ones.

Blade assembly replacement (Tridon blades)

Refer to illustration 13.5

4   Park the wiper blades in a convenient position to be worked on. To do this, run the wipers, then turn the ignition key to Off when the wiper blades reach the desired position.

5   Lift the blade slightly from the windshield. Pull up on the spring lock to release the blade **(see illustration)** and take the blade off. **Caution:** *Do not pull too hard on the spring lock or it will be distorted.*

6   Push the new blade assembly onto the arm pivot pin. Make sure the spring lock secures the blade to the pin.

Blade element replacement (Tridon blades)

7   Remove the wiper blade from the arm (see above).

8   Locate one of the 7/16-inch removal notches in the blade assembly. There is a notch at each end of the blade, approximately one inch from the end **(see illustration 13.5)**.

9   Stand the blade on a non-slippery surface, then press down on the upper end of the blade enough to bow it slightly. **Caution:** *Do not press down hard enough to break the blade.*

10   Take firm hold of the blade element's plastic backing strip. Pull up on the element and twist it counterclockwise at the same time, so the plastic backing strip snaps out of the retaining tab on the end of the blade.

11   Lift the blade off the surface and let it hang slack.

12   Slide the plastic backing strip down the blade until the removal notch aligns with the next retaining tab. Twist the element slightly to pop it out of the blade.

13   Repeat Step 12 with the remaining tabs to remove the blade.

14   To install, reverse Steps 12 and 13. Be sure the element engages all six retaining tabs in the wiper blade.

Blade assembly replacement (Trico blades)

Refer to illustration 13.17

15   Trico metal blades have a rectangular release hole above the wiper arm mounting pin.

16   Park the wiper blades in a convenient position to be worked on. To do this, run the wipers, then turn the ignition key to Off when the blades reach the desired position.

Trico—Tempo/Topaz/Escort

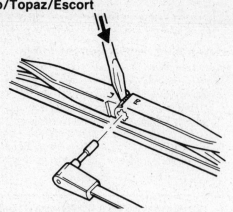

1. CYCLE ARM AND BLADE ASSEMBLY TO UP POSITION ON THE WINDSHIELD WHERE REMOVAL OF BLADE ASSEMBLY CAN BE PERFORMED WITHOUT DIFFICULTY. TURN IGNITION KEY OFF AT DESIRED POSITION.

2. TO REMOVE BLADE ASSEMBLY, INSERT SCREWDRIVER IN SLOT, PUSH DOWN ON SPRING LOCK AND PULL BLADE ASSEMBLY FROM PIN (VIEW A)

3. TO INSTALL, PUSH THE BLADE ASSEMBLY ON THE PIN SO THAT THE SPRING LOCK ENGAGES THE PIN (VIEW A). BE SURE THE BLADE ASSEMBLY IS SECURELY ATTACHED TO PIN.

VIEW A

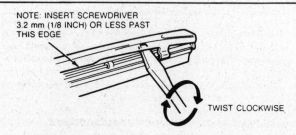

NOTE: INSERT SCREWDRIVER 3.2 mm (1/8 INCH) OR LESS PAST THIS EDGE

TWIST CLOCKWISE

ELEMENT REPLACEMENT

1. INSERT SCREWDRIVER BETWEEN THE EDGE OF THE SUPER STRUCTURE AND THE BLADE BACKING DRIP (VIEW B). TWIST SCREWDRIVER SLOWLY UNTIL ELEMENT CLEARS ONE SIDE OF THE SUPER STRUC-TURE CLAW.

2. SLIDE THE ELEMENT INTO THE SUPER STRUCTURE CLAWS.

VIEW B

4. INSERT ELEMENT INTO ONE SIDE OF THE END CLAWS (VIEW D) AND WITH A ROCKING MOTION PUSH ELEMENT UPWARD UNTIL IT SNAPS IN (VIEW E).

VIEW D

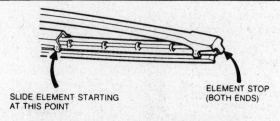

SLIDE ELEMENT STARTING AT THIS POINT

ELEMENT STOP (BOTH ENDS)

3. SLIDE THE ELEMENT INTO THE SUPER STRUCTURE CLAWS, STARTING WITH SECOND SET FROM EITHER END (VIEW C) AND CONTINUE TO SLIDE THE BLADE ELEMENT INTO ALL THE SUPER STRUCTURE CLAWS TO THE ELEMENT STOP (VIEW C).

VIEW C

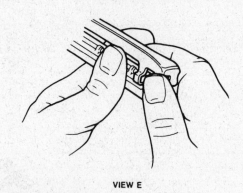

VIEW E

13.17   Wiper blade and element replacement – Trico blades

17   Let the blade assembly rest on the windshield and insert a small flat-bladed screwdriver into the release hole **(see illustration)**. Push down on the coil spring inside the hole and pull the wiper blade from the arm.
18   Push the new blade onto the pivot pin until it locks.

Blade element replacement (Trico blades)
19   Remove the wiper blade from the arm (see Step 17 above).
20   Insert a flat-bladed screwdriver 1/8-inch or less into the space be-tween the element and rubber backing strip **(see illustration 13.17)**. While pressing the screwdriver down and inward, twist it clockwise to sep-arate the element from the retaining tab.
21   Slide the element out of the other retaining tabs.
22   Slide the new element into four of the five retaining tabs. Twist the ele-ment into the fifth retaining tab to secure it.

23   Make sure the new element is secured by all five tabs, then install the wiper blade on the arm.

14   Air filter – replacement

1   The air filter cannot be cleaned. If it's dirty, replace it.

Carbureted and Central Fuel Injection (CFI) models
Refer to illustration 14.2
2   Remove the air cleaner housing cover wing nut(s) and grommet(s) **(see illustration)**. On CFI models, lift the cover off.
3   On carbureted models, remove the cover clips and cover. On all mod-els, lift the element out.

14.2   After removing the cover, lift the air cleaner element out

4   Check the inner sealing surface of the cover for evidence of leakage past the air filter. Place a light on the inside (clean side) of the filter and look through the filter at the light. If the light cannot be seen or if there are holes in the element, no matter how small, replace it with a new one.
5   Clean the inner sealing surface between the air filter housing and cover.
6   Before installing the new air filter, check it for deformed seals and holes in the paper. If the filter is marked TOP, be sure the marked side faces up.

7   To replace the crankcase ventilation filter, see Section 15.
8   Reverse Steps 2 and 3 to complete the installation.

Multi-point fuel injection models
Refer to illustration 14.9

9   Disconnect the air inlet hose from the air cleaner cover (models so equipped) **(see illustration)**.
10   Detach the air cleaner cover clips and remove the cover.
11   Lift the filter element out of the air cleaner.
12   Inspect and install as described in Steps 4 through 6 above.
13   Reverse Steps 9 through 11 to complete the installation. If one side of the filter element is marked TOP, make sure it is up.

---

15   Crankcase emission filter replacement and PCV valve check and replacement

---

1   Some models are not equipped with a PCV valve. If yours has a PCV valve, it will be mounted in the valve cover. Some models have a crankcase emission filter mounted in the air cleaner; others have the filter mounted in the oil filler cap. Still other models do not have a crankcase emission filter. To determine which type of crankcase emission filter you have (if any), look at your vehicle's engine.

Crankcase emission filter replacement
Filter in air cleaner
Refer to illustration 15.3

2   Remove the air cleaner cover (see Section 14).

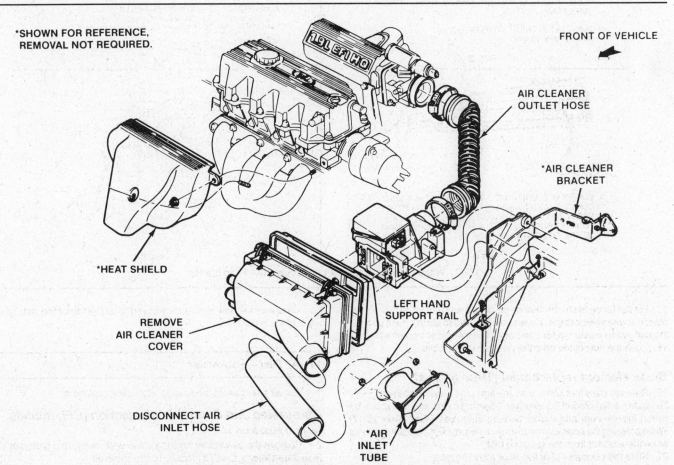

14.9   Air cleaner details – Multi-point fuel injection (HO models shown; others similar)

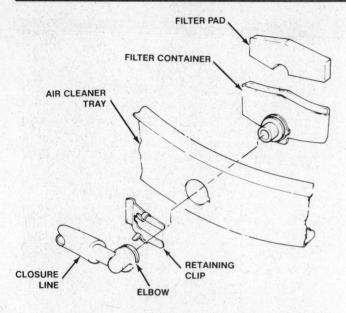

15.3   Typical crankcase emission filter installation details

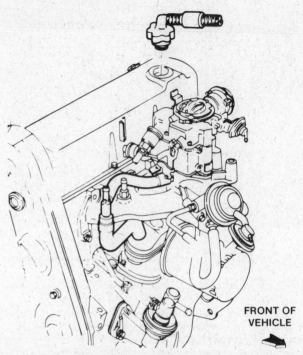

15.6   On some models, the crankcase ventilation filter is an integral part of the oil filler cap

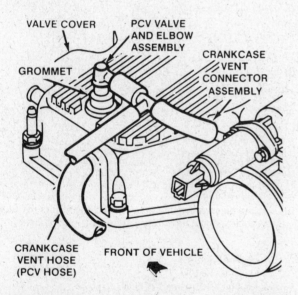

15.10   Pull the PCV valve out and shake it – a rattling sound indicates it is not clogged

3   Disconnect the hose from the filter pocket in the side of the air cleaner. Unclip the filter pocket from the air cleaner and take it out. Pull the old filter out of the pocket **(see illustration)**.
4   Wipe the inside of the pocket clean. Apply a light coat of clean engine oil to a new filter and install it in the pocket.
5   Install the pocket in the air cleaner, reconnect the hose and install the air cleaner cover.

Filter in oil filler cap

Refer to illustration 15.6
6   Disconnect the ventilation hose from the oil filler cap and air cleaner **(see illustration)**.
7   Unscrew the oil filler cap from the engine. The oil filler cap and ventilation filter are replaced as a unit.
8   Clean the hose with solvent.
9   Install the oil filler cap and filter assembly, then connect the hose.

PCV valve check and replacement

Refer to illustration 15.10
10   Pull the PCV valve out of the valve cover **(see illustration)**.
11   Shake the valve. It should rattle. If not, replace it.
12   Check the valve for built-up deposits. If these are present, the PCV hoses should be removed and cleaned.
13   To replace the valve, disconnect the PCV valve and elbow from the hose(s). If the new valve comes with an elbow, install it. If not, reuse the old one. **Caution:** *Do not force the elbow onto the valve or you'll break it. If it is difficult to install, soak it in warm water; you may have to soak it for an hour.*
14   Connect the PCV system hose(s).

16   Fuel system check

Warning: *Gasoline is extremely flammable, so take extra precautions when you work on any part of the fuel system. Don't smoke or allow open flames or bare light bulbs near the work area, and don't work in a garage where a natural gas-type appliance (such as a water heater or clothes dryer) with a pilot light is present. If you spill any fuel on your skin, rinse it off immediately with soap and water. When you perform any kind of work on the fuel system, wear safety glasses and have a Class B type fire extinguisher on hand.*

1   If you smell gasoline while driving or after the vehicle has been sitting in the sun, inspect the fuel system immediately.
2   Remove the gas filler cap and inspect if for damage and corrosion. The gasket should have an unbroken sealing imprint. If the gasket is damaged or corroded, install a new cap.
3   Inspect the fuel feed and return lines for cracks. Make sure that the connections between the fuel lines and carburetor or fuel injection system and between the fuel lines and the in-line fuel filter are tight. Warning: You must relieve fuel system pressure before servicing fuel injection system components. The fuel system pressure relief procedure is outlined in Chapter 4.
4   Since some components of the fuel system – the fuel tank and part of the fuel feed and return lines, for example – are underneath the vehicle, they can be inspected more easily with the vehicle raised on a hoist. If a hoist is unavailable, raise the vehicle and support it on jackstands.

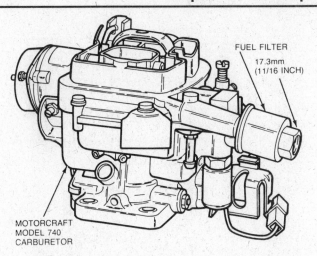

17.1   The fuel filter on carbureted models is threaded into the carburetor body

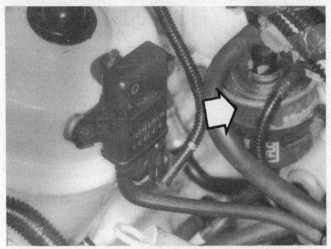

17.9   The fuel filter on fuel-injected models is mounted in the engine compartment – note the direction of the "flow" arrow before removing it

5   With the vehicle raised and safely supported, inspect the gas tank and filler neck for punctures, cracks and other damage. The connection between the filler neck and the tank is particularly critical. Sometimes a rubber filler neck will leak because of loose clamps or deteriorated rubber. Inspect all fuel tank mounting brackets and straps to be sure that the tank is securely attached to the vehicle. Warning: Do not, under any circumstances, try to repair a fuel tank (except rubber components). A welding torch or any open flame can easily cause fuel vapors inside the tank to explode.

6   Carefully check all rubber hoses and metal lines leading away from the fuel tank. Check for loose connections, deteriorated hoses, crimped lines and other damage. Repair or replace damaged sections as necessary (see Chapter 4).

17   Fuel filter replacement

Warning: *Gasoline is extremely flammable, so take extra precautions when you work on any part of the fuel system. Don't smoke or allow open flames or bare light bulbs near the work area, and don't work in a garage where a natural gas-type appliance (such as a water heater or clothes dryer) with a pilot light is present. If you spill any fuel on your skin, rinse it off immediately with soap and water. When you perform any kind of work on the fuel system, wear safety glasses and have a Class B type fire extinguisher on hand.*
Caution: *Before removing the fuel filter on fuel-injected models, the fuel system pressure must be relieved (See Chapter 4).*

Carbureted models

Refer to illustration 17.1

1   Remove the air cleaner housing on top of the carburetor to gain access to the filter **(see illustration)**.

2   Place a rag under the filter, then unscrew the line from the filter while holding the filter hex with a back-up wrench. A flare-nut wrench should be used if available – it will prevent rounding off the fuel line fitting hex.

3   Unscrew the filter or fuel inlet fitting from the carburetor.

4   Apply one drop of Threadlock and Sealer (part No. EOAZ-19554-A) or equivalent to the filter threads.

5   Screw the filter into the carburetor by hand, then tighten it snugly with a wrench.

6   Apply motor oil to the fuel line fitting threads. Thread the line into the filter by hand, hold the filter with a back-up wrench and tighten the fuel line securely.

7   Reinstall the air cleaner housing.

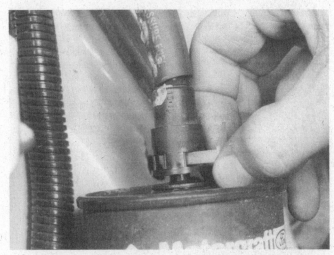

17.10   Before disengaging the hose from either end of the fuel filter, remove the hairpin clip as described in the text

Fuel-injected models

Refer to illustrations 17.9 and 17.10

8   Relieve the fuel system pressure (see Chapter 4).

9   Locate the fuel filter in the right rear corner of the engine compartment **(see illustration)**. Inspect the hose fittings at both ends of the filter to see if they're clean. If more than a light coating of dust is present, clean the fittings before proceeding.

10   Remove the hairpin clips. To disengage a hairpin clip **(see illustration)** from a fitting, spread the two clip legs apart about 1/8-inch and simultaneously push on them. Once the clip is halfway off, grasp the other end of the clip and pull it off. **Caution:** *Don't use any tools to remove the hairpin clips. Tools may damage the clips, and you may have to re-use them (particularly if there aren't any new ones with the new filter).*

11   Once both hairpin clips are removed, grasp the fuel hoses, one at a time, and pull them off the filter. Plug both hoses to prevent leakage and contamination.

12   Check the hairpin clips for damage and distortion. If they were damaged or distorted in any way during removal, new ones must be used when the hoses are reattached to the new filter (if new clips are packaged with the filter, be sure to use them in place of the originals).

13   Note which way the arrow on the filter is pointing – the new filter must be installed the same way. Loosen the clamp screw and detach the filter from the bracket.

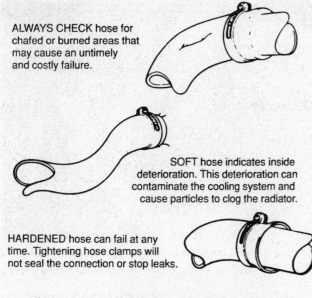

ALWAYS CHECK hose for chafed or burned areas that may cause an untimely and costly failure.

SOFT hose indicates inside deterioration. This deterioration can contaminate the cooling system and cause particles to clog the radiator.

HARDENED hose can fail at any time. Tightening hose clamps will not seal the connection or stop leaks.

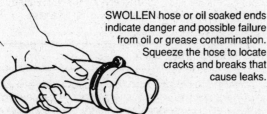

SWOLLEN hose or oil soaked ends indicate danger and possible failure from oil or grease contamination. Squeeze the hose to locate cracks and breaks that cause leaks.

18.4   Hoses, like drivebelts, have a habit of failing at the worst possible time – to prevent the inconvenience of a blown radiator or heater hose, inspect them carefully, as shown here

14   Install the new filter in the bracket with the arrow pointing in the right direction. Tighten the clamp screw securely.
15   Unplug each hose, then carefully push it onto the filter until it's seated against the collar on the fitting. Install the hairpin clips – the triangular part should point away from the filter. **Warning:** *Make sure the clips are securely attached to the hose fittings – if they come off, the hoses could back off the filter and a fire could result!*
16   Start the engine and check for fuel leaks.

18   Cooling system check

Refer to illustrations 18.4

1   Many major engine failures can be attributed to a faulty cooling system. If the vehicle is equipped with an automatic transaxle, the cooling system also plays an important role in prolonging transaxle life because it cools the transmission fluid.
2   The engine should be cold for the cooling system check, so perform the following procedure before the vehicle is driven for the day or after it has been shut off for at least three hours.
3   Remove the radiator cap and clean it thoroughly, inside and out, with clean water. Also clean the filler neck on the radiator. The presence of rust or corrosion in the filler neck means the coolant should be changed (see Section 28). The coolant inside the radiator should be relatively clean and transparent. If it's rust colored, drain the system and refill it with new coolant.
4   Carefully check the radiator hoses and the smaller diameter heater hoses **(see illustration)**. Inspect each coolant hose along its entire length, replacing any hose which is cracked, swollen or deteriorated. Cracks will show up better if the hose is squeezed. Pay close attention to hose clamps that secure the hoses to cooling system components. Hose

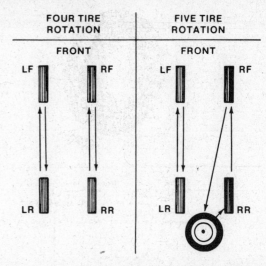

20.2   The recommended rotation pattern for radial tires

clamps can pinch and puncture hoses, resulting in coolant leaks.
5   Make sure that all hose connections are tight. A leak in the cooling system will usually show up as white or rust colored deposits on the area adjoining the leak. If wire-type clamps are used on the hoses, it may be a good idea to replace them with screw-type clamps.
6   Clean the front of the radiator and air conditioning condenser with compressed air, if available, or a soft brush. Remove all bugs, leaves, etc. embedded in the radiator fins. Be extremely careful not to damage the cooling fins or cut your fingers on them.
7   If the coolant level has been dropping consistently and no leaks are detectable, have the radiator cap and cooling system pressure checked at a service station.

19   Exhaust system check

1   With the engine cold (at least three hours after the vehicle has been driven), check the complete exhaust system from the engine to the end of the tailpipe. Ideally, the inspection should be done with the vehicle on a hoist to permit unrestricted access. If a hoist is not available, raise the vehicle and support it securely on jackstands.
2   Check the exhaust pipes and connections for evidence of leaks, severe corrosion and damage. Make sure that all brackets and hangers are in good condition and tight.
3   At the same time, inspect the underside of the body for holes, corrosion, open seams, etc. which may allow exhaust gases to enter the passenger compartment. Seal all body openings with silicone sealant or body putty.
4   Rattles and other noises can often be traced to the exhaust system, especially the mounts and hangers. Try to move the pipes, muffler and catalytic converter. If the components can come in contact with the body or suspension parts, secure the exhaust system with new mounts.
5   Check the running condition of the engine by inspecting inside the end of the tailpipe. The exhaust deposits here are an indication of engine state-of-tune. If the pipe is black and sooty or coated with white deposits, the engine is in need of a tune-up, including a thorough fuel system inspection and adjustment.

20   Tire rotation

Refer to illustration 20.2

1   The tires should be rotated at the specified intervals and whenever uneven wear is noticed. Since the vehicle will be raised and the tires removed anyway, check the brakes also (see Section 22).
2   Radial tires must be rotated in a specific pattern **(see illustration)**.

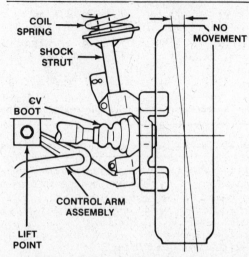

21.10a   To check the balljoints, try to move the lower edge of each front wheel in and out while watching or feeling for movement at the top of the tire. . .

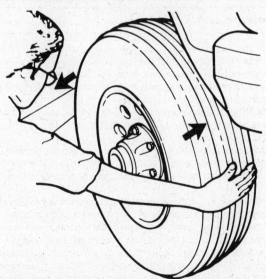

21.11   To check the steering gear mounts and tie-rod connections for play, grasp each front tire like this and try to move it back and forth – if play is noted, check the steering gear mounts and make sure they're tight; if either tie-rod is worn or bent, replace it

3   Refer to the information in *Jacking and towing* at the front of this manual for the proper procedure to follow when raising the vehicle and changing a tire. If the brakes are to be checked, do not apply the parking brake, as stated.
4   The vehicle must be raised on a hoist or supported on jackstands to

21.10b   . . . and at the balljoint-to-steering knuckle joint (arrow)

get two wheels at a time off the ground. Make sure the vehicle is safely supported!
5   After the rotation procedure is finished, check and adjust the tire pressures as necessary and be sure to check the lug nut tightness.

21   Suspension and steering check

Note: *The steering linkage and suspension components should be checked periodically. Worn or damaged suspension and steering linkage components can result in excessive and abnormal tire wear, poor ride quality and vehicle handling and reduced fuel economy. For detailed illustrations of the steering and suspension components, refer to Chapter 10.*

Strut check
1   Park the vehicle on level ground, turn the engine off and set the parking brake. Check the tire pressures.
2   Push down at one corner of the vehicle, then release it while noting the movement of the body. It should stop moving and come to rest in a level position within one or two bounces.
3   If the vehicle continues to move up and down or if it fails to return to its original position, a worn or weak strut is probably the reason.
4   Repeat the above check at each of the three remaining corners of the vehicle.
5   Raise the vehicle and support it on jackstands.
6   Check the shock struts for evidence of fluid leakage. A light film of fluid on the shaft is no cause for concern. Make sure that any fluid noted is from the shocks and not from some other source. If leakage is noted, replace both struts at that end of the vehicle (front or rear).
7   Check the struts to be sure that they are securely mounted and undamaged. Check the upper mounts for damage and wear. If damage or wear is noted, replace both struts on that end of the vehicle.
8   If struts must be replaced, refer to Chapter 10 for the procedure.

Front suspension and steering check
Refer to illustrations 21.10a, 21.10b and 21.11
9   Visually inspect the steering system components for damage and distortion. Look for leaks and damaged seals, boots and fittings.
10   Wipe off the lower end of the steering knuckle and control arm assembly. Have an assistant grasp the lower edge of the tire and move the wheel in and out while you look for movement at the balljoint-to-steering knuckle joint **(see illustrations)**. If there is any movement, the balljoints must be replaced (see Chapter 10).
11   Grasp each front tire at the front and rear edges, push in at the rear, pull out at the front and feel for play in the steering system components **(see illustration)**. If any freeplay is noted, check the steering gear mounts and the tie-rod ends for looseness. If the steering gear mounts are loose, tighten them. If the tie-rod ends are loose, they will probably need to be replaced (see Chapter 10).

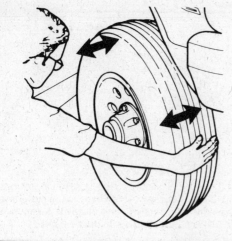

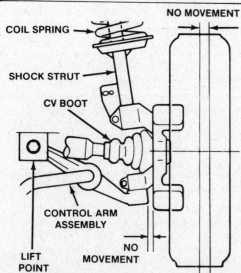

21.12   To check the wheel bearings, try to move the tire in and out – if any play is noted, or if the bearings feel rough or sound noisy when the tire is rotated, the bearings need to be replaced

Front wheel bearing check

Refer to illustration 21.12

Note: *The front wheel bearings are a "cartridge" design and are permanently lubricated and sealed at the factory. They require no scheduled maintenance or adjustment. They can, however, be checked for excessive play. If the following check indicates that either of the front bearings is faulty, replace both bearings (see Chapter 10).*

12   Grasp each front tire at the front and rear edges, then push in and out on the wheel and feel for play **(see illustration)**. There should be no noticeable movement. Turn the wheel and listen for noise from the bearings. If either of these conditions is noted, refer to Chapter 10 for the bearing replacement procedure.

Driveaxle Constant Velocity (CV) joint boot check

13   If the driveaxle rubber boots are damaged or deteriorated, serious and costly damage can occur to the CV joints.

14   It is very important that the boots be kept clean, so wipe them off before inspection. Check the four boots (two on each driveaxle) for cracks, tears, holes, deteriorated rubber and loose or missing clamps. Pushing on the boot surface can reveal cracks not ordinarily visible **(see illustration 21.12)**.

15   If damage or deterioration is evident, check the CV joints for damage (see Chapter 8) and replace the boot(s) with new ones.

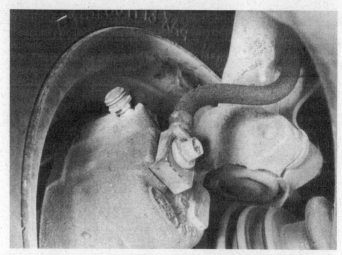

22.7   Check the flexible rubber brake hoses at all four wheels for cracks, swelling, leaks and chafing

22   Brake check

Note: *In addition to the specified intervals, the brake system should be inspected each time the wheels are removed or a malfunction is indicated. Because of the obvious safety considerations, the following brake system checks are some of the most important maintenance procedures you can perform on your vehicle.*

Symptoms of brake system problems

1   The disc brake pads have built-in wear indicators which should make a high-pitched squealing or scraping noise when they are worn to the replacement point. When you hear this noise, replace the pads immediately or expensive damage to the rotors could result.

2   Any of the following symptoms could indicate a brake system defect: the vehicle pulls to one side when the brake pedal is depressed, the brakes make squealing or dragging noises when applied, brake pedal travel is excessive, the pedal pulsates or brake fluid leaks are noted (usually on the inner side of the tire or wheel). If any of these conditions are noted, inspect the brake system immediately.

Brake lines and hoses

Refer to illustration 22.7

Note: *Steel tubing is used throughout the brake system, with the exception of flexible, reinforced hoses at the front and rear wheels. Periodic inspection of these lines is very important.*

3   Park the vehicle on level ground and turn the engine off.

4   Remove the wheel covers. Loosen, but do not remove, the lug nuts.

5   Raise the vehicle and support it securely on jackstands.

6   Remove the wheels (see *Jacking and towing* at the front of this manual, or refer to your owner's manual, if necessary).

7   Check all brake hoses and lines for cracks, chafing of the outer cover, leaks, blisters and distortion **(see illustration)**. Check all threaded fittings for leaks and make sure the brake hose mounting bolts and clips are secure.

8   If leaks or damage are discovered, they must be fixed immediately. Refer to Chapter 9 for detailed information on brake system repair procedures.

Front disc brakes

Refer to illustration 22.11

9   If it hasn't already been done, raise the front of the vehicle and support it securely on jackstands. Apply the parking brake and remove the front wheels.

10   The disc brake calipers, which contain the pads, are now visible. Each caliper has an outer and an inner pad – all pads should be checked.

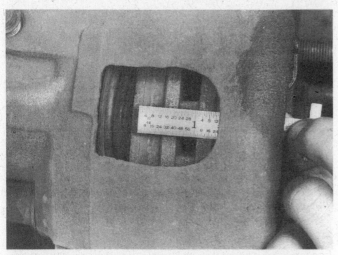

22.11 The front disc brake pads can be checked easily through the inspection hole in each caliper – position a six-inch steel rule against the pads and measure the lining thickness

11   Note the pad thickness by looking through the inspection hole in the caliper **(see illustration)**. If the lining material is 1/8-inch thick or less, or if it is tapered from end to end, the pads should be replaced (see Chapter 9). Keep in mind that the lining material is riveted or bonded to a metal plate or shoe – the metal portion is not included in this measurement.

12   Check the condition of the brake disc. Look for score marks, deep scratches and overheated areas (they will appear blue or discolored). If damage or wear is noted, the disc can be removed and resurfaced by an automotive machine shop or replaced with a new one. Refer to Chapter 9 for more detailed inspection and repair procedures.

Rear drum brakes
Refer to illustration 22.15

13   Refer to Chapter 9 and remove the rear brake drums.

14   Warning: Brake dust produced by lining wear and deposited on brake components may contain asbestos, which is hazardous to your health. DO NOT blow it out with compressed air and DO NOT inhale it! DO NOT use gasoline or solvents to remove the dust. Brake system cleaner should be used to flush the dust into a drain pan. After the brake components are wiped clean with a damp rag, dispose of the contaminated rag(s) and solvent in a covered and labelled container.

15   Note the thickness of the lining material on the rear brake shoes **(see illustration)** and look for signs of contamination by brake fluid and grease. If the lining material is within 1/16-inch of the recessed rivets or metal shoes, replace the brake shoes with new ones. The shoes should also be replaced if they are cracked, glazed (shiny lining surfaces) or contaminated with brake fluid or grease. See Chapter 9 for the replacement procedure.

16   Check the shoe return and hold-down springs and the adjusting mechanism to make sure they are installed correctly and in good condition. Deteriorated or distorted springs, if not replaced, could allow the linings to drag and wear prematurely.

17   Check the wheel cylinders for leakage by carefully peeling back the rubber boots. If brake fluid is noted behind the boots, the wheel cylinders must be replaced (see Chapter 9).

18   Check the drums for cracks, score marks, deep scratches and hard spots, which will appear as small discolored areas. If imperfections cannot be removed with emery cloth, the drums must be resurfaced by an automotive machine shop (see Chapter 9 for more detailed information).

19   Refer to Chapter 9 and install the brake drums.

20   Install the wheels, but do not lower the vehicle yet.

Parking brake lubrication and check
Refer to illustration 22.22

Note: *The parking brake cable and linkage should be periodically checked and lubricated. This maintenance procedure helps prevent the parking*

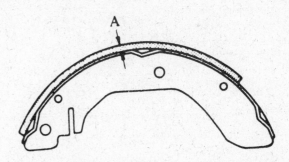

22.15   If the lining is bonded to the brake shoe, measure the lining thickness from the outer surface to the metal shoe, as shown here; if the lining is riveted to the shoe, measure from the lining outer surface to the rivet head

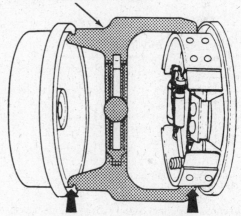

BRAKE ADJUSTMENT GAUGE

SET TO DRUM DIAMETER HERE   FIND CORRECT SHOE DIAMETER HERE

22.22   Parking brake cable lubrication points

brake cable adjuster or the linkage from binding and adversely affecting the operation or adjustment of the parking brake.

Lubrication

21   Set the parking brake.

22   Apply multi-purpose grease to the parking brake linkage, adjuster assembly, connectors and the areas of the parking brake cable that come in contact with the other parts of the vehicle **(see illustration)**.

23   Release the parking brake and repeat the lubrication procedure.

24   Remove the jackstands and lower the vehicle.

25   Tighten the wheel lug nuts to the torque listed in this Chapter's Specifications and install the wheel covers.

Check

26   The easiest, and perhaps most obvious, method of checking the parking brake is to park the vehicle on a steep hill with the parking brake set and the transaxle in Neutral. If the parking brake cannot prevent the vehicle from rolling, refer to Chapter 9 and adjust it.

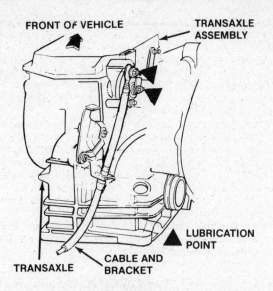

23.3   Lubricate the automatic transaxle shift linkage at the points indicated

23   Automatic transaxle shift linkage lubrication

Refer to illustration 23.3

1   Open the hood and locate the shift cable running up the backside of the transaxle on the left side.
2   Clean the linkage and pivot points at the upper end of the cable.

3   Lubricate the shift linkage and pivot points with multi-purpose grease **(see illustration)**.

24   Clutch linkage lubrication

Refer to illustration 24.1

1   Open the hood and locate the clutch cable to the left of the brake master cylinder **(see illustration)**.
2   Follow the cable to its contact point with the release fork. Clean the cable ball pocket and lubricate it with multi-purpose grease. DO NOT lubricate the inner clutch cable.

25   Manual transaxle lubricant level check and change

Refer to illustrations 25.1 and 25.4
Note: *The transaxle lubricant should not deteriorate under normal driving conditions. However, it is recommended that you check the level occasionally. The most convenient time is when the vehicle is raised for another reason, such as an engine oil change.*

Lubricant level check

1   Park the vehicle on a level surface. Turn the engine off, apply the parking brake and block the wheels. Open the hood and locate the filler plug **(see illustration)**.
2   To protect the transaxle from contamination, wipe off any dirt or grease in the area around the plug.
3   Unscrew the plug. If the plug has a protruding square head, use an open-end wrench of the correct size. If it has a recessed square head, use a 3/8-inch drive ratchet without a socket **(see illustration 25.1)**.
4   Check the lubricant level with a finger **(see illustration)**. It should be up to the bottom of the filler hole. If it is low, add the lubricant listed in this Chapter's Specifications with a syringe or hand pump until it begins to flow out the hole.

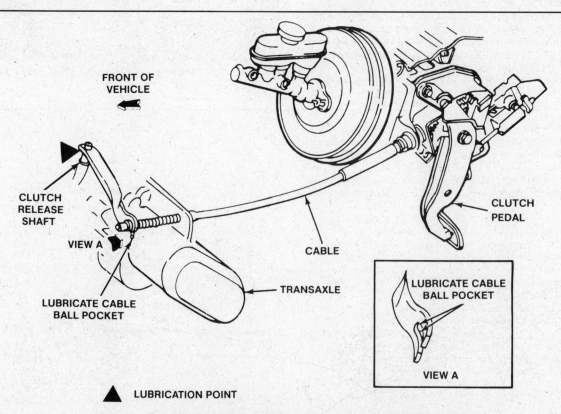

24.1   Lubricate the clutch cable end where it rests in the ball pocket on the release fork – do not lubricate the inner clutch cable

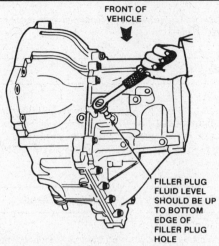

FRONT OF VEHICLE

FILLER PLUG
FLUID LEVEL
SHOULD BE UP
TO BOTTOM
EDGE OF
FILLER PLUG
HOLE

25.1   The manual transaxle filler plug is located on the side of the transaxle

5   Clean the plug threads and reinstall the plug in the hole. Tighten it securely.

Lubricant change

6   Changing the manual transaxle lubricant shouldn't be necessary under normal circumstances. To change the lubricant, remove the filler plug (see Steps 2 and 3) and pump the old lubricant through the filler plug hole with a hand pump. Fill the transaxle to the bottom of the filler plug hole with the specified lubricant.

26   Spark plug replacement

Refer to illustrations 26.1, 26.2, 26.5a, 26.5b, 26.6 and 26.10
Note: *Every time a spark plug wire is detached from a spark plug, the distributor cap or the coil, silicone dielectric compound (a special grease available at auto parts stores) must be applied to the inside of each boot before reconnection. Use a small standard screwdriver to coat the entire inside surface of each boot with a thin layer of the compound.*

1   The spark plugs are located on the front (radiator) side of the engine **(see illustration)**.

2   In most cases, the tools necessary for spark plug replacement include a spark plug socket which fits onto a ratchet (spark plug sockets are padded inside to prevent damage to the porcelain insulators on the new plugs), various extensions and a gap gauge to check and adjust the gaps on the new plugs **(see illustration)**. A special plug wire removal tool is available for separating the wire boots from the spark plugs, but it isn't absolutely necessary. A torque wrench should be used to tighten the new plugs.
3   The best approach when replacing the spark plugs is to purchase the new ones in advance, adjust them to the proper gap and replace the plugs one at a time. When buying the new spark plugs, be sure to obtain the correct plug type for your particular engine. This information can be found on the Vehicle Emission Control Information label located under the hood and in the factory owner's manual. If differences exist between the plug specified on the emissions label and in the owner's manual, assume that the emissions label is correct.
4   Allow the engine to cool completely before attempting to remove any of the plugs. While you are waiting for the engine to cool, check the new plugs for defects and adjust the gaps.

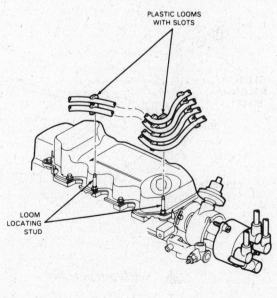

FILL THE TRANSAXLE
TO THE BOTTOM OF THE
FILLER PLUG HOLE

25.4   The lubricant level should be up to the bottom of the filler plug hole

**26.1   Spark plug wire layout
(1.6L engine shown; 1.9L similar)**

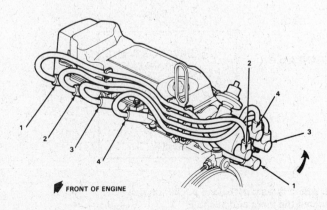

FRONT OF ENGINE

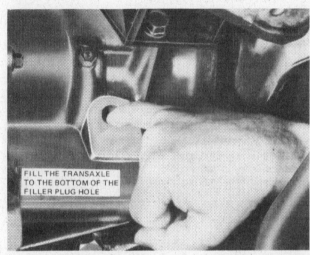

PLASTIC LOOMS
WITH SLOTS

LOOM
LOCATING
STUD

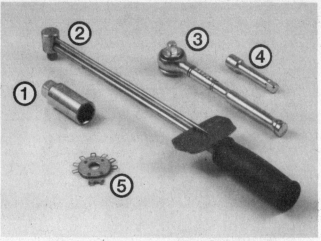

26.2   Tools required for changing spark plugs

1 *Spark plug socket* – *This will have special padding inside to protect the spark plug's porcelain insulator*
2 *Torque wrench* – *Although not mandatory, using this tool is the best way to ensure the plugs are tightened properly*
3 *Ratchet* – *Standard hand tool to fit the spark plug socket*
4 *Extension* – *Depending on model and accessories, you may need special extensions and universal joints to reach one or more of the plugs*
5 *Spark plug gap gauge* – *This gauge for checking the gap comes in a variety of styles. Make sure the gap for your engine is included.*

26.5b   To change the gap, bend the *side* electrode only, as indicated by the arrows, and be very careful not to crack or chip the porcelain insulator surrounding the center electrode

26.5a   Spark plug manufacturers recommend using a wire-type gauge when checking the gap – if the wire does not slide between the electrodes with a slight drag, adjustment is required

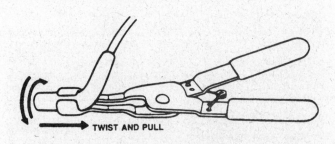

26.6   When removing the spark plug wires, pull only on the boot and twist it back-and-forth

26.10   A length of 3/16-inch ID rubber hose will save time and prevent damaged threads when installing the spark plugs

5   The gap is checked by inserting the proper thickness gauge between the electrodes at the tip of the plug **(see illustration)**. The gap between the electrodes should be the same as the one specified on the Vehicle Emissions Control Information label. The wire should just slide between the electrodes with a slight amount of drag. If the gap is incorrect, use the adjuster on the gauge body to bend the curved side electrode slightly until the proper gap is obtained **(see illustration)**. If the side electrode is not exactly over the center electrode, bend it with the adjuster until it is. Check for cracks in the porcelain insulator (if any are found, the plug should not be used).

6   With the engine cool, remove the spark plug wire from one spark plug. Pull only on the boot at the end of the wire – do not pull on the wire. A plug wire removal tool should be used if available **(see illustration)**.

7   If compressed air is available, use it to blow any dirt or foreign material away from the spark plug hole. A common bicycle pump will also work. The idea here is to eliminate the possibility of debris falling into the cylinder as the spark plug is removed.

8   Place the spark plug socket over the plug and remove it from the engine by turning it in a counterclockwise direction.

9   Compare the spark plug to those shown in the accompanying photos to get an indication of the general running condition of the engine.

10   Thread one of the new plugs into the hole until you can no longer turn it with your fingers, then tighten it with a torque wrench (if available) or the ratchet. It might be a good idea to slip a short length of rubber hose over the end of the plug to use as a tool to thread it into place **(see illustration)**. The hose will grip the plug well enough to turn it, but will start to slip if the plug begins to cross-thread in the hole – this will prevent damaged threads and the accompanying repair costs.

11   Before pushing the spark plug wire onto the end of the plug, inspect it following the procedures outlined in Section 27.

CARBON DEPOSITS

Symptoms: Dry sooty deposits indicate a rich mixture or weak ignition. Causes misfiring, hard starting and hesitation.

Recommendation: Check for a clogged air cleaner, high float level, sticky choke and worn ignition points. Use a spark plug with a longer core nose for greater anti-fouling protection.

OIL DEPOSITS

Symptoms: Oily coating caused by poor oil control. Oil is leaking past worn valve guides or piston rings into the combustion chamber. Causes hard starting, misfiring and hesition.

Recommendation: Correct the mechanical condition with necessary repairs and install new plugs.

TOO HOT

Symptoms: Blistered, white insulator, eroded electrode and absence of deposits. Results in shortened plug life.

Recommendation: Check for the correct plug heat range, over-advanced ignition timing, lean fuel mixture, intake manifold vacuum leaks and sticking valves. Check the coolant level and make sure the radiator is not clogged.

PREIGNITION

Symptoms: Melted electrodes. Insulators are white, but may be dirty due to misfiring or flying debris in the combustion chamber. Can lead to engine damage.

Recommendation: Check for the correct plug heat range, over-advanced ignition timing, lean fuel mixture, clogged cooling system and lack of lubrication.

HIGH SPEED GLAZING

Symptoms: Insulator has yellowish, glazed appearance. Indicates that combustion chamber temperatures have risen suddenly during hard acceleration. Normal deposits melt to form a conductive coating. Causes misfiring at high speeds.

Recommendation: Install new plugs. Consider using a colder plug if driving habits warrant.

GAP BRIDGING

Symptoms: Combustion deposits lodge between the electrodes. Heavy deposits accumulate and bridge the electrode gap. The plug ceases to fire, resulting in a dead cylinder.

Recommendation: Locate the faulty plug and remove the deposits from between the electrodes.

NORMAL

Symptoms: Brown to grayish-tan color and slight electrode wear. Correct heat range for engine and operating conditions.

Recommendation: When new spark plugs are installed, replace with plugs of the same heat range.

ASH DEPOSITS

Symptoms: Light brown deposits encrusted on the side or center electrodes or both. Derived from oil and/or fuel additives. Excessive amounts may mask the spark, causing misfiring and hesitation during acceleration.

Recommendation: If excessive deposits accumulate over a short time or low mileage, install new valve guide seals to prevent seepage of oil into the combustion chambers. Also try changing gasoline brands.

WORN

Symptoms: Rounded electrodes with a small amount of deposits on the firing end. Normal color. Causes hard starting in damp or cold weather and poor fuel economy.

Recommendation: Replace with new plugs of the same heat range.

DETONATION

Symptoms: Insulators may be cracked or chipped. Improper gap setting techniques can also result in a fractured insulator tip. Can lead to piston damage.

Recommendation: Make sure the fuel anti-knock values meet engine requirements. Use care when setting the gaps on new plugs. Avoid lugging the engine.

SPLASHED DEPOSITS

Symptoms: After long periods of misfiring, deposits can loosen when normal combustion temperature is restored by an overdue tune-up. At high speeds, deposits flake off the piston and are thrown against the hot insulator, causing misfiring.

Recommendation: Replace the plugs with new ones or clean and reinstall the originals.

MECHANICAL DAMAGE

Symptoms: May be caused by a foreign object in the combustion chamber or the piston striking an incorrect reach (too long) plug. Causes a dead cylinder and could result in piston damage.

Recommendation: Remove the foreign object from the engine and/or install the correct reach plug.

1

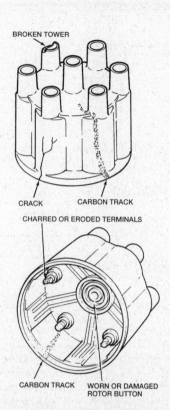

27.11   Shown here are some of the common defects to look for when inspecting the distributor cap (if in doubt about its condition, install a new one)

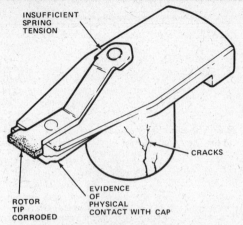

27.12   The ignition rotor should be checked for wear and corrosion as indicated here (if in doubt about its condition, buy a new one)

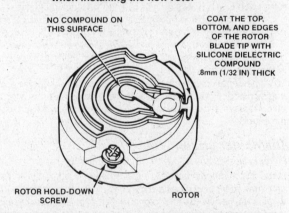

27.13a   On rotors like this, be sure to align the square peg on the rotor (arrow) with the square hole in the distributor shaft mount when installing the new rotor

27.13b   Apply silicone dielectric compound (grease) to single-blade rotors as shown here before installing the distributor cap – do not apply dielectric compound to multipoint rotors

12   Attach the plug wire to the new spark plug, again using a twisting motion on the boot until it is seated on the spark plug.

13   Repeat the procedure for the remaining spark plugs, replacing them one at a time to prevent mixing up the spark plug wires.

27   Spark plug wire, distributor cap and rotor check and replacement

Spark plug wires

Note: *Every time a spark plug wire is detached from a spark plug, the distributor cap or the coil, silicone dielectric compound (a special grease available at auto parts stores) must be applied to the inside of each boot before reconnection. Use a small standard screwdriver to coat the entire inside surface of each boot with a thin layer of the compound.*

1   The spark plug wires should be checked and, if necessary, replaced at the same time new spark plugs are installed. **Warning:** *Don't touch the spark plug or coil wires with the engine running. The moisture on your skin can conduct high ignition voltage even through good wires, causing serious electrical shocks.*

2   The easiest way to identify bad wires is to make a visual check while the engine is running. In a dark, well-ventilated garage, start the engine and look at each plug wire. Be careful not to come into
contact with any moving engine parts. If there is a break in the wire, you will see arcing or a small spark at the damaged area. If arcing is noticed, make a note to obtain new wires.

3   The spark plug wires should be inspected one at a time, beginning with the spark plug for the number one cylinder (the one nearest the right end of the engine), to prevent confusion. Clearly label each original plug wire with a piece of tape marked with the correct number. The plug wires must be reinstalled in the correct order to ensure proper engine operation.

4   Disconnect the plug wire from the first spark plug. A removal tool can be used **(see illustration 26.6)**, or you can grab the wire boot, twist it slightly and pull the wire free. Do not pull on the wire itself, only on the rubber boot.

5   Push the wire and boot back onto the end of the spark plug. It should fit snugly. If it doesn't, detach the wire and boot once more and use a pair of pliers to carefully crimp the metal connector inside the wire boot until it does.

6   Using a clean rag that's damp with solvent, wipe the entire length of the wire to remove built-up dirt and grease.

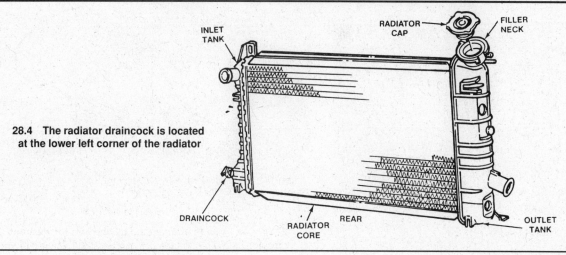

28.4   The radiator draincock is located at the lower left corner of the radiator

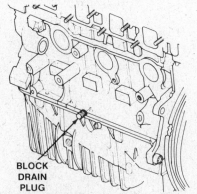

28.5   The engine block drain plug is located on the side of the cylinder block

7   Once the wire is clean, check for burns, cracks and other damage. Do not bend the wire sharply or you might break the conductor.

8   Disconnect the wire from the distributor. Again, pull only on the rubber boot. Check for corrosion and a tight fit. Reinstall the wire in the distributor.

9   Inspect each of the remaining spark plug wires, making sure that each one is securely fastened at the distributor and spark plug when the check is complete.

10   If new spark plug wires are required, purchase a set for your specific engine model. Pre-cut wire sets with the boots already installed are available. Remove and replace the wires one at a time to avoid mixups in the firing order.

Distributor cap and rotor

Refer to illustrations 27.11, 27.12, 27.13a and 27.13b

Note: *It is common practice to install a new distributor cap and rotor each time new spark plug wires are installed. If you're planning to install new wires, install a new cap and rotor also. But if you are planning to reuse the existing wires, be sure to inspect the cap and rotor to make sure that they are in good condition.*

11   Remove the mounting screws and detach the cap from the distributor. Check it for cracks, carbon tracks and worn, burned or loose terminals **(see illustration)**.

12   Check the rotor for cracks and carbon tracks. Make sure the center terminal spring tension is adequate and look for corrosion and wear on the rotor tip **(see illustration)**. **Note:** *the silicone dielectric compound used on single-point rotors darkens with age and may look like dirt or corrosion. Do not replace a rotor just because of the dielectric compound's appearance.*

13   Replace the cap and rotor if damage or defects are found. Note that the rotor is indexed so it can only be installed one way **(see illustration)**. On some models, the rotor is secured by two screws; on others, it can be pulled straight off of the distributor shaft. If the vehicle has a single-point rotor, apply a 1/32-inch coat of silicone dielectric compound to the rotor tip before installing the distributor cap **(see illustration)**. Do not apply dielectric compound to multi-point rotors.

14   When installing a new cap, remove the wires from the old cap one at a time and attach them to the new cap in the exact same location – do not simultaneously remove all the wires from the old cap or firing order mixups may occur.

28   Cooling system servicing (draining, flushing and refilling)

Warning: *Do not allow antifreeze to come in contact with your skin or painted surfaces of the vehicle. Rinse off spills immediately with plenty of water. Antifreeze is highly toxic if ingested. Never leave antifreeze lying around in an open container or in puddles on the floor; children and pets are attracted by it's sweet smell and may drink it. Check with local authorities about disposing of used antifreeze. Many communities have collection centers which will see that antifreeze is disposed of safely.*

1   Periodically, the cooling system should be drained, flushed and refilled to replenish the antifreeze mixture and prevent formation of rust and corrosion, which can impair the performance of the cooling system and cause engine damage. When the cooling system is serviced, all hoses and the radiator cap should be checked and replaced if necessary.

Draining

Refer to illustrations 28.4 and 28.5

2   Apply the parking brake and block the wheels. If the vehicle has just been driven, wait several hours to allow the engine to cool down before beginning this procedure.

3   Once the engine is completely cool, remove the radiator cap to vent the cooling system.

4   Move a large container under the radiator drain to catch the coolant and open the draincock **(see illustration)**.

5   After the coolant stops flowing out of the radiator, move the container under the engine block drain plug **(see illustration)**. Remove the plug and allow the coolant in the block to drain.

6   While the coolant is draining, check the condition of the radiator hoses, heater hoses and clamps (see Section 18 if necessary).

7   Replace any damaged clamps or hoses (see Chapter 3 for detailed replacement procedures).

Flushing

8   Once the system is completely drained, flush the radiator with fresh water from a garden hose until water runs clear at the drain. The flushing action of the water will remove sediments from the radiator but will not remove rust and scale from the engine and cooling tube surfaces.

9   These deposits can be removed by the chemical action of a cleaner such as Ford Cooling System Fast Flush. Follow the procedure outlined in the manufacturer's instructions. If the radiator is severely corroded, damaged or leaking, it should be removed (see Chapter 3) and taken to a radiator repair shop.

1

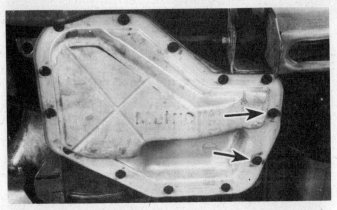

29.5   Remove all the pan bolts except two of the rear ones (arrows), then carefully pry the pan loose from the transaxle case – be careful; too much force could damage the flange and cause leaks

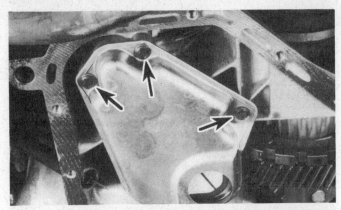

29.8   On most models, the filter is held in place by three bolts (arrows)

29.9   Be sure to install the new seal before bolting the new filter to the transaxle

29.10   Tighten the transaxle pan bolts with a torque wrench – follow a criss-cross pattern and work up to the final torque in three steps to avoid warping the pan flange

10   Remove the overflow hose from the coolant recovery reservoir. Drain the reservoir and flush it with clean water, then reconnect the hose.

Refilling

11   Close and tighten the radiator drain. Install and tighten the block drain plug.

12   Place the heater temperature control in the maximum heat position.

13   Slowly add new coolant (a 50/50 mixture of water and antifreeze) to the radiator until it is full. Add coolant to the reservoir up to the lower mark.

14   Leave the radiator cap off and run the engine in a well-ventilated area until the thermostat opens (coolant will begin flowing through the radiator and the upper radiator hose will become hot).

15   Turn the engine off and let it cool. Add more coolant mixture to bring the level back up to the lip on the radiator filler neck.

16   Squeeze the upper radiator hose to expel air, then add more coolant mixture if necessary. Replace the radiator cap.

17   Start the engine, allow it to reach normal operating temperature and check for leaks.

---

29   Automatic transaxle fluid and filter change

Refer to illustrations 29.5, 29.8, 29.9 and 29.10

1   Before beginning work, purchase the specified transmission fluid (see Recommended lubricants and fluids at the beginning of this Chapter) and a new filter. The filter will come with a new pan gasket and seal.

2   The fluid should be drained immediately after the vehicle has been driven. More sediment and contaminants will be removed with the fluid if it's hot. **Warning:** *Fluid temperature can exceed 350-degrees F in a hot transaxle, so wear gloves when draining the fluid.*

3   After the vehicle has been driven to warm up the fluid, raise it and support it on jackstands.

4   Position a drain pan capable of holding four quarts under the transaxle. Be careful not to touch any of the hot exhaust components.

5   Remove all of the pan bolts except for the two at the rear corners **(see illustration)**. Unscrew the two remaining bolts two turns, but leave them in place to support the pan.

6   Carefully separate the pan from the transaxle case and allow the fluid to drain out. Try not to splash fluid as the gasket seal is broken and the pan is detached. Once the fluid has drained, remove the two bolts and detach the pan.

7   Scrape all traces of the old gasket from the pan and the transaxle case, then clean the pan with solvent and dry it with compressed air – DO NOT use a rag to wipe out the pan (lint from the rag could contaminate the transaxle). Also, be careful when scraping the gasket surface on the transaxle case; the aluminum gouges easily.

8   Remove the filter bolts or clip and detach the filter **(see illustration)**. Discard the filter and the seal.

9   Attach the new seal to the new filter **(see illustration)**, then bolt the filter to the transaxle.

10   Position the new gasket on the pan, then hold the pan against the transaxle case and install the bolts **(see illustration)**.

11   Tighten the pan bolts to the torque listed in this Chapter's Specifications in a criss-cross pattern. Work up to the final torque in three steps. **Caution:** *Don't overtighten the bolts or the pan flange could be distorted and leaks could result.*

12   Lower the vehicle. With the engine off, fill the transaxle with fluid (see Section 7 if necessary). Use a funnel to prevent spills. It is best to add a little fluid at a time, continually checking the level with the dipstick. Allow the fluid time to drain into the pan.

13   Start the engine and shift the selector into all positions from Park through Low, then shift into Park and apply the parking brake.

14   With the engine idling, check the fluid level. Lower the vehicle, drive it for several miles, then recheck the fluid level and look for leaks at the transaxle pan.

Chapter 2 Part A Engine

Contents

2A

Specifications

General

Type	Inline four-cylinder
Displacement	1.3, 1.6 or 1.9 liter
Bore and stroke	
1.3L	3.13 inch x 2.4 inch
1.6L	3.13 inch x 3.13 inch
1.9L	3.23 inch x 3.46 inch
Firing order	1-3-4-2
Cylinder numbers (timing belt end to transaxle end)	1–2–3–4

0754H

1.3L engine

0758H

1.9L engine

0755H

1.6L engine

Cylinder location and distributor rotation

Hydraulic valve lifter clearance

1981 through 1986	0.059 to 0.194 inch
1987 and 1988	
CFI engine	0.047 to 0.138 inch
EFI engine	0.059 to 0.150 inch
1989	
Non-HO engine	0.047 to 0.138 inch
HO engine	0.059 to 0.150 inch

Hydraulic valve lifter clearance (continued)

1990
  HO engine
    Flat lifter
      Minimum .... 0.047 inch
      Normal .... 0.13 inch
      Maximum .... 0.22 inch
    Roller lifter
      Minimum .... 0.02 inch
      Normal .... 0.1 inch
      Maximum .... 0.193 inch
  Non-HO engine
    Flat lifter
      Minimum .... 0.028 inch
      Normal .... 0.114 inch
      Maximum .... 0.205 inch
    Roller lifter
      Minimum .... 0 inch
      Normal .... 0.087 inch
      Maximum .... 0.177 inch

Cylinder head and valve train

Cylinder head-to-piston "squish" height
  Non-HO engine .... 0.046 to 0.060 inch
  HO engine .... 0.039 to 0.070 inch
Valve tappet, hydraulic
  Diameter (standard) .... 0.874 inch
  Clearance in bore .... 0.0009 to 0.0026 inch
  Service limit .... 0.005 inch
Distributor shaft bearing bore diameter .... 1.852 to 1.854 inch
Lifter bore diameter .... 0.8676 +/- 0.0006 inch
Camshaft bearing inside diameter
1981 through 1984
  No. 1 (from timing belt end of engine) .... 1.763 to 1.803 inch
  No. 2 .... 1.773 to 1.774 inch
  No. 3 .... 1.783 to 1.784 inch
  No. 4 .... 1.793 to 1.794 inch
  No. 5 .... 1.802 to 1.803 inch
1985
  No. 1 .... 1.7636 to 1.7646 inch
  No. 2 .... 1.7735 to 1.7745 inch
  No. 3 .... 1.7833 to 1.7843 inch
  No. 4 .... 1.7931 to 1.7941 inch
  No. 5 .... 1.8030 to 1.8040 inch
1986
  No. 1, 2, 3, 4 and 5 .... 1.8030 to 1.8040 inch
1985 and 1986 – oversize (not applicable to HO, EFI and Turbo)
  No. 1 .... 1.7786 to 1.7796 inch
  No. 2 .... 1.7884 to 1.7894 inch
  No. 3 .... 1.7983 to 1.7993 inch
  No. 4 .... 1.8081 to 1.8091 inch
  No. 5 .... 1.8179 to 1.8189 inch
1987 through 1990
  No. 1, 2, 3, 4 and 5 .... 1.8030 to 1.8040 inch
1987 through 1990 – oversize (not applicable to EFI engine)
  No. 1 .... 1.7786 to 1.7796 inch
  No. 2 .... 1.7884 to 1.7894 inch
  No. 3 .... 1.7983 to 1.7993 inch
  No. 4 .... 1.8081 to 1.8091 inch
  No. 5 .... 1.8179 to 1.8189 inch

Camshaft

Lobe lift
  HO and EFI
    Intake .... 0.240 inch
    Exhaust .... 0.240 inch
    Allowable lobe loss .... 0.005 inch
  All other models
    Intake .... 0.229 inch

Exhaust .... 0.229 inch
   Allowable lobe loss .... 0.005 inch
Theoretical valve lift @ zero lash
   HO and EFI (intake and exhaust) .... 0.436 inch
   All other models (intake and exhaust) .... 0.376 inch
Endplay
   HO and EFI .... 0.0018 to 0.006 inch
   All other models .... 0.0059 to 0.009 inch
Endplay service limit .... 0.0078 inch
Journal-to-bearing (oil) clearance
   1981 and 1982 .... 0.0009 to 0.0027 inch
   1983 through 1985 .... 0.0008 to 0.0028 inch
   1986 through 1990 .... 0.0013 to 0.0033 inch
Journal diameter
   1981 through 1985
     No. 1 .... 1.761 to 1.762 inch
     No. 2 .... 1.771 to 1.772 inch
     No. 3 .... 1.781 to 1.782 inch
     No. 4 .... 1.792 to 1.798 inch
     No. 5 .... 1.801 to 1.802 inch
   1983 through 1985 – oversize (not applicable to HO)
     No. 1 .... 1.7763 to 1.7773 inch
     No. 2 .... 1.7861 to 1.7871 inch
     No. 3 .... 1.7960 to 1.7969 inch
     No. 4 .... 1.8058 to 1.8068 inch
     No. 5 .... 1.8156 to 1.8166 inch
   1986 through 1990
     Standard .... 1.8007 to 1.8017 inch
     Oversize (not applicable to EFI engine) .... 1.8156 to 1.8166 inch
Camshaft runout limit .... 0.005 inch (runout of center bearing relative to No. 1 and No. 5)
Journal out-of-round limit .... 0.0003 inch

Oil pump

Relief valve spring tension
   1981 through 1983 .... 9.6 to 10.6 ft-lbs at 0.921 inch
   1984 .... 8.0 to 8.8 lbs @ 1.1 inch
   1985 .... 4.7 to 5.3 lbs @ 1.65 inch
   1986 through 1990 .... 9.3 to 10.3 lbs @ 1.1 inch
Relief valve-to-bore clearance .... 0.0007 to 0.0031 inch
Rotor outer race assembly end clearance (assembled) .... 0.0016 to 0.0025 inch
Outer race-to-housing clearance .... 0.0027 to 0.0055 inch
Outer gear-to-housing clearance .... 0.003 to 0.0065 inch
Inner and outer gear-to-cover clearance (endplay)
   1983 .... 0.000 to 0.003 inch
   1984 .... 0.000 to 0.0035 inch
   1985 through 1990 .... 0.0005 to 0.0035 inch
Inner-to-outer gear tip clearance (1984 through 1990) .... 0.002 to 0.007 inch

Torque specifications   **Ft-lbs** (unless otherwise indicated)

Timing belt tensioner attaching bolt .... 17 to 20
Camshaft sprocket-to-cam bolt .... 37 to 46
Camshaft thrust plate-to-head bolts .... 84 to 132 in-lbs
Crankshaft pulley bolt
   1988 and earlier .... 74 to 90
   1989 on .... 81 to 96
Cylinder head bolts
   1981 through 1984
     Step 1 44
     Step 2 .... 1/4 turn from Step 1
     Step 3 .... 1/4 turn from Step 2
   1985 on
     Step 1 44
     Step 2 .... Loosen all bolts 2 turns
     Step 3 44
     Step 4 .... 1/4 turn from Step 3
     Step 5 .... 1/4 turn from Step 4
Exhaust manifold-to-head nuts .... 15 to 20
Flywheel/driveplate-to-crankshaft bolts
   1981 through 1983 .... 59 to 69
   1984 through 1990 .... 54 to 63

Intake manifold-to-block nut	
1981 through 1983	12 to 16
1984 through 1990	12 to 15
Monolithic timing plug	15 to 25
Oil filter adaptor-to-block	21 to 26
Oil filter	12 to 16
Oil pan drain plug	16
Oil pan-to-block bolts	
1981 through 1985	6 to 8
1986 through 1990	15
Oil pan-to-transaxle bolts (1986 on)	29
Oil pump-to-block bolts	72 to 96 in-lbs
Oil pump tube support-to-block bolt	120 to 156 in-lbs
Oil pump cover bolts (1984 through 1990)	72 to 108 in-lbs
Oil pump main discharge plug (1984 on)	72 to 108 in-lbs
Oil pump relief valve plug (1984 on)	144 to 180 in-lbs
Oil gallery pipe plugs	96 to 144 in-lbs
Oil pick-up and screen-to-pump bolts	72 to 96 in-lbs
Rocker arm stud-to-head	84 to 132 in-lbs
Rocker arm-to-head stud nut	15 to 19
Rocker arm-to-head bolt (1987 and later 1.9L engine)	15 to 19
Valve cover-to-head bolt	72 to 96 in-lbs
Timing belt tensioning torque	
1981	
1.3L engine	44 to 48
1.6L engine	41 to 44
1982 through 1988	
New belt	27 to 32
Used belt*	120 in-lbs
Timing belt cover stud-to-block	84 to 108 in-lbs
Timing belt cover-to-block nuts	60 to 84 in-lbs

*A belt is considered used after 30 days of service.

1   General information

This Part of Chapter 2 is devoted to in-vehicle repair procedures for the engine. All information concerning engine removal and installation and engine block and cylinder head overhaul can be found in Part B of this Chapter.

The following repair procedures are based on the assumption that the engine is installed in the vehicle. If the engine has been removed from the vehicle and mounted on a stand, many of the steps outlined in this Part of Chapter 2 will not apply.

The Specifications included in this Part of Chapter 2 apply only to the procedures contained in this Part. Part B of Chapter 2 contains the Specifications necessary for cylinder head and engine block rebuilding.

2   Repair operations possible with the engine in the vehicle

Many major repair operations can be accomplished without removing the engine from the vehicle.

Clean the engine compartment and the exterior of the engine with some type of degreaser before any work is done. It will make the job easier and help keep dirt out of the internal areas of the engine.

Depending on the components involved, it may be helpful to remove the hood to improve access to the engine as repairs are performed (refer to Chapter 11 if necessary). Cover the fenders to prevent damage to the paint. Special pads are available, but an old bedspread or blanket will also work.

If vacuum, exhaust, oil or coolant leaks develop, indicating a need for gasket or seal replacement, the repairs can generally be made with the engine in the vehicle. The intake and exhaust manifold gaskets, timing cover gasket, oil pan gasket, crankshaft oil seals and cylinder head gasket are all accessible with the engine in place.

Exterior engine components, such as the intake and exhaust manifolds, the oil pan, the water pump, the starter motor, the alternator, the distributor and the fuel system components can be removed for repair with the engine in place.

Since the cylinder head can be removed without pulling the engine, valve component servicing can also be accomplished with the engine in the vehicle. Replacement of the timing belt is also possible with the engine in the vehicle.

In extreme cases caused by a lack of necessary equipment, repair or replacement of piston rings, pistons, connecting rods and rod bearings is possible with the engine in the vehicle. However, this practice is not recommended because of the cleaning and preparation work that must be done to the components involved.

3   Top Dead Center (TDC) for number one piston – locating

Refer to illustration 3.8

Note: *The following procedure is based on the assumption that the distributor is correctly installed. If you are trying to locate TDC to install the distributor correctly, piston position must be determined by feeling for compression at the number one spark plug hole, then aligning the ignition timing marks as described in step 8.*

1   Top Dead Center (TDC) is the highest point in the cylinder that each piston reaches as it travels up-and-down when the crankshaft turns. Each piston reaches TDC on the compression stroke and again on the exhaust stroke, but TDC generally refers to piston position on the compression stroke.

2   Positioning the piston(s) at TDC is an essential part of many procedures such as rocker arm removal, camshaft and timing belt removal and distributor removal.

3   Before beginning this procedure, be sure to place the transaxle in Neutral and apply the parking brake or block the rear wheels. Also, disable the ignition system by detaching the coil wire from the center terminal of the distributor cap and grounding it on the block with a jumper wire. Remove the spark plugs (see Chapter 1).

3.8 Locations of the timing marks

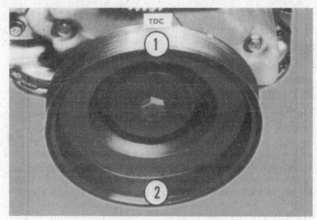

4.3 Marking the crankshaft pulley

2A

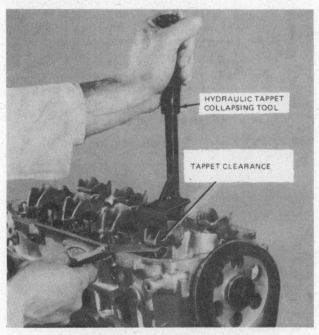

HYDRAULIC TAPPET COLLAPSING TOOL

TAPPET CLEARANCE

4.4 Checking collapsed tappet clearance

4   In order to bring any piston to TDC, the crankshaft must be turned using one of the methods outlined below. When looking at the front of the engine, normal crankshaft rotation is clockwise.

   a) The preferred method is to turn the crankshaft with a socket and ratchet attached to the bolt threaded into the front of the crankshaft.

   b) A remote starter switch, which may save some time, can also be used. Follow the instructions included with the switch. Once the piston is close to TDC, use a socket and ratchet as described in the previous paragraph.

   c) If an assistant is available to turn the ignition switch to the Start position in short bursts, you can get the piston close to TDC without a remote starter switch. Make sure your assistant is out of the vehicle, away from the ignition switch, then use a socket and ratchet as described above to complete the procedure.

5   Note the position of the terminal for the number one spark plug wire on the distributor cap. If the terminal isn't marked, follow the plug wire from the number one cylinder spark plug to the cap. **Note:** *The position of the number one terminal varies with different models. However, all models have a 1-3-4-2 firing order and counterclockwise distributor rotation.*

6   Use a felt-tip pen or chalk to make a mark on the distributor body directly under the terminal.

7   Detach the cap from the distributor and set it aside (see Chapter 1 if necessary).

8   Turn the crankshaft (see Step 3) until the notch in the crankshaft pulley is aligned with the 0 on the timing plate (located at the front of the engine) **(see illustration)**.

9   Look at the distributor rotor – it should be pointing directly at the mark you made on the distributor body.

10   If the rotor is 180-degrees off, the number one piston is at TDC on the exhaust stroke.

11   To get the piston to TDC on the compression stroke, turn the crankshaft one complete turn (360-degrees) clockwise. The rotor should now be pointing at the mark on the distributor. When the rotor is pointing at the number one spark plug wire terminal in the distributor cap and the ignition timing marks are aligned, the number one piston is at TDC on the compression stroke.

12   After the number one piston has been positioned at TDC on the compression stroke, TDC for any of the remaining pistons can be located by turning the crankshaft and following the firing order. Mark the remaining spark plug wire terminal locations on the distributor body just like you did for the number one terminal, then number the marks to correspond with the cylinder numbers. As you turn the crankshaft, the rotor will also turn. When it's pointing directly at one of the marks on the distributor, the piston for that particular cylinder is at TDC on the compression stroke.

---

4   Hydraulic valve lifter clearance – checking

Refer to illustrations 4.3 and 4.4

1   The valve stem-to-rocker arm clearance must be within specification with the valve lifter completely collapsed.

2   To check the clearance, crank the engine with the ignition off until the number one cylinder is at Top Dead Center (TDC) on the compression stoke.

3   Mark the crankshaft pulley with chalk or white paint at TDC (position 1) and 180-degrees opposite (position 2) **(see illustration)**.

4   Using a special tool, each hydraulic lifter should be slowly bled down until it is completely collapsed, following the order in Steps 5, 6 and 7 **(see illustration)**. Check the clearance between the valve stem and rocker arm and compare it to this Chapter's Specifications. The following should be checked against this Chapter's Specifications for wear:

   a) Fulcrum
   b) Hydraulic lifter
   c) Cam lobe

5   With the crankshaft pulley in position 1 (TDC), check the following valves:

   No. 1 intake
   No. 1 exhaust
   No. 2 intake

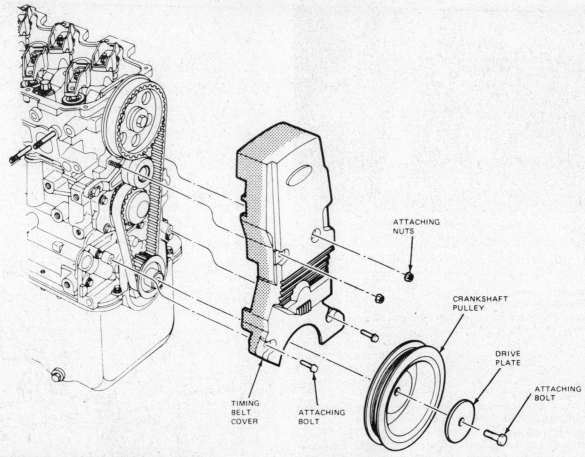

ATTACHING
NUTS

CRANKSHAFT
PULLEY

DRIVE
PLATE

ATTACHING
BOLT

TIMING
BELT
COVER

ATTACHING
BOLT

5.3 Timing belt cover and pulley components

5.4a Camshaft sprocket timing marks

5.4b Crankshaft sprocket timing marks

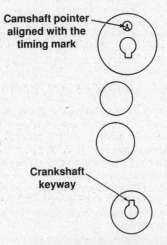

Camshaft pointer aligned with the timing mark

Crankshaft keyway

5.4c The proper relationship of the upper and lower pulleys

6   Rotate the crankshaft pulley (in a clockwise direction) to position 2 and check the following valves:
    No. 3 intake
    No. 3 exhaust
7   Rotate the pulley (in a clockwise direction) 180-degrees and back to position 1 to check the following valves:
    No. 4 intake
    No. 4 exhaust
    No. 2 exhaust
8   If any components are worn out of specification, they must be replaced to bring the valve gear back into proper relationship.

5   Timing belt – replacement

Refer to illustrations 5.3, 5.4a, 5.4b, 5.4c, 5.5 and 5.6
Note: *The manufacturer recommends that the timing belt be replaced with a new one any time the tension is released or it is removed. This normally occurs when the water pump is removed or when timing belt replacement is called for in the maintenance schedule (see Chapter 1). This procedure must be done with the engine cold. DO NOT set timing belt tension with the engine warm.*
1   Disconnect the battery negative cable.

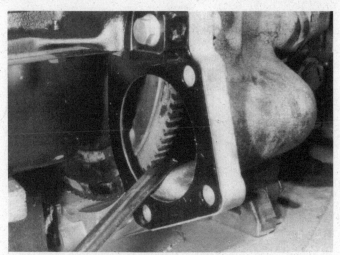

5.5   Lock the flywheel ring gear with a large screwdriver

5.6   Removing timing belt tension (at arrow)

2   Remove the accessory drivebelts (see Chapter 1).

3   Remove the timing belt cover **(see illustration)**.

4   Use a wrench on the crankshaft pulley bolt and rotate the engine until the timing mark on the camshaft pulley is aligned with the one on the cylinder head. Reinstall the front cover just long enough to check that the crankshaft pulley mark is aligned with the TDC mark on the cover **(see illustrations)**. Remove the front cover.

5   Remove the starter and lock the flywheel ring gear with a screwdriver **(see illustration)**. Remove the crankshaft pulley bolt.

6   Loosen the belt tensioner bolts, pry the tensioner to one side and then retighten the bolts to hold it in position **(see illustration)**.

7   Remove the crankshaft pulley and the timing belt.

8   Starting at the crankshaft, install a new belt in a counterclockwise direction over the pulleys, making sure the camshaft and crankshaft timing marks are aligned **(see illustrations 5.4a and 5.4b)**. Be sure to keep the belt span from the crankshaft to the camshaft tight while installing it over the remaining pulleys.

9   Loosen the belt tensioner attaching bolts so the tensioner snaps into place against the belt. Tighten one of the tensioner bolts.

10   Install the crankshaft pulley and bolt and tighten it to the torque listed in this Chapter's Specifications. Lock the flywheel ring gear in place with a screwdriver through the starter motor opening. Afterwards, reinstall the starter.

11   Rotate the crankshaft two complete revolutions and stop on the second revolution at the point where the crankshaft sprocket returns to the TDC position **(see illustration 5.4b)**. Verify that the cam sprocket is also at TDC **(see illustration 5.4a)**. On 1989 and later models, temporarily install the timing belt cover and verify the pulley and timing cover marks are aligned. **Caution:** *If resistance is felt while turning the crankshaft, the valves may be hitting the pistons because the timing is incorrect. Stop and check the timing again. Forcing the crankshaft will damage the engine! Also, only turn the engine in the normal direction of rotation or you may damage the engine.*

12   On 1982 and later models, re-connect the battery negative cable and crank the engine to seat the belt, then disconnect the negative cable once again.

13   Loosen the timing belt tensioner bolt tightened earlier.

14   On 1988 and earlier models, have an assistant hold a wrench on the crankshaft bolt so it can't turn. Apply tension to the timing belt as follows: Using a torque wrench, turn the camshaft sprocket counterclockwise until the tensioning torque reaches the reading listed in this Chapter's Specifications. **Caution:** *Don't use the camshaft sprocket bolt to turn the camshaft – use a special tool such as KD-3254 or equivalent to turn the large hex on the sprocket only!* Hold this reading and tighten the belt tensioner attaching bolts to the torque listed in this Chapter's Specifications.

15   On 1989 and later models, loosen the timing belt tensioner bolts and allow the tensioner to snap against the belt (this will set the belt to the proper tension). Tighten the belt tensioner bolts to the torque listed in this

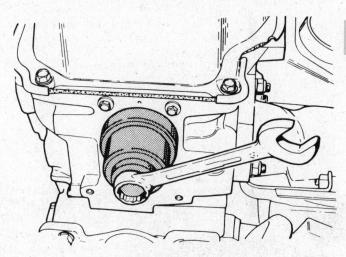

6.5   Installing the camshaft oil seal

Chapter's Specifications.

16   Install the timing belt cover.

17   Install and adjust the drivebelts (see Chapter 1).

18   Reconnect the negative battery cable.

6   Camshaft oil seal – replacement

Refer to illustration 6.5

1   Disconnect the battery negative cable.

2   Remove the timing belt (see Section 5). **Note:** *If you want to save time by not removing and installing the timing belt and re-timing the engine, you can unfasten the camshaft sprocket and suspend it out of the way – with the belt still attached – by a piece of rope. Be sure the rope keeps firm tension on the belt so the belt won't become disengaged from any of the sprockets.*

3   Insert a suitable bar through the camshaft sprocket to lock it, remove the retaining bolt and withdraw the sprocket.

4   Using a suitable hooked tool, pry the seal out. Be careful not to damage the seal bore with the tool or oil leaks could develop.

5   Apply a light coat of grease around the outer edge of the new seal. Apply a film of engine oil to the seal lips. Place the seal in position and draw it into its bore, using the sprocket bolt and a suitable spacer piece such as a large socket **(see illustration)**.

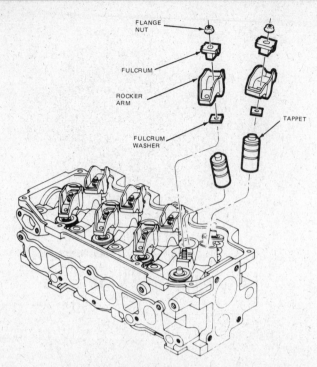

7.13a   An exploded view of the rocker arms and lifters (tappets) used on early models

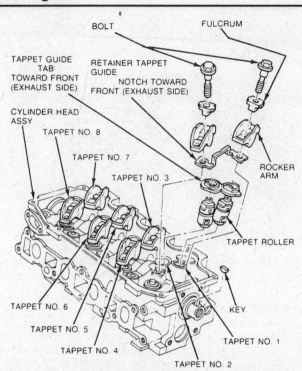

7.13b   An exploded view of the rocker arms and lifters (tappets) used on later models

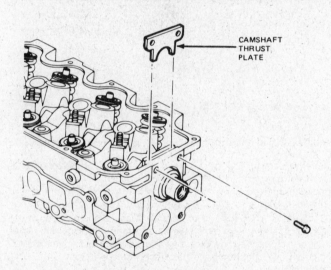

7.19   Camshaft thrust plate removal

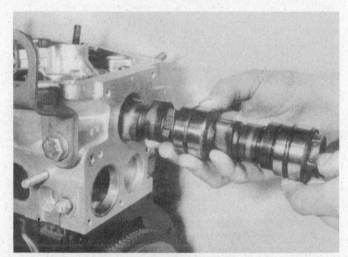

7.20   When removing the camshaft, support it close to the cylinder head and be careful not to contact the camshaft bearing surfaces in the cylinder head

6   Reinstall the sprocket and tighten the bolt to the torque listed in this Chapter's Specifications.
7   Install the timing belt and adjust the tension as described in Section 5.
8   Connect the battery negative cable.

7   Valve cover, camshaft, lifters and rocker arms – removal, inspection and installation

Valve cover

1   Disconnect the battery negative cable.
2   Disconnect the crankcase ventilation hose from the intake manifold and valve cover.

3   Remove the air cleaner (see Chapter 4).
4   Detach the throttle cable (see Chapter 4).
5   Remove the bolts and detach the valve cover.
6   Installation is basically the reverse of removal, but observe the following points:
   a) Use a scraper to remove all traces of old gasket material from the cylinder head and valve cover mating surfaces, then wipe them with a rag soaked in lacquer thinner or acetone. When scraping, be careful not to gouge the gasket mating surfaces or leaks will result.
   b) On engines equipped with a valve cover gasket, install a new gasket. Do not use sealant with silicone rubber gaskets. On engines that use RTV sealant instead of a valve cover gasket, remove all traces of old sealant and apply a ring of RTV sealant to the valve cover mating surface. Be sure to apply the sealant to the inside of the bolt holes or leaks will develop at the bolt holes.

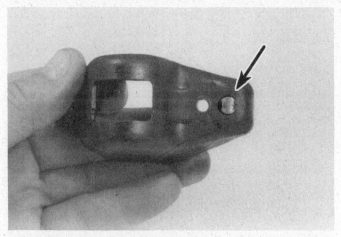

7.23a Check the rocker arm surfaces that contact the valve stem and lifter (arrow), ...

7.23b ... the fulcrum seats in the rocker arms ...

Camshaft, lifters and rocker arms
Removal
Refer to illustrations 7.13a, 7.13b, 7.19 and 7.20

7   Remove the valve cover, as described above.

8   If the windshield washer fluid reservoir will prevent the camshaft from sliding out of the engine, disconnect the pipes and remove the reservoir from the engine compartment.

9   On carbureted models, unbolt and remove the fuel pump (see Chapter 4).

10   On carbureted models, remove the fuel pump insulating spacer and operating pushrod.

11   Disconnect the wires from the spark plugs, then remove the distributor cap and secure it to the left side of the engine compartment.

12   Remove the distributor from the cylinder head (see Chapter 5).

13   Unscrew the securing nuts or bolts and remove the rocker arms, fulcrums and lifter (tappet) guide retainers (models equipped with roller lifters) **(see illustrations)**. Keep the components in their originally installed sequence by marking them with a piece of numbered tape or by using a suitable sub-divided box.

14   Withdraw the hydraulic lifters (and lifter guides, if so equipped), again keeping them in their originally installed sequence.

15   Remove the drivebelts (see Chapter 1).

16   On later models, remove the ignition coil and bracket, if necessary to provide clearance for the camshaft to slide out of the engine (see Chapter 5).

17   Remove the timing belt (see Section 5). **Note:** *If you want to save time by not removing and installing the timing belt and re-timing the engine, you can unfasten the camshaft sprocket and suspend it out of the way – with the belt still attached – by a piece of rope. Be sure the rope keeps firm tension on the belt so the belt won't become disengaged from any of the sprockets.*

18   Pass a rod or large screwdriver through one of the holes in the camshaft sprocket to lock it, then unscrew the sprocket bolt. Remove the sprocket.

19   Remove the two bolts and pull out the camshaft thrust plate **(see illustration)**.

20   Slowly withdraw the camshaft from the distributor end of the cylinder head **(see illustration)**.

Inspection
Lifters
21   Inspect each lifter for wear on the foot (the end that rides on the camshaft). If roller lifters are used, check that each roller turns freely and smoothly. Also check for wear on the end that contacts the rocker arm. Replace any lifters that show excessive wear.

22   On models with non-roller lifters, the foot should be slightly convex, but it's so slightly convex that it's impossible to tell by looking at it. Place the foot of each lifter against the side of another lifter (which is flat) and

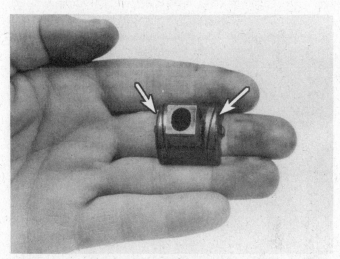

7.23c ... and the fulcrums themselves for wear and galling

move the lifter back and forth slightly. If the lifter does not move slightly, its foot is not convex and the lifter should be replaced.

Rocker arms
Refer to illustrations 7.23a, 7.23b and 7.23c

23   Inspect each rocker arm for wear at the points where it rides on the lifter, fulcrum and valve stem **(see illustrations)**. Replace any rocker arms or fulcrums that show excessive wear. Replace rocker arms and fulcrums as pairs. Do not replace just a rocker arm or fulcrum.

Camshaft
Refer to illustration 7.28

24   Inspect the camshaft for wear, particularly on the lobes. Look for places where the hardened surface of the lobe is flaking off, scored or showing excessive wear. Replace the camshaft if any of these conditions exist.

25   Using a micrometer, measure the camshaft bearing journals (the raised round areas). Compare your measurements with this Chapter's Specifications. If the measurements are out of specification, replace the camshaft.

26   Using an inside micrometer or telescoping gauge and micrometer, measure the inside diameter of the camshaft bearing surfaces in the cylinder head. Compare the measurements to this Chapter's Specifications. If the measurements are not within specification, remove the cylinder head (see Section 14 or 15) and take it to an automotive engine rebuilding shop.

27   To obtain the camshaft journal-to-bearing (oil) clearance, subtract the measurement you recorded for each bearing journal in Step 25 from the measurement you recorded for the corresponding bearing surface in Step 26. Compare the figure to this Chapter's Specifications.

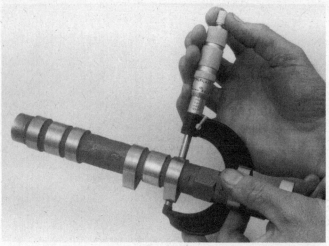

7.28   Measure the lobe height of each lobe on the camshaft, then measure 90-degrees from this measurement, at the base circle of the lobe

8.4   This is the air hose adapter that threads into the spark plug hole – they're commonly available from auto supply stores

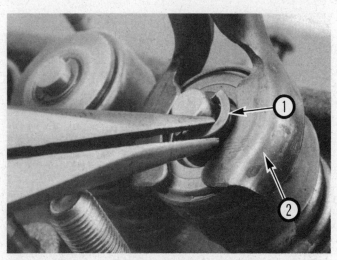

8.9   Valve spring compressor (2) releasing the valve keepers (1)

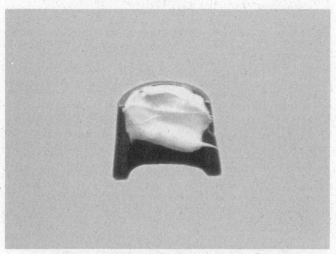

8.17   Apply a small dab of grease onto each keeper before installation to hold it in place on the valve stem until the spring is released

28   To obtain the camshaft lobe lift measurement, measure each camshaft lobe at its highest point **(see illustration)**, then measure it 90-degrees from this point, at its lowest point. Subtract the lowest-point measurement from the highest-point measurement and compare the figure to this Chapter's Specifications. If any lobe lifts are not within specification, replace the camshaft.

Installation

29   Installing the camshaft, lifters and rocker arms is the reverse of removal, but observe the following points:

30   Lubricate the camshaft bearing surfaces before inserting the camshaft into the cylinder head.

31   A new oil seal should always be installed after the camshaft has been installed (see Section 6). Apply thread locking compound to the sprocket bolt threads. Reinstall the sprocket and tighten the bolt to the torque listed in this Chapter's Specifications.

32   Install and adjust the timing belt as described in Section 5.

33   Lubricate the hydraulic lifters with engine oil before inserting them into their original bores.

34   Replace the rocker arms and guides in their original sequence. Use new nuts and tighten them to the torque listed in this Chapter's Specifications. It is essential that before each rocker arm is installed and its nut tightened, the respective lifter is positioned at its lowest point (in contact with the cam base circle). Turn the camshaft (by means of the crankshaft pulley bolt) as necessary to achieve this.

8   Valve springs, retainers and seals – replacement

Refer to illustrations 8.4, 8.9 and 8.17

Note: *Broken valve springs and defective valve stem seals can be replaced without removing the cylinder head. Two special tools and a compressed air source are normally required to perform this operation, so read through this Section carefully and rent or buy the tools before beginning the job. If compressed air isn't available, a length of nylon rope can be used to keep the valves from falling into the cylinder during this procedure.*

1   Refer to Section 7 and remove the valve cover from the cylinder head.

2   Remove the spark plug from the cylinder which has the defective component. If all of the valve stem seals are being replaced, all of the spark plugs should be removed.

3   Turn the crankshaft until the piston in the affected cylinder is at top dead center on the compression stroke (refer to Section 3 for instructions). If you're replacing all of the valve stem seals, begin with cylinder number one and work on the valves for one cylinder at a time. Move from cylinder-to-cylinder following the firing order sequence (see this Chapter's Specifications).

4   Thread an adapter into the spark plug hole **(see illustration)** and connect an air hose from a compressed air source to it. Most auto parts stores

9.12 Intake manifold installation – carbureted models

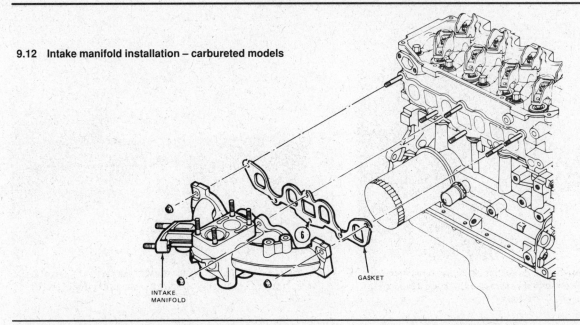

INTAKE
MANIFOLD

GASKET

can supply the air hose adapter. **Note:** *Many cylinder compression gauges utilize a screw-in fitting that may work with your air hose quick-disconnect fitting.*

5   Remove the nut, fulcrum and rocker arm for the valve with the defective part. If all of the valve stem seals are being replaced, all of the rocker arms should be removed (refer to Section 7).

6   Apply compressed air to the cylinder. **Warning:** *The piston may be forced down by compressed air, causing the crankshaft to turn suddenly. If the wrench used when positioning the number one piston at TDC is still attached to the bolt in the crankshaft nose, it could cause damage or injury when the crankshaft moves.*

7   The valves should be held in place by the air pressure. If the valve faces or seats are in poor condition, leaks may prevent air pressure from retaining the valves – refer to the alternative procedure following.

8   If you don't have access to compressed air, an alternative method can be used. Position the piston at a point approximately 45-degrees before TDC on the compression stroke, then feed a long piece of nylon rope through the spark plug hole until it fills the combustion chamber. Be sure to leave the end of the rope hanging out of the engine so it can be removed easily. Use a large ratchet and socket to rotate the crankshaft in the normal direction of rotation until slight resistance is felt.

9   Stuff shop rags into the cylinder head holes above and below the valves to prevent parts and tools from falling into the engine, then use a valve spring compressor to compress the spring. Remove the keepers with small needle-nose pliers or a magnet **(see illustration)**. **Note:** *A couple of different types of tools are available for compressing the valve springs with the head in place. One type, shown here, grips the lower spring coils and presses on the retainer as the knob is turned, while the other type utilizes the rocker arm stud and nut for leverage. Both types work very well, although the lever type is usually less expensive.*

10   Remove the spring retainer, shield and valve spring, then remove the umbrella type guide seal. **Note:** *If air pressure fails to hold the valve in the closed position during this operation, the valve face or seat is probably damaged. If so, the cylinder head will have to be removed for additional repair operations.*

11   Wrap a rubber band or tape around the top of the valve stem so the valve won't fall into the combustion chamber, then release the air pressure.

12   Inspect the valve stem for damage. Rotate the valve in the guide and check the end for eccentric movement, which would indicate that the valve is bent.

13   Move the valve up-and-down in the guide and make sure it doesn't bind. If the valve stem binds, either the valve is bent or the guide is damaged. In either case, the head will have to be removed for repair.

14   Reapply air pressure to the cylinder to retain the valve in the closed

position, then remove the tape or rubber band from the valve stem. If a rope was used instead of air pressure, rotate the crankshaft in the normal direction of rotation until slight resistance is felt.

15   Lubricate the valve stem with engine oil and install a new guide seal.

16   Install the spring and shield in position over the valve.

17   Install the valve spring retainer. Compress the valve spring and carefully position the keepers in the groove. Apply a small dab of grease to the inside of each keeper to hold it in place **(see illustration)**.

18   Remove the pressure from the spring tool and make sure the keepers are seated.

19   Disconnect the air hose and remove the adapter from the spark plug hole. If a rope was used in place of air pressure, pull it out of the cylinder.

20   Refer to Section 7 and install the rocker arm(s).

21   Install the spark plug(s) and hook up the wire(s).

22   Refer to Section 7 and install the valve cover.

23   Start and run the engine, then check for oil leaks and unusual sounds coming from the valve cover area.

9   Intake manifold (carbureted models) – removal and installation

Refer to illustration 9.12

Removal

1   Disconnect the battery negative cable.

2   Drain the cooling system partially and disconnect the heater hoses from the manifold.

3   Remove the air cleaner assembly (see Chapter 4) and disconnect and label any vacuum hoses which would interfere with removal.

4   Disconnect the carburetor bowl vent, choke cap and idle fuel solenoid wires.

5   Remove the EGR supply tube (see Chapter 6).

6   Raise the vehicle and support it securely on jackstands.

7   Remove and label the ported vacuum switch connectors.

8   Remove the bottom three intake manifold nuts.

9   Lower the vehicle and disconnect the fuel line from the filter and the return line from the carburetor.

10   Disconnect the accelerator cable (see Chapter 4), cruise control cable (if equipped) and Throttle Valve (TV) linkage (automatic transaxle models only) (see Chapter 7B). Remove the cable bracket bolts.

11   Remove the fuel pump (see Chapter 4).

12   Remove the remaining attachment nuts and the intake manifold **(see illustration)**. **Note:** *To avoid damage to the machined surface do not lay the intake manifold on the gasket surface.*

2A

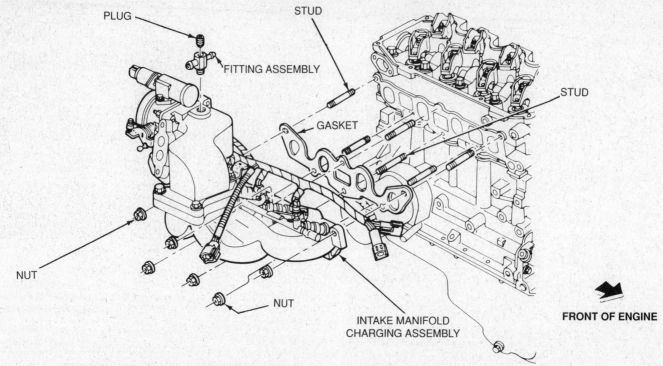

10.11   Intake manifold and related components (turbo and 1983 through 1985 fuel-injected models)

Installation

13   Use a scraper to remove all traces of old gasket material from the manifold and cylinder head mating surfaces, then clean the surfaces with a rag soaked in lacquer thinner or acetone. Be careful not to gouge the mating surfaces while scraping. Install a new gasket, place the manifold in position and install the upper and lower retaining nuts and tighten them to the torque listed in this Chapter's Specifications.
14   Install the fuel pump (see Chapter 4).
15   Connect all throttle cables and brackets that were removed.
16   Connect the fuel lines.
17   Connect the ported vacuum switch and heater hoses.
18   Connect the wires to the choke cap, bowl vent and idle fuel solenoid.
19   Install the EGR supply tube (see Chapter 6).
20   Lower the vehicle.
21   Reconnect any vacuum hoses which were removed and install the air cleaner assembly.
22   Fill the cooling system with the specified coolant (see Chapter 3).
23   Connect the battery negative cable.

10   Intake manifold (turbo and 1983 through 1985 fuel-injected models) – removal and installation

Refer to illustration 10.11

Removal

1   Relieve the fuel system pressure (see Chapter 4), then disconnect the battery negative cable.
2   Remove the air intake from the throttle body (see Chapter 4).
3   Disconnect and label the vacuum hoses connected to the intake manifold.
4   Remove the EGR tube (see Chapter 6).
5   Disconnect the electrical connector at the air bypass valve and the engine wiring harness at the shock absorber tower.
6   Raise the vehicle and support it securely on jackstands.
7   Remove the bottom three intake manifold nuts.
8   Lower the vehicle and disconnect the fuel lines (inlet and return) at the manifold.

9   Disconnect the accelerator cable from the throttle body (see Chapter 4).
10   Remove the PCV orifice and hose from the intake manifold and valve cover.
11   Remove the three remaining attachment nuts and carefully detach the intake manifold **(see illustration)**. **Note:** *To avoid damage to the machined surface do not lay the intake manifold on the gasket surface.*

Installation

12   Installation is the reverse of removal. Use a scraper to remove all traces of old gasket material from the manifold and cylinder head mating surfaces, then clean the surfaces with a rag soaked in lacquer thinner or acetone. Be careful not to gouge the mating surfaces while scraping. Install a new gasket and tighten the nuts to the torque listed in this Chapter's Specifications.

11   Intake manifold (1986 and later fuel-injected models) – removal and installation

Multi-port fuel-injected (EFI) models
Refer to illustration 11.10

1   Disconnect the battery negative cable.
2   Depressurize the fuel system. Remove the air cleaner assembly and disconnect and label any vacuum hoses which would interfere with removal.
3   Disconnect the accelerator cable and cruise control cable (if so equipped).
4   Disconnect the vacuum lines from the manifold and the EGR valve.
5   Disconnect the EGR supply tube by unscrewing the upper tube nut while holding the lower nut with a wrench.
6   Remove the upper support bracket bolt.
7   Unplug the electrical connectors from the wire harness and the sensor located near the heater supply tube.
8   Disconnect the fuel return and supply lines.
9   Remove the upper of the two bracket-to-block retaining bolts. Remove the six intake manifold retaining nuts.

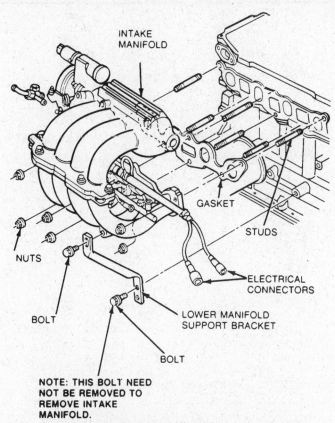

11.10   Intake manifold details (1986 and later multi-port fuel-injected models)

12.4   EGR supply tube (CFI manifold shown, others similar)

27   Installation is the reverse of the removal Steps. Use a new gasket. Tighten the manifold nuts to the torque listed in this Chapter's Specifications. Use torque wrench adapter T81P-9245-A or equivalent to tighten the top center nut.

2A

10   Remove the intake manifold from the engine, complete with wiring harness **(see illustration)**. **Note:** *To avoid damage to the machined surface do not lay the intake manifold on the gasket surface.*
11   Installation is the reverse of removal. Use a scraper to remove all traces of old gasket material from the manifold and cylinder head mating surfaces, then clean the surfaces with a rag soaked in lacquer thinner or acetone. Be careful not to gouge the mating surfaces while scraping. Install a new gasket and tighten the nuts to the torque listed in this Chapter's Specifications.

Central Fuel Injection (CFI) models

12   Disconnect the negative cable from the battery.
13   Drain part of the coolant and disconnect the heater hose from the fitting at the side of the intakle manifold.
14   Remove the air cleaner (see Chapter 4).
15   Label the vacuum hoses that attach to the intake manifold, then disconnect them.
16   Unplug the electrical connectors from the air charge temperature sensor and coolant temperature sensor **(see illustration 2.5 in Chapter 6).**
17   Disconnect the EGR supply tube from the intake manifold.
18   Raise the front of the vehicle and support it securely on jackstands.
19   Label and disconnect the vacuum lines from the bottom of the manifold.
20   Remove the lower four intake manifold attaching nuts.
21   Remove the jackstands and lower the vehicle.
22   Disconnect the fuel lines from the throttle body (see Chapter 4).
23   Disconnect the accelerator cable (and speed control cable, if equipped).
24   If equipped with an automatic transaxle, disconnect the throttle valve linkage and remove the cable bracket.
25   Remove the remaining intake manifold nuts. Use torque wrench adapter T81P-9245-A or equivalent on the top center nut.
26   Remove the manifold and gasket. Don't set the manifold down on the gasket surface or it may be damaged.

12   Exhaust manifold (non-turbo models) – removal and installation

Refer to illustrations 12.4 and 12.8

1   Disconnect the battery negative cable.
2   If the air cleaner obstructs manifold removal, remove it (see Chapter 4).
3   Remove the hot air tube and shroud assembly (if equipped).
4   Disconnect the exhaust gas oxygen sensor and EGR supply tube at the exhaust manifold **(see illustration)**.
5   Unbolt the exhaust pipe from the manifold.
6   Remove the attaching nuts and remove the manifold. It may be necessary to rock the manifold up and down to break it loose from the cylinder head. Do not attempt to use a screwdriver or prybar to pry on the manifold as this could damage the mating surfaces on manifold and cylinder head.
7   Use a scraper to remove all traces of old gasket material from the manifold and cylinder head mating surfaces, then clean the surfaces with a rag soaked in lacquer thinner or acetone. Be careful not to gouge the mating surfaces while scraping.
8   To install, place the manifold and new gasket (except CFI models) in position, install the attaching nuts and tighten them to the torque listed in this Chapter's Specifications **(see illustration)**.
9   Reinstall the removed components and connect the battery negative cable.

13   Exhaust manifold (turbo models) – removal and installation

The exhaust manifold is removed together with the turbocharger (refer to Chapter 4).

14   Cylinder head (non-turbo models) – removal and installation

Refer to illustrations 14.14 and 14.18

Removal

1   Disconnect the battery negative cable.
2   Remove the air cleaner and detach the connecting hoses.
3   Drain the cooling system (see Chapter 3).

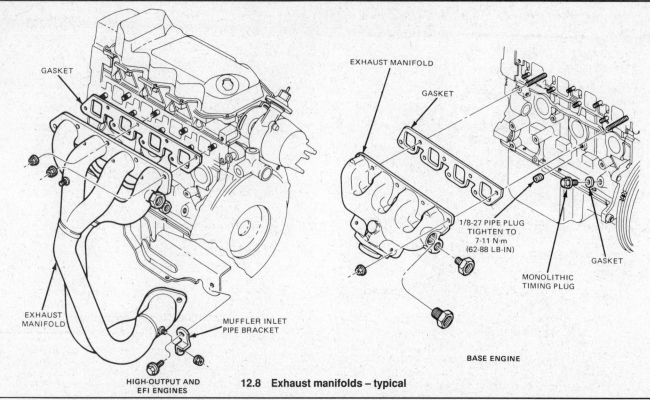

12.8   Exhaust manifolds – typical

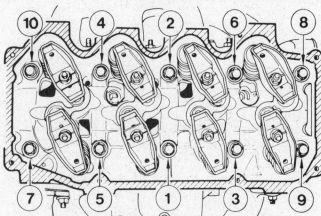

14.14   Cylinder head bolt TIGHTENING sequence – when loosening the bolts, reverse this sequence

4   Disconnect the coolant hoses from the thermostat housing and from the heater fitting under the manifold (if equipped).

5   Disconnect the throttle cable from the carburetor or throttle body (see Chapter 4). Disconnect the cruise control cable and automatic transaxle Throttle Valve (TV) linkage (if equipped) (see Chapter 7B).

6   On carbureted models, disconnect the fuel pipe from the fuel pump.

7   Disconnect the vacuum servo pipe (power brakes) from the intake manifold.

8   Disconnect the EGR supply tube from the exhaust manifold **(see illustration 12.4).**

9   Disconnect the leads from the coolant temperature sender, the ignition coil and the anti-run-on solenoid valve at the carburetor (if equipped).

10   Unbolt the exhaust downpipe from the manifold by unscrewing the flange bolts. Support the exhaust pipe by tying it up with wire.

11   Set the No. 1 piston to TDC (see Section 3) and remove the timing belt (see Section 5). **Note:** *If you want to save time by not removing and installing the timing belt and re-timing the engine, you can unfasten the camshaft sprocket and suspend it out of the way – with the belt still attached – by a*

piece of rope. Be sure the rope keeps firm tension on the belt so the belt won't become disengaged from any of the sprockets.

12   Disconnect the leads from the spark plugs and unscrew and remove the spark plugs.

13   Remove the valve cover (see Section 7).

14   Unscrew the cylinder head bolts, progressively and in the reverse sequence to that given for tightening **(see illustration)**. Discard the bolts, as new ones must be used during installation.

15   Remove the cylinder head complete with the manifolds. Use the manifolds if necessary as levers to rock the head from the block. Do not attempt to tap the head sideways off the block as it is located on dowels, and do not attempt to lever between the head and the block or damage will result.

Installation

16   Before installing the cylinder head, make sure the mating surfaces of the cylinder head and block are perfectly clean with the head locating dowels in position. Clean the bolt holes free from oil. In extreme cases it is possible that oil left in the holes could crack the block.

17   On all 1.9L engines, check the piston "squish" height (see Section 15, Steps 12 through 17).

18   If either the crankshaft or camshaft was disturbed after cylinder head removal, position the crankshaft keyway at 9 o'clock and the camshaft keyway at 6 o'clock **(see illustration)**.

19   Use a scraper to remove all traces of old gasket material from the head and cylinder block mating surfaces. Clean the surfaces with a rag soaked in lacquer thinner or acetone. Place a new head gasket on the cylinder block and then locate the cylinder head on the locating dowels **(see illustration 14.18)**. The upper surface of most gaskets is marked "UP" or "TOP." Be sure this side faces up.

20   Install and tighten the cylinder head bolts as described in this Chapter's specifications. In order to measure the 1/4-turn tightening stages accurately, mark each bolt head with a spot of quick-drying paint (with the paint spots all pointing in the same direction). Tighten all bolts at each stage in the proper sequence before going to the next stage **(see illustration 14.14)**.

21   Install the timing belt as described in Section 5.

22   Installation and reconnecting of all other components is a reversal of removal.

23   Refill the cooling system (see Chapter 3).

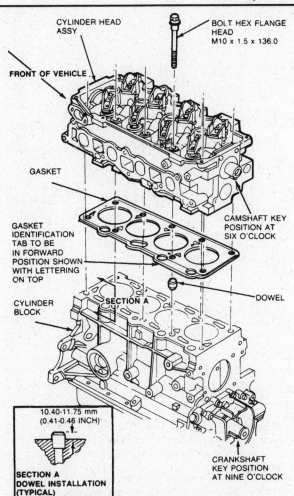

14.18 Cylinder head removal and installation

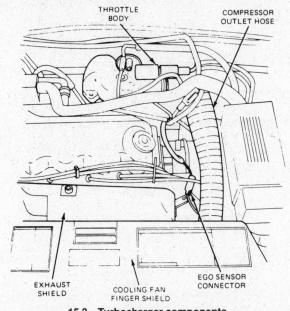

15.3 Turbocharger components

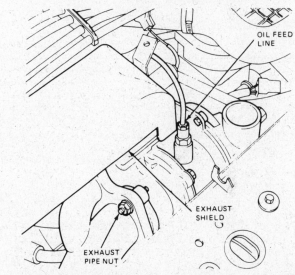

15.9a Turbocharger oil feed line and exhaust pipe connections

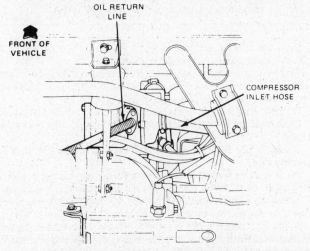

15.9b Turbocharger oil return line location

2A

15 Cylinder head (turbo models) – removal and installation

Refer to illustrations 15.3, 15.9a, 15.9b and 15.13

1   The procedure in Section 14 should be followed with the addition of the following steps:

2   Disconnect the upper radiator hose at the cylinder head.

3   Disconnect the cooling fan switch lead and any EFI-related wires that may interfere with removal **(see illustration)**. **Note:** *When disconnecting EFI wires, each should be marked to simplify reconnection.*

4   Remove the air intake hose at the throttle body (see Chapter 4).

5   Remove the PCV oil separator system.

6   Disconnect the EGO sensor and the EGR valve vacuum hose.

7   Remove the turbocharger air inlet hose.

8   Disconnect and remove the oil supply tube at the turbocharger coolant outlet and the engine block.

9   Disconnect the exhaust pipe from the turbocharger, then disconnect the oil return line at the turbocharger **(see illustrations)**.

10   Remove the cylinder head with the turbocharger attached. Use a scraper to remove all traces of old gasket material from the head and cylinder block mating surfaces. Clean the surfaces with a rag soaked in lacquer thinner or acetone. **Note:** *Before installing the cylinder head, the piston "squish" height must be checked (see Steps 12 through 17). Try to keep the head gasket in good condition during removal, as a used head gasket is preferred for the squish height measurement.*

11   Place a new head gasket on the cylinder block and then locate the cylinder head on the locating dowels. The upper surface of most gaskets is marked "UP" or "TOP". Be sure this side faces up. **Note:** *The cylinder head*

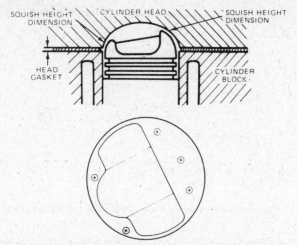

15.13   Position small pieces of solder at the points indicated when checking piston "squish" height

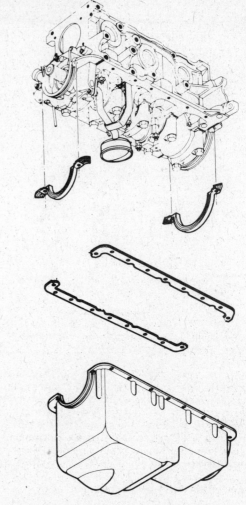

16.8   Oil pan installation

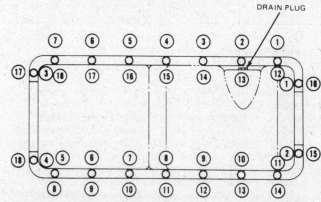

16.9   Oil pan bolt tightening sequence – use the inner number sequence for initial tightening and the outer sequence for final tightening

gasket on a turbo engine is different than the one on a non-turbo engine. Be sure the correct gasket is installed. The remainder of installation is the reverse of the removal procedure.

Piston "squish" height (all turbo and 1.9L models) – checking

Note: *Any replacement of parts (crankshaft, pistons and connecting rods) or modification to the cylinder head causing the "squish" height to be out of specification are not permitted. If no parts other than a head gasket are replaced, the piston "squish" height should be within this Chapter's Specifications. If parts other than the head gasket are replaced the "squish" height must be checked.*

12   Clean both gasket surfaces (cylinder head and engine block) to remove all old gasket material.

13   Place a small amount of solder on the piston in the areas shown in the illustration **(see illustration).**

14   Rotate the crankshaft to lower the piston and install the head gasket and the cylinder head. **Note:** *A compressed (used) head gasket is preferred.*

15   Install the head bolts and tighten them to 30 to 44 ft-lbs in the proper tightening sequence **(see illustration 14.14). Note:** *This specification is solely for the purpose of checking the position squish height. When reinstalling the cylinder head, be sure to use the torque values listed in this Chapter's Specifications.*

16   Rotate the crankshaft to move the piston through the TDC position.

17   Remove the cylinder head and measure the thickness of the solder to determine the "squish" height. It should be as listed in this Chapter's Specifications. If it is not, double-check to make sure that any new parts installed which might affect "squish" height, such as the head gasket or pistons, are the parts specified for this engine. If you have the correct parts and the "squish" height is still not within this Chapter's Specifications, consult your Ford dealer service department.

16   Oil pan (1981 through 1985 non-turbo models) – removal and installation

Refer to illustrations 16.8 and 16.9

Removal

1   Disconnect the battery negative cable.
2   Drain the engine oil (see Chapter 1).
3   Remove the starter motor (see Chapter 5).
4   Remove the cover plate from the flywheel housing.
5   Unscrew the plastic timing belt trim guard from the front of the engine (two bolts).

6   Unscrew the oil pan securing bolts progressively and remove them.
7   Remove the oil pan and remove the gasket and sealing strips.

Installation

8   Using a scraper, remove all traces of old gasket material from the oil pan and cylinder block mating surfaces. Clean the surfaces with a rag soaked in lacquer thinner or acetone. While scraping, be careful not to gouge the mating surfaces or oil leaks will develop. Make sure the sealing

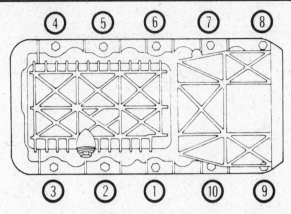

17.9 Oil pan tightening sequence – 1986 through 1990 models

11   Tighten the pan-to-transaxle bolts to the torque listed in this Chapter's Specifications.
12   The remainder of installation is the reverse of the removal procedure.

18   Oil pan (turbo models) – removal and installation

1   The procedure in Section 16 should be followed with the addition of the following steps.
2   Remove the knee braces at the transaxle.
3   Remove the EGR tube at the exhaust inlet and disconnect the exhaust pipe between the turbocharger and the converter.
4   The remainder of installation is the reverse of the removal procedure.

19   Flywheel/driveplate – removal and installation

Removal

1   Raise the vehicle and support it securely on jackstands, then refer to Chapter 7 and remove the transaxle. If it's leaking, now would be a very good time to replace the front pump seal/O-ring (automatic transaxle only).
2   Remove the pressure plate and clutch disc (see Chapter 8) (manual transaxle equipped vehicles). Now is a good time to check/replace the clutch components and pilot bearing.
3   Use a center-punch to make alignment marks on the flywheel/driveplate and crankshaft to ensure correct alignment during reinstallation.
4   Remove the bolts that secure the flywheel/driveplate to the crankshaft. If the crankshaft turns, wedge a screwdriver through the starter opening to jam the flywheel.
5   Remove the flywheel/driveplate from the crankshaft. Since the flywheel is fairly heavy, be sure to support it while removing the last bolt.

Installation

6   Clean the flywheel to remove grease and oil. Inspect the surface for cracks, rivet grooves, burned areas and score marks. Light scoring can be removed with emery cloth. Check for cracked and broken ring gear teeth. Lay the flywheel on a flat surface and use a straightedge to check for warpage.
7   Clean and inspect the mating surfaces of the flywheel/driveplate and the crankshaft. If the crankshaft rear seal is leaking, replace it before reinstalling the flywheel/driveplate.
8   Position the flywheel/driveplate against the crankshaft. Be sure to align the marks made during removal. Note that some models have an alignment dowel or staggered bolt holes to ensure correct installation. Before installing the bolts, apply thread locking compound to the threads.
9   Wedge a screwdriver through the starter motor opening to keep the flywheel/driveplate from turning as you tighten the bolts to the torque listed in this Chapter's Specifications.
10   The remainder of installation is the reverse of the removal procedure.

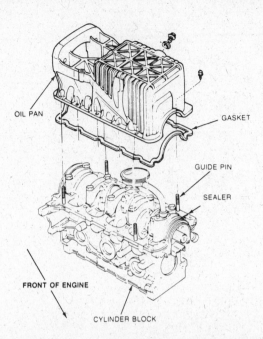

17.7 Oil pan installation details – 1986 through 1990 models

surfaces of the oil pan and the block are clean, then install new end sealing strips into their grooves and stick new side gaskets into position using an adhesive gasket sealer to hold them in place. Press the front seal into the retainer and the rear seal into the oil pump slot. Apply adhesive to the oil pump flange and the mating surface of the oil pan gaskets. The end of the side gaskets should overlap the end sealing strips **(see illustration)**.
9   Install the oil pan, taking care not to displace the gaskets. Then insert the securing bolts and tighten them in the sequence shown **(see illustration)**.
10   Install the cover plate to the flywheel housing.
11   Install the starter motor.
12   Fill the engine with oil (see Chapter 1) and connect the battery negative cable.

17   Oil pan (1986 through 1990 non-turbo models) – removal and installation

Refer to illustrations 17.7 and 17.9

1   The procedure in Section 16 should be followed with the addition of the following steps:
2   Remove the two bolts attaching the oil pan to the transaxle.
3   Remove the exhaust pipe at the manifold and catalytic converter.
4   Prior to installation, remove the oil pump pickup tube and screen. Clean the screen and install the assembly using a new gasket.
5   Clean the gasket mating surface of the pan and engine block and apply a bead of Ford silicone rubber gasket sealant (D6AZ-19562-B) or equivalent at the corners of the block, at the oil pump seating joint and at the rear seal retainer joint.
6   Clean the oil pan rail with solvent to remove all traces of oil.
7   Install the gasket in the oil pan **(see illustration)**. Be sure to press the tabs securely into the channel.
8   Place the oil pan in position and install the bolts finger tight. **Note:** *If the pan is being installed with the engine out of the vehicle, the transaxle or a similar fixture must be in place so the pan will line up flush with the engine block.*
9   Tighten the pan bolts enough to allow the two 10 mm pan-to-transaxle bolts to be installed. Tighten the bolts to the torque listed in this Chapter's Specifications in the sequence shown **(see illustration)**.
10   Tighten the pan-to-block bolts to the torque listed in this Chapter's Specifications.

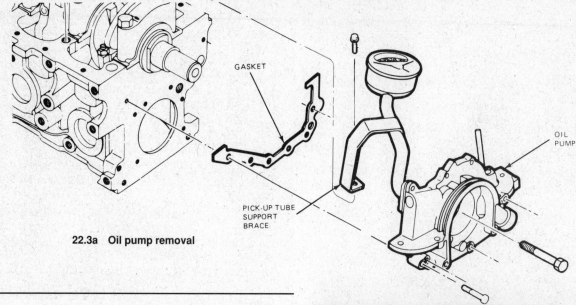

22.3a   Oil pump removal

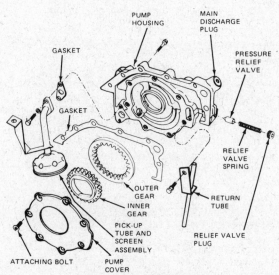

22.3b   Oil pump components

22.5   Wrap tape around the front end of the crankshaft to prevent damage to the oil pump seal during installation

3   Unbolt and remove the rear cover plate.
4   Remove the flywheel/driveplate (see section 19).
5   Using a suitable hooked tool, pry out the oil seal from the cylinder block. **Note:** *Use caution to avoid damage to the oil seal bore in the engine block.*
6   Grease the lips of the new seal and press the new seal into position, using special tool T81P-6701-A or equivalent. If the special tool is unavailable, you may be able to tap the seal into position squarely with a blunt punch and a hammer. If you must use this method, be very careful not to damage the seal or crankshaft. As you install the seal, work the seal lip over the end of the crankshaft with the rounded end of a socket extension or a similar tool.
7   Installation is the reverse of the removal procedure.
8   Run the engine and check for oil leaks.

20   Crankshaft front oil seal – replacement

1   Remove the timing belt (see Section 5).
2   Pull off the crankshaft sprocket. If it is tight, use a two-jaw puller.
3   Remove the dished washer from the crankshaft, noting that the concave side is against the oil seal.
4   Using a suitable hooked tool, pry out the oil seal from the oil pump housing.
5   Grease the lips of the new seal and press it into position using the pulley bolt, a large washer and a suitable distance piece made from a piece of pipe.
6   Install the dished washer (concave side to the oil seal), the belt sprocket and the pulley to the crankshaft.
7   Install and adjust the timing belt by the method described in Section 5.

21   Crankshaft rear oil seal – replacement

1   Disconnect the battery negative cable.
2   Remove the transaxle (see Chapter 7).

22   Oil pump – removal and installation

Refer to illustrations 22.3a, 22.3b, 22.5, 22.6, 22.9a and 22.9b
1   Remove the timing belt cover, timing chain and pulleys (see Section 5).
2   Remove the water pump (see Chapter 3) and the oil pan (see Section 16, 17 or 18).
3   Remove the oil pump and support brace attaching bolts and remove the oil pump **(see illustrations)**.

22.6 Prime the oil pump prior to installation

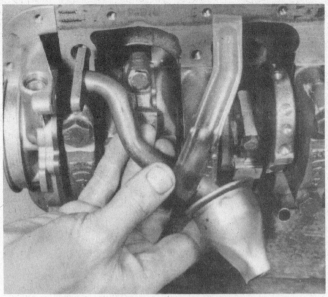

22.9a Installing the oil pump pick-up tube

2A

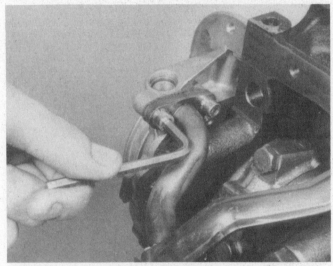

22.9b Use an Allen wrench to tighten the oil pick-up tube bolt

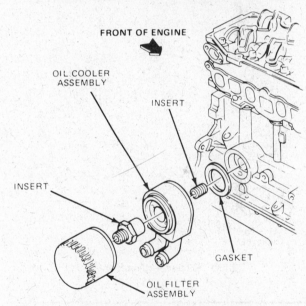

FRONT OF ENGINE

OIL COOLER
ASSEMBLY

INSERT

INSERT

GASKET

OIL FILTER
ASSEMBLY

23.5 Oil cooler installation details

4   Clean the oil pump with solvent and inspect it for wear, grooving or scoring of the mating surface and the rotor for nicks or burrs. Check the gears for damage, wear or looseness. Use a feeler gauge to check if gear-to-housing clearances are within specification. Check the relief valve spring for free movement and to see if it is collapsed or worn. The oil pump cannot be rebuilt and a suspected unit should be replaced with a new one.

5   Before installing the oil pump, the crankshaft must be wrapped to prevent damage to the oil seal from the step on the front of the crankshaft. First remove the Woodruff key and then build up the front end of the crankshaft using adhesive tape to form a smooth inclined surface to permit the pump seal to slide over the step without its lip turning back or the seal spring being displaced during installation **(see illustration)**.

6   If the oil pump is new pour some oil into it before installation in order to prime it and rotate its driving gear a few times **(see illustration)**.

7   Align the pump gear flats with those on the crankshaft and install the oil pump complete with a new gasket. Tighten the bolts to the torque listed in this Chapter's Specifications

8   Remove the adhesive tape from the crankshaft and install the Woodruff key into its groove.

9   Bolt the oil pick-up tube into position and tighten it securely **(see illustrations)**.

10   Install a new crankshaft front oil seal (see Section 20).

11   Install the water pump (see Chapter 3) and the oil pan (see Section 16, 17 or 18).

12   Install the timing belt cover, timing chain and pulleys (see Section 5).

23   Oil cooler (turbo models) – removal and installation

Refer to illustration 23.5

1   Disconnect the battery negative lead.

2   Drain the engine oil and remove the oil filter (see Chapter 1).

3   Drain the engine coolant (see Chapter 3).

4   Disconnect the two coolant hoses at the oil cooler.

5   Remove the oil filter insert from the cooler and detach the oil cooler **(see illustration)**.

6   Installation is the reverse of the removal procedure. Use a new oil cooler gasket and refill the cooling system with the proper mixture of water and coolant (see Chapter 3).

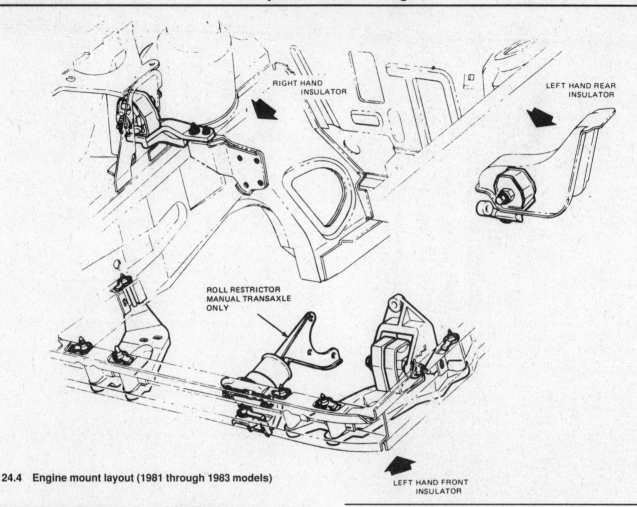

24.4   Engine mount layout (1981 through 1983 models)

24   Engine mounts – check and replacement

Refer to illustrations 24.4, 24.8a, 24.8b, 24.8c, 24.8d, 24.8e and 24.8f

1   Engine mounts seldom require attention, but broken or deteriorated mounts should be replaced immediately or the added strain placed on the driveline components may cause damage or wear.

Check

2   During the check, the engine must be raised slightly to remove the weight from the mounts.
3   Raise the vehicle and support it securely on jackstands, then position a jack under the engine oil pan. Place a large block of wood between the jack head and the oil pan, then carefully raise the engine just enough to take the weight off the mounts. **Warning:** *DO NOT place any part of your body under the engine when it's supported only by a jack!*
4   Check the mounts to see if the rubber is cracked, hardened or separated from the metal plates **(see illustration)**. Sometimes the rubber will split right down the center.
5   Check for relative movement between the mount plates and the engine or frame (use a large screwdriver or pry bar to attempt to move the mounts). If movement is noted, lower the engine and tighten the mount fasteners.
6   Rubber preservative should be applied to the mounts to slow deterioration.

Replacement

7   Disconnect the negative battery cable from the battery, then raise the vehicle and support it securely on jackstands (if not already done).
8   Remove the fasteners and detach the mount from the frame bracket **(see illustrations)**.

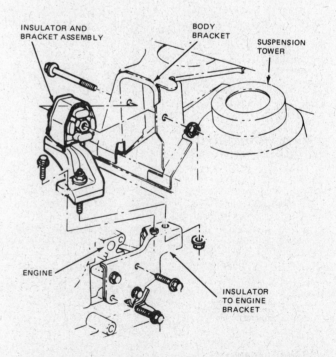

24.8a   Right (number 3A) engine mount and insulator (1981 through 1983 models)

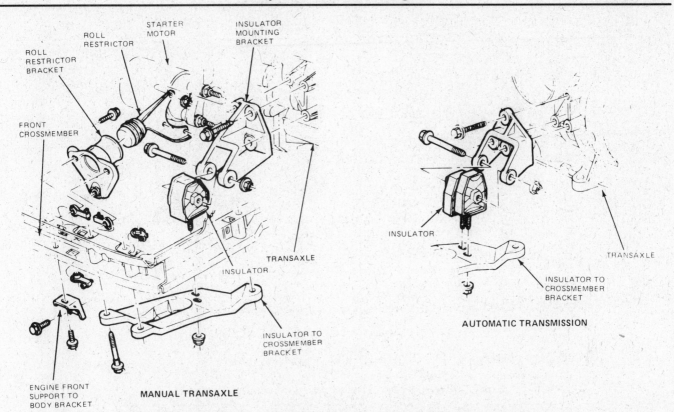

24.8b Left front (number 1) engine mount and insulator (1981 through 1983 models)

2A

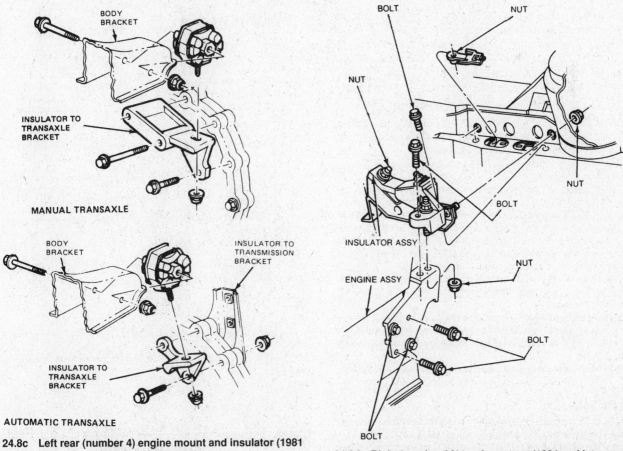

24.8c Left rear (number 4) engine mount and insulator (1981 through 1983 models)

24.8d Right (number 3A) engine mount (1984 and later models)

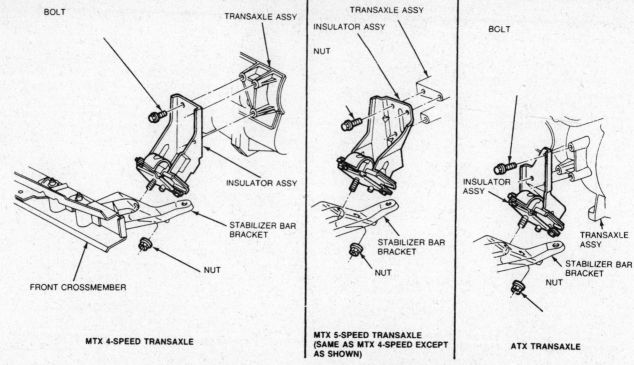

24.8e   Left front (number 1) engine mount (1984 and later models)

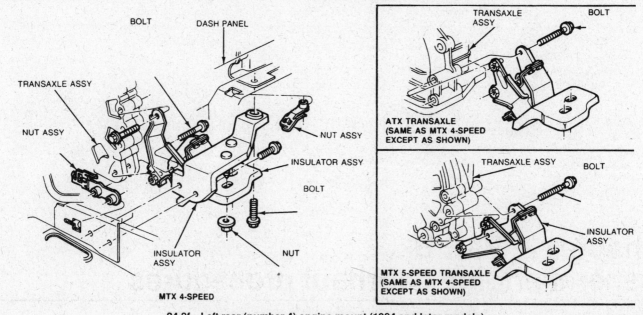

24.8f   Left rear (number 4) engine mount (1984 and later models)

9   Raise the engine slightly with a jack or hoist (make sure the fan doesn't hit the radiator or shroud). Remove the mount-to-block bolts and detach the mount.

10   Installation is the reverse of the removal procedures with the following additions:

11   The right insulator must be installed with the word "Front" facing the transaxle bracket.

12   Use thread locking compound on the mount bolts and tighten the bolts securely.

Chapter 2 Part B
General engine overhaul procedures

Contents

Specifications

General

Oil pressure (at 2000 rpm) .... 35 to 65 psi
Compression pressure .... The lowest-reading cylinder must be within 75-percent of the highest-reading cylinder (see chart below)

COMPRESSION TEST PERCENTAGE CHART

Maximum PSI	Minimum PSI	Maximum PSI	Minimum PSI	Maximum PSI	Minimum PSI
134	101	174	131	214	160
136	102	176	132	216	162
138	104	178	133	218	163
140	105	180	135	220	165
142	107	182	136	222	166
144	108	184	138	224	168
146	110	186	140	226	169
148	111	188	141	228	171
150	113	190	142	230	172
152	114	192	144	232	174
154	115	194	145	234	175
156	117	196	147	236	177
158	118	198	148	238	178
160	120	200	150	240	180
162	121	202	151	242	181
164	123	204	153	244	183
166	124	206	154	246	184
168	126	208	156	248	186
170	127	210	157	250	187
172	129	212	158		

Find the reading for the highest cylinder in the Maximum PSI column, then look across to the Minimum PSI column to find the lowest acceptable reading for the lowest cylinder

Cylinder head and valves

Valve seats (intake and exhaust)
  Width .... 0.069 to 0.091 inch
  Angle 45-degrees
  Runout (total indicator reading) .... 0.003 inch max
Cylinder head warpage limits
  Per inch .... 0.0016 inch
  Per six inches .... 0.003 inch
  Total .... 0.059 inch
Valve stem-to-guide clearance
  1981 through 1983
    Intake .... 0.0008 to 0.0027 inch
    Exhaust .... 0.0015 to 0.0032 inch
  1984 on
    Intake .... 0.0008 to 0.0027 inch
    Exhaust .... 0.0018 to 0.0037 inch
Valve head diameter
  Intake .... 1.654 inch
  Exhaust .... 1.457 inch
Valve face runout limit .... 0.002 inch
Valve stem diameter
  Standard
    Intake .... 0.316 inch
    Exhaust .... 0.315 inch
  Oversize 1
    Intake .... 0.331 inch
    Exhaust .... 0.330 inch

Oversize 2
    Intake . . . .   0.348 inch
    Exhaust . . . .   0.348 inch
Valve springs (1981 through 1983)
    Compression pressure @ specified length
        Loaded . . . .   180 lbs @ 1.09 inch
        Unloaded . . . .   75 lbs @ 1.461 inch
    Free length (approximate) . . . .   1.742 inch
        Assembled height . . . .   1.417 to 1.504 inch
        Out-of-square limit . . . .   0.060 inch
Valve springs (1987 and later EFI engine)
    Compression pressure @ specified length
        Loaded . . . .   216 lbs @ 1.016 inch
        Unloaded . . . .   94 lbs @ 1.461 inch
    Free length . . . .   1.90 inch
    Assembled height . . . .   1.417 to 1.504 inch
    Out-of-square limit . . . .   0.060 inch
Valve springs (all others)
    Compression pressure @ specified length
        Loaded . . . .   200 lbs @ 1.09 inch
        Unloaded . . . .   95 lbs @ 1.461 inch
    Free length . . . .   1.86 inch
    Assembled height . . . .   1.48 to 1.44 inch
    Out-of-square limit . . . .   0.060 inch
Valve lifter, hydraulic
    Diameter (standard) . . . .   0.874 inch
    Clearance in bore
        Standard . . . .   0.0009 to 0.0026 inch
        Service limit . . . .   0.005 inch

Cylinder block

Head gasket surface flatness . . . .   0.003 inch overall, 0.002 inch per 6 inches
Cylinder bore
    Diameter
        1.3L and 1.6L . . . .   3.15 inch
        1.9L . . . .   3.23 inch
    Out-of-round limit
        Standard . . . .   0.0015 inch
        Service limit . . . .   0.005 inch
    Taper service limit . . . .   0.01 inch
Main bearing bore diameter . . . .   2.452 + 0.0005 inch, – 0.0003 inch

Crankshaft and flywheel

Main bearing journal
    Diameter . . . .   2.2826 to 2.2834 inch
    Out-of-round limit
        1.3L and 1.6L . . . .   0.0005 inch
        1.9L . . . .   0.008 inch
    Taper limit . . . .   0.0003 inch per inch
    Runout limit . . . .   0.005 inch
    Thrust bearing journal length . . . .   1.135 to 1.136 inch
Connecting rod journal
    Diameter . . . .   1.885 to 1.886 inch
    Out-of-round limit
        1.3L and 1.6L . . . .   0.0005 inch
        1.9L . . . .   0.008 inch
    Taper limit . . . .   0.0003 inch per inch
Main bearing thrust face runout limit . . . .   0.001 inch
Flywheel clutch face runout limit . . . .   0.007 inch
Flywheel/driveplate ring gear lateral runout
    Manual transaxle (flywheel) . . . .   0.025 inch
    Automatic transaxle (driveplate) . . . .   0.005 inch
Crankshaft endplay . . . .   0.004 to 0.008 inch
Connecting rod bearings
    Journal-to-bearing (oil) clearance
        Desired . . . .   0.0008 to 0.0015 inch
        Allowable . . . .   0.0008 to 0.0026 inch

Crankshaft and flywheel (continued)

Main bearings
Journal-to-bearing (oil) clearance
    Desired . . . . 0.0008 to 0.0015 inch
    Allowable . . . . 0.0008 to 0.0026 inch

Connecting rods

Piston pin bore diameter . . . . 0.8106 to 0.8114 inch
Crankshaft bearing bore diameter . . . . 2.0035 to 2.0043 inch
Out-of-round limit, piston pin bore
    1981 through 1983 . . . . 0.0004 inch
    1984 on . . . . 0.0003 inch
Taper limit – piston pin bore
    1981 through 1983 . . . . 0.0004 inch
    1984 on . . . . 0.0015 inch per inch
Length (bore center-to-bore center)
    1.3L . . . . 4.285 to 4.288 inch
    1.6L and 1.9L . . . . 5.193 to 5.196 inch
Alignment (bore-to-bore max. diff.)
    Twist
        1981 through 1983 . . . . 0.003 inch per inch
        1984 on . . . . 0.002 inch
    Bend
        1981 through 1983 . . . . 0.0015 inch per inch
        1984 on . . . . 0.0015 inch
Side clearance (endplay)
    Standard . . . . 0.004 to 0.01 inch
    Service limit . . . . 0.014 inch

Pistons and piston rings (1.3L and 1981 through 1983 1.6L engines)

Piston diameter
    Coded red . . . . 3.1461 to 3.1466 inch
    Coded blue . . . . 3.1472 to 3.1478 inch
    0.004 in oversize . . . . 3.1500 to 3.1506 inch
Piston-to-bore clearance . . . . 0.0008 to 0.0016 inch
Pin bore diameter . . . . 0.8122 to 0.8127 inch
Ring groove width
    Top compression ring . . . . 0.0645 to 0.0653 inch
    Bottom Compression ring . . . . 0.0802 to 0.0812 inch
    Oil ring . . . . 0.1578 to 0.1587 inch
Piston pin
    Length . . . . 2.606 to 2.638 inch
    Standard diameter . . . . 0.8119 to 0.8124 inch
    Piston-to-pin clearance . . . . 0.0002 to 0.0004 inch
    Pin-to-rod clearance . . . . press fit
Piston rings
    Width
        Top compression ring . . . . 0.0621 to 0.0634 inch
        Bottom compression ring . . . . 0.078 to 0.0786 inch
        Oil ring . . . . Side seal (snug fit)
    Gap
        Both compression rings . . . . 0.012 to 0.020 inch
        Oil ring (steel rail) . . . . 0.016 to 0.055 inch
    Side clearance
        Top compression ring . . . . 0.001 to 0.003 inch
        Bottom compression ring . . . . 0.002 to 0.003 inch

Pistons and piston rings (1984 and later 1.6L engines)

Piston diameter
    Coded red . . . . 3.1463 to 3.157 inch
    Coded blue . . . . 3.1468 to 3.1474 inch
    0.004 in oversize . . . . 3.1496 to 3.1502 inch
Piston-to-bore clearance . . . . 0.0018 to 0.0026 inch
Pin bore diameter . . . . 0.8123 to 0.8128 inch
Ring groove width
    Top compression ring . . . . 0.0621 to 0.0626 inch
    Bottom compression ring . . . . 0.0802 to 0.0812 inch
    Oil ring . . . . 0.1578 to 0.1587 inch

Piston pin

Length	2.606 to 2.638 inch
Standard diameter	0.8119 to 0.8124 inch
Piston-to-pin clearance	0.0003 to 0.0005 inch
Pin-to-rod clearance	press fit

Piston rings

Width

Top compression ring	0.0621 to 0.0634 inch
Bottom compression ring	0.078 to 0.0786 inch
Oil ring	Side seal (snug fit)

Gap

Both compression rings	0.012 to 0.020 inch
Oil ring (steel rail)	0.016 to 0.055 inch

Side clearance

Top compression ring	0.002 to 0.0032 inch
Bottom compression ring	0.0016 to 0.0032 inch

Pistons and piston rings (1.9L engines)

Piston diameter

Coded red	3.224 to 3.225 inch
Coded blue	3.225 to 3.226 inch
0.004 in oversize	3.226 to 3.227 inch
Piston-to-bore clearance	0.0016 to 0.0024 inch
Pin bore diameter	0.8123 to 0.8128 inch

Ring groove width

Top compression ring	0.0602 to 0.061 inch
Bottom compression ring	0.0602 to 0.061 inch
Oil ring	0.1578 to 0.1587 inch

Piston pin

Length	2.606 to 2.638 inch
Standard diameter	0.8119 to 0.8125 inch
Piston-to-pin clearance	0.0002 to 0.0004 inch
Pin-to-rod clearance	press fit

Piston rings

Width

Top compression ring	0.0578 to 0.0582 inch
Bottom compression ring	0.0574 to 0.0586 inch
Oil ring	Side seal (snug fit)

Gap

Top compression ring	0.010 to 0.020 inch
Bottom compression ring	0.010 to 0.020 inch
Oil ring (steel rail)	0.016 to 0.055 inch

Side clearance

Top compression ring	0.0015 to 0.0032 inch
Bottom compression ring	0.0015 to 0.0035 inch

Torque specifications* .... **Ft-lb** (unless otherwise indicated)

Connecting rod cap nut

1988 and earlier	19 to 25
1989 on	26 to 30
Crankshaft rear oil seal retainer bolts	72 to 96 in-lbs

Crankshaft pulley bolt

1988 and earlier	74 to 90
1989 on	81 to 96
Main bearing cap-to-block bolts	67 to 80

Refer to Part A for additional torque specifications

---

1 General information

Included in this portion of Chapter 2 are the general overhaul procedures for the cylinder head and internal engine components.

The information ranges from advice concerning preparation for an overhaul and the purchase of replacement parts to detailed, step-by-step procedures covering removal and installation of internal engine components and the inspection of parts.

The following Sections have been written based on the assumption that the engine has been removed from the vehicle. For information concerning in-vehicle engine repair, as well as removal and installation of the external components necessary for the overhaul, see Part A of this Chapter and Sections 5 and 6 of this Part.

The Specifications included in this Part are only those necessary for the inspection and overhaul procedures which follow. Refer to Part A for additional Specifications.

2 Engine overhaul – general information

Refer to illustration 2.1a and 2.1b

It's not always easy to determine when, or if, an engine should be completely overhauled, as a number of factors must be considered **(see illustrations)**.

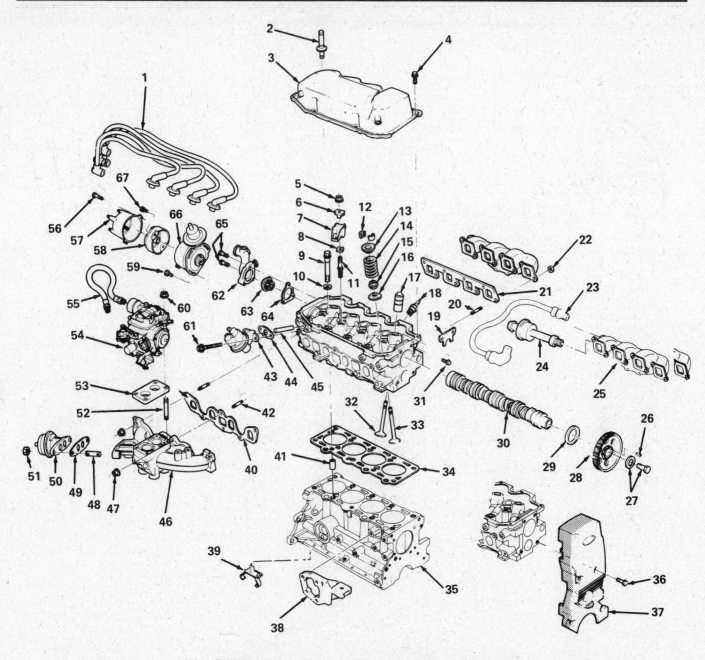

2.1a   Cylinder head and upper engine components – exploded view

1	Spark plug cable set	18	Spark plug	35	Cylinder block	51	Valve nut
2	Cover bolt and stud	19	Camshaft thrust plate	36	Cover bolts and nuts	52	Carburetor stud
3	Valve cover	20	Manifold stud	37	Timing belt cover	53	Carburetor mounting gasket
4	Cover screw	21	Exhaust manifold gasket	38	Engine mount	54	Carburetor
5	Fulcrum nut	22	Manifold nut	39	Crankcase ventilation baffle	55	Fuel line
6	Rocker arm fulcrum	23	EGR tube	40	Intake manifold gasket	56	Cap screw
7	Rocker arm	24	Air injection check valve	41	Cylinder head alignment	57	Distributor cap
8	Fulcrum washer	25	Exhaust manifold		dowel	58	Rotor
9	Cylinder head bolt	26	Cam sprocket shaft key	42	Manifold stud	59	Distributor bolt
10	Cylinder head bolt washer	27	Sprocket bolt and washer	43	Fuel pump	60	Distributor nut
11	Fulcrum stud	28	Camshaft sprocket	44	Fuel pump gasket	61	Pump bolt
12	Valve spring retainer keys	29	Camshaft seal	45	Fuel pump push rod	62	Thermostat housing
13	Valve spring retainer	30	Camshaft	46	Intake manifold	63	Thermostat
14	Valve spring	31	Thrust plate bolt	47	Manifold nut	64	Housing gasket
15	Valve stem seal	32	Intake valve	48	Valve stud	65	Housing bolt
16	Valve spring seat	33	Exhaust valve	49	EGR valve gasket	66	Distributor
17	Hydraulic lifter	34	Cylinder head gasket	50	EGR valve	67	Rotor screw

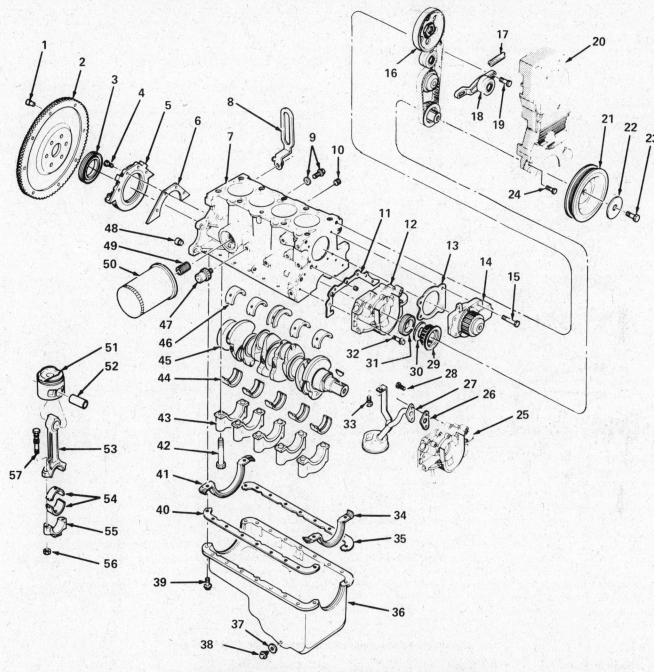

2.1b Cylinder block and lower engine components – exploded view

1	Pressure plate alignment dowel	14	Water pump	29	Crankshaft sprocket	44	Lower main bearing insets
2	Flywheel	15	Water pump bolt	30	Timing belt guide	45	Crankshaft
3	Crankshaft rear seal	16	Timing belt – installed view	31	Crankshaft front seal	46	Upper main bearing inserts
4	Retainer bolt	17	Tensioner spring	32	Oil pump bolt	47	Oil pressure sending unit
5	Seal retainer	18	Tensioner bracket and idler	33	Brace bolt	48	Transmission alignment dowel
6	Retainer gasket	19	Tensioner bolt	34	Oil pan front seal	49	Oil filter adapter
7	Cylinder block	20	Timing belt cover	35	Oil pan side gasket	50	Oil filter
8	Engine lifting eye	21	Crankshaft pulley	36	Oil pan	51	Piston
9	Monolithic timing plug and gasket	22	Pulley bolt washer	37	Drain plug seal	52	Piston pin
10	Coolant drain plug	23	Pulley bolt	38	Oil pan drain plug	53	Connecting rod
11	Oil pump gasket	24	Cover bolt	39	Oil pan bolt	54	Connecting rod bearings
12	Oil pump	25	Oil pump	40	Oil pan side gasket	55	Connecting rod cap
13	Water pump gasket	26	Pick-up tube gasket	41	Oil pan rear seal	56	Cap nut
		27	Pick-up tube	42	Cap bolt	57	Cap bolt
		28	Pick-up tube bolt	43	Main bearing caps		

High mileage is not necessarily an indication that an overhaul is needed, while low mileage doesn't preclude the need for an overhaul. Frequency of servicing is probably the most important consideration. An engine that's had regular and frequent oil and filter changes, as well as other required maintenance, will most likely give many thousands of miles of reliable service. Conversely, a neglected engine may require an overhaul very early in its life.

Excessive oil consumption is an indication that piston rings, valve seals and/or valve guides are in need of attention. Make sure that oil leaks aren't responsible before deciding that the rings and/or guides are bad. Perform a cylinder compression check to determine the extent of the work required (see Section 3).

Check the oil pressure with a gauge installed in place of the oil pressure sending unit and compare it to this Chapter's Specifications. If it's extremely low, the bearings and/or oil pump are probably worn out.

Loss of power, rough running, knocking or metallic engine noises, excessive valve train noise and high fuel consumption rates may also point to the need for an overhaul, especially if they're all present at the same time. If a complete tune-up doesn't remedy the situation, major mechanical work is the only solution.

An engine overhaul involves restoring the internal parts to the specifications of a new engine. During an overhaul, the piston rings are replaced and the cylinder walls are reconditioned (rebored and/or honed). If a rebore is done by an automotive machine shop, new oversize pistons will also be installed. The main bearings, connecting rod bearings and camshaft bearings are generally replaced with new ones and, if necessary, the crankshaft may be reground to restore the journals. Generally, the valves are serviced as well, since they're usually in less-than-perfect condition at this point. While the engine is being overhauled, other components, such as the distributor, starter and alternator, can be rebuilt as well. The end result should be a like-new engine that will give many thousands of trouble-free miles. **Note:** *Critical cooling system components such as the hoses, drivebelts, thermostat and water pump MUST be replaced with new parts when an engine is overhauled. The radiator should be checked carefully to ensure that it isn't clogged or leaking (see Chapter 3). Also, be sure to check the oil pump as described in Part A of this Chapter.*

Before beginning the engine overhaul, read through the entire procedure to familiarize yourself with the scope and requirements of the job. Overhauling an engine isn't difficult if you follow all of the instructions carefully, have the necessary tools and equipment and pay close attention to all specifications; however, it is time consuming. Plan on the vehicle being tied up for a minimum of two weeks, especially if parts must be taken to an automotive machine shop for repair or reconditioning. Check on availability of parts and make sure that any necessary special tools and equipment are obtained in advance. Most work can be done with typical hand tools, although a number of precision measuring tools are required for inspecting parts to determine if they must be replaced. Often an automotive machine shop will handle the inspection of parts and offer advice concerning reconditioning and replacement. **Note:** *Always wait until the engine has been completely disassembled and all components, especially the engine block, have been inspected before deciding what service and repair operations must be performed by an automotive machine shop. Since the block's condition will be the major factor to consider when determining whether to overhaul the original engine or buy a rebuilt one, never purchase parts or have machine work done on other components until the block has been thoroughly inspected. As a general rule, time is the primary cost of an overhaul, so it doesn't pay to install worn or substandard parts.*

As a final note, to ensure maximum life and minimum trouble from a rebuilt engine, everything must be assembled with care in a spotlessly clean environment.

3   Compression check

1 A compression check will tell you what mechanical condition the upper end (pistons, rings, valves, head gaskets) of your engine is in. Specifically, it can tell you if the compression is down due to leakage caused by worn piston rings, defective valves and seats or a blown head gasket. **Note:** *The engine must be at normal operating temperature and the bat-*

tery must be fully charged for this check. Also, if the engine is equipped with a carburetor, the choke valve must be all the way open to get an accurate compression reading (if the engine's warm, the choke should be open).

2 Begin by cleaning the area around the spark plugs before you remove them (compressed air should be used, if available, otherwise a small brush or even a bicycle tire pump will work). The idea is to prevent dirt from getting into the cylinders as the compression check is being done.

3 Remove all of the spark plugs from the engine (see Chapter 1).

4 Block the throttle wide open.

5 Detach the coil wire from the center of the distributor cap and ground it on the engine block. Use a jumper wire with alligator clips on each end to ensure a good ground. On fuel injected models, the fuel pump circuit should also be disabled at the inertia switch (see Chapter 4).

6 Install the compression gauge in the number one spark plug hole.

7 Crank the engine over at least seven compression strokes and watch the gauge. The compression should build up quickly in a healthy engine. Low compression on the first stroke, followed by gradually increasing pressure on successive strokes, indicates worn piston rings. A low compression reading on the first stroke, which doesn't build up during successive strokes, indicates leaking valves or a blown head gasket (a cracked head could also be the cause). Deposits on the undersides of the valve heads can also cause low compression. Record the highest gauge reading obtained.

8 Repeat the procedure for the remaining cylinders and compare the results to this Chapter's Specifications.

9 Add some engine oil (about three squirts from a plunger-type oil can) to each cylinder, through the spark plug hole, and repeat the test.

10 If the compression increases after the oil is added, the piston rings are definitely worn. If the compression doesn't increase significantly, the leakage is occurring at the valves or head gasket. Leakage past the valves may be caused by burned valve seats and/or faces or warped, cracked or bent valves.

11 If two adjacent cylinders have equally low compression, there's a strong possibility that the head gasket between them is blown. The appearance of coolant in the combustion chambers or the crankcase would verify this condition.

12 If one cylinder is 20-percent lower than the others, and the engine has a slightly rough idle, a worn exhaust lobe on the camshaft could be the cause. Generally, there's something seriously wrong with the engine anytime one cylinder is 20-percent or more below the others

13 If the compression is unusually high, the combustion chambers are probably coated with carbon deposits. If that's the case, the cylinder head should be removed and decarbonized.

14 If compression is way down or varies greatly between cylinders, it would be a good idea to have a leak-down test performed by an automotive repair shop. This test will pinpoint exactly where the leakage is occurring and how severe it is.

4   Engine removal – methods and precautions

If you've decided that an engine must be removed for overhaul or major repair work, several preliminary steps should be taken.

Locating a suitable place to work is extremely important. Adequate work space, along with storage space for the vehicle, will be needed. If a shop or garage isn't available, at the very least a flat, level, clean work surface made of concrete or asphalt is required.

Cleaning the engine compartment and engine before beginning the removal procedure will help keep tools clean and organized.

An engine hoist or A-frame will also be necessary. Make sure the equipment is rated in excess of the combined weight of the engine and accessories. Safety is of primary importance, considering the potential hazards involved in lifting the engine out of the vehicle.

If the engine is being removed by a novice, a helper should be available. Advice and aid from someone more experienced would also be helpful. There are many instances when one person cannot simultaneously perform all of the operations required when lifting the engine out of the vehicle.

Plan the operation ahead of time. Arrange for or obtain all of the tools and equipment you'll need prior to beginning the job. Some of the equipment necessary to perform engine removal and installation safely and with relative ease are (in addition to an engine hoist) a heavy duty floor jack, complete sets of wrenches and sockets as described in the front of this manual, wooden blocks and plenty of rags and cleaning solvent for mopping up spilled oil, coolant and gasoline. If the hoist must be rented, make sure that you arrange for it in advance and perform all of the operations possible without it beforehand. This will save you money and time.

Plan for the vehicle to be out of use for quite a while. A machine shop will be required to perform some of the work which the do-it-yourselfer can't accomplish without special equipment. These shops often have a busy schedule, so it would be a good idea to consult them before removing the engine in order to accurately estimate the amount of time required to rebuild or repair components that may need work.

Always be extremely careful when removing and installing the engine. Serious injury can result from careless actions. Plan ahead, take your time and a job of this nature, although major, can be accomplished successfully.

5   Engine (non-turbo models) – removal and installation

Refer to illustration 5.5

Warning: *The air conditioning system is under high pressure! Have a dealer service department or service station discharge the system before disconnecting any air conditioning system hoses or fittings.*

Note: *On 1981 models, the engine and transaxle must be removed as an assembly; you cannot separate the two until they're out of the vehicle. On 1982 and later models, the engine can be removed separately.*

Removal
All models

1   Refer to Chapter 4 and relieve the fuel system pressure (fuel-injected models only), then disconnect the negative cable from the battery.
2   Cover the fenders and cowl and remove the hood (see Chapter 11). Special pads are available to protect the fenders, but an old bedspread or blanket will also work.
3   Remove the air cleaner assembly, together with the air intake duct and the heat tube, if equipped (see Chapter 4).
4   Drain the cooling system (see Chapter 1).
5   Label the vacuum lines, emissions system hoses, wiring connectors, ground straps and fuel lines, to ensure correct reinstallation, then detach them. Pieces of masking tape with numbers or letters written on them work well **(see illustration)**. If there's any possibility of confusion, make a sketch of the engine compartment and clearly label the lines, hoses and wires.
6   Label and detach all coolant hoses from the engine.
7   Remove the cooling fan, shroud and radiator (see Chapter 3).
8   Remove the drivebelts (see Chapter 1).

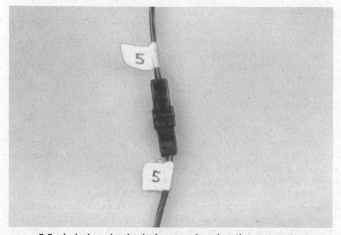

5.5   Label each wire before unplugging the connector

9   **Warning:** *Gasoline is extremely flammable, so extra precautions must be taken when working on any part of the fuel system. DO NOT smoke or allow open flames or bare light bulbs near the vehicle. Also, don't work in a garage if a natural gas appliance with a pilot light is present. Disconnect the fuel lines running from the engine to the chassis (see Chapter 4). Plug or cap all open fittings/lines.*
10   Disconnect the throttle linkage (and TV linkage/speed control cable, if equipped) from the engine (see Chapter 4).
11   If equipped with cruise control, unbolt the cruise control servo and set it aside.
12   On power steering equipped models, unbolt the power steering pump (see Chapter 10). Leave the lines/hoses attached and make sure the pump is kept in an upright position in the engine compartment (use wire or rope to restrain it out of the way).
13   On air conditioned models, unbolt the compressor (see Chapter 3) and set it aside. Do not disconnect the hoses.
14   Drain the engine oil (see Chapter 1) and remove the oil filter.
15   Remove the starter motor (see Chapter 5).
16   Remove the alternator (see Chapter 5).
17   Unbolt the exhaust system from the engine (see Chapter 4).
18   Remove the alternator air intake tube, if equipped.
19   Remove the secondary wire from the ignition coil.

1981 models

20   If you'll be using an engine support bar, remove the Thermactor pump bracket bolt.
21   If an engine support bar (Ford tool no. T81P-6000-A or equivalent) is available, hook it up to the engine using a short piece of chain. Attach the chain to the engine using the 10 mm bolt hole at the transaxle end, the exhaust manifold side of the cylinder head and the thermactor bracket hole. Tighten the J-bolt on the bar to take up the slack in the chain.
22   If an engine support bar is not available, attach lifting brackets to the engine and hook up an engine sling or a length of chain to the brackets. Attach an engine hoist to the sling or chain and take up the slack. Do not lift the engine.
23   On manual transaxle models, remove the roll restrictor at the engine and body.
24   Remove the stabilizer bar.
25   Remove the lower control arm through bolts at the body brackets.
26   Disconnect the left tie-rod from the steering knuckle (see Chapter 10, if necessary).
27   Disconnect the driveaxles from the transaxle (see Chapter 8). Support the driveaxles with wire, out of the way. **Caution:** *Do not let the driveaxles hang or damage to the outer CV joints may occur. Install 15/16-inch dowels in the driveaxle holes to keep the differential side gears from falling while the driveaxles are disconnected. If the side gears fall, a dealer service department or other qualified shop will have to disassemble the differential to reposition them.*
28   Disconnect the speedometer cable from the transaxle.
29   On manual transaxle models, disconnect the shift control rod at the transaxle (see Chapter 7A).
30   On automatic transaxle models, disconnect the shift selector cable at the transaxle. Also, remove the torque converter-to-driveplate attaching nuts (see Chapter 7B, if necessary).
31   If equipped with power steering, disconnect the pump return line at the pump and the pressure line at the intermediate fitting.
32   Remove the left front (no. 1) mount insulator attaching bracket and insulator with its thru-bolts. **Note:** *See Chapter 2A for additional information on the engine mounts.*
33   Remove the left rear (no. 4) mount insulator stud nut.
34   Loosen the J-bolt (if you're using an engine support bar) or lower the hoist slightly until the left rear mount insulator stud clears the mounting bracket.
35   Remove the left rear mount-to-transaxle case attaching bracket.
36   If you're using a support bar, attach an engine hoist and remove the support bar.
37   Disconnect the 3A (front) engine mount
38   Lift the engine and transaxle assembly from the vehicle. Set the assembly on the ground. Remove the transaxle-to-engine bolts and separate the engine and transaxle.

2B

1982 and later models

39   Remove the Thermactor air pump.

40   Remove the support bracket located in front of the torque converter cover (automatic transaxle) or inspection cover (manual transaxle). Remove the converter cover or inspection cover.

41   Remove the crankshaft pulley.

42   On automatic transaxle models, remove the torque converter-to-driveplate attaching nuts (see Chapter 7B, if necessary).

43   On manual transaxle models, remove the lower bolts from the timing belt cover.

44   Remove the lower bolts from the torque converter housing (automatic transaxle) or flywheel housing (manual transaxle).

45   Support the transaxle with a jack. Position a block of wood between the transaxle and jack to prevent damage to the transaxle. Special transaxle jacks with safety chains are available – use one if possible.

46   Install lifting brackets on the engine. Attach an engine sling or a length of chain to the lifting brackets.

47   Roll the hoist into position and connect the sling to it. Take up the slack in the sling or chain, but don't lift the engine. **Warning:** *DO NOT place any part of your body under the engine when it's supported only by a hoist or other lifting device.*

48   Remove the two oil pan-to-transaxle bolts, if equipped.

49   On manual transaxle models, remove the remaining timing belt cover bolts and remove the cover.

50   Remove the transaxle-to-engine block bolts.

51   Remove the engine mount bolts (see Chapter 2A, if necessary).

52   Recheck to be sure nothing is still connecting the engine to the transaxle or vehicle. Disconnect anything still remaining.

53   Raise the engine slightly. Carefully work it to one side to separate it from the transaxle. If you're working on a vehicle with an automatic transaxle, be sure the torque converter stays in the transaxle (clamp a pair of vise-grips to the housing to keep the converter from sliding out). If you're working on a vehicle with a manual transaxle, the input shaft must be completely disengaged from the clutch. Slowly raise the engine out of the engine compartment. Check carefully to make sure nothing is hanging up.

54   Remove the flywheel/driveplate and mount the engine on an engine stand.

Installation

55   Check the engine and transaxle mounts. If they're worn or damaged, replace them.

56   If you're working on a manual transaxle equipped vehicle, install the clutch and pressure plate (see Chapter 7). Now is a good time to install a new clutch.

57   On 1981 models, join the engine and transaxle and install and tighten the transaxle-to-engine bolts. If you're working on an automatic transaxle-equipped model, be sure the studs on the torque converter engage with the holes in the driveplate.

58   Carefully lower the engine or engine/transaxle assembly into the engine compartment – make sure the engine mounts line up.

59   If you're working on an automatic transaxle-equipped vehicle, attach the torque converter to the driveplate (see Chapter 7B).

60   On 1982 and later models, if you're working on a manual transaxle equipped vehicle, guide the input shaft into the clutch hub.

61   On 1982 and later models, install the transaxle-to-engine bolts and tighten them securely. **Caution:** *DO NOT use the bolts to force the transaxle and engine together!*

62   Reinstall the remaining components in the reverse order of removal.

63   Add coolant, oil, power steering and transaxle fluid as needed.

64   Run the engine and check for leaks and proper operation of all accessories, then install the hood and test drive the vehicle.

65   Have the air conditioning system recharged and leak tested.

---

6   Engine (turbo models) – removal and installation

---

1   The procedure in Section 5 should be followed with the addition of the following steps:

2   After the vehicle is raised, remove the oil cooler (see Chapter 2A,

Section 23).

3   After disconnecting the exhaust pipe from the turbocharger, remove the exhaust pipe support bracket.

4   Installation is the reverse of the removal procedure.

---

7   Engine rebuilding alternatives

The do-it-yourselfer is faced with a number of options when performing an engine overhaul. The decision to replace the engine block, piston/connecting rod assemblies and crankshaft depends on a number of factors, with the number one consideration being the condition of the block. Other considerations are cost, access to machine shop facilities, parts availability, time required to complete the project and the extent of prior mechanical experience on the part of the do-it-yourselfer.

Some of the rebuilding alternatives include:

Individual parts – If the inspection procedures reveal that the engine block and most engine components are in reusable condition, purchasing individual parts may be the most economical alternative. The block, crankshaft and piston/connecting rod assemblies should all be inspected carefully. Even if the block shows little wear, the cylinder bores should be surface honed.

Short block – A short block consists of an engine block with a crankshaft and piston/connecting rod assemblies already installed. All new bearings are incorporated and all clearances will be correct. The existing camshaft, valve train components, cylinder head and external parts can be bolted to the short block with little or no machine shop work necessary.

Long block – A long block consists of a short block plus an oil pump, oil pan, cylinder head, camshaft and valve train components, timing sprockets and belt and timing cover. All components are installed with new bearings, seals and gaskets incorporated throughout. The installation of manifolds and external parts is all that's necessary.

Give careful thought to which alternative is best for you and discuss the situation with local automotive machine shops, auto parts dealers and experienced rebuilders before ordering or purchasing replacement parts.

---

8   Engine overhaul – disassembly sequence

---

1   It's much easier to disassemble and work on the engine if it's mounted on a portable engine stand. A stand can often be rented quite cheaply from an equipment rental yard. Before the engine is mounted on a stand, the flywheel/driveplate should be removed from the engine.

2   If a stand isn't available, it's possible to disassemble the engine with it blocked up on the floor. Be extra careful not to tip or drop the engine when working without a stand.

3   If you're going to obtain a rebuilt engine, all external components must come off first, to be transferred to the replacement engine, just as they will if you're doing a complete engine overhaul yourself. These include:

> *Alternator and brackets*
> *Emissions control components*
> *Distributor, spark plug wires and spark plugs*
> *Thermostat and housing cover*
> *Power steering pump*
> *Fuel injection components or carburetor*
> *Intake/exhaust manifolds*
> *Oil filter (and oil cooler on turbocharged engines)*
> *Engine mounts*
> *Clutch and flywheel/driveplate*
> *Engine rear plate*

Note: *When removing the external components from the engine, pay close attention to details that may be helpful or important during installation. Note the installed position of gaskets, seals, spacers, pins, brackets, washers, bolts and other small items.*

4   If you're obtaining a short block, which consists of the engine block, crankshaft, pistons and connecting rods all assembled, then the cylinder head, oil pan and oil pump will have to be removed as well. See *Engine*

rebuilding alternatives for additional information regarding the different possibilities to be considered.

5   If you're planning a complete overhaul, the engine must be disassembled and the internal components removed in the following order:

Valve cover
Intake and exhaust manifolds
Rocker arms
Valve lifters
Camshaft
Cylinder head
Timing cover
Timing belt
Water pump
Oil pan
Oil pump
Piston/connecting rod assemblies
Crankshaft and main bearings

6   Before beginning the disassembly and overhaul procedures, make sure the following items are available. Also, refer to *Engine overhaul – reassembly sequence* for a list of tools and materials needed for engine reassembly.

Common hand tools
Small cardboard boxes or plastic bags for storing parts
Gasket scraper
Ridge reamer
Vibration damper puller
Micrometers
Telescoping gauges
Dial indicator set
Valve spring compressor
Cylinder surfacing hone
Piston ring groove cleaning tool
Electric drill motor
Tap and die set
Wire brushes
Oil gallery brushes
Cleaning solvent

9   Cylinder head – disassembly

Refer to illustrations 9.3, 9.4 and 9.5

Note: *New and rebuilt cylinder heads are commonly available for most engines at dealerships and auto parts stores. Due to the fact that some specialized tools are necessary for the disassembly and inspection procedures, and replacement parts may not be readily available, it may be* more practical and economical for the home mechanic to purchase a replacement head rather than taking the time to disassemble, inspect and recondition the original.

1   Cylinder head disassembly involves removal of the intake and exhaust valves and related components. If they're still in place, remove the rocker arm nuts (or bolts), fulcrums, rocker arms and fulcrum washers (if equipped) from the cylinder head. Remove the hydraulic lifters (tappets) from the cylinder head. Label the parts or store them separately so they can be reinstalled in their original locations. **Note:** *On models with roller lifters (1989 and later), remove the lifter guides and guide retainers before removing the lifters. Be sure to store these parts so they can be returned to their original locations – they must not be mixed up.*

2   Before the valves are removed, arrange to label and store them, along with their related components, so they can be kept separate and reinstalled in the same valve guides they are removed from.

3   Compress the springs on the first valve with a spring compressor and remove the keepers **(see illustration)**. Carefully release the valve spring compressor and remove the retainer, the spring and the spring seat.

4   Pull the valve out of the head, then remove the oil seal from the guide. If the valve binds in the guide (won't pull through), push it back into the head and deburr the area around the keeper groove with a fine file or whetstone **(see illustration)**.

5   Repeat the procedure for the remaining valves. Remember to keep all the parts for each valve together so they can be reinstalled in the same locations **(see illustration)**.

9.3   Use a valve spring compressor to compress the spring, then remove the keepers from the valve stem

9.4   If the valve won't pull through the guide, deburr the edge of the stem end and the area around the top of the keeper groove with a file or whetstone

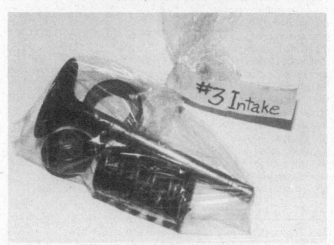

9.5   A small plastic bag, with an appropriate label, can be used to store the valve train components so they can be kept together and reinstalled in the original location

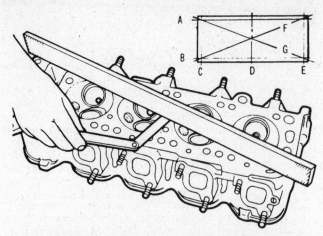

10.12   Check the cylinder head gasket surface for warpage by trying to slip a feeler gauge under the straightedge (see this Chapter's Specifications for the maximum warpage allowed and use a feeler gauge of that thickness)

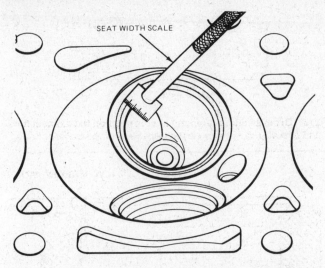

10.13   Measuring valve seat width with a special scale

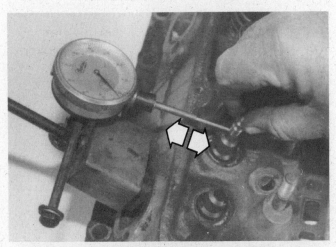

10.14   A dial indicator can be used to determine the valve stem-to-guide clearance (move the valve stem as indicated by the arrows)

6   Once the valves and related components have been removed and stored in an organized manner, the head should be thoroughly cleaned and inspected. If a complete engine overhaul is being done, finish the engine disassembly procedures before beginning the cylinder head cleaning and inspection process.

10   Cylinder head – cleaning and inspection

Refer to illustrations 10.12, 10.13, 10.14, 10.15, 10.16, 10.17, 10.18 and 10.19

1   Thorough cleaning of the cylinder head and related valve train components, followed by a detailed inspection, will enable you to decide how much valve service work must be done during the engine overhaul. **Note:** *If the engine was severely overheated, the cylinder head is probably warped (see Step 12).*

Cleaning

2   Scrape all traces of old gasket material and sealing compound off the head gasket, intake manifold and exhaust manifold sealing surfaces. Be very careful not to gouge the cylinder head. Special gasket removal solvents that soften gaskets and make removal much easier are available at auto parts stores.
3   Remove all built-up scale from the coolant passages.

4   Run a stiff wire brush through the various holes to remove deposits that may have formed in them.
5   Run an appropriate size tap into each of the threaded holes to remove corrosion and thread sealant that may be present. If compressed air is available, use it to clear the holes of debris produced by this operation. **Warning:** *Wear eye protection when using compressed air!*
6   If equipped, clean the rocker arm pivot stud threads with a wire brush.
7   Clean the cylinder head with solvent and dry it thoroughly. Compressed air will speed the drying process and ensure that all holes and recessed areas are clean. **Note:** *Decarbonizing chemicals are available and may prove very useful when cleaning cylinder heads and valve train components. They are very caustic and should be used with caution. Be sure to follow the instructions on the container.*
8   Clean the rocker arms, fulcrums, fulcrum washers (if equipped), nuts (or bolts) and hydraulic lifters with solvent and dry them thoroughly (don't mix them up during the cleaning process). Compressed air will speed the drying process and can be used to clean out the oil passages.
9   Clean all the valve springs, spring seats, keepers and retainers with solvent and dry them thoroughly. Do the components from one valve at a time to avoid mixing up the parts.
10   Scrape off any heavy deposits that may have formed on the valves, then use a motorized wire brush to remove deposits from the valve heads and stems. Again, make sure the valves don't get mixed up.

Inspection

Note: *Be sure to perform all of the following inspection procedures before concluding that machine shop work is required. Make a list of the items that need attention.*

Cylinder head

11   Inspect the head very carefully for cracks, evidence of coolant leakage and other damage. If cracks are found, check with an automotive machine shop concerning repair. If repair isn't possible, a new cylinder head should be purchased.
12   Using a straightedge and feeler gauge, check the head gasket mating surface for warpage **(see illustration)**. If the warpage exceeds the limit listed in this Chapter's Specifications, it can be resurfaced at an automotive machine shop.
13   Examine the valve seats in each of the combustion chambers and measure the width **(see illustration)**. If they're pitted, cracked or burned or the width is not within the specifications in this Chapter, the head will require valve service that's beyond the scope of the home mechanic.
14   Check the valve stem-to-guide clearance by measuring the lateral movement of the valve stem with a dial indicator attached securely to the head **(see illustration)**. The valve must be in the guide and approximately 1/16-inch off the seat. The total valve stem movement indicated by the gauge needle must be divided by two to obtain the actual clearance. After

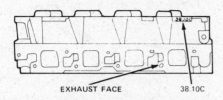

EXHAUST FACE   38.10C

10.15   Oversize lifters (tappets) are stamped on the exhaust face and oversize camshafts on the upper end of the cylinder head

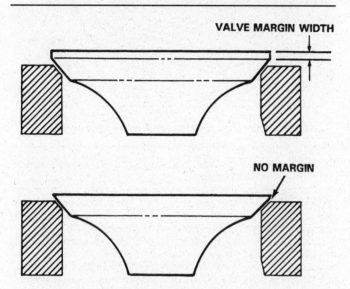

VALVE MARGIN WIDTH

NO MARGIN

10.17   Each valve must have a substantial margin – if no margin exists, the valve cannot be reused

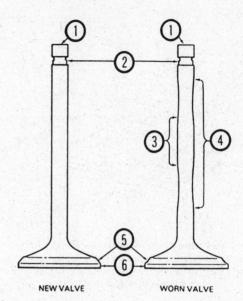

NEW VALVE   WORN VALVE

10.16   Check for valve wear at the points shown here

1 Valve tip	4 Stem (most worn area)
2 Keeper groove	5 Valve face
3 Stem (least worn area)	6 Margin

2B

10.19   Check each valve spring for squareness

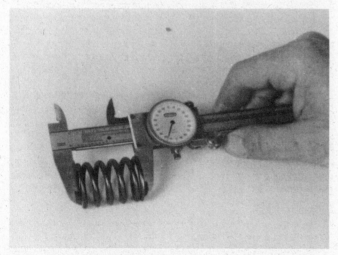

10.18   Measure the free length of each valve spring with a dial or vernier caliper

this is done, if there's still some doubt regarding the condition of the valve guides they should be checked by an automotive machine shop (the cost should be minimal).

15   It is seldom that the hydraulic type valve lifters (tappets) wear in their cylinder head bores. If the bores are worn, then a new cylinder head should be installed. Some models have oversize lifters and this will be noted by a stamping on the cylinder head **(see illustration)**.

Valves

16   Carefully inspect each valve face for uneven wear, deformation, cracks, pits and burned areas. Check the valve stem for scuffing and gall-ing and the neck for cracks **(see illustration)**. Rotate the valve and check for any obvious indication that it's bent. Look for pits and excessive wear on the end of the stem. The presence of any of these conditions indicates the need for valve service by an automotive machine shop.

17   Check to be sure there is a substantial margin on each valve **(see illustration)**. If any valves don't have a margin or have a small margin, they will have to be replaced with new ones.

Valve components

18   Check each valve spring for wear (on the ends) and pits. Measure the free length and compare it to this Chapter's Specifications **(see illustration)**. Any springs that are shorter than specified have sagged and should not be reused. The tension of all springs should be checked with a special fixture before deciding that they're suitable for use in a rebuilt engine (take the springs to an automotive machine shop for this check).

19   Stand each spring on a flat surface and check it for squareness **(see illustration)**. If any of the springs are distorted or sagged, replace all of them with new parts.

12.3   Installing a valve stem oil seal using a socket

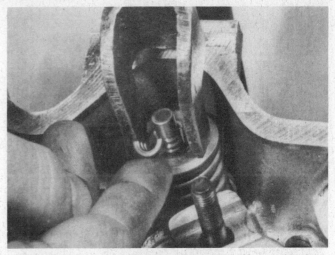

12.6   Make sure the valve keepers are securely seated in the valve stem grooves

12.8a   Valve rocker arm and lifter (tappet) installation

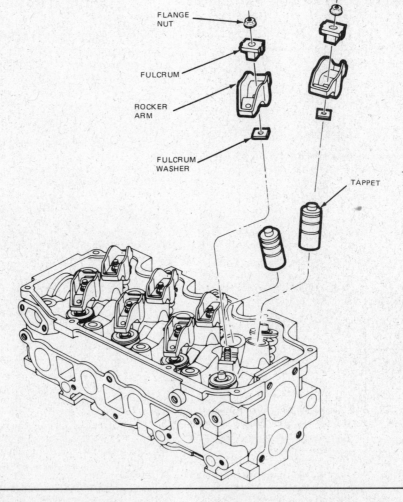

FLANGE NUT

FULCRUM

ROCKER ARM

FULCRUM WASHER

TAPPET

20   Check the spring retainers and keepers for obvious wear and cracks. Any questionable parts should be replaced with new ones, as extensive damage will occur if they fail during engine operation.

Rocker arm components

21   Check the rocker arm faces (the areas that contact the hydraulic lifters and valve stems) for pits, wear, galling, score marks and rough spots. Check the rocker arm pivot contact areas and fulcrums as well. Look for cracks in each rocker arm and nut or bolt.

22   Inspect the hydraulic lifters (tappets) for scuffing and excessive wear. See Chapter 2A for inspection procedures.

23   Check the rocker arm studs (if equipped) in the cylinder heads for damaged threads and secure installation.

24   Any damaged or excessively worn parts must be replaced with new ones.

25   If the inspection process indicates that the valve components are in

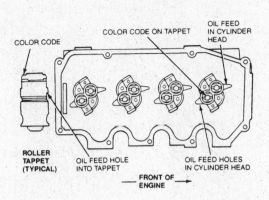

12.8b   Roller lifter installation details (1989 and later models)

generally poor condition and worn beyond the limits specified in this Chapter's Specifications, which is usually the case in an engine that's being overhauled, reassemble the valves in the cylinder head and refer to Section 11 for valve servicing recommendations.

11   Valves – servicing

1   Because of the complex nature of the job and the special tools and equipment needed, servicing of the valves, the valve seats and the valve guides, commonly known as a valve job, should be done by a professional.
2   The home mechanic can remove and disassemble the head, do the initial cleaning and inspection, then reassemble and deliver it to a dealer service department or an automotive machine shop for the actual service work. Doing the inspection will enable you to see what condition the head and valve train components are in and will ensure that you know what work and new parts are required when dealing with an automotive machine shop.
3   The dealer service department, or automotive machine shop, will remove the valves and springs, recondition or replace the valves and valve seats, recondition the valve guides, check and replace the valve springs, spring retainers and keepers (as necessary), replace the valve seals with new ones, reassemble the valve components and make sure the installed spring height is correct. The cylinder head gasket surface will also be resurfaced if it's warped.
4   After the valve job has been performed by a professional, the head will be in like-new condition. When the head is returned, be sure to clean it again before installation on the engine to remove any metal particles and abrasive grit that may still be present from the valve service or head resurfacing operations. Use compressed air, if available, to blow out all the oil holes and passages.

12   Cylinder head – reassembly

Refer to illustrations 12.3, 12.6, 12.8a and 12.8b

1   Regardless of whether or not the head was sent to an automotive repair shop for valve servicing, make sure it's clean before beginning reassembly.
2   If the head was sent out for valve servicing, the valves and related components will already be in place. Begin the reassembly procedure with Step 8.
3   Install new seals on each of the intake valve guides. Using a hammer and a deep socket or seal installation tool, gently tap each seal into place until it's completely seated on the guide **(see illustration)**. Don't twist or cock the seals during installation or they won't seal properly on the valve stems. The umbrella-type seals (if used) are installed over the valves after

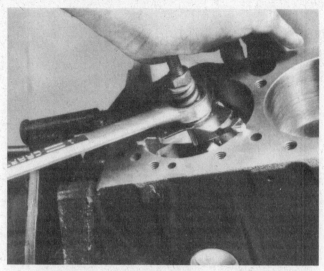

13.1   A ridge reamer is required to remove the ridge from the top of each cylinder – do this before removing the pistons!

the valves are in place.
4   Beginning at one end of the head, lubricate and install the first valve. Apply moly-base grease or clean engine oil to the valve stem.
5   Drop the spring seat over the valve guide and set the valve spring (closer coils to the cylinder head) and retainer in place.
6   Compress the springs with a valve spring compressor and carefully install the keepers in the upper groove, then slowly release the compressor and make sure the keepers seat properly **(see illustration)**. Apply a small dab of grease to each keeper to hold it in place if necessary.
7   Repeat the procedure for the remaining valves. Be sure to return the components to their original locations – don't mix them up!
8   Install the lifters into their receptacles in the cylinder head **(see illustration)**. If the vehicle is equipped with roller lifters, note the following important points:

    a) Lubricate each lifter bore with clean, 40 or 50-weight engine oil (type SG).
    b) Install each lifter with the roller down and the guide flats parallel to the camshaft centerline. The color dots on the lifters must be opposite the oil feed holes in the cylinder head **(see illustration)**.
    c) Install each lifter guide with the tab on the exhaust side.
    d) Lubricate the tops of the lifters and the ends of the valve stems with clean, 40 or 50-weight engine oil (type SG).
    e) Position the guide retainers in the fulcrum slots with the notch on the exhaust valve side.

9   Apply moly-base grease to the rocker arm faces and the fulcrums, then install the rocker arms and fulcrums on the cylinder head studs.

13   Pistons/connecting rods – removal

Refer to illustrations 13.1, 13.3, 13.4 and 13.6

Note: *Prior to removing the piston/connecting rod assemblies, remove the cylinder head and the oil pan by referring to the appropriate Sections in Chapter 2A.*

1   Use your fingernail to feel if a ridge has formed at the upper limit of ring travel (about 1/4-inch down from the top of each cylinder). If carbon deposits or cylinder wear have produced ridges, they must be completely removed with a special tool **(see illustration)**. Follow the manufacturer's instructions provided with the tool. Failure to remove the ridges before attempting to remove the piston/connecting rod assemblies may result in piston breakage.
2   After the cylinder ridges have been removed, turn the engine upside-down so the crankshaft is facing up.
3   Before the connecting rods are removed, check the endplay with

13.3   Check the connecting rod side clearance with a feeler gauge as shown

13.4   Mark the rod bearing caps in order from the front of the engine to the rear (one mark for the front cap, two for the second one and so on)

13.6   To prevent damage to the crankshaft journals and cylinder walls, slip sections of rubber or plastic hose over the rod bolts before removing the pistons

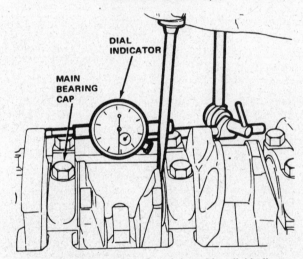

14.1   Checking crankshaft endplay with a dial indicator

feeler gauges **(see illustration)**. Slide them between the first connecting rod and the crankshaft throw until the play is removed. The endplay is equal to the thickness of the feeler gauge(s). If the endplay exceeds the service limit in this Chapter's Specifications, new connecting rods will be required. If new rods (or a new crankshaft) are installed, the endplay may fall under the specified minimum (if it does, the rods will have to be machined to restore it – consult an automotive machine shop for advice if necessary). Repeat the procedure for the remaining connecting rods.

4   Check the connecting rods and caps for identification marks. If they aren't plainly marked, use a small center-punch to make the appropriate number of indentations on each rod and cap (1, 2, 3 or 4, depending on the cylinder they're associated with) **(see illustration)**.

5   Loosen each of the connecting rod cap nuts 1/2-turn at a time until they can be removed by hand. Remove the number one connecting rod cap and bearing insert. Don't drop the bearing insert out of the cap.

6   Slip a short length of plastic or rubber hose over each connecting rod cap bolt to protect the crankshaft journal and cylinder wall as the piston is removed **(see illustration)**.

7   Remove the bearing insert and push the connecting rod/piston assembly out through the top of the engine. Use a wooden hammer handle to push on the upper bearing surface in the connecting rod. If resistance is felt, double-check to make sure that all of the ridge was removed from the cylinder.

8   Repeat the procedure for the remaining cylinders.

9   After removal, reassemble the connecting rod caps and bearing inserts in their respective connecting rods and install the cap nuts finger tight. Leaving the old bearing inserts in place until reassembly will help prevent the connecting rod bearing surfaces from being accidentally nicked or gouged.

10   Don't separate the pistons from the connecting rods (see Section 18 for additional information).

14   Crankshaft – removal

Refer to illustrations 14.1, 14.3, 14.4a and 14.4b
Note: *The crankshaft can be removed only after the engine has been removed from the vehicle. It's assumed that the flywheel or driveplate, crankshaft pulley, timing belt and crankshaft sprocket, oil pan, oil pump and all piston/connecting rod assemblies have already been removed. The crankshaft rear oil seal housing must be unbolted and separated from the block before proceeding with crankshaft removal.*

1   Before the crankshaft is removed, check the endplay. Mount a dial indicator with the stem in line with the crankshaft and just touching one of the crank throws **(see illustration)**.

2   Push the crankshaft all the way to the rear and zero the dial indicator. Next, pry the crankshaft to the front as far as possible and check the read-

14.3   Checking the crankshaft endplay with a feeler gauge

14.4a   Use a center punch or number stamping dies to mark the main bearing caps to ensure installation in their original locations on the block (make the punch marks near one of the bolt heads)

14.4b   The arrow on the main bearing cap indicates the front of the engine

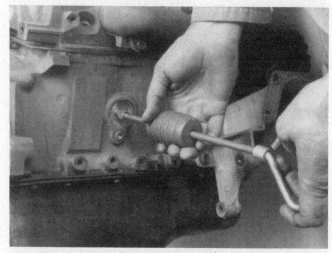

15.1   The core plugs should be removed with a puller – if they're driven into the block, they may be impossible to retrieve

2B

ing on the dial indicator. The distance that it moves is the endplay. If it's greater than the limit listed in this Chapter's Specifications, check the crankshaft thrust surfaces for wear. If no wear is evident, new main bearings should correct the endplay.

3   If a dial indicator isn't available, feeler gauges can be used. Gently pry or push the crankshaft all the way to the front of the engine. Slip feeler gauges between the crankshaft and the front face of the thrust main bearing to determine the clearance **(see illustration)**.

4   Check the main bearing caps to see if they're marked to indicate their locations. They should be numbered consecutively from the front of the engine to the rear. If they aren't, mark them with number-stamping dies or a center-punch **(see illustration)**. Main bearing caps generally have a cast-in arrow, which points to the front of the engine **(see illustration)**. Loosen the main bearing cap bolts 1/4-turn at a time each, until they can be removed by hand. Note if any stud bolts are used and make sure they're returned to their original locations when the crankshaft is reinstalled.

5   Gently tap the caps with a soft-face hammer, then separate them from the engine block. If necessary, use the bolts as levers to remove the caps. Try not to drop the bearing inserts if they come out with the caps.

6   Carefully lift the crankshaft out of the engine. It may be a good idea to have an assistant available, since the crankshaft is quite heavy. With the bearing inserts in place in the engine block and main bearing caps, return the caps to their respective locations on the engine block and tighten the bolts finger tight.

15   Engine block – cleaning

Refer to illustrations 15.1, 15.8 and 15.10
Caution: *The core plugs (also known as freeze plugs or soft plugs) may be difficult or impossible to retrieve if they're driven into the block coolant passages.*

1   Drill a small hole in the center of each core plug and pull them out with an auto body type dent puller **(see illustration)**.

2   Using a gasket scraper, remove all traces of gasket material from the engine block. Be very careful not to nick or gouge the gasket sealing surfaces.

3   Remove the main bearing caps and separate the bearing inserts from the caps and the engine block. Tag the bearings, indicating which cylinder they were removed from and whether they were in the cap or the block, then set them aside.

4   Remove all of the threaded oil gallery plugs from the block. The plugs are usually very tight – they may have to be drilled out and the holes retapped. Install new plugs when the engine is reassembled.

5   If the engine is extremely dirty it should be taken to an automotive machine shop to be steam cleaned or hot tanked.

6   After the block is returned, clean all oil holes and oil galleries one more time. Brushes specifically designed for this purpose are available at most

15.8   All bolt holes in the block – particularly the main bearing cap and head bolt holes – should be cleaned and restored with a tap (be sure to remove debris from the holes after this is done)

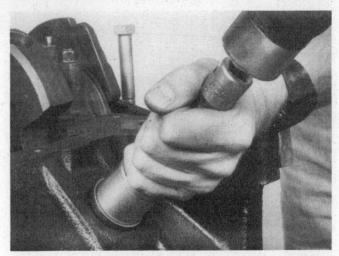

15.10   A large socket on an extension can be used to drive the new core plugs into the bores

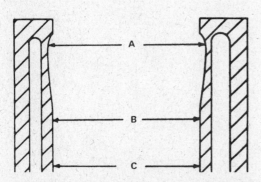

16.4a   Measure the diameter of each cylinder just under the wear ridge (A), at the center (B) and at the bottom (C)

16.4b   The ability to "feel" when the telescoping gauge is at the correct point will be developed over time, so work slowly and repeat the check until you're satisfied the bore measurement is accurate

auto parts stores. Flush the passages with warm water until the water runs clear, dry the block thoroughly and wipe all machined surfaces with a light, rust preventive oil. If you have access to compressed air, use it to speed the drying process and to blow out all the oil holes and galleries. **Warning:** *Wear eye protection when using compressed air!*

7   If the block isn't extremely dirty or covered with sludge, you can do an adequate cleaning job with hot soapy water and a stiff brush. Take plenty of time and do a thorough job. Regardless of the cleaning method used, be sure to clean all oil holes and galleries very thoroughly, dry the block completely and coat all machined surfaces with light oil to prevent rust.

8   The threaded holes in the block must be clean to ensure accurate torque readings during reassembly. Run the proper size tap into each of the holes to remove rust, corrosion, thread sealant or sludge and restore damaged threads **(see illustration)**. If possible, use compressed air to clear the holes of debris produced by this operation. Now is a good time to clean the threads on the head bolts and the main bearing cap bolts as well.

9   Reinstall the main bearing caps and tighten the bolts finger tight.

10   After coating the sealing surfaces of the new core plugs with Permatex no. 2 sealant, install them in the engine block **(see illustration)**. Make sure they're driven in straight and seated properly or leakage could result. Special tools are available for this purpose, but a large socket, with an outside diameter that will just slip into the core plug, a 1/2-inch drive extension and a hammer will work just as well.

11   Apply non-hardening sealant (such as Permatex no. 2 or Teflon pipe sealant) to the new oil gallery plugs and thread them into the holes in the block. Make sure they're tightened securely.

12   If the engine isn't going to be reassembled right away, cover it with a large plastic trash bag to keep it clean and dry.

16   Engine block – inspection

Refer to illustration 16.4a, 16.4b and 16.4c

1   Before the block is inspected, it should be cleaned as described in Section 15.

2   Visually check the block for cracks, rust and corrosion. Look for stripped threads in the threaded holes. It's also a good idea to have the block checked for hidden cracks by an automotive machine shop that has the special equipment to do this type of work. If defects are found, have the block repaired, if possible, or replaced.

3   Check the cylinder bores for scuffing and scoring.

4   Measure the diameter of each cylinder at the top (just under the ridge area), center and bottom of the cylinder bore, parallel to the crankshaft axis **(see illustrations)**.

5   Next, measure each cylinder's diameter at the same three locations across the crankshaft axis. Compare the results to this Chapter's Specifications.

6   If the required precision measuring tools aren't available, the piston-to-cylinder clearances can be obtained, though not quite as accurately, using feeler gauge stock. Feeler gauge stock comes in 12-inch lengths and various thicknesses and is generally available at auto parts stores.

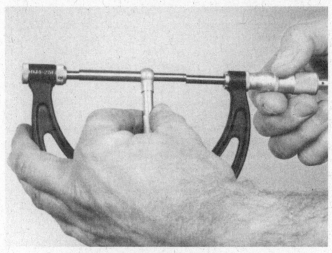

16.4c   The gauge is then measured with a micrometer to determine the bore size

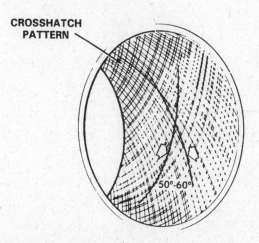

17.3a   The cylinder hone should leave a smooth, crosshatch pattern with the lines intersecting at approximately a 60-degree angle

2B

7   To check the clearance, select a feeler gauge and slip it into the cylinder along with the matching piston. The piston must be positioned exactly as it normally would be. The feeler gauge must be between the piston and cylinder on one of the thrust faces (90-degrees to the piston pin bore).

8   The piston should slip through the cylinder (with the feeler gauge in place) with moderate pressure.

9   If it falls through or slides through easily, the clearance is excessive and a new piston will be required. If the piston binds at the lower end of the cylinder and is loose toward the top, the cylinder is tapered. If tight spots are encountered as the piston/feeler gauge is rotated in the cylinder, the cylinder is out-of-round.

10   Repeat the procedure for the remaining pistons and cylinders.

11   If the cylinder walls are badly scuffed or scored, or if they're out-of-round or tapered beyond the limits given in this Chapter's Specifications, have the engine block rebored and honed at an automotive machine shop. If a rebore is done, oversize pistons and rings will be required.

12   If the cylinders are in reasonably good condition and not worn to the outside of the limits, and if the piston-to-cylinder clearances can be maintained properly, then they don't have to be rebored. Honing is all that's necessary (see Section 17).

17.3b   A "bottle brush" hone will produce better results if you've never honed cylinders before

17   Cylinder honing

Refer to illustrations 17.3a and 17.3b

1   Prior to engine reassembly, the cylinder bores must be honed so the new piston rings will seat correctly and provide the best possible combustion chamber seal. **Note:** *If you don't have the tools or don't want to tackle the honing operation, most automotive machine shops will do it for a reasonable fee.*

2   Before honing the cylinders, install the main bearing caps and tighten the bolts to the torque listed in this Chapter's Specifications.

3   Two types of cylinder hones are commonly available – the flex hone or "bottle brush" type and the more traditional surfacing hone with spring-loaded stones. Both will do the job, but for the less experienced mechanic the "bottle brush" hone will probably be easier to use. You'll also need some kerosene or honing oil, rags and an electric drill motor. Proceed as follows:

   a)   Mount the hone in the drill motor, compress the stones and slip it into the first cylinder. Be sure to wear safety goggles or a face shield!

   b)   Lubricate the cylinder with plenty of honing oil, turn on the drill and move the hone up-and-down in the cylinder at a pace that will produce a fine crosshatch pattern on the cylinder walls. Ideally, the crosshatch lines should intersect at approximately a 60-degree

angle **(see illustrations)**. Be sure to use plenty of lubricant and don't take off any more material than is absolutely necessary to produce the desired finish. **Note:** *Piston ring manufacturers may specify a smaller crosshatch angle than the traditional 60-degrees – read and follow any instructions included with the new piston rings.*

   c)   Don't withdraw the hone from the cylinder while it's running. Instead, shut off the drill and continue moving the hone up-and-down in the cylinder until it comes to a complete stop, then compress the stones and withdraw the hone. If you're using a "bottle brush" type hone, stop the drill motor, then turn the chuck in the normal direction of rotation while withdrawing the hone from the cylinder.

   d)   Wipe the oil out of the cylinder and repeat the procedure for the remaining cylinders.

4   After the honing job is complete, chamfer the top edges of the cylinder bores with a small file so the rings won't catch when the pistons are installed. Be very careful not to nick the cylinder walls with the end of the file.

5   The entire engine block must be washed again very thoroughly with warm, soapy water to remove all traces of the abrasive grit produced during the honing operation. **Note:** *The bores can be considered clean when a lint-free white cloth – dampened with clean engine oil- used to wipe them out doesn't pick up any more honing residue, which will show up as gray areas on the cloth. Be sure to run a brush through all oil holes and galleries and flush them with running water.*

18.4a   The piston ring grooves can be cleaned with a special tool, as shown here, . . .

18.4b   . . . or a section of a broken ring

6   After rinsing, dry the block and apply a coat of light rust preventive oil to all machined surfaces. Wrap the block in a plastic trash bag to keep it clean and dry and set it aside until reassembly.

18   Pistons/connecting rods – inspection

Refer to illustrations 18.4a, 18.4b, 18.10 and 18.11

1   Before the inspection process can be carried out, the piston/connecting rod assemblies must be cleaned and the original piston rings removed from the pistons. **Note:** *Always use new piston rings when the engine is reassembled.*

2   Using a piston ring installation tool, carefully remove the rings from the pistons. Be careful not to nick or gouge the pistons in the process.

3   Scrape all traces of carbon from the top of the piston. A hand-held wire brush or a piece of fine emery cloth can be used once the majority of the deposits have been scraped away. Do not, under any circumstances, use a wire brush mounted in a drill motor to remove deposits from the pistons. The piston material is soft and may be eroded away by the wire brush.

4   Use a piston ring groove cleaning tool to remove carbon deposits from the ring grooves **(see illustration)**. If a tool isn't available, a piece broken off the old ring will do the job. Be very careful to remove only the carbon deposits – don't remove any metal and do not nick or scratch the sides of the ring grooves **(see illustration)**.

5   Once the deposits have been removed, clean the piston/rod assemblies with solvent and dry them with compressed air (if available). Make sure the oil return holes in the back sides of the ring grooves are clear.

6   If the pistons and cylinder walls aren't damaged or worn excessively, and if the engine block is not rebored, new pistons won't be necessary. Normal piston wear appears as even vertical wear on the piston thrust surfaces and slight looseness of the top ring in its groove. New piston rings, however, should always be used when an engine is rebuilt.

7   Carefully inspect each piston for cracks around the skirt, at the pin bosses and at the ring lands.

8   Look for scoring and scuffing on the thrust faces of the skirt, holes in the piston crown and burned areas at the edge of the crown. If the skirt is scored or scuffed, the engine may have been suffering from overheating and/or abnormal combustion, which caused excessively high operating temperatures. The cooling and lubrication systems should be checked thoroughly. A hole in the piston crown is an indication that abnormal combustion (preignition) was occurring. Burned areas at the edge of the piston crown are usually evidence of spark knock (detonation). If any of the above problems exist, the causes must be corrected or the damage will occur again. The causes may include intake air leaks, incorrect fuel/air mixture, incorrect ignition timing and EGR system malfunctions.

9   Corrosion of the piston, in the form of small pits, indicates that coolant

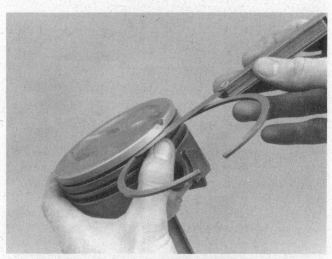

18.10   Check the ring side clearance with a feeler gauge at several points around the groove

18.11   Measure the piston diameter at a 90-degree angle to the piston pin and in line with it

is leaking into the combustion chamber and/or the crankcase. Again, the cause must be corrected or the problem may persist in the rebuilt engine.

10   Measure the piston ring side clearance by laying a new piston ring in each ring groove and slipping a feeler gauge in beside it **(see illustration)**.

19.2   Rubbing a penny lengthwise on each journal will reveal its condition – if copper rubs off and is embedded in the crankshaft, the journals should be reground

19.3   The oil holes should be chamfered so sharp edges don't gouge or scratch the new bearings

19.4   Use a wire or stiff plastic bristle brush to clean the oil passages in the crankshaft

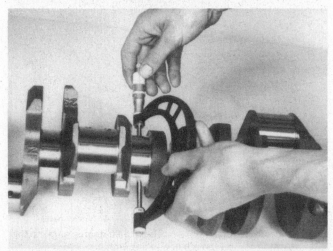

19.6   Measure the diameter of each crankshaft journal at several points to detect taper and out-of-round conditions

Check the clearance at three or four locations around each groove. Be sure to use the correct ring for each groove – they are different. If the side

clearance is greater than the figure listed in this Chapter's Specifications, new pistons will have to be used.

11   Check the piston-to-bore clearance by measuring the bore (see Section 16) and the piston diameter. Make sure the pistons and bores are correctly matched. Measure the piston across the skirt, at a 90-degree angle to and in line with the piston pin **(see illustration)**. Subtract the piston diameter from the bore diameter to obtain the clearance. If it's greater than specified, the block will have to be rebored and new pistons and rings installed.

12   Check the piston-to-rod clearance by twisting the piston and rod in opposite directions. Any noticeable play indicates excessive wear, which must be corrected. The piston/connecting rod assemblies should be taken to an automotive machine shop to have the pistons and rods resized and new pins installed.

13   If the pistons must be removed from the connecting rods for any reason, they should be taken to an automotive machine shop. While they are there have the connecting rods checked for bend and twist, since automotive machine shops have special equipment for this purpose. **Note:** *Unless new pistons and/or connecting rods must be installed, do not disassemble the pistons and connecting rods.*

14   Check the connecting rods for cracks and other damage. Temporarily remove the rod caps, lift out the old bearing inserts, wipe the rod and cap bearing surfaces clean and inspect them for nicks, gouges and scratches. After checking the rods, replace the old bearings, slip the caps into place and tighten the nuts finger tight. **Note:** *If the engine is being rebuilt because of a connecting rod knock, be sure to install new rods.*

19   Crankshaft – inspection

Refer to illustrations 19.2, 19.3, 19.4, 19.6 and 19.8

1   Check the main and connecting rod bearing journals for uneven wear, scoring, pits and cracks.

2   Rub a penny across each journal several times **(see illustration)**. If a journal picks up copper from the penny, it's too rough and must be reground.

3   Remove all burrs from the crankshaft oil holes with a stone, file or scraper **(see illustration)**.

4   Clean the crankshaft with solvent and dry it with compressed air (if available). Be sure to clean the oil holes with a stiff brush and flush them with solvent **(see illustration)**.

5   Check the rest of the crankshaft for cracks and other damage. It should be magnafluxed to reveal hidden cracks – an automotive machine shop can handle the procedure.

6   Using a micrometer, measure the diameter of the main and connecting rod journals and compare the results to this Chapter's Specifications **(see illustration)**. By measuring the diameter at a number of points

19.8   If the seals have worn grooves in the crankshaft journals, or if the seal contact surfaces are nicked or scratched, the new seals will leak

around each journal's circumference, you'll be able to determine whether or not the journal is out-of-round. Take the measurement at each end of the journal, near the crank throws, to determine if the journal is tapered.

7   If the crankshaft journals are damaged, tapered, out-of-round or worn beyond the limits given in this Chapter's Specifications, have the crankshaft reground by an automotive machine shop. Be sure to use the correct size bearing inserts if the crankshaft is reconditioned.

8   Check the oil seal journals at each end of the crankshaft for wear and damage **(see illustration)**. If the seal has worn a groove in the journal, or if it's nicked or scratched, the new seal may leak when the engine is reassembled. In some cases, an automotive machine shop may be able to repair the journal by pressing on a thin sleeve. If repair isn't feasible, a new or different crankshaft should be installed.

9   Refer to Section 20 and examine the main and rod bearing inserts.

20   Main and connecting rod bearings – inspection

Refer to illustration 20.1

1   Even though the main and connecting rod bearings should be replaced with new ones during the engine overhaul, the old bearings should be retained for close examination, as they may reveal valuable information about the condition of the engine **(see illustration)**.

2   Bearing failure occurs because of lack of lubrication, the presence of dirt or other foreign particles, overloading the engine and corrosion. Regardless of the cause of bearing failure, it must be corrected before the engine is reassembled to prevent it from happening again.

3   When examining the bearings, remove them from the engine block, the main bearing caps, the connecting rods and the rod caps and lay them out on a clean surface in the same general position as their location in the engine. This will enable you to match any bearing problems with the corresponding crankshaft journal.

4   Dirt and other foreign particles get into the engine in a variety of ways. It may be left in the engine during assembly, or it may pass through filters or the PCV system. It may get into the oil, and from there into the bearings. Metal chips from machining operations and normal engine wear are often present. Abrasives are sometimes left in engine components after reconditioning, especially when parts are not thoroughly cleaned using the proper cleaning methods. Whatever the source, these foreign objects often end up embedded in the soft bearing material and are easily recognized. Large particles will not embed in the bearing and will score or gouge the bearing and journal. The best prevention for this cause of bearing failure is to clean all parts thoroughly and keep everything spotlessly clean during engine assembly. Frequent and regular engine oil and filter changes are also recommended.

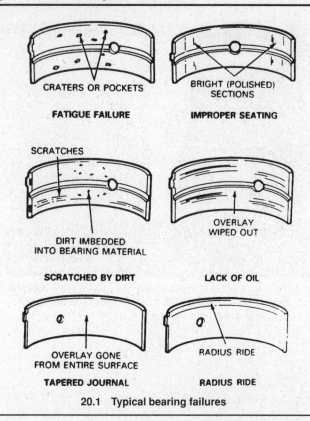

20.1   Typical bearing failures

5   Lack of lubrication (or lubrication breakdown) has a number of interrelated causes. Excessive heat (which thins the oil), overloading (which squeezes the oil from the bearing face) and oil leakage or throw off (from excessive bearing clearances, worn oil pump or high engine speeds) all contribute to lubrication breakdown. Blocked oil passages, which usually are the result of misaligned oil holes in a bearing shell, will also oil starve a bearing and destroy it. When lack of lubrication is the cause of bearing failure, the bearing material is wiped or extruded from the steel backing of the bearing. Temperatures may increase to the point where the steel backing turns blue from overheating.

6   Driving habits can have a definite effect on bearing life. Full throttle, low speed operation (lugging the engine) puts very high loads on bearings, which tends to squeeze out the oil film. These loads cause the bearings to flex, which produces fine cracks in the bearing face (fatigue failure). Eventually the bearing material will loosen in pieces and tear away from the steel backing. Short trip driving leads to corrosion of bearings because insufficient engine heat is produced to drive off the condensed water and corrosive gases. These products collect in the engine oil, forming acid and sludge. As the oil is carried to the engine bearings, the acid attacks and corrodes the bearing material.

7   Incorrect bearing installation during engine assembly will lead to bearing failure as well. Tight fitting bearings leave insufficient bearing oil clearance and will result in oil starvation. Dirt or foreign particles trapped behind a bearing insert result in high spots on the bearing which lead to failure.

21   Engine overhaul – reassembly sequence

1   Before beginning engine reassembly, make sure you have all the necessary new parts, gaskets and seals as well as the following items on hand:

Common hand tools
A 1/2-inch drive torque wrench
Piston ring installation tool

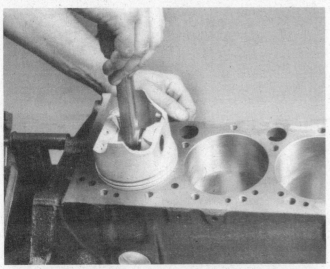

22.3 When checking piston ring end gap, the ring must be square in the cylinder bore (this is done by pushing the ring down with the top of a piston as shown)

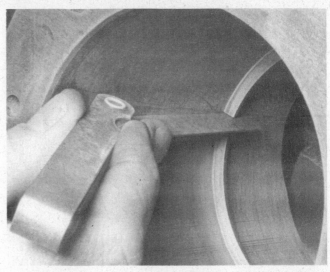

22.4 With the ring square in the cylinder, measure the end gap with a feeler gauge

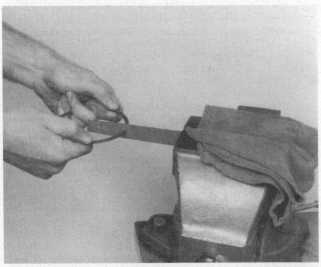

22.5 If the end gap is too small, clamp a file in a vise and file the ring ends (from the outside in only) to enlarge the gap slightly

Piston ring compressor
Vibration damper installation tool
Short lengths of rubber or plastic hose to fit over connecting rod bolts
Plastigage
Feeler gauges
A fine-tooth file
New engine oil and filter
Engine assembly lube or moly-base grease
Gasket sealant
Thread locking compound

2   In order to save time and avoid problems, engine reassembly must be done in the following general order:

Piston rings
Crankshaft, main bearings and rear main oil seal
Piston/connecting rod assemblies
Oil pump
Oil pan
Cylinder head
Camshaft, lifters and rocker arms

Water pump
Timing belt and sprockets
Timing cover
Intake and exhaust manifolds
Valve cover
Flywheel/driveplate

2B

---

22   Piston rings – installation

Refer to illustrations 22.3, 22.4, 22.5, 22.9a, 22.9b and 22 12

1   Before installing the new piston rings, the ring end gaps must be checked. It's assumed that the piston ring side clearance has been checked and verified correct (see Section 18).

2   Lay out the piston/connecting rod assemblies and the new ring sets so the ring sets will be matched with the same piston and cylinder during the end gap measurement and engine assembly.

3   Insert the top (number one) ring into the first cylinder and square it up with the cylinder walls by pushing it in with the top of the piston **(see illustration)**. The ring should be near the bottom of the cylinder, at the lower limit of ring travel.

4   To measure the end gap, slip feeler gauges between the ends of the ring until a gauge equal to the gap width is found **(see illustration)**. The feeler gauge should slide between the ring ends with a slight amount of drag. Compare the measurement to this Chapter's Specifications. If the gap is larger or smaller than specified, double-check to make sure you have the correct rings before proceeding.

5   If the gap is too small, it must be enlarged or the ring ends may come in contact with each other during engine operation, which can cause serious damage to the engine. The end gap can be increased by filing the ring ends very carefully with a fine file. Mount the file in a vise equipped with soft jaws, slip the ring over the file with the ends contacting the file face and slowly move the ring to remove material from the ends **(see illustration)**. When performing this operation, file only from the outside in.

6   Excess end gap isn't critical unless it's greater than 0.040-inch. Again, double-check to make sure you have the correct rings for your engine.

7   Repeat the procedure for each ring that will be installed in the first cylinder and for each ring in the remaining cylinders. Remember to keep rings, pistons and cylinders matched up.

8   Once the ring end gaps have been checked/corrected, the rings can be installed on the pistons.

22.9a   Installing the spacer/expander in the oil control ring groove

22.9b   DO NOT use a piston ring installation tool when installing the oil ring side rails

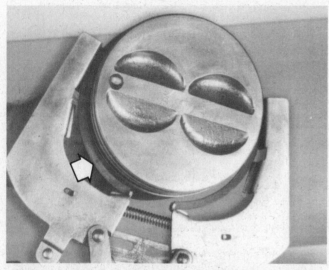

22.12   Installing the compression rings with a ring expander – the mark (arrow) must face up

9   The oil control ring (lowest one on the piston) is usually installed first. It's composed of three separate components. Slip the spacer/expander into the groove **(see illustration)**. If an anti-rotation tang is used, make sure it's inserted into the drilled hole in the ring groove. Next, install the lower side rail **(see illustration)**. Don't use a piston ring installation tool on the oil ring side rails, as they may be damaged. Instead, place one end of the side rail into the groove between the spacer/expander and the ring land, hold it firmly in place and slide a finger around the piston while pushing the rail into the groove. Next, install the upper side rail in the same manner.

10   After the three oil ring components have been installed, check to make sure that both the upper and lower side rails can be turned smoothly in the ring groove.

11   The number two (middle) ring is installed next. It's usually stamped with a mark which must face up, toward the top of the piston. **Note:** *Always follow the instructions printed on the ring package or box – different manufacturers may require different approaches. Do not mix up the top and middle rings, as they have different cross sections.*

12   Use a piston ring installation tool and make sure the identification mark is facing the top of the piston, then slip the ring into the middle groove on the piston **(see illustration)**. Don't expand the ring any more than necessary to slide it over the piston.

13   Install the number one (top) ring in the same manner. Make sure the mark is facing up. Be careful not to confuse the number one and number two rings.

14   Repeat the procedure for the remaining pistons and rings.

---

23   Crankshaft – installation and main bearing oil clearance check

Refer to illustrations 23.10, 23.14 and 23.18

1   Crankshaft installation is the first step in engine reassembly. It's assumed at this point that the engine block and crankshaft have been cleaned, inspected and repaired or reconditioned.

2   Position the engine with the oil pan mating surface facing up.

3   Remove the main bearing cap bolts and lift out the caps. Lay them out in the proper order to ensure correct installation.

4   If they're still in place, remove the original bearing inserts from the block and the main bearing caps. Wipe the bearing surfaces of the block and caps with a clean, lint-free cloth. They must be kept spotlessly clean.

Main bearing oil clearance check

5   Clean the back sides of the new main bearing inserts and lay one in each main bearing saddle in the block. The cylinder block half of the center bearing is flanged to control crankshaft endplay. Lay the other bearing from each set in the corresponding main bearing cap. Make sure the tab on the bearing insert fits into the recess in the block or cap. **Caution:** *The oil holes in the block must line up with the oil holes in the bearing insert. Do not hammer the bearing into place and don't nick or gouge the bearing faces. No lubrication should be used at this time.*

6   Clean the faces of the bearings in the block and the crankshaft main bearing journals with a clean, lint-free cloth.

7   Check or clean the oil holes in the crankshaft, as any dirt here can go only one way – straight into the new bearings.

8   Once you're certain the crankshaft is clean, carefully lay it in position in the main bearings.

9   Before the crankshaft can be permanently installed, the main bearing oil clearance must be checked.

10   Cut several pieces of the appropriate size Plastigage (they must be slightly shorter than the width of the main bearings) and place one piece on each crankshaft main bearing journal, parallel with the journal axis **(see illustration)**.

11   Clean the faces of the bearings in the caps and install the caps in their respective positions (don't mix them up) with the arrows pointing toward the front of the engine. Don't disturb the Plastigage.

23.10 Lay the Plastigage strips (arrow) on the main bearing journals, parallel to the crankshaft centerline

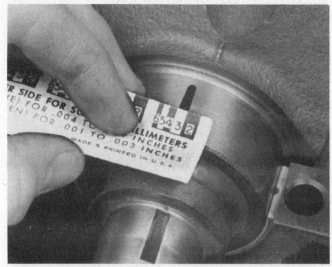

23.14   Compare the width of the crushed Plastigage to the scale on the envelope to determine the main bearing oil clearance (always take the measurement at the widest point of the Plastigage); be sure to use the correct scale – standard and metric ones are included

2B

Final crankshaft installation

17   Carefully lift the crankshaft out of the engine.

18   Clean the bearing faces in the block, then apply a thin, uniform layer of moly-base grease or engine assembly lube to each of the bearing surfaces **(see illustration)**. Be sure to coat the thrust faces as well as the journal face of the thrust bearing.

19   Make sure the crankshaft journals are clean, then lay the crankshaft back in place in the block.

20   Clean the faces of the bearings in the caps, then apply lubricant to them.

21   Install the caps in their respective positions with the arrows pointing toward the timing belt end of the engine.

22   Install the bolts.

23   Tighten bearing cap bolts to the torque listed in this Chapter's Specifications (work from the center out and approach the final torque in three steps).

24   Tap the ends of the crankshaft forward and backward with a lead or brass hammer to line up the main bearing and crankshaft thrust surfaces.

25   Retighten all main bearing cap bolts to the specified torque, starting with the center main and working out toward the ends.

26   Rotate the crankshaft a number of times by hand to check for any obvious binding.

27   The final step is to check the crankshaft endplay with a feeler gauge or a dial indicator as described in Section 14. The endplay should be correct if the crankshaft thrust faces aren't worn or damaged and new bearings have been installed.

28   Install a new rear main oil seal and bolt the seal retainer to the block.

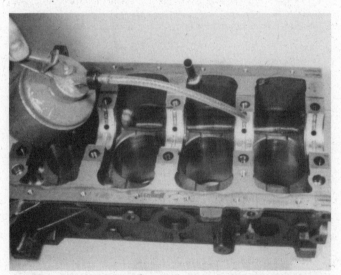

23.18   Lubricate the bearings prior to installing the crankshaft

12   Starting with the center main and working out toward the ends, tighten the main bearing cap bolts, in three steps, to the torque listed in this Chapter's Specifications. Don't rotate the crankshaft at any time during this operation.

13   Remove the bolts and carefully lift off the main bearing caps. Keep them in order. Don't disturb the Plastigage or rotate the crankshaft. If any of the main bearing caps are difficult to remove, tap them gently from side-to-side with a soft-face hammer to loosen them.

14   Compare the width of the crushed Plastigage on each journal to the scale printed on the Plastigage envelope to obtain the main bearing oil clearance **(see illustration)**. Check this Chapter's Specifications to make sure it's correct.

15   If the clearance is not as specified, the bearing inserts may be the wrong size (which means different ones will be required). Before deciding that different inserts are needed, make sure that no dirt or oil was between the bearing inserts and the caps or block when the clearance was measured. If the Plastigage was wider at one end than the other, the journal may be tapered (refer to Section 19).

16   Carefully scrape all traces of the Plastigage material off the main bearing journals and/or the bearing faces. Use your fingernail or the edge of a credit card – don't nick or scratch the bearing faces.

---

24   Pistons/connecting rods – installation and rod bearing oil clearance check

Refer to illustrations 24.5, 24.9, 24.11, 24.13 and 24.17

1   Before installing the piston/connecting rod assemblies, the cylinder walls must be perfectly clean, the top edge of each cylinder must be chamfered, and the crankshaft must be in place.

2   Remove the cap from the end of the number one connecting rod (refer to the marks made during removal). Remove the original bearing inserts and wipe the bearing surfaces of the connecting rod and cap with a clean, lint-free cloth. They must be kept spotlessly clean.

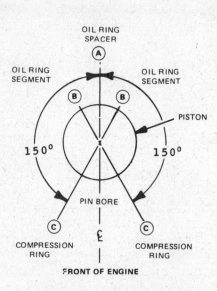

24.5   **Piston ring gap spacing diagram**

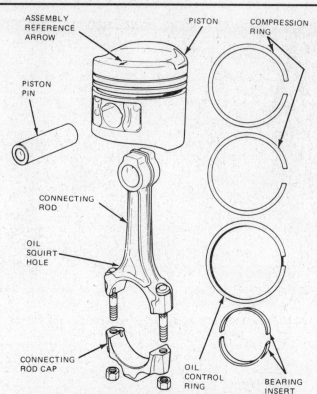

24.9   **Piston and connecting rod components – note the assembly reference (directional) arrow on the top of the piston**

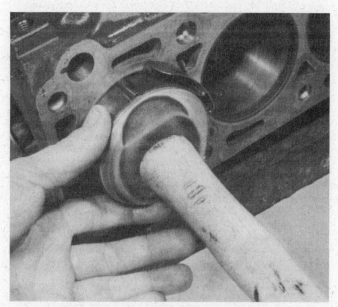

24.11   **Installing the piston with a ring compressor**

Connecting rod bearing oil clearance check

3   Clean the back side of the new upper bearing insert, then lay it in place in the connecting rod. Make sure the tab on the bearing fits into the recess in the rod. Don't hammer the bearing insert into place and be very careful not to nick or gouge the bearing face. Don't lubricate the bearing at this time.

4   Clean the back side of the other bearing insert and install it in the rod cap. Again, make sure the tab on the bearing fits into the recess in the cap, and don't apply any lubricant. It's critically important that the mating surfaces of the bearing and connecting rod are perfectly clean and oil free when they're assembled.

5   Position the piston ring gaps around the piston as shown (**see illustration**).

6   Slip a section of plastic or rubber hose over each connecting rod cap bolt.

7   Lubricate the piston and rings with clean engine oil and attach a piston ring compressor to the piston. Leave the skirt protruding about 1/4-inch to guide the piston into the cylinder. The rings must be compressed until they're flush with the piston.

8   Rotate the crankshaft until the number one connecting rod journal is at BDC (bottom dead center) and apply a coat of engine oil to the cylinder walls.

9   With the directional arrow on top of the piston (**see illustration**) facing toward the timing belt end of the engine, gently insert the piston/connecting rod assembly into the number one cylinder bore and rest the bottom edge of the ring compressor on the engine block.

10   Tap the top edge of the ring compressor to make sure it's contacting the block around its entire circumference.

11   Gently tap on the top of the piston with the end of a wooden hammer handle (**see illustration**) while guiding the end of the connecting rod into place on the crankshaft journal. The piston rings may try to pop out of the ring compressor just before entering the cylinder bore, so keep some downward pressure on the ring compressor. Work slowly, and if any resistance is felt as the piston enters the cylinder, stop immediately. Find out what's hanging up and fix it before proceeding. Do not, for any reason, force the piston into the cylinder – you might break a ring and/or the piston.

12   Once the piston/connecting rod assembly is installed, the connecting rod bearing oil clearance must be checked before the rod cap is permanently bolted in place.

13   Cut a piece of the appropriate size Plastigage slightly shorter than the width of the connecting rod bearing and lay it in place on the number one connecting rod journal, parallel with the journal axis (**see illustration**).

14   Clean the connecting rod cap bearing face, remove the protective hoses from the connecting rod bolts and install the rod cap. Make sure the mating mark on the cap is on the same side as the mark on the connecting rod.

15   Install the nuts and tighten them to the torque listed in this Chapter's Specifications, working up to it in three steps. **Note:** *Use a thin-wall socket to avoid erroneous torque readings that can result if the socket is wedged between the rod cap and nut. If the socket tends to wedge itself between the nut and the cap, lift up on it slightly until it no longer contacts the cap. Do not rotate the crankshaft at any time during this operation.*

16   Remove the nuts and detach the rod cap, being very careful not to disturb the Plastigage.

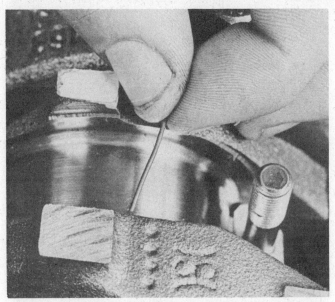

24.13 Lay the Plastigage strips on each rod bearing journal, parallel to the crankshaft centerline

24.17 Measuring the width of the crushed Plastigage to determine the rod bearing oil clearance (be sure to use the correct scale – standard and metric ones are included)

2B

17   Compare the width of the crushed Plastigage to the scale printed on the Plastigage envelope to obtain the oil clearance **(see illustration)**. Compare it to this Chapter's Specifications to make sure the clearance is correct.

18   If the clearance is not as specified, the bearing inserts may be the wrong size (which means different ones will be required). Before deciding that different inserts are needed, make sure that no dirt or oil was between the bearing inserts and the connecting rod or cap when the clearance was measured. Also, recheck the journal diameter. If the Plastigage was wider at one end than the other, the journal may be tapered (refer to Section 19).

Final connecting rod installation

19   Carefully scrape all traces of the Plastigage material off the rod journal and/or bearing face. Be very careful not to scratch the bearing – use your fingernail or the edge of a credit card.

20   Make sure the bearing faces are perfectly clean, then apply a uniform layer of clean moly-base grease or engine assembly lube to both of them. You'll have to push the piston into the cylinder to expose the face of the bearing insert in the connecting rod – be sure to slip the protective hoses over the rod bolts first.

21   Slide the connecting rod back into place on the journal, remove the protective hoses from the rod cap bolts, install the rod cap and tighten the nuts to the torque listed in this Chapter's Specifications. Again, work up to the torque in three steps.

22   Repeat the entire procedure for the remaining pistons/connecting rods.

23   The important points to remember are:
   a) Keep the back sides of the bearing inserts and the insides of the connecting rods and caps perfectly clean when assembling them.
   b) Make sure you have the correct piston/rod assembly for each cylinder.
   c) The directional arrow on top of the piston must face toward the timing belt end of the engine.
   d) Lubricate the cylinder walls with clean oil.
   e) Lubricate the bearing faces when installing the rod caps after the oil clearance has been checked.

24   After all the piston/connecting rod assemblies have been properly installed, rotate the crankshaft a number of times by hand to check for any obvious binding.

25   As a final step, the connecting rod endplay must be checked. Refer to Section 12 for this procedure.

26   Compare the measured endplay to the this Chapter's Specifications to make sure it's correct. If it was correct before disassembly and the original crankshaft and rods were reinstalled, it should still be right. If new rods or a new crankshaft were installed, the endplay may be inadequate. If so, the rods will have to be removed and taken to an automotive machine shop for resizing.

---

25   Initial start-up and break-in after overhaul

Warning: *Have a fire extinguisher handy when starting the engine for the first time.*

1   Once the engine has been installed in the vehicle, double-check the engine oil and coolant levels.

2   With the spark plugs out of the engine and the ignition system disabled (see Section 3), crank the engine until oil pressure registers on the gauge or the light goes out.

3   Install the spark plugs, hook up the plug wires and restore the ignition system functions (see Section 3).

4   Start the engine. It may take a few moments for the fuel system to build up pressure, but the engine should start without a great deal of effort. **Note:** *If backfiring occurs through the carburetor or throttle body, recheck the valve timing and ignition timing.*

5   After the engine starts, it should be allowed to warm up to normal operating temperature. While the engine is warming up, make a thorough check for fuel, oil and coolant leaks.

6   Shut the engine off and recheck the engine oil and coolant levels.

7   Drive the vehicle to an area with minimum traffic, accelerate at full throttle from 30 to 50 mph, then allow the vehicle to slow to 30 mph with the throttle closed. Repeat the procedure 10 or 12 times. This will load the piston rings and cause them to seat properly against the cylinder walls. Check again for oil and coolant leaks.

8   Drive the vehicle gently for the first 500 miles (no sustained high speeds) and keep a constant check on the oil level. It is not unusual for an engine to use oil during the break-in period.

9   At approximately 500 to 600 miles, change the oil and filter.

10   For the next few hundred miles, drive the vehicle normally. Do not pamper it or abuse it.

11   After 2000 miles, change the oil and filter again and consider the engine broken in.

Chapter 3 Cooling, heating and air conditioning systems

Contents

Specifications

General

System type	Pressurized, assisted by a belt-driven water pump and electric fan
Thermostat type	Wax pellet
Radiator	Corrugated fin, copper/brass or aluminum construction with removable plastic tanks, crossflow type
Radiator pressure test	16 to 18 psi
Radiator cap operating pressure	16 psi
Electric fan operating temperatures	Fan cuts in at 221-degrees F and runs until temperature drops to 201-degrees F
Water pump type	Belt-driven impeller
Refrigerant capacity	2-1/2 lbs

Torque specifications

	Ft-lbs (unless otherwise indicated)
Air conditioning compressor-to-bracket bolts	25 to 35
Air conditioning bracket-to-block bolts	31 to 43
Thermostat housing bolts	12 to 15
Water pump bolts	60 to 84 in-lbs
Water pump inlet tube-to-cylinder block	30 to 40
Water pump inlet tube-to-water pump	
1981 through 1983	48 to 60 in-lbs
1984 through 1990	60 to 84 in-lbs
Water pump pulley-to-hub bolts	72 to 96 in-lbs

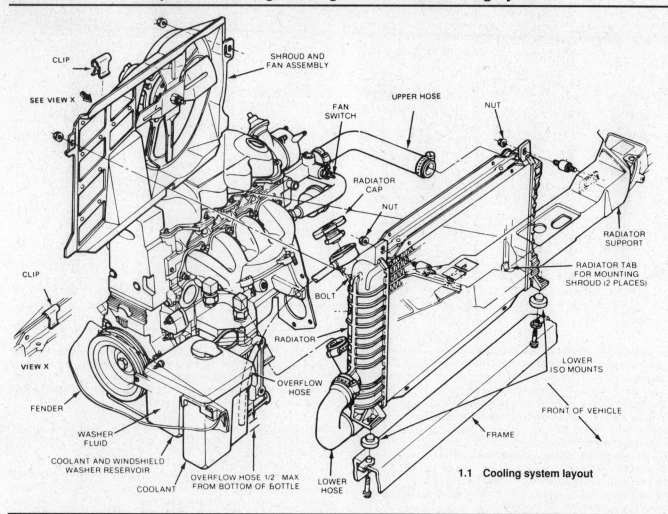

1.1   Cooling system layout

1   General information

Refer to illustration 1.1

Engine cooling system

All vehicles covered by this manual employ a pressurized engine cooling system with thermostatically controlled coolant circulation **(see illustration)**. An impeller-type water pump mounted on the front of the block pumps coolant through the engine. The coolant flows around each cylinder and toward the rear of the engine. Cast-in coolant passages direct coolant around the intake and exhaust manifolds ports, near the spark plug areas and in close proximity to the exhaust valve guides.

A wax pellet-type of thermostat is located in the housing near the front of the engine. During warm up, the closed thermostat prevents the coolant from circulating through the radiator. As the engine nears normal operating temperature, the thermostat opens and allows hot coolant to travel trough the radiator, where it's cooled before returning to the engine.

The cooling system is sealed by a pressure type radiator cap, which raises the boiling point of the coolant and increases the cooling efficiency of the radiator. If the system pressure exceeds the cap pressure relief valve value, the excess pressure in the system forces the spring-loaded valve inside the cap off its seat and allows the coolant to escape through an overflow tube into the coolant reservoir. When the system cools the excess coolant is automatically drawn from the reservoir back into the radiator.

The coolant reservoir does double duty as both the point at which fresh coolant is added to the cooling system to maintain the proper fluid level and as a holding tank for overheated coolant.

This type of cooling system is known as a closed design because coolant that escapes past the pressure cap is saved and reused.

Heating system

The heating system consists of a blower fan and heater core located in the heater case, the hoses connecting the heater core to the engine cooling system and the heater/air conditioning control head on the instrument panel. Hot engine coolant is circulated through the heater core. When the heater mode is activated, a flap door opens to expose the heater case to the passenger compartment. A fan switch on the control head activates the blower motor, which forces air through the core, heating the air.

Air conditioning system

The air conditioning system consists of a condenser mounted in front of the radiator, an evaporator mounted adjacent to the heater core, a compressor mounted on the engine, an accumulator/drier contains a high-pressure relief valve and the plumbing connecting all of the above components.

A blower fan forces the warmer air of the passenger compartment through the evaporator core (sort of a radiator-in-reverse), transferring the heat from the air to the refrigerant. The liquid refrigerant boils off into low pressure vapor, taking the heat with it when it leaves the evaporator.

2   Antifreeze – general information

Warning: *Do not allow antifreeze to come in contact with your skin or painted surfaces of the vehicle. Rinse off spills immediately with plenty of water. Antifreeze is highly toxic if ingested. Never leave antifreeze lying*

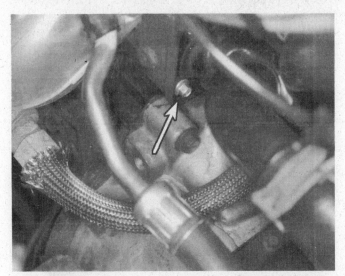

3.10 The thermostat housing is bolted to the flywheel (driver's) side of the engine – one bolt is hidden in this photo

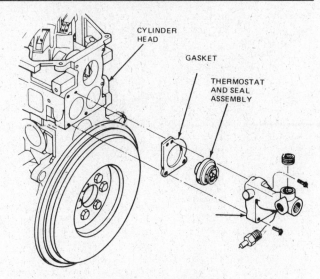

3.11 Thermostat installation

around in an open container or in puddles on the floor; children and pets are attracted by its sweet smell and may drink it. Check with local authorities about disposing of used antifreeze. Many communities have collection centers which will see the antifreeze is disposed of safely.

The cooling system should be filled with water/ethylene glycol based antifreeze solution, which will prevent freezing down to at least -20-degrees F, or lower if the local climate requires it. It also provides protection against corrosion and increases the coolant boiling point.

The cooling system should be drained, flushed and refilled at least every year (see Chapter 1). The use of antifreeze solutions for periods of longer than two years is likely to cause damage and encourage the formation of rust and scale in the system. If your tap water is "hard," use distilled water with the antifreeze.

Before adding antifreeze to the system, check all coolant and heater hose connections, because antifreeze tends to search out and leak through very minute openings. Engines do not normally consume coolant. Therefore, if the level goes down find the cause and correct it.

The exact mixture of antifreeze-to-water which you should use depends on the relative weather conditions. The mixture should contain at least 50-percent antifreeze, but should never contain more than 70-percent antifreeze. Consult the mixture ratio on the carton the antifreeze container before adding coolant. Hydrometers are available at most auto parts stores to test the ratio of antifreeze to water. Use antifreeze which meets specifications ESE-M97B44-A (Ford Cooling System Fluid, part No. E2FZ-19549-A) or equivalent.

3   Thermostat – check and replacement

Warning: *Do not remove the radiator cap, drain the coolant or replace the thermostat until the engine has cooled completely.*

Check

1   Before assuming the thermostat is to blame for a cooling system problem, check the coolant level, drivebelt tension (see Chapter 1) and temperature gauge (or light) operation.
2   If the engine seems to be taking a long time to warm up (based on heater output or temperature gauge operation), the thermostat is probably stuck in the open position. Replace the thermostat with a new one.
3   If the engine runs hot, use your hand to check the temperature of the upper radiator hose. If the hose isn't hot but the engine is, the thermostat is probably stuck in the closed position, preventing the coolant inside the engine from escaping to the radiator. Replace the thermostat. **Caution:**

Don't drive the vehicle without a thermostat. The computer may stay in the open loop and emissions and fuel economy will suffer.
4   If the upper radiator hose is hot, it means that the coolant is flowing and the thermostat is open. Consult the *Troubleshooting* Section at the front of this manual for cooling system diagnosis.

Replacement

Refer to illustrations 3.10 and 3.11
5   Disconnect the negative battery cable from the battery.
6   Drain the cooling system (see Chapter 1). If the coolant is relatively new or in good condition (see Chapter 1), save it and reuse it. **Warning:** *Do not leave the drained coolant lying around in an open container or in puddles on the floor where it is accessible to children and pets – they are attracted by its sweet smell and may drink it. Ingesting even a small amount of coolant can be fatal!*
7   Follow the upper radiator hose to the engine to locate the thermostat housing.
8   Loosen the hose clamp, then detach the hose from the thermostat fitting. If it is stuck, grasp it near the end with a pair of Channelock pliers and carefully twist it to break the seal, then pull it off. If the hose is old or deteriorated, cut it off and install a new upper hose.
9   If the large fitting that mates with the hose is deteriorated (corroded, pitted, etc.) it may be damaged further by hose removal.
10   Remove the bolts and detach the thermostat housing **(see illustration)**. If it is stuck, tap it with a soft-face hammer to jar it loose. Be prepared for some coolant to spill as the gasket seal is broken.
11   Turn the thermostat counterclockwise and remove it from the thermostat housing **(see illustration)**.
12   Stuff a rag into the engine opening, then remove all traces of old gasket material and sealant from the thermostat housing with a gasket scraper. Remove the rag from the engine opening and clean the gasket mating surface with lacquer thinner or acetone.
13   Insert the thermostat into the housing, compress the seal and rotate the thermostat clockwise to lock it in place. The thermostat locking tabs must be 90-degrees from the heater hose inlet.
14   Gaskets may be plain or pre-coated with adhesive. On pre-coated gaskets, peel the protective paper away from the adhesive. Coat plain gaskets on both sides with a thin, even layer of gasket sealant.
15   Install the thermostat housing and bolts. Tighten the bolts to the torque listed in this Chapter's Specifications.
16   Reattach the upper hose to the fitting and tighten the hose clamp securely.
17   Refill the cooling system (see Chapter 1).
18   Connect the negative battery cable onto the battery.

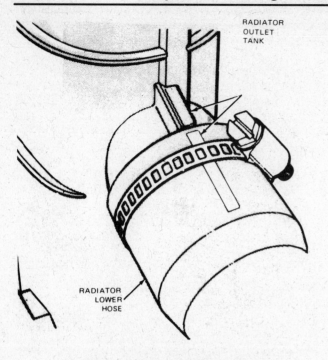

RADIATOR
OUTLET
TANK

RADIATOR
LOWER
HOSE

4.15   Radiator hose alignment mark

19   Start the engine and allow it to reach normal operating temperature, then check for leaks and proper thermostat operation (as described in Steps 2 through 4).

4   Radiator – removal and installation

Refer to illustration 4.15

Warning: *Wait until the engine is completely cool before beginning this procedure.*

1   Disconnect the negative battery cable from the battery.

2   Drain the cooling system (see Chapter 1). If the coolant is relatively new or in good condition (see Chapter 1), save it and reuse it. **Warning:** *Be sure to store coolant where children and pets can't get to it. It's sweet smell attracts them and they may drink it. Ingesting even a small amount of coolant can be fatal!*

3   Remove the alternator air tube (if equipped) and carburetor air intake from the radiator support.

4   Loosen the hose clamps, then detach the hoses from the radiator fittings. If they're stuck, grasp each hose near the end with a pair of adjustable pliers and carefully twist it to break the seal, then pull it off – be careful not to distort the radiator fittings! If the hoses are old or deteriorated, cut them off and install new hoses.

5   Disconnect the reservoir hose from the radiator filler neck.

6   Remove the screws that secure the shroud to the radiator and slide the shroud toward the engine.

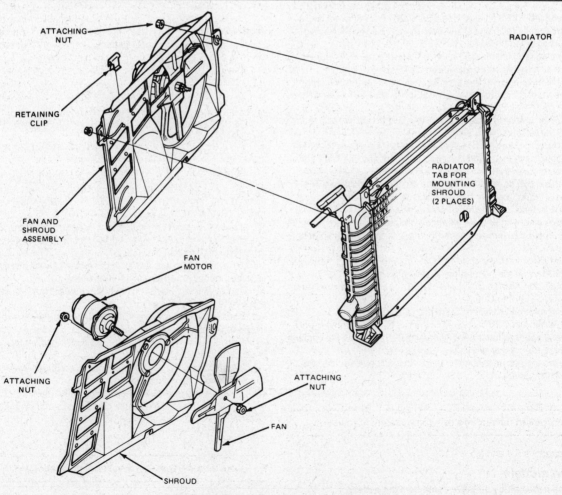

ATTACHING
NUT

RETAINING
CLIP

FAN AND
SHROUD
ASSEMBLY

FAN
MOTOR

ATTACHING
NUT

ATTACHING
NUT

FAN

SHROUD

RADIATOR

RADIATOR
TAB FOR
MOUNTING
SHROUD
(2 PLACES)

5.4   Fan shroud and motor installation

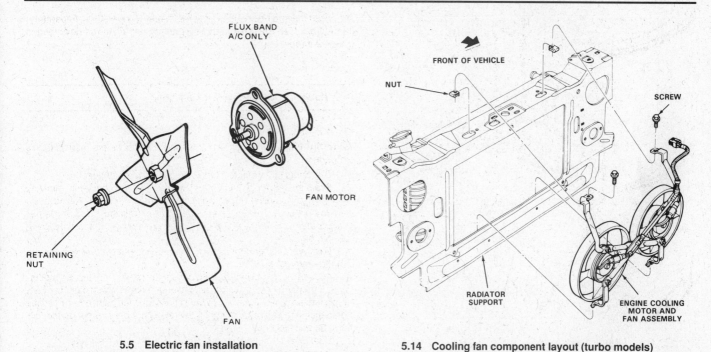

5.5   Electric fan installation

5.14   Cooling fan component layout (turbo models)

7   If the vehicle is equipped with an automatic transaxle, disconnect the fluid cooler lines from the radiator. Use a flare-nut wrench so the nut isn't rounded off and hold the fitting with a backup wrench so it isn't damaged. Use a drip pan to catch the spilled fluid.

8   Plug the lines and fittings with golf tees, or equivalent. A very small amount of dirt can cause automatic transaxle failure.

9   Remove the two nuts securing the top of the radiator to the support.

10   Tip it rearward for clearance of the mounting studs and remove the radiator from the vehicle. Don't spill coolant on the vehicle or scratch the paint. If the lower rubber mounts have come out with the radiator, return them to their proper location.

11   With the radiator removed, it can be inspected for leaks and damage. If it needs repair, have the a radiator shop or dealer service department perform the work as special techniques are required.

12   Bugs and dirt can be removed from the radiator with compressed air and a soft brush. Don't bend the cooling fins as this is done.

13   Check the radiator mounts for deterioration and make sure they're in place and there's nothing in them when the radiator is installed.

14   Installation is the reverse of the removal procedure with the addition of the following.

15   Install the lower radiator hose onto the radiator aligning the white mark on the hose with the outlet tank rib **(see illustration)**.

16   After installation, fill the cooling system with the proper mixture of anti-freeze and water. Refer to Chapter 1.

17   Connect the negative battery cable onto the battery.

18   Start the engine and allow it to reach normal operating temperature, indicated by the upper radiator hose becoming hot. Recheck the coolant level and add more if required.

19   If you're working on an automatic transaxle equipped vehicle, check and add fluid as needed.

---

5   Electric cooling fan and motor – removal and installation

Refer to illustrations 5.4 and 5.5

Non-turbo models

1   Disconnect the battery negative cable from the battery.
2   Disconnect the wiring connector from the fan motor.
3   Disconnect the wiring loom from the shroud by pushing down on the

two lock fingers and then pulling the connector from the end of the motor.

4   Remove the two nuts securing the motor and shroud and lift the motor and shroud assembly from the engine compartment **(see illustration)**.

5   Remove the nut securing the fan to the motor shaft and remove the fan **(see illustration)**. The nut has left-hand threads.

6   Remove the three nuts and remove the motor from the shroud.

7   To install, place the fan motor in the shroud and install the nuts.

8   Install the fan onto the motor shaft and install the retaining nut (turn the nut counterclockwise).

9   Place the fan motor and shroud assembly in the vehicle and install the retaining nuts.

10   Install the fan motor wiring loom and connect the wiring connector to the motor. Make sure the lock fingers snap in place.

11   Connect the battery negative cable onto the battery.

Turbo models

Refer to illustration 5.14

12   Disconnect the negative battery cable from the battery.

13   Remove the radiator fan shield and disconnect the electrical connector from the fan motor.

14   Remove the two bolts from the fan motor bracket and detach the fan assembly from the vehicle **(see illustration)**.

15   Remove the four retaining nuts and separate the fan motors from the brackets.

16   Installation is the reverse of the removal procedures with the addition of the following.

17   After installing the four retaining nuts on the fan motors, tighten them to 44 to 66 in-lb.

18   After installing the fan motor bracket assembly in the vehicle, tighten the remaining bolts to 35 to 45 in-lb.

19   Thread the fan motor wire loom through the radiator support. Reconnect the wire connector to the vehicle harness, making sure the two fingers on the connector snap securely into lace.

---

6   Coolant reservoir – removal and installation

Refer to illustration 6.2

1   Disconnect the overflow hose at the radiator neck.

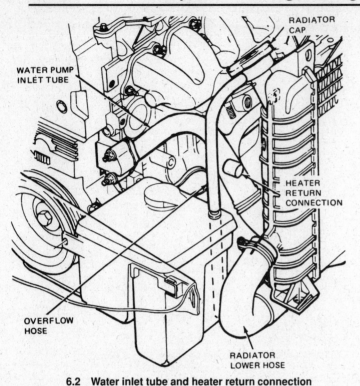

6.2   Water inlet tube and heater return connection

2   Detach the reservoir from the inner fender panel **(see illustration)**.
3   Pull the reservoir away from the locating tab.
4   Lift the reservoir out of the engine compartment.
5   Installation is the reverse of removal.

7   Water pump – check and replacement

1   A failure in the water pump can cause serious engine damage due to overheating.

Check

2   There are three ways to check the operation of the water pump while it's installed on the engine. If the pump is defective, it should be replaced with a new or rebuilt unit.
3   With the engine running at normal operating temperature, squeeze the upper radiator hose. If the water pump is working properly, a pressure surge should be felt as the hose is released. **Warning:** *Keep your hands away from the fan blades.*
4   Water pumps are equipped with weep or vent holes. If a failure occurs in the pump seal, coolant will leak from the hole.
5   If the water pump shaft bearings fail there may be a howling sound at the front of the engine while it's running. Shaft wear can be felt if the water pump pulley is rocked up and down.

Replacement

Refer to illustrations 7.13 and 7.21
Warning: *Wait until the engine is completely cool before beginning this procedure.*
6   Disconnect the negative battery cable from the battery.
7   Drain the cooling system (see Chapter 1). If the coolant is relatively new or in good condition (see Chapter 1), save it and reuse it. **Warning:** *Be sure to store coolant where children and pets can't get to it. Its sweet smell attracts them and they may drink it. Ingesting even a small amount of coolant can be fatal!*
8   Remove the cooling fan and shroud (Section 5).
9   Remove the drivebelt (see Chapter 1) and the pulley at the end of the water pump shaft.
10   Remove the engine timing belt cover and set the number one cylinder at TDC (see Chapter 2).
11   Remove the timing belt, tensioner assembly and camshaft sprocket (see Chapter 2).
12   Remove the timing belt rear stud.

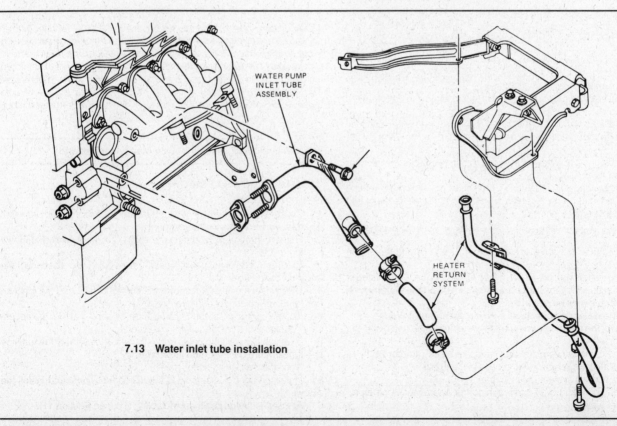

7.13   Water inlet tube installation

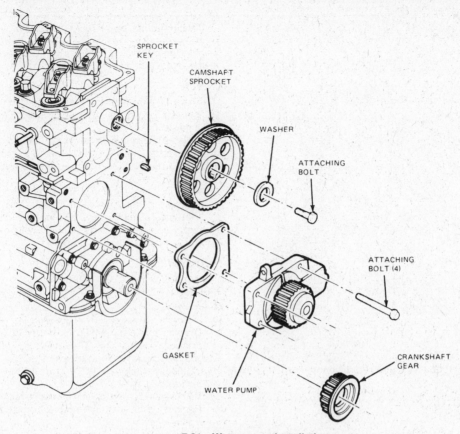

7.21 Water pump installation

SPROCKET KEY

CAMSHAFT SPROCKET

WASHER

ATTACHING BOLT

ATTACHING BOLT (4)

GASKET

WATER PUMP

CRANKSHAFT GEAR

13   Loosen the clamps and detach the hoses from the water pump and inlet tube **(see illustration)**. If they're stuck, grasp each hose near the end with a pair of adjustable pliers and carefully twist it to break the seal, then pull it off. If the hoses are old or deteriorated, cut them off and install a new hoses.

14   Remove the bolts and detach the water pump from the engine. Note the locations of the various lengths and different types of bolts as they're removed to ensure correct installation.

15   Clean the bolt threads and the threaded holes in the engine to remove corrosion and sealant.

17   Compare the new pump to the old one to make sure they're identical.

16   Remove all traces of old gasket material from the engine with a gasket scraper.

18   Clean the engine and new water pump mating surfaces with lacquer thinner or acetone.

19   Apply a thin coat of RTV sealant to both sides of the new gasket and install it on the water pump. Coat the water pump bolts with sealant and install the water pump.

20   Slip a couple of bolts through the water pump to hold the gasket in place.

21   Carefully attach the pump and gasket to the engine and thread the bolts into the holes finger tight **(see illustration)**.

22   Install the remaining bolts, then tighten all bolts to the torque listed in this Chapter's Specifications in 1/4-turn increments. Don't overtighten them as the pump may be distorted.

23   Rotate the water pump to make sure it rotates freely.

24   Reconnect the heater return tube and water inlet pipe and install the timing cover stud.

25   Install the camshaft sprocket and timing belt (see Chapter 2).

26   Reinstall all parts removed for access to the pump.

27   Refill the cooling system (see Chapter 1).

28   Start the engine and allow it to reach normal operating temperature, then check for leaks.

8   Heater – general information

The heater circulates engine coolant through a small radiator (heater core) in the passenger compartment. Air is drawn in through an opening in the cowl, then blown (by the blower motor) through the heater core to pick up heat. The heated air is blended with varying amounts of unheated air to regulate the temperature. The heated air is then blown into the passenger compartment. Various doors in the heater control the flow of air to the floor and through the instrument panel louvers and defroster outlets.

9   Heater control assembly – removal and installation

1981 through 1983 models
Refer to illustrations 9.6a and 9.6b

1   Remove the two screws securing the center finish panel, unsnap it and remove it from the instrument panel.

2   Remove the screws attaching the control assembly and disconnect the control cables.

3   Pull the control panel out of the instrument panel and disconnect the electrical connectors.

4   Disconnect the lever arms from the control cables and the function and temperature control end retainers.

5   If a new control assembly is going to be installed, transfer the necessary components from the old control assembly.

6   To install, connect the cable end retainers and connect the function and temperature controls **(see illustrations)**.

7   Reconnect all wiring connectors.

8   Install the control assembly in the instrument panel and install the screws.

9   Adjust the control cable self-adjusting clip (see Section 11).

3

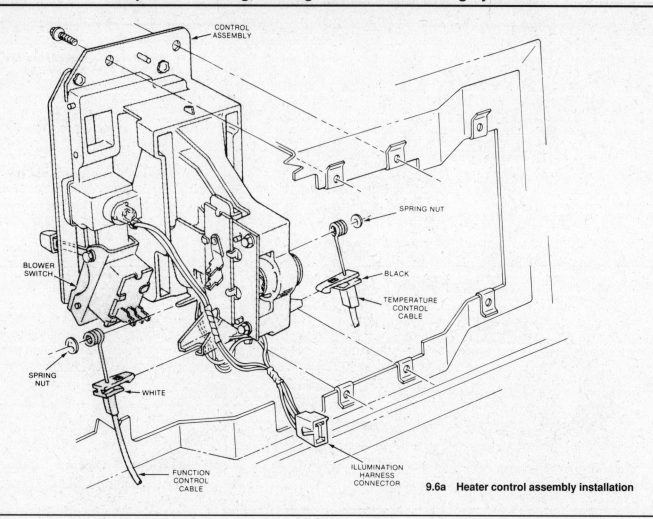

CONTROL ASSEMBLY

SPRING NUT

BLOWER SWITCH

BLACK

TEMPERATURE CONTROL CABLE

SPRING NUT

WHITE

FUNCTION CONTROL CABLE

ILLUMINATION HARNESS CONNECTOR

9.6a   Heater control assembly installation

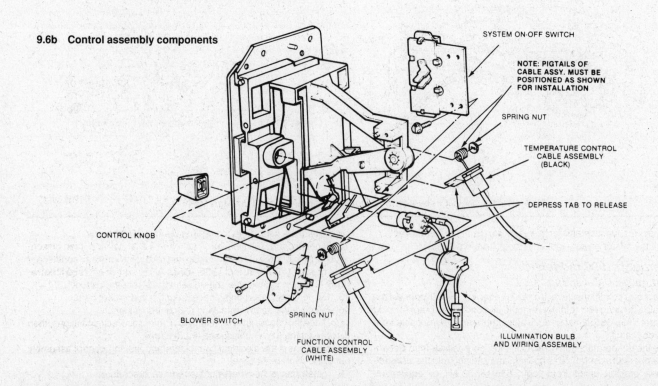

9.6b   Control assembly components

SYSTEM ON-OFF SWITCH

NOTE: PIGTAILS OF CABLE ASSY. MUST BE POSITIONED AS SHOWN FOR INSTALLATION

SPRING NUT

TEMPERATURE CONTROL CABLE ASSEMBLY (BLACK)

DEPRESS TAB TO RELEASE

CONTROL KNOB

BLOWER SWITCH

SPRING NUT

FUNCTION CONTROL CABLE ASSEMBLY (WHITE)

ILLUMINATION BULB AND WIRING ASSEMBLY

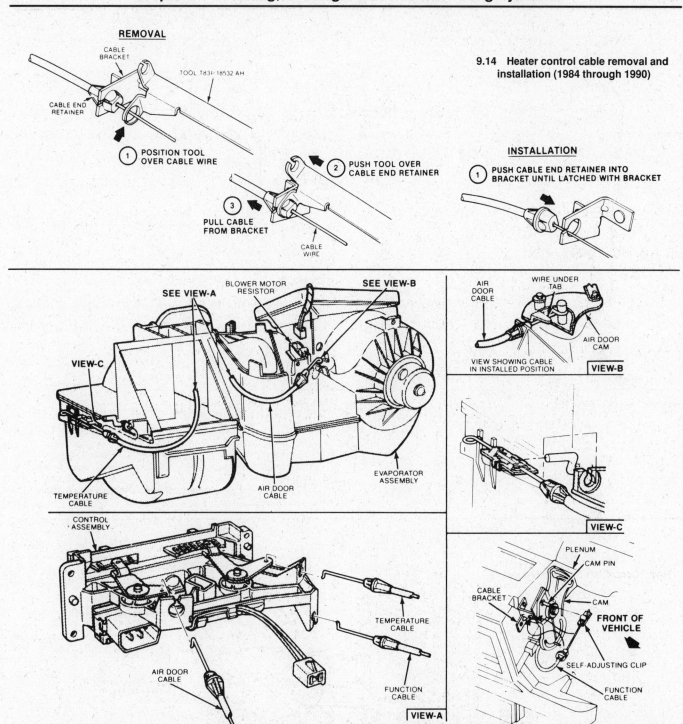

9.14 Heater control cable removal and installation (1984 through 1990)

9.17 Heater control assembly and installation details (1984 through 1990)

10   Connect the function and temperature cables to the heater case.
11   Install the center finish panel onto the instrument panel.

1984 through 1990 models

Refer to illustrations 9.14 and 9.17

12   Place the air conditioner lever in the Max position, then disconnect the air inlet cable housing end retainer from the air conditioner bracket using the Ford tool T83p-18532-AH or equivalent, then remove the cable from the inlet door cam.
13   Place the temperature control lever in the Cool position, then disconnect the temperature control cable housing and retainer from the air conditioner case bracket using Ford tool T83p-18532-AH or equivalent.

Disconnect the cable from the temperature door crank arm.
14   Place the function selector lever in the Panel position, then disconnect the function select cable housing end retainer from the air conditioner case bracket using Ford tool T83p-18532-AH or equivalent **(see illustration)**. Disconnect the cable self-adjusting clip from the cam pin.
15   Remove the center finish panel from the instrument panel.
16   Remove the screws attaching the control assembly.
17   Place the control levers in the Cool, Panel and Recirc positions, then disconnect the three cables **(see illustration)**.
18   Disconnect the electrical connectors and pull the control assembly out of the instrument panel.
19   Installation is the reverse of the removal procedure.

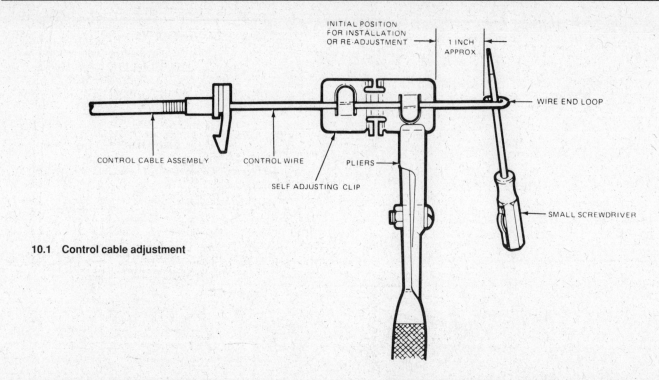

10.1   Control cable adjustment

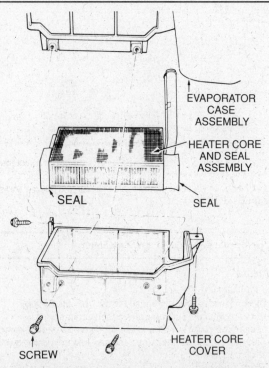

12.6   Later model high-output heater core installation details

10   Heater control cable – adjustment

Refer to illustration 10.1

1   Before installing the cable:
  a) Slip a small screwdriver blade into the wire coil on the end of the cable **(see illustration)**.
  b) Use pliers to slide the self-adjusting clip along the cable until it is about one inch from the wire loop.

  c) Install the cable.
2   If the cable is already installed:
  a) Move the control lever or knob to the Cool position or the function lever to the Off position.
  b) Hold the crank arm firmly in place, insert the blade of a small screwdriver in the wire loop and pull the cable through the self-adjusting clip until there is approximately one inch of space between it and the loop **(see illustration 10.1).**
  c) Push the control lever to the top of the slot to position the self-adjusting clip.
  d) Check for proper operation.

11   Heater blower motor and wheel – removal and installation

1   Remove the right ventilator assembly (see Section 15).
2   Remove the hub clamp from the blower motor hub and withdraw the wheel assembly. Discard the hub clamp.
3   Remove the screws securing the blower motor to the inside of the housing. Withdraw the motor and disconnect the motor's electrical connectors.
4   Installation is the reverse of the removal Steps with the addition of the following.
5   Align the flat on the wheel hub with the flat on the motor shaft and install the blower wheel. Install a new hub clamp.

12   Heater core – replacement

Refer to illustrations 12.6 and 12.7

1984 and 1985 high output heater models

1   Partially drain the cooling system (see Chapter 1).
2   Loosen the clamps on the heater hose at the engine compartment side of the firewall. Twist the hoses and carefully separate them from the heater core tubes.
3   Plug or cap the heater core tubes to prevent coolant from spilling into the passenger compartment when the heater core is removed.
4   From underneath the glove box remove the two screws securing the floor duct, the instrument panel screw and the evaporator assembly.

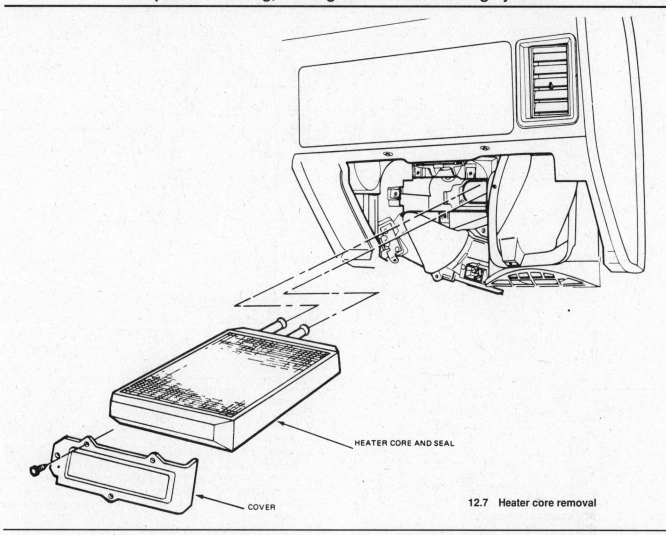

HEATER CORE AND SEAL

COVER

12.7   Heater core removal

5   Place a plastic sheet on the vehicle floor to prevent stains in case the coolant spills.
6   Remove two screws and the heater core cover **(see illustration)**.
7   Working in the passenger compartment, pull the heater core through the glovebox opening **(see illustration)**.
8   Installation is the reverse of the removal procedure.

All other models

9   Partially drain the cooling system (see Chapter 1).
10   Loosen the clamps on the heater hose at the engine compartment side of the firewall. Twist the hoses and carefully separate them from the heater core tubes.
11   Plug or cap the heater core tubes to prevent coolant from spilling into the passenger compartment when the heater core is removed.
12   Place a plastic sheet on the vehicle floor to prevent stains in case the coolant spills.
13   Remove the glovebox door, liner and lower reinforcement (see Chapter 12).
14   Place the temperature control in the Warm position.
15   Remove the heater cover.
16   Working in the engine compartment, loosen the two nuts securing the heater case assembly to the instrument panel. Loosen the heater core by pushing the core tubes inward, toward the passenger compartment.
17   Working in the passenger compartment, pull the heater core through the glovebox opening **(see illustration 12.7)**.
18   To install, place the heater core with the tubes on top, then slide it through the glovebox opening into the heater case.
19   Install the heater core cover and tighten the retaining screws.
20   Install and tighten the heater core-to-instrument panel nuts.

21   Uncap or unplug the heater core tubes, then reconnect the hoses.
22   Install the glovebox door, liner and lower reinforcement.
23   Fill the cooling system (see Chapter 1). Run the engine and check for leaks and test the heater.

13   Heater case – removal and installation

Removal

Refer to illustration 13.17
1   Disconnect the battery negative cable from the battery.
2   Partially drain the cooling system (see Chapter 1).
3   Loosen the clamps on the heater hose at the engine compartment side of the firewall. Twist the hoses and carefully separate them from the heater core tubes.
4   Plug or cap the heater core tubes to prevent coolant from spilling into the passenger compartment when the heater core is removed.
5   Remove the steering column cover and lower shroud. Disconnect the column bracket and lower the steering column to the seat.
6   Remove the radio covers and speakers (see Chapter 10).
7   Remove the instrument panel center bracket.
8   Disconnect the ventilator control handles.
9   Disconnect the speedometer cable at the transaxle.
10   Disconnect the heater blower resistor wiring harness and (if so equipped) the right door courtesy light switch at the A pillar.
11   Disconnect the function and temperature control cables from the heater case (see Section 10).
12   Remove the bolts securing the instrument panel center brace, then

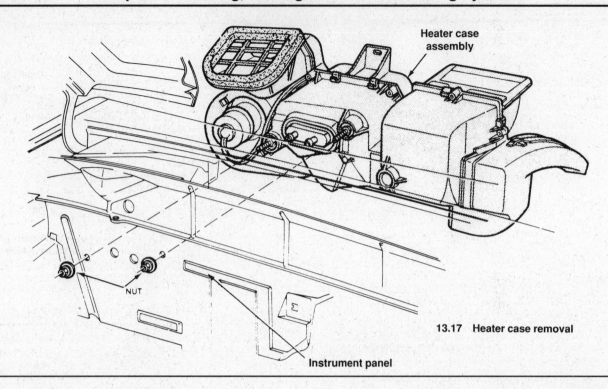

13.17   Heater case removal

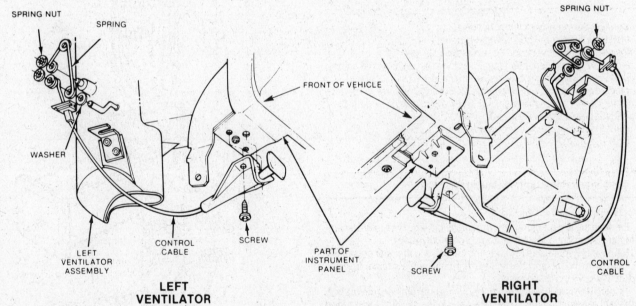

14.1   Ventilator control cable installation

remove the brace. Pull the instrument panel toward the rear to gain access to the heater case.

13   Remove the nut securing the heater case top support to the heater case.

14   Working in the engine compartment, remove the two nuts securing the heater case to the firewall.

15   Loosen the insulation around the air inlet opening of the top of the control panel and remove the heater case from the firewall.

Installation

16   To install, place the heater case in position on the firewall and install the nut securing the heater case top support.

17   Working in the engine compartment, install the two nuts securing the heater case to the firewall **(see illustration)**.

18   Reposition the insulation around the air inlet opening.

19   Install the instrument panel center brace and bolts.

20   Connect the function and temperature control cables onto the heater case (see Section 10).

21   Move the instrument panel back into position and install and tighten the bolts (see Chapter 12).

22   Connect the function and temperature control cables onto the heater case (see Section 10 and Section 11).

23   Connect the heater blower resistor wiring harness and (if so equipped) the right door courtesy light switch at the A pillar.

24   Connect the speedometer cable to the transaxle.

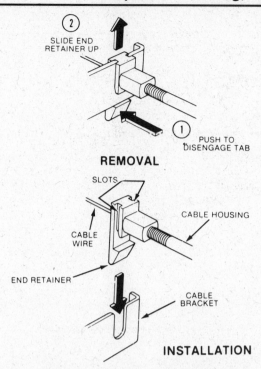

14.4 Control cable end retainer details

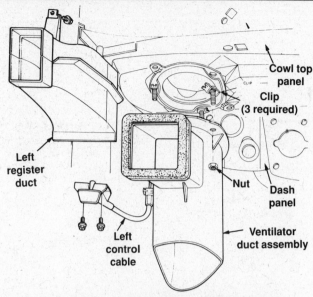

15.1 Left ventilator and register installation

25 Connect the ventilator control handles.
26 Install the instrument panel center bracket.
27 Install the radio covers and speakers (see Chapter 10).
28 Move the steering column up into position and connect the column bracket. Install the steering column cover and lower shroud.
29 Unplug or uncap the heater core tubes and install the heater hoses to the heater case. Tighten the hose clamps on the heater hoses at the engine compartment side of the firewall.
30 Refill the cooling system (see Chapter 1).
31 Connect the battery negative cable onto the battery.

14 Ventilator cable – removal and installation

Refer to illustrations 14.1 and 14.4

1 Remove the two retaining screws attaching the control cable assembly to the instrument panel lower edge **(see illustration)**.
2 Remove the spring cap nut securing the cable to the door crank arm.
3 Push in on the tab and disengage the control cable retainer from the bracket. Remove the cable assembly.
4 To install the cable, align the cable housing and retainer grooves with the bracket assembly and slide the retainer into the slot until it locks **(see illustration)**.
5 Install the cable loop onto the ventilator door arm.
6 Locate the control cable knob housing in place on the lower edge of the instrument panel and align the holes. Install and tighten the retaining screws.
7 Check for proper operation.

15 Left ventilator assembly – removal and installation

Refer to illustration 15.1

1 Remove the screws securing the left ventilator assembly to the instrument panel, then remove the nuts securing the left ventilator to the cowl panel. Remove the left ventilator assembly **(see illustration)**.
2 Remove the ventilator cable from the left ventilator assembly (see Section 14).

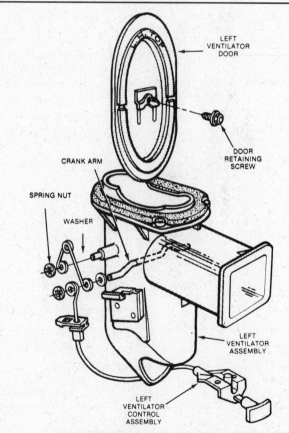

16.2 Left ventilator door installation

3 Installation is the reverse of the removal procedure with the addition of the following.
4 Check for proper operation.

16 Left ventilator door – removal and installation

Refer to illustration 16.2

1 Remove the left ventilator assembly (see Section 13).
2 Remove the screw securing the door **(see illustration)**.

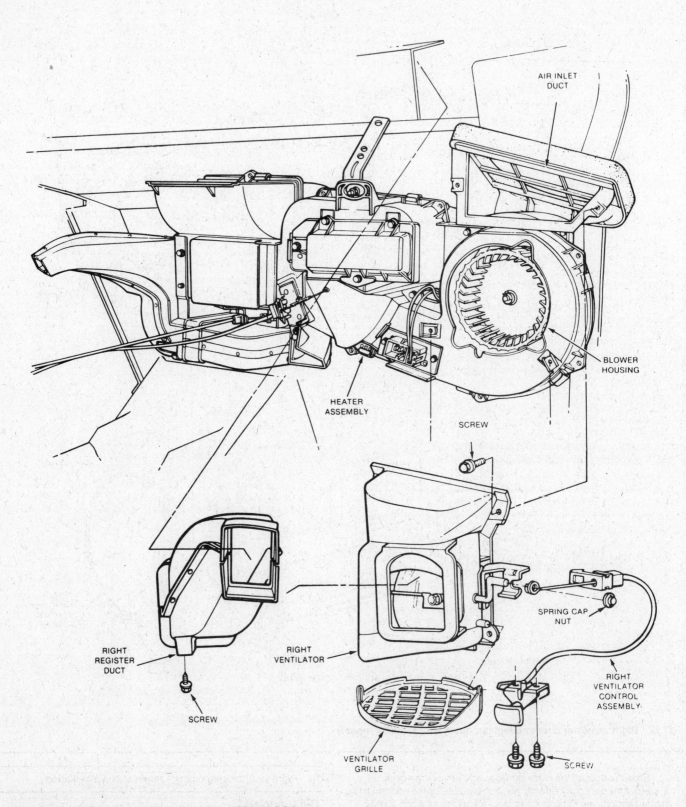

17.5   Right ventilator door and register duct (1981 models)

3

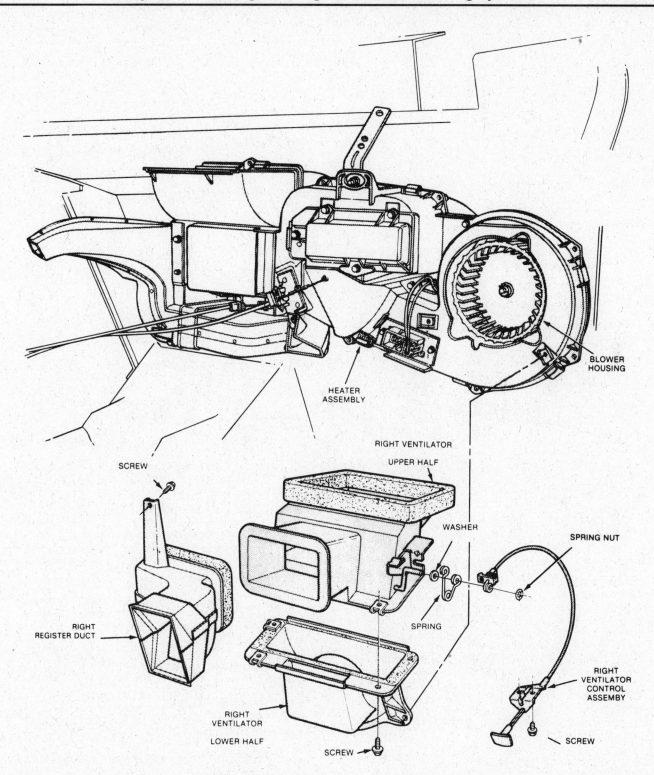

17.17 Right ventilator door and register duct (1982 and later models)

3   Slide the door off the crank arm loop and remove the door.
4   Move the door crank arm into position and position the door mounting bracket pocket over the crank arm loop. Install the retaining screw.
5   Install the left ventilator assembly.
6   Check for proper operation.

17   Right ventilator assembly – removal and installation

1981 models

Refer to illustration 17.5
1   Remove the glovebox door and hinge (see Chapter 12).

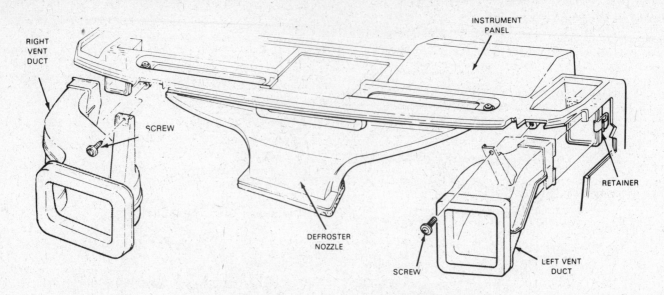

19.2   Register duct and ventilator installation

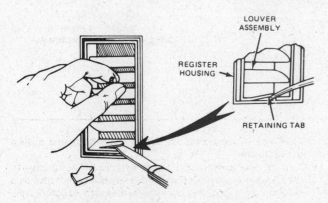

20.1   Register louver removal

3   To install the duct(s), make sure the duct's retainers are in place prior to installing the ducts.
2   Remove the two screws securing the control cable to the instrument panel and remove the cable assembly.
3   Remove the right register duct assembly from the instrument panel.
4   Disengage the ventilator grill from the mounting pins on the side of the ventilator and remove the grille from the right ventilator assembly.
5   Remove the screws securing the right ventilator assembly **(see illustration)**.
6   Remove the spring cap nut and disengage the control cable loop from the ventilator door crank arm.
7   To install, connect the control cable loop to the crank arm and install the spring cap nut.
8   Install the control cable housing retainer to the cable bracket.
9   Install the grille and retaining clip onto the ventilator assembly.
10   Place the register duct into position between the register opening and the ventilator assembly.
11   Install the glovebox door and hinge.
12   Install the screw securing the register duct.
13   Install the control cable to the instrument panel and secure with the screws.
14   Check for proper operation.

1982 and later models
Refer to illustration 17.17
15   Remove the glovebox door and hinge (see Chapter 12).

16   Remove the spring cap nut and disengage the control cable loop from the ventilator door crank arm.
17   Remove the six screws securing the ventilator duct to the blower housing and remove the ventilator assembly **(see illustration)**.
18   To install, place the ventilator in position on the heater blower and install the retaining screws.
19   Connect the control cable loop to the crank arm and install the spring cap nut.
20   Install the control cable housing retainer to the cable bracket.
21   Install the glovebox door and hinge.
22   Check for proper operation.

18   Right ventilator door – removal and installation

1   Remove the right ventilator assembly (see Section 15).

1981 models
2   Disengage the ventilator grill from the mounting pins on the side of ventilator and remove the grille from the right ventilator assembly.
3   Remove the screw securing the door.
4   Slide the door off the crank arm loop and remove the door.
5   Move the door crank arm into position and position the door mounting bracket pocket over the crank arm loop. Install the retaining screw.
6   Install the right ventilator assembly (see Section 15).

1982 and later models
7   Use a screwdriver and disengage the door from the crank arm shaft.
8   To install, place the door on the ventilator on the crank arm shaft and push it on until it locks in place.
9   On all models, move the door several times and check for proper operation.
10   Install the right ventilator assembly (see Section 15).

19   Vent ducts and defroster nozzle – removal and installation

Refer to illustration 19.2
1   To gain access on some models, it is necessary to remove the instrument panel (see Chapter 12).
2   Remove the screws securing the vent duct(s) or defroster nozzle and remove the duct(s) or nozzle **(see illustration)**.

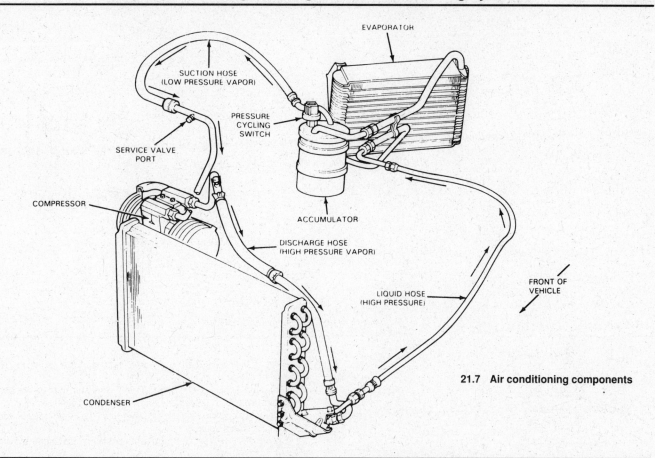

21.7 Air conditioning components

3

---

3   Move the vent duct into place and push it in until it engages the clips, then install the retaining screw.
4   Move the defroster nozzle into place and install the retaining screw.
5   If removed, install the instrument panel.

20   Register louver – removal and installation

Refer to illustration 20.1
1   Insert a knifeblade or thin screwdriver blade under the louver retaining tab and carefully pry the tab up toward the louver until it clears the locking hole in the instrument panel **(see illustration)**.
2   Pull out on the end of the register that has been released so it will not move back and become locked again.
3   Repeat Step 1 for the retaining tab on the other end of the louver and remove it from the instrument panel. Mark the louver so it will be reinstalled in the correct location in the instrument panel.
4   Locate the louver in the correct location in the instrument panel and make sure it is right side up. Press the louver into place until both retaining tabs have locked into place.

21   Air conditioning system – check and maintenance

Refer to illustration 21.7
Warning: *The air conditioning system is under high pressure. Do not loosen any hose fittings or remove any components until after the system has been discharged by a dealer service department or service station. Always wear eye protection when disconnecting air conditioning system fittings.*

1   The following maintenance checks should be performed on a regular basis to ensure that the air conditioner continues to operate at peak efficiency.

a) Check the compressor drivebelt. If it's worn or deteriorated, replace it (see Chapter 1).
b) Check drivebelt tension and, if necessary, adjust it (see Chapter 1).
c) Check the system hoses. Look for cracks, bubbles, hard spots and deterioration. Inspect the hoses and all fittings for oil bubbles and seepage. If there's any evidence of wear, damage or leaks, replace the hose(s).
d) Inspect the condenser for leaves, bugs and other debris. Use a "fin comb" or compressed air to clean the condenser.
e) Make sure the system has the correct refrigerant charge.
2   It's a good idea to operate the system for about 10 minutes at least once a month particularly during the winter. Long term non-use can cause hardening, and subsequent failure, of the seals.
3   Because of the complexity of the air conditioning system and the special equipment necessary to service it, in-depth troubleshooting and repairs are not included in this manual. However, simple checks and component replacement procedure are provided in this Chapter. For more complete information on the air conditioning system, refer to the *Haynes Automotive Heating and Air Conditioning Manual*.
4   The most common cause of poor cooling is simply a low system refrigerant charge. If a noticeable drop in cool air output occurs, one of the following quick checks will help you determine if the refrigerant level is low.

Checking the refrigerant charge

5   Warm the engine up to normal operating temperature.
6   Place the air conditioning temperature selector at the coldest setting and put the blower at the highest setting. Open the doors (to make sure the air conditioning system doesn't cycle off as soon as it cools the passenger compartment).
7   With the compressor engaged, the clutch will make an audible click and the center of the clutch will rotate. Working in the engine compartment, feel the evaporator inlet pipe between the orifice and the accumulator with one hand while placing the other hand on the surface of the accumulator housing **(see illustration)**.

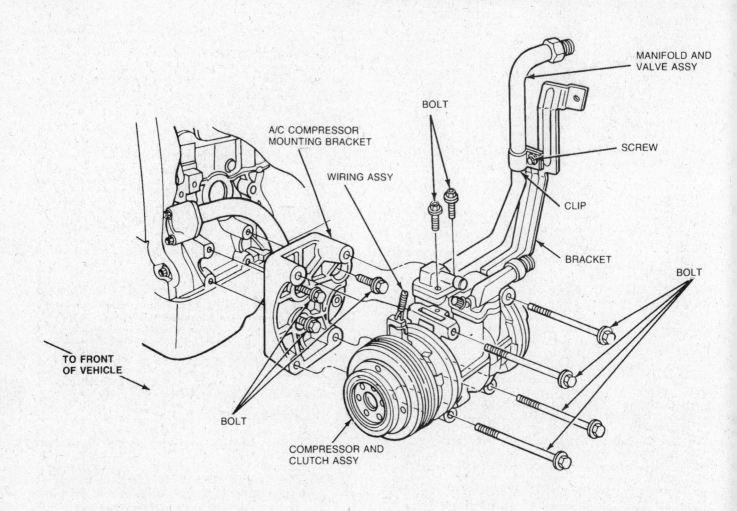

MANIFOLD AND
VALVE ASSY

BOLT

A/C COMPRESSOR
MOUNTING BRACKET

SCREW

WIRING ASSY

CLIP

BRACKET

BOLT

TO FRONT
OF VEHICLE

BOLT

COMPRESSOR AND
CLUTCH ASSY

22.5   Air conditioning compressor installation (typical)

8   If both surfaces feel about the same temperature and if both feel a little cooler than the surrounding air, the refrigerant level is probable okay.

9   If the inlet pipe has frost accumulation or feels cooler than the accumulator surface, the refrigerant charge is low.

10   If a low refrigerant charge is suspected, take your vehicle to a dealer or automotive air conditioning shop for service or repair.

22   Air conditioning system compressor – removal and installation

Refer to illustration 22.5

Warning: *The air conditioning system is under high pressure. Do not loosen any hose fittings or remove any components until after the system has been discharged by a dealer service department or service station. Always wear eye protection when disconnecting air conditioning system fittings.*

Note: *The accumulator should be replaced whenever the compressor is replaced (see Section 24).*

1   Have the air conditioning system discharged (see Warning above).

2   Disconnect the negative battery cable from the battery.

3   Disconnect the compressor clutch wiring harness.

4   Remove the compressor drivebelt (see Chapter 1).

5   Disconnect the refrigerant lines from the compressor manifolds use a backup wrench to prevent twisting the tubing **(see illustration)**. Plug the openings to prevent the entry of dirt and moisture.

6   Unbolt the compressor from the mounting bracket and lift it out of the vehicle.

7   If a new compressor is being installed, follow the directions with the compressor regarding the draining of excess oil prior to installation.

8   The clutch may have to be transferred from the original to the new compressor.

9   Installation is the reverse of the removal procedure with the addition of the following.

10   Replace all O-rings with new ones specially made for air conditioning system use and lubricate them with refrigerant oil.

11   Have the system evacuated, recharged and leak tested by the shop that discharged it.

12   Adjust the drivebelt (see Chapter 1).

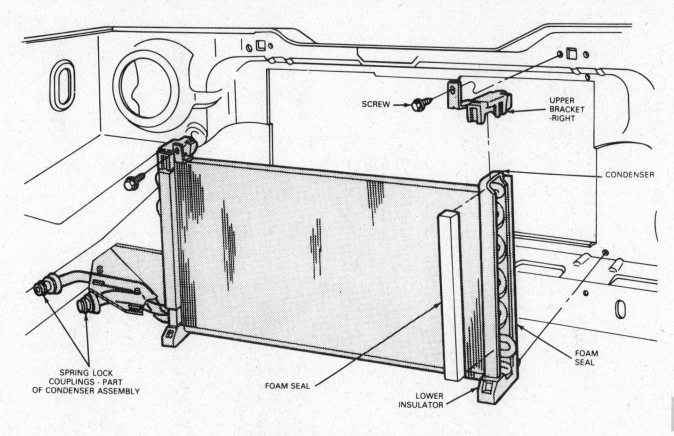

23.5 Air conditioning condenser installation (typical)

Labels on illustration:
SCREW
UPPER BRACKET -RIGHT
CONDENSER
FOAM SEAL
LOWER INSULATOR
FOAM SEAL
SPRING LOCK COUPLINGS - PART OF CONDENSER ASSEMBLY

---

23 Air conditioning system condenser – removal and installation

Refer to illustration 23.5

Warning: *The air conditioning system is under high pressure. Do not loosen any hose fittings or remove any components until after the system has been discharged by a dealer service department or service station. Always wear eye protection when disconnecting air conditioning system fittings.*

Note: *The accumulator should be replaced whenever the compressor is replaced (see Section 24).*

Removal

1   Have the air conditioning system discharged (see Warning above).
2   Remove battery (see Chapter 5).
3   Drain the cooling system (see Chapter 1).
4   Remove the radiator (see Section 4).
5   Disconnect the refrigerant lines from the condenser **(see illustration)**. The lines use spring-lock couplings, which require a special Ford tool for connection and reconnection.
6   Remove the mounting bolts from the condenser brackets.
7   Grasp the upper corners of the condenser and move the top of the condenser toward the engine. Lift the condenser out of the vehicle and plug the lines to prevent the entry of dirt and moisture.
8   If the original condenser is going to be reinstalled, store it with the line fittings on top to prevent oil from draining out.
9   Prior to installing a new condenser, pour one ounce of refrigerant oil into it prior to installation.

Installation

10   Installation is the reverse of the removal procedure with the addition of the following.
11   Replace all O-rings with new ones specially made for air conditioning system use and lubricate them with refrigerant oil.
12   If necessary, replace the foam seals on each side.
13   Lubricate the upper rubber mounts with rubber lubricant or silicone.
14   Position the condenser into the lower mounts, then move the top portion forward until it snaps into place in the rubber mounts.
15   Have the system evacuated, recharged and leak tested by the shop that discharged it.

---

24 Air conditioning system accumulator/drier – removal and installation

Warning: *The air conditioning system is under high pressure. Do not loosen any hose fittings or remove any components until after the system has been discharged by a dealer service department or service station. Always wear eye protection when disconnecting air conditioning system fittings.*

Removal

1   Have the air conditioning system discharged (see Warning above).
2   Disconnect the battery negative cable from the battery.
3   If the vehicle is equipped with power steering, remove the air pump from the engine (see Chapter 6).
4   Unplug the electrical connector from the pressure switch near the top of the accumulator/drier.
5   Disconnect the refrigerant lines from the accumulator/drier. Use a backup wrench to prevent twisting the tubing.

3

6   Plug the lines to prevent the entry of dirt and moisture.

7   Remove the two screws securing the two strap clamps and remove the accumulator/drier.

8   If a new accumulator/drier is being installed, remove the Schrader valve and pour the existing oil out into a measuring cup, note the amount. Add fresh refrigerant oil to the new accumulator/drier equal to the amount removed from the old unit plus one ounce.

Installation

9   Installation is the reverse of the removal procedure with the addition of the following.

10   Replace all O-rings with new ones specially made for A/C system use and lubricate them with refrigerant oil.

11   Have the system evacuated, recharged and leak tested by the shop that discharged it.

Chapter 4   Fuel and exhaust systems

Contents

Specifications

Fuel pressure

Carbureted	4.5 to 6.5 psi
Central Fuel Injection (CFI)	14.5 psi
Multi-point fuel injection (EFI)	39 psi

Torque specifications

Ft-lbs (unless otherwise indicated)

Carburetor-to-intake manifold nuts/bolts	
1981 through 1984	12 to 15
1985 and 1986	15 to 25
Mechanical fuel pump-to-block bolts	
1981 through 1984	14 to 21
1985 and 1986	11 to 19
Central Fuel Injection (CFI)	
Fuel charging assembly-to-intake manifold studs	
First stage	5 to 11
Second stage	13 to 19
Fuel fitting to main body	14 to 17
Fuel pressure regulator cover screws	28 to 32 in-lbs
Throttle position sensor screws	11 to 16 in-lbs
ISC bracket-to-throttle body screws	40 to 49 in-lbs
ISC motor-to-mounting bracket screws	44 to 50 in-lbs
Main body-to-throttle body screws	38 to 43 in-lbs

Multi-point fuel injection (EFI)

Lower intake manifold mounting nuts	12 to 15
Upper intake manifold-to-lower	
intake manifold bolts	15 to 22
Throttle body-to-upper intake manifold nuts/bolts	
1984 through 1988	12 to 15
1989 and 1990	15 to 22
Air bypass valve-to-throttle body screws	71 to 97 in-lbs
Throttle position sensor-to-throttle body screws	
1984 through 1988	14 to 16 in-lbs
1989 and 1990	25 to 30 in-lbs
Fuel rail assembly-to-fuel charging assembly bolts	15 to 22
Fuel pressure regulator-to-fuel rail screws	27 to 40 in-lbs
Vane air meter-to-bracket screws	72 to 108 in-lbs
Air cleaner tray-to-vane air meter screws	
1984 and 1985	72 to 108 in-lbs
1986 through 1990	33 to 49 in-lbs
Turbocharger	
Exhaust manifold-to-cylinder head nuts	16 to 19
Turbocharger-to-exhaust manifold nuts	16 to 19
Exhaust shield-to-water outlet bracket bolts	70 to 97 in-lbs
Exhaust pipe-to-turbocharger nuts	14 to 22
Oil return line-to-turbocharger	70 to 97 in-lbs

---

1   General information

Fuel system

The fuel system consists of the fuel tank, the fuel pump, an air cleaner assembly, either a carburetor or a fuel injection system and the various steel, plastic and/or nylon lines and fittings connecting everything together.

Models covered by this manual are equipped with one of three general types of fuel systems: carburetor; Central Fuel Injection (CFI); or multi-point electronic fuel injection (EFI). To identify the system which applies to your vehicle, refer to Sections 8, 10 and 11.

The fuel pump on carburetor-equipped models is a mechanical type mounted on the cylinder head and driven off the camshaft by an eccentric lobe and pushrod. Early fuel-injected models have a high-pressure pump mounted on the chassis. In later years, fuel-injected models have a high-pressure pump installed inside the fuel tank.

The turbocharger used on some 1.6L engine models forces air into an electronic fuel injection system.

Exhaust system

All vehicles are equipped with an exhaust manifold, a catalytic converter, an exhaust pipe and a muffler. Any component of the exhaust system can be replaced. The "dual brick underbody" type converter utilizes both a three-way catalyst and a conventional oxidation catalyst. See Chapter 6 for further details regarding the catalytic converter.

---

2   Fuel pressure relief procedure (fuel-injected models)

Refer to illustrations 2.1a, 2.1b and 2.1c

1   The fuel pump switch – sometimes called the "inertia switch"- which shuts off fuel to the engine in the event of a collision, affords a simple and convenient means by which fuel pressure can be relieved before servicing fuel injection components. The switch is located in the luggage compartment **(see illustrations)**.

2   Unplug the inertia switch electrical connector.

3   Crank the engine with the starter for 15 seconds.

4   The fuel system pressure is now relieved. When you're finished working on the fuel system, simply plug the electrical connector back into the switch and push the reset button on the top of the switch **(see illustration 2.1a)**.

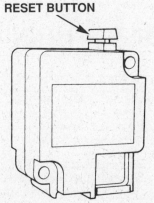

2.1a   On fuel-injected models, the fuel pump switch assembly is located in the luggage compartment – the reset button must be pushed in to reactivate the switch/pump

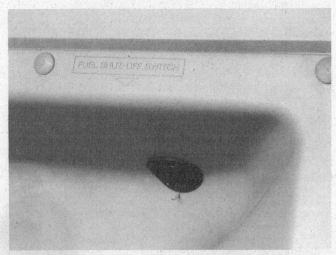

2.1b   The switch can be reached on some models by removing a rubber plug . . .

2.1c   . . . which provides access to the reset button on top of the switch (shown here with the interior panel removed for clarity)

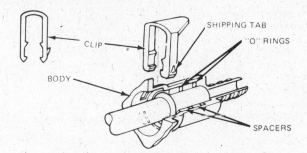

3.5   An exploded view of the hairpin clip type push-connect fitting

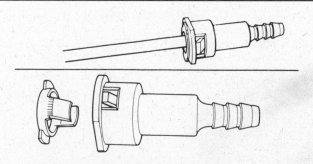

3.10   A push-connect fitting with a duck-bill clip

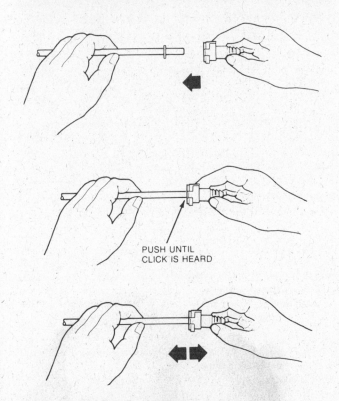

PUSH UNTIL
CLICK IS HEARD

3.9   Reassembling push-connect fittings

3   Fuel lines and fittings – disassembly and reassembly

Refer to illustrations 3.5, 3.9, 3.10, 3.13, 3.14, 3.26a and 3.26b

Warning: *The fuel system pressure must be relieved before disconnecting fuel lines and fittings on fuel-injected models (see Section 2). Gasoline is extremely flammable, so take extra precautions when you work on any part of the fuel system. Don't smoke or allow open flames or bare light bulbs near the work area, and don't work in a garage where a natural gas-type appliance (such as a water heater or clothes dryer) with a pilot light is present. If you spill any fuel on your skin, rinse it off immediately with soap and water. When you perform any kind of work on the fuel system, wear safety glasses and have a Class B type fire extinguisher on hand.*

Push-connect fittings

1   Ford uses two different push-connect fitting designs. Fittings used with 3/8 and 5/16-inch diameter lines have a "hairpin" type clip; fittings used with 1/4-inch diameter lines have a "duck bill" type clip. The procedure used for releasing each type of fitting is different. The clips should be replaced whenever a connector is disassembled.

2   Disconnect all push-connect fittings from fuel system components such as the fuel filter, the carburetor/fuel charging assembly, the fuel tank, etc. before removing the assembly.

3/8 and 5/16-inch fittings (hairpin clip)

3   Inspect the internal portion of the fitting for accumulations of dirt. If more than a light coating of dust is present, clean the fitting before disassembly.

4   Some adhesion between the seals in the fitting and the line will occur over a period of time. Twist the fitting on the line, then push and pull the fitting until it moves freely.

5   Remove the hairpin clip from the fitting by bending the shipping tab down until it clears the body **(see illustration)**. Then, using nothing but your hands, spread each leg about 1/8-inch to disengage the body and push the legs through the fitting. Finally, pull lightly on the triangular end of the clip and work it clear of the line and fitting. Remember, don't use any tools to perform this part of the procedure.

6   Grasp the fitting and hose and pull it straight off the line.

7   Do not reuse the original clip in the fitting. A new clip must be used.

8   Before reinstalling the fitting on the line, wipe the line end with a clean cloth. Inspect the inside of the fitting to ensure that it's free of dirt and/or obstructions.

9   To reinstall the fitting on the line, align them and push the fitting into place. When the fitting is engaged, a definite click will be heard. Pull on the fitting to ensure that it's completely engaged **(see illustration)**. To install the new clip, insert it into any two adjacent openings in the fitting with the triangular portion of the clip pointing away from the fitting opening. Using your index finger, push the clip in until the legs are locked on the outside of the fitting.

1/4-inch fittings (duck-bill clip)

10   The duck bill clip type fitting consists of a body, spacers, O-rings and the retaining clip **(see illustration)**. The clip holds the fitting securely in

4

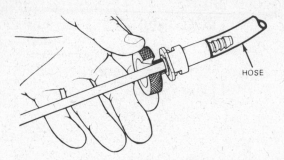

3.13   Disassembling a duck-bill clip fitting using the special Ford tool

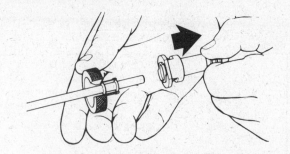

3.14   Pulling off the duck-bill clip type push-connect fitting

place on the line. One of the two following methods must be used to disconnect this type of fitting.

11   Before attempting to disconnect the fitting, check the visible internal portion of the fitting for accumulations of dirt. If more than a light coating of dust is evident, clean the fitting before disassembly.

12   Some adhesion between the seals in the fitting and line will occur over a period of time. Twist the fitting on the line, then push and pull the fitting until it moves freely.

13   The preferred method used to disconnect the fitting requires a special tool. To disengage the line from the fitting, align the slot in the push-connect disassembly tool (Ford Part No. T82L-9500-AH or equivalent tool) with either tab on the clip (90-degrees from the slots on the side of the fitting) and insert the tool **(see illustration)**. This disengages the duck bill from the line. **Note:** *Some fuel lines have a secondary bead which aligns with the outer surface of the clip. The bead can make tool insertion difficult. If necessary, use the alternative disassembly method described in Step 16.*

14   Holding the tool and the line with one hand, pull the fitting off **(see illustration)**. **Note:** *Only moderate effort is necessary if the clip is properly disengaged. The use of anything other than your hands should not be required.*

15   After disassembly, inspect and clean the line sealing surface. Also inspect the inside of the fitting and the line for any internal parts that may have been dislodged from the fitting. Any loose internal parts should be immediately reinstalled (use the line to insert the parts).

16   The alternative disassembly procedure requires a pair of small adjustable pliers. The pliers must have a jaw width of 3/16-inch or less.

17   Align the jaws of the pliers with the openings in the side of the fitting and compress the portion of the retaining clip that engages the body. This disengages the retaining clip from the body (often one side of the clip will disengage before the other – both sides must be disengaged).

18   Pull the fitting off the line. **Note:** *Only moderate effort is required if the retaining clip has been properly disengaged. Do not use any tools for this procedure.*

19   Once the fitting is removed from the line end, check the fitting and line for any internal parts that may have been dislodged from the fitting. Any loose internal parts should be immediately reinstalled (use the line to insert the parts).

20   The retaining clip will remain on the line. Disengage the clip from the line bead to remove it. Do not reuse the retaining clip – install a new one!

21   Before reinstalling the fitting, wipe the line end with a clean cloth. Check the inside of the fitting to make sure that it's free of dirt and/or obstructions.

22   To reinstall the fitting, align it with the line and push it into place. When the fitting is engaged, a definite click will be heard. Pull on the fitting to ensure that it's fully engaged.

23   Install the new replacement clip by inserting one of the serrated edges on the duck bill portion into one of the openings. Push on the other side until the clip snaps into place.

Spring-lock couplings

24   The fuel supply and return lines used on EFI engines utilize spring-lock couplings at the engine fuel rail end instead of plastic push-connect fittings. The male end of the spring-lock coupling, which is girded by two

3.26a   Some fuel-injection fittings use spring-lock couplings, which require special tools to disconnect and reconnect – later models use a clip and tether for extra security

O-rings, is inserted into a female flared end engine fitting. The coupling is secured by a garter spring which prevents disengagement by gripping the flared end of the female fitting. On later models, a clip-tether assembly provides additional security.

25   To disconnect the 1/2-inch (12.7mm) spring-lock coupling supply fitting, you will need to obtain a spring lock coupling tool D87L-9280-B or its equivalent; for the 3/8-inch (9.52mm) return fitting, get tool D87L-9280-A or its equivalent.

26   Study the accompanying illustrations carefully before detaching either spring-lock coupling fitting.

---

4   Fuel pump – check

Mechanical fuel pump (carburetor-equipped models)

1   If a problem occurs in the fuel pump itself, it will normally either deliver no fuel at all or not enough to sustain high engine speeds or loads.

2   When an engine develops a lean (fuel starved) condition, the fuel pump is often to blame, but the same symptoms will be evident if the carburetor float bowl filter is clogged. A lean condition will also occur if the carburetor is malfunctioning, the fuel lines and hoses are leaking, kinked or restricted or the electrical system is shorting out or malfunctioning.

General check

3   If the fuel pump is noisy:
   a) Check for loose fuel pump mounting bolts and, if necessary, tighten them to the torque listed in this Chapter's Specifications. Replace the gasket if necessary.

TO DISCONNECT COUPLING

CAUTION — RELIEVE FUEL PRESSURE BEFORE DISCONNECTING COUPLING

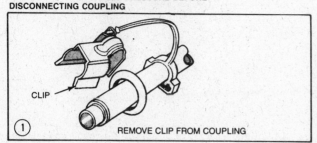

CLIP

1 REMOVE CLIP FROM COUPLING

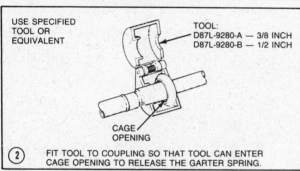

USE SPECIFIED TOOL OR EQUIVALENT

TOOL:
D87L-9280-A — 3/8 INCH
D87L-9280-B — 1/2 INCH

CAGE OPENING

2 FIT TOOL TO COUPLING SO THAT TOOL CAN ENTER CAGE OPENING TO RELEASE THE GARTER SPRING.

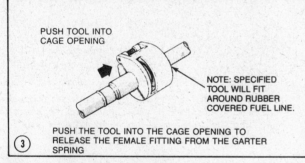

PUSH TOOL INTO CAGE OPENING

NOTE: SPECIFIED TOOL WILL FIT AROUND RUBBER COVERED FUEL LINE.

3 PUSH THE TOOL INTO THE CAGE OPENING TO RELEASE THE FEMALE FITTING FROM THE GARTER SPRING

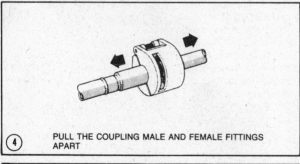

4 PULL THE COUPLING MALE AND FEMALE FITTINGS APART

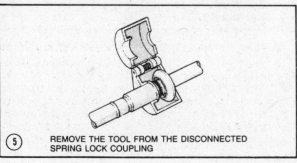

5 REMOVE THE TOOL FROM THE DISCONNECTED SPRING LOCK COUPLING

TO CONNECT COUPLING

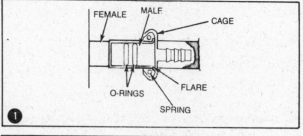

FEMALE   MALE   CAGE

O-RINGS   FLARE   SPRING

1

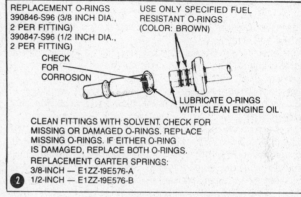

REPLACEMENT O-RINGS
390846-S96 (3/8 INCH DIA., 2 PER FITTING)
390847-S96 (1/2 INCH DIA., 2 PER FITTING)

USE ONLY SPECIFIED FUEL RESISTANT O-RINGS (COLOR: BROWN)

CHECK FOR CORROSION

LUBRICATE O-RINGS WITH CLEAN ENGINE OIL

CLEAN FITTINGS WITH SOLVENT. CHECK FOR MISSING OR DAMAGED O-RINGS. REPLACE MISSING O-RINGS. IF EITHER O-RING IS DAMAGED, REPLACE BOTH O-RINGS.
REPLACEMENT GARTER SPRINGS:
3/8-INCH — E1ZZ-19E576-A
1/2-INCH — E1ZZ-19E576-B

2

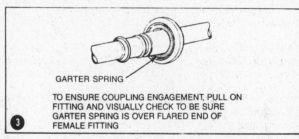

GARTER SPRING

3 TO ENSURE COUPLING ENGAGEMENT, PULL ON FITTING AND VISUALLY CHECK TO BE SURE GARTER SPRING IS OVER FLARED END OF FEMALE FITTING

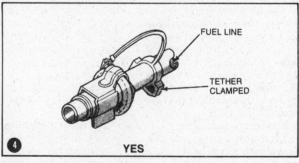

FUEL LINE

TETHER CLAMPED

4 **YES**

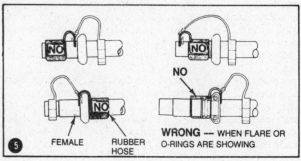

NO   NO

NO

FEMALE   RUBBER HOSE

NO

5 **WRONG** — WHEN FLARE OR O-RINGS ARE SHOWING

3.26b Connecting and disconnecting spring-lock coupling fittings – later models use a clip and tether to secure the lines

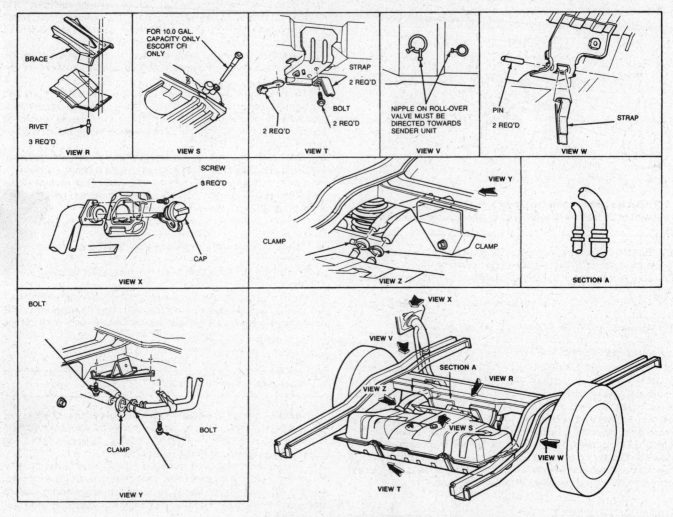

5.5   A typical fuel tank and fittings

b) Check for loose or missing fuel line mounting clips. Loose or missing clips will sound louder when you are sitting inside the vehicle than when standing outside of it. Tighten the clips on the fuel lines if necessary.

c) Check for a worn, or sticking fuel pump pushrod.

4   Before assuming a fuel pump is defective:

a) Be sure the tank has fuel in it.

b) Be sure the fuel filter is not plugged. If it hasn't been changed recently, install a new one.

c) Inspect all rubber hoses from the fuel pump to the fuel tank for kinks and cracks. With the engine idling, check all fuel lines and rubber hoses and connections from the fuel pump to the fuel tank for fuel leaks. Tighten any loose connections and replace kinked, cracked or leaking fuel lines or hoses as required. Leaking or kinked lines or hoses will severely affect fuel pump performance.

d) Inspect the fuel pump inlet and outlet connections for fuel leaks. Tighten them if necessary.

e) Inspect the fuel pump diaphragm crimp (the area where the stamped steel section is attached to the casting) and the breather hole(s) in the casting for evidence of fuel or oil leakage. Replace the pump if it's leaking.

Output (capacity) test

Warning: *Gasoline is extremely flammable, so take extra precautions when you work on any part of the fuel system. Don't smoke or allow open flames or bare light bulbs near the work area, and don't work in a garage where a natural gas-type appliance (such as a water heater or clothes dry-er) with a pilot light is present. If you spill any fuel on your skin, rinse it off immediately with soap and water. When you perform any kind of work on the fuel system, wear safety glasses and have a Class B type fire extin-guisher on hand.*

5   Remove the air cleaner assembly (see Section 8).

6   Carefully disconnect the fuel line at the fuel filter inlet (see Chapter 1).

7   Attach a section of rubber fuel hose to the end of the disconnected line with hose clamps and route the end of the hose into an approved gasoline container (1/2-liter or 1 pint minimum). **Note:** *It may be necessary to attach a section of hose to the disconnected fuel line in order to reach the contain-er.* Disconnect the high-tension wire from the coil and ground it on the en-gine with a jumper wire. Crank the engine over about 10 revolutions. The fuel pump should deliver at least 1/3-pint of fuel.

8   If the output is adequate, perform the pressure test below.

9   If the output is less than specified, repeat the test with a remote fuel supply. Detach the hose from the fuel pump inlet line and attach a separate section of fuel hose to the line with a hose clamp. Route the end of the hose into the remote fuel supply (an approved gasoline container at least half full of fuel) and repeat the procedure in Step 7. If the output is now as speci-fied, the problem is either a plugged in-tank filter or a kinked or leaking fuel hose. Make the necessary repairs. If output is still not as specified, replace the fuel pump.

Pressure test

10   Connect a fuel pressure gauge (0 to 15 psi) to the fuel filter end of the line.

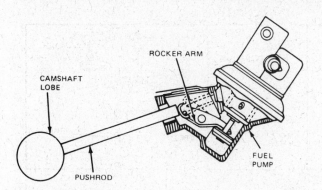

CAMSHAFT LOBE

ROCKER ARM

PUSHROD

FUEL PUMP

7.2   Before removing the fuel pump, turn the engine so the low point of the camshaft lobe rests on the fuel pump pushrod

11   Start the engine – it should be able to run for over 30 seconds on the fuel in the carburetor bowl – and read the pressure after ten seconds. Compare your reading to the pressure listed in this Chapter's Specifications.
12   If pump pressure is not as specified, install a new fuel pump (refer to Section 7).
13   Reconnect the fuel lines and install the air cleaner.

Electric fuel pump

14   An electric fuel pump malfunction will usually result in a loss of fuel flow and/or pressure that is often reflected by a corresponding drop in performance. If you suspect an electric fuel pump problem, disconnect the wire harness from the pump(s) (see Section 7), attach a fused jumper wire between the battery and the pump and carefully listen to the pump. If it's not running, replace it. If it is running, the pressure may be low (see Section 12) or the problem may lie within the fuel pump circuit or elsewhere (see Troubleshooting at the front of this manual). Diagnosis of this circuit is beyond the scope of the home mechanic. Take the vehicle to a dealer and have the fuel pump circuit checked by a professional.

5   Fuel tank – removal and installation

Refer to illustration 5.5
Warning: *Gasoline is extremely flammable, so take extra precautions when you work on any part of the fuel system. Don't smoke or allow open flames or bare light bulbs near the work area, and don't work in a garage where a natural gas-type appliance (such as a water heater or clothes dryer) with a pilot light is present. If you spill any fuel on your skin, rinse it off immediately with soap and water. When you perform any kind of work on the fuel system, wear safety glasses and have a Class B type fire extinguisher on hand. Don't use an electrically-powered siphon pump to siphon fuel, and don't siphon by mouth. Inexpensive hand-powered siphon pumps are available at auto parts stores.*
Note: *Don't begin this procedure until the gauge indicates that the tank is empty or nearly empty. If the tank must be removed when it's full (for example, if the fuel pump malfunctions), siphon any remaining fuel from the tank prior to removal.*

1   On fuel-injected models, relieve the fuel pressure (see Section 2).
2   Detach the cable from the negative terminal of the battery.
3   Raise the vehicle and support it securely on jackstands.
4   Unless the vehicle has been driven far enough to completely empty the tank, it's a good idea to siphon the residual fuel out before removing the tank from the vehicle. Siphon or pump the fuel out through the fuel filler pipe. On US vehicles, a small diameter hose may be necessary because of the small trap door installed in the fuel filler pipe to prevent vapors from escaping during refueling. Fuel-injected models have reservoirs inside the tank to maintain fuel near the pump pick-up during vehicle cornering maneuvers and when the fuel level is low. The reservoirs could prevent si-

phon tubes or hoses from reaching the bottom of the fuel tank. This situation can be overcome by repositioning the siphon hose several times.
5   Remove the filler neck bracket bolt securing the fuel filler neck hose and the breather hose to the fuel tank **(see illustration)**.
6   If possible, disconnect the fuel and vapor lines (on some models, the fittings are on top of the tank and cannot be reached until the tank is partially lowered).
7   Remove the electric fuel pump (if equipped) and sending unit wire harness clips with a screwdriver. On some models, the harness connector is on top of the tank and inaccessible. Since no intermediate connection point is provided, the harness cannot be disconnected until the tank is partially lowered.
8   Place a floor jack under the tank and position a block of wood between the jack pad and the tank. Raise the jack until it's supporting the tank.
9   Remove the bolts or nuts from the front ends of the fuel tank straps **(see illustration 5.5)**. The straps are hinged at the other end so you can swing them out of the way.
10   Lower the tank far enough to unplug the wiring harness, if not already unplugged.
11   Slowly lower the jack while steadying the tank. Remove the tank from the vehicle.
12   If you're replacing the tank, or having it cleaned or repaired, refer to Section 6.
13   Refer to Section 7 to remove and install the fuel pump/sending unit.
14   Installation is the reverse of removal. SAE 10W-40 engine oil can be used as an assembly aid when pushing the fuel filler neck back into the tank.

6   Fuel tank – cleaning and repair

1   Repairs to the fuel tank or filler neck should be performed by a professional with the proper training to carry out this critical and potentially dangerous work. Even after cleaning and flushing, explosive fumes can remain and could explode during repair of the tank.
2   If the fuel tank is removed from the vehicle, it should not be placed in an area where sparks or open flames could ignite the fumes coming out of the tank. **Warning:** *Be especially careful inside a garage where a natural gas appliance is located because the pilot light could cause an explosion!*

7   Fuel pump – removal and installation

Warning: *Gasoline is extremely flammable, so take extra precautions when you work on any part of the fuel system. Don't smoke or allow open flames or bare light bulbs near the work area, and don't work in a garage where a natural gas-type appliance (such as a water heater or clothes dryer) with a pilot light is present. If you spill any fuel on your skin, rinse it off immediately with soap and water. When you perform any kind of work on the fuel system, wear safety glasses and have a Class B type fire extinguisher on hand.*

Mechanical fuel pump (carburetor-equipped models)
Refer to illustrations 7.2 and 7.4

1   Loosen the threaded fuel line fittings (at the pump) with the proper size wrench (a flare nut wrench is recommended), then retighten them until they're just snug. Don't remove the lines at this time. The outlet line is pressurized, so protect your eyes with safety goggles or wrap the fitting with a shop rag, then loosen it carefully.
2   Loosen the mounting bolts two turns. Use your hands to loosen the fuel pump if it's stuck to the block (do not use a tool – you could damage the pump). If you cannot loosen the pump by hand, have an assistant operate the starter while you keep one hand on the pump. As the camshaft turns, it will operate the pump – when the pump feels loose, stop turning the engine over **(see illustration)**.
3   Disconnect the fuel lines from the pump. Be sure to use a back-up wrench.

4

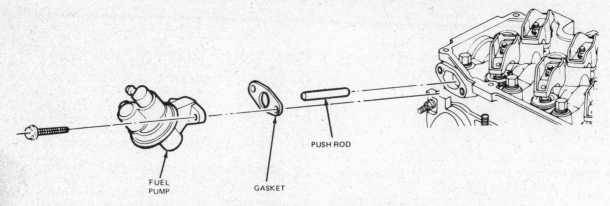

PUSH ROD

FUEL
PUMP

GASKET

**7.4   Loosen the mounting bolts two turns, then break the pump loose from the engine with
hand pressure, if necessary, before removing the bolts the rest of the way**

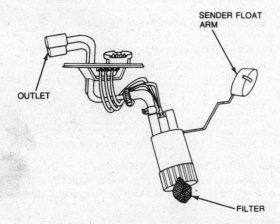

SENDER FLOAT
ARM

OUTLET

FILTER

**7.13   In-tank electric fuel pump and fuel gauge sending unit
assembly – typical**

4   Remove the fuel pump bolts and detach the pump and gasket **(see
illustration)**. Discard the old gasket.
5   Using a gasket scraper, remove all old gasket material and sealant
from the engine block. If you're installing the original pump, remove all the
old gasket material from the pump mating surface as well. Wipe the mating
surfaces of the block and pump with a cloth saturated with lacquer thinner
or acetone.
6   Insert the bolts through the pump (to use as a guides for the new gasket) and place the gasket in position on the fuel pump mounting flange.
Position the fuel pump on the block (make sure the pump pushrod engages the camshaft properly) **(see illustration 7.2)**. Tighten the bolts a

little at a time until they're at the specified torque.
7   Attach the fuel lines to the pump. Start the threaded fitting by hand to
avoid cross-threading it. Tighten the outlet nut securely. If any of the hoses
are cracked, hardened or otherwise deteriorated, replace them at this
time.
8   Start the engine and check for fuel leaks for two minutes.
9   Stop the engine and check the fuel line connections for leaks by running a finger under each fitting. Check for oil leaks at the fuel pump mounting gasket.

Electric in-tank fuel pump (later fuel-injected models)
Refer to illustration 7.13
10   Relieve the fuel system pressure (see Section 2).
11   Remove the fuel tank (see Section 5).
12   Using hammer and a brass punch or wood dowel only, tap the lock
ring counterclockwise until it's loose.
13   Carefully pull the fuel pump/sending unit assembly from the tank **(see
illustration)**.
14   Remove the old lock ring gasket and discard it.
15   Clean the fuel pump mounting flange and the tank mounting surface
and seal ring groove.
16   Installation is the reverse of removal. Apply a thin coat of heavy
grease to the new lock ring gasket to hold it in place during assembly. Be
sure the locating tabs on the fuel pump are correctly positioned in their
notches. Be sure the gasket stays in its groove.

Electric chassis-mount fuel pump (early fuel-injected models)
Refer to illustration 7.18
17   Depressurize the fuel system as outlined in Section 2 and raise the
rear of the vehicle, supporting it safely on the jackstands.

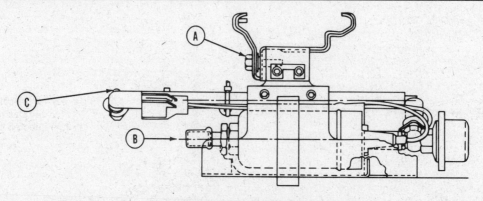

7.18   Chassis-mounted electric fuel pump

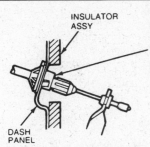

9.2a   The throttle cable is secured to the dash panel by retainer prongs – to remove the cable, pry the snap-in nylon bushing from the top of the pedal . . .

9.2b   . . . and compress the retainer prongs so the cable can be pushed through the firewall into the engine compartment

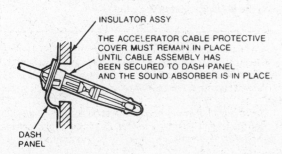

9.2c   To install the cable, push it in, let the prongs expand and make sure they're secured against the dash panel, then snap the cable bushing into the pedal – don't remove the protective cover supplied with a new cable until after the cable is installed

18   Loosen the mounting bolt at point A **(see illustration)**. Detach the pump from the bracket and unclip the parking brake cable from the pump.
19   Disconnect the electrical connector from the pump, which is located near the fuel tank. Disconnect the inlet and outlet hoses **(see illustration 7.18)** and take the pump out.
20   Install the fuel pump in its bracket, then attach the parking brake cable to its clip.
21   Connect the fuel inlet hose to point B **(see illustration 7.18)**. Connect the outlet hose to point C.
22   Lower the vehicle.
23   Connect a fuel pressure gauge to the fitting on the fuel rail. Turn the ignition key on, then Off, in two-second bursts until fuel pressure reaches 35 psi.
24   Run the engine and check for fuel leaks.

8   Air cleaner housing – removal and installation

Carburetor and CFI equipped models
1   Remove the air filter (see Chapter 1).
2   Disconnect the fresh air inlet duct from the end of the air cleaner snorkel.
3   Disconnect the heated air duct from the underside of the air cleaner snorkel.
4   Disconnect all hoses connecting the air cleaner to the engine.
5   Lift the housing from the engine. Installation is the reverse of removal.

Multi-point fuel injection models
6   Remove the cover and filter element (see Chapter 1).
7   Detach and remove components as necessary, referring to the illustrations in Chapter 1.
8   Installation is the reverse of the removal steps.

9   Throttle cable – removal and installation

Refer to illustrations 9.2a, 9.2b, 9.2c and 9.5
1   Remove the air intake duct (see Section 8), if necessary for access.
2   Detach the cable snap-in nylon bushing from the accelerator pedal arm **(see illustrations)**.
3   Remove the cable housing from the firewall by compressing the two prongs and pushing the cable through the firewall into the engine compartment.
4   Detach the cruise control cable (if equipped) from the throttle cable.
5   Detach the cable from the bracket on the engine **(see illustration)**.

4

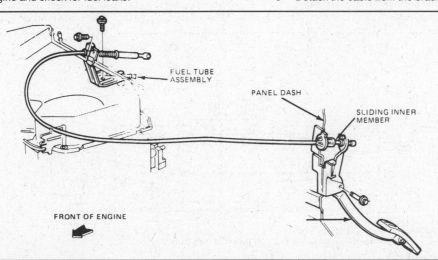

9.5   A typical throttle cable (carbureted model shown, fuel-injected models similar)

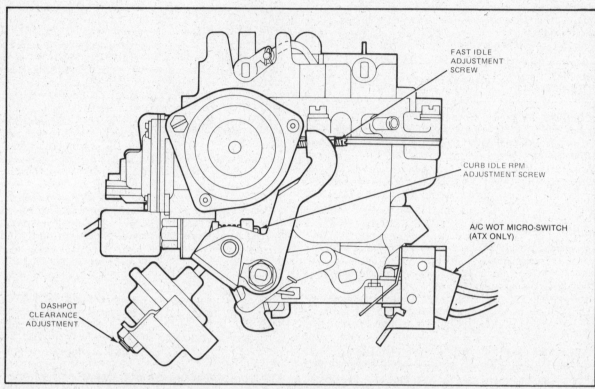

FAST IDLE
ADJUSTMENT
SCREW

CURB IDLE RPM
ADJUSTMENT SCREW

A/C WOT MICRO-SWITCH
(ATX ONLY)

DASHPOT
CLEARANCE
ADJUSTMENT

Figure 1   1.6L with 740-2V Carburetor — Fast Idle RPM and Curb Idle RPM

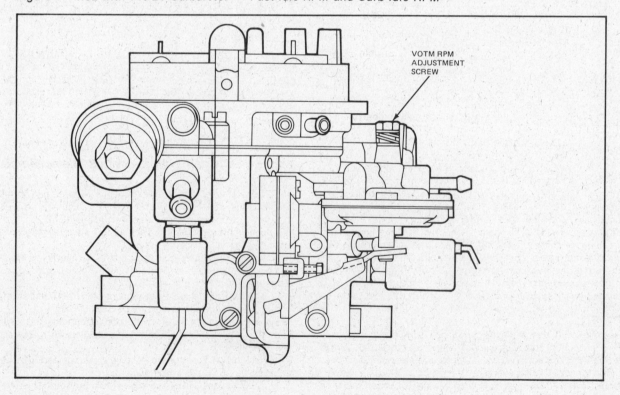

VOTM RPM
ADJUSTMENT
SCREW

10.21   Idle speed adjustment points – carburetor without idle speed control

6   Detach the throttle cable from the throttle lever by inserting a screwdriver between the cable assembly and the throttle lever and twisting the screwdriver.

7   Installation is the reverse of removal. If the new cable has a protective cover on the pedal end, don't remove the cover until after the cable is pushed through the firewall.

---

10   Carburetor – diagnosis, removal, overhaul, installation and adjustment

Warning: *Gasoline is extremely flammable, so take extra precautions when you work on any part of the fuel system. Don't smoke or allow open flames or bare light bulbs near the work area, and don't work in a garage where a natural gas-type appliance (such as a water heater or clothes dryer) with a pilot light is present. If you spill any fuel on your skin, rinse it off immediately with soap and water. When you perform any kind of work on the fuel system, wear safety glasses and have a Class B type fire extinguisher on hand.*

Diagnosis

1   A thorough road test and check of carburetor adjustments should be done before any major carburetor service work. Specifications for some adjustments are listed on the Vehicle Emissions Control Information label found in the engine compartment.

2   Some performance complaints directed at the carburetor are actually a result of loose, out-of-adjustment or malfunctioning engine or electrical components. Others develop when vacuum hoses leak, are disconnected or are incorrectly routed. The proper approach to analyzing carburetor problems should include a routine check of the following items.

  a) Inspect all vacuum hoses and actuators for leaks and correct installation (see Chapter 6).
  b) Tighten the intake manifold nuts/bolts and carburetor mounting nuts evenly and securely.
  c) Perform a cylinder compression test (see Chapter 2B).
  d) Clean or replace the spark plugs as necessary.
  e) Check the spark plug wires.
  f) Inspect the ignition primary wires and check the vacuum advance operation. Replace any defective parts.
  g) Check the ignition timing according to the instructions printed on the Vehicle Emissions Control Information label.
  h) Check the fuel pump pressure.
  i) Check the heat control valve in the air cleaner for proper operation (see Chapter 6).
  j) Check/replace the air filter element.
  k) Check the PCV system (see Chapter 6).

3   Carburetor problems usually show up as flooding, hard starting, stalling, severe backfiring, poor acceleration and lack of response to idle mixture screw adjustments. A carburetor that is leaking fuel and/or covered with wet-looking deposits definitely needs attention.

4   Diagnosing carburetor problems may require that the engine be started and run with the air cleaner off. While running the engine without the air cleaner, backfires are possible. This situation is likely to occur if the carburetor is malfunctioning, but just the removal of the air cleaner can lean the fuel/air mixture enough to produce an engine backfire. **Warning:** *Do not position any part of your body, especially your face, directly over the carburetor during inspection and servicing procedures!*

Removal

5   Remove the air cleaner housing assembly (see Section 8).

6   Disconnect the throttle cable from the throttle lever (see Section 9).

7   If your vehicle is equipped with an automatic transaxle, disconnect the TV rod from the throttle lever (see Chapter 7B).

8   **Note:** *To simplify installation, label all vacuum hoses and fittings before removing them.* Disconnect all vacuum hoses and the fuel line from the carburetor. Use a back-up wrench on the fuel inlet fitting when removing the fuel line to avoid changing the float level.

9   Label the wires and terminals, then unplug all wire harness connectors at the carburetor.

10   Remove the mounting nuts and detach the carburetor from the intake manifold. Remove the carburetor mounting gasket and, if equipped, spacer. Place a rag inside the intake manifold cavity to prevent dirt and debris from falling down into the engine while the carburetor is removed.

Overhaul

11   Once it's determined that the carburetor needs adjustment or an overhaul, several options are available. If you're going to attempt to overhaul the carburetor yourself, first obtain a good quality carburetor rebuild kit (which will include all necessary gaskets, internal parts, instructions and a parts list). You'll also need some special solvent and a means of blowing out the internal passages of the carburetor with air.

12   Because carburetor designs are constantly modified by the manufacturer in order to meet increasingly more stringent emissions regulations, it isn't feasible for us to do a step-by-step overhaul of each type. You'll receive a detailed, well illustrated set of instructions with any carburetor overhaul kit; they will apply in a more specific manner to the carburetor on your vehicle.

13   Another alternative is to obtain a new or rebuilt carburetor. They are available from dealers and auto parts stores. Make absolutely sure the exchange carburetor is identical to the original. A tag is usually attached to the top of the carburetor. It will aid in determining the exact type of carburetor you have. When obtaining a rebuilt carburetor or a rebuild kit, take time to make sure that the kit or carburetor matches your application exactly. Seemingly insignificant differences can make a large difference in the performance of your engine.

14   If you choose to overhaul your own carburetor, allow enough time to disassemble the carburetor carefully, soak the necessary parts in the cleaning solvent (usually for at least one-half day or according to the instructions listed on the carburetor cleaner) and reassemble it, which will usually take much longer than disassembly. When disassembling the carburetor, match each part with the illustration in the carburetor kit and lay the parts out in order on a clean work surface. Overhauls by inexperienced mechanics can result in an engine which runs poorly or not at all. To avoid this, use care and patience when disassembling the carburetor so you can reassemble it correctly.

Installation

15   Clean the gasket mating surfaces of the intake manifold and the carburetor to remove all traces of the old gasket. Remove the rag from the manifold. Place the spacer, if equipped, and a new gasket on the intake manifold. Position the carburetor on the gasket and spacer and install the mounting nuts. To prevent distortion or damage to the carburetor body flange, tighten the nuts to the torque listed in this Chapter's Specifications in several steps.

16   The remaining installation steps are the reverse of removal.

Adjustment – carburetors without idle speed control

Refer to illustration 10.21

17   Major adjustments, such as float level, are done as part of carburetor overhaul. Curb idle and fast idle should be adjusted after an overhaul.

18   Warm the engine to normal operating temperature.

19   Connect a tachometer to the engine, following the instructions of the tachometer manufacturer.

20   Locate the air supply valve and follow its vacuum line. If the line connects to the carburetor, disconnect it at the Thermactor air control valve bypass section and plug it.

21   Place the fast idle cam on the second step **(see illustration)**.

22   Disconnect and plug the EGR valve vacuum line.

23   Start the engine and run it until the cooling fan starts to run. **Warning:** *Stay out of the way of rotating engine components when working on the running engine.*

24   Check fast idle speed on the tachometer and compare it to the specification on the VECI label under the hood.

25   If fast idle speed is incorrect, loosen the locknut on the fast idle screw, turn the screw to make the adjustment and retighten the locknut. **Note:** *The cooling fan must be running during fast idle adjustment. If necessary, apply power to the fan with jumper wires.*

26   With fast idle set correctly, tap the accelerator so the fast idle cam releases and idle speed drops to normal.

4

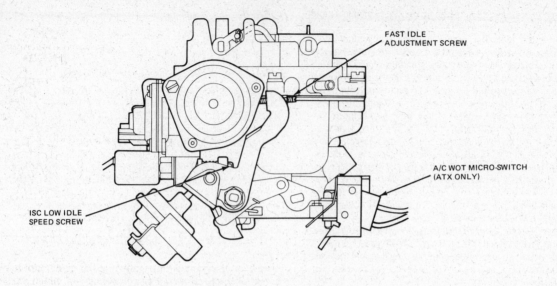

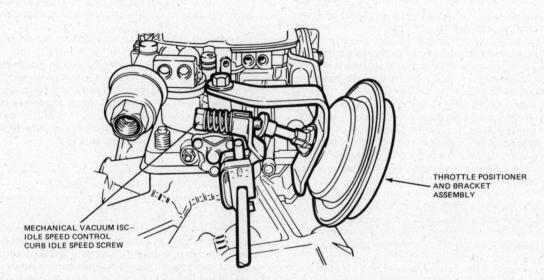

10.35   Idle speed adjustment points – carburetor with idle speed control

27   Place the transaxle in the gear specified on the VECI label. Check the idle speed and compare it to the VECI label. Adjust it, if necessary, by turning the curb idle screw.

28   Check and adjust the dashpot (if equipped) clearance. The tip of the dashpot plunger should be about 0.020-inch from the lever.

29   If equipped with an automatic transaxle, the throttle linkage must be adjusted if idle speed is changed more than 50 rpm (see Chapter 7B).

30   Turn off the engine. Remove the bypass plug (if used) and reconnect all vacuum hose(s).

Adjustment – carburetors with idle speed control

Refer to illustration 10.35

31   Perform Steps 18 through 21 and 23 through 26 above.

32   With the cooling fan on and the transaxle in Drive, check idle speed and compare it to the VECI label.

33   If adjustment is necessary, place the transaxle in the specified gear (see VECI label).

34   Disconnect and plug the idle speed control vacuum hose.

35   Connect a hand vacuum pump to the idle speed control throttle positioner. Apply vacuum until the throttle positioner retracts its plunger clear of the adjusting screw **(see illustration)**.

36   Place the transaxle in Drive and check idle speed. It should be at the

"ISC retracted" speed on the VECI label. If not, adjust by turning the throttle stop adjusting screw **(see illustration 10.35).**

37   Place the transaxle in Park. Disconnect the vacuum pump, then unplug and reconnect the throttle positioner vacuum line.

38   Place the transaxle in Drive and make sure the cooling fan is on.

39   Check curb idle speed and compare to the VECI label. Adjust it, if necessary, with the curb idle screw.

40   Place the transaxle in Neutral or Park. Rev the engine briefly and let engine speed drop back to idle.

41   Place the transaxle in the specified gear and recheck curb idle. Readjust if necessary.

42   Unplug and reconnect the Thermactor bypass hose.

43   If idle speed was changed more than 50 rpm, adjust the throttle linkage (refer to Chapter 7B).

---

11   Fuel injection systems – general information

Central Fuel Injection (CFI) system

The Central Fuel Injection (CFI) system is a single-point, pulse time modulated injection system. Fuel is metered into the air intake stream in accordance with engine demands by a solenoid injection valve mounted in a throttle body on the intake manifold.

Fuel is supplied to the injector by a low pressure, electric fuel pump mounted in the fuel tank. The fuel is filtered and sent to the fuel charging assembly, then to a regulator which maintains the fuel delivery pressure at a nominal value of 14.5 psi. Excess fuel supplied by the pump but not needed by the engine is returned to the fuel tank by a steel fuel return line. The single injector nozzle is mounted vertically above the throttle plate.

The fuel charging assembly consists of five individual components which perform the fuel and air metering function. The throttle body assembly is attached to the conventional carburetor mounting pad on the intake manifold and houses the air control system, fuel injector nozzle, fuel pressure regulator, idle speed control motor and throttle position sensor.

Air flow to the engine is controlled by the throttle body. This consists of a housing and butterfly valve, which opens and closes to admit or restrict air. The butterfly valve, which resembles a carburetor throttle valve, is controlled by the throttle pedal and cable.

Fuel flow to the engine is controlled by the injector. The amount of fuel flowing to the engine varies directly according to how long the injector remains open (pulse width). This in turn is controlled by a signal from the EEC electronic processor. The size of the injector opening is fixed and fuel pressure to the injector is constant.

The pressure regulator is built into the fuel charging main body near the rear of the air horn surface. The regulator prevents any drop in fuel pressure from affecting the fuel pressure at the injector.

The pressure regulator also maintains fuel pressure when the engine is off. The regulator functions as a downstream check valve and traps the fuel between itself and the fuel pump. This prevents fuel from vaporizing in the lines after engine shutdown, which can cause hard restarts and an unstable idle with a hot engine.

The idle speed control system regulates idle speed by modulating the throttle lever for the required airflow to maintain the desired engine rpm for any operating condition, from an idling cold engine to a warm engine at normal operating temperature. An idle tracking switch (ITS) determines when the throttle lever has contacted the actuator, signalling the need to control engine rpm. The ISC motor extends or retracts a shaft through a gear reduction system to move the throttle lever.

A non-adjustable throttle position sensor, mounted to the throttle shaft on the side of the fuel charging assembly, sends a voltage signal to the EEC processor that varies with throttle position. The processor uses this signal to determine whether the engine is at closed, part or full throttle. The processor uses the information to regulate fuel mixture, ignition timing and EGR flow.

Electronic Fuel Injection (EFI) system

The Electronic Fuel Injection (EFI) system is a multi-point, pulse time, speed density control design. Fuel is metered into the intake air stream in accordance with engine demand through four injectors mounted on a tuned intake manifold. A blow-through turbocharger system used on some 1984 and 1985 models pumps compressed air through a hose into the throttle body.

An Electronic Engine Control (EEC-IV) computer accepts inputs from various engine sensors to compute the required fuel flow rate necessary to maintain a prescribed air/fuel ratio throughout the entire engine operational range. The computer then outputs a command to the fuel injectors to meter the approximate quantity of fuel.

The EEC-IV engine control system also determines and compensates for the age of the vehicle and its uniqueness. The system automatically senses and compensates for changes in altitude and, on vehicles with a manual transmission, permits push-starting, should it become necessary.

An electric high-pressure fuel pump forces pressurized fuel through a series of metal and plastic lines and an inline fuel filter/reservoir to the fuel charging manifold assembly. The pump is mounted outside the tank on early models and in the tank on later models.

The fuel charging manifold assembly incorporates electrically actuated fuel injectors directly above each intake port. When energized, the injectors spray a metered quantity of fuel into the intake air stream.

A pressure regulator maintains a constant fuel pressure at the injectors. The regulator is positioned downstream from the fuel injectors. Ex-

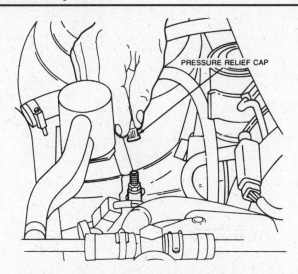

12.3   The Schrader valve fitting on the multi-point fuel rail assembly is protected by a threaded cap, which must be unscrewed to connect the fuel pressure gauge to the valve

cess fuel passes through the regulator and returns to the fuel tank through a fuel return line.

All four injectors are energized simultaneously, once every crankshaft revolution. The period of time that the injectors are energized (known as "on time" or "pulse width") is controlled by the EEC computer. Air entering the engine is sensed by speed, pressure and temperature sensors. The outputs of these sensors are processed by the EEC-IV computer. The computer uses the information to regulate injector pulse width, thus controlling the amount of fuel that enters the engine.

12   Fuel injection system – pressure check

Refer to illustration 12.3

Warning: *Gasoline is extremely flammable, so take extra precautions when you work on any part of the fuel system. Don't smoke or allow open flames or bare light bulbs near the work area, and don't work in a garage where a natural gas-type appliance (such as a water heater or clothes dryer) with a pilot light is present. If you spill any fuel on your skin, rinse it off immediately with soap and water. When you perform any kind of work on the fuel system, wear safety glasses and have a Class B type fire extinguisher on hand.*

1   Fuel pressure is measured with a Ford T80L-9974-B fuel pressure gauge (or equivalent) on all fuel-injected vehicles covered by this manual. Adapter T85L-9974-A (or equivalent) is required for multi-point fuel injection (EFI) and adapter T85L-9974-C (or equivalent) is required for Central Fuel Injection. On multi-point fuel-injected versions of this vehicle, the pressure gauge is connected to a Schrader valve. On Central Fuel Injection-equipped versions, the fuel pressure gauge is connected into the fuel line to the throttle body.

2   The special Ford fuel pressure gauge/adapter assembly is designed to relieve fuel pressure, as well as measure it, through the Schrader valve (EFI models only). If you have this gauge, you can use this method on EFI models as an alternative to the procedure for fuel pressure relief outlined in Section 2. **Warning:** *DO NOT attempt to relieve fuel pressure through the Schrader valve without this special setup!*

3   To attach the gauge to multi-point injection vehicles, simply remove the valve cap **(see illustration)**, screw on the adapter and attach the gauge to the adapter.

4   To attach the gauge to Central Fuel Injection vehicles, first relieve fuel system pressure as described in Section 2. Then disconnect the fuel inlet line from the throttle body and connect adapter T85L-9974-C in series with it.

5   Connect pressure gauge T80L-9974-B to the adapter.

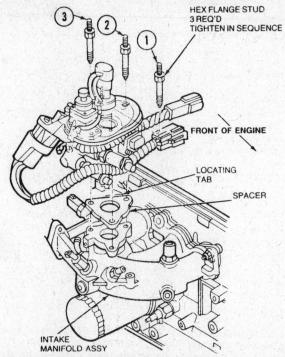

HEX FLANGE STUD
3 REQ'D
TIGHTEN IN SEQUENCE

FRONT OF ENGINE

LOCATING
TAB

SPACER

INTAKE
MANIFOLD ASSY

13.6   An assembled view of a typical fuel charging assembly

6   On all models, start the engine and allow it to reach a steady idle. Note the indicated fuel pressure reading and compare it to the specified pressure.

7   If the indicated fuel pressure is lower than specified, the problem is probably a leaking fuel line, a malfunctioning fuel pump or a leaking injector. If the pressure is higher than specified, the cause could be a blocked fuel line or a stuck fuel pressure regulator.

13   Central Fuel Injection (CFI) system – component replacement

Warning: *Gasoline is extremely flammable, so take extra precautions when you work on any part of the fuel system. Don't smoke or allow open flames or bare light bulbs near the work area, and don't work in a garage where a natural gas-type appliance (such as a water heater or clothes dryer) with a pilot light is present. If you spill any fuel on your skin, rinse it off immediately with soap and water. When you perform any kind of work on the fuel system, wear safety glasses and have a Class B type fire extinguisher on hand.*

Fuel charging assembly

Refer to illustration 13.6

1   When buying replacement parts for the fuel charging assembly, always check the number on the identification tag underneath the fuel charging assembly to make sure that you are getting the right parts. If the assembly is installed on the vehicle, you'll need a mirror to read the number.

2   Relieve the fuel system pressure (see Section 2). Detach the cable from the negative terminal of the battery.

3   Remove the air cleaner housing assembly (see Section 8).

4   Detach the throttle cable and, if equipped, cruise control cable fitting from the throttle lever (see Section 9).

5   If your vehicle is equipped with an automatic transaxle, detach the throttle valve linkage (see Chapter 7B).

6   Unplug the electrical connectors to the fuel injector, the Idle Speed Control (ISC) and the Throttle Position (TP) sensor **(see illustration)**.

7   Remove the fuel line bracket bolt.

8   Disconnect the fuel inlet and return lines (see Section 3).

9   Detach the EGR valve vacuum hose.

10   Remove the three mounting studs.

11   Installation is the reverse of removal. Using a scraper, remove all traces of old gasket material from the mating surfaces, then clean the surfaces with a rag soaked in lacquer thinner or acetone. Be careful not to gouge the mating surfaces while scraping. Tighten the three mounting studs in sequence (1, 2 and 3, illustration 13.6) to the initial torque setting in this Chapter's Specifications, then tighten them again in the same sequence to the final torque setting.

Idle Speed Control (ISC) motor

Refer to illustration 13.13

12   Remove the fuel charging assembly as described above.

13   Turn the assembly upside down and detach the ISC motor and bracket assembly from the fuel charging assembly **(see illustration)**.

14   If necessary, remove the three screws and detach the bracket from the ISC motor.

15   Installation is the reverse of the removal steps.

Throttle Position (TP) sensor

Note: *It is not necessary to remove the fuel charging assembly to replace the TP sensor.*

Removal

16   Detach the cable from the negative terminal of the battery.

17   Unplug the wire harness electrical connector from the TP sensor connector.

18   Remove the TP sensor retaining screws **(see illustration 13.13)**.

19   Slide the throttle position sensor off the throttle shaft.

Installation

20   Slide the throttle position sensor onto the throttle shaft. Rotate it counterclockwise only until it's aligned with the screw holes on the throttle body. Install the retaining screws and tighten them securely.

21   Connect the throttle position sensor wiring harness.

22   The remainder of installation is the reverse of removal.

Fuel injector

23   Remove the fuel charging assembly from the intake manifold (see above).

24   Remove the fuel injector retainer screws and retainer **(see illustration 13.13)**.

25   Carefully pull up on the injector while using a twisting motion. Remove the injector and its O-ring.

26   Discard the old O-ring and replace it with a new one. Use clean engine oil (not transmission oil) to lubricate the new O-ring before installing it.

27   Installation is the reverse of removal.

Fuel pressure regulator

28   Press down on the pressure regulator cover so its spring won't push the parts out when the cover is removed.

29   Remove four retaining screws, release the spring tension and remove the regulator parts **(see illustration 13.13)**.

30   Installation is the reverse of the removal steps.

14   Multi-point fuel injection (EFI) – component replacement

1   Most EFI sub-assemblies can be removed without removing the entire fuel charging assembly from the engine. In this case, however, the following steps must be taken:

   a) Make sure the ignition key is in the Off position.

   b) Drain the radiator (see Chapter 3).

   c) Disconnect the battery ground cable from the battery. Tie it back out of the way so it can't accidentally swing back and contact the battery terminal.

   d) Relieve the fuel system pressure (see Section 2).

   e) To disconnect the injector wiring harness, disconnect the ECT sensor in the heater line under the lower intake manifold and EEC harness.

   f) Disconnect the air bypass electrical connector from the EEC harness.

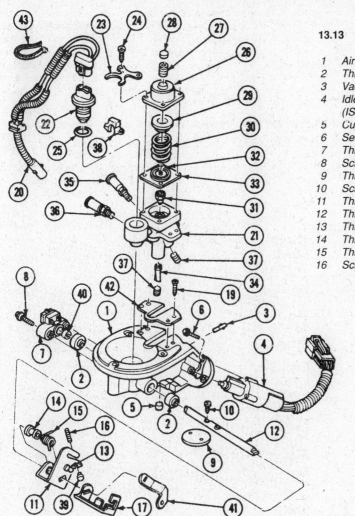

13.13 An exploded view of a typical fuel charging assembly

1	Air intake throttle body	17	Automatic transaxle linkage lever
2	Throttle shaft bearing	18	Fuel charging assembly main gasket
3	Vacuum transfer tube		
4	Idle speed control (ISC) motor	19	Screw
5	Cup plug	20	Wiring harness
6	Self-tapping screw	21	Fuel charging assembly main body
7	Throttle position sensor		
8	Screw	22	Fuel injector
9	Throttle plate	23	Fuel injector retainer
10	Screw	24	Screw
11	Throttle lever	25	O-ring
12	Throttle shaft	26	Pressure regulator cover
13	Throttle lever ball	27	Fuel pressure regulator adjusting screw (do not adjust)
14	Throttle linkage bearing		
15	Throttle return spring		
16	Screw	28	Expansion plug
		29	Fuel pressure regulator diaphragm cup
		30	Fuel pressure regulator diaphragm spring
		31	Fuel pressure regulator outlet tube
		32	Fuel pressure regulator body
		33	Fuel pressure regulator diaphragm
		34	Filter screen
		35	Fuel inlet line connector
		36	Fuel outlet line connector
		37	Plug
		38	Plug
		39	Locknut
		40	Spacer
		41	Throttle shaft lever
		42	Fuel charging body gasket
		43	Wiring harness retainer

4

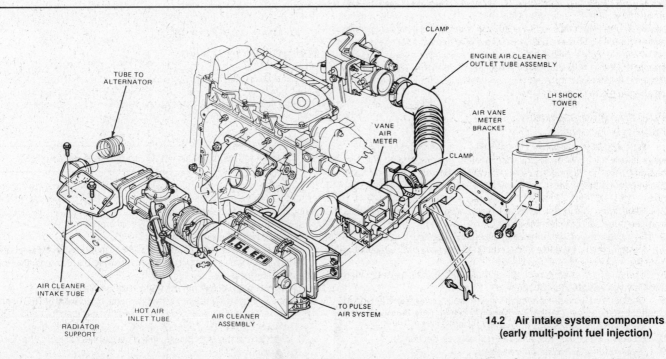

14.2 Air intake system components (early multi-point fuel injection)

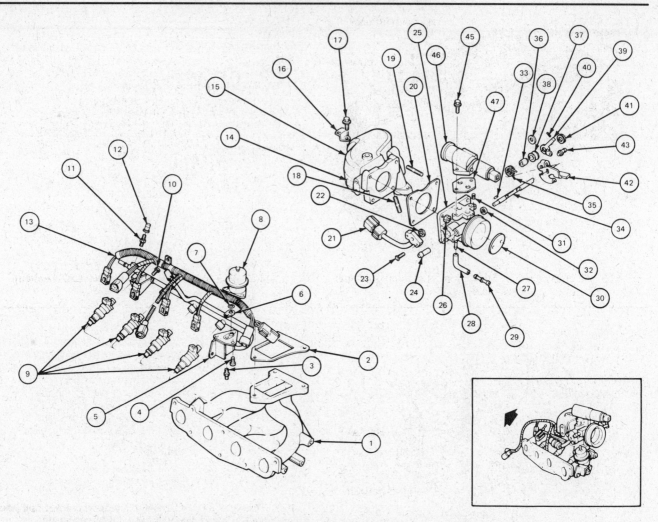

14.9   An exploded view of the early multi-point fuel injection system

1	Lower intake manifold	17	Bolt			
2	Upper intake manifold gasket	18	Stud	33	Pin	
3	Connector	19	Stud	34	Shaft	
4	Screw	20	Gasket	35	Throttle return spring	
5	Fuel rail assembly	21	Throttle position sensor	36	Bushing	
6	Fuel pressure regulator gasket	22	Throttle shaft bushing	37	Throttle linkage bearing	
7	O-ring	23	Screw and washer assembly	38	Throttle spring spacer	
8	Fuel pressure regulator	24	Emission inlet tube		(manual transaxle only)	
9	Fuel injector	25	Air intake throttle body	39	Transmission linkage lever	
10	Bolt	26	Nut	40	Screw	
11	Fuel pressure relief valve	27	Tube	41	Throttle shaft spacer	
12	Fuel pressure relief valve cap	28	Vacuum hose	42	Throttle lever	
13	Fuel charging assembly wiring harness	29	Connector	43	Throttle lever ball	
14	Identification decal	30	Air intake throttle plate	45	Bolt	
15	Upper intake manifold	31	Screw	46	Throttle air bypass valve	
16	Wiring harness retainer	32	Throttle shaft seal	47	Air bypass valve gasket	

Fuel charging/intake manifold assembly (early models)

Removal

Refer to illustrations 14.2 and 14.9

2   Loosen the clamps and detach the air cleaner outlet tube from the air intake throttle body **(see illustration)**.

3   Detach the throttle cable (and cruise control cable, if equipped) (refer to Section 9).

4   Label and disconnect the front and rear vacuum lines at the top of the manifold.

5   Remove the PCV system. To do this, label and remove the hoses, then unbolt the PCV separator bracket from the cylinder and take the PCV system off of the engine.

6   Label and disconnect the EGR valve vacuum line. Remove the two nuts that secure the EGR tube to the upper intake manifold and disconnect the tube.

7   Remove the dipstick, then remove the dipstick tube mounting nut and pull the dipstick tube out of the engine.

8   Disconnect the fuel return line.

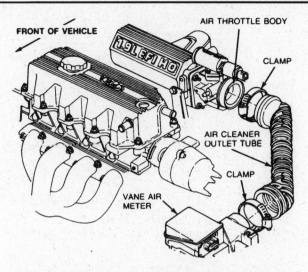

14.25 Air intake system components (later multi-point fuel injection system)

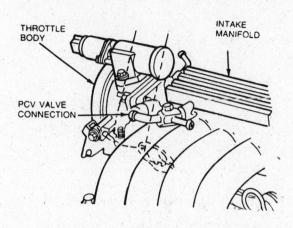

14.28 PCV system fitting (multi-point fuel injection)

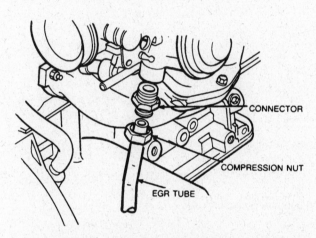

14.30 Hold the connector nut with a back-up wrench and disconnect the compression nut

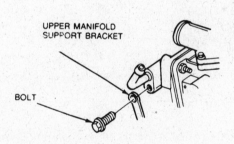

14.31 Remove the upper manifold support bracket bolt (shown) – the lower bolt need not be removed

4

9 Remove the manifold mounting nuts and take the fuel charging assembly off of the engine **(see illustration)**. Using a gasket scraper, remove all traces of old gasket material from the gasket mating surfaces, then clean the surfaces with a rag soaked in lacquer thinner or acetone. Be careful not to gouge the mating surfaces with the scraper.

Installation

10 Make sure the gasket surfaces on the cylinder head and fuel charging assembly are completely clean and free of warpage.
11 Clean the threads on the manifold studs and lubricate them lightly with clean engine oil.
12 Install a new gasket over the studs.
13 Place the fuel charging assembly over the studs. Install the top center nut only and tighten it finger-tight.
14 Connect the fuel return line to the fuel rail.
15 Install two more manifold nuts and tighten them finger-tight.
16 Install the dipstick tube in the engine. Install its attaching nut finger-tight.
17 Install the last three manifold nuts and tighten them finger-tight. Tighten all the manifold nuts in several stages to the torque listed in this Chapter's Specifications.
18 Coat the threads of the EGR tube nuts with oil and install the EGR tube.
19 The remainder of installation is the reverse of the removal steps.

Upper intake manifold (early models)

20 Loosen the clamps and detach the air cleaner outlet tube from the air intake throttle body **(see illustration 14.2)**.
21 Disconnect the electrical connectors from the throttle position sensor and air bypass valve.
22 Remove the three bolts that secure the upper intake manifold to the lower manifold, then lift the upper manifold off.
23 Using a gasket scraper, remove all traces of old gasket from the upper and lower manifolds, being careful not to gouge the gasket surfaces. Then wipe the surfaces clean with a cloth soaked in lacquer thinner or acetone.
24 Installation is the reverse of the removal steps. Tighten the manifold bolts to the torque listed in this Chapter's Specifications.

Fuel charging/intake manifold assembly (later models)

Refer to illustrations 14.25, 14.28, 14.30, 14.31 and 14.34
25 Loosen the clamps and detach the air cleaner outlet tube from the air intake throttle body **(see illustration)**.
26 Disconnect the throttle cable (and cruise control cable, if equipped) (see Section 9).
27 Label and disconnect the vacuum lines at the top of the manifold.
28 Disconnect the PCV system at the intake manifold and remove it **(see illustration)**.
29 Label and disconnect the EGR valve vacuum line.
30 Hold the EGR tube connector with a back-up wrench and loosen the compression nut **(see illustration)**. Disconnect the EGR tube.
31 Remove the top bolt (not the bottom bolt) that secures the upper manifold support bracket **(see illustration)**.

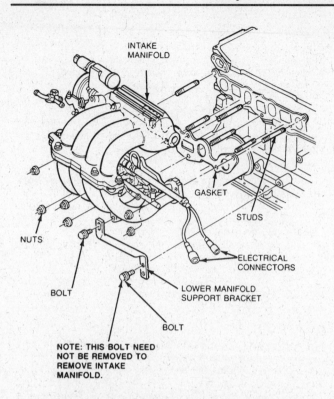

14.34   Intake manifold assembly (later multi-point fuel injection models)

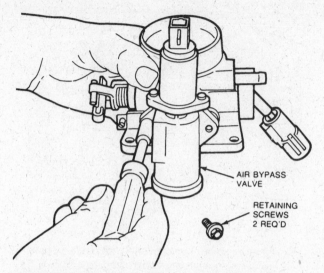

14.44   Remove the air bypass valve attaching screws . . .

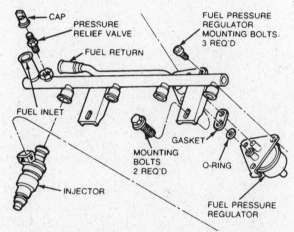

14.56   An exploded view of the fuel rail assembly

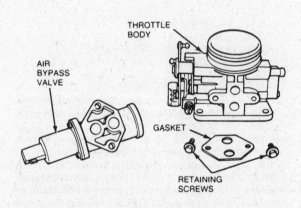

14.45   . . . then remove the valve and its gasket

32   Disconnect the electrical connectors at the main harness (near the intake manifold runner for No. 1 cylinder) and at the ECT sensor in the heater tube.

33   Disconnect the fuel inlet and return lines (see Section 3).

34   Remove the lower manifold mounting nuts **(see illustration)**. Remove the top bolt (not the bottom bolt) that secures the lower manifold support bracket, then take the fuel charging assembly off. Installation is the reverse of removal. Remove all traces of old gasket material with a scraper and wipe the gasket surfaces clean with a rag soaked in lacquer thinner or acetone. Install a new gasket.

Air intake throttle body
Removal
35   Detach the cable from the negative terminal of the battery.

36   Detach the throttle position sensor and throttle air bypass valve connectors. Loosen the hose clamps and disconnect the air cleaner outlet hose.

37   If equipped, remove the PCV vent closure hose at the throttle body.

38   Remove the throttle body mounting nuts or bolts **(see illustration 14.2 or 14.25)**

39   Carefully separate the throttle body from the upper intake manifold.

40   Remove and discard the gasket between the throttle body and the upper intake manifold.

Installation
41   Clean the gasket mating surfaces. If scraping is necessary, be careful not to damage the gasket surfaces or allow material to drop into the manifold. Installation is the reverse of removal. Be sure to tighten the throttle body mounting nuts to the torque listed in this Chapter's Specifications.

Air bypass valve assembly
Refer to illustrations 14.44 and 14.45

42   Detach the cable from the negative terminal of the battery.

43   Detach the air bypass valve assembly from the wiring harness.

44   Remove the two air bypass valve retaining screws **(see illustration)**.

45   Remove the air bypass valve and gasket **(see illustration)**.

46   Clean the gasket mating surface. If scraping is necessary, be careful not to damage the air bypass valve or throttle body gasket surfaces or drop material into the throttle body.

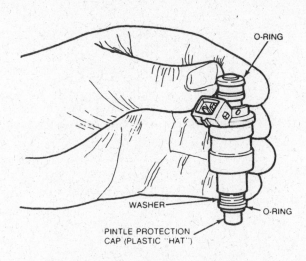

14.81 Note the proper location of the two injector O-rings, the washer and the plastic hat that protects the pintle

47 Installation is essentially the reverse of removal. Be sure to tighten the bolts securely.

Throttle Position (TP) sensor

48 Detach the cable from the negative terminal of the battery.
49 Detach the wiring harness from the throttle position sensor.
50 Remove the two throttle position sensor mounting screws.
51 Remove the throttle position sensor.
52 To install the sensor, position it on the throttle body with its wires pointing downward. Position its tangs over the blade on the throttle shaft, then turn the TPS clockwise (not counterclockwise) to align the mounting screw holes. If this procedure isn't followed exactly, idle speed may be too high.
53 The remainder of installation is the reverse of removal. Be sure to tighten the screws securely.

Fuel rail assembly

Refer to illustration 14.56

Removal

54 Relieve the fuel pressure (see Section 2).
55 Detach the cable from the negative terminal of the battery.
56 Disconnect the fuel inlet and return lines (see Section 3). Remove the two fuel rail assembly retaining bolts **(see illustration)**.
57 Disconnect the injector electrical connectors.
58 Carefully disengage the fuel rail from the fuel injectors and remove the fuel rail.
59 Use a rocking, side-to-side motion while lifting to separate the fuel rail from the injectors.

Installation

60 Ensure that the injector caps are clean and free of contamination.
61 Place the fuel injector fuel rail assembly over each of the injectors and seat the injectors into the fuel rail. Ensure that the injectors are well seated in the fuel rail assembly.
62 Hold the fuel rail down and secure it with the two retaining bolts. Tighten the bolts to the torque listed in this Chapter's Specifications.
63 Connect the fuel lines (Section 3).
64 Before you connect the injector wiring, turn the ignition key to Run so the fuel pump can pressurize the fuel injection system.
65 Wipe around the injectors and fuel line connections with a clean rag to check for leaks.
66 Connect the fuel injector connectors and run the engine for two minutes.
67 Turn the engine off and check for fuel leaks.

Fuel pressure regulator

Removal

68 Relieve the system fuel pressure (see Section 2).
69 Detach the cable from the negative terminal of the battery.
70 Remove the vacuum line at the pressure regulator.
71 Remove the three Allen retaining screws from the regulator housing.
72 Remove the pressure regulator assembly, gasket and O-ring. Discard the gasket and inspect the O-ring for signs of cracks or deterioration.
73 If scraping is necessary, be careful not to damage the fuel pressure regulator or fuel supply line gasket surfaces.

Installation

74 Lubricate the fuel pressure regulator O-ring with engine oil. **Note:** *Never use silicone grease. It will clog the injectors.*
75 Ensure that the gasket surfaces of the fuel pressure regulator and fuel rail assembly are clean.
76 Install the O-ring and new gasket on the regulator.
77 Install the fuel pressure regulator on the fuel rail assembly with new Allen screws. Tighten the three screws securely.
78 The remainder of installation is the reverse of removal.

Fuel injector

Refer to illustration 14.81

Removal

79 Relieve the system fuel pressure (see Section 2).
80 Remove the fuel rail assembly (see above).
81 Grasping the injector body, pull up while gently rocking the injector from side-to-side **(see illustration)**.
82 Check the two O-rings on each injector for signs of deterioration or damage. Replace any O-rings that are less than perfect.
83 Inspect the injector plastic "hat" (covering the injector pintle) and washer for signs of deterioration. Replace as required. If the hat is missing, look for it in the intake manifold.

Installation

84 Lubricate new O-rings with light grade oil ESE-M2C39-F or equivalent and install two on each injector. **Note:** *Do not use silicone grease. It will clog the injectors.*
85 Using a light, twisting motion, install the injector(s).
86 The remainder of installation is the reverse of removal.

Vane air meter

87 Loosen the hose clamp and detach the air intake tube from the vane air meter **(see illustration 14.2 for early models or 14.25 for later models)**.
88 Disconnect the air inlet tube from the air cleaner. Release the cover clips, then remove the air cleaner cover and filter element.
89 Remove the four screws and washers that secure the air cleaner tray to the vane air meter, then take the tray off. Check the gasket between air cleaner tray and vane air meter for damage or deterioration and replace as required. Remove all old gasket material, but don't damage the gasket surfaces if you have to scrape them.
90 Disconnect the vane air meter electrical connector.
91 Support the vane air meter so it won't fall and remove its three mounting screws. **Note:** *One of the screws is a different size from the other two. Label it so it can be reinstalled in the correct hole.*
92 Installation is the reverse of the removal steps.

---

15 Turbocharger

Removal and installation

Refer to illustrations 15.1, 15.3, 15.5, 15.10 and 15.13

1 The turbocharger is mounted low on the forward side of the engine **(see illustration)**. Make sure the engine has cooled overnight (or for several hours) before beginning work on the turbocharger.
2 Detach the cable from the negative terminal of the battery.

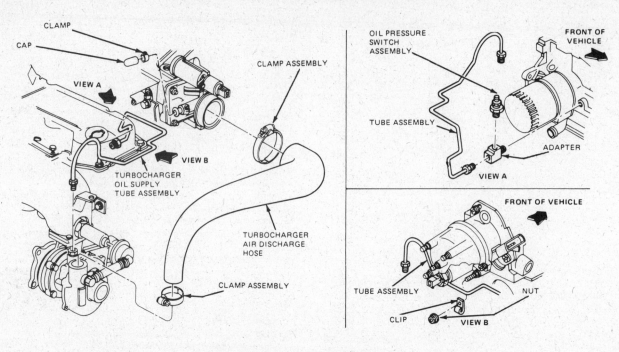

15.1   Turbocharger system components

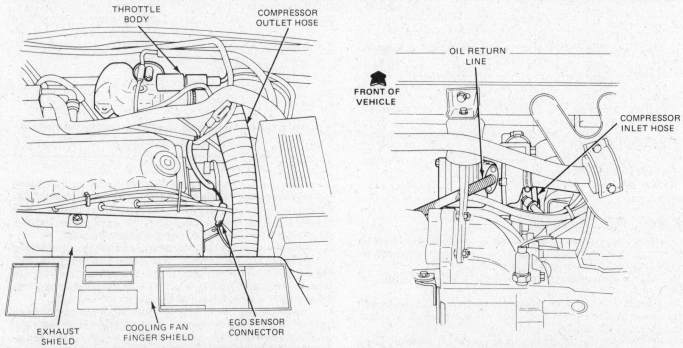

15.3   The cooling fan finger shield must be removed to gain access to the turbocharger mounting nuts

15.5   Disconnect the compressor inlet hose and oil return line – plug the line to keep it free of contaminants

3   Remove the cooling fan finger shield **(see illustration)**.
4   Loosen the clamps and disconnect the air discharge hose **(see illustration 15.1)**.
5   Loosen the clamp and disconnect the compressor inlet hose **(see illustration)**.
6   Remove the alternator and its mounting bracket (see Chapter 5).
7   Disconnect the oxygen (EGO) sensor electrical connector **(see illustration 15.3)**.
8   Jack up the vehicle and support it securely on jackstands. Disconnect the oil return line from the bottom of the turbocharger **(see illustra-**

tion 15.5).
9   Remove the jackstands and lower the vehicle.
10   Remove the nuts that secure the exhaust pipe to the turbocharger **(see illustration)**.
11   Unbolt the exhaust shield from the water outlet connector **(see illustration 15.3)**.
12   Detach the oil feed line from the top of the turbocharger **(see illustration 15.10)**.
13   Detach the exhaust manifold from the cylinder head **(see illustration)**. Separate the manifold from the head far enough to

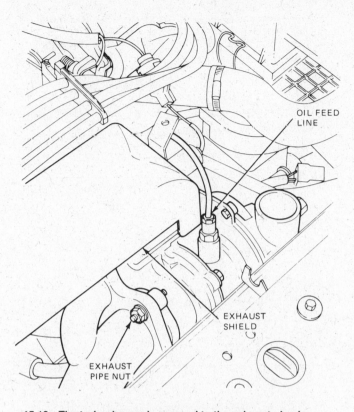

15.10 The turbocharger is secured to the exhaust pipe by three nuts

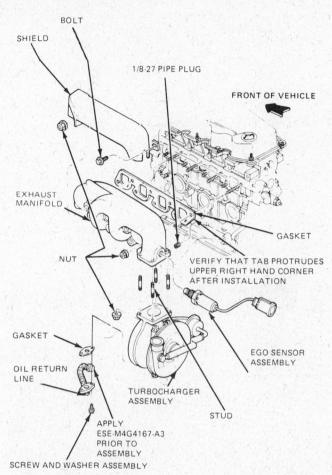

15.13 Exhaust manifold components (turbocharged models)

provide removal clearance for the exhaust shield. Lift off the shield, then remove the exhaust manifold and turbocharger as an assembly.

14 Remove four turbocharger-to-manifold nuts, then take the turbocharger off the manifold.

15 Installation is the reverse of the removal steps. Use a new exhaust manifold-to-cylinder head gasket.

16 After installation, run the engine for 30 to 60 seconds. Check for oil, water, intake and exhaust leaks.

Bearing clearance check

17 Use your fingers to push the turbocharger blade shaft assembly as far as it will go in one direction. Spin the shaft by hand and listen for metal-to-metal rubbing sounds inside the turbocharger.

18 Push the shaft in the opposite direction as far as it will go. Again, spin the shaft and listen for rubbing sounds.

19 Rubbing sounds indicate that the turbine blade or the compressor blade is touching the inside of its housing due to worn bearings. The turbocharger should be replaced.

20 If neither blade comes in contact with the housing, the bearings are good.

---

16 Exhaust system components – replacement

Warning: *Never attempt to service any part of the exhaust system until it has cooled. Be especially careful when working around the catalytic converter. The temperature of the converter rises to a high level after only a few minutes of engine operation and, once the engine reaches its operating temperature, can remain high enough to cause burns for a long time after the engine is shut off. Also, when working under the vehicle, make sure you support it securely with jackstands.*

1 The exhaust system consists of the exhaust manifold, the catalytic converter, the muffler, the tailpipe and connecting pipes, brackets, hangers and clamps. The exhaust system is attached to the body with mounting brackets and rubber hangers. If any of the parts are improperly installed, excessive noise and vibration will be transferred to the body.

2 Conduct regular inspections of the exhaust system to keep it safe and quiet. Look for any damaged or bent parts, open seams, holes, loose connections, excessive corrosion or other defects which could allow exhaust fumes to enter the vehicle. Deteriorated exhaust system components should not be repaired; they should be replaced with new parts.

3 If the exhaust system components are extremely corroded or rusted together, welding equipment will probably be required to remove them. The convenient way to accomplish this is to have a muffler repair shop remove the corroded sections with a cutting torch. If, however, you want to save money by doing yourself (and you don't have a welding outfit with a cutting torch), simply cut off the old components with a hacksaw. If you have compressed air, special pneumatic cutting chisels can also be used. If you decide to tackle the job at home, be sure to wear safety goggles to protect your eyes from metal chips and work gloves to protect your hands.

4 Here are some simple guidelines to follow when repairing the exhaust system:

   a) Work from the back to the front when removing exhaust system components.
   b) Apply penetrating oil to the exhaust system components fasteners to make them easier to remove.
   c) Use new gaskets, hangers and clamps when installing exhaust system components.

d) Apply anti-seize compound to the threads of all exhaust system fasteners during reassembly.

e) Be sure to allow sufficient clearance between newly installed parts and all points on the underbody to avoid overheating the floor pan and possibly damaging the interior carpet and insulation. Pay particularly close attention to the catalytic converter and heat shield.

Chapter 5   Engine electrical systems

Contents

Specifications

Drivebelt deflection .... See Chapter 1

Battery voltage

Engine off	12 volts (approximately)
Engine running	
With external voltage regulator	Battery voltage plus 2 volts maximum
With internal voltage regulator	Battery voltage plus 2.5 volts maximum

Ignition coil

Ignition coil-to-distributor cap wire resistance
Duraspark II and TFI-I systems .... 5000 ohms per inch
TFI-IV system .... 5000 ohms per foot
Ignition coil resistance
Duraspark II system
1981
Primary resistance .... 1 to 2 ohms
Secondary resistance .... 7.7 to 9.6 K-ohms
1982 and 1983
Primary resistance .... 0.8 to 1.6 ohms
Secondary resistance .... 7.7 to 10.5 K-ohms
Ballast resistor .... 0.8 to 1.6 ohms
TFI-I and TFI-IV systems
Primary resistance .... 0.3 to 1.0 ohms
Secondary resistance .... 8.0 to 11.5 K-ohms

Distributor

Stator assembly wiring harness to ground
resistance (Duraspark II) .... 70,000 ohms minimum
Stator assembly and wiring harness
resistance (Duraspark II) .... 400 to 1300 ohms
Stator assembly resistance (Duraspark II) .... 650 to 1300 ohms
Stator assembly and module resistance (TFI-I) .... 650 to 1300 ohms

Alternator/voltage regulator

Resistance at regulator F terminal (external regulator)
1981 through 1983 .... 3 ohms minimum
1984 and later .... 2.4 ohms minimum
Resistance at regulator A and F terminal
screws (internal regulator) .... 2.4 ohms minimum

---

1   General information

The engine electrical systems include all ignition, charging and starting components. Because of their engine-related functions, these components are considered separately from chassis electrical devices like the lights, instruments, etc.

2.2   The battery hold-down clamp and bolt (arrow) are located alongside the battery in the left front corner of the engine compartment – always disconnect the negative cable first, as shown here, and reconnect it last to prevent a possible battery explosion

Be very careful when working on the engine electrical components. They are easily damaged if checked, connected or handled improperly. The alternator is driven by an engine drivebelt which could cause serious injury if your hands, hair or clothes become entangled in it with the engine running. Both the starter and alternator are connected directly to the battery and could arc or even cause a fire if mishandled, overloaded or shorted out.

Never leave the ignition switch on for long periods of time with the engine off. Don't disconnect the battery cables while the engine is running. Correct polarity must be maintained when connecting battery cables from another source, such as another vehicle, during jump starting. Always disconnect the negative cable first and hook it up last. Connecting the positive cable when the negative cable is already hooked up can cause a spark, which could ignite hydrogen gas around the battery, causing the battery to explode.

Additional safety related information on the engine electrical systems can be found in *Safety first* near the front of this manual. It should be referred to before beginning any operation included in this Chapter.

2   Battery – removal and installation

Refer to illustration 2.2

1   Disconnect both cables from the battery terminals. **Caution:** *Always disconnect the negative cable first and hook it up last or the battery may explode.*

2   Locate the battery hold-down clamp in the left front corner of the engine compartment **(see illustration)**. Remove the bolt and the hold-down clamp.

3   Lift out the battery. Special straps that attach to the battery posts are available – lifting and moving the battery is much easier if you use one. **Caution:** *Don't let battery acid drip on your clothes; it will stain or eat holes in them.*

4   Installation is the reverse of removal.

3 Battery – emergency jump starting

Refer to the *Booster battery (jump) starting* procedure at the front of this manual.

4 Battery cables – check and replacement

1   Periodically inspect the entire length of each battery cable for damage, cracked or burned insulation and corrosion. Poor battery cable connections can cause starting problems and decreased engine performance.

2   Check the cable-to-terminal connections at the ends of the cables for cracks, loose wire strands and corrosion. The presence of white, fluffy deposits under the insulation at the cable terminal connection is a sign that the cable is corroded and should be replaced. Check the terminals for distortion, missing mounting bolts and corrosion.

3   When replacing the cables, always disconnect the negative cable first and hook it up last. **Warning:** *Connecting the positive cable with the negative cable already connected can cause a spark, which can ignite hydrogen gas around the battery and cause the battery to explode. Even if only the positive cable is being replaced, be sure to disconnect the negative cable from the battery first.*

4   Disconnect and remove the cable. Make sure the replacement cable is the same length and diameter.

5   Clean the threads of the relay or ground connection with a wire brush to remove rust and corrosion. Apply a light coat of petroleum jelly to the threads to prevent future corrosion.

6   Attach the cable to the relay or ground connection and tighten the mounting nut/bolt securely.

7   Before connecting the new cable to the battery, make sure it reaches the battery post without having to be stretched.

8   Connect the positive cable first, followed by the negative cable.

5 Ignition system – general information

The Duraspark II ignition system is used on all 1981 models, as well as on 1982 models with manual transaxles. The TFI-I ignition system is used on 1982 automatic transaxle models as well as 1983 and later carbureted models. The TFI-IV ignition system is used on 1983 through 1986 fuel-injected models, as well as all 1987 and later models.

All Escort/Lynx ignition systems are solid state electronic designs consisting of an ignition module, coil, distributor, the spark plug wires and the spark plugs. Mechanically, the system is similar to a breaker point system, except that the distributor cam and ignition points are replaced by an armature and magnetic pickup unit (Duraspark II and TFI-I ignition) or Hall effect switch (TFI-IV ignition).

When the ignition is switched on, the ignition primary circuit is energized. When the rotating armature spokes approach the magnetic coil assembly or the Hall effect switch vanes approach the permanent magnet, a voltage is induced which signals the amplifier to turn off the coil primary current.

When it's on, current flows from the battery through the ignition switch, the coil primary winding, the ignition module and then to ground. When the current is interrupted, the magnetic field in the ignition coil collapses, inducing a high voltage in the coil secondary windings. The voltage is conducted to the distributor where the rotor directs it to the appropriate spark plug. This process is repeated continuously.

The TFI-IV type distributor is similar to the Duraspark II and TFI-I models but has neither a centrifugal nor a vacuum advance mechanism (advance is handled by the computer instead). The TFI-IV module does, however, include a "push start" mode that allows push starting of the vehicle if necessary.

Vehicles equipped with the Duraspark II ignition module have an oil filled coil; vehicles equipped with the TFI-I or TFI-IV module use the "E-core" type ignition coil.

6.2 To use a calibrated ignition tester (available at most auto parts stores), simply disconnect a spark plug wire, attach the wire to the tester, clip the tester to a convenient ground (like a valve cover bolt) and operate the starter – if there's enough power to fire the plug, sparks will be visible between the electrode tip and the tester body

6 Ignition system – check

Refer to illustration 6.2

Warning: *Because of the very high secondary (spark plug) voltage generated by the ignition system, extreme care should be taken when this check is done.*

1   If the engine turns over but won't start, disconnect the spark plug lead from any spark plug and attach it to a calibrated ignition tester (available at most auto parts stores). If you don't have a tester, go to the next Step.

2   Connect the clip on the tester to a bolt or metal bracket on the engine **(see illustration)**, crank the engine and watch the end of the tester to see if bright blue, well-defined sparks occur. If a calibrated tester isn't available, remove the wire from one of the spark plugs. Pull back the spark plug boot and, using an insulated tool, hold the wire about 1/4-inch from a good ground and have an assistant crank the engine.

3   If sparks occur, sufficient voltage is reaching the plug to fire it (repeat the check at the remaining plug wires to verify that the distributor cap and rotor are OK). However, the plugs themselves may be fouled, so remove and check them as described in Chapter 1 or install new ones.

4   If no sparks or intermittent sparks occur, remove the distributor cap and check the cap and rotor as described in Chapter 1. If moisture is present, use WD-40 (or something similar) to dry out the cap and rotor, then reinstall the cap and repeat the spark test.

5   If there's still no spark, detach the secondary coil wire from the distributor cap and hook it up to the tester (reattach the plug wire to the spark plug), then repeat the spark check.

6   If no sparks occur, check the primary (small) wire connections at the coil to make sure they're clean and tight. Refer to Section 7 and check the ignition coil supply voltage circuit. Make any necessary repairs, then repeat the check again.

7   If sparks now occur, the distributor cap, rotor, plug wire(s) or spark plug(s) (or all of them) may be defective.

8   If there's still no spark, the coil-to-cap wire may be bad (check the resistance with an ohmmeter and compare it to the Specifications). If a known good wire doesn't make any difference in the test results, the ignition coil, module or other internal components may be defective.

5

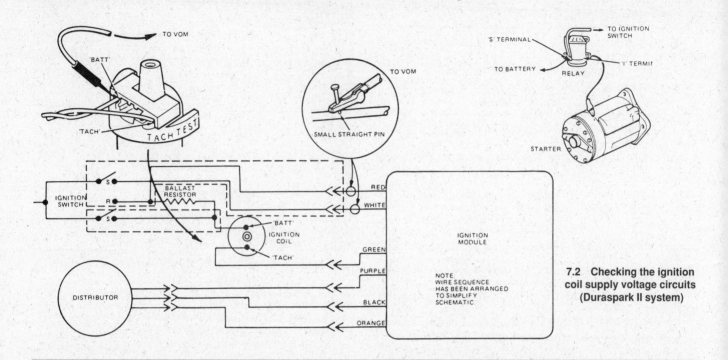

7.2   Checking the ignition coil supply voltage circuits (Duraspark II system)

---

7   Ignition coil and circuits – check and coil replacement

Duraspark II system

Supply voltage circuits

Refer to illustrations 7.2 and 7.6

1   If you've been referred to this Section from the preliminary ignition system check in Section 6, remove the spark tester if you have not already done so and reconnect the spark plug wire to the spark plug.

2   If the starter relay has a terminal labeled I, detach the cable from the starter relay to the starter motor **(see illustration)**.

3   If the starter relay doesn't have a terminal labeled I, detach the wire to the S terminal of the relay.

4   Carefully insert small straight pins into the red and white module wires. **Caution:** *Don't allow the pins to ground on anything.*

5   Check the battery voltage with a voltmeter and record it for reference later.

6   Check the voltage at the points indicated with the ignition switch in various positions **(see illustration)**. **Note:** *Attach the negative lead of the voltmeter to the distributor base and wiggle the wires in the wiring harness when performing the voltage checks.*

7   If the indicated voltage readings are 90-percent or more of battery voltage, the supply voltage circuit is okay. Refer to Step 12.

8   If the indicated voltage readings are less than 90-percent of battery voltage, check the wiring harness and connector(s). Inspect the ignition switch for wear and/or damage (see Chapter 12).

9   Turn the ignition switch to the Off position.

10   Remove the straight pins.

11   Reattach any cables/wires removed from the starter relay.

Ignition coil supply voltage

Refer to illustration 7.12

12   Attach the negative lead of a voltmeter to the distributor base **(see illustration)**.

13   Turn the ignition switch to the Run position.

14   Attach the positive lead of the voltmeter to the BATT terminal on the ignition coil.

WIRE/ TERMINAL	CIRCUIT	IGNITION SWITCH TEST POSITION
RED	RUN	RUN
WHITE	START	START
'BATT' TERMINAL IGNITION COIL	BALLAST RESISTOR BYPASS	START

7.6   Check the supply voltage circuit terminals with the switch in the indicated positions (Duraspark II system)

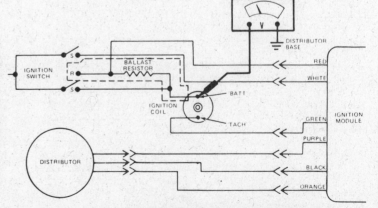

7.12   Checking the ignition coil supply voltage (Duraspark II system)

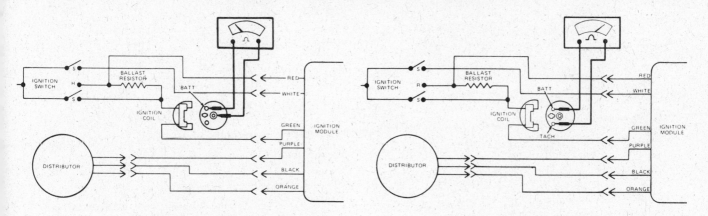

7.19   Checking ignition coil secondary resistance (Duraspark II system)

7.24   Checking the ignition coil primary resistance (Duraspark II system)

15   If the indicated voltage is six-to-eight volts, refer to the distributor stator assembly and wiring harness check in Section 11.

16   If the indicated voltage is less than six or more than eight volts, refer to Step 23.

17   Turn the ignition switch to the Off position.

Ignition coil secondary resistance

Refer to illustration 7.19

18   Disconnect and inspect the ignition coil wires and connector.

19   Using an ohmmeter, check the resistance between the BATT terminal and the center terminal of the coil **(see illustration).**

20   If the resistance is correct (refer to this Chapter's Specifications), the coil secondary circuit is normal. Refer to the ignition module check in Section 10.

21   If the indicated resistance is less or more than the specified resistance, replace the ignition coil (see Step 89).

22   Reconnect the coil wires.

Ignition coil primary resistance

Refer to illustration 7.24

23   Detach the ignition coil wires.

24   Using an ohmmeter, measure the primary resistance between the BATT and TACH terminals **(see illustration).**

25   If the resistance is as listed in this Chapter's Specifications, the ignition coil primary resistance is normal. Check the primary circuit continuity (see Step 28).

26   If the indicated resistance is less or more than the specified resis-

tance, replace the ignition coil (see Step 89).

27   Reconnect the coil wire.

Primary circuit continuity

Refer to illustration 7.28

28   Carefully insert a small straight pin into the ignition module green wire **(see illustration)**. Refer to Section 10 for a more detailed illustration of the module terminals. **Caution:** *Don't allow the straight pin to ground against anything.*

29   Attach the negative lead of a voltmeter to the distributor base.

30   Turn the ignition switch to the Run position.

31   Measure the voltage at the green module wire.

32   If the indicated voltage is greater than 1.5-volts, check the module (see Section 10).

33   If the indicated voltage is 1.5-volts or less, inspect the wiring harness and the connectors between the ignition module and the coil.

34   Turn the ignition switch to the Off position.

35   Remove the straight pin.

Ballast resistor

Refer to illustration 7.38

36   Separate and inspect the ignition module two-wire connector with the red and white wires.

37   Unplug and inspect the ignition coil connector.

38   Attach the leads from an ohmmeter to the BATT terminal of the ignition coil and the red wire in the module connector **(see illustration).**

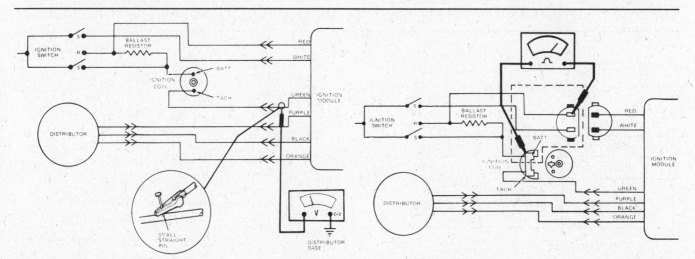

7.28   Checking primary circuit continuity (Duraspark II system)

7.38   Checking the ballast resistor (Duraspark II system)

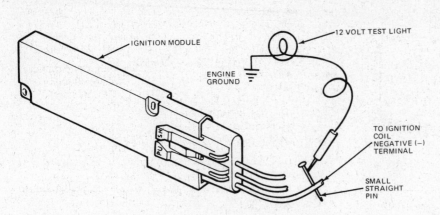

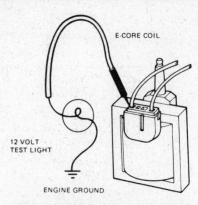

7.42a   Checking ignition coil primary circuit switching (TFI-I system)

7.42b   Checking ignition coil primary circuit switching (TFI-IV system) – the test light should blink on-and-off when the engine is cranked

39   If the indicated resistance is the same as the specified primary resistance, the problem is either intermittent or not in the ignition system.

40   If the indicated resistance is less or more than the specified primary resistance, replace the ballast resistor.

TFI-I and TFI-IV systems

Ignition coil primary circuit

Refer to illustrations 7.42a and 7.42b

41   TFI-IV only: Unplug the electrical connector from the ignition module. Inspect it for dirt, corrosion and damage (refer to Section 10 for a detailed illustration of the connector terminals), then plug it back in.

42   On TFI-I systems, insert a small straight pin through the ignition coil negative terminal wire about one-inch from the ignition module. Connect a 12-volt DC test light between the pin and a good ground **(see illustration)**. On TFI-IV systems, connect a 12-volt DC test light between the coil TACH terminal and a good engine ground **(see illustration)**.

43   Crank the engine.

44   If the light flashes, or comes on but doesn't flash, refer to Step 47.

45   If the light stays off or is very dim, refer to Step 56.

46   Remove the test light.

Ignition coil primary resistance

Refer to illustration 7.49

47   Turn the ignition switch to Off.

48   Unplug the ignition coil electrical connector. Inspect it for dirt, corrosion and damage.

49   Using an ohmmeter, measure the resistance between the primary terminals of the ignition coil **(see illustration)**.

50   If the indicated resistance is within the limits listed in this Chapter's Specifications, proceed to Step 52.

51   If the indicated resistance is less or more than specified, replace the ignition coil (see Step 89).

Ignition coil secondary resistance

Refer to illustration 7.52

52   Measure the resistance from the negative primary terminal to the secondary terminal of the ignition coil **(see illustration)**.

53   If the indicated resistance is within the limits listed in this Chapter's Specifications, proceed to Step 65.

54   If the indicated resistance is less or more than the specified resistance, replace the ignition coil (see Step 89).

55   Reconnect the ignition coil wires.

Primary circuit continuity

Refer to illustrations 7.59a and 7.59b

56   Unplug the electrical connector from the ignition module. Inspect it for dirt, corrosion and damage.

57   Attach the negative lead of a voltmeter to the distributor base.

58   Measure battery voltage and record it for future reference.

59   Attach the positive lead of the voltmeter to a small straight pin inserted into connector terminal 1 (TFI) or 2 (TFI-IV) **(see illustrations)**. **Caution:** *Don't allow the straight pin to ground against anything.*

60   Turn the ignition switch to the Run position and measure the terminal 2 voltage.

61   If the measured voltage is 90-percent of battery voltage, proceed to the wiring harness check (see Step 65).

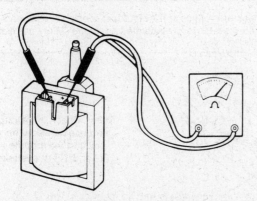

7.49   Measuring ignition coil primary resistance (TFI-I and TFI-IV systems)

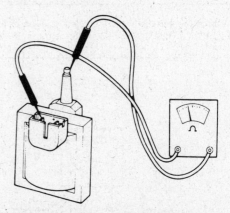

7.52   Measuring ignition coil secondary resistance (TFI-I and TFI-IV systems)

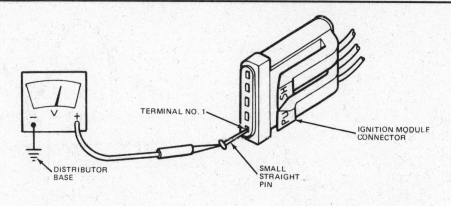

7.59a   Checking primary circuit continuity (TFI-I system)

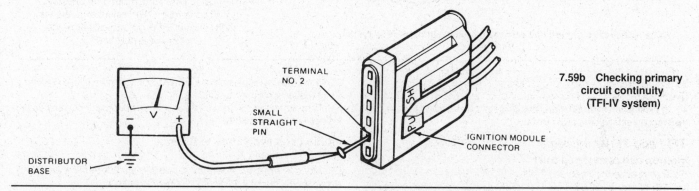

7.59b   Checking primary circuit continuity (TFI-IV system)

62   If the measured voltage is less than 90-percent of battery voltage, proceed to Step 75.

63   Turn the ignition switch to the Off position.

64   Remove the straight pin.

Wiring harness

Refer to illustrations 7.69a, 7.69b and 7.69c

65   Unplug the electrical connector from the ignition module. Inspect it for dirt, corrosion and damage.

66   Disconnect the wire at the S terminal of the starter relay.

67   Attach the negative lead of a voltmeter to the distributor base.

68   Measure battery voltage and record it for future reference.

69   Using the accompanying table (**see illustrations**), measure the connector terminal voltage by attaching the positive lead of the voltmeter to a small straight pin inserted into the connector terminals, one at a time, with the ignition switch in the position shown in the table (**see illustration**).

5

CONNECTOR TERMINAL	WIRE/CIRCUIT	IGNITION SWITCH TEST POSITION
#1	TO IGNITION COIL (–) TERMINAL	RUN
#2	RUN CIRCUIT	RUN AND START
#3	START CIRCUIT	START

7.69a   Check the voltage at the electrical connector terminals with the ignition switch in the indicated positions (TFI-I system)

CONNECTOR TERMINAL	WIRE/CIRCUIT	IGNITION SWITCH TEST POSITION
#2	TO IGNITION COIL (–) TERMINAL	RUN
#3	RUN CIRCUIT	RUN AND START
#4	START CIRCUIT	START

7.69b   Check the voltage at the electrical connector terminals with the ignition switch in the indicated positions (TFI-IV system)

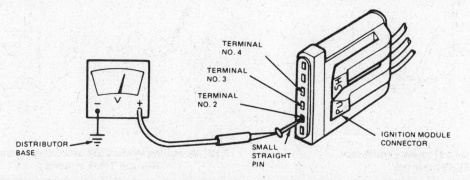

7.69c   Check the wiring harness between the coil and the module (TFI-I and TFI-IV systems)

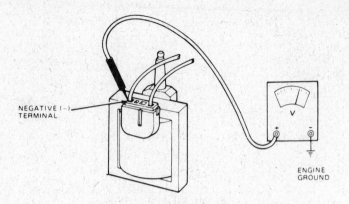

**7.78   Measuring ignition coil primary voltage
(TFI-I and TFI-IV systems)**

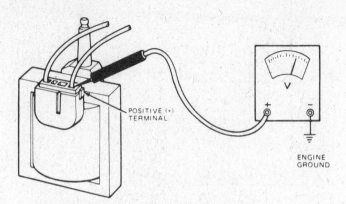

**7.86   Measuring ignition coil supply voltage
(TFI-I and TFI-IV systems)**

70   If the indicated voltage is 90-percent of battery voltage at all three terminals:

   a)   TFI-I system: Check the stator and ignition module (see Section 10).

   b)   TFI-IV system: Refer to the EEC-IV/TFI-IV check in Section 10.

71   If the indicated voltage is less than 90-percent of battery voltage, inspect the wiring harness and the connectors. Check the ignition switch for damage or wear (refer to Chapter 12).

72   Turn the ignition switch to the Off position.

73   Remove the straight pin.

74   Reconnect the wire to the S terminal of the starter relay.

Ignition coil primary voltage

Refer to illustration 7.78

75   Attach the negative lead of a voltmeter to the distributor base.

76   Measure battery voltage and record it.

77   Turn the ignition switch to the Run position.

78   Measure the voltage at the negative terminal of the ignition coil **(see illustration)**.

79   If the indicated voltage is 90-percent of battery voltage, inspect the wiring harness between the ignition module and the coil negative terminal.

80   If the indicated voltage is less than 90-percent of battery voltage, inspect the wiring harness between the ignition module and the coil negative terminal, then proceed to Step 82.

81   Turn the ignition switch to the Off position.

Ignition coil supply voltage

Refer to illustration 7.86

82   Unplug the ignition coil wire harness.

83   Attach the negative lead of a voltmeter to the distributor base.

84   Measure battery voltage.

85   Turn the ignition switch to the Run position.

86   Measure the voltage at the positive terminal of the ignition coil **(see illustration)**.

87   If the indicated voltage is 90-percent of battery voltage, inspect the ignition coil connector and terminals for dirt, corrosion and damage. If both the connector and terminals are clean, replace the ignition coil (see Step 89).

88   If the indicated voltage is less than 90-percent of battery voltage. inspect and repair the circuit between the ignition coil and the ignition switch. Check the ignition switch for damage and wear (see Chapter 12).

Ignition coil replacement

89   Detach the cable from the negative terminal of the battery.

90   Detach the wires from the primary terminals on the coil (some coils have a single connector for the primary wires).

91   Unplug the coil secondary lead.

92   Remove both bracket bolts and detach the coil.

93   Installation is the reverse of removal.

---

8   Distributor – removal and installation

Refer to illustrations 8.3, 8.4, 8.5a and 8.5b

Removal

1   Detach the cable from the negative terminal of the battery.

2   Unhook the rubber shield that surrounds the distributor cap (if equipped) and unwrap it from the distributor. Detach the coil secondary wire from the coil and the wires from the plugs, then remove the distributor cap and wires as an assembly (see Chapter 1).

3   Unplug the module electrical connector **(see illustration)**.

4   Make a mark on the edge of the distributor base directly below the rotor tip and in line with it (if the rotor on your engine has more than one tip, use the center one for reference). Also, mark the distributor base and the engine block to ensure that the distributor is installed correctly **(see illustration)**.

8.3   Unplug the module electrical connector (arrow) from the base of the distributor (TFI-IV ignition shown, others similar)

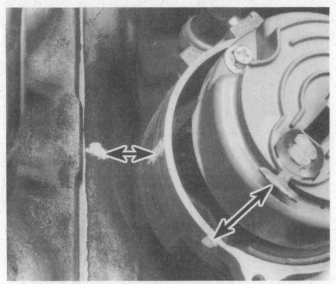

8.4   Mark the position of the rotor on the edge of the distributor base (arrow) and paint or scribe alignment marks on the distributor base and the block to ensure proper reinstallation

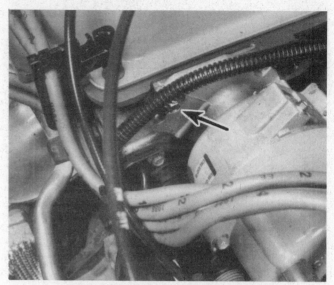

8.5a   Remove the distributor hold-down bolts (arrow)

5   Remove the distributor hold-down bolts **(see illustrations)**, then pull the distributor straight out to remove it. **Caution:** *If the crankshaft is turned while the distributor is removed, or if a new distributor is required, the alignment marks will be useless.*

Installation

Crankshaft not turned after distributor removal

6   Before installation, rotate the distributor shaft by hand to make sure it spins freely. Make sure the distributor shaft O-ring and drive coupling spring are installed.

7   Insert the distributor into the engine in exactly the same relationship to the block that it was in when removed. The tang on the end of the distributor shaft is offset so it will only go in one way. If the distributor shaft is 180-degrees out of position, the tang won't fit into the end of the camshaft.

Crankshaft turned after distributor removal

8   Refer to Chapter 2 and position the number one piston at TDC on the compression stroke.

9   Position the offset tang on the distributor shaft to align with the slot in the end of the camshaft.

10   Lower the distributor into place.

Final installation

11   With the base of the distributor seated against the block, turn the distributor to align the marks made on the distributor base and the block.

12   With the distributor marks aligned, the rotor should be pointing at the alignment mark you made on the distributor housing before removal.

13   Install the hold-down bolts and tighten them until the distributor body can just be rotated by hand.

14   Install the distributor cap and tighten the cap screws securely.

15   Plug in the module electrical connector.

16   Reattach the spark plug wires to the plugs.

17   Connect the cable to the negative terminal of the battery.

18   Check the ignition timing (see Section 9) and tighten the distributor hold-down bolts securely.

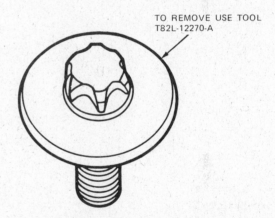

TO REMOVE USE TOOL
T82L-12270-A

8.5b   Some models use security type hold-down bolts – a special tool is required to remove them

ditional steps or a different procedure. If it does, follow the label instructions.

1   Apply the parking brake and block the wheels. Place the transaxle in Park (automatic) or Neutral (manual). Turn off all accessories (heater, air conditioner, etc.).

2   Start the engine and warm it up. Once it has reached operating temperature, turn it off.

3   If the distributor has a vacuum advance line, disconnect and plug the hose (not the fitting on the distributor).

4   If the vehicle has a barometric pressure switch (early models), disconnect it from the ignition module and connect a jumper wire between its terminals (yellow and black wires) at the ignition module connector.

5   Disconnect the single white or black wire at the connector near the distributor (if equipped).

6   Connect an inductive timing light and a tachometer in accordance with the manufacturer's instructions. **Caution:** *Make sure that the timing light and tach wires don't hang anywhere near the electric cooling fan or they may become entangled in the fan blades when it comes on.*

---

9   Ignition timing – check and adjustment

Refer to illustration 9.7

Note: *This procedure applies to all models. However, check the Vehicle Emission Control Information label on your vehicle to see if it specifies ad-*

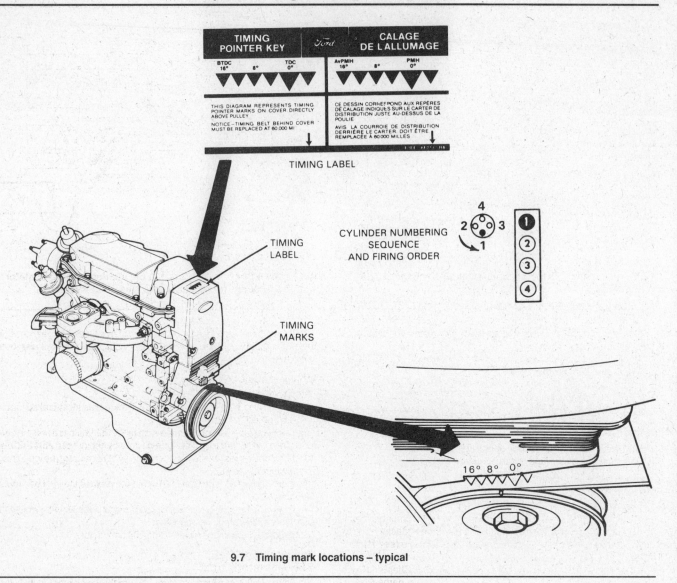

9.7 Timing mark locations – typical

7   Locate the timing notch in the crankshaft pulley and the timing scale on the front of the engine **(see illustration)**. If the timing scale is dirty, wipe it off with a rag soaked in solvent.

8   Start the engine again.

9   Point the timing light at the timing marks and note whether the timing notch is aligned with the correct mark on the scale.

10   If the proper mark isn't aligned with the stationary pointer, loosen the distributor hold down bolts. Turn the distributor to change timing until the correct timing mark on the flywheel/driveplate is aligned with the stationary pointer. Tighten the distributor hold-down bolts securely when the timing is correct and recheck it to make sure it didn't change when the bolt was tightened.

11   Turn off the engine.

12   Plug in the single wire connector, attach the vacuum hoses, remove the jumper wire and reconnect the barometric pressure switch (if equipped).

13   Restart the engine and check the idle speed. Note that the specified rpm for automatic and manual transaxle equipped vehicles is different. If it's incorrect on carbureted models, adjust it (see Chapter 4). Because fuel-injected models are equipped with automatic idle speed control, idle rpm is not adjustable. If the idle rpm is not within the specified range, take the vehicle to a dealer service department or other repair shop. Adjustment requires specialized test equipment and procedures that are beyond the scope of the home mechanic.

14   Turn off the engine.

15   Remove the timing light and tachometer.

---

10   Ignition module and circuits – check and module replacement

Caution: *The ignition module is a delicate and relatively expensive electronic component. The following tests must be done with the right equipment by someone that knows how to use it properly. Failure to follow the step-by-step procedures could result in damage to the module and/or other electronic devices, including the EEC-IV microprocessor itself (in TFI-IV vehicles). Additionally, all devices under computer control are protected by a Federally mandated extended warranty. Check with your dealer before attempting to diagnose them yourself.*

Check

Duraspark II system

Ignition module voltage

Refer to illustration 10.2

1   Turn the ignition switch off.

2   Carefully insert a small straight pin into the red module wire **(see illustration)**. **Caution:** *Don't allow the straight pin to ground against anything.*

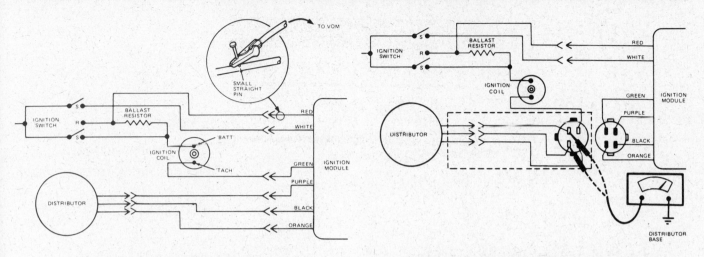

10.2   Checking ignition module voltage (Duraspark II system)

10.11   Measuring the resistance of the ignition module-to-stator assembly wiring harness (Duraspark II system)

3   Attach the negative lead of a voltmeter to the distributor base.

4   Measure battery voltage.

5   Attach the positive voltmeter lead to the pin in the red module wire with the ignition switch in the Run position.

6   If the measured voltage is 90-percent of battery voltage, check the ballast resistor (see Section 7).

7   If the measured voltage is less than 90-percent of the battery voltage, inspect the wiring harness between the module and the ignition switch. Also inspect the ignition switch for wear and damage (see Chapter 12).

8   Turn the ignition switch to the Off position.

9   Detach the voltmeter and remove the straight pin.

Ignition module wiring harness
Refer to illustration 10.11

10   Attach one lead of an ohmmeter to the distributor base.

11   Check the resistance between the wiring harness terminals mating with the black and purple module wires and ground by attaching the remaining ohmmeter lead to the wire terminals one at a time **(see illustration)**.

12   If the resistance is greater than the value listed in this Chapter's Specifications, the ignition module-to-distributor stator wiring harness resistance is normal. Check the ignition coil secondary resistance (see Section 7).

13   If the resistance is less than specified, inspect the wiring harness between the module connector and the distributor, including the distributor grommet.

Ignition module-to-coil wire
Refer to illustration 10.15

14   Unplug and inspect the four-wire ignition module electrical connector and the ignition coil connector.

15   Connect one lead of an ohmmeter to the distributor base and the other lead to the TACH terminal of the ignition coil connector **(see illustration)**.

16   Measure the resistance between the TACH terminal of the ignition coil connector and ground.

17   If the resistance is greater than one ohm, replace the ignition module (see Step 43).

18   If the resistance is less than one ohm, inspect the wiring harness between the ignition module and the coil.

19   Reattach the ignition module and coil connectors.

Ground circuit
Refer to illustration 10.20

20   Carefully insert a small straight pin into the black module wire **(see illustration)**. **Caution:** *Don't allow the straight pin to ground against anything.*

5

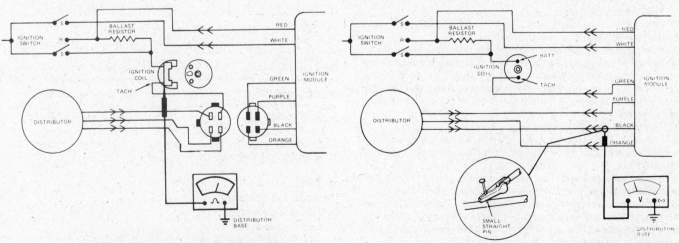

10.15   Measuring the resistance of the ignition module-to-coil wire (Duraspark II system)

10.20   Checking ground circuit continuity (Duraspark II system)

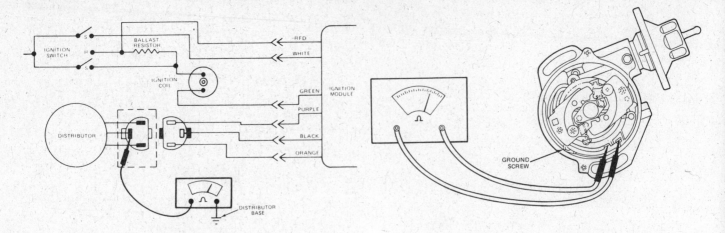

10.30   Checking distributor ground circuit continuity (Duraspark II system)

10.36   Checking stator resistance (TFI-I system)

21 Attach the negative lead of a voltmeter to the distributor base.

22 Turn the ignition switch to the Run position.

23 Measure the voltage at the black wire.

24 If the voltage is greater than 0.5 volt, check the distributor ground circuit (see Step 28).

25 If the voltage is less than 0.5 volt, replace the ignition module (see Step 43).

26 Turn the ignition switch to the Off position.

27 Remove the straight pin and detach the voltmeter.

Distributor ground circuit
Refer to illustration 10.30

28 Unplug the electrical connector from the distributor and inspect it for dirt, corrosion and damage.

29 Attach one lead of an ohmmeter to the distributor base.

30 Attach the other lead to the black wire in the distributor connector **(see illustration)**. Measure the resistance in the distributor ground circuit. **Note:** *Wiggle the distributor grommet when making this check.*

31 If the resistance is less than 1 ohm, the distributor ground circuit is okay. Inspect the wiring harness and the connectors between the distributor and the ignition module.

32 If the resistance is greater than 1 ohm, check the ground screw in the distributor.

TFI-I system
Ignition module and stator
Refer to illustration 10.36

33 Remove the distributor (see Section 8).

34 Remove the ignition module from the distributor (see Step 51).

35 Check the condition of the distributor ground screw, stator wires and connector terminals. Clean or repair as needed.

36 Connect an ohmmeter between the stator terminals **(see illustration)**. If resistance is within the value listed in this Chapter's Specifications, the stator is good (the ignition module may be defective). If not, the ignition module is good (the stator may be defective).

TFI-IV system
EEC-IV/TFI-IV

37 Unplug the wiring harness connector from the ignition module. Inspect it for dirt, corrosion and/or damage, then plug it back in.

38 Using a calibrated spark tester, check for spark (see Section 6 if necessary).

39 If there is no spark, proceed to the distributor/TFI-IV module check (see Step 42 and 46).

40 If there is spark, the problem lies either with the inferred mileage sensor (IMS) or within the EEC-IV electronic control module (ECM). Diagno-

sis of these items is beyond the scope of the home mechanic. Take the vehicle to a dealer service department or other repair shop.

41 If you're proceeding to Step 42, leave the spark tester connected. If not, remove it.

Distributor/TFI-IV module – 1984 through 1987 models
Note: *You must purchase a new ignition module before performing the following check. Since the check can result in only one of two possibilities (you will need a new module, or you won't), the odds are 50/50 that you'll be buying a new module that you may not need. Electronic components can't be returned once they're purchased, so if you're unwilling to invest in a new module that you may need now or you may not use until later, stop here. Take the vehicle to a dealer service department or other repair shop and have the module checked out.*

42 Remove the distributor (see Section 8).

43 Install a new module on the distributor (see Step 51 below). Connect the body harness to the TFI-IV. Make sure the unit is grounded with a jumper lead from the distributor to the engine. Rotate the distributor shaft by hand and check for spark at the secondary coil wire with the ignition tester (see Section 6).

44 If there is spark, the old module has failed. Leave the new module on the distributor and install the distributor (see Section 8).

45 If there is no spark, the sensor has failed. Your old module is okay but you need a new or rebuilt distributor. Install the new/rebuilt distributor with the old module (and put your new module on the shelf for another day!).

Distributor/TFI-IV module – 1987 through 1990 models
Refer to illustrations 10.47a and 10.47b

46 Remove the ignition module (see Step 54).

47 Measure resistance between the ignition module terminals in the various ignition switch positions **(see illustrations)**.

Measure Between These Terminals	Resistor Should Be
● GND - PIP In	Greater than 500 Ohms
● PIP PWR - PIP In	Less than 2K Ohms
● PIP PWR - TFI PWR	Less than 200 Ohms
● GND - IGN GND	Less than 2 Ohms
● PIP In - PIP	Less than 200 Ohms

10.47a   Check the resistance between the ignition module terminals with the ignition switch in the indicated positions (TFI-IV system)

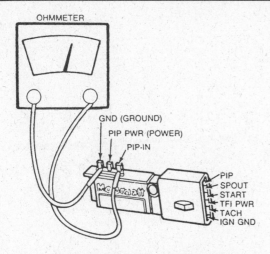

10.47b   Checking the resistance between the ignition module terminals (TFI-IV system)

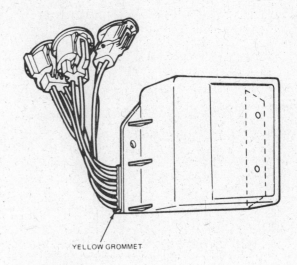

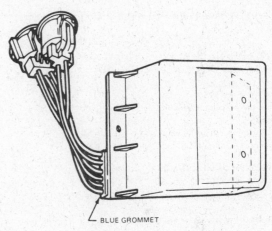

48   If resistance is as listed in the table **(see illustration 10.47a)**, the module is good and the stator is defective. Because the TFI-IV stator can't be replaced separately, the entire distributor must be replaced.

49   If resistance is incorrect, replace the module.

Module replacement

Duraspark II system

Refer to illustration 10.51

50   Detach the cable from the negative terminal of the battery.

51   Vehicles equipped with a Duraspark II system may have either the standard Duraspark II module or the universal ignition module **(see illustration)**. If your vehicle is equipped with the standard module, unplug both connectors; if your vehicle is equipped with the universal module, unplug all three connectors.

52   Remove the mounting screws and detach the module.

53   Installation is the reverse of removal.

TFI-I and TFI-IV systems

Refer to illustrations 10.55, 10.56 and 10.57

54   Remove the distributor from the engine (see Section 8).

55   Remove the two module mounting screws with a 1/4-inch drive deep socket **(see illustration)**.

56   Pull straight down on the module to disconnect the spade connectors from the stator connector **(see illustration)**.

10.51   Duraspark II ignition systems will have one of two different ignition modules – the one on the top, known as a universal ignition module (UIM), has three electrical connectors and a yellow grommet; the one on the bottom is the standard Duraspark II module with two connectors and a blue grommet

10.55   To remove the TFI-I or TFI-IV ignition module from the distributor base, remove the two screws (arrows) . . .

10.56   . . . then pull the module straight down to detach the spade terminals from the stator connector

5

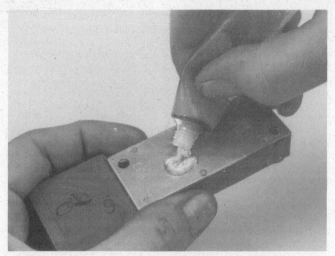

10.57   Be sure to wipe the back side of the module clean and apply a film of dielectric grease (essential for cool operation of the module) – DO NOT use any other type of grease!

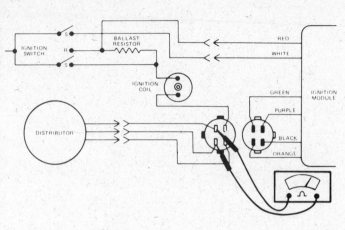

11.2   Measuring the resistance of the stator assembly and wiring harness (Duraspark II system)

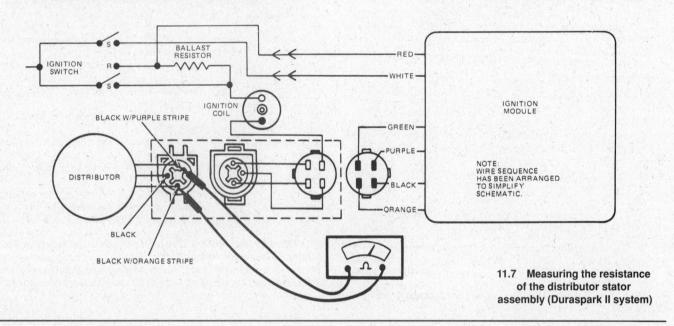

11.7   Measuring the resistance of the distributor stator assembly (Duraspark II system)

.57   Whether you are installing the old module or a new one, wipe the back side of the module clean with a soft, clean shop rag and apply a film of silicone dielectric grease to the back side of the module **(see illustration)**. If this is not done, the module will overheat and fail prematurely.

58   Installation is the reverse of removal. When plugging in the module, make sure the three terminals are inserted all the way into the stator connector.

11   Distributor stator assembly – check and replacement

Check

Duraspark II system

Stator assembly and wiring harness

Refer to illustration 11.2

1   Unplug the ignition module four-wire connector. Inspect it for dirt, corrosion and/or damage.

2   Attach the leads of an ohmmeter to the black and purple wire terminals of the electrical connector **(see illustration)**.

3   Measure the resistance between the terminals. **Note:** *Wiggle the wires in the harness when making the check.*

4   If the resistance is as listed in this Chapter's Specifications, the distributor stator assembly and wiring harness is okay. Measure the ignition module-to-distributor stator assembly wiring harness resistance (see Section 10).

5   If the resistance is less or more than the specified resistance, measure the resistance of the distributor stator assembly itself (see Step 6).

Stator assembly

Refer to illustration 11.7

Note: *This is not the same test as the one above.*

6   Unplug the electrical connector from the distributor. Inspect it for dirt, corrosion and damage.

7   Remove either the connector hold-down plate or the distributor cap so the wire colors can be seen. Attach the leads of an ohmmeter to the connector terminals of the orange and purple wires **(see illustration)**.

8   If the resistance is as listed in this Chapter's Specifications, the distributor stator is okay. Inspect the wiring harness between the distributor and the ignition module.

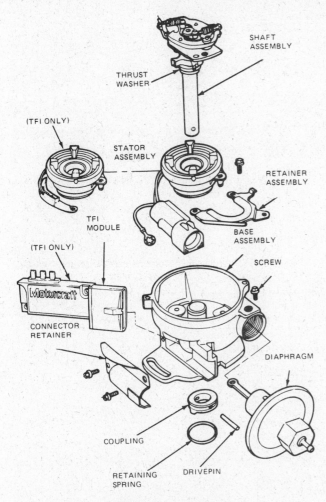

11.15   An exploded view of the Duraspark II and TFI-I distributor components

9   If the resistance is less or more than the specified resistance, replace the stator assembly (see Step 12).

10   Detach the ohmmeter and reconnect the distributor and ignition module connectors.

TFI-I system

11   The stator and module are checked in the same test (see Section 10).

TFI-IV system

12   The factory doesn't specify a check for the TFI-IV system stator (sensor). If the ignition module is good, but the system won't function normally, the distributor must be replaced with a new one, since the stator can't be replaced as a separate unit.

Replacement

Duraspark II and TFI-I systems

Refer to illustrations 11.15 and 11.22

13   Remove the distributor cap (without disconnecting the wires) and place it out of the way.

14   Remove the distributor rotor, then remove the distributor from the engine (see Section 8).

15   Remove the diaphragm attaching screw. Pull the diaphragm out until it's clear of the distributor, then disengage the diaphragm rod from the stator pivot pin and take the diaphragm out **(see illustration)**.

16   Remove the retaining spring from the drive coupling with a small screwdriver or pointed tool. **Caution:** *Don't damage the spring or coupling.*

17   Clean all dirt and oil from the drive end of the distributor.

18   Make match marks on the drive coupling and the end of the shaft so they can be reassembled in the correct relationship.

19   Support the distributor in a padded vise or similar holding fixture. Take care not to damage it.

20   Align the drive pin with the slot in the distributor base, then tap the drive pin out of the distributor with a hammer and punch.

21   Take the drive coupling off the distributor shaft and set it aside, together with the pin.

22   Before removing the shaft from the distributor, check it for burrs or built up residue, particularly around the drive tang roll pin hole **(see illustration)**. If burrs or residue are evident, polish the shaft with emery paper and wipe it clean to prevent damage to the lip seal and bushing in the distributor base.

23   Carefully lift up on the shaft plate to pull the shaft out of the distributor base. Note the position of the thrust washer **(see illustration 11.15)**, then lift it out.

24   Hold the shaft from moving with one hand and twist the shaft plate with the other. The plate should rotate freely and return to its original position when released. If not, replace the distributor as an assembly.

25   Remove both stator connector retaining screws and save them for use during reassembly.

26   On TFI-I distributors only, detach the connector from the top of the ignition module.

27   Remove three screws that secure the stator retainer. Lift the retainer and stator out of the distributor, then carefully pull them apart.

28   Check the stator bumper for wear and replace as needed.

29   Check the diaphragm O-ring and distributor base O-ring for brittleness, wear, or breakage. Replace as needed.

30   Check the distributor base bushing for wear or heat damage. Replace the entire distributor if these conditions are found.

31   Check the shaft oil seal for wear or damage. Replace the entire distributor if these conditions are found.

32   Check the shaft oil seal's spring retainer for wear or damage. Replace the spring retainer if worn or damaged.

33   Check the distributor base casting for wear or damage. Replace the entire distributor if these conditions are found.

34   Slide the stator retainer into the groove on the bottom of the stator and position the open end of the retainer toward the diaphragm rod pivot pin.

35   On TFI-I distributors only, align the ignition module connector pins, then press the connector onto the module.

36   Place the stator assembly in the distributor so the diaphragm rod pivot pin is opposite the diaphragm mounting hole. Use a small screwdriver or similar tool to line up the stator retainer holes with the screw holes in the distributor base, then install the retaining screws and tighten them securely.

5

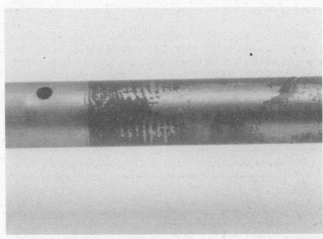

11.22   Inspect the distributor shaft for burrs or residue buildup like this in the vicinity of the hole for the drive coupling roll pin (remove it with emery cloth to prevent damage to the distributor shaft bushing when removing and installing the shaft)

11.56   As soon as you remove the distributor shaft, note how the washer is installed before removing it (it could easily fall out and get lost)

11.57   To detach the octane rod from the distributor, remove the retaining screw – note the condition of the small square rubber grommet that seals the octane rod hole when you pull the rod out (it seals the interior of the distributor to prevent moisture from damaging the electronics)

11.58   To remove the octane rod, lift the inner end of the rod off the stator assembly post (A) – to remove the stator assembly, remove both mounting screws (B) and lift the stator straight up off the posts

TFI-IV distributor stator

Refer to illustrations 11.56, 11.57, 11.58 and 11.62

46   Remove the distributor cap and position it out of the way with the wires attached.

47   Disconnect the TFI-I module from the wire harness.

48   Remove the distributor (see Section 8).

49   Remove the rotor (see Chapter 1 if necessary).

50   Although not absolutely necessary, it's a good idea to remove the ignition module (see Section 10) to prevent possible damage to the module while the distributor is being disassembled.

51   Clamp the lower end of the distributor housing in a vise. Place a shop rag in the vise jaws to prevent damage to the distributor and don't overtighten the vise.

52   Before removing the drive tang, make paint marks on the drive tang and distributor shaft so the drive tang can be reinstalled in the correct orientation.

53   With an assistant holding the distributor steady in the vise, use a pin punch of the appropriate diameter to hammer the roll pin out of the shaft.

54   Take the drive tang off the shaft and set it aside.

55   Before removing the shaft from the distributor, check it for burrs or built up residue, particularly around the drive tang roll pin hole **(see illustration 11.22)**. If burrs or residue are evident, polish the shaft with emery paper and wipe it clean to prevent damage to the lip seal and bushing in the distributor base.

56   After removing any burrs/residue, remove the shaft assembly by gently pulling on the plate. Note the relationship of the spacer washer to the distributor base before removing the washer **(see illustration)**.

57   Remove the octane rod retaining screw **(see illustration)**.

58   Lift the inner end of the rod off the stator retaining post **(see illustration)** and pull the octane rod from the distributor base. **Note:** *Don't lose the grommet installed in the octane rod hole. The grommet protects the electronic components of the distributor from moisture.*

59   Remove the two stator screws **(see illustration 11.58)**.

60   Gently lift the stator assembly straight up and remove it from the distributor.

61   Check the shaft bushing in the distributor base for wear or signs of excessive heat buildup. If signs of wear and/or damage are evident, replace the complete distributor assembly.

62   Inspect the O-ring at the base of the distributor. If it's damaged, remove it and install a new one **(see illustration)**.

63   Inspect the base casting for cracks and wear. If any damage is evident, replace the distributor assembly.

64   Place the stator assembly in position over the shaft bushing and press

37   Make sure the stator rotates easily within the limits allowed by its electrical wiring (the diaphragm rod will rotate it slightly to change ignition timing when the distributor is in operation). If it doesn't, stop and find out why before continuing with assembly.

38   Install the connector retainer to the base with the two screws. Position the two stator wires behind the wire guard portion of the connector retainer, making sure they're not tangled or twisted.

39   Insert the diaphragm into the distributor base. Hook its rod over the pivot pin, then install the diaphragm retaining screw.

40   Apply a small amount of clean engine oil (not too much) to the distributor shaft beneath the armature. Install the distributor shaft in the base.

41   Align the match marks on the drive coupling and distributor shaft, then install the drive coupling with the match marks aligned. Push the drive pin in part way, place the distributor on a vise or other support and tap the pin in the rest of the way. The pin should be flush with the groove in the coupling when installed. Neither end of the pin should protrude past the groove.

42   Make sure the distributor shaft turns freely.

43   Install the drive pin retainer spring in the coupling groove.

44   Install the distributor in the engine (see Section 8).

45   Install the distributor rotor and cap (see Chapter 1).

11.62 If the O-ring at the base of the distributor is damaged, replace it with a new one

it down onto the distributor base until it's completely seated on the posts.

65 Install the stator screws and tighten them securely.

66 Insert the octane rod through the hole in the distributor base and push the inner end of the rod onto the post. **Note:** *Make sure that the octane rod hole is properly sealed by the grommet.*

67 Reinstall the octane rod screw and tighten it securely.

68 Apply a light coat of engine oil (not too much) to the distributor shaft and insert the shaft through the bushing.

69 Align the paint marks on the distributor drive coupling and shaft, then install the coupling.

70 Install the roll pin and tap it in with a hammer and appropriate size punch. Make sure neither end of the pin protrudes from the drive coupling.

71 Check the distributor shaft for smooth rotation, then remove the distributor assembly from the vise.

72 Install the retainer spring in the groove on the drive coupling.

73 Install the TFI-IV module (see Section 10).

74 Install the rotor (see Chapter 1 if necessary).

75 Install the distributor.

12 Charging system – general information and precautions

The charging system includes the alternator, either an internal or an external voltage regulator, a charge indicator, the battery, a fusible link and the wiring between all the components. The charging system supplies electrical power for the ignition system, the lights, the radio, etc. The alternator is driven by a drivebelt at the front (right end) of the engine.

The purpose of the voltage regulator is to limit the alternator's voltage to a preset value. This prevents power surges, circuit overloads, etc., during peak voltage output. On EVR (external voltage regulator) systems, the regulator is mounted on the right fender apron of the vehicle. On IAR (integral alternator/regulator) systems, a solid state regulator is housed inside the alternator itself.

The fusible link is a short length of insulated wire integral with the engine compartment wiring harness. The link is several wire gauges smaller in diameter than the circuit it protects. Production fusible links and their identification flags are identified by the flag color. Refer to Chapter 12 for more information on the fusible links.

The charging system doesn't ordinarily require periodic maintenance. However, the drivebelt, battery and wires and connections should be inspected at the intervals outlined in Chapter 1.

Be very careful when making electrical circuit connections to a vehicle equipped with an alternator and note the following:

a) When reconnecting wires to the alternator from the battery, be sure to note the polarity.

b) Before using arc welding equipment to repair any part of the vehicle, disconnect the wires from the alternator and the battery terminals.

c) Never start the engine with a battery charger connected.

d) Always disconnect both battery cables before using a battery charger.

13 Charging system – check

1 If a malfunction occurs in the charging circuit, don't automatically assume that the alternator is causing the problem. First check the following items:

a) The battery cables where they connect to the battery. Make sure the connections are clean and tight (see Chapter 1).

b) Check the external alternator wiring harness and the connectors at the alternator and voltage regulator. They must be in good condition, clean and tight.

c) Check the drivebelt condition and tension (see Chapter 1).

d) Make sure the alternator mounting and adjustment bolts are tight.

e) Check the fusible link located between the starter relay (on the left inner fender well – see Section 19) and the alternator. If it's burned, determine the cause, repair the circuit and replace the link (see Chapter 12).

f) Run the engine and check the alternator for abnormal noise.

2 Connect a voltmeter between the battery terminals and check the battery voltage with the engine off. It should be approximately 12-volts.

3 Run the engine at a fast idle (approximately 1500 rpm) and check the battery voltage again after the voltage stops rising. This may take a few minutes. It should now be higher than battery voltage, but not more than 2-volts higher (EVR) or 2.5-volts higher (IAR).

4 If the voltage reading is less than the specified charging voltage, perform the Under-voltage test for the vehicle's charging system in this section. If it is higher, perform the Over-voltage test.

5 Turn on the high beam headlights and turn the heater or air conditioner blower to its highest setting. Run the engine at 2,000 rpm and check the voltage reading. It should now be at least 0.5 volt higher than battery voltage. If not, perform the appropriate Under-voltage test.

6 If the voltage readings are correct in the preceding Steps, the charging system is working properly. Use a 12-volt test light and the wiring diagrams (see Chapter 12) to check for a battery drain.

External voltage regulator models
Under-voltage test

Refer to illustrations 13.7, 13.8 and 13.11

7 Unplug the electrical connector from the regulator. Temporarily install a blade terminal in the wiring harness F terminal, then measure resistance between the F terminal and ground with an ohmmeter **(see illustration)**.

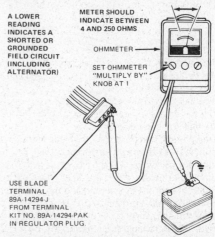

13.7 To measure field circuit resistance in models equipped with an external regulator, unplug the regulator electrical connector and temporarily install a blade terminal in the F terminal socket of the connector

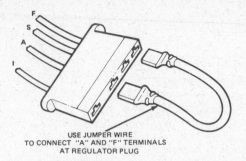

13.8   To check the regulator and wiring, bypass the regulator with a jumper wire between the A and F terminals in the regulator connector

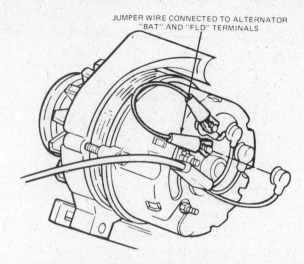

13.11   Disconnect the FLD terminal wire from the alternator, pull back the BAT terminal cover and connect a jumper wire between the FLD and BAT terminals

a) If it is less than listed in this Chapter's Specifications, repair the shorted or grounded field circuit in the alternator or wiring harness, then repeat the load test (see Step 5).

b) If the ohmmeter reading is correct, proceed with Step 8.

8   Remove the blade terminal. Connect a jumper wire between terminals A and F **(see illustration)**.

9   Repeat the load test (see Step 5) with the jumper wire connected.

a) If the reading is more than 0.5-volt above battery voltage, the problem is in the wiring or regulator. Perform the S circuit test (ammeter equipped models) or S and I circuit tests indicator light equipped models) to isolate the problem.

b) If the reading is still too low, continue with Step 10.

10   Remove the jumper wire from the electrical connector, but leave the connector unplugged for now.

11   Disconnect the FLD terminal wire at the back of the alternator. Pull back the cover from the BAT terminal and connect a jumper wire between the FLD and BAT terminals **(see illustration)**.

12   Repeat the load test (see Step 5).

a) If voltage is now 0.5-volt or more above battery voltage, perform the S and I circuit tests.

b) If voltage is still too low, proceed to Step 13.

13   Turn off the engine and move the positive voltmeter lead to the BAT terminal on the alternator.

a) If the voltmeter now indicates battery voltage, replace the alternator.

b) If the voltmeter indicates zero, check the wire between the alternator and starter relay for breaks or bad connections and repair as needed.

Over-voltage test

14   Start this test with the regulator electrical connector plugged in.

15   Connect a jumper wire between the base of the voltage regulator and the alternator frame casting.

16   Repeat the no-load test (see Step 3).

a) If the voltage reading drops to within the specified range, check for a poor ground at the alternator, at the regulator, between the engine and firewall, or at either end of the negative battery cable.

b) If the voltage is still too high, perform Step 16.

17   Unplug the wiring connector from the voltage regulator and repeat the no-load test (see Step 3).

a) If the voltage reading is now correct, replace the voltage regulator.

b) If the voltage reading is still too high, check for a short between the A and F circuits.

S circuit test (ammeter-equipped vehicles)

18   Unplug the electrical connector from the voltage regulator. Connect the voltmeter positive lead to the S terminal in the connector. Connect the negative lead to the battery negative terminal.

19   Check the voltmeter reading with the engine off. It should be zero.

20   Turn the ignition key to the On position, but don't start the engine. The voltmeter should indicate battery voltage.

a) If there is no voltage with the key On, check the S wire between the ignition switch and electrical connector for a break or bad connection.

b) If the voltage readings are as specified, replace the voltage regulator.

21   Repeat the load test (see Step 5).

S and I circuit test (indicator light-equipped vehicles)

22   Unplug the electrical connector from the regulator, then connect a jumper wire between the A and F terminals **(see illustration 13.8)**.

23   Connect the voltmeter negative lead to battery negative terminal.

24   Start the engine and let it idle.

25   Connect the voltmeter positive lead to the S terminal, then the I terminal in the regulator connector. The I terminal voltage reading should be approximately twice as high as the S terminal voltage reading.

a) If the voltage readings are correct, replace the voltage regulator.

b) If there is no voltage, check the S and I circuit wiring for breaks or bad connections.

Integral voltage regulator models
Under-voltage test

Refer to illustrations 13.26a, 13.26b, 13.27, 13.29 and 13.31

26   Unplug the electrical connector from the regulator **(see illustration)**.

13.26a   The integral regulator used on later models is installed on the back of the alternator (arrow)

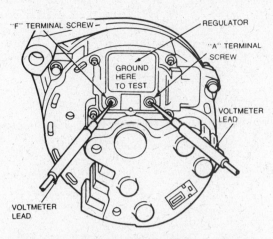

13.26b To check regulator resistance on integral regulator models, connect an ohmmeter between the regulator A and F terminals

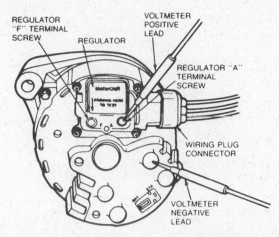

13.27 To check A circuit voltage on integral regulator models, connect the voltmeter negative lead to the alternator housing and the positive lead to the A terminal screw

Connect an ohmmeter between the A and F terminal screws **(see illustration)**. The ohmmeter should indicate at least 2.4-ohms.

  a) If the ohmmeter reading is too low, the regulator is defective. **Caution:** *The regulator failure may have been caused by a shorted rotor or field circuit. These must be checked before replacing the regulator or the new regulator may fail as well. Checking the rotor and field circuit requires disassembly of the alternator and should be done by a dealer or electrical shop. It may be less expensive to replace the alternator with a rebuilt unit.*

  b) If the ohmmeter reading is within specifications, reconnect the electrical connector to the regulator and perform Step 27.

27   Connect the voltmeter negative lead to the alternator rear housing and the positive lead to the regulator A terminal screw **(see illustration)**. The voltmeter should indicate battery voltage. If not, check the A circuit for breaks or bad connections.

28   Repeat the load test (see Step 5).

29   If the voltmeter indicates battery voltage in Step 27, place the ignition key in the Off position. Connect the voltmeter negative lead to the alternator frame and the positive lead to the F terminal screw **(see illustration)**.

  a) If the voltmeter indicates no voltage, replace the alternator.

  b) If the voltmeter indicates battery voltage, proceed to Step 30.

30   Turn the ignition key to the Run position, but don't start the engine. Touch the voltmeter negative lead to the rear of the alternator and the positive lead to the F terminal screw on the regulator.

  a) If the voltmeter indicates more than 1.5-volts, perform the I circuit test – integral regulator in this Section.

  b) If the voltmeter indicates 1.5-volts or less, proceed to Step 31.

31   Disconnect the alternator electrical connector. Connect 12-gauge jumper wires between the alternator B+ terminals and their corresponding terminals in the electrical connector **(see illustration)**. Perform the load test (see Step 5) with the voltmeter positive terminal connected to one of the B+ jumper wire terminals.

  a) If voltage increases to more than 0.5-volt above battery voltage, check the wiring from alternator to starter relay for breaks or bad connections.

  b) If the voltage does not increase to more than 0.5-volt above battery voltage, perform Step 32.

32   Connect a jumper wire between the alternator rear housing and the regulator F terminal screw **(see illustration 13.29)**. Repeat the load test (see Step 5) with the voltmeter positive lead connected to one of the B+ jumper wire terminals.

  a) If voltage increases by more than 0.5-volt, replace the regulator.

  b) If voltage doesn't increase by more than 0.5-volt, replace the alternator.

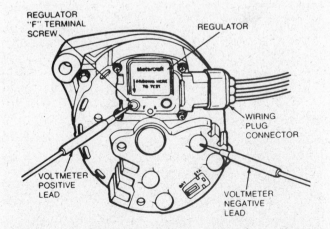

13.29 To check F terminal voltage on integral regulator models, connect the voltmeter negative lead to the alternator housing and the positive lead to the F terminal screw

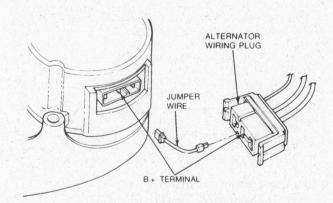

13.31 To check the wire from alternator to starter relay, connect jumper wires between the alternator wiring connector and the alternator B+ terminals – measure voltage from one of the B+ terminals to the battery negative terminal with the engine running

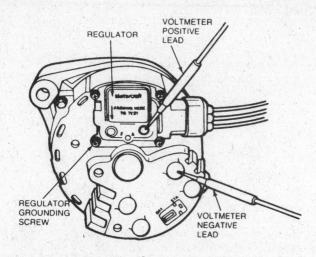

13.34   To isolate the cause of over-voltage on integral regulator models, connect the voltmeter negative lead to the alternator housing and the positive lead to the A terminal screw and regulator grounding screw, in turn

Over-voltage test

Refer to illustration 13.34

33   Turn the key to the On position but leave the engine off.

34   Connect the voltmeter negative lead to the alternator rear housing, then connect the positive lead to the A terminal screw and the regulator grounding screw in turn **(see illustration)**. If the voltage readings differ by more than 0.5-volt, check the A circuit for breaks or bad connections.

35   Check for loose regulator grounding screws and tighten them as needed.

36   If the voltage reading is still too high, place the ignition key in the Off position. Connect the voltmeter negative lead to the alternator frame. Connect the voltmeter positive lead to the A terminal screw, then to the F terminal screw **(see illustration 13.27)**.

    a)   If the voltage readings at the two screw heads are different, replace the alternator.

    b)   If the voltage readings at the two screw heads are the same, replace the regulator.

S and I circuit test

Refer to illustration 13.38

37   Disconnect the alternator electrical connector.

38   Connect one jumper wire from the alternator A terminal to its corresponding terminal in the electrical connector. Connect another jumper wire from the regulator F screw to the alternator housing **(see illustration)**.

39   Start the engine and let it idle.

40   Connect the voltmeter negative lead to the alternator housing. Connect the positive lead to the connector S terminal and I terminal in turn **(see illustration 13.38)**. Voltage at the I terminal should be approximately double the reading at the S terminal.

    a)   If the readings are as specified, replace the regulator.

    b)   If there is no voltage, check the wiring for breaks or bad connections. If the wiring is good, replace the alternator.

14   Alternator – removal and installation

1   Detach the cable from the negative terminal of the battery.

2   Unplug the electrical connectors from the alternator.

3   Loosen the alternator adjustment and pivot bolts and detach the

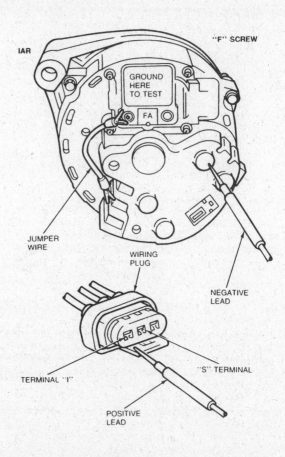

13.38   To check the S and I circuits on integral regulator models, connect a jumper wire between the regulator A terminal screw and alternator housing – then connect the voltmeter negative lead to the alternator housing and the positive lead to the connector S and I terminals, in turn

drivebelt (see Chapter 1).

4   Remove the adjustment and pivot bolts and separate the alternator from the engine.

5   Installation is the reverse of removal.

6   After the alternator is installed, adjust the drivebelt tension (see Chapter 1).

15   Voltage regulator/alternator brushes – replacement

Integral regulator

Refer to illustrations 15.3, 15.5a, 15.5b, 15.7, 15.8a, 15.8b and 15.10

1   Remove the alternator (see Section 14).

2   Set the alternator on a clean workbench.

3   Remove the four voltage regulator mounting screws **(see illustration)**. Note that these have T20 Torx heads and require a special screwdriver.

4   Detach the voltage regulator.

5   If you're working on an early model, remove the insulator from the A terminal screw **(see illustration)**. If you're working on a later model, break off the tab that covers the A screw head with a screwdriver **(see illustration)**.

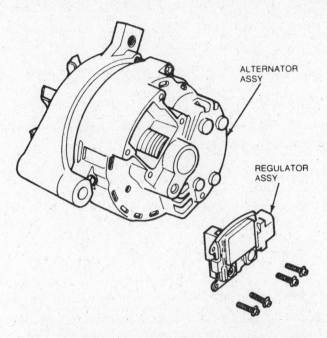

15.3   The regulator is secured to the alternator by four T20 Torx screws, which must be removed with a special screwdriver – don't try to use an Allen wrench (the holes will be rounded out)

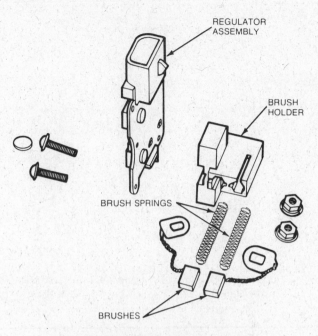

15.5a   Brush older and voltage regulator assembly – exploded view

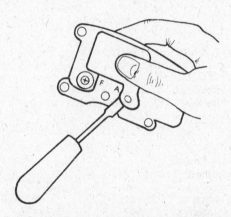

15.5b   On later model regulators, the A terminal screw is covered by a tab – break this off with a screwdriver

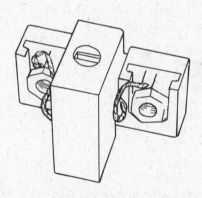

15.7   Insert the brush holder nuts into their slots, then insert the brush lead terminals between the nuts and the holder

6   Remove the A terminal insulator and the two Torx screws that secure the brush holder to the regulator. Remove the regulator from the brush holder, then remove the nuts, brushes and springs.

7   Install the brush holder nuts into their slots **(see illustration)**. Tip the brush holder to one side so the flanged portions of the nuts fall away from the brush holder, leaving a small gap between the nuts and the brush holder. Insert the brush lead terminals in the slots between the wide part of the nuts and the brush holder.

8   The brushes must be retained in their holder while the regulator and brush assembly is installed in the alternator. There are two ways to do this:

a) For early models, Ford recommends installing a short length of stiff wire (such as a paper clip) in the brush holder **(see illustration)**. When the brush holder is installed on the regulator, the piece of wire protrudes through a hole in the regulator made for this purpose.

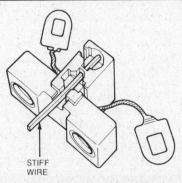

15.8a   One recommended method of retaining brushes in the holder is to insert a piece of stiff wire as shown . . .

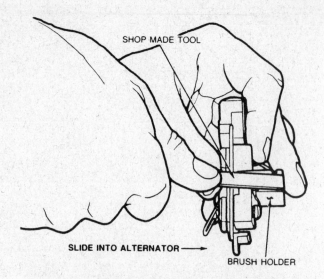

15.8b ... the other recommended method is to press the
brushes into their holder with a flat, thin piece of steel while
you're installing the brush holder in the alternator

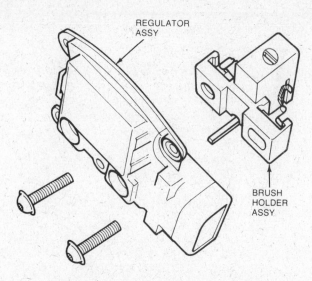

15.10   Be sure the brush and regulator assembly mating
surfaces are clean before assembling them to each other

b) For later models, Ford recommends using a piece of flat, thin steel
to retain the brushes while the brush holder and regulator are being
installed in the alternator **(see illustration)**. A feeler gauge will
work.

9   Carefully remove all contamination from the regulator base plate with
a clean shop rag.

10   Assemble the regulator and brush holder **(see illustration)**, then install and tighten the mounting screws.

11   If there was an insulator on the A terminal screw head, install it. If you
broke off the tab that covered the A terminal screw, cover the screw head
with a small piece of electrical tape.

12   Install the regulator and brush assembly on the alternator. Be sure the
brushes don't hang up during installation.

13   Remove the brush retainer (piece of wire or flat steel). **Caution:** *If current is supplied to the alternator while the retainer is still in position, the
resulting short circuit will destroy the voltage regulator.*

14   Install the alternator (see Section 14).

External regulator

Refer to illustration 15.15

15   Remove the negative cable from the battery terminal, then disconnect the wire harness from the regulator. Use a screwdriver to unplug the
harness connector – do not pull on the wires **(see illustration)**.

16   Remove the mounting bolts and detach the regulator.

17   Installation is the reverse of removal.

16   Starting system – general information

The function of the starting system is to crank the engine to start it. The
system is composed of the starter motor, starter relay, battery, switch and
connecting wires.

Turning the ignition key to the Start position actuates the starter relay
through the starter control circuit. The starter relay then connects the battery to the starter. The battery supplies the electrical energy to the starter
motor, which does the actual work of cranking the engine.

Vehicles equipped with an automatic transaxle have a Neutral start
switch in the starter control circuit, which prevents operation of the starter
unless the shift lever is in Neutral or Park. The circuit on vehicles with a
manual transaxle prevents operation of the starter motor unless the clutch
pedal is depressed.

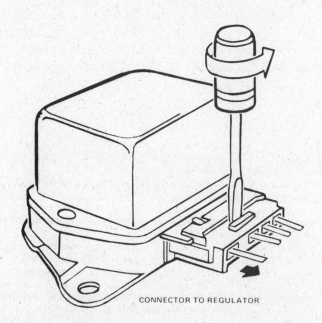

15.15   To detach the wire harness from the external voltage
regulator, position the tip of a screwdriver as shown and twist
it – the screwdriver will push the connector off the regulator

Never operate the starter motor for more than 15-seconds at a time
without pausing to allow it to cool for at least two minutes. Excessive
cranking can cause overheating, which can seriously damage the starter.

17   Starter motor and circuit – in-vehicle check

*Note: Before diagnosing starter problems, make sure the battery is fully
charged.*

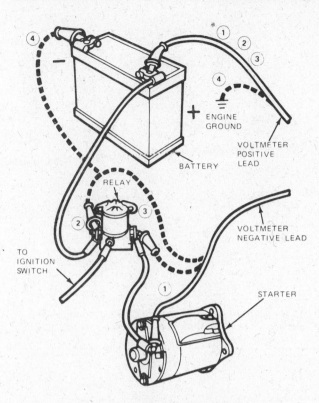

17.11   The four test lead connections for the starter cranking circuit test

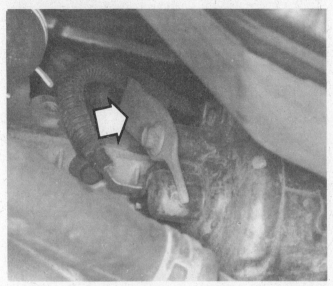

18.4   If the starter has a brace like the one shown here, remove it

General check

1   If the starter motor doesn't turn at all when the switch is operated, make sure the shift lever is in Neutral or Park (automatic transaxle) or the clutch pedal is depressed (manual transaxle).

2   Make sure the battery is charged and that all cables at the battery and starter relay terminals are secure.

3   If the starter motor spins but the engine doesn't turn over, then the drive assembly in the starter motor is slipping and the starter motor must be replaced (see Section 18).

4   If, when the switch is actuated, the starter motor doesn't operate at all but the starter relay operates (clicks), then the problem lies with either the battery, the starter relay contacts or the starter motor connections.

5   If the starter relay doesn't click when the ignition switch is actuated, either the starter relay circuit is open or the relay itself is defective. Check the starter relay circuit or replace the relay (see Section 19).

6   To check the starter relay circuit, remove the push-on connector from the relay wire (the red one with a blue stripe). Make sure that the connection is clean and secure and the relay bracket is grounded. If the connections are good, check the operation of the relay with a jumper wire. To do this, place the transaxle in Park (automatic) or Neutral (manual). Remove the push-on connector from the relay. Connect a jumper wire between the battery positive terminal and the exposed terminal on the relay. If the starter motor now operates, the starter relay is okay. The problem is in the ignition switch, Neutral start switch or in the starting circuit wiring (look for open or loose connections).

7   If the starter motor still doesn't operate, replace the starter relay (see Section 19).

8   If the starter motor cranks the engine at an abnormally slow speed, first make sure the battery is fully charged and all terminal connections are clean and tight. Also check the connections at the starter relay and battery ground. Eyelet terminals should not be easily rotated by hand. Also check for a short to ground. If the engine is partially seized, or has the wrong viscosity oil in it, it will crank slowly.

Starter cranking circuit test

Refer to illustration 17.11

Note: *To determine the location of excessive resistance in the starter circuit, perform the following simple series of tests.*

9   Disconnect the ignition coil wire from the distributor cap and ground it on the engine.

10   Connect a remote control starter switch from the battery terminal of the starter relay to the S terminal of the relay.

11   Make the test connections as shown **(see illustration)**. Refer to this illustration as you perform the following four tests.

12   Operate the ignition switch and take the voltmeter readings as soon as a steady figure is indicated. Don't allow the starter motor to turn for more than 15-seconds at a time.

13   The voltage drop in the circuit will be indicated by the voltmeter (put the voltmeter on the 0-to-2 volt range). The maximum allowable voltage drop should be:

   a) 0.5-volt with the voltmeter negative lead connected to the starter terminal and the positive lead connected to the battery positive terminal **(Connection 1 in illustration 17.11)**.

   b) 0.1-volt with the voltmeter negative lead connected to the starter relay (battery side) and the positive lead connected to the positive terminal of the battery **(Connection 2 in illustration 17.11)**.

   c) 0.3-volt with the voltmeter negative lead connected to the starter relay (starter side) and the positive lead connected to the positive terminal of the battery **(Connection 3 in illustration 17.11)**.

   d) 0.3-volt with the voltmeter negative lead connected to the negative terminal of the battery and the positive lead connected to the engine ground **(Connection 4 in illustration 17.11)**.

18   Starter motor – removal and installation

Refer to illustrations 18.4 and 18.7

1   Detach the cable from the negative terminal of the battery.

2   Raise the vehicle and support it securely on jackstands.

3   Disconnect the large cable from the terminal on the starter motor.

4   Remove the starter support brace (if equipped) **(see illustration)**.

5   If your vehicle is equipped with a roll restrictor (manual transaxle equipped vehicles only), remove the three nuts that attach the brace to the transmission housing and remove the brace.

5

6   On automatic transaxle models so equipped, remove two nuts that secure the hose bracket to the starter studs, then remove the bracket.

7   Remove the three starter fasteners **(see illustration)** and remove the starter.

8   Installation is the reverse of removal.

19   Starter relay – removal and installation

1   Detach the cable from the negative terminal of the battery.

2   Label the wires and the terminals, then disconnect the Neutral safety switch wire (automatic transaxle models only), the battery cable, the fusible link and the starter cable from the relay terminals.

3   Remove the mounting bolts and detach the relay.

4   Installation is the reverse of removal.

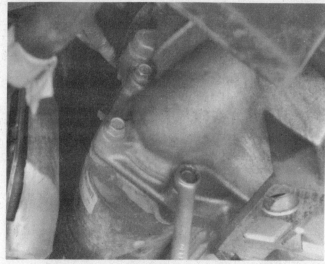

18.7   Disconnect the starter fasteners – some models use three nuts and studs, while others use two nuts and studs and one bolt

Chapter 6   Emissions control systems

Contents

1   General information

Refer to illustration 1.6

To prevent pollution of the atmosphere from incompletely burned and evaporating gases, and to maintain good driveability and fuel economy, a number of emission control systems are incorporated. They include the:

Electronic Engine Control (EEC-IV) system (fuel-injected models only)
Exhaust Gas Recirculation (EGR) system
Managed air thermactor system
Fuel evaporative emission control system
Positive Crankcase Ventilation (PCV) system
Inlet air temperature control system
Catalytic converter

The Sections in this Chapter include general descriptions, checking procedures within the scope of the home mechanic and component replacement procedures (when possible) for each of the systems listed above.

Before assuming that an emissions control system is malfunctioning, check the fuel and ignition systems carefully. The diagnosis of some emission control devices requires specialized tools, equipment and training. If checking and servicing become too difficult or if a procedure is beyond your ability, consult a dealer service department.

This doesn't mean, however, that emission control systems are particularly difficult to maintain and repair. You can quickly and easily perform many checks and do most (if not all) of the regular maintenance at home with common tune-up and hand tools. **Note:** *The most frequent cause of emissions problems is simply a loose, broken or misrouted vacuum hose or wire, so always check the hose and wiring connections first.* Pay close attention to any special precautions outlined in this Chapter. It should be noted that the illustrations of the various systems may not exactly match

the system installed on your vehicle because of changes made by the manufacturer during production or from year-to-year.

A Vehicle Emissions Control Information label is located in the engine compartment **(see illustration)**. This label contains important emissions specifications and adjustment information, as well as a vacuum hose schematic with emissions components identified. When servicing the engine or emissions systems, the VECI label in your particular vehicle should always be checked for up-to-date information.

1.6   The Vehicle Emission Control Information (VECI) label located in the engine compartment contains essential information (like the spark plug type, the ignition timing procedure and a vacuum hose routing diagram)

2   Electronic Engine Control (EEC-IV) system

Refer to illustrations 2.1a, 2.1b, 2.5, 2.7, 2.9, 2.14 and 2.15

General description

1   The Electronic Engine Control (EEC-IV) system consists of an on-board computer, known as the Electronic Control Assembly (ECA), and the information sensors, which monitor various functions of the engine and send data to the ECA **(see illustrations)**. Based on the data and the information programmed into the computer's memory, the ECA generates output signals to control various engine functions.

2   The ECA, located inside the dashboard to the left of the steering column, is the "brain" of the EEC-IV system. It receives data from a number of sensors and other electronic components (switches, relays, etc.). Based on the information it receives, the ECA generates output signals to control various relays, solenoids and other actuators (see below). The ECA is specifically calibrated to optimize the emissions, fuel economy and drive-ability of your vehicle.

3   Because of a Federally-mandated 5 year/50,000 mile extended warranty which covers the ECA, the information sensors and all components under its control, and because any damage to the ECA, the sensors and/or the control devices may void the warranty, it isn't a good idea to attempt diagnosis or replacement of the ECA at home. Take your vehicle to a dealer service department if the ECA or a system component malfunctions.

Information input sensors

4   When battery voltage is applied to the compressor clutch, a signal is sent to the ECA, which interprets the signal as an added load created by the A/C compressor and increases engine idle speed accordingly to compensate.

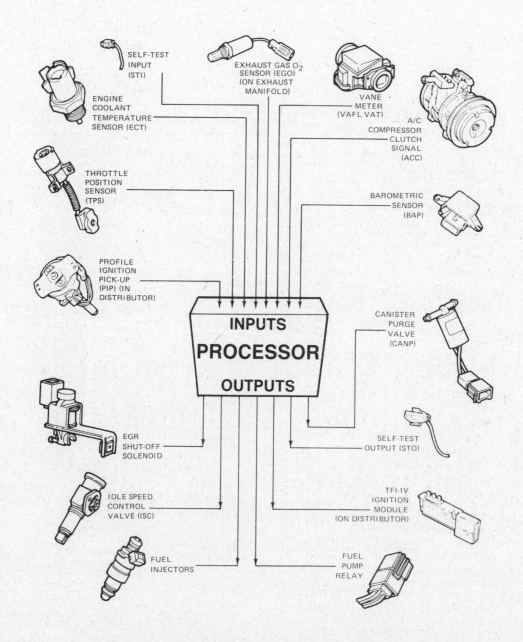

2.1a   EEC-IV system input and output devices (typical multi-point fuel injection)

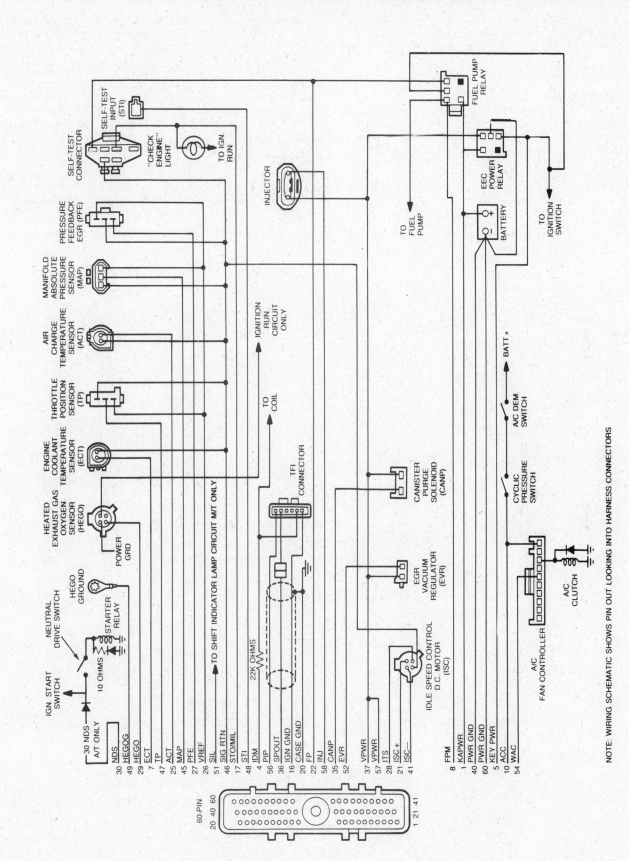

2.1b EEC–IV system schematic (typical Central Fuel Injection)

NOTE: WIRING SCHEMATIC SHOWS PIN OUT LOOKING INTO HARNESS CONNECTORS

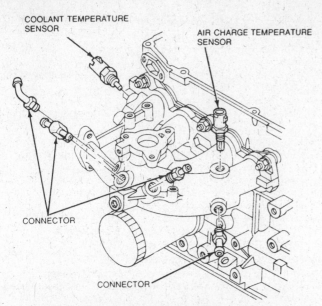

2.5   Engine Coolant Temperature sensor and Air Charge Temperature sensor (CFI engine shown, multi-point fuel injected engines similar)

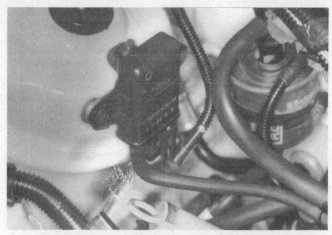

2.7   Typical Manifold Absolute Pressure (MAP) sensor

2.9   The oxygen sensor is threaded into the exhaust manifold

2.14   A typical canister purge solenoid valve

2.15   A typical EGR solenoid

5   The Air Charge Temperature sensor (ACT), threaded into a runner of the intake manifold **(see illustration)**, provides the ECA with fuel/air mixture temperature information. The ECA uses this information to correct fuel flow and control fuel flow during cold enrichment (cold starts).

6   The Engine Coolant Temperature (ECT) sensor, which is threaded into the intake manifold **(see illustration 2.5),** monitors engine coolant temperature. The ECT sends the ECA a constantly varying voltage signal that influences ECA control of the fuel mixture, ignition timing and EGR operation.

7   The Manifold Absolute Pressure (MAP) sensor, used with CFI systems, is mounted on the firewall **(see illustration)**. It measures the absolute pressure of the mixture in the intake manifold and sends a signal to the ECA that is proportional to absolute pressure.

8   The barometric pressure sensor, used with multi-point fuel injection systems, measures barometric (atmospheric) pressure. This information, together with other inputs, is used by the ECA to regulate the air-fuel ratio, ignition timing and EGR flow.

9   The oxygen sensor (EGO), which is threaded into the exhaust manifold **(see illustration)**, constantly monitors the oxygen content of the exhaust gases. A voltage signal which varies in accordance with the difference between the oxygen content of the exhaust gases and the sur-

rounding atmosphere is sent to the ECA. The ECA translates this exhaust gas oxygen content signal to fuel/air ratio, then alters it to the ideal ratio for current engine operating conditions. The oxygen sensor on some models is electrically heated.

10   The Profile Ignition Pick-up (PIP), integral with the distributor, informs the ECA of crankshaft position and speed. The PIP assembly consists of an armature with four windows and four metal tabs that rotate past a stator assembly (the Hall effect switch).

11   The Throttle Position Sensor (TPS), which is mounted on the side of the throttle body and connected directly to the throttle shaft, senses throttle movement and position, then transmits an electrical signal to the

ECA. This signal enables the ECA to determine when the throttle is closed, in its normal cruise condition or wide open.

Output devices

12   The A/C and cooling fan controller module is operated by the ECA, the coolant temperature switch and the brake light switch. The controller module provides an output signal which controls operation of the A/C compressor clutch and the engine cooling fan.

13   The EEC power relay, which is activated by the ignition switch, supplies battery voltage to the ECA when the switch is on.

14   The canister purge solenoid (CANP), located on the left fender well (see Illustration), switches manifold vacuum to operate the canister purge valve when a signal is received from the ECA. Vacuum opens the purge valve when the solenoid is energized.

15   The EGR control solenoid, used with 1.9L multi-point fuel injected engines (see illustration), switches manifold vacuum to operate the EGR valve on command from the ECA. Vacuum opens the EGR valve when the solenoid is energized.

16   The four fuel injectors on multi-point fuel-injected engines are mounted in the lower intake manifold. The single fuel injector on Central Fuel Injection models is located in the throttle body. The ECA controls the length of time the injector(s) remain open. The "open" time of the injector(s) determines the amount of fuel delivered. For information regarding injector replacement, refer to Chapter 4.

17   The fuel pump relay (used on fuel-injected models) is activated by the ECA with the ignition switch in the On position. When the ignition switch is turned to the On position, the relay is activated to supply initial line pressure to the system. For information regarding fuel pump check and replacement, refer to Chapter 4.

18   The Idle Speed Control (ISC) motor changes idle speed in accordance with signals from the ECA. For information regarding ISC replacement, refer to Chapter 4.

19   The TFI ignition module, mounted on the side of the distributor base, triggers the ignition coil and determines dwell. The ECA uses a signal from the Profile Ignition Pick-Up to determine crankshaft position. Ignition timing is determined by the ECA, which then signals the module to fire the coil. For further information regarding the TFI module, refer to the appropriate Section in Chapter 5.

Checking

20   Because of the specialized test equipment needed to check the sensors and output devices, diagnosis is well beyond the scope of the home mechanic. If engine driveability deteriorates, take the vehicle to a dealer service department to have the EEC-IV system checked.

Component replacement

Note: *Because of the Federally-mandated extended warranty which covers the ECA, the information sensors and the devices it controls, there's no point in replacing any of the following components yourself unless the warranty has expired. However, once the warranty has expired, you may wish to perform some of the following component replacement procedures yourself after having the problem diagnosed by a dealer service department or repair shop.*

Air Charge Temperature (ACT) sensor

21   Detach the cable from the negative terminal of the battery.

22   Locate the ACT sensor in the intake manifold (see illustration 2.5).

23   Unplug the electrical connector from the sensor.

24   Remove the sensor with a wrench.

25   Wrap the threads of the new sensor with teflon tape to prevent air leaks.

26   Installation is the reverse of removal.

Manifold Absolute Pressure (MAP) sensor or barometric pressure sensor

27   Detach the cable from the negative terminal of the battery.

28   Locate the sensor on the firewall (see illustration 2.7).

29   Unplug the electrical connector from the sensor.

30   Detach the vacuum line from the sensor (MAP sensor only).

31   Remove the two mounting bolts and detach the sensor.

32   Installation is the reverse of removal.

Exhaust Gas Oxygen (EGO) sensor

33   Detach the cable from the negative terminal of the battery.

34   Locate the EGO sensor on the exhaust manifold (see illustration 2.9).

35   Unplug the electrical connector from the sensor.

36   Remove the sensor with a wrench.

37   Coat the threads of the new sensor with anti-seize compound to prevent the threads from welding themselves to the manifold.

38   Installation is the reverse of removal.

Throttle Position Sensor (TPS) switch

39   Don't attempt to replace the TPS switch! Specialized calibration equipment is necessary to adjust the switch once it's installed, making adjustment (and therefore replacement) beyond the scope of the home mechanic.

Canister Purge Solenoid

40   Detach the cable from the negative terminal of the battery.

41   Locate the canister purge solenoid on the left side of the engine compartment, next to the left wheel well (see illustration 2.14).

42   Unplug the electrical connector from the solenoid.

43   Label the vacuum hoses and ports, then detach the hoses.

44   Remove the solenoid.

45   Installation is the reverse of removal.

---

3   Exhaust Gas Recirculation (EGR) system

Refer to illustrations 3.1a, 3.1b and 3.12

General description

1   The EGR system is designed to reintroduce small amounts of exhaust gas into the combustion cycle, thus reducing the generation of nitrogen oxide emissions (see illustrations). The amount of exhaust gas

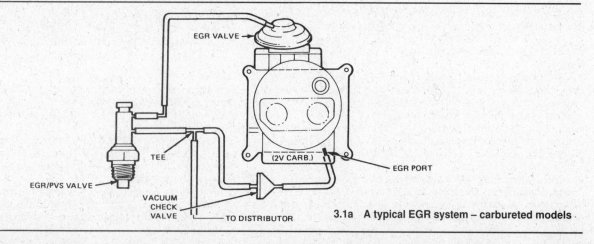

3.1a   A typical EGR system – carbureted models

6

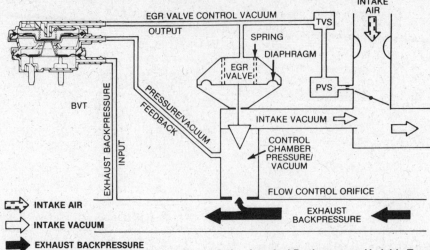

3.1b   A typical Backpressure Variable Transducer (BVT) EGR system

3.12   To remove the EGR valve, disconnect the threaded fitting between the EGR pipe and the valve and remove the valve mounting bolts

reintroduced and the timing of the cycle is controlled by various factors such as engine speed, altitude, manifold vacuum, exhaust system backpressure, coolant temperature and throttle angle. All EGR valves are vacuum actuated and the vacuum diagram for your particular vehicle is shown on the Emissions Control Information label in the engine compartment.

2   Escort/Lynx vehicles use either the ported type or integral back-pressure transducer type EGR valves.

3   The ported EGR valve is operated by a vacuum signal from the throttle body or intake manifold EGR port, which actuates the valve diaphragm. As the vacuum increases sufficiently to overcome the spring, the valve is opened, allowing EGR flow. The amount of flow is contingent upon the tapered pintle or the poppet position, which is affected by the vacuum signal. The vacuum signal is controlled by a Backpressure Variable Transducer (BVT) on most models.

Checking

4   Make sure that all vacuum lines are properly routed, secure and in good condition (not cracked, kinked or broken off).

5   When the engine is cold, there should be no vacuum to operate the EGR valve. If there is vacuum, check the ported vacuum switch (PVS) or temperature vacuum switch (TVS) and replace them as required.

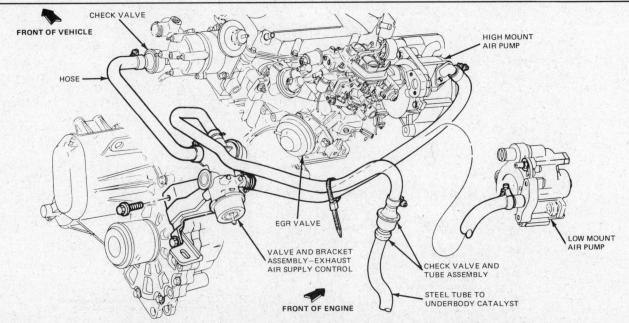

4.1   Managed air thermactor system – carbureted engine shown, others similar

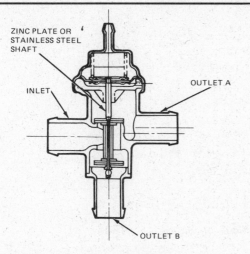

ZINC PLATE OR
STAINLESS STEEL
SHAFT

INLET

OUTLET A

OUTLET B

4.3a   A typical air control valve

6   There should be no vacuum to the valve at curb idle (engine warm).

7   There should be vacuum to the valve at 4000 rpm. If there is no vacuum, check the TVS and PVS and replace them as required.

8   With the engine at idle, apply 8 in-Hg vacuum to the valve. The valve stem should move, opening the valve, and the engine should stall or run roughly. If the valve stem moves but the engine doesn't respond, remove and clean the inlet and outlet ports with a wire brush. Do not sandblast or clean the valve with gasoline or damage will result!

9   With the engine at idle, trap 4 in-Hg vacuum in the valve. Vacuum shouldn't drop more than 1 in-Hg in 30 seconds. If it does, replace the valve.

10   When the valve is suspected of leaking (indicated by a rough idle or stalling) perform the following simple check:

a) Insert a blocking gasket (no flow holes) between the valve and

base and reinstall the valve.

b) If the engine idle improves, replace the valve and remove the blocking gasket. If the idle doesn't improve, take the vehicle to a dealer service department.

Component replacement

11   Detach the cable from negative terminal of the battery.

12   Unscrew the threaded fitting that attaches the EGR pipe to the EGR valve (**see illustration**).

13   Remove the two mounting bolts and detach the valve.

14   Remove all traces of old gasket material, using a scraper, if necessary.

15   Installation is the reverse of removal.

---

4   Managed air Thermactor system

General description

Refer to illustrations 4.1, 4.3a, 4.3b and 4.4

1   The thermactor exhaust emission control system (**see illustration**) reduces carbon monoxide and hydrocarbon content in the exhaust gases by directing fresh air into the hot exhaust gases leaving the exhaust ports. When fresh air is mixed with hot exhaust gases, oxidation is increased, reducing the concentration of hydrocarbons and carbon monoxide and converting them into harmless carbon dioxide and water.

2   Most Escort/Lynx vehicles utilize a "managed air" thermactor system, which diverts thermactor air either upstream to the exhaust manifold check valve or downstream to the rear section check valve and dual-bed catalyst (catalytic converter).

3   An air control valve is used to direct the air upstream or downstream (**see illustration**). An air bypass valve is used to dump air to the atmosphere when it's not required. In some applications, the two valves are combined into a single air bypass/control valve (**see illustration**).

6

4.3b   A typical exhaust air bypass/control valve

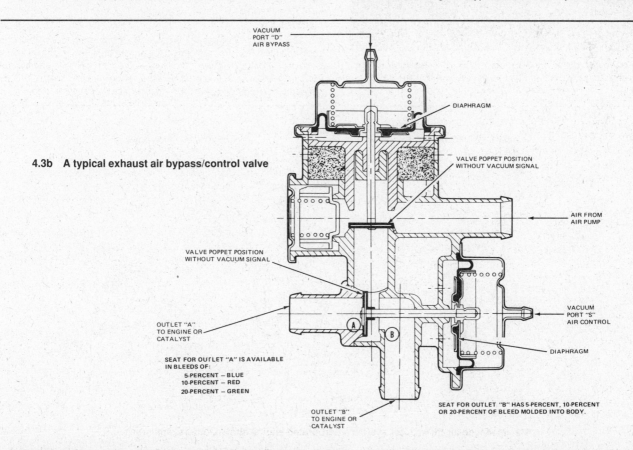

VACUUM
PORT "D"
AIR BYPASS

DIAPHRAGM

VALVE POPPET POSITION
WITHOUT VACUUM SIGNAL

AIR FROM
AIR PUMP

VALVE POPPET POSITION
WITHOUT VACUUM SIGNAL

OUTLET "A"
TO ENGINE OR
CATALYST

VACUUM
PORT "S"
AIR CONTROL

DIAPHRAGM

SEAT FOR OUTLET "A" IS AVAILABLE
IN BLEEDS OF:
    5-PERCENT — BLUE
    10-PERCENT — RED
    20-PERCENT — GREEN

OUTLET "B"
TO ENGINE OR
CATALYST

SEAT FOR OUTLET "B" HAS 5-PERCENT, 10-PERCENT
OR 20-PERCENT OF BLEED MOLDED INTO BODY.

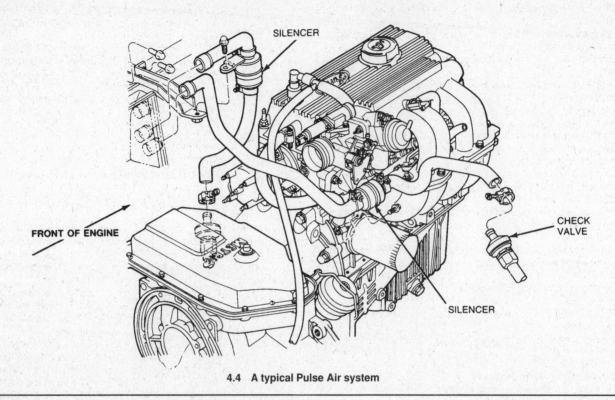

4.4   A typical Pulse Air system

4   Some engines are equipped with an air induction system called Pulse Air or Thermactor II **(see illustration)**. Instead of forcing air into the engine with a pump, this system uses the suction from exhaust system pulses to pull air into the exhaust manifold through pulse air valves. The pulse air valve is connected to the exhaust manifold with a long tube and to the air cleaner or silencer with a hose.

Checking
Thermactor system
Air supply pump
5   Check and adjust the drivebelt tension (see Chapter 1).
6   Disconnect the air supply hose at the air bypass valve inlet.
7   The pump is operating satisfactorily if air flow is felt at the pump outlet with the engine running at idle, increasing as the engine speed is increased.
8   If the air pump doesn't pass the above tests, replace it with a new or rebuilt unit.

Air bypass valve
9   With the engine running at idle, disconnect the hose from the valve outlet.
10   Remove the vacuum hose from the port and remove or bypass any restrictors or delay valves in the vacuum hose.
11   Verify that vacuum is present in the vacuum hose by putting your finger over the end. If vacuum is not present, trace the hose to its source, looking for cracks, disconnections or kinks.
12   Reconnect the vacuum hose to the port.
13   With the engine running at 1500 rpm, the air pump supply air should be felt or heard at the air bypass valve outlet.
14   With the engine running at 1500 rpm, disconnect the vacuum hose. Air at the valve outlet should be decreased or shut off and air pump supply air should be felt or heard at the silencer ports.
15   Reconnect all hoses.
16   If the normally closed air bypass valve doesn't successfully pass the above tests, check the air pump (refer to Steps 5 through 7).
17   If the air pump is operating satisfactorily, replace the air bypass valve with a new one.

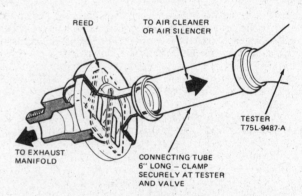

4.47   When testing a Pulse Air valve, connect a piece of hose, at least six inches long, between the valve and tester

Air supply control valve
18   With the engine running at 1500 rpm, disconnect the hose at the air supply control valve inlet and verify that air is flowing through the hose. If not, the pump is malfunctioning or a hose is disconnected or damaged.
19   Reconnect the hose to the valve inlet.
20   Disconnect the hoses at the vacuum port and at outlets A and B **(see illustration 4.3a)**.
21   With the engine running at 1500 rpm, air flow should be felt at outlet B with little or no air flow at outlet A.
22   With the engine running at 1500 rpm, connect a line from any manifold vacuum fitting to the vacuum port.
23   Air flow should be present at outlet A with little or no air flow at outlet B.
24   Reconnect all hoses.
25   If all conditions above are not met, replace the air control valve with a new one.

Combination air bypass/air control valve
26   Disconnect the hoses from outlets A and B **(see illustration 4.3b)**.
27   Disconnect the vacuum hose at port D and plug the hose.

28   With the engine running at 1500 rpm, verify that air flows from the by-pass vents.

29   Unplug and reconnect the vacuum hose at port D, then disconnect and plug the hose attached to port S.

30   Verify that vacuum is present in the hose to port D by momentarily disconnecting it.

31   Reconnect the vacuum hose to port D.

32   With the engine running at 1500 rpm, verify that air is flowing out of outlet B with no air flow present at outlet A.

33   Attach a length of hose to port S.

34   With the engine running at 1500 rpm, apply vacuum to the hose and verify that air is flowing out of outlet A. With bleed type valves, a small amount of air will flow from port A or B and the rate of air flow from the main port will change when vacuum is applied to port S.

35   Reconnect all hoses. Be sure to unplug the hose to Port S before reconnecting it.

36   If all conditions above are not met, replace the combination valve with a new one.

Check valve

37   Disconnect the hose(s) from the check valve **(see illustration 4.1)**. If the check valve is threaded into the exhaust manifold, unscrew it and take it out.

38   Blow through both ends of the check valve, verifying that air flows in one direction only.

39   If air flows in both directions or not at all, replace the check valve with a new one.

40   When reconnecting the valve, make sure it is installed in the proper direction.

Thermactor system noise test

41   The thermactor system is not completely noiseless. Under normal conditions, noise rises in pitch as the engine speed increases. To determine if noise is the fault of the air injection system, detach the drivebelt (after verifying that the belt tension is correct) and operate the engine. If the noise disappears, proceed with the following diagnosis. **Caution:** *The pump must accumulate 500 miles (vehicle miles) before the following check is valid.*

42   If the belt noise is excessive:
   a)   Check for a loose belt and tighten as necessary (refer to Chapter 1).
   b)   Check for a seized pump and replace it if necessary.
   c)   Check for a loose pulley. Tighten the mounting bolts as required.
   d)   Check for loose, broken or missing mounting brackets or bolts. Tighten or replace as necessary.

43   If there is excessive mechanical noise:
   a)   Check for an overtightened mounting bolt.
   b)   Check for an overtightened drivebelt (refer to Chapter 1).
   c)   Check for excessive flash on the air pump adjusting arm boss and remove as necessary.
   d)   Check for a distorted adjusting arm and, if necessary, replace the arm.

44   If there is excessive thermactor system noise (whirring or hissing sounds):
   a)   Check for a leak in the hoses (use a soap and water solution to find the leaks) and replace the hose(s) as necessary
   b)   Check for a loose, pinched or kinked hose and reassemble, straighten or replace the hose and/or clamps as required.
   c)   Check for a hose touching other engine parts and adjust or reroute the hose to prevent further contact.
   d)   Check for an inoperative bypass valve (refer to Step 12) and replace if necessary.
   e)   Check for an inoperative check valve (refer to Step 40) and replace if necessary.
   f)   Check for loose pump or pulley mounting fasteners and tighten as necessary.
   g)   Check for a restricted or bent pump outlet fitting. Inspect the fitting and remove any casting flash blocking the air passageway. Replace bent fittings.
   h)   Check for air dumping through the bypass valve (only at idle). On many vehicles, the thermactor system has been designed to dump

air at idle to prevent overheating the catalytic converter. This condition is normal. Determine that the noise persists at higher speeds before proceeding.
   i)   Check for air dumping through the bypass valve (the decel and idle dump). On many vehicles, the thermactor air is dumped into the air cleaner or the remote silencer. Make sure that the hoses are connected properly and not cracked.

45   If there is excessive pump noise, make sure the pump has had sufficient break-in time (at least 500 miles). Check for a worn or damaged pump and replace as necessary.

Pulse Air or Thermactor II system

Refer to illustration 4.47

Warning: *The engine should be shut off and completely cooled down before beginning this procedure.*

46   Inspect all the hoses and tubes for leaks, since leaks will cause the system to malfunction.

47   With the engine off, check the Pulse Air valve for leaks, as follows:
   a)   Disconnect the hose on the inlet side of the valve and connect the Ford Check Valve Tester (T75L-9487-A) or equivalent as shown **(see illustration)**. Be sure to connect a six-inch length of hose, securely clamped, between the valve and the tester.
   b)   Squeeze the rubber bulb on the tester as flat as possible, then release it. The bulb should remain creased for eight seconds and should not return to normal shape until after 15 seconds. If the valve does not pass this test, replace the valve.
   c)   If the above tester is not available, blow through the check valve, toward the exhaust manifold, then attempt to suck back through the valve. The valve should free flow in the direction of the exhaust manifold only. If the valve is attached to the engine and difficult to reach, attach a long length of hose to the valve inlet or unscrew and remove the valve from the engine.

48   Disconnect the hose from the Pulse Air valve inlet, then start the engine and set the parking brake.

49   With the engine idling in Park, place a piece of paper over the valve inlet. The paper should be drawn onto the valve inlet by the light suction of the system. If the valve is not drawn down or it is blown away, the Pulse Air valve is faulty. Replace it.

Component replacement

50   To replace the air bypass valve, air supply control valve, check valve, combination air bypass/air control valve or the silencer, label and disconnect the hoses leading to them, replace the faulty component and reattach the hoses to the proper ports. Make sure the hoses are in good condition. If not, replace them with new ones.

51   To replace the air supply pump, first loosen the appropriate engine drivebelts (refer to Chapter 1), then remove the faulty pump from the mounting bracket. Label all wires and hoses as they're removed to facilitate installation of the new unit.

52   If you're replacing the Pulse Air valve on a Pulse Air System (Thermactor II), be sure to use a back-up wrench.

53   After the new pump is installed, adjust the drivebelts to the specified tension (refer to Chapter 1).

---

5   Fuel evaporative emissions control system

Refer to illustrations 5.2a, 5.2b, 5.4, 5.5, 5.6, 5.7 and 5.21

General description

1   This system is designed to prevent hydrocarbons from being released into the atmosphere by trapping and storing fuel vapor from the fuel tank and the carburetor or the fuel injection system in a charcoal-filled canister. The vapor is then vented to the intake manifold or air cleaner to be burned by normal combustion.

2   The serviceable parts of the system include a charcoal-filled canister and the connecting lines between the fuel tank, fuel tank filler tube and the

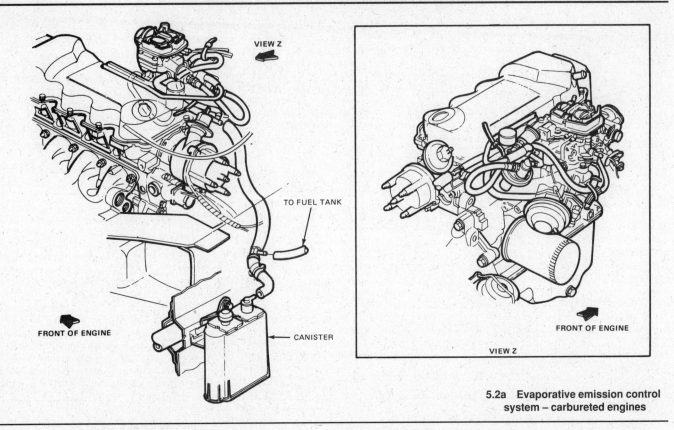

VIEW Z

TO FUEL TANK

FRONT OF ENGINE

CANISTER

FRONT OF ENGINE

VIEW Z

5.2a   Evaporative emission control system – carbureted engines

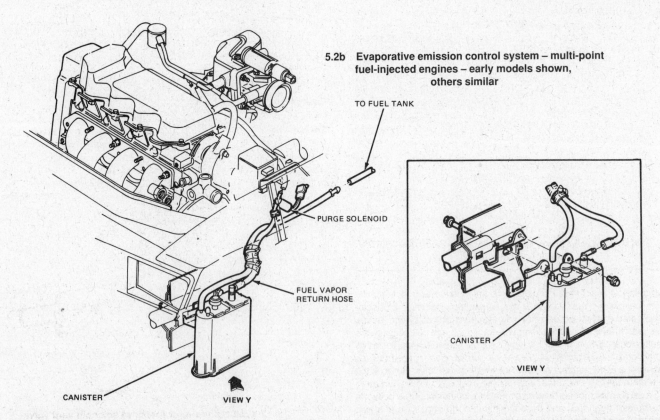

5.2b   Evaporative emission control system – multi-point fuel-injected engines – early models shown, others similar

TO FUEL TANK

PURGE SOLENOID

FUEL VAPOR RETURN HOSE

CANISTER

CANISTER

VIEW Y

VIEW Y

carburetor or fuel injection system **(see illustrations)**.
3   Vapor trapped in the fuel tank is vented through a valve in the top of the tank. The vapor leaves the valve through a single line and is routed to a charcoal canister located between the left front wheel well and the front bumper, where it's stored until the next time the engine is started.
4   On carbureted models, a canister purge valve **(see illustration)** con-

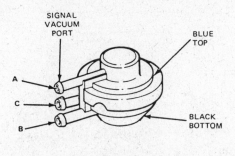

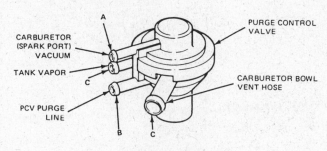

REMOTE MOUNTED

CANISTER MOUNTED

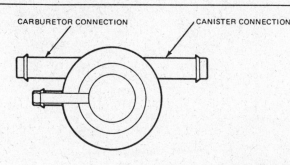

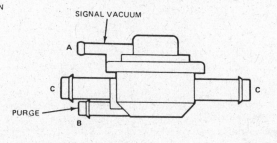

IN-LINE PURGE VALVE

5.4   A typical inline canister purge valve used on carbureted engines

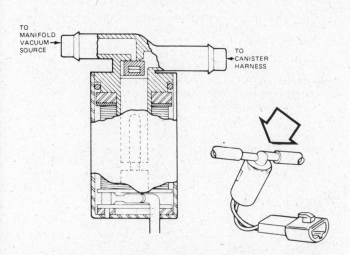

5.5   A typical canister purge solenoid (arrow) used on all EEC-IV equipped vehicles

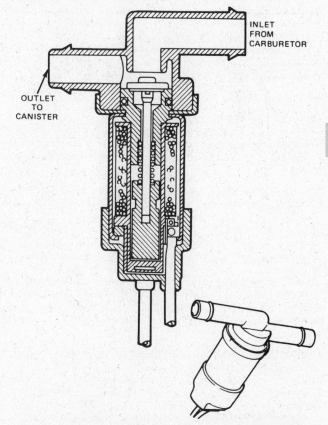

trols the flow of vapor from the canister to the intake manifold.

5   On fuel-injected models, the canister outlet is connected to an electrically actuated canister purge solenoid (**see illustration**) that is, in turn, connected to the air cleaner housing. The canister purge solenoid valve is normally closed. When the engine is started, the solenoid is energized by a signal from the ECA and allows intake vacuum to open the line between the canister and the air cleaner housing, which draws vapor stored in the canister through the air cleaner and into the engine where it's burned.

6   On carbureted models, vaporized fuel that would otherwise collect in the carburetor float bowl and pass directly into the atmosphere is also vented to the charcoal canister when the engine is stopped. Vapor flow is controlled by a fuel bowl solenoid vent valve (**see illustration**), which is normally open when the engine is off but closes the line to the canister when the engine is started. The valve returns to its normally open position when the engine is turned off. **Note:** *If the valve leaks or doesn't close, the*

5.6   A typical carburetor fuel bowl solenoid vent valve

fuel/air mixture will be leaned out. If a lean fuel mixture is suspected as the cause of a problem, check the bowl vent solenoid valve for proper closing during engine operation (refer to Step 16).

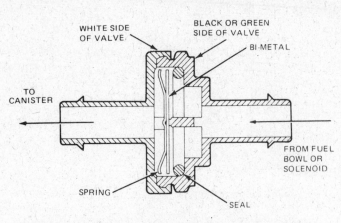

5.7   A typical carburetor fuel bowl thermal vent valve

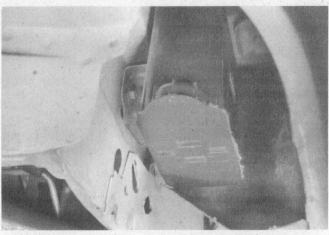

5.21   To remove the charcoal canister, detach the vacuum hose and remove the mounting bolt (hidden above the canister)

7   The thermal vent valve **(see illustration)** is a temperature actuated off/on valve in the carburetor-to-canister vent line and is closed when the engine compartment is cold. This prevents fuel tank vapor (generated when the engine heats up before the engine compartment does) from being vented through the carburetor float bowl and forces it instead into the carbon canister. This effect can occur, for example, when sunlight strikes a vehicle that has been sitting out all night and begins to warm the fuel tank. With the thermal vent valve closed, the vapor cannot enter the carburetor float bowl vent valve, but is routed instead to the charcoal canister. As the engine compartment warms up during normal engine operation, the thermal vent valve opens. When the engine is again turned off, the thermal vent valve (now open because underhood temperature is above 120-degrees F) allows fuel vapor generated in the carburetor float bowl to pass through the valve and be stored in the carbon canister. As the thermal vent valve cools, it closes and the cycle begins again.

Checking
Charcoal canister
8   There are no moving parts and nothing to wear in the canister. Check for loose, missing, cracked or broken fittings and inspect the canister for cracks and other damage. If the canister is damaged, replace it (refer to Step 20).

Canister purge valve (carburetor-equipped models)
9   Clearly label all vacuum hoses and ports, then detach the hoses from the valve.
10   Remove the valve.
11   Apply vacuum to port B **(see illustration 5.4).** The valve should be closed (no air flows through it). If it does, the valve is open. Replace it with a new one.
12   After applying and maintaining 16 in-Hg vacuum to port A, apply vacuum to port B again. Air should pass through (the valve should open). If no air flows, the valve is closed. Replace it. **Caution:** *Never apply vacuum to port C. Doing so may dislodge the internal diaphragm and the valve will be permanently damaged.*

Canister purge solenoid (fuel-injected models)
13   Remove the solenoid (refer to Step 24).
14   With the solenoid de-energized, apply 5 in-Hg to the vacuum source port **(see illustration 5.5).** The valve should not pass air. If it does, replace the valve.
15   Apply 9-to-14 volts to the valve electrical connector terminals with jumper wires. The valve should open and pass air. If it doesn't, replace the valve.

Carburetor fuel bowl solenoid vent valve
16   Remove the valve (refer to Step 24).
17   Apply 9-to-14 volts to the valve electrical connector terminals with jumper wires. The valve should close, preventing air from passing through. If the valve doesn't close, replace it.

Carburetor fuel bowl thermal vent valve
Note: *You'll need an oven and an accurate pyrometer or thermometer to test the fuel bowl thermal vent valve.*
18   Remove the valve (refer to Step 24).
19   The vent should be fully closed at 90-degrees F and below and at 120-degrees F and above. If it isn't, replace it.

Component replacement
Charcoal canister
20   Locate the canister in the engine compartment.
21   Reach up above the canister and remove the single mounting bolt **(see illustration)**.
22   Lower the canister, detach the hose from the purge valve or purge solenoid valve and remove the canister.
23   Installation is the reverse of removal.

All other components
24   Referring to the VECI label of your vehicle, locate the component to be replaced.
25   Label the hoses and fittings, then detach the hoses and remove the component.
26   Installation is the reverse of removal.

---

6   Positive Crankcase Ventilation (PCV) system

Refer to illustrations 6.3a, 6.3b and 6.3c

General description
1   The Positive Crankcase Ventilation (PCV) system cycles crankcase vapors (blow-by) back through the engine where they are burned. The valve or fixed orifice regulates the amount of blow-by gas to the intake manifold.
2   The PCV system on 1.9L multi-point fuel injected engines consists of a replaceable PCV valve, a crankcase ventilation filter and the connecting hoses.
3   The PCV system on carbureted, 1.6L multi-point and 1.9L CFI models doesn't use a conventional PCV valve. Instead, it uses a fixed orifice (two fixed orifices on 1.9L CFI models) to regulate the flow of blow-by gases from the crankcase **(see illustrations)**. Intake manifold vacuum pulls the blow-by gases through the orifice into the manifold. At idle, where only a small amount of blow-by is produced, the system also pulls air through the orifice. At high engine speeds, where a large amount of blow-by is produced, any excess that won't go through the orifice is routed to the

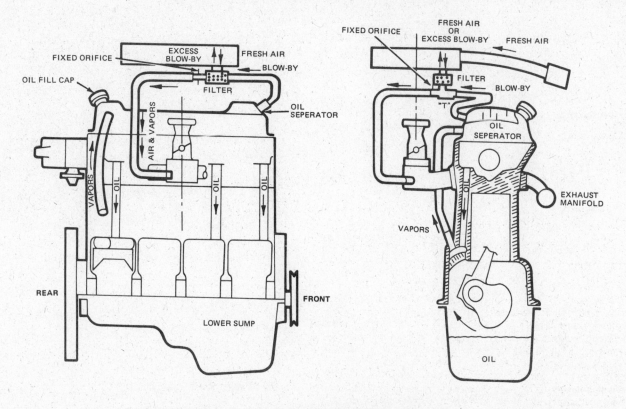

6.3a Positive crankcase ventilation system – carbureted engines

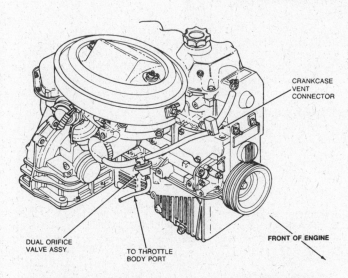

6.3b Positive crankcase ventilation system – CFI engines

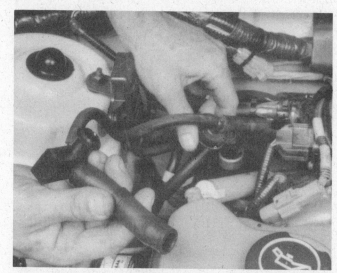

6.3c The PCV system components on CFI engines are located at the timing belt end of the engine

air cleaner. On 1.9L CFI engines, the smaller of the dual orifices is open to the intake manifold at all times. The larger orifice opens during part throttle and full throttle operation.

Checking

4   Checking procedures for the PCV system components are included in Chapter 1.
Component replacement
5   Component replacement involves simply installing a new valve or hose in place of the one removed during the checking procedure.

7   Inlet air temperature control system

Refer to illustrations 7.3a, 7.3b, 7.4, 7.20, 7.24 and 7.27

General description

1   The inlet air temperature control system provides heated intake air during warm-up, then maintains the inlet air temperature within a 70-degree F to 105-degree F operating range by mixing warm and cool air. This allows leaner fuel/air mixture settings for the carburetor or fuel injection system, which reduces emissions and improves driveability.

6

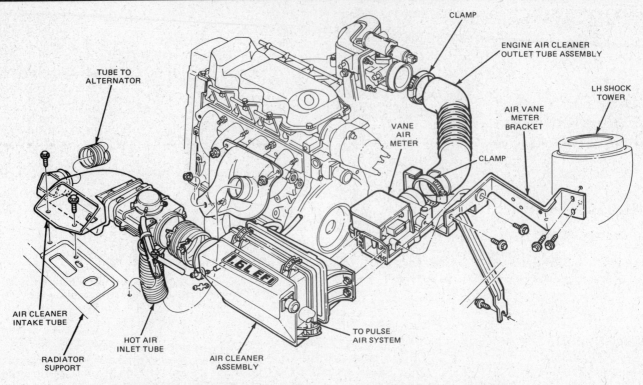

7.3a   Inlet air temperature control system – 1.6L multi-point fuel injected engines

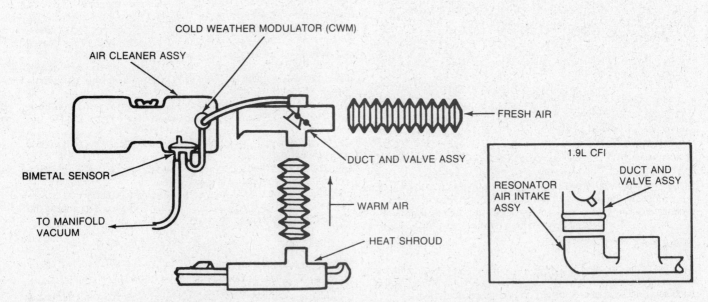

7.3b   Inlet air temperature control system – CFI engines (carbureted engines similar)

2   Two fresh air inlets – one warm and one cold – are used. The balance between the two is controlled by intake manifold vacuum, a temperature vacuum switch and a time delay valve (some models). A vacuum motor, which operates a heat duct valve in the air cleaner, is controlled by the vacuum switch.

3   When the underhood temperature is cold, warm air radiating off the exhaust manifold is routed by a shroud which fits over the manifold up through a hot air inlet tube and into the air cleaner (**see illustrations**). This provides warm air for the carburetor or fuel injection system, resulting in better driveability and faster warm-up. As the underhood temperature

rises, a heat duct valve is gradually closed by a vacuum motor and the air cleaner draws air through a cold air duct instead. The result is a consistent intake air temperature.

4   A temperature vacuum switch (**see illustration**) mounted on the air cleaner housing monitors the temperature of the inlet air heated by the exhaust manifold. A bimetal disc in the temperature vacuum switch orients itself in one of two positions, depending on the temperature. One position allows vacuum through a hose to the motor; the other position blocks vacuum.

5   The vacuum motor itself is regulated by a cold weather modulator

7.4   A typical air cleaner temperature vacuum switch (arrow)

7.20   To remove the TVS from the air cleaner housing cover, pry the retaining clip off with a small screwdriver

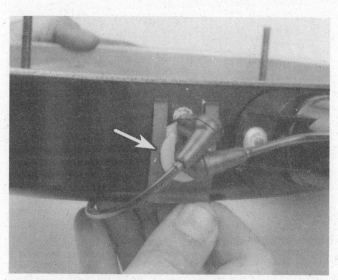

7.24   The cold weather modulator (CWM) (arrow) is located in the vacuum line between the TVS and the vacuum motor underneath the air cleaner housing – to remove it from the side of the air cleaner, disconnect the vacuum lines, pull out the clip and push the CWM into the air cleaner housing

the hinge. If it fails to work properly after servicing, replace it.

10   If the vacuum motor door is okay but the motor still fails to operate correctly, check carefully for a leak in the hose leading to it. Check the vacuum source to and from the bimetal sensor and the time delay valve as well (if equipped). If no leak is found, replace the vacuum motor (refer to Step 26).

11   Start the engine. If the duct door has moved or moves to the "heat on" (closed to fresh air) position, go to Step 15.

12   If the door stays in the "heat off" (closed to warm air) position, place a finger over the bimetal sensor bleed. The duct door must move rapidly to the "heat on" position. If the door doesn't move to the "heat on" position, stop the engine and replace the vacuum motor (refer to Step 26). Repeat this Step with the new vacuum motor.

13   With the engine off, cool the bimetal sensor and the cold weather modulator (CWM) with ice (wait for 20 seconds after the ice contacts the sensor and CWM).

14   Restart the engine. The duct door should move to the "heat on" position. If the door doesn't move or moves only partially, replace the TVS (refer to Step 18).

15   Start and run the engine briefly (less than 15 seconds). The duct door should move to the "heat on" position.

16   Shut off the engine and watch the duct door. It should stay in the "heat on" position for at least two minutes.

17   If it doesn't stay in the "heat on" position for at least two minutes, replace the CWM (refer to Step 23) and repeat this Step after cooling the CWM and bimetal sensor again with ice.

(CWM) on some models. The CWM is mounted between the temperature vacuum switch and the motor, which provides the motor with a range of graduated positions between fully open and fully closed.

Checking

Note: *Make sure that the engine is cold before beginning this test.*

6   Always check the vacuum source and the condition of all vacuum hoses between the source and the vacuum motor before beginning the following test. Do not proceed until they're okay.

7   Apply the parking brake and block the wheels.

8   Detach, but do not remove, the air cleaner housing and element (see Chapter 4).

9   Turn the air cleaner housing upside down so the vacuum motor door is visible. The door should be open. If it isn't, it may be binding or sticking. Make sure that it's not rusted in an open or closed position by attempting to move it by hand. If it's rusted, it can usually be freed by cleaning and oiling

Component replacement

Temperature Vacuum Switch (TVS)

18   Clearly label, then detach both vacuum hoses from the TVS (one is coming from the vacuum source at the manifold and the other is going to the vacuum motor underneath the air cleaner housing).

19   Remove the air cleaner housing cover assembly (refer to Chapter 1 or 4 if necessary).

20   Pry the TVS retaining clip off with a screwdriver **(see illustration)**.

21   Remove the TVS.

22   Installation is the reverse of removal.

Cold Weather Modulator (CWM)

23   Detach the air cleaner housing assembly (refer to Chapter 1 or 4).

24   Detach both vacuum hoses from the CWM, then pull out its clip and push it into the air cleaner housing **(see illustration)**.

25   Installation is the reverse of removal.

7.27   The vacuum motor is mounted on the top of the air cleaner intake – to remove it, detach the housing, detach the vacuum hose from the motor and drill out the rivet (arrow) or remove both mounting screws

Vacuum motor

26   Detach the air cleaner housing assembly (refer to Chapter 1 or 4).
27   Locate the vacuum motor **(see illustration)**.
28   Detach the vacuum hose and remove both motor mounting screws (if equipped) or drill out the rivet.
29   Remove the motor.
30   Installation is the reverse of removal.

8   Catalytic converter

Refer to illustrations 8.1, 8.8 and 8.11

General description

1   The catalytic converter **(see illustration)** is designed to reduce hydrocarbon, carbon monoxide and nitrogen oxide pollutants in the exhaust. The converter "oxidizes" these components (speeds up the heat-producing chemical reaction between the exhaust gas constituents) and converts them to water and carbon dioxide.
2   The converter, which closely resembles a muffler, is located in the exhaust system, either close to the exhaust manifold or underneath the vehicle (you'll need to raise the vehicle to inspect or replace it).
3   **Warning:** *If large amounts of unburned gasoline enter the converter, it may overheat and cause a fire. Always observe the following precautions:*

> *Use only unleaded gasoline*
> *Avoid prolonged idling*
> *Do not run the engine with a nearly empty fuel tank*
> *Avoid coasting with the ignition turned off*

Checking

Note: *An infrared sensor is required to check the actual operation of the catalytic converter. Such a device is prohibitively expensive. Take the vehicle to a dealer service department or a service station for this procedure. However, there are a few things you should check whenever the vehicle is raised for any reason.*

4   Check the bolts at the flange between the exhaust pipe front section and the front end of the catalytic converter and at the U-bolt that secures the rear end of the converter to the main exhaust pipe for a tight fit. Also check the hose clamps that seal the ends of both thermactor hoses (if equipped) to the catalytic converter for tightness.
5   Check the converter itself for dents (maximum 3/4-inch deep) and other damage that could affect its performance.
6   Inspect the heat insulator plates above and below underbody catalytic converters for damage and loose fasteners.

Component replacement

Warning: *Don't attempt to remove the catalytic converter until the complete exhaust system is cool.*

7   Raise the vehicle and support it securely on jackstands. Apply penetrating oil to the flange and clamp bolts and allow it to soak in.

Underbody converter

8   Remove the flange bolts at the front of the converter and the U-bolt at the rear **(see illustration)**.
9   Detach the air hoses from the converter.
10   Detach the converter from the inlet and outlet pipes and remove it from the vehicle. Installation is the reverse of removal. After installation, start the engine and check carefully for exhaust leaks.

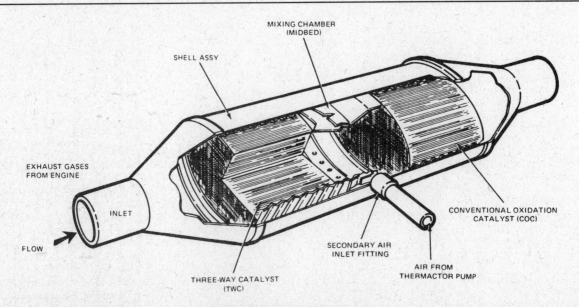

MIXING CHAMBER
(MIDBED)

SHELL ASSY

EXHAUST GASES
FROM ENGINE

INLET

FLOW

THREE-WAY CATALYST
(TWC)

SECONDARY AIR
INLET FITTING

AIR FROM
THERMACTOR PUMP

CONVENTIONAL OXIDATION
CATALYST (COC)

8.1   A typical dual catalytic converter

EFI

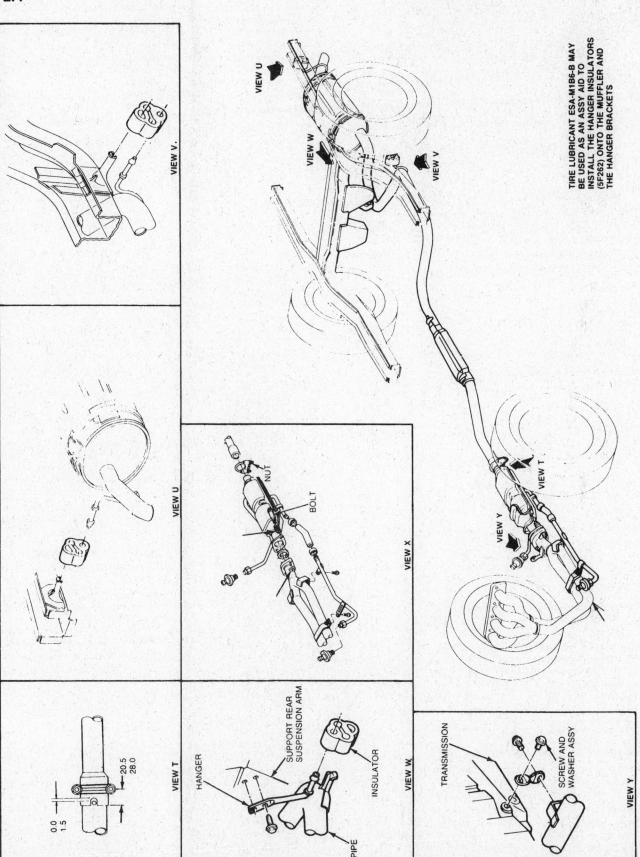

VIEW V

VIEW U

VIEW W

VIEW V

VIEW U

NUT

BOLT

VIEW X

VIEW T

20.5
28.0

0.0
1.5

VIEW T

HANGER

SUPPORT REAR
SUSPENSION ARM

INSULATOR

VIEW W

PIPE

TRANSMISSION

SCREW AND
WASHER ASSY

VIEW Y

VIEW T

VIEW Y

TIRE LUBRICANT ESA-M1B6-B MAY
BE USED AS AN ASSY AID TO
INSTALL THE HANGER INSULATORS
(5F262) ONTO THE MUFFLER AND
THE HANGER BRACKETS

8.8   A typical underbody catalytic (multi-point fuel injected models shown; carbreted models similar)

6

8.11   To detach the converter from the exhaust manifold, remove these two bolts (arrows)

Close-mount converter

11   Remove the flange bolts **(see illustration)** that attach the converter inlet pipe to the exhaust manifold.

12   Release the hose clamps (if equipped) and detach the hoses from the thermactor pipe inlets (if equipped) at the converter.

13   Remove the bolts and nuts that attach the converter outlet pipe to the exhaust pipe. Unbolt the converter support bracket and the engine ground strap.

14   Remove the catalytic converter.

15   Installation of the converter is the reverse of removal.

16   Start the engine and check carefully for exhaust leaks.

Chapter 7 Part A Manual transaxle

Contents

7A

Specifications

Torque specifications

Ft-lbs (unless otherwise indicated)

Transaxle-to-engine bolts	
1981 through 1983	28 to 31
1984 on	25 to 35
Shift lever-to-control assembly bolts	15 to 20
Speedometer retainer screw	12 to 24 in-lbs

---

1 General information

The vehicles covered by this manual are equipped with either a four- or five-speed manual transaxle or a three speed automatic transaxle. Information on the manual transaxle is included in this Part of Chapter 7. Service procedures for the automatic transaxle are contained in Chapter 7, Part B.

The manual transaxle is a compact, two piece, lightweight aluminum alloy housing containing both the transmission and differential assemblies.

Because of the complexity, unavailability of replacement parts and special tools necessary, internal repair procedures for the manual transaxle are not recommended for the home mechanic. For readers who wish to tackle a transaxle rebuild, exploded views and a brief *Transaxle overhaul – general information* Section are provided. The bulk of information in this Chapter is devoted to removal and installation procedures.

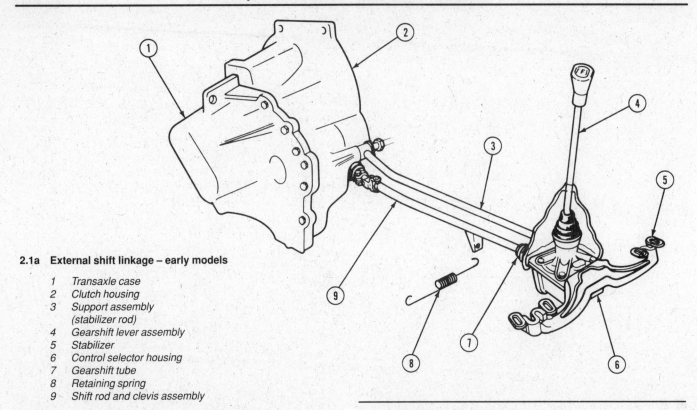

2.1a   External shift linkage – early models

1   Transaxle case
2   Clutch housing
3   Support assembly
    (stabilizer rod)
4   Gearshift lever assembly
5   Stabilizer
6   Control selector housing
7   Gearshift tube
8   Retaining spring
9   Shift rod and clevis assembly

2   Shift linkage – removal and installation

Refer to illustrations 2.1a, 2.1b, 2.1c and 2.1d
1   The external gearshift mechanism **(see illustrations)** consists of a shift lever, transaxle shift rod, stabilizer rod and shift housing. The shift housing provides for shift lever mounting and connection to the shift rod. The housing is bolted to the stabilizer, which is rubber mounted and attached to the floor pan. On the transaxle end, the stabilizer rod is mounted through a rubber insulator to a boss on the clutch housing. The function of the stabilizer rod is to equalize the movement of the engine with the shift mechanism and prevent engine movement from pulling the transaxle out of gear. Rubber boots are provided for protection of the shafts and for sound insulation. Adjustment of the external linkage is not required.

Shift lever assembly
Removal
2   Remove the console (if equipped) (see Chapter 11).
3   On early models, loosen the shift knob locking nut located under the shift knob **(see illustration 2.1b).** Remove the shift knob by rotating it counterclockwise on the shift lever, then remove the shift knob locking nut.
4   Remove the four screws that hold the boot assembly to the floor pan. Slide the boot up to uncover the tunnel opening. On early models, the boot can be lifted completely off the shift lever.
5   Through the tunnel opening, remove the four bolts that hold the shift lever assembly to the control assembly mounting bracket. Lift the shift lever assembly out of the mounting bracket and tunnel opening.
6   To remove the boot and knob from the lever on later models, secure the lever in a vise and pull the knob off. This requires approximately 80-lbs of force.

Installation
7   If you removed the boot and knob from the lever on a later model, tap it back on with light blows from a rubber mallet.
8   Insert the shift lever assembly through the tunnel opening into the control assembly. Make sure the lower plastic pivot ball on the shift lever is inserted into the bushing on the end of the shift rod.
9   Fasten the shift lever to the control assembly with the four bolts. Tighten the bolts to the torque listed in this Chapter's Specifications.

10   Depress the clutch and operate the shift lever to check the function and tightness of all fasteners.
11   Position the boot assembly over its bolt holes and secure it to the floor pan.
12   On early models, install the shift knob as follows:
   a)   Thread the locking nut down as far as it will go.
   b)   Thread the shift knob down until it reaches the locking nut and back it off until the shift pattern on top of the knob is in the correct position.
   c)   Tighten the locking nut against the shift knob.

Gearshift stabilizer bar bushing
Removal
13   Raise the vehicle and support it securely on jackstands.
14   Detach the electrical connector from the transmission control selector indicator switch.
15   Disconnect the stabilizer bar from the transaxle case by removing the bolt, the two washers and the switch and bracket **(see illustrations 2.1b and 2.1d).**
16   Push the metal sleeve out of the center of the rubber bushing.
17   Pull the rubber bushing out of the stabilizer bar ring with a pair of pliers.

Installation
18   Lubricate the bushing with rubber grease or silicone spray lubricant and push it into the stabilizer bar ring with a pair of pliers.
19   Lubricate the metal sleeve and install it in the bushing (center it in the bushing).
20   Line up the stabilizer bar bushing with the boss on the transaxle case and attach it with the bolt, washer, switch and bracket assembly.

Support assembly and shift rod/clevis assembly
Removal
21   Remove the shift lever assembly (see Step 2 above).
22   Raise the vehicle and support it securely on jackstands.
23   Remove the bolt and two washers that hold the stabilizer bar to the transaxle. Disconnect and remove the transaxle control selector indicator switch and bracket.

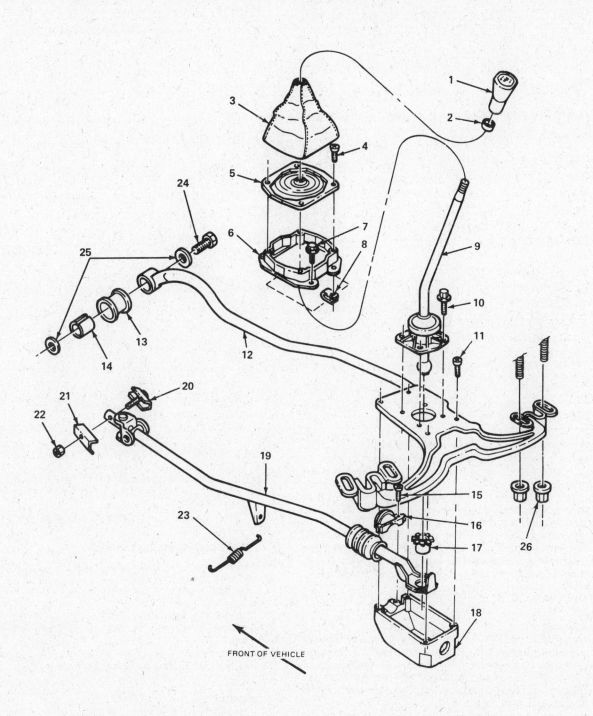

2.1b An exploded view of a typical manual transaxle shift linkage – early models

1	Gearshift lever knob	10	Bolt	19	Shift rod and clevis assembly
2	Shift knob locking nut	11	Screw	20	Gearshift lever clamp assembly
3	Upper gearshift lever boot assembly	12	Shift stabilizer bar support assembly	21	Gearshift lever clamp (2 required)
4	Screw	13	Stabilizer bar bushing	22	Nut
5	Lower shifting boot assembly	14	Gearshift rod sleeve	23	Gearshift tube retaining spring
6	Shift boot retaining assembly	15	Screw	24	Stabilizer bar attaching bolt
7	Shift boot retaining bolt	16	Control selector cover	25	Flat washers
8	Spring nut	17	Bushing	26	Nut and washer assembly
9	Gearshift lever assembly	18	Control selector housing		

7A

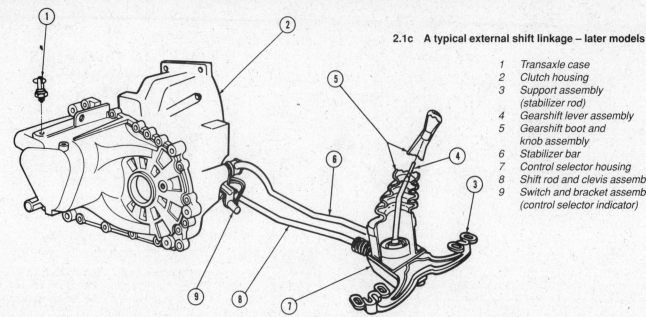

2.1c   A typical external shift linkage – later models

1   Transaxle case
2   Clutch housing
3   Support assembly
      (stabilizer rod)
4   Gearshift lever assembly
5   Gearshift boot and
      knob assembly
6   Stabilizer bar
7   Control selector housing
8   Shift rod and clevis assembly
9   Switch and bracket assembly
      (control selector indicator)

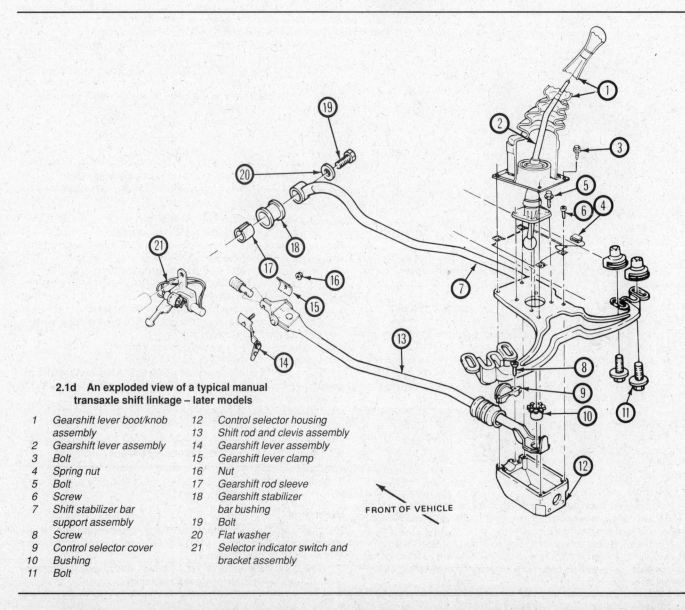

**2.1d   An exploded view of a typical manual
transaxle shift linkage – later models**

1	Gearshift lever boot/knob assembly	12	Control selector housing
2	Gearshift lever assembly	13	Shift rod and clevis assembly
3	Bolt	14	Gearshift lever assembly
4	Spring nut	15	Gearshift lever clamp
5	Bolt	16	Nut
6	Screw	17	Gearshift rod sleeve
7	Shift stabilizer bar support assembly	18	Gearshift stabilizer bar bushing
8	Screw	19	Bolt
9	Control selector cover	20	Flat washer
10	Bushing	21	Selector indicator switch and bracket assembly
11	Bolt		

FRONT OF VEHICLE

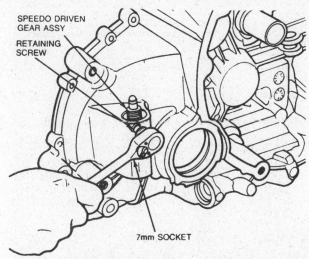

3.2   Remove the driven gear retaining screw – this illustration shows the speedometer cable disconnected from the driven gear

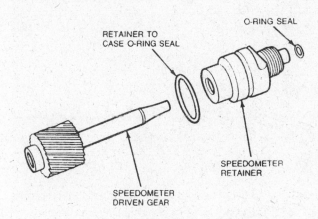

3.5   The speedometer driven gear components

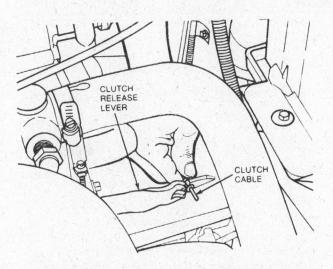

4.2   Separate the clutch cable from the release lever

24   On early models, remove the retaining spring from the shift rod and clevis assembly.

25   Loosen the shift rod clamp nut and remove the clamp and clamp assembly from the shift rod.

26   Support the support assembly and remove the four bolts or nuts that hold the support assembly to the body. **Note:** It may be necessary to lower the exhaust system (see Chapter 4) in order to remove the support assembly from between the exhaust pipe and the body.

27   Remove the four screws that hold the control selector housing and the shift rod assembly to the support assembly.

28   Remove the two screws that hold the control selector cover to the control selector housing.

29   Remove the shift rod/clevis assembly from the control selector housing.

Installation

30   Install the shift rod/clevis assembly in the control selector housing.

31   Fasten the control selector lever cover to the housing and slide the rubber boot over the mating surfaces.

32   Fasten the control selector housing to the support assembly.

33   Position the support assembly under the vehicle so the mounting bracket slots line up with the body bolts or nuts and loosely attach the assembly with the nuts or bolts.

34   Slide the shift rod over the transaxle input shaft and rotate the shift rod until the horizontal hole in the input shaft lines up with the holes in the shift rod U-joint. Install and tighten the bolt/lever assembly, the clamp and the nut.

35   Line up the stabilizer bar bushing and the transmission control selector indicator switch with the boss on the transaxle case and bolt it in place. Locate the washer on the passenger's side of the stabilizer bar and the switch and bracket on the driver's side of the stabilizer bar. Attach the connector to the switch.

36   Tighten the four nuts or bolts holding the support assembly to the body.

37   On early models, attach the retainer spring to the shift rod and clevis assembly.

38   Lower the vehicle.

39   Install the shift lever assembly (see Step 7 above).

3   Speedometer driven gear – removal and installation

Refer to illustrations 3.2 and 3.5

1   Clean off the top of the speedometer retainer.

2   Remove the retaining screw **(see illustration)**.

3   Carefully pull up on the cable to withdraw the speedometer retainer and the driven gear assembly from the bore.

4   Unscrew the speedometer cable from the retainer.

5   Carefully remove the small O-ring from the stem end of the speedometer driven gear **(see illustration)**.

6   Slide the speedometer driven gear from the retainer.

7   Carefully remove the large O-ring from the groove in the retainer.

8   Replace the O-rings with new ones.

9   Reassembly is the reverse of disassembly.

10   Lightly grease the O-ring on the retainer.

11   Using a 13/16-inch deep socket, gently tap the retainer and gear assembly into the bore while aligning the groove in the retainer with the screw hole in the side of the clutch housing case.

12   Install the screw and tighten it securely.

4   Manual transaxle – removal and installation

Refer to illustrations 4.2, 4.4a, 4.4b, 4.7, 4.8, 4.9, 4.13, 4.16, 4.17, 4.18, 4.21, 4.22, 4.26a, 4.26b and 4.27

Removal

1   Drain the transaxle lubricant (see Chapter 1) and wedge a wood block approximately seven-inches long under the clutch pedal to hold it up slightly above its normal position.

2   Grasp the clutch cable and pull forward, disconnecting it from the clutch release lever assembly **(see illustration)**.

7A

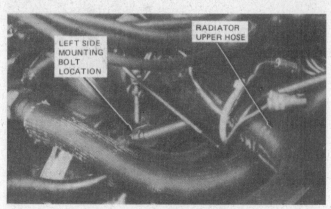

4.4a   There are two upper transaxle mounting bolts: one on the left side . . .

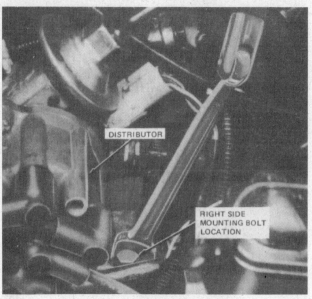

4.4b   . . . and one on the right

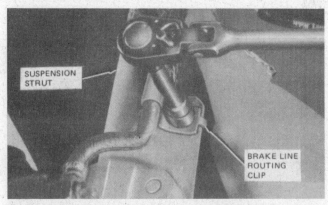

4.7   On 1981 through 1984 models, unbolt the brake hose clip from the suspension strut on each side

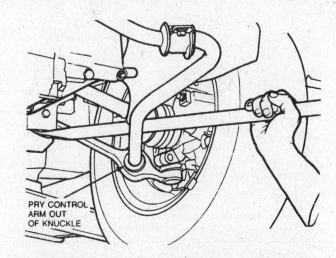

4.9   Pry downward against the stabilizer bar to separate the lower arm from the knuckle – DO NOT pry against the lower arm

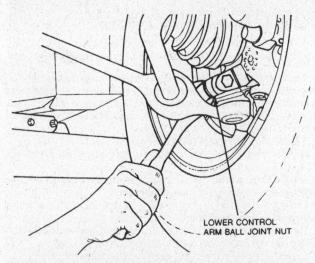

4.8   The lower control arm balljoint is secured by a nut and bolt – the nut and bolt must be discarded once removed

3   Remove the clutch cable from the rib on the upper surface of the transaxle case. Remove the starter ground cable and wiring clip from the upper transaxle-to-stud bolt.

4   Remove the two upper transaxle-to-engine bolts **(see illustrations)**.

5   Remove the upper bolt that secures the air management valve (if equipped) to the transaxle case.

6   Raise the vehicle and support it securely on jackstands.

7   On 1981 through 1984 models, unbolt the brake hose clip from the bracket on the suspension strut **(see illustration)**.

8   Remove the nut and bolt securing the lower control arm balljoint to the steering knuckle assembly **(see illustration)**. Discard the nut and bolt and install new ones on reassembly. Repeat this procedure on the other side.

9   Using a large prybar, pry against the stabilizer bar to separate the lower control arm away from the knuckle **(see illustration)**. **Caution:** *Do not pinch or cut the balljoint boot.* The prybar must not contact the lower arm. Repeat this procedure on the other side.

10   Pry the left inner driveaxle CV joint assembly from the transaxle (refer to Chapter 8). Be very careful when using a prybar to remove the CV joint assembly. Carelessness can result in damage to the differential oil seal.

11   Remove the inner CV joint from the transaxle (refer to Chapter 8) by grasping the left steering knuckle and swinging the knuckle and shaft out from the transaxle.

12   If the CV joint assembly cannot be pried from the transaxle, a special tool known as a differential rotator (Ford tool no. T81P-4026-A, or its equivalent), must be inserted through the left side so the joint can be tapped out. The tool can be used from either side of the transaxle.

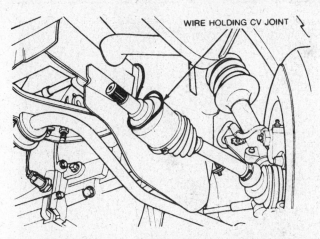

4.13 Secure both driveaxles in a near-horizontal position with wire – don't let them hang by their own weight or CV joint damage could result

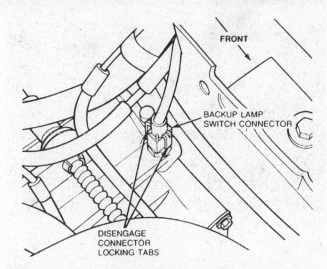

4.16 Disengage the locking tabs and unplug the electrical connector for the back-up light switch . . .

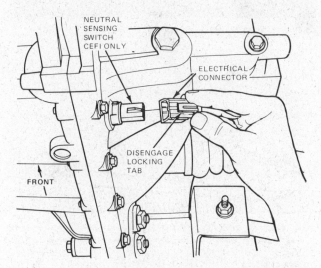

4.17 . . . on early EFI models, do the same for the neutral sensing switch

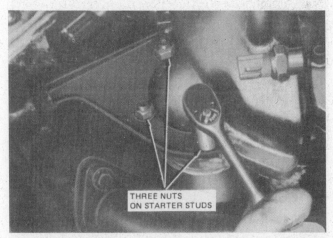

4.18 If the vehicle is equipped with a roll restrictor, remove the three nuts that secure it – these thread onto the starter stud bolts

7A

13   Tie the shaft assembly in a near-level position to prevent damage during the remaining operations (see illustration). Insert a 15/16-inch wood dowel into the transaxle opening from which the driveaxle was removed. This will keep the differential side gear from dropping while the driveaxle is removed.

14   Repeat Steps 7 through 13 on the opposite side.

15   On 1981 through 1984 models, remove the stabilizer bar (see Chapter 10).

16   Using a small screwdriver, remove the electrical connector from the transaxle back-up light switch (see illustration).

17   On early EFI models, unplug the electrical connector from the neutral sensing switch (see illustration).

18   Remove the engine roll restrictor (if equipped) (see illustration).

19   Remove the starter nuts and studs or bolts (see Chapter 5).

20   On early models, remove the shift mechanism retainer spring.

21   Remove the mechanism-to-shift shaft nut and bolt and the control selector indicator switch arm (see illustration). Remove the shift shaft.

22   Remove the shift mechanism stabilizer bar-to-transaxle mounting bolt (see illustration). Remove the screw and detach the control selector indicator switch and bracket assembly.

23   Using a large crowfoot wrench, remove the speedometer cable from the transaxle (see Section 3).

24   Remove the two stiffener brace bolts from the lower part of the clutch housing.

25   Position a transmission jack under the transaxle.

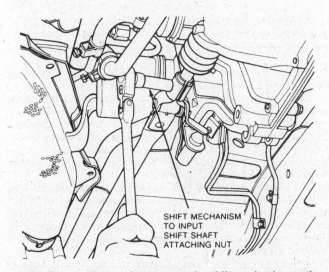

4.21 Remove the nut that secures the shift mechanism to the shift shaft

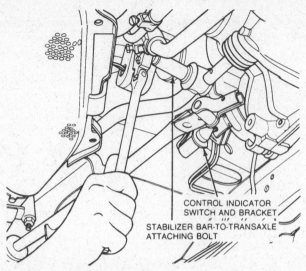

4.22   Unbolt the shift stabilizer bar from the transaxle

4.26a   On early models, remove the nut from the rear mount stud . . .

4.26b   . . . then remove the lower attaching bolt from the rear mount and loosen the two upper bolts

4.27   On early models, note the position of the wiring harness clip, then unbolt the front mount from the transaxle

26   On 1981 through 1984 models, loosen the rear mount nut **(see illustration)**. Remove the mount bottom bolt and loosen the two mount top bolts **(see illustration)**.

27   On 1981 through 1984 models, note the location of the wiring harness clip **(see illustration)**, then remove the three bolts that secure the front mount to the transaxle.

28   On 1985 and later models, remove the two nuts that secure the rear insulator to the body bracket.

29   On 1985 and later models, remove the bolts that secure the front insulator to the body bracket.

30   Make a final check that all wires and hoses have been disconnected from the transaxle, then remove the remaining transaxle-to-engine bolts and lower the transaxle jack until the transaxle clears the rear insulator. Support the engine with a jack under the oil pan. Position a block of wood between the oil pan and the jack. The jack must remain in place the entire time the transaxle is out of the vehicle.

31   Slide the transaxle away from the engine until the input shaft clears the clutch assembly. Lower the transaxle from the vehicle. The transaxle casting may have sharp edges, so wear gloves when handling the it. **Caution:** *Do not depress the clutch pedal while the transaxle is out of the vehicle.*

32   With the transaxle removed, the clutch components are now accessible and can be inspected (see Chapter 8). In most cases, new clutch components should be routinely installed when the transaxle is removed.

Installation

33   If removed, install the clutch components (see Chapter 8).

34   With the transaxle secured to the jack with a chain, raise it into position behind the engine, then carefully slide it forward, engaging the input shaft with the clutch plate hub splines. Do not use excessive force to install the transaxle – if the input shaft does not slide into place, readjust the angle of the transaxle so it is level and/or turn the input shaft so the splines engage properly with the clutch plate hub.

35   Install the lower transaxle-to-engine bolts. Tighten them securely.

36   The remainder of installation is the reverse of removal. Fill the transaxle with lubricant to the proper level (see Chapter 1).

---

5   Transaxle overhaul – general information

Refer to illustrations 5.4a, 5.4b, 5.4c and 5.4d

Overhauling a manual transaxle is a difficult job for the do-it-yourselfer. It involves the disassembly and reassembly of many small parts. Numerous clearances must be precisely measured and, if necessary, changed with select-fit spacers and snap-rings. As a result, if transaxle problems arise, it can be removed and installed by a competent do-it-yourselfer, but overhaul should be left to a transmission repair shop. Rebuilt transaxles may be available – check with your dealer parts department and auto parts stores. At any rate, the time and money involved in an overhaul is almost sure to exceed the cost of a rebuilt unit.

Nevertheless, it's not impossible for an inexperienced mechanic to rebuild a transaxle if the special tools are available and the job is done in a deliberate step-by-step manner so nothing is overlooked.

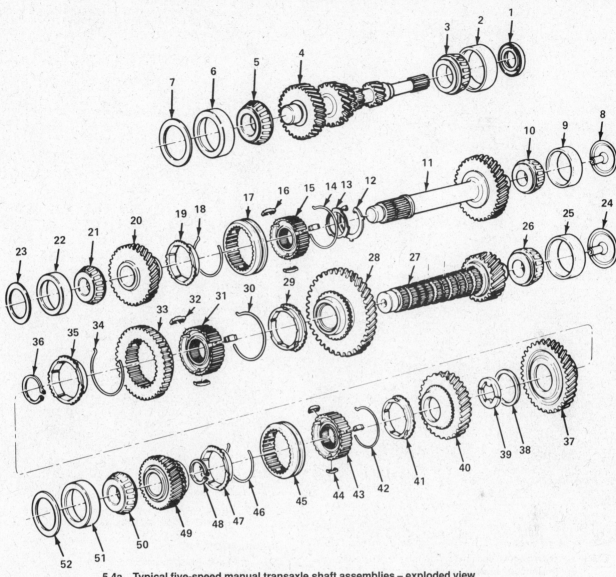

5.4a Typical five-speed manual transaxle shaft assemblies – exploded view

1	Input shaft seal assembly	19	Synchronizer blocking ring
2	Roller bearing race	20	Fifth speed gear
3	Input shaft front bearing	21	Fifth gear shaft rear bearing
4	Input cluster shaft	22	Roller bearing race
5	Input shaft rear bearing	23	Bearing preload shim
6	Roller bearing race	24	Mainshaft funnel
7	Bearing preload shim	25	Roller bearing race
8	Fifth gear funnel	26	Mainshaft front bearing
9	Roller bearing race	27	Mainshaft
10	Fifth gear shaft front bearing	28	First speed gear
11	Fifth gear drive shaft	29	Synchronizer blocking ring
12	Synchronizer insert retainer	30	Synchronizer spring
13	Synchronizer retaining spacer	31	First/second synchronizer hub
14	Synchronizer spring	32	Synchronizer hub first/second insert
15	Fifth gear synchronizer hub	33	Reverse sliding gear
16	Fifth gear synchronizer hub insert	34	Synchronizer spring
17	Fifth gear synchronizer sleeve	35	Synchronizer blocking ring
18	Synchronizer spring	36	First/second synchronizer retaining ring

37	Second speed gear
38	Second/third thrust washer retaining ring
39	Second/third gear thrust washer
40	Third speed gear
41	Synchronizer blocking ring
42	Synchronizer spring
43	Third/fourth synchronizer hub
44	Synchronizer hub third/fourth insert
45	Third/fourth synchronizer sleeve
46	Synchronizer spring
47	Synchronizer blocking ring
48	Third/fourth synchronizer ring
49	Fourth speed gear
50	Mainshaft rear bearing
51	Roller bearing race
52	Bearing preload shim

The tools necessary for an overhaul include internal and external snap-ring pliers, a bearing puller, a slide hammer, a set of pin punches, a dial indicator and possibly a hydraulic press. In addition, a large, sturdy workbench and a vise or transaxle stand will be required.

During disassembly of the transaxle, make careful notes of how each piece comes off, where it fits in relation to other pieces and what holds it in place. Exploded views are included **(see illustrations)** to show where the parts go – but actually noting how they are installed when you remove the parts will make it much easier to get the transaxle back together.

Before taking the transaxle apart for repair, it will help if you have some

5.4b Typical five-speed manual transaxle case and related components – exploded view

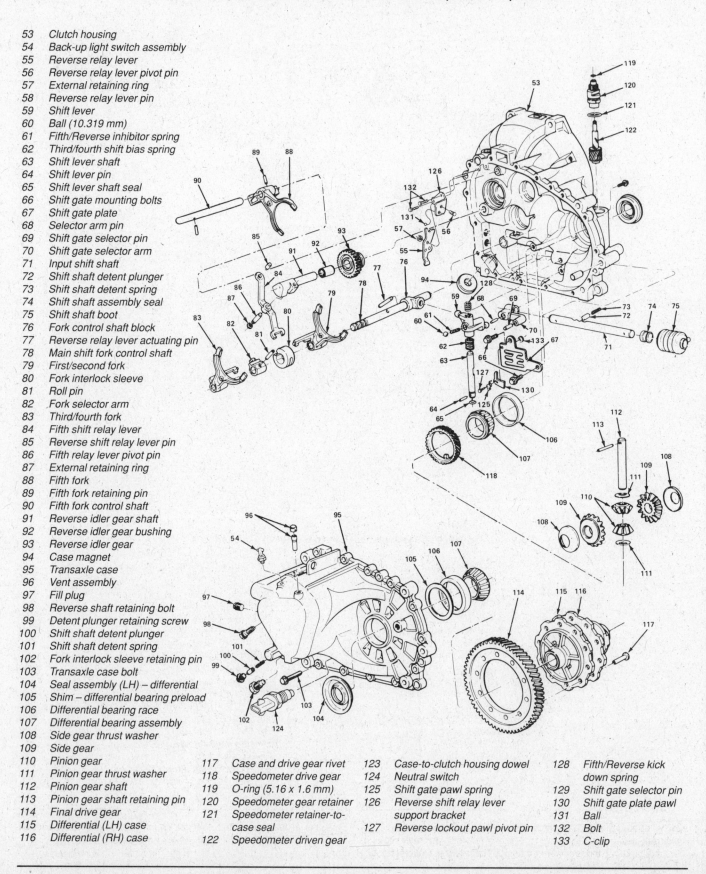

53 Clutch housing
54 Back-up light switch assembly
55 Reverse relay lever
56 Reverse relay lever pivot pin
57 External retaining ring
58 Reverse relay lever pin
59 Shift lever
60 Ball (10.319 mm)
61 Fifth/Reverse inhibitor spring
62 Third/fourth shift bias spring
63 Shift lever shaft
64 Shift lever pin
65 Shift lever shaft seal
66 Shift gate mounting bolts
67 Shift gate plate
68 Selector arm pin
69 Shift gate selector pin
70 Shift gate selector arm
71 Input shift shaft
72 Shift shaft detent plunger
73 Shift shaft detent spring
74 Shift shaft assembly seal
75 Shift shaft boot
76 Fork control shaft block
77 Reverse relay lever actuating pin
78 Main shift fork control shaft
79 First/second fork
80 Fork interlock sleeve
81 Roll pin
82 Fork selector arm
83 Third/fourth fork
84 Fifth shift relay lever
85 Reverse shift relay lever pin
86 Fifth relay lever pivot pin
87 External retaining ring
88 Fifth fork
89 Fifth fork retaining pin
90 Fifth fork control shaft
91 Reverse idler gear shaft
92 Reverse idler gear bushing
93 Reverse idler gear
94 Case magnet
95 Transaxle case
96 Vent assembly
97 Fill plug
98 Reverse shaft retaining bolt
99 Detent plunger retaining screw
100 Shift shaft detent plunger
101 Shift shaft detent spring
102 Fork interlock sleeve retaining pin
103 Transaxle case bolt
104 Seal assembly (LH) – differential
105 Shim – differential bearing preload
106 Differential bearing race
107 Differential bearing assembly
108 Side gear thrust washer
109 Side gear
110 Pinion gear
111 Pinion gear thrust washer
112 Pinion gear shaft
113 Pinion gear shaft retaining pin
114 Final drive gear
115 Differential (LH) case
116 Differential (RH) case

117 Case and drive gear rivet
118 Speedometer drive gear
119 O-ring (5.16 x 1.6 mm)
120 Speedometer gear retainer
121 Speedometer retainer-to-case seal
122 Speedometer driven gear

123 Case-to-clutch housing dowel
124 Neutral switch
125 Shift gate pawl spring
126 Reverse shift relay lever support bracket
127 Reverse lockout pawl pivot pin

128 Fifth/Reverse kick down spring
129 Shift gate selector pin
130 Shift gate plate pawl
131 Ball
132 Bolt
133 C-clip

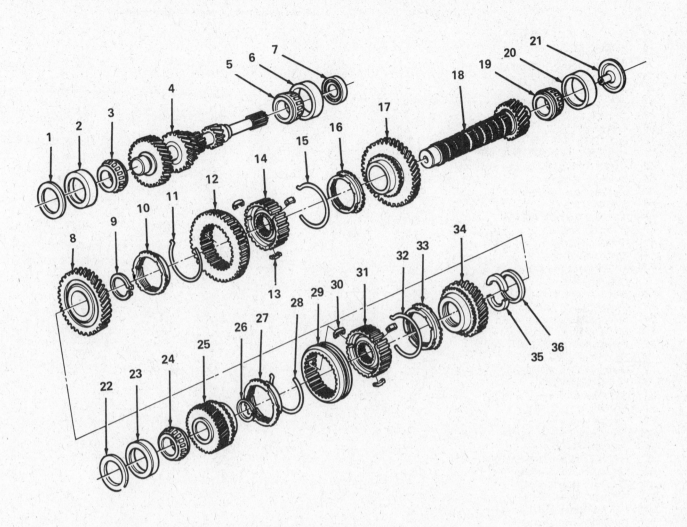

5.4c Typical four-speed manual transaxle shafts – exploded view

1	Bearing preload shim
2	Roller bearing race
3	Input shaft rear bearing
4	Input cluster shaft
5	Input shaft front bearing
6	Roller bearing race
7	Input shaft seal assembly
8	Second speed gear
9	First/second synchro retaining ring
10	Synchro blocking ring
11	Synchronizer spring
12	Reverse sliding gear
13	Synchro hub/first/second insert
14	First/second synchro hub
15	Synchronizer spring
16	Synchro blocking ring
17	First speed gear
18	Mainshaft
19	Mainshaft front bearing
20	Roller bearing race
21	Mainshaft funnel
22	Bearing preload shim
23	Roller bearing race
24	Mainshaft rear bearing
25	Fourth speed gear
26	Third/fourth synchro retaining ring
27	Synchro blocking ring
28	Synchronizer spring
29	Third/fourth synchro sleeve
30	Synchro hub third/fourth insert
31	Third/fourth synchro
32	Synchronizer spring
33	Synchro blocking ring
34	Third speed gear
35	Second/third gear thrust washer
36	Second/third thrust washer retaining ring

7A

idea what area of the transaxle is malfunctioning. Certain problems can be closely tied to specific areas in the transaxle, which can make component examination and replacement easier. Refer to the Troubleshooting section at the front of this manual for information regarding possible sources of trouble.

**5.4d   Typical four-speed manual transaxle case and
related components – exploded view**

37   Clutch housing
38   Transaxle-to-engine bolt
39   Dowel
40   Reverse relay lever pivot pin
41   Reverse relay lever
42   Back-up light switch assembly
43   External retaining ring
44   Reverse inhibitor spring and
     retaining assembly
A   Pin
B   Washer
C   Spring
D   Ring
45   Reverse inhibitor plunger
46   Shift lever shaft
47   Selector plate mounting bolt
48   Selector plate
49   Shift lever
50   Shift lever shaft set screw
51   Roll pin
52   Input shift shaft selector plate arm
53   Expansion plug
54   Input shift shaft detent plunger
55   Input shift shaft detent spring
56   Ceramic case magnet
57   Input shift shaft
58   O-ring seal (5.16 x 1.6 mm)
59   Speedometer driven gear
     retainer
60   Speedometer retainer-to-case
     seal
61   Speedometer driven gear
62   Speedometer retaining screw
63   Right differential seal assembly
64   Dowel
65   Shift shaft oil seal assembly
66   Input shift shaft boot
67   Differential bearing race
68   Transaxle identification tag
69   Case vent
70   Third/fourth fork

71   Fork selector arm
72   Spring pin
73   Fork interlock sleeve
74   First/second fork
75   Reverse idler shaft
76   Reverse idler gear
77   Fill plug

78   Reverse shaft retaining bolt
79   Main shift shaft detent plunger
80   Main shift shaft detent spring
81   Detent plunger retaining screw
82   Fork interlock sleeve retaining pin
83   Seal assembly (LH) – differential
84   Bolt

85   Case
86   Differential bearing preload shim
87   Differential bearing race
88   Main shift shaft
89   Reverse relay actuating lever pin
90   Differential and final drive ring gear
91   Third/fourth shift bias spring

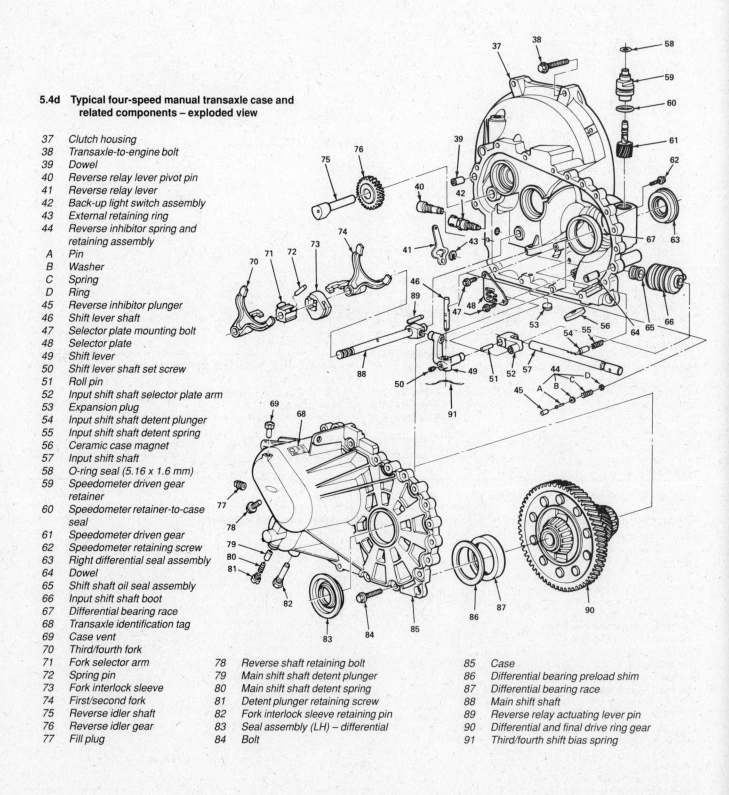

Chapter 7 Part B Automatic transaxle

Contents

Specifications

Transaxle fluid type and capacity . . . .   See Chapter 1

Torque specifications . . . .   Ft-lbs (unless otherwise indicated)

Gearshift linkage
  Manual lever-to-control cable nut
    1981 through 1987 . . . . 10 to 15
    1988 on . . . . 10 to 20
  Shift lever and housing assembly bolts . . . . 36 to 84 in-lbs
  Control cable bracket bolts . . . . 15 to 25
  Selector lever pivot bolt . . . . 13 to 20
Transaxle removal and installation
  Transaxle-to-engine bolts
    1981 . . . . 40 to 50
    1982 on . . . . 25 to 33
  Brake hose routing clip . . . . 96 in-lbs
  Manual lever bracket-to-transaxle case bolts . . . . 10 to 20
  Torque converter dust cover bolts
    1981 . . . . 12 to 16
    1982 on . . . . 15 to 21
  Torque converter-to-flywheel bolts
    1981 . . . . 17 to 29
    1982 on . . . . 23 to 39
  Insulator-to-bracket nuts . . . . 55 to 70
  Insulator bracket-to-frame bolts . . . . 40 to 50
  Insulator mount-to-transaxle bolts
    1981 . . . . 40 to 50
    1982 on . . . . 25 to 33

1   General information

Due to its complexity and because of the special tools and skills required to overhaul an automatic transaxle, all major repairs should be done by a dealer service department or a transmission shop. The troubleshooting procedures are complex and well beyond the scope of the home mechanic. Therefore, the procedures in this Chapter are limited to general diagnosis, routine adjustments, on-vehicle replacement of a few components and transaxle removal and installation.

You can adjust the throttle valve cable, shift control cable and Neutral start switch and replace a worn or damaged differential oil seal. But if the transaxle requires internal repairs or an overhaul, take it to a dealer service department or a transmission repair shop.

2   Diagnosis – general

Note: *Automatic transmission malfunctions may be caused by five general conditions: poor engine performance, improper adjustments, hydraulic malfunctions or mechanical malfunctions. Diagnosis of these problems should always begin with a check of the easily repaired items: fluid level and condition (see Chapter 1), gearshift linkage adjustment and Throttle Valve (TV) linkage adjustment. Next, perform a road test to determine if the problem has been corrected or if more diagnosis is necessary. If the problem persists after the preliminary tests and corrections are completed, additional diagnosis should be done by a dealer service department or transmission repair shop.*

Preliminary checks

1   Drive the vehicle to warm the transaxle to normal operating temperature.
2   Check the fluid level as described in Chapter 1:
   a) If the fluid level is unusually low, add enough fluid to bring the level within the SAFE area of the dipstick, then check for external leaks.
   b) If the fluid level is abnormally high, drain off the excess, then check the drained fluid for contamination by coolant.
   c) If the fluid is foaming, drain it and refill the transaxle, then check for coolant in the fluid or a high fluid level.
3   Check the engine idle speed. **Note:** *If the engine is malfunctioning, do not proceed with the preliminary checks until it has been repaired and runs normally.*
4   Check the Throttle Valve (TV) linkage for freedom of movement. Adjust it if necessary (see Section 3). **Note:** *The cable may function properly when the engine is shut off and cold, but it may malfunction once the engine is hot. Check it cold and at normal engine operating temperature.*
5   Inspect the gearshift cable (see Section 4). Make sure that it's properly adjusted and that the linkage operates smoothly.

Fluid leak diagnosis

6   Most fluid leaks are easy to locate visually. Repair usually consists of replacing a seal or gasket. If a leak is difficult to find, the following procedure may help.
7   Identify the fluid. Make sure it's transmission fluid and not engine oil or brake fluid.
8   Try to pinpoint the source of the leak. Drive the vehicle several miles, then park it over a large sheet of cardboard. After a minute or two, you should be able to locate the leak by determining the source of the fluid dripping onto the cardboard.
9   Make a careful visual inspection of the suspected component and the area immediately around it. Pay particular attention to gasket mating surfaces. A mirror is often helpful for finding leaks in areas that are hard to see.
10 If the leak still cannot be found, clean the suspected area thoroughly with a degreaser or solvent, then dry it.
11 Drive the vehicle for several miles at normal operating temperature and varying speeds. After driving the vehicle, visually inspect the suspected component again.

12 Once the leak has been located, the cause must be determined before it can be properly repaired. If a gasket is replaced but the sealing flange is bent, the new gasket will not stop the leak. The bent flange must be straightened.
13 Before attempting to repair a leak, check to make sure that the following conditions are corrected or they may cause another leak. **Note:** *Some of the following conditions (a leaking torque converter, for instance) cannot be fixed without highly specialized tools and expertise. Such problems must be referred to a transmission shop or a dealer service department.*

Gasket leaks
14 Check the pan periodically. Make sure the bolts are tight, no bolts are missing, the gasket is in good condition and the pan is flat (large dents in the pan may indicate damage to the valve body inside).
15 If the pan gasket is leaking, the fluid level or the fluid pressure may be too high, the vent may be plugged, the pan bolts may be too tight, the pan sealing flange may be warped, the sealing surface of the transaxle housing may be damaged, the gasket may be damaged or the transaxle casting may be cracked or porous. If sealant instead of gasket material has been used to form a seal between the pan and the transaxle housing, it may be the wrong sealant.

Seal leaks
16 If a transaxle seal is leaking, the fluid level or pressure may be too high, the vent may be plugged, the seal bore may be damaged, the seal itself may be damaged or improperly installed, the surface of the shaft protruding through the seal may be damaged or a loose bearing may be causing excessive shaft movement.
17 Make sure the dipstick tube seal is in good condition and the tube is properly seated. Periodically check the area around the speed sensor for leakage. If transmission fluid is evident, check the speedometer driven gear O-rings for damage. Also inspect the differential oil seals for leakage.

Case leaks
18 If the case itself appears to be leaking, the casting is porous and will have to be repaired or replaced.
19 Make sure the oil cooler hose fittings are tight and in good condition.

Fluid comes out vent pipe or fill tube
20 If this condition occurs, the transaxle is overfilled, there is coolant in the fluid, the case is porous, the dipstick is incorrect, the vent is plugged or the drain back holes are plugged.

3   Throttle Valve (TV) linkage – check and adjustment

Refer to illustrations 3.16 and 3.19

General description

1   The TV linkage on carburetor-equipped engines consists of the coupling lever on the carburetor, the shaft assembly, the transaxle control rod assembly, the external control lever on the transaxle and a linkage return spring. The coupling lever follows the motion of the carburetor throttle lever. The TV linkage shaft and control rod transmits motion between the coupling lever on the carburetor and the TV control lever on the transaxle.
2   The TV linkage on fuel-injected engines consists of a coupling lever on the throttle body, the rod assembly, the bellcrank assembly, the transaxle control rod assembly, the external TV control lever on the transaxle and a linkage return spring. The coupling lever follows the motion of the throttle body shaft. The control rod, the bellcrank assembly and the control rod transmit motion between the coupling lever on the throttle body and the TV control lever on the transaxle.
3   On all engines, the control rod assembly is adjusted to proper length during initial assembly. The external TV control lever actuates the control mechanism which regulates the control pressure. The external TV control lever motion is controlled by internal transaxle stops at idle and beyond wide open throttle. The linkage return spring must overcome the transaxle lever load (due to spring loading to WOT).

3.16   To adjust the TV control linkage, loosen the bolt on the sliding trunnion block at least one turn . . .

4   The TV control is set to the proper length during initial assembly using the sliding trunnion block on the TV control rod assembly. Any required adjustment of the TV linkage can be accomplished at the sliding trunnion block.

5   On fuel-injected engines, when the linkage is properly adjusted, the TV control lever on the transaxle will just contact the internal idle stop (lever rotated clockwise as far as it will travel when viewed from the left side of the vehicle) when the throttle lever is in the closed throttle position (idle speed control plunger retracted).

6   On all engines, at wide open throttle, the TV control lever on the transmission will not be at the wide open stop. The wide open throttle position must not be used as the reference point for adjusting the linkage.

Shift trouble diagnosis related to throttle linkage adjustment

7   If the transmission shifts early and/or softly with or without a slip/bump feel, or if there is no forced downshift (kickdown) function at the appropriate speeds, the TV linkage is set too short.

8   If shifts are extremely delayed, upshifts are harsh or idle engagement is harsh, the TV control linkage is set too long. Adjust the linkage as described in this Section.

9   If idle engagement is harsh after engine warm-up, there's a shift clunk when the throttle is backed off after heavy acceleration, the coasting downshifts from 3rd to 2nd, or 2nd to 1st in the D range are harsh, or upshifts are delayed during light acceleration, either:
  a) The TV control rod or linkage shaft isn't returning properly. Remove the cause of the interference, then check and/or reset the linkage as described in this Section.
  b) Excessive friction due to binding of the grommets is preventing the TV control linkage from returning. Check for bent/twisted rods or levers causing misalignment of the grommets. Repair or replace the defective components (replace the grommets if they're damaged). Reset the TV control linkage as described in this Section.

10   If upshifts are erratic and/or delayed, there is no kickdown or engagements are harsh, the clamping bolt on the trunnion at the upper end of the TV control rod is loose. Reset the TV control linkage as described in this Section.

11   If there are no upshifts and/or engagements are harsh, either:
  a) The TV control rod is disconnected (leaving the transaxle at maximum TV pressure). Reconnect the TV control rod. If the disconnected rod is caused by defective grommets, replace the grommets.
  b) The linkage return spring is broken or disconnected. Reconnect or replace the spring.

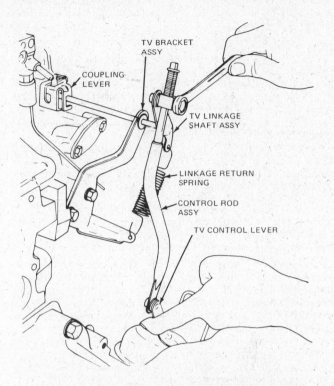

3.19   . . . then, using one finger, rotate the TV control lever at the transaxle up against the internal idle stop and tighten the bolt on the trunnion block

Linkage adjustment

Manual linkage

12   This is a critical adjustment. Be sure that the D detent in the transaxle corresponds exactly with the stop in the console. If not, adjust the gearshift linkage (see Section 4). Hydraulic leakage at the manual valve can cause delays in engagement and/or slipping if the linkage is not correctly adjusted.

TV linkage

13   Start the engine and warm it up to normal operating temperature. Turn off all accessories. Verify the curb idle speed is correct and the choke, if equipped, is off. **Note:** *On carbureted models, the linkage cannot be properly set if the throttle lever is on the choke fast idle cam.* **Warning:** *The following steps require working near the EGR system. Care must be taken to avoid contact with hot parts.*

14   Set the parking brake and place the transaxle in Park

15   On 1981 through 1983 models, set the adjustment screw on the coupling lever to its approximate midrange position and insure that the TV linkage shaft assembly is fully seated upward into the coupling lever.

16   Loosen the bolt on the sliding trunnion block on the TV control rod assembly at least one turn **(see illustration)**.

17   Remove any corrosion from the control rod and free up the trunnion block so it slides freely.

18   On 1988 and later models, connect a jumper wire between the STI connector and the signal return ground on the self-test connector. Turn the ignition key to the RUN position. Do not start the engine. The ISC plunger will retract. Wait until the plunger is fully retracted (about ten seconds). Shut off the key and remove the jumper wire.

19   With the engine idling and the transaxle in Park, rotate the transaxle TV control lever up using one finger and a light force (about one pound) to make sure the TV control lever is against the internal idle stop. Without relaxing the force on the TV control lever, tighten the bolt on the trunnion block securely **(see illustration)**.

7B

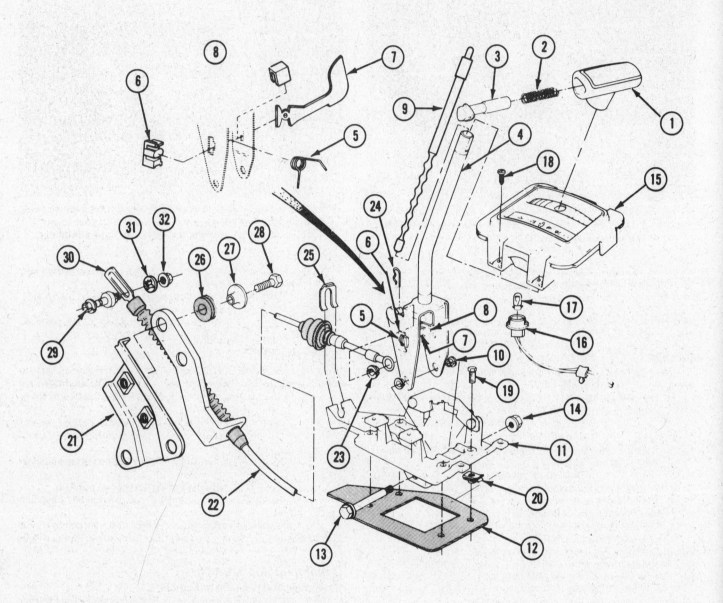

4.4 Automatic transaxle shifter assembly components – exploded view

1	Shift lever knob	11	Housing assembly	22	Cable and bracket assembly
2	Shift rod spring	12	Seal	23	Shift lever bushing
3	Release button	13	Pilot bolt (M8 X 1.25 flange)	24	Retaining pin
4	Shift lever assembly	14	Nut	25	Brake cable spring lock clip
5	Park gear lockout	15	Bezel assembly	26	Cable bracket insulator
	return spring	16	Indicator light	27	Cable bracket spacer
6	Spacer	17	Bulb	28	Bolt
7	Shift lever pawl	18	Screw	29	Shift arm insulator
8	Shift lever sleeve	19	Bolt	30	Shift connecting rod
9	Selector rod	20	Nut		adjusting stud
10	Shift lever shaft	21	Cable bracket	31	Nut (M8 push-on)
	clevis bushing		retainer assembly	32	Nut and washer

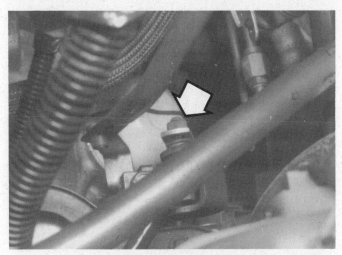

4.7   To adjust the control linkage, place the shift lever in Drive, loosen the manual lever-to-control cable retaining nut (arrow), move the transaxle lever to the second detent from the rear position and tighten the nut

4.12   To remove the knob from the shift lever, put the lever in any gear that places the lever at an angle in line with your forearm, grip the knob firmly, depress the button and pull straight up

---

4   Gearshift linkage – check, adjustment and replacement

Refer to illustrations 4.4, 4.7, 4.12, 4.14, 4.15, 4.16, 4.17, 4.18, 4.25, 4.30, 4.31, 4.32 and 4.35

Check

1   If the engine won't start in Park and/or Neutral, any of the following problems could be the cause:
   a) The transaxle Neutral start switch is out of adjustment. Readjust it (see Chapter 12).
   b) The transaxle cable retainer bracket is loose. Secure the bracket by tightening the two bolts (see Step 32).
   c) The cable bracket attached to the transmission retainer bracket is loose. Tighten it (see Step 32).
   d) The shift linkage requires adjustment (see Step 6).
2   If the gear position indicator doesn't correspond to the transaxle gear:
   a) The transaxle cable retainer bracket is loose. Tighten the bolts holding the bracket (see Step 32).
   b) The cable bracket attached to the transmission retainer bracket is loose. Tighten it (see Step 32).
   c) The shift linkage requires adjustment (see Step 6).
   d) The clip securing the cable to the housing or the clip securing the cable to the lever assembly is loose. Install the clip(s) properly (see Step 16).
3   If the gear position indicator doesn't light up:
   a) The bulb is burned out. Replace the bulb (see Chapter 12).
   b) The wiring harness is damaged. Repair or replace the harness (refer to Chapter 12 and the wiring diagrams at the end of this book).
4   If there's a rattle, noise, buzz, etc.:
   a) The shift knob is loose. Tighten the locking nut on the upper end of the shift lever (see Step 25).
   b) The lever and housing assembly is not bolted tightly to the floor pan. Tighten the mounting nuts (see Step 19).
   c) The park gear lockout spring is not hooked. Attach the spring properly **(see illustration)**.
   d) The bezel assembly is loose. Tighten the bezel assembly mounting screws (see Step 14).
   e) The transaxle gear shift lever cable bushing is missing. Install the bushing (see Step 17).
   f) The transaxle control shift rod clevis bushing is missing. Install the bushing **(see illustration 4.4)**.
5   If water enters the inside of the vehicle:
   a) The cable assembly grommet is not secured to the floor pan. Secure the grommet to the floor pan (see Step 29).

   b) The cable assembly grommet is torn. Install a new cable assembly (see Steps 28 through 46).
   c) The lever and housing assembly is loose. Tighten the bolts that attach the housing to the floor pan (see Step 18).
   d) The lever and housing assembly seal is missing or torn **(see illustration 4.4)**. Refer to Step 19.

Adjustment

Note: *The control linkage adjustments must be performed in the order in which they appear. Refer to the exploded view* **(see illustration 4.4)** *when necessary for the following adjustment and component replacement procedures.*

6   Position the shift lever on the transaxle in the Drive position, against the rear stop. The shift lever must be held in the rear position while the linkage is being adjusted.
7   Loosen the manual lever-to-control cable retaining nut **(see illustration)**.
8   Move the shift lever inside the vehicle to the Drive position.
9   Tighten the control cable nut to the torque listed in this Chapter's Specifications.
10   Check the operation of the transaxle in each shift lever position (try to start the engine in each gear – the starter should operate in Park and Neutral only).

Component replacement
Shift lever and housing assembly

11   Place the shift lever in a position (D, 2 or 1) that will incline the lever towards you.
12   To detach the shift knob, grasp it securely, depress the release button and pull up **(see illustration)**. **Note:** *The release button is spring-loaded. Make sure that it doesn't pop out of the shift knob and get lost.*
13   Remove the console/consolette assembly (see Chapter 11).
14   Remove the four screws from the bezel assembly **(see illustration)**.
15   Lift the bezel assembly slightly, disconnect the indicator light harness **(see illustration)** and remove the bezel assembly.
16   Remove the cable retaining clips from the shift lever and the housing assembly **(see illustration)**. Place the control cable assembly and bushing aside.
17   Remove the four bolts which attach the shift lever and lever housing assembly to the floor pan **(see illustration)** and remove the assembly.
18   Remove the selector lever pilot bolt nut, slide the pilot bolt out and separate the lever from the housing. Remove the pilot bolt bushings from the selector lever clevis **(see illustration)** and inspect them for damage and wear. If either bushing is worn or damaged, replace the pair and reassemble the selector lever and housing assembly. Be sure to coat the new bushings with multi-purpose grease to prevent squeaking and wear.

7B

4.14   The shift lever bezel housing screws (arrows)

4.15   Unplug the shift indicator light harness connector before attempting to remove the shift lever bezel housing

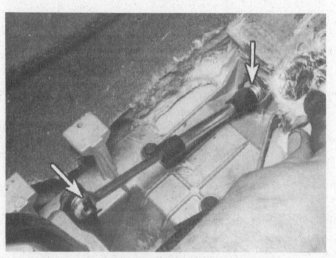

4.16   To detach the shift cable from the shift lever, remove the retaining pin and the clip (arrows)

4.17   The shift lever housing assembly mounting bolts (arrows)

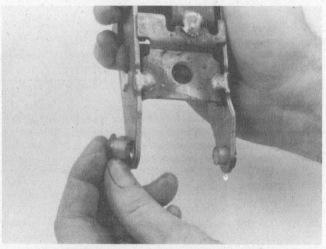

4.18   To get at the shift lever clevis bushings, remove the pilot bolt and nut and pull the lever from the housing – if the bushings are worn or damaged, replace them

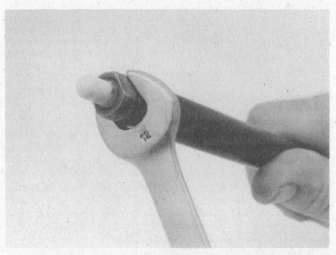

4.25   Make sure the locking nut on top of the shift lever is tight

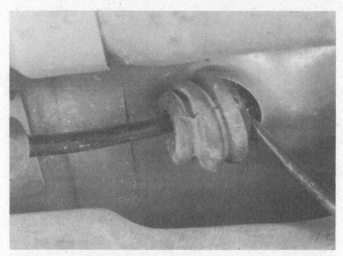

4.30 Before detaching the shift cable, pry the rubber grommet out – if it's worn, cracked or torn, replace it (or water will get into the passenger compartment)

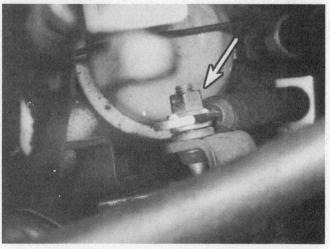

4.31 To detach the shift cable from the transaxle lever, remove the retaining nut (arrow)

19 Check the selector lever housing seal, then install the lever and housing assembly and secure it with the four bolts. Tighten the bolts securely.

20 Inspect the control cable bushing for wear and damage. Replace it if necessary. Slide the control cable assembly and bushing onto the shaft. Be sure to lubricate the bushing with multi-purpose grease to prevent squeaking and wear.

21 Secure the cable assembly and bushing to the selector lever by installing the retainer pin **(see illustration 4.16)**.

22 Position the control cable assembly in the lever and housing assembly and secure it by installing the cable retaining clip **(see illustration 4.16)**.

23 Install the bezel assembly over the shift lever, connect the indicator light harness and secure the bezel assembly to the selector housing with the four screws.

24 Install the console on the lever and housing assembly and attach it with the four screws (see Chapter 11 if necessary).

25 Make sure that the locking nut on the upper end of the shift lever is tight **(see illustration)**.

26 Assemble the shift knob, spring and button.

27 Hold the shift knob securely and depress the button all the way, then firmly push the shift knob onto the lever until it's seated.

Cable and bracket assembly

28 Remove the shift knob, console, bezel assembly, control cable clip and cable retaining pin (see Steps 11 through 18).

29 Raise the vehicle and place it securely on jackstands.

30 Disengage the rubber grommet from the floor pan by pushing it towards the engine compartment **(see illustration)**. Be careful not to tear it.

31 Remove the retaining nut and control cable assembly from the transaxle lever **(see illustration)**.

32 Remove the control cable assembly bracket bolts **(see illustration)**.

33 Pull the cable through the floor pan.

34 Feed the round end of the new control cable assembly through the floor pan.

35 Press the rubber boot on the control cable assembly into the body panel opening **(see illustration)**.

36 Position the control cable assembly in the selector lever housing assembly and install the spring clip.

37 Install the bushing and control cable assembly on the selector lever and housing assembly shaft and secure it with the retaining pin.

38 Install the bezel assembly, console and shift knob (see Steps 19 through 27).

39 Position the shift lever in the Drive position. The lever must be held in this position while attaching the other end of the control cable assembly.

40 Position the control cable bracket on the retainer bracket and secure it with the two bolts, then tighten both bolts securely.

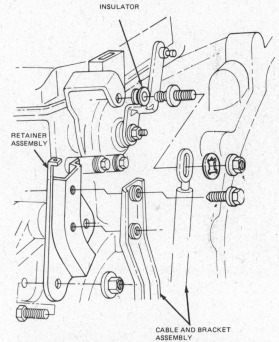

4.32 Shift control cable bracket and related components – exploded view

7B

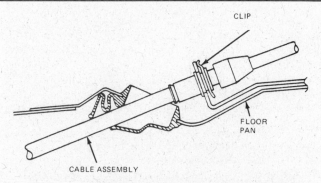

4.35 Be sure the rubber grommet is properly installed in the opening in the floor pan (if it isn't, water may get into the vehicle through the hole)

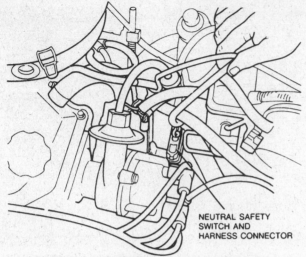

5.3   Unplug the electrical connector for the neutral
safety switch . . .

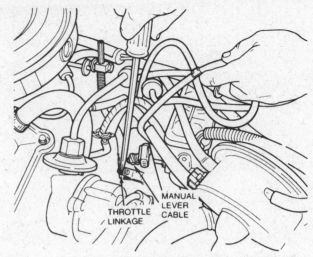

5.4   . . . then disconnect the throttle linkage and manual
lever cables

5.6   Some models are equipped with a managed air valve –
unbolt it from the top of the transaxle

41   Shift the transaxle manual lever into Drive (the second detent from the rear position).
42   Place the cable end on the transaxle manual lever stud, using care not to align the flats on the stud with the slot in the cable. Start the attaching nut.
43   Make sure the shift lever hasn't moved from the Drive detent, then tighten the nut securely.
44   Lower the vehicle and make sure the engine starts in Park and Neutral only.

Retainer bracket assembly

45   Raise the vehicle and place it securely on jackstands.
46   Remove the bolts securing the cable bracket to the retainer bracket assembly.
47   Remove the two nuts which attach the retainer bracket assembly to the engine mount bracket. Do not remove the two bolts.
48   Slide the retainer bracket assembly off.
49   Place the retainer bracket assembly on the engine mount bolts and secure it by installing the two nuts.
50   Position the cable assembly bracket on the retainer bracket and install the bolts.
51   Lower the vehicle and check the shift lever operation.

Lever and adapter assembly

52   Remove the shift knob, console and bezel assembly (see Steps 11 through 18) and disconnect the control cable assembly from the shift lever and housing assemblies (see Steps 28 through 33).
53   Remove the lever, adapter and housing assemblies (see Steps 11 through 18).
54   Unscrew the lever and adapter assembly pivot nut and remove the pivot bolt.
55   Pull the shift lever assembly out of the selector housing.
56   Remove the pivot bushings from the lever and adapter assembly.
57   Install the pivot bushings in the lever and adapter assembly. Apply silicone grease to the lever assembly park pawl, park pawl slot and the bushings.
58   Insert the lever and adapter assembly into the housing and align the bolt holes.
59   Install the pivot bolt and nut and tighten the nut securely.
60   Install the lever and housing assembly (see Steps 19 through 27).
61   Install the control cable assembly, bezel assembly, console and shift knob (see Steps 19 through 27).
62   Adjust the control linkage (see Steps 6 through 10).

---

5   Automatic transaxle – removal and installation

Refer to illustrations 5.3, 5.4, 5.6, 5.9a, 5.9b, 5.19, 5.20, 5.21, 5.22, 5.23, 5.24, 5.25 and 5.27

1   Disconnect the negative battery cable from the battery.
2   Remove the air cleaner if necessary to provide access for transaxle removal.
3   Disconnect the electrical connector from the neutral safety switch **(see illustration)**.
4   Disconnect the transaxle throttle linkage at the transaxle levers **(see illustration)**.
5   On models with a timing window in the torque converter housing, cover it with duct tape or equivalent to keep dirt from falling in.
6   If the vehicle has a managed air thermactor valve attached to the transaxle top cover, unbolt it **(see illustration)**. Remove the thermactor hose retaining bolts as needed and position the hoses out of the way.
7   Remove the ground strap above the upper engine mount (if equipped).
8   Remove the ignition coil and bracket (see Chapter 5).
9   Remove both upper transaxle-to-engine bolts **(see illustrations)**.
10   Loosen the front wheel nuts. Raise the vehicle and position it securely on jackstands. DO NOT get under a vehicle that is supported only by a jack! Remove the front wheels and drain the transaxle fluid (see Chapter 1).

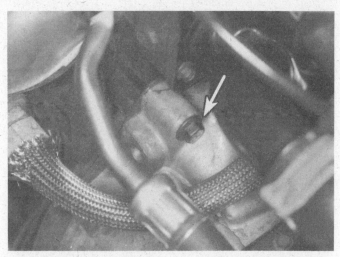

5.9a The upper front transaxle mounting bolt is located on one side of and slightly below the distributor . . .

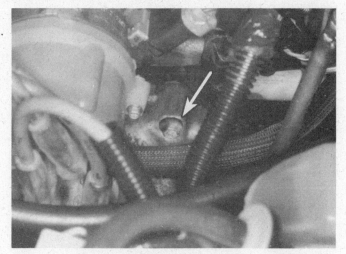

5.9b . . . while the upper rear transaxle mounting bolt is located on the other side of and slightly below the distributor

11 Remove and discard the balljoint clamp bolt on each side of the vehicle, then disengage the suspension arms from the steering knuckles (see Chapter 10).

12 Remove the stabilizer bar (see Chapter 10).

13 Unbolt the brake hose clip from the suspension strut on each side of the vehicle.

14 Remove the steering gear tie-rod nuts and detach the tie rods from the steering knuckles (see Chapter 10).

15 Detach the right-hand driveaxle from the transaxle (see Chapter 8) and support it with wire. Do not allow it to hang by its own weight.

16 Separate the left-hand driveaxle from the transaxle with Ford tool T81P-4026-A or equivalent (see Chapter 8). Support the driveaxle with wire; do not allow it to hang by its own weight.

17 Install seal plugs (Ford tool T81P-1177-B or equivalent) in the driveaxle holes. If the plugs are not available, install 15/16-inch wood dowels. Plugs or dowels must be installed or the differential side gears could drop, meaning you'll have to tow the vehicle to a dealer service department (or other qualified shop) to have the side gears re-positioned.

18 Remove the starter (see Chapter 5).

19 Unbolt and remove the transaxle support bracket (see illustration).

20 Remove the torque converter housing dust cover (see illustration).

21 Turn the crankshaft with a socket on the pulley bolt to bring each of the torque converter-to-flywheel nuts into view (see illustration). Remove the nuts.

22 Place a transmission jack beneath the transaxle. Make sure the transaxle is securely supported, then remove the rear support bracket nuts (see illustration).

23 Remove the attaching nuts and bolts and take out the left front mounting insulator bracket (see illustration).

24 Disconnect the transaxle cooler lines (see illustration).

25 Unbolt the manual lever bracket from the transaxle case (see illustration).

26 Securely support the engine with a jack. Use a block of wood between the jack and oil pan to prevent damage.

27 Remove the four transaxle-to-engine bolts (two on each side) that haven't yet been removed (see illustration).

28 Carefully insert a screwdriver between the driveplate and torque converter and pry the engine and transaxle apart until the torque converter studs clear the driveplate.

29 Lower the transaxle 2 to 3 inches and disconnect the speedometer cable.

30 Check to be sure all hoses and wires are disconnected, then lower the transaxle the rest of the way. While you're lowering, keep an eye on the left front mounting insulator. If it's in the way, remove it.

31 Installation is the reverse of the removal steps. Refer to Chapter 10 for suspension and driveaxle installation procedures. Refill the transaxle with fluid (see Chapter 1).

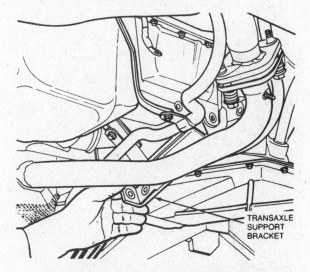

5.19 With the vehicle securely supported on jackstands, remove the transaxle support bracket

7B

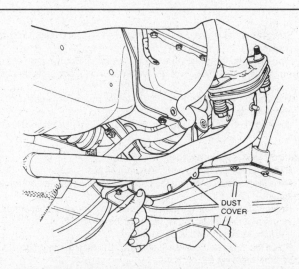

5.20 Access to the torque converter-to-flywheel bolts is gained by removing the torque converter housing dust cover

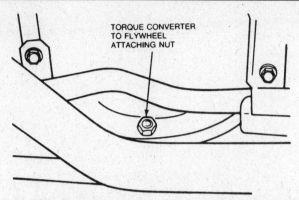

5.21   Turn the crankshaft pulley with a wrench on the pulley bolt to bring each of the torque converter-to-flywheel bolts to an accessible position – if you remove the spark plugs, you may be able to turn the pulley with your bare hands, but be careful not to cut yourself on any sharp edges

5.22   With the transaxle securely supported on a transmission jack, remove the transaxle support nuts

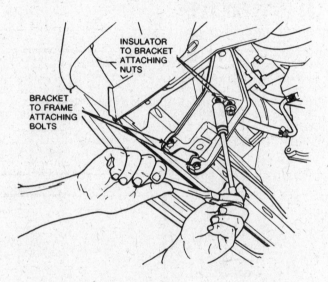

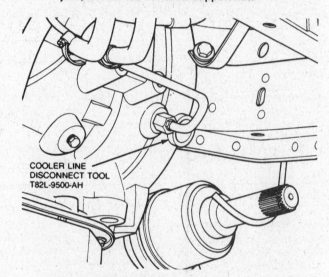

5.23   Remove the left front mounting insulator bracket

5.24   Disconnect the transaxle cooler lines from the transaxle – for lines that use flare-nut fittings, use a flare-nut wrench (Ford tool T82L-9500-AH or equivalent)

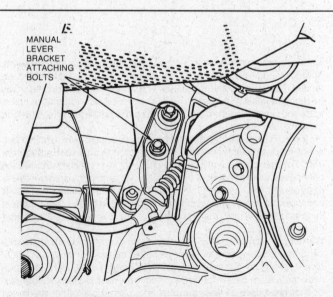

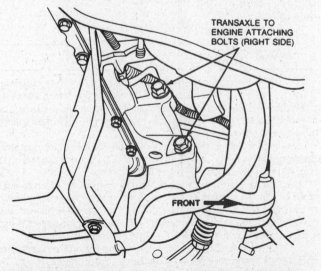

5.25   Remove the manual lever bracket attaching bolts

5.27   In addition to the upper two transaxle mounting bolts, there are two mounting bolts on each side of the transaxle

Chapter 8   Clutch and driveaxles

Contents

Specifications

Torque specifications   Ft-lbs

Pressure plate-to-flywheel bolts	12 to 24
Clutch release lever-to-shaft bolt	
1981 and 1982	12 to 24
1983	30
1984 on	30 to 40
Clutch pedal pivot bolt nut	
1981 through 1985	15 to 25
1986 on	25 to 30
Clutch pedal stop mounting bracket nuts	15 to 25
Driveaxle hub nut	180 to 200

---

1   General information

All vehicles with a manual transaxle have a single dry plate, diaphragm spring type clutch. The clutch plate has a splined hub which allows it to slide along the splines on the input shaft. The clutch and pressure plate are held in contact by spring pressure exerted by the diaphragm spring in the pressure plate.

During gear shifting, the clutch pedal is depressed, which operates a cable, pulling on the release lever so the release bearing pushes on the diaphragm spring fingers, disengaging the clutch.

The clutch pedal incorporates a self-adjusting device which compensates for clutch wear. A spring in the clutch pedal arm maintains tension on the cable and the adjuster pawl grabs a ratcheting mechanism when the pedal is depressed and the clutch is released. Consequently the slack is always taken up in the cable, making adjustment unnecessary.

Power from the engine passes through the clutch and transaxle to the front wheels by two driveaxles. The driveaxles are of unequal length. The driveaxles consist of three sections: the inner splined ends which are held in the differential by clips or springs, two constant velocity (CV) joints and outer splined ends which are held in the hub by a nut. The CV joints are internally splined and contain ball bearings which allow them to operate at various lengths and angles as the suspension is compressed and extended. The CV joints are lubricated with special grease and are protected by rubber boots which must be inspected periodically for cracks, holes, tears and signs of leakage, which could lead to damage of the joints and failure of the driveaxle.

It should be noted that the terms used in this manual to describe various clutch components may vary somewhat from those used by parts vendors. For example, such terms as clutch plate, pressure plate and release bearing are used throughout this Chapter. An auto parts store or dealer parts department, however, might use the terms clutch disc, clutch cover and throwout bearing, respectively, for the above parts. The important thing is to keep in mind that the terms are interchangeable – they mean the same thing.

Warning: *Dust produced by clutch wear and deposited on clutch components may contain asbestos, which is hazardous to your health. DO NOT blow it out with compressed air and DO NOT inhale it. DO NOT use gasoline or petroleum-based solvents to remove the dust. Brake system cleaner should be used to flush the dust into a drain pan. After the clutch components are wiped clean with a rag, dispose of the contaminated rags and cleaner in a covered container.*

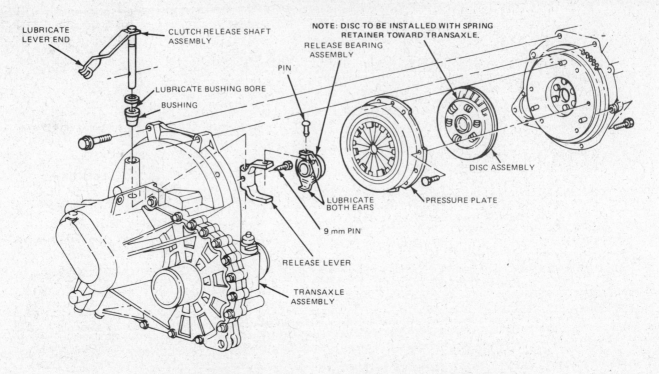

3.4   An exploded view of the clutch assembly and related components

2   Clutch operation – check

Other than to replace components with obvious damage, some preliminary checks should be done to diagnose clutch problems.

a) With the engine running and the brake applied, hold the clutch pedal 1/2-inch from the floor and shift back-and-forth between First and Second gear several times. If the shifts are smooth, the clutch is releasing properly. If they aren't, the clutch is not releasing completely. Check the pedal, cable, lever and throwout bearing.

b) To check clutch "spin down" time, run the engine at normal idle speed with the transaxle in Neutral (clutch pedal up – engaged). Disengage the clutch (pedal down), wait several seconds and shift the transaxle into Reverse. No grinding noise should be heard. A grinding noise would indicate component failure in the clutch plate or pressure plate.

c) A clutch pedal that's binding is most likely caused by a faulty clutch cable or dry clutch release shaft bushing. Lubricate the bushing with SAE 10W-30 motor oil. Check the cable where it enters the case for rust and corrosion. If it looks good, lubricate the cable with penetrating oil. If pedal operation improves, the cable is worn out and should be replaced.

3   Clutch components – removal, inspection and installation

Refer to illustrations 3.4, 3.6, 3.9 and 3.11

Warning: *Dust produced by clutch wear and deposited on clutch components may contain asbestos, which is hazardous to your health. DO NOT blow it out with compressed air and DO NOT inhale it. DO NOT use gasoline or petroleum-based solvents to remove the dust. Brake system cleaner should be used to flush the dust into a drain pan. After the clutch components are wiped clean with a rag, dispose of the contaminated rags and cleaner in a covered container.*

Removal

1   Remove the engine/transaxle assembly from the vehicle (Chapter 2, part B). Remove the bolts and separate the engine from the transaxle.

2   Use a center punch to mark the position of the pressure plate assembly on the flywheel so it can be installed in the same position.

3   Loosen the pressure plate bolts a little at a time, in a criss-cross pattern, to prevent warping the pressure plate.

4   Remove the bolts and detach the pressure plate and disc assembly from the flywheel **(see illustration)**.

5   Handle the clutch carefully, trying not to touch the lining surface, and set it aside.

Inspection

6   Inspect the friction surfaces of the disc assembly, pressure plate and flywheel for signs of uneven contact, indicating improper installation or damaged clutch springs. Also look for score marks, burned areas, deep grooves, cracks and other types of wear and damage. If the flywheel is worn or damaged, remove it and take it to an automotive machine shop to see if it can be resurfaced (if it can't, a new one will be required). If the flywheel is glazed, rough it up with fine emery cloth. To see how worn the disc assembly is, measure the distance from the rivet heads to the lining surface **(see illustration)**. There should be at least 1/16-inch of lining above the rivet heads. However, the disc assembly is ordinarily replaced with a new one whenever it's removed for any reason (due to the relatively low cost of the part and the work involved to get to it).

7   Check the lining for contamination by oil or grease and replace the disc assembly with a new one if any is present. Check the hub for cracks, blue discolored areas, broken springs and contamination by grease or oil. Slide the disc assembly onto the input shaft to make sure the fit is snug and the splines are not burred or worn.

8   Remove and inspect the release bearing and release lever as described in Section 4.

9   Check the flatness of the pressure plate with a straightedge. Look for signs of overheating, cracks, deep grooves and ridges. The inner end of the diaphragm spring fingers should not show any signs of uneven wear. Replace the pressure plate with a new one if its condition is in doubt **(see illustration)**.

10   Make sure the pressure plate fits snugly on the flywheel dowels. Replace it with a new one if it fits loosely on the dowels.

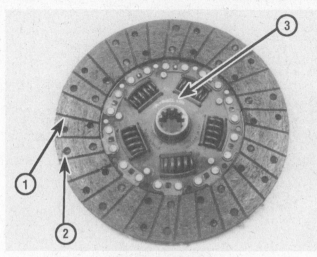

3.6 The clutch plate

1 Lining – this will wear down in use
2 Rivets – these secure the lining and will damage the
   flywheel or pressure plate if allowed to contact the surfaces
3 Markings – "Flywheel side" or something similar

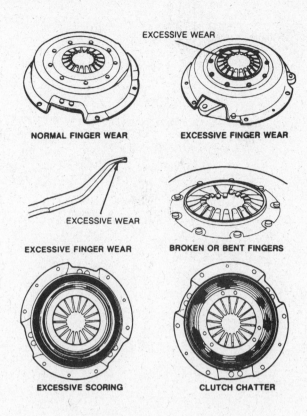

3.9 Replace the pressure plate if excessive wear is noted

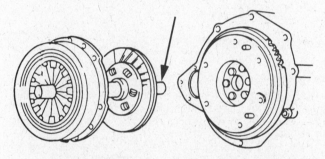

**3.11 A special tool (arrow) – available at auto parts stores
– is needed to align the clutch plate with the transaxle input
shaft and hold it in place as the pressure plate is installed**

Installation

11 Position the disc assembly on the flywheel, centering it with an alignment tool **(see illustration)**.
12 With the clutch plate held in place by the alignment tool, place the pressure plate in position on the flywheel dowels, aligning it with the marks made at the time of removal.
13 Install the bolts and tighten them in a criss-cross pattern, one or two turns at a time, until they're at the torque listed in this Chapter's Specifications.
14 Install the release lever and release bearing (see Section 4).
15 Attach the transaxle to the engine (see Chapter 2, Part B).

4 Clutch release bearing and lever – removal, inspection and installation

Refer to illustration 4.2
Warning: *Dust produced by clutch wear and deposited on clutch components may contain asbestos, which is hazardous to your health. DO NOT blow it out with compressed air and DO NOT inhale it. DO NOT use gasoline or petroleum-based solvents to remove the dust. Brake system cleaner should be used to flush the dust into a drain pan. After the clutch components are wiped clean with a rag, dispose of the contaminated rags and cleaner in a covered container.*

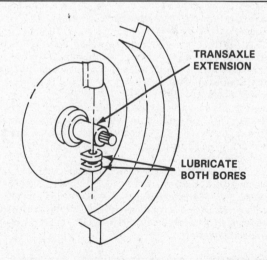

4.2 The release bearing rides on the transaxle extension

Removal

1 Remove the engine/transaxle assembly from the vehicle, separate the transaxle from the engine and clean the clutch housing as described in the Warning above.
2 Remove the release bearing retaining pin **(see illustration 3.4)** from the release lever and slide the bearing off the transaxle extension **(see illustration)**.
3 To remove the release lever from the shaft, remove the lever-to-shaft bolt **(9mm pin in illustration 3.4)**. Pull the shaft up through the clutch housing and lift out the lever.

8

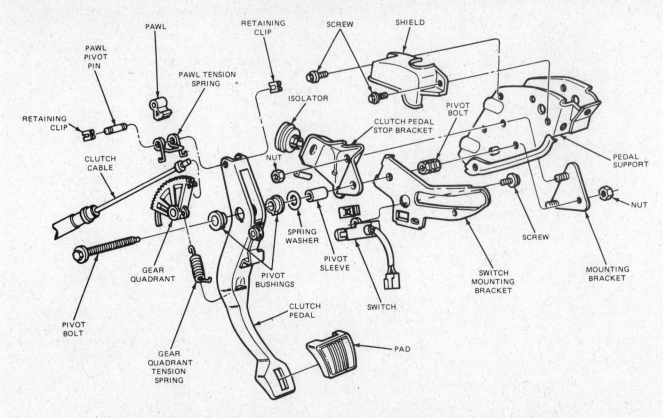

5.2   An exploded view of the clutch pedal, self adjuster mechanism and related components

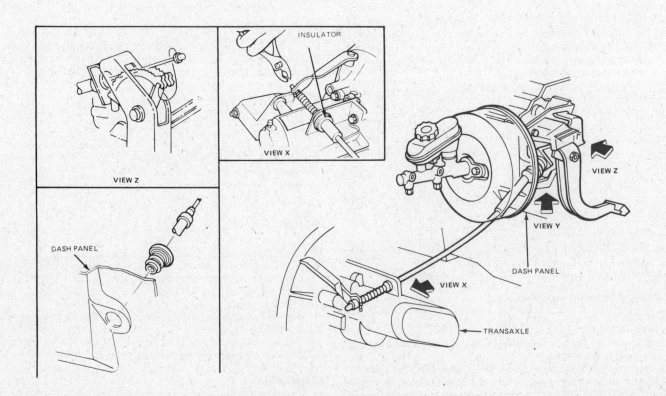

5.3   Clutch cable installation details

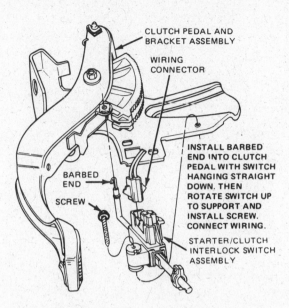

CLUTCH PEDAL AND
BRACKET ASSEMBLY

WIRING
CONNECTOR

BARBED
END

SCREW

INSTALL BARBED
END INTO CLUTCH
PEDAL WITH SWITCH
HANGING STRAIGHT
DOWN. THEN
ROTATE SWITCH UP
TO SUPPORT AND
INSTALL SCREW.
CONNECT WIRING.

STARTER/CLUTCH
INTERLOCK SWITCH
ASSEMBLY

6.3   Starter/clutch interlock switch mounting details

Inspection

4   Check the lever arms and shaft for excessive wear and galling.
5   Inspect the bearing for damage, wear and cracks. Hold the center of the bearing and spin the outer race, putting pressure against it. If the bearing doesn't turn smoothly or if it's noisy, replace it with a new one. It's common practice to replace the bearing with a new one whenever a clutch job is performed, to decrease the possibility of a bearing failure in the future.

Installation

6   Wipe the old grease from the release bearing if the bearing is to be reused. Do not clean it by immersing it in solvent; it's sealed at the factory and would be ruined if solvent got into it. Fill the cavities and coat the inner surface, as well as the transaxle extension, with high-temperature multi-purpose grease.
7   Lubricate the release shaft bushings, position the release lever in the clutch housing and slide the shaft down through the lever and into the bottom bushing. Install the lever-to-shaft bolt and tighten it to the torque listed in this Chapter's Specifications. Lubricate the release lever arms where they contact the bearing with high-temperature multi-purpose grease.
8   Slide the release bearing onto the transaxle extension and position it in the release lever arms with the ears on the bearing straddling the lever arms. Insert the locating pin through the top ear and into the release lever.
9   Work the clutch release shaft lever by hand to verify smooth operation of the release bearing and shaft.

5   Clutch cable – removal and installation

Refer to illustrations 5.2 and 5.3

Removal

1   Remove the left side under-dash panel.
2   Using a small screwdriver, disengage the adjuster pawl from the gear quadrant (**see illustration**).
3   Remove the air cleaner assembly for access to the clutch cable (see Chapter 4). Pull the clutch cable from the clutch release lever with a pair of pliers. Grip the cable end, not the cable itself (**see illustration**).
4   Pull the cable and housing through the insulator on the transaxle (**see illustration 5.3**).

5   Loosen the front clutch pedal shield screw, remove the rear screw and swing the shield up and out of the way. Tighten the front screw to hold the shield up (**see illustration 5.2**).
6   With the pawl released from the gear quadrant, rotate the quadrant forward and unhook the cable. The quadrant is under spring tension – don't let it snap back into position.
7   Pull the cable from the clutch pedal assembly and push it through the firewall into the engine compartment.

Installation

8   Insert the cable through the firewall from the engine compartment side.
9   Working under the dash, guide the cable through the isolator on the pedal stop bracket (**see illustration 5.2**). Have an assistant lift up on the clutch pedal to release the pawl. Rotate the quadrant forward. Hook the cable end into the quadrant.
10   Swing the shield back into place and tighten the two screws.
11   Route the cable through the insulator on the transaxle housing.
12   Have an assistant pull back on the clutch pedal and hold it there. Connect the cable to the clutch release lever.
13   Depress the clutch pedal a few times to adjust the cable.
14   Install the under-dash panel.
15   Install the air cleaner assembly.

6   Starter/clutch interlock switch – removal and installation

Refer to illustration 6.3

Removal

1   Remove the left side under-dash panel.
2   Detach the wire harness connector from the interlock switch.
3   Remove the interlock switch-to-bracket screw and rotate the switch down (**see illustration**).
4   Compress the barb at the end of the switch rod and remove the switch from the clutch pedal.

Installation

5   Position the adjuster clip approximately 1-inch from the end of the rod.
6   Insert the barbed end of the rod into the bushing on the clutch pedal.
7   With the clutch pedal all the way up, swing the switch into place. Install the mounting screw and tighten it securely.
8   Push the clutch pedal to the floor to adjust the switch.
9   Install the under-dash panel.

7   Clutch pedal and self-adjusting mechanism – removal and installation

Refer to illustrations 7.9a, 7.9b, 7.10 and 7.11

Removal

1   Remove the clutch cable (see Section 5).
2   Disconnect the clutch switch electrical connectors.
3   Remove three nuts and detach the clutch pedal stop bracket from the brake pedal support (**see illustration 5.2**). Take the clutch pedal assembly out of the vehicle.
4   Remove the pedal pivot bolt nut, pivot bolt and pedal.
5   Remove the quadrant tension spring, pivot sleeve, bushings and gear quadrant from the pedal.
6   Remove the clip from the pawl pivot pin, then remove the pin, pawl and tension spring (**see illustration 5.2**).

Installation

7   Check all parts for wear or damage and replace as necessary.
8   Apply a thin coat of multi-purpose grease to the pivot bore of the quadrant and pawl, as well as to the quadrant pivot pin and sleeve.

8

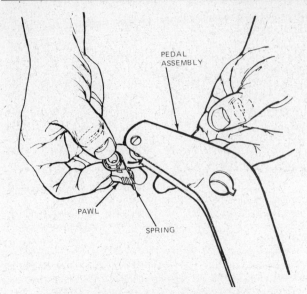

7.9a   **Install the pawl and spring on the pedal, then secure them with the pivot pin and clip . . .**

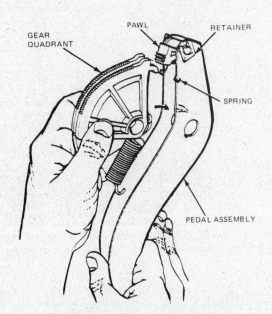

7.10   **Hook the quadrant spring into the quadrant so its free end is positioned as shown, then insert the quadrant into the pedal**

7.9b   **. . . so the spring and pawl are oriented as shown**

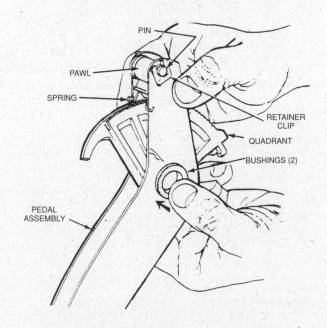

7.11   **Engage the pawl with the quadrant teeth, then install the pivot sleeve and bushings**

15   Position the clutch pedal on the brake pedal support. Install the three mounting nuts and tighten them to the torque listed in this Chapter's Specifications.
16   The remainder of installation is the reverse of the removal Steps.

8   Driveaxles, constant velocity (CV) joints and boots – check

1   The driveaxles, CV joints and boots should be inspected periodically and whenever the vehicle is raised for any reason. The most common symptom of driveaxle or CV joint failure is knocking or clicking noises when turning.
2   Raise the vehicle and support it securely on jackstands.
3   Inspect the CV joint boot for cracks, leaks and broken retaining bands. If lubricant leaks out through a hole or crack in the boot, the CV joint will wear prematurely and require replacement. Replace any damaged boots immediately (see Section 10). It's a good idea to disassemble, clean, inspect and repack the CV joint whenever replacing a CV joint boot, to ensure that the joint is not contaminated with moisture or dirt, which could cause premature CV joint failure.
4   Check the entire length of each axle to make sure they aren't cracked, dented, twisted or bent.
5   Grasp each axle and rotate it in both directions while holding the CV joint housings to check for excessive movement, indicating worn splines or loose CV joints.

9   Install the pawl and tension spring in the pedal. Install the pawl pivot pin and secure it with the clip **(see illustration)**. Be sure the pawl and spring are positioned correctly **(see illustration)**.
10   Hook the quadrant tension spring to the quadrant with its free end positioned as shown in the accompanying illustration.
11   Insert the tension spring in the pedal past the bracket, then rotate the quadrant and engage the pawl with the quadrant teeth **(see illustration)**.
12   Install the two bushings and pivot sleeve in the pedal **(see illustration 7.11)**.
13   Hook the tension spring to its recess in the clutch pedal.
14   Install the pivot bolt, spring washer and stop mounting bracket. Be sure the spring washer works as it should and don't let it get it trapped under the pivot sleeve. Install the pivot bolt nut and tighten it to the torque listed in this Chapter's Specifications.

9.6 Use a large screwdriver or prybar (arrow) to carefully pry the CV joint out of the transaxle

9.7 A gear puller can be used to push the driveaxle from the hub – DO NOT hammer on the axle! (the puller jaws are hooked behind the hub flange; as the screw is tightened, force is applied to the end of the driveaxle to push it out)

6   If a boot is damaged or loose, remove the driveaxle as described in Section 8. Disassemble and inspect the CV joint as outlined in Section 9. **Note:** *Some auto parts stores carry "split" type replacement boots, which can be installed without removing the driveaxle from the vehicle. This is a convenient alternative; however, it's recommended that the driveaxle be removed and the CV joint disassembled and cleaned to ensure that the joint is free from contaminants such as moisture and dirt, which will accelerate CV joint wear.*

9   Driveaxles – removal and installation

Refer to illustrations 9.6, 9.7, 9.8, 9.9, 9.11, 9.14, 9.16, 9.17, 9.18, 9.19 and 9.21

Warning: *Ford recommends that whenever any of the suspension or steering fasteners are loosened or removed, they be replaced with new ones – discard the originals and don't reuse them. They must be replaced with new ones of the same part number or of original equipment quality and design. Torque specifications must be followed for proper reassembly and component retention.*

Caution: *Whenever both the right and left driveaxles are removed at the same time, the differential side gears must be supported so they don't fall into the case. A wooden dowel, approximately 15/16-inch in diameter, inserted into each side gear will work. If this precaution is not heeded and the side gears do drop, the differential will have to be removed from the transaxle to realign the gears (which will necessitate towing the vehicle to a Ford dealer service department or a repair shop). Also, this procedure requires a special puller and adapters to install the driveaxle in the hub (due to the interference fit designed into the mating splines on the axle and in the hub). The use of the correct Ford factory tool is highly recommended if available. However, an alternative tool can be fabricated from a bearing puller and materials available at a hardware store. Read the entire procedure before beginning any work to decide whether or not you want to undertake a job of this nature.*

Removal

Right driveaxle only on automatic transaxle models; both driveaxles on manual transaxle models

1   Loosen the wheel lug nuts, raise the vehicle and support it securely on jackstands. Remove the wheel(s).
2   Remove the caliper and brake disc as outlined in Chapter 9.

9.8 After the driveaxle has been pushed out of the hub, pull out on the strut/knuckle assembly and free the stub shaft from the hub

3   Remove the driveaxle hub nut from the end of the axle, in the center of the wheel hub (if you have a automatic transaxle equipped vehicle and both driveaxles are being removed, work on the right one first). Place a prybar between two of the wheel studs to prevent the hub from turning while loosening the nut.
4   Remove the brake hose support bracket-to-strut bolt.
5   Remove the lower control arm-to-steering knuckle bolt and separate the control arm from the knuckle (see to Chapter 10, Section 4)
6   Using a large screwdriver or prybar, pry the inner CV joint assembly from the transaxle (**see illustration**). Be careful not to damage the case or the oil pan. Suspend the axle with a piece of wire – don't let it hang or damage to the outer CV joint may occur.
7   Push the driveaxle out of the hub with a gear puller (**see illustration**).
8   Once the driveaxle is loose from the hub splines, pull out on the strut/knuckle assembly and guide the outer CV joint out of the hub. Remove the support wire and carefully detach the driveaxle from the vehicle (**see illustration**).
9   If both driveaxles are being removed on a vehicle equipped with a manual transaxle, insert a snug-fitting wooden dowel (15/16-inch diameter) into the right differential side gear (**see illustration**), then repeat the procedure in Steps 1 through 8 to remove the left driveaxle (manual transaxle models only). Support the left side gear also.

8

9.9   If both driveaxles are being removed on a manual transaxle model, insert a wooden dowel (arrow) into the differential side gear to keep the gears from falling into the case

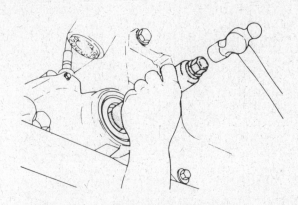

9.11   Driving the left driveaxle from the differential side gear with Ford tool number T81P-4026-A (a narrow screwdriver may be used in place of the special tool if extreme care is taken)

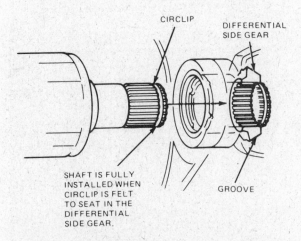

9.14   The inner CV joint stub shaft is completely seated when the circlip on the shaft snaps into the groove in the differential side gear

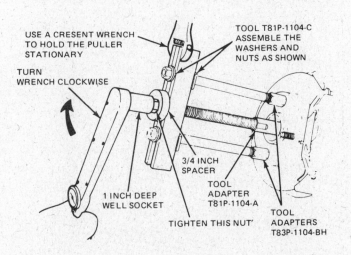

9.16   Using the special Ford tool to pull the stub shaft into the hub

Left driveaxle on automatic transaxle models

10   Remove the right driveaxle as described above.

11   Using Ford tool T81P-4026-A or a narrow screwdriver inserted through the right hand differential side gear, drive the left driveaxle stud shaft out of the left differential side gear just far enough to unseat the circlip on the stub shaft from the side gear **(see illustration)**. Insert a snug-fitting wooden dowel (15/16-inch diameter) into the right differential side gear to prevent it from falling when the left driveaxle is removed.

12   Follow the procedure in Steps 1 through 8 to remove the left driveaxle from the vehicle. Insert a wooden dowel into the left side gear.

Installation (both driveaxles)

Note: *If both driveaxles were removed, install one at a time, removing the wooden dowel from each side only when the driveaxle is ready for insertion into the transaxle.*

13   Install a new circlip on the inner stub shaft splines.

14   Coat the differential seal lips with multi-purpose grease and insert the stub shaft into the differential side gear until the shaft is seated and the circlip snaps into place **(see illustration)**.

15   Pull out on the strut/knuckle assembly and insert the outer CV joint stub shaft in the hub (make sure the splines are aligned). Push the shaft as

far into the hub as possible by hand.

16   Use Ford tool T81P-1104-C with adapters T83P-1104-BH and adapter T81P-1104-A (if available) to pull the stub shaft into the hub until it's seated **(see illustration)**, then proceed to Step 23. If the special Ford tools aren't available, fabricate a tool as described in the following Steps.

17   Obtain the following items from a hardware store **(see illustration)**:
   Two 1-1/2 inch long 1/2-inch pipe unions
   One 1-1/4 inch long 1/2-inch pipe coupler
   One 3-1/2 inch long by 5/16-inch diameter bolt and nut
   Small and large washers
   A small bearing puller
   Two 4-1/2 inch long Grade 8 bolts (the correct diameter and thread pitch to thread into the puller holes)

18   Assemble the pipe coupler to one pipe union. Insert the 3-1/2 inch long 5/16-inch diameter bolt, with a small washer under the bolt head, through the coupler and union, then install the large washer and nut on the union side **(see illustration)**. Now thread the remaining union onto the exposed portion of the coupler.

19   Grind the ends of each 4-1/2 inch long bolt to a point and thread them into the bearing puller. It may be necessary to install spacers between the bearing puller halves so the bolts will straddle the raised portion of the hub flange **(see illustration)**.

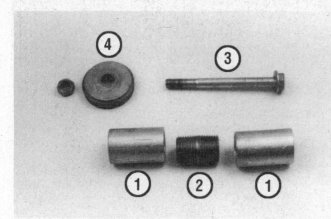

9.17   The hardware required to construct the center portion of the home-built driveaxle installation tool

1   *Pipe unions (1/2-inch)*   3   *5/16 x 3-1/2-inch bolt*
2   *Pipe coupler*   4   *Washers*

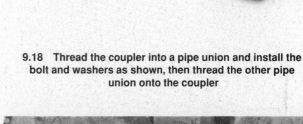

9.18   Thread the coupler into a pipe union and install the bolt and washers as shown, then thread the other pipe union onto the coupler

9.19   The completed center portion and the bearing puller with the modified bolts and spacers (use Grade 8 bolts to prevent bending)

1   *Bearing puller*   2   *4-1/2 inch bolts (Grade 8)*

9.21   Thread the center portion of the tool onto the driveaxle stub shaft and slowly tighten the two puller bolts, a little at a time, until the shaft is completely seated in the hub

20   Place the previously assembled tubular portion of the tool through the bearing puller, into the hub, and thread it onto the end of the stub axle with a pair of pliers. Although the thread pitch is not exactly the same, the pipe union metal is relatively soft in comparison to the axle, so no damage to the axle threads will occur. be sure the union goes on straight and don't over-tighten it. The large washer should bear against the puller.

21   Thread the two bolts through the bearing puller until they contact the hub flange. They must be exactly perpendicular to the flange, or the bolts will "walk" when tightened **(see illustration)**.

22   Tighten the bolts 1/2-turn at a time, alternating between the two, until the stub axle is pulled into the hub.

23   Remove the tool and install the axle washer and a *new* nut. Tighten the nut to the torque listed in this Chapter's Specifications while preventing the hub from turning by placing a screwdriver between two wheel studs.

24   Pry down on the lower control arm and insert the balljoint stud into the steering knuckle. Install a *new* pinch bolt and tighten it to the torque speci-fied in Chapter 10.

25   Install the brake rotor and caliper (Chapter 9).

26   Install the brake hose support bracket bolt.

27   Install the wheel and lug nuts and lower the vehicle. Tighten the lug nuts to the torque specified in Chapter 1.

---

10   Constant velocity (CV) joints and boots – disassembly, inspection and reassembly

Inner CV joint and boot – ball and cage type CV joint

Refer to illustrations 10.3, 10.4a, 10.4b, 10.5, 10.6, 10.7, 10.9, 10.10, 10.11, 10.12a, 10.12b, 10.14, 10.15, 10.17, 10.18, 10.19, 10.20, 10.22a, 10.22b, 10.23, 10.24 and 10.25

Disassembly

1   Remove the driveaxle from the vehicle (see Section 9).

2   Mount the driveaxle in a vise. The jaws of the vise should be lined with wood or rags to prevent damage to the driveaxle.

8

10.3   Cut the boot clamps off and discard them

10.4a   Pry the wire ring from the outer race with a small screwdriver

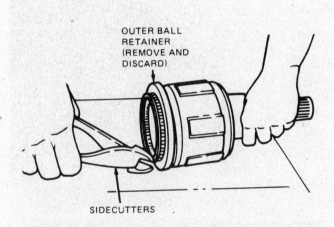

10.4b   If the CV joint is equipped with a "roll crimp" ball retainer, cut the retainer and pry it from the outer race

10.5   With the retainer removed, the outer race can be pulled off the inner race

10.6   Spread the stop ring and slide it back on the unsplined portion of the axleshaft . . .

10.7   . . . then push the inner race and cage assembly back and pry the circlip off the shaft

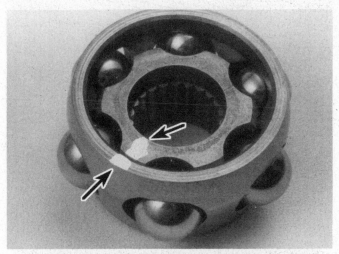

10.9   Make index marks on the inner race and cage so they'll both be facing the same direction when reassembled

10.10   Pry the balls from the cage with a screwdriver (be careful not to nick or scratch them)

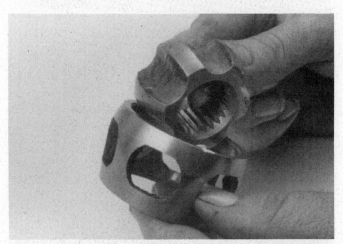

10.11   Tilt the inner race 90-degrees and rotate it out of the cage

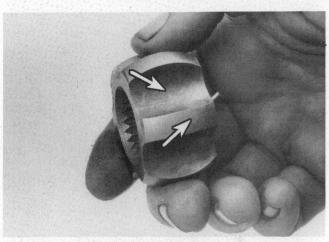

10.12a   Check the inner race lands and grooves for pitting and score marks

3   Cut the boot clamps from the boot and discard them **(see illustration)**.

4   Slide the boot back on the axleshaft and pry the wire ring ball retainer from the outer race **(see illustration)**. Some inner CV joints use a "roll crimp" type ball retainer, which must be cut to remove it **(see illustration)**. A retainer is not necessary for reassembly. The reassembly procedure for the wire ring ball retainer should be followed.

5   Pull the outer race off the inner bearing assembly **(see illustration)**.

6   Remove the stop ring from the groove in the axleshaft with a pair of snap-ring pliers and slide the stop ring back on the axle **(see illustration)**.

7   Push the inner assembly toward the end of the axleshaft far enough to gain access to the circlip. Remove the circlip with a small screwdriver and discard it **(see illustration)**.

8   Slide the inner bearing assembly off the axleshaft.

9   Mark the inner race and cage to ensure that they are reassembled with the correct sides facing out **(see illustration)**.

10   Using a screwdriver or piece of wood, pry the balls from the cage **(see illustration)**. Be careful not to scratch the inner race, the balls or the cage.

11   Rotate inner race 90-degrees, align the inner race lands with the cage windows and rotate the race out of the cage **(see illustration)**.

Inspection

12   Clean the components with solvent to remove all traces of grease. Inspect the cage and races for pitting, score marks, cracks and other signs of wear and damage. Shiny, polished spots are normal and will not adversely affect CV joint performance **(see illustrations)**.

8

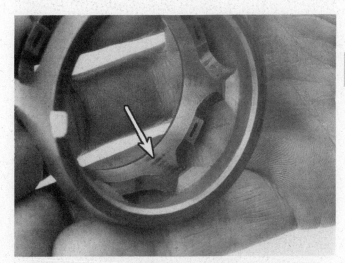

10.12b   Check the cage for cracks, pitting and score marks (shiny spots are normal and don't affect operation)

10.14   Press the balls into the cage through the windows

10.15   Wrap the splined area of the axle with tape to prevent damage to the boot when installing it

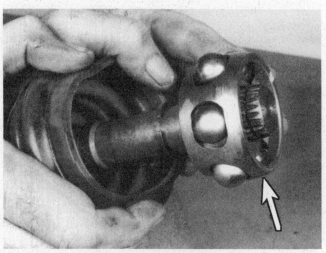

10.17   Install the inner race and cage assembly with the "bulge" (arrow) facing the axleshaft end

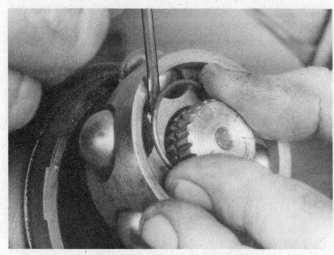

10.18   Install the circlip . . .

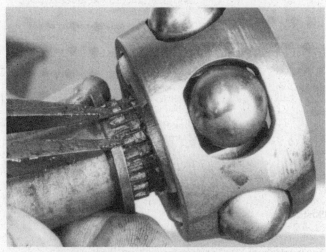

10.19   . . . then seat the stop ring in the groove

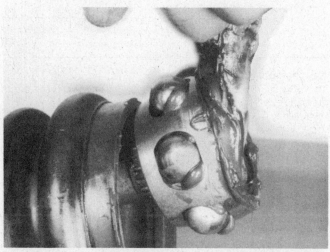

10.20   Pack grease into the bearing until it's completely full

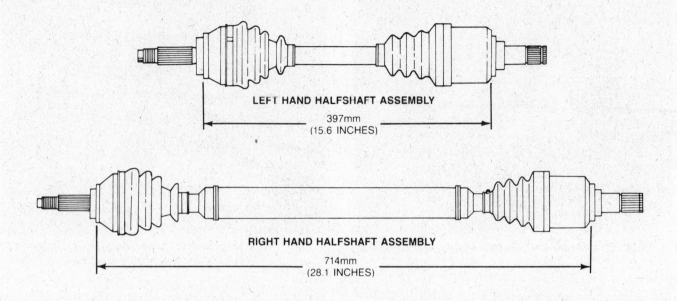

10.22a   Adjust the driveaxle to the proper length using this diagram for 1981 through 1983 models . . .

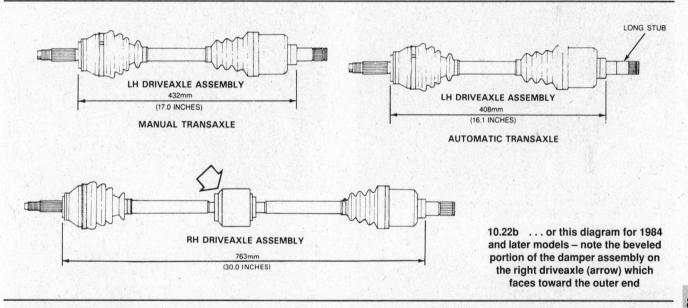

10.22b   . . . or this diagram for 1984 and later models – note the beveled portion of the damper assembly on the right driveaxle (arrow) which faces toward the outer end

8

Reassembly

13   Insert the inner race into the cage. Verify that the matchmarks are on the same side. However, it's not necessary for them to be in direct alignment with each other.

14   Press the balls into the cage windows with your thumbs **(see illustration)**.

15   Wrap the axleshaft splines with tape to avoid damaging the boot. Slide the small boot clamp and boot onto the axleshaft, then remove the tape **(see illustration)**.

16   Install a new stop ring on the axleshaft. Don't seat it in the groove at this time, but slide it past the splined area.

17   Install the inner race and cage assembly on the axleshaft with the larger diameter side or "bulge" of the cage facing the axleshaft end **(see illustration)**.

18   Install the circlip and slide the inner race and cage assembly out until the inner race contacts the circlip **(see illustration)**.

19   Install the stop ring in the groove **(see illustration)**. Make sure it's completely seated by pushing on the inner race and cage assembly.

20   Fill the outer race and boot with the specified type and quantity of CV joint grease (normally included with the new boot kit). Pack the inner race and cage assembly with grease, by hand, until grease is worked completely into the assembly **(see illustration)**.

21   Slide the outer race down onto the inner race and install the wire ring retainer.

22   Wipe any excess grease from the axle boot groove on the outer race. Seat the small diameter of the boot in the recessed area on the axleshaft and install the clamp. Push the other end of the boot onto the outer race and move the race in-or-out to adjust the axle to the proper length **(see illustrations)**.

23   With the axle set to the proper length, equalize the pressure in the boot by inserting a dull screwdriver between the boot and the outer race **(see illustration)**. Don't damage the boot with the tool.

24   Install the boot clamp. A pair of special clamp-crimping pliers is used to tighten the clamp. The pliers are available at most auto parts stores **(see illustration)**.

10.23   Equalize the pressure inside the boot by inserting a small screwdriver between the boot and the outer race

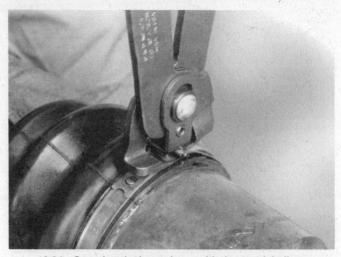

10.24   Securing the boot clamp with the special pliers (available at auto parts stores)

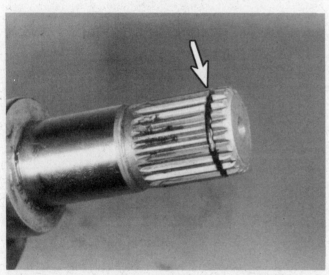

10.25   Always replace the circlip on the inner stub axle

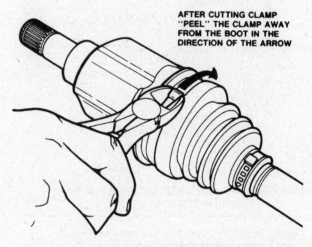

AFTER CUTTING CLAMP "PEEL" THE CLAMP AWAY FROM THE BOOT IN THE DIRECTION OF THE ARROW

10.27   Cut the large clamp and peel it off the boot – don't cut the small clamp unless the boot needs to be replaced

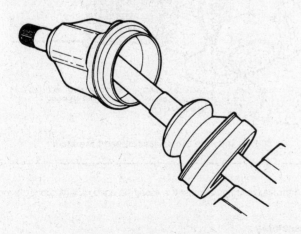

10.28   Separate the boot from the shaft and wipe off any excess grease

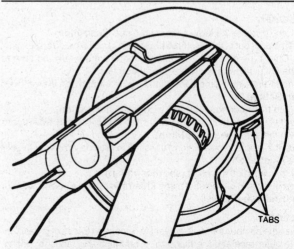

TABS

10.29   There are six retaining tabs that secure the tripod – bend these back slightly, but don't break them – they will be reused

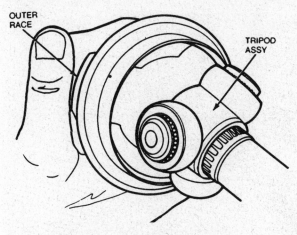

10.30 Slip the outer race off the tripod

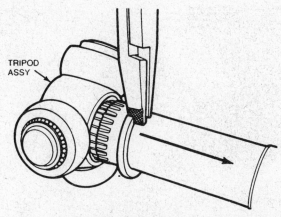

10.31 Carefully spread the stop ring with heavy-duty snap-ring pliers – don't bend the stop ring, as it will be reused

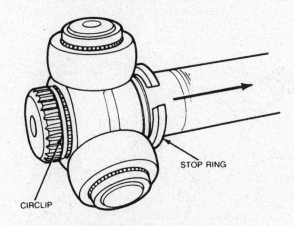

10.32 Slide the tripod away from the circlip so it can be removed . . .

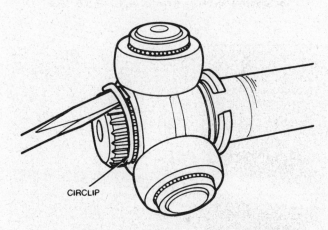

10.33 Then pry the circlip off the shaft and discard it

25 Install a new circlip on the stub axle **(see illustration)**.
26 Install the driveaxle as described in Section 9.

Inner CV joint and boot – tripod type CV joint

Refer to illustrations 10.27, 10.28, 10.29, 10.30, 10.31, 10.32, 10.33, 10.34, 10.37, 10.38, 10.39, 10.40, 10.41, 10.42 and 10.43

Disassembly
27 Cut and remove the large boot clamp **(see illustration)**.
28 Pull the boot out of the way **(see illustration)** and wipe off any excess grease. Check the grease for contamination; if there is any, be sure to check the CV joint parts very carefully for damage.
29 Bend the retaining tabs back slightly so the tripod can be removed **(see illustration)**.
30 Detach the outer race from the tripod **(see illustration)**.
31 Carefully spread the stop-ring with snap-ring pliers and slide it part-way down the shaft **(see illustration)**.
32 Slide the tripod part-way along the shaft to provide access to the circlip **(see illustration)**.
33 Pry the circlip off the shaft **(see illustration)**.
34 Slide the tripod off the shaft **(see illustration)**. If the boot is worn or damaged, remove it as well.

Inspection
35 Clean the components with solvent to remove all traces of grease. Inspect the outer race and the tripod roller bearings and races for pitting, score marks, cracks and other signs of wear and damage. Shiny, polished spots are normal and will not adversely affect CV joint performance. Grease the tripod and races. When reassembling the tripod, grease will

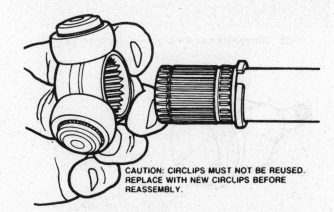

CAUTION: CIRCLIPS MUST NOT BE REUSED. REPLACE WITH NEW CIRCLIPS BEFORE REASSEMBLY.

10.34 Slide the tripod assembly off the shaft

hold the roller bearings against the tripod as each race is slipped over them.

Reassembly
36 If the boot was removed, install it on the shaft and make sure it is seated in its groove. To prevent boot damage, wrap the shaft splines with electrical tape before sliding on the boot.

8

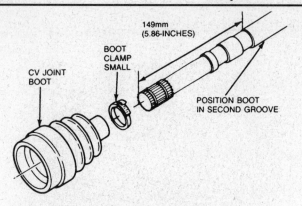

10.37   If the boot requires replacement, cut the small clamp and take the boot off

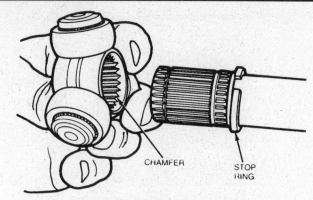

10.38   The chamfered side of the tripod faces onto the shaft

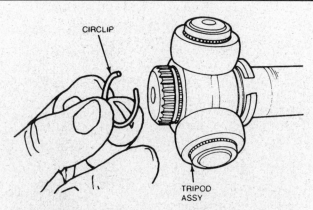

10.39   Push the tripod on and secure it with a new circlip

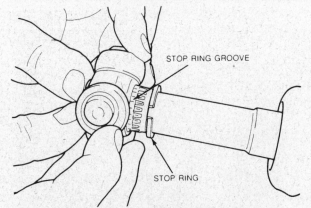

10.40   Compress the circlip and slide the tripod over it . . .

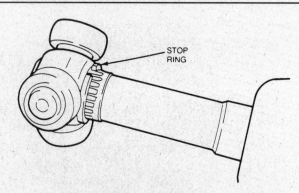

10.41   . . . then install the stop ring securely in its groove

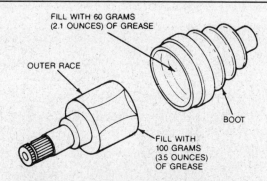

10.42   Fill the outer race with the specified amount of special grease

37   Install the small boot clamp **(see illustration)**. A pair of special clamp-crimping pliers is used to tighten the clamp. The pliers are available at most auto parts stores.

38   Slide the tripod onto the shaft with its chamfered side toward the stop ring **(see illustration)**. Slide it on far enough so the circlip can be installed.

39   Install a new circlip in the shaft groove **(see illustration)**.

40   Squeeze the circlip and slide the tripod over it far enough to uncover the stop ring groove **(see illustration)**.

41   Carefully spread the stop ring with snap ring pliers and install it in its groove **(see illustration)**. Make sure the stop ring is fully seated in the groove.

42   Fill the outer race with about 3-1/2 oz (100 grams) of special grease (usually included in the joint boot kit). Fill the boot with 2.1 oz (60 grams) of grease **(see illustration)**.

43   Install the outer race over the tripod, then bend back the six retaining tabs to secure it **(see illustration)**.

44   Perform Steps 22 through 26 above.

Outer CV joint and boot

Refer to illustrations 10.47, 10.49, 10.50, 10.51, 10.52, 10.55, 10.56, 10.57 and 10.61

Disassembly

45   Remove the driveaxle from the vehicle (see Section 9).

46   Follow the procedure in Steps 2 and 3 of this Section.

47   Slide the boot back off the outer race. With a *brass drift* positioned on the *inner race*, dislodge the CV joint assembly from the axle **(see illustration)**. A lot of force will be required, as the inner race must overcome a circlip on the axleshaft. Do not let the CV joint assembly fall.

48   Mount the assembly in a vise lined with wood or rags.

49   Press down on the inner race far enough to allow a ball bearing to be removed. If it's difficult to tilt, tap the inner race with a brass drift and hammer **(see illustration)**.

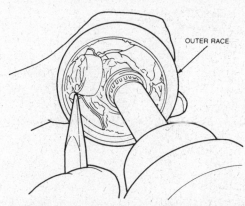

10.43 Install the outer race on the tripod, then bend the six retaining tabs into their original positions

10.47 Dislodge the CV joint assembly with a brass drift and hammer (be careful not to let the joint fall!)

10.49 Tilt the inner race far enough to allow ball removal – a brass punch can be used if the inner race is difficult to move

10.50 If necessary, pry the balls out with a screwdriver

10.51 Tilt the inner race and cage 90-degrees, then align the windows in the cage with the lands and rotate the inner race up and out of the outer race

10.52 Align the inner race lands with the cage windows and rotate the inner race out of the cage

50   Pry the balls from the cage, one at a time, with a blunt screwdriver or wooden tool **(see illustration)**.

51   With all of the balls removed from the cage and the cage/inner race assembly tilted 90-degrees, align the cage windows with the outer race lands and remove the assembly from the outer race **(see illustration)**.

52   Remove the inner race from the cage by turning the inner race 90-degrees in the cage, aligning the inner lands with the cage windows and rotating the inner race out of the cage **(see illustration)**.

Inspection

53   Wash all of the parts in solvent. Inspect the components as described in Step 12.

Reassembly

54   Install the inner race in the cage by reversing the technique described in Step 52.

55   Install the inner race and cage assembly in the outer race by reversing the removal method used in Step 51. The beveled edge of the inner race splined area must face out after it's installed in the outer race **(see illustration)**.

56   Press the balls into the cage windows **(see illustration)**.

57   Pack the CV joint assembly with the specified lubricant through the inner splined hole. Force the grease into the bearing by inserting a wooden dowel through the splined hole and pushing it to the bottom of the joint. Repeat this procedure until the bearing is completely packed **(see illustration)**.

8

10.55   The beveled edge of the inner race (arrow) must face out when assembled

10.56   Align the cage windows and the inner and outer race grooves, then tilt the cage and inner race to insert the balls

10.57   Apply grease through the splined hole, then insert a wooden dowel (approximately 15/16-inch diameter) into the hole and push down – the dowel will force the grease into the joint

10.61   Line up the splines of the inner race with the axleshaft splines, then tap the CV joint assembly onto the shaft with a brass or plastic hammer until the inner race is seated against the stop ring

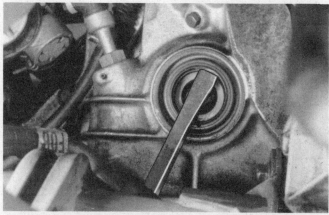

11.2   Carefully pry the old seal from the case with a prybar or screwdriver

58   Install the boot on the axleshaft as described in Step 15. Apply a liberal amount of grease to the inside of the boot.

59   Install a new stop ring and position it in the groove on the axleshaft.

60   Install a new circlip on the end of the axleshaft.

61   Position the CV joint assembly on the axleshaft, aligning the splines. Using a brass or plastic tip hammer, drive the CV joint onto the axleshaft until it seats against the stop ring **(see illustration)**.

62   Adjust the driveaxle length and install the boot. Refer to Steps 22 through 24.

63   Install the driveaxle as described in Section 8.

11   Differential seals – replacement

Refer to illustrations 11.2 and 11.3

Caution: *Whenever both the right and left driveaxles are removed at the same time, the differential side gears must be supported so they don't fall into the case. A wooden dowel, approximately 15/16-inch in diameter, inserted into each side gear will work. If this precaution is not heeded and the side gears do drop, the differential will have to be removed from the transaxle to realign the gears (which will necessitate towing the vehicle to a Ford dealer service department or a repair shop).*

1   Refer to Section 9 and remove the driveaxle.

2   Pry the seal from the transaxle case with a large screwdriver or prybar

11.3   Drive the new seal into the case with a large socket (arrow) or piece of pipe – be careful not to cock the seal in the bore

(see illustration). Be careful not to damage the case.

3   Coat the outer edge of the new seal with oil or grease, then position it in the bore and carefully drive it in with a hammer and large socket (if a socket isn't available, a section of pipe will also work) **(see illustration).**

4   Lubricate the seal lip with moly-base grease, then install the driveaxle (see Section 9).

Chapter 9   Brakes

Contents

Specifications

Brake fluid type . . . .   See Chapter 1

Disc brakes

Brake disc thickness
   Standard . . . .   0.945 in (24.0 mm)
   Minimum* . . . .   0.882 in (22.4 mm)
Brake disc thickness variation
   limit (1-inch from edge) . . . .   0.0005 in (0.013 mm)
Brake disc runout limit . . . .   0.003 in (0.076 mm)
Minimum brake pad thickness . . . .   See Chapter 1

* Refer to marks stamped on the disc (they supersede information printed here).

Drum brakes

Standard drum diameter
   7-inch brakes . . . .   7 in (180.0 mm)
   8-inch brakes
      1981 through 1985 . . . .   8.006 in (203.2 mm)
      1986 through 1990 . . . .   8.065 in (204.7 mm)
Maximum drum diameter* . . . .   Standard diameter plus 0.059 in (1.5 mm)
Out-of-round limit . . . .   0.005 in (0.127 mm)
Minimum brake lining thickness . . . .   See Chapter 1

*Refer to marks cast into drum (they supersede information printed here)

9

Torque specifications

	Ft-lbs (unless otherwise indicated)
Disc brake caliper mounting pins	18 to 25
Brake hose-to-caliper bolt	
1981	20 to 30
1982 through 1990	30 to 40
Master cylinder mounting nuts	13 to 25
Brake booster mounting nuts	
1981 through 1988	13 to 25
1989 and 1990	20 to 30
Wheel cylinder bolts	
1981	84 to 132 in-lbs
1982 through 1990	108 to 156 in-lbs
Wheel lug nuts	See Chapter 1
Brake drum retaining nut	
Initial torque	17 to 25
Final torque	
1981 through 1986	10 to 15 in-lbs
1987 and 1988	10 to 12 in-lbs
1989 and 1990	24 to 28 in-lbs

1   General information

Description

All models are equipped with disc-type front and drum-type rear brakes which are hydraulically operated and vacuum assisted.

The front brakes feature a single piston, floating caliper design. The rear drum brakes are leading/trailing shoe types with a single pivot.

The front disc brakes automatically compensate for pad wear during usage. The rear drum brakes also feature automatic adjustment.

Front drive vehicles tend to wear the front brake pads at a faster rate than rear drive vehicles. Consequently, it's important to inspect the brake pads frequently to make sure they haven't worn to the point where the disc itself is scored or damaged.

All models are equipped with a cable actuated parking brake which operates the rear brakes.

The hydraulic system is a dual line type with a dual master cylinder and is diagonally split (the left front and the right rear brakes are on the same circuit, and the right front and the left rear are on the other circuit). In the event of brake line or seal failure, half the brake system will still operate. The master cylinder also incorporates two pressure control valves that reduce the pressure to the rear brakes in order to limit rear wheel lockup during hard braking.

Precautions

Use only DOT 3 brake fluid.

The brake pads and linings may contain asbestos fibers, which are hazardous to your health if inhaled. When working on brake system components, carefully clean all parts with denatured alcohol or brake cleaner. Don't allow the fine dust to become airborne. It's a good idea to wear an approved filtering mask whenever you work on or around the brakes.

Safety should be paramount when working on brake system components. Don't use parts or fasteners that aren't in perfect condition and be sure that all clearances and torque specifications are adhered to. If you're at all unsure about a certain procedure, seek professional advice. When finished working on the brakes, test them carefully under controlled conditions before driving the vehicle in traffic. If a problem is suspected in the brake system, don't drive the vehicle until the fault is corrected.

2   Disc brake pads – replacement

Refer to illustrations 2.4a through 2.4i
Warning: *Disc brake pads must be replaced on both front wheels at the same time – never replace the pads on only one wheel. Also, the dust created by the brake system may contain asbestos, which is harmful to your health. Never blow it out with compressed air and don't inhale any of*

it. *An approved filtering mask should be worn when working on the brakes. Do not, under any circumstances, use petroleum-based solvents to clean brake parts. Use brake cleaner or denatured alcohol only! When servicing the disc brakes, use only high quality, nationally recognized brand name pads.*

1   Remove about two-thirds of the fluid from the master cylinder reservoir.

2   Loosen the wheel lug nuts, raise the vehicle and support it securely on jackstands. Remove the front wheels.

3   Check the disc carefully as outlined in Section 4. If machining is necessary, follow the procedure in Section 4 to remove the disc.

4   Follow the accompanying photos, beginning with **illustration 2.4a**, for the actual pad replacement procedure. Be sure to stay in order and read the information in the caption under each illustration.

5   Once the new pads are in place and the caliper pins have been installed and properly tightened, install the wheels and lower the vehicle to the ground. **Note:** *If the brake hose was disconnected from the caliper for any reason, the brake system must be bled as described in Section 10.*

6   Fill the master cylinder reservoir(s) with new brake fluid and slowly pump the brakes a few times to seat the pads against the disc.

7   Check the fluid level in the master cylinder reservoir(s) one more time and then road test the vehicle carefully before driving it in traffic.

2.4a   Using a large C-clamp, push the piston back into the caliper bore just enough to allow the caliper to slide off the disc easily – note that one end of the clamp is on the flat area near the brake hose fitting and the other end (screw end) is pressing on the outer pad

2.4b   Remove the two caliper pins that hold the caliper to the steering knuckle (this will require a special TORX bit)

2.4c   Rotate the bottom of the caliper up and off the brake disc (don't put excessive strain on the brake hose or damage could result)

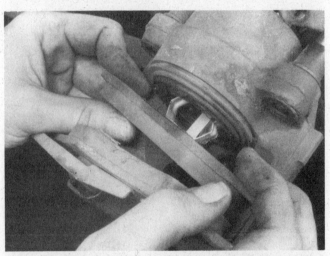

2.4d   Pull the inner brake pad straight out of the caliper piston (inspect the piston for cracks and signs of leakage, which will warrant replacement of the caliper)

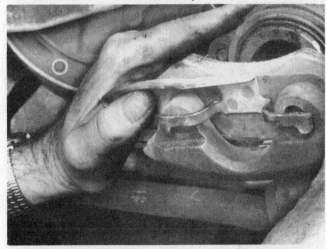

2.4e   Push the outer pad toward the piston to dislodge the locating lugs from the caliper frame, then lift out the pad

2.4f   Push the piston into the cylinder bore to provide room for the new pads to fit over the disc – use a block of wood and a C-clamp, but don't use excessive force or damage to the plastic piston will result

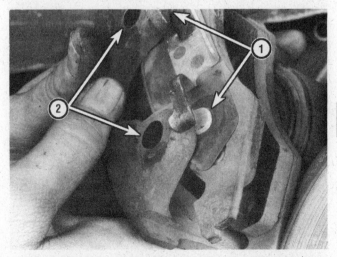

2.4g   To install the new pads in the caliper, carefully push the inner pad retaining clips straight into the piston until the brake pad backing plate rests on the piston face – slide the outer pad into the caliper as shown (be sure the locating lugs on the pad [1] seat into the mounting holes in the caliper frame [2])

9

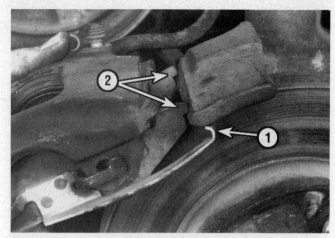

2.4h　Position the anti-rattle spring on the outer pad (1) under the upper arm of the steering knuckle with the notches in the upper edge of both pads resting on the upper arm of the knuckle (2), rotate the caliper down until the notches in the opposite end of the pads seat against the lower arm of the steering knuckle (make sure the brake hose is not twisted)

2.4i　Apply silicone grease to the caliper pins and to the inside of the pin insulators and insert the pins through the caliper housing into the steering knuckle arms (tighten them by hand first, then to the torque listed in this Chapter's Specifications)

3.2a　Removing the brake hose fitting bolt (be sure to use new sealing washers on each side of the fitting to prevent fluid leaks)

3.2b　To avoid damage to the brake hose, suspend the caliper with a piece of wire

3　Disc brake caliper – removal, overhaul and installation

Warning: *The dust created by the brake system may contain asbestos, which is harmful to your health. Never blow it out with compressed air and don't inhale any of it. An approved filtering mask should be worn when working on the brakes. Do not, under any circumstances, use petroleum-based solvents to clean brake parts. Use brake cleaner or denatured alcohol only!*

Note: *The brake calipers on this vehicle feature cast iron caliper housings with one piston per cylinder. The pistons are made of aluminum (early models) or plastic (later models). If service is required (usually because of fluid leakage) it's recommended that the caliper be replaced rather than rebuilt. New and factory-rebuilt calipers are available on an exchange basis, which makes this job quite easy and will ensure that the caliper is in top condition. Always rebuild or replace the calipers in pairs – never rebuild or replace just one of them.*

Removal

Refer to illustrations 3.2a and 3.2b

1　Loosen the wheel lug nuts, raise the vehicle and support it securely on jackstands. Remove the wheel.

2　Disconnect the brake hose from the back of the caliper **(see illustra-**

tion). Have a rag handy for fluid spills and wrap a plastic bag around the end of the hose to prevent fluid loss and contamination. Discard the fitting washers – new ones should be used during installation. If the caliper is only being removed to get at the disc, don't detach the hose (this will save the trouble of bleeding the brake system). Suspend the caliper with a piece of wire from the strut **(see illustration)**.

3　Refer to the first few Steps in Section 2 to separate the caliper from the steering knuckle – it's part of the brake pad replacement procedure.

Overhaul

Refer to illustrations 3.6, 3.7, 3.8, 3.9a, 3.9b, 3.13, 3.14 and 3.16

4　Refer to Section 2 and remove the brake pads from the caliper.

5　Clean the exterior of the caliper with brake cleaner or denatured alcohol. **Warning:** *Never use gasoline, kerosene or petroleum-based cleaning solvents. Place the caliper on a clean workbench.*

6　Position a wood block or several shop rags in the caliper as a cushion, then use compressed air to remove the piston from the caliper **(see illustration)**. Use only enough air pressure to ease the piston out of the bore. If the piston is blown out, even with the cushion in place, it may be damaged. **Warning:** *Never place your fingers in front of the piston in an attempt to catch or protect it when applying compressed air, as serious injury could occur.*

3.6   With the caliper padded to catch the piston, use compressed air to force the piston out of the bore – make sure your fingers are out of the way!

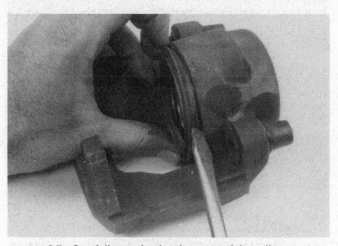

3.7   Carefully pry the dust boot out of the caliper

3.8   To avoid damage to the caliper bore or seal groove, remove the seal with a wood or plastic tool – a pencil works well

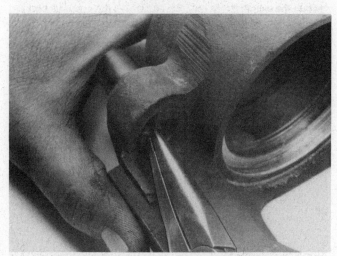

3.9a   To remove a caliper pin insulator, grab it with a pair of needle-nose pliers, twist it and push it through the caliper frame

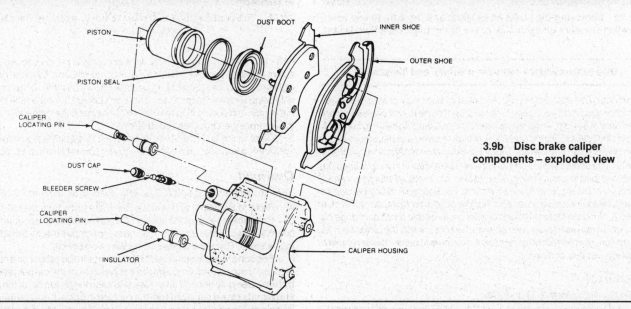

PISTON
DUST BOOT
INNER SHOE
PISTON SEAL
OUTER SHOE
CALIPER LOCATING PIN
DUST CAP
BLEEDER SCREW
CALIPER LOCATING PIN
INSULATOR
CALIPER HOUSING

3.9b   Disc brake caliper components – exploded view

9

7   Carefully pry the dust boot out of the caliper bore **(see illustration)**.

8   Using a wood or plastic tool, remove the piston seal from the groove in the caliper bore **(see illustration)**. Metal tools may cause bore damage.

9   Remove the caliper bleeder screw, then remove and discard the insulators from the caliper ears. Discard all rubber parts **(see illustrations)**.

10   Clean the remaining parts with brake system cleaner or denatured al-

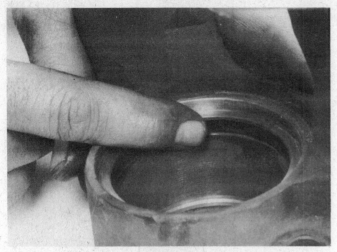

3.13   Position the seal in the caliper bore, making sure it isn't twisted

3.14   Stretch the new boot over the top of the piston, making sure it rests in the piston groove – the flange must be nearest to the top of the piston

3.16   Use a punch to carefully seat the dust boot

4.2   The brake pads on this vehicle were obviously neglected, as they wore down to the rivets and cut deep grooves into the disc – wear this severe will require replacement of the disc

cohol then blow them dry with compressed air.

11   Carefully examine the piston for nicks, burrs, cracks and (on aluminum pistons) loss of plating. If any of these defects are present, the parts must be replaced.

12   Check the caliper bore in a similar way. Light polishing with crocus cloth is permissible to remove light corrosion and stains. Discard the caliper pins if they're corroded or damaged.

13   When assembling, lubricate the piston bore and seal with clean brake fluid. Position the seal in the caliper bore groove **(see illustration)**.

14   Lubricate the piston with clean brake fluid, then install a new boot in the piston groove, with the flange facing up **(see illustration)**.

15   Insert the piston squarely into the caliper bore, then apply force to bottom the piston in the bore **(see illustration 2.4f)**.

16   Position the dust boot in the caliper counterbore, then use a blunt punch to drive it into position **(see illustration)**. Make sure the boot is seated evenly.

17   Install the bleeder screw. Tighten it securely, but don't overtighten it.

18   Install new insulators in the caliper ears and fill the area between the insulators with the silicone grease supplied in the rebuild kit. Push the caliper locating pins into the insulators.

Installation

19   Install the brake pads in the caliper (see Section 2).

20   Place the caliper in position over the brake disc, thread the caliper pins in by hand, then tighten them to the torque listed in this Chapter's Specifications.

21   Install the brake hose and inlet fitting bolt, using new copper washers, then tighten the bolt to the torque listed in this Chapter's Specifications. Be sure to bleed the brakes (see Section 10). (This isn't necessary if the brake hose was left connected to the caliper.)

22   Install the wheels and lower the vehicle, then tighten the lug nuts to the torque listed in the Chapter 1 Specifications.

23   After the job has been completed, firmly depress the brake pedal a few times to bring the pads into contact with the disc. Check brake operation carefully before driving the vehicle in traffic.

---

4   Brake disc – inspection, removal and installation

Refer to illustrations 4.2, 4.3a, 4.3b, 4.4a and 4.4b

Inspection

1   Loosen the wheel lug nuts, raise the vehicle and support it securely on jackstands. Remove the wheel and install two lug nuts to hold the disc in place.

4.3a   With two lug nuts installed to hold the disc in place, check disc runout with a dial indicator – if the reading exceeds the maximum allowable runout limit, the disc will have to be machined or replaced

4.3b   Using a swirling motion, remove the glaze from the disc with emery cloth or sandpaper

4.4a   The minimum allowable disc thickness is cast into the inside of the disc

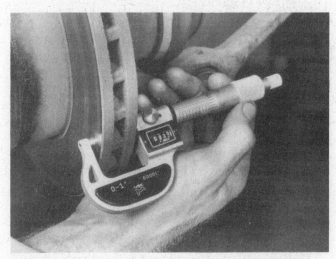

4.4b   A micrometer is used to measure disc thickness

2   Visually inspect the disc surface for score marks and other damage. Light scratches and shallow grooves are normal after use and may not be detrimental to brake operation. Deep score marks – over 0.015-inch (0.38 mm) – require disc removal and refinishing by an automotive machine shop. Be sure to check both sides of the disc (**see illustration**).

3   To check disc runout, attach a dial indicator to the brake caliper and locate the stem about 1-inch from the outer edge of the disc (**see illustration**). Set the indicator to zero and turn the disc. The indicator reading should not exceed that listed in this Chapter's Specifications. If it does, the disc should be resurfaced by an automotive machine shop. **Note:** *Professionals recommend resurfacing of brake discs regardless of the dial indicator reading (to produce a smooth, flat surface that will eliminate brake pedal pulsations and other undesirable symptoms related to questionable discs). At the very least, if you elect not to have the discs resurfaced, de-glaze the brake pad surface with emery cloth or sandpaper (use a swirling motion to ensure a non-directional finish)* (**see illustration**).

4   The disc should never be machined to a thickness under the specified minimum allowable thickness, which is cast into the disc itself (**see illustration**). The disc thickness can be checked with a micrometer (**see illustration**).

Removal and installation

5   Refer to Section 3 and remove the brake caliper. **Caution:** *Don't allow the caliper to hang by the brake hose and don't disconnect the hose from the caliper.*

6   Remove the two lug nuts that were put on to hold the disc in place and detach the disc from the hub.

7   Installation is the reverse of removal.

---

5   Rear brake drum – removal, inspection and installation

Refer to illustrations 5.2, 5.3, 5.4, 5.5, 5.8a, 5.8b and 5.11

Removal

1   Loosen the wheel lug nuts, raise the rear of the vehicle and support it securely on jackstands. Block the front wheels, then remove the rear wheel.

9

5.2   A hammer and chisel can be used to gently tap the grease cap from the hub/drum assembly

5.3   After the cotter pin and nut lock have been removed, pull the drum out to dislodge the bearing – be careful not to drop it

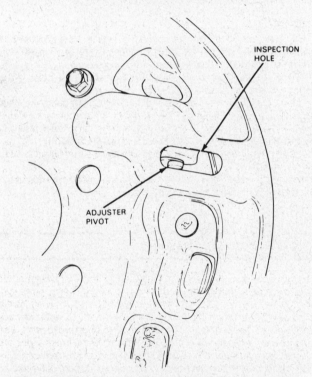

5.4   Location of the adjuster pivot on the 7-inch rear brake

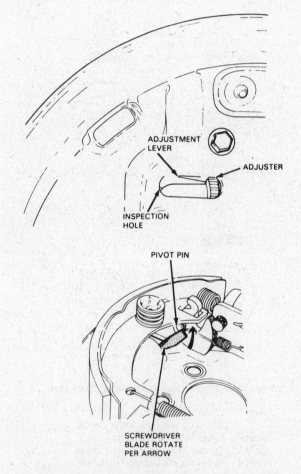

5.5   Backing-off the adjuster on the 8-inch brake

2   Remove the grease cap, cotter pin, nut lock and retaining nut **(see illustration)**.

3   Grasp the brake drum and pull it out far enough to dislodge the outer bearing and washer **(see illustration)**. If the drum is stuck, loosen the brake adjuster as described in the next Steps.

4   7-inch brakes: Remove the rubber plug from the adjusting hole in the backing plate. Insert a thin-bladed screwdriver in the hole and press the adjuster assembly pivot sideways so the adjuster quadrant can release the brake adjustment **(see illustration)**.

5   8-inch brakes: Remove the bracket that secures the brake line to the axle. Remove the rubber plug from the adjusting hole in the backing plate. Hold the adjustment lever away from the star wheel with a thin-bladed screwdriver and turn the star wheel with a brake tool to retract the brake shoes **(see illustration)**.

6   Remove the bearing.

7   Pull the hub/drum assembly off the axle.

Inspection

8   Check the drum for cracks, score marks, deep grooves and signs of overheating of the shoe contact surface. If the drums have blue spots, indicating overheated areas, they should be replaced. Also, look for grease or brake fluid on the shoe contact surface. Grease and brake fluid can be removed with denatured alcohol or brake cleaner, but the brake shoes must

5.8a   Remove glaze from the drum surface with emery cloth or sandpaper

5.8b   The maximum allowable diameter is cast into the drum

WITH WHEEL ROTATING
TIGHTEN ADJUSTING NUT.
TO 23-34 N·m (17-25 LB-FT)

BACK ADJUSTING
NUT OFF 1/2 TURN

TIGHTEN ADJUSTING
NUT

INSTALL THE RETAINER
AND A NEW COTTER PIN

5.11   Rear wheel bearing adjusting procedure

*Step 1:   While rotating the drum, tighten the
adjusting nut to the initial torque*
Step 2:   Loosen the nut 1/2-turn
Step 3:   Tighten the nut to the final torque
Step 4:   Install the nut lock and cotter pin

be replaced if they are contaminated. Surface glazing, which is a glossy, highly polished finish, can be removed with emery cloth or sandpaper **(see illustration)**. **Note:** *Professionals recommend resurfacing the drums whenever a brake job is done. Resurfacing will eliminate the possibility of out-of-round drums. If the drums are worn so much that they can't be resurfaced without exceeding the maximum allowable diameter stamped into the drum* **(see illustration)**, *new ones will be required.*

Installation

9   While the hub/drum assembly is off the vehicle, it's a good idea to clean, inspect and repack or, if necessary, replace the rear wheel bearings. Refer to Chapter 10 for rear wheel bearing service.
10   Place the hub/drum assembly on the axle, install the outer wheel bearing and washer and push the assembly into place.
11   Install the retaining nut and washer and tighten the nut to the initial torque (listed in this Chapter's Specifications) while rotating the drum. Back off the adjusting nut 1/2-turn, then tighten the nut to the final torque (also listed in this Chapter's Specifications) **(see illustration)**.
12   Install the nut lock, cotter pin and grease cap. Be careful not to damage the grease cap.
13   Install the wheel, lower the vehicle and tighten the lug nuts to the torque listed in this Chapter's Specifications.

6   Rear brake shoes – replacement

Warning: *The brake shoes must be replaced on both rear wheels at the same time – never replace the shoes on only one wheel. Also, brake system dust may contain asbestos, which is harmful to your health. Never blow it out with compressed air and don't inhale any of it. Do not, under any circumstances, use petroleum-based solvents to clean brake parts. Use brake cleaner or denatured alcohol only. Whenever the brake shoes are replaced, the return and hold-down springs should also be replaced. Due to the continuous heating/cooling cycle that the springs are subjected to, they lose their tension over a period of time and may allow the shoes to drag on the drum and wear at a much faster rate than normal. When replacing the rear brake shoes, use only high quality, nationally recognized brand-name parts.*

1   Some two-door models use 7-inch rear brakes. All others use 8-inch rear brakes. Service procedures differ for the two designs.

7-inch brakes

Refer to illustrations 6.6a through 6.6r and 6.7

2   Remove about two-thirds of the brake fluid from the master cylinder reservoir.
3   Loosen the wheel lug nuts, raise the rear of the vehicle and support it on jackstands. Block the front wheels and remove the rear wheels from the vehicle.
4   Refer to Section 5 in this Chapter and remove the brake drums.
5   Carefully inspect the brake drums as outlined in Section 5 of this Chapter. Also inspect the wheel cylinder for fluid leakage as described in Chapter 1.

9

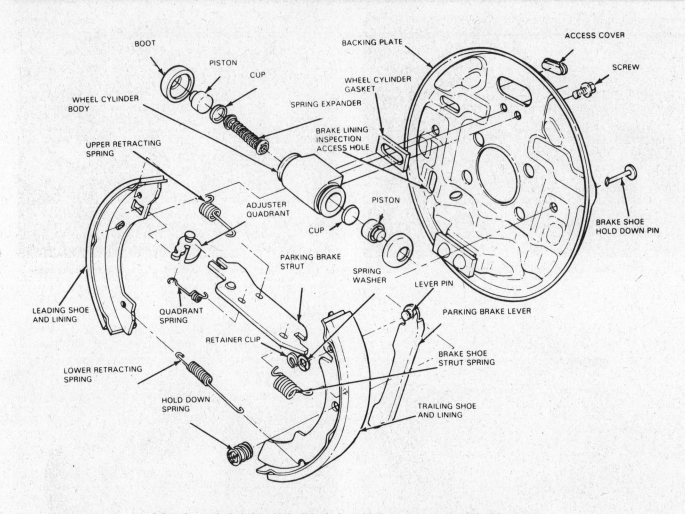

BOOT

PISTON

CUP

WHEEL CYLINDER BODY

BACKING PLATE

WHEEL CYLINDER GASKET

SPRING EXPANDER

BRAKE LINING INSPECTION ACCESS HOLE

ACCESS COVER

SCREW

UPPER RETRACTING SPRING

ADJUSTER QUADRANT

PISTON

CUP

PARKING BRAKE STRUT

SPRING WASHER

LEVER PIN

PARKING BRAKE LEVER

BRAKE SHOE HOLD DOWN PIN

LEADING SHOE AND LINING

QUADRANT SPRING

RETAINER CLIP

BRAKE SHOE STRUT SPRING

LOWER RETRACTING SPRING

HOLD DOWN SPRING

TRAILING SHOE AND LINING

6.6a   An exploded view of the 7-inch drum brake components – left side shown

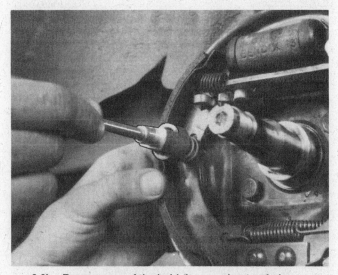

6.6b   Remove one of the hold down springs and pins . . .

6.6c   . . . then the other – the special tool shown is helpful, but a pair of pliers will work

6   Clean the brake assembly with brake system cleaner and allow the components to dry (be sure to place a drain pan under the brake). Follow the accompanying photographs (**illustra-** **tions 6.6a through 6.6r**) to remove the shoes. Be sure to stay in order and read the information in the caption under each illustration.

6.6d   Lift off the brake assembly . . .

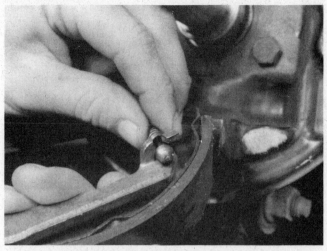

6.6e   . . . then turn it over and detach the parking brake cable

6.6f   Unhook the lower retracting spring and take it off

6.6g   Rotate the leading shoe to release the retracting spring tension, then take the spring off – DO NOT pry the spring off, or you'll damage it

6.6h   To separate the parking brake mechanism from the shoe, pull it straight out from the shoe and twist it downward . . .

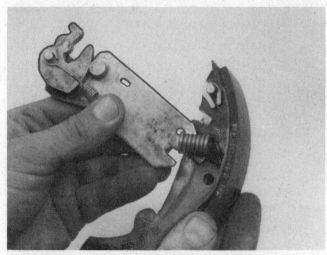

6.6i   . . . rotate the strut toward you to release the spring tension . . .

9

6.6j   . . . then unhook and remove the spring

6.6k   To separate the parking brake lever from the shoe, pry open the clip, then slip the lever pin out of the shoe

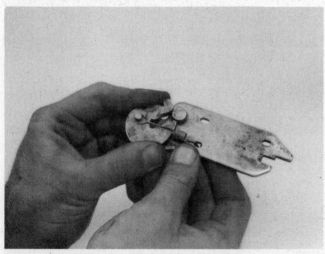

6.6l   To disassemble the adjuster, pull the quadrant straight away from the knurled pin and rotate it so the quadrant is out of mesh with the pin . . .

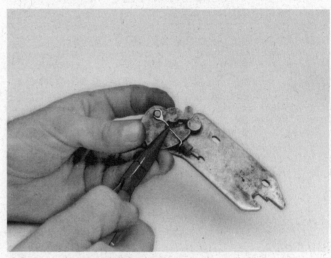

6.6m   . . . then carefully unhook the spring – don't bend it – and separate the quadrant from the strut

6.6n   To reassemble, slide the quadrant pin into the slot in the strut, then turn it over and install the spring

6.6o   Use a new clip to attach the parking brake lever to the shoe – squeeze the clip with pliers until it holds the pin securely

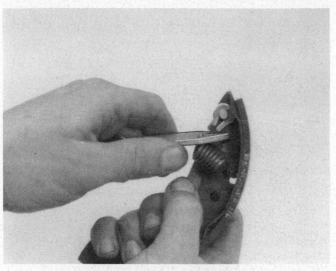

6.6p   Hook the spring to the parking brake strut, then position the strut on the shoe

6.6q   Apply high-temperature brake grease to the shoe and backing plate friction points, then reverse the removal steps to complete installation

7   Position the adjusting quadrant **(see illustration)** in a notch that will allow the shoes to just clear the drum when it's installed.
8   Once the new shoes are in place and adjusted, install the hub/drum assembly as outlined in Section 5.
9   Repeat the adjustment on the opposite wheel.
10   Install the plugs in the backing plate access holes.
11   Install the wheels and lower the vehicle. Tighten the lug nuts to the torque listed in the Chapter 1 Specifications.
12   Adjust the parking brake as described in Section 11 of this Chapter.
13   Top up the master cylinder with brake fluid and pump the pedal several times. Lower the vehicle and check brake operation before driving the vehicle in traffic.

8-inch brakes

Refer to illustrations 6.18a through 6.18n, 6.21, 6.22a and 6.22b

14   Remove about two-thirds of the brake fluid from the master cylinder reservoir.

15   Loosen the wheel lug nuts, raise the rear of the vehicle and support it on jackstands. Block the front wheels and remove the rear wheels from the vehicle.
16   Refer to Section 5 in this Chapter and remove the brake drums.
17   Carefully inspect the brake drums as outlined in Section 5 of this Chapter. Also inspect the wheel cylinder for fluid leakage as described in Chapter 1.
18   Follow the accompanying photos **(illustrations 6.18a through 6.18n)** for the actual shoe replacement procedure. Be sure to stay in order and read the information in the caption under each illustration.
19   Once the new shoes are in place, install the hub/drum assembly as outlined in Section 5.
20   Remove the rubber plug from the brake backing plate.

6.6r   The brakes should look like this when they are assembled

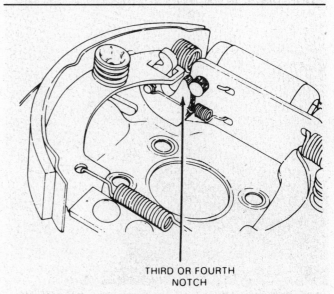

THIRD OR FOURTH NOTCH

6.7   Adjust the quadrant so the drum is just able to slide over the shoes

9

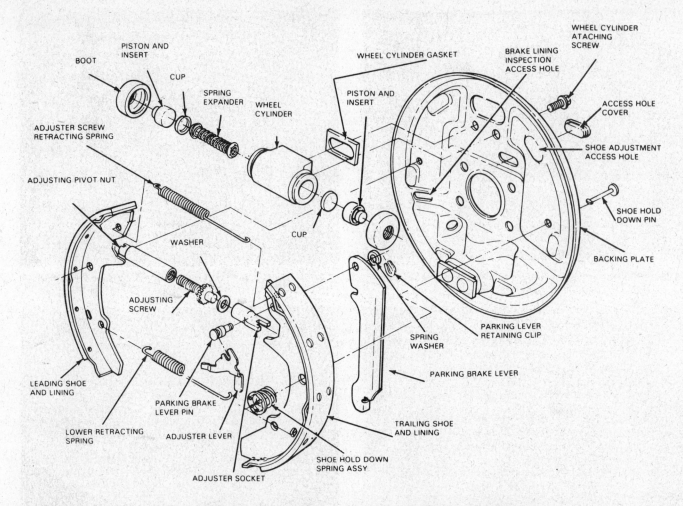

PISTON AND INSERT

BOOT

CUP

SPRING EXPANDER

WHEEL CYLINDER

WHEEL CYLINDER GASKET

PISTON AND INSERT

BRAKE LINING INSPECTION ACCESS HOLE

WHEEL CYLINDER ATACHING SCREW

WHEEL CYLINDER ATACHING SCREW

ACCESS HOLE COVER

ADJUSTER SCREW RETRACTING SPRING

SHOE ADJUSTMENT ACCESS HOLE

ADJUSTING PIVOT NUT

SHOE HOLD DOWN PIN

CUP

BACKING PLATE

WASHER

ADJUSTING SCREW

SPRING WASHER

PARKING LEVER RETAINING CLIP

LEADING SHOE AND LINING

PARKING BRAKE LEVER

PARKING BRAKE LEVER PIN

TRAILING SHOE AND LINING

LOWER RETRACTING SPRING

ADJUSTER LEVER

SHOE HOLD DOWN SPRING ASSY

ADJUSTER SOCKET

6.18a   An exploded view of the 8-inch drum brake components – left side shown

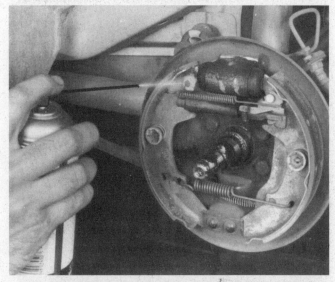

6.18b   Before removing any internal drum brake components, wash them off with brake cleaner and allow them to dry – position a drain pan under the brake to catch the residue – DO NOT USE COMPRESSED AIR TO BLOW THE BRAKE DUST FROM THE PARTS!

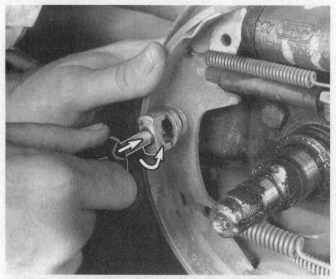

6.18c   Depress and turn the spring retainers and remove the hold-down springs and pins

6.18d   Slide the entire assembly up and off the shoe retaining plate (be careful not to bend the adjusting lever)

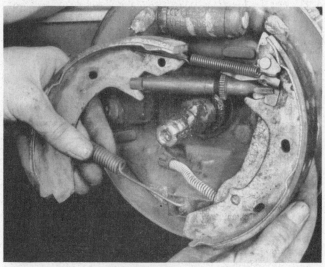

6.18e   Unhook the lower retracting spring from the trailing brake shoe, . . .

6.18f   . . . then remove the adjuster screw retracting spring from the adjuster lever (at which time the adjuster lever, adjuster screw assembly and the leading brake shoe can also be removed)

6.18g   Unclip the parking brake cable end from the parking brake lever on the trailing shoe, then remove the shoe and lever assembly

6.18h   Spread the parking brake lever retaining clip with a screwdriver and remove the clip and spring washer (note that the lever mounts to the BACK SIDE of the trailing shoe)

6.18i   Attach the parking brake lever to the new shoe, inserting the pivot pin through the front of the shoe, then through the lever – install the spring washer and retaining clip and crimp it closed with a pair of pliers

9

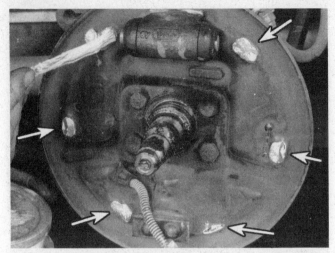

6.18j   Lubricate the brake shoe contact areas (arrows) with high-temperature grease

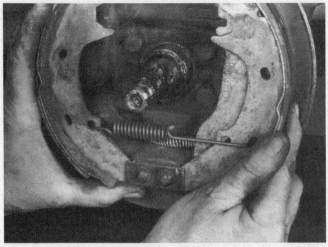

6.18k   Install the parking brake cable in the lever, hook the lower retracting spring between the two shoes and slide the shoes down on the shoe retaining plate

6.18l   Install the trailing shoe hold-down pin, spring and retainer, then insert the adjuster screw assembly into the trailing shoe as shown (be sure the correct letter is facing up, depending on the side of the vehicle you are working on)

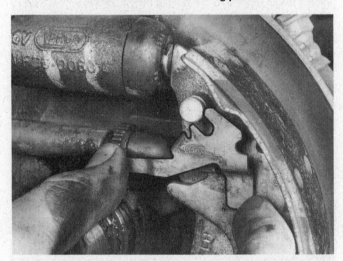

6.18m   Position the adjuster lever on the parking brake lever pivot pin, . . .

6.18n   . . . then install the new leading shoe, hold-down pin, spring and retainer – stretch the adjuster screw retracting spring and hook it in the notch on the adjuster lever (arrow)

6.21   Turn the star wheel on the adjuster screw assembly until the brake shoes drag on the drum, . . .

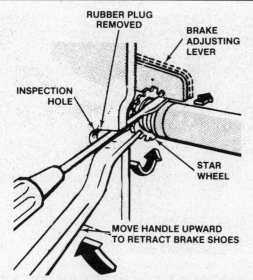

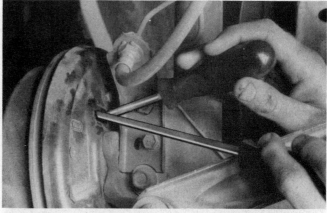

6.22b   Two screwdrivers may also be used to adjust the brakes

23   Repeat the adjustment on the opposite wheel.
24   Install the plugs in the backing plate access holes.
25   Install the wheels and lower the vehicle. Tighten the lug nuts to the torque listed in the Chapter 1 Specifications.
26   Adjust the parking brake as described in Section 11 of this Chapter.
27   Top up the master cylinder with brake fluid and pump the pedal several times. Lower the vehicle and check brake operation before driving the vehicle in traffic.

6.22a   . . . then back off the star wheel with a brake tool while holding the adjuster lever away from the star wheel until the brake shoes drag just slightly on the drum (the drum must still be able to rotate freely)

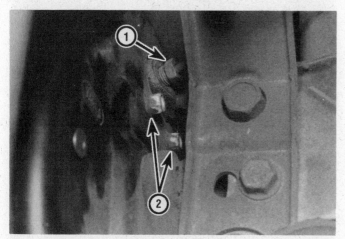

7.3   Unscrew the brake line fitting (1), then remove the two wheel cylinder bolts (2)

21   Insert a narrow screwdriver or brake adjusting tool through the adjustment hole and turn the star wheel until the brakes drag slightly as the drum is turned (**see illustration**).
22   Turn the star wheel in the opposite direction until the drum turns freely. Keep the adjuster lever from contacting the star wheel or it won't turn (**see illustrations**).

7   Wheel cylinder – removal, overhaul and installation

Refer to illustrations 7.3 and 7.5
Note: *If an overhaul is indicated (usually because of fluid leakage or sticky operation) explore all options before beginning the job. It is recommended that new wheel cylinders be installed, which makes this job quite easy. If you decide to rebuild the wheel cylinder, make sure that rebuild kits are available before proceeding. Never overhaul only one wheel cylinder – always rebuild both of them at the same time.*

Removal

1   Loosen the wheel lug nuts, raise the rear of the vehicle and support it on jackstands, then block the front wheels. Remove the rear wheel(s).
2   Remove the rear hub/drum (see Section 5) and brake shoes (see Section 6).
3   Disconnect the brake line from the back of the wheel cylinder and plug it (**see illustration**).
4   Unbolt the wheel cylinder and remove it from the backing plate. Clean the backing plate and wheel cylinder mating surfaces.

Overhaul

5   Remove the bleeder valve, cups (seals), pistons, boots and spring assembly from the wheel cylinder housing (**see illustration**).

9

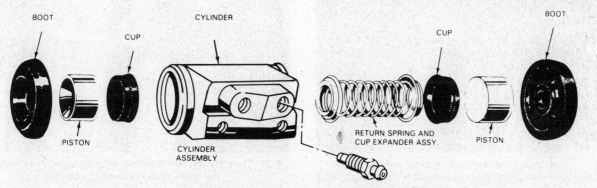

7.5   Wheel cylinder components – exploded view

8.2   Unscrew the brake line fittings from the master cylinder – a flare nut wrench is recommended (aluminum and plastic master cylinder shown – cast iron master cylinder similar)

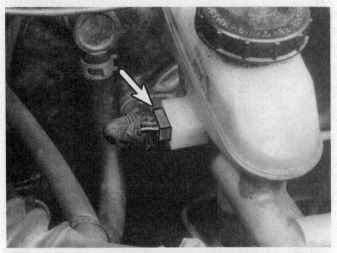

8.4a   Unplug the electrical connector from the master cylinder reservoir (if equipped) (dislodge the locking tab on the underside of the connector to allow removal)

6   Clean the wheel cylinder with brake fluid, denatured alcohol or brake system cleaner. **Warning:** *Do not, under any circumstances, use petroleum-based solvents to clean brake parts!*

7   Use compressed air to remove excess fluid from the wheel cylinder and to blow out the passages.

8   Check the cylinder bore for corrosion and score marks. Crocus cloth can be used to remove light corrosion and stains, but the cylinder must be replaced with a new one if the defects cannot be removed easily, or if the bore is scored.

9   Lubricate the new cups with brake fluid.

10   Assemble the brake cylinder components. Make sure the cup lips face in.

Installation

11   Place the wheel cylinder in position and install the bolts, but don't tighten them yet.

12   Connect the brake line to the wheel cylinder, but don't tighten it yet. Tighten the wheel cylinder mounting bolts to the torque listed in this Chapter's Specifications, then tighten the brake line fitting securely.

13   Install the brake shoe assembly (see Section 6). Install the brake drum and adjust the wheel bearing as described in Section 5.

14   Bleed the brakes (see Section 10).

---

8   Master cylinder – removal and installation

Refer to illustrations 8.2, 8.4a and 8.4b

Note: *The master cylinder installed on early models has a cast iron body; the master cylinder on later models features a plastic reservoir mated to an aluminum body. If service is indicated (usually because of insufficient pedal resistance or no resistance at all, or external fluid leakage) it's recommended that the master cylinder be replaced rather than attempting to rebuild it. New and factory rebuilt units are available on an exchange basis, which makes this job quite easy and will ensure that the master cylinder is in top condition.*

Removal

1   Place rags under the fittings and prepare caps or plastic bags to cover the ends of the lines once they are disconnected. Remove as much fluid as possible with a suction gun before starting this procedure. **Caution:** *Brake fluid will damage paint. Cover all body parts and be careful not to spill fluid during this procedure.*

2   Loosen the tube nuts at the ends of the brake lines where they enter the master cylinder **(see illustration)**. To prevent rounding off the flats, use a flare-nut wrench, which wraps around the nut.

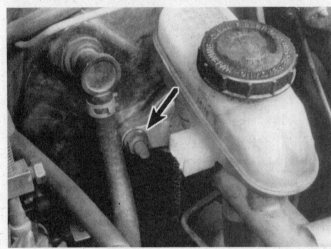

8.4b   Remove the two master cylinder mounting nuts and pull the master cylinder off the power booster or firewall

3   Pull the brake lines away from the master cylinder slightly and plug the ends to prevent contamination.

4   Unplug the electrical connector at the master cylinder (if equipped), then remove the two nuts attaching the master cylinder to the power booster **(see illustrations)**. Pull the master cylinder off the studs and lift it out of the engine compartment. Again, be careful not to spill the fluid as this is done.

Installation

5   Install the master cylinder over the studs on the power brake booster and tighten the nuts only finger tight at this time.

6   Using your fingers, thread the brake line fittings into the master cylinder. Since the master cylinder is still a bit loose, it can be moved slightly in order for the fittings to thread in easily. Don't strip the threads as the fittings are tightened.

7   Tighten the brake line fittings and the two mounting nuts.

8   Fill the master cylinder reservoir with brake fluid. It will be necessary to bleed the master cylinder to remove any air that may be present.

9   Place plenty of rags or newspapers under and around the master cylinder to absorb the brake fluid that will escape during the bleeding process. It is also recommended that eye protection be worn while performing the bleeding procedure.

10   With an assistant seated in the driver's seat, loosen the upper secondary brake line fitting (the one closest to the front of the vehicle) approxi-

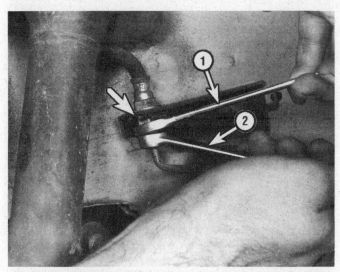

9.3 To disconnect the brake hose from the steel brake line, place a back-up wrench (1) on the hose fitting and loosen the tube nut with a flare nut wrench (2) (the U-clip [arrow] can now be removed)

mately 3/4-turn. Have your assistant push the brake pedal slowly to the floor and hold it there. Tighten the fitting and have the assistant slowly return the pedal to the released position. Wait five seconds, then repeat this operation until the stream of fluid from the loosened fitting is free of air bubbles.

11 Repeat the procedure at the upper primary brake line fitting (the one closest to the power booster). Be sure to keep an eye on the fluid level.

12 Fill the reservoir to the MAX indicator and install the filler cap.

13 Remove the newspapers or rags. Be careful not to let any brake fluid drip on the vehicle's paint. Rinse the area around the master cylinder with water immediately to wash away residual fluid that will damage the engine compartment paint.

14 Refer to Section 10 for further brake hydraulic system bleeding.

---

9 Brake hoses and lines – inspection and replacement

Refer to illustration 9.3

Inspection

1 About every six months, with the vehicle raised and supported securely on jackstands, the rubber hoses which connect the steel brake lines with the front and rear brake assemblies should be inspected for cracks, chafing of the outer cover, leaks, blisters and other damage. These are important and vulnerable parts of the brake system and inspection should be complete. A light and mirror will be helpful for a thorough check. If a hose exhibits any of the above conditions, replace it with a new one.

Flexible hose replacement

2 Clean all dirt away from the ends of the hose.

3 Disconnect the brake line from the hose fitting using a back-up wrench on the fitting **(see illustration)**. Be careful not to bend the frame bracket or line. If necessary, soak the connections with penetrating oil.

4 Unbolt the hose bracket from the strut assembly.

5 Remove the U-clip from the female fitting at the bracket **(see illustration 9.3)** and remove the hose from the bracket.

6 Disconnect the hose from the caliper, discarding the copper washers on either side of the fitting block.

7 Using new copper washers, attach the new brake hose to the caliper.

8 Pass the female fitting through the frame bracket. With the least amount of twist in the hose, install the fitting in this position (use the paint stripe on the hose to help determine twist). **Note:** *The weight of the vehicle should be on the suspension, so the vehicle should not be raised while positioning the hose.*

9 Install the U-clip in the female fitting at the frame bracket.

10 Attach the brake line to the hose fitting using a back-up wrench on the fitting.

11 Mount the brake hose bracket to the strut assembly.

12 Carefully check to make sure the suspension or steering components don't make contact with the hose. Have an assistant push on the vehicle and also turn the steering wheel from lock-to-lock during inspection.

13 Bleed the brake system as described in Section 10.

Rigid brake line replacement

14 When replacing brake lines, be sure to use the correct parts. Don't use copper tubing for any brake system components. Purchase steel brake lines from a dealer or auto parts store.

15 Prefabricated brake line, with the tube ends already flared and fittings installed, is available at auto parts stores and dealers. These lines are also bent to the proper shapes.

16 If prefabricated lines aren't available, obtain the recommended steel tubing and fittings to match the line to be replaced. Determine the correct length by measuring the old brake line (a piece of string can usually be used for this) and cut the new tubing to length, allowing about 1/2-inch extra for flaring the ends.

17 Install the fitting over the cut tubing and flare the ends of the line with a flaring tool.

18 If necessary, carefully bend the line to the proper shape. A tube bender is recommended for this. **Warning:** *Do not crimp or damage the line.*

19 When installing the new line, make sure it's securely supported in the brackets and has plenty of clearance between moving or hot components.

20 After installation, check the master cylinder fluid level and add fluid as necessary. Bleed the brake system as outlined in the next Section and test the brakes carefully before driving the vehicle in traffic.

---

10 Brake hydraulic system – bleeding

Refer to illustration 10.8

Warning: *Wear eye protection when bleeding the brake system. If the fluid comes in contact with your eyes, immediately rinse them with water and seek medical attention.*

1 Bleeding the hydraulic system is necessary to remove any air that manages to find its way into the system as a result of removal and installation of a hose, line, caliper or master cylinder. Use only the specified fluid in this system or extensive damage could result. It will probably be necessary to bleed the system at all four brakes if air has entered the system due to low fluid level, or if the brake lines have been disconnected at the master cylinder.

2 If a brake line was disconnected only at one wheel, then only that caliper (or wheel cylinder) must be bled.

3 If a brake line is disconnected at a fitting located between the master cylinder and any of the brakes, that part of the system served by the disconnected line must be bled.

4 Remove any residual vacuum from the power brake booster by applying the brake several times with the engine off.

5 Remove the master cylinder reservoir cover and fill the reservoir with brake fluid. Reinstall the cover. **Note:** *Check the fluid level often during the bleeding operation and add fluid as necessary to prevent the level from falling low enough to allow air bubbles into the master cylinder.*

6 Have an assistant on hand, as well as a supply of new brake fluid, an empty clear plastic container, a length of 3/16-inch clear plastic or vinyl tubing to fit over the bleeder screw and a wrench to open and close the bleeder screw.

7 Beginning at the right rear wheel, loosen the bleeder screw slightly, then tighten it to a point where it's snug but can still be loosened quickly and easily.

9

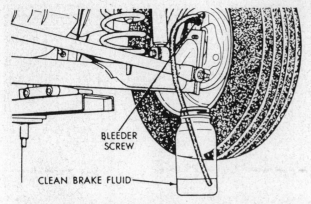

10.8   When bleeding the brakes, a hose is connected to the bleeder screw and then submerged in brake fluid – air will be seen as bubbles in the container and the hose (all air must be removed before continuing to the next wheel)

8   Place one end of the tubing over the bleeder screw and submerge the other end in brake fluid in the container **(see illustration)**.
9   Have an assistant pump the brakes a few times to get pressure in the system, then hold the pedal down.
10   While the pedal is held down, open the bleeder screw until brake fluid begins to flow. Watch for air bubbles to exit the submerged end of the tube. When the fluid flow slows after a couple of seconds, tighten the screw and have your assistant release the pedal.
11   Repeat Steps 9 and 10 until no more air is seen leaving the tube, then tighten the bleeder screw and proceed to the left front wheel, the left rear wheel and the right front wheel, in that order, and perform the same procedure. Be sure to check the fluid in the master cylinder reservoir frequently.
12   Never use old brake fluid. It contains moisture which will deteriorate the brake system components.
13   Refill the master cylinder with fluid at the end of the operation.
14   Check the operation of the brakes. The pedal should feel solid when depressed, with no sponginess. If necessary, repeat the entire process.
Warning: *DO NOT operate the vehicle if you are in doubt about the effectiveness of the brake system.*

---

11   Parking brake – adjustment

Refer to illustration 11.5

1   Start the engine and firmly depress the brake pedal several times to seat the shoes in the brake drum. Turn off the engine.
2   Raise the rear of the vehicle and support it securely on jackstands. Block the front wheels.
3   Remove the console trim surrounding the parking brake lever (see Chapter 11).
4   Pull up on the parking brake lever until the twelfth notch is engaged (listen for the clicks).
5   Tighten the adjusting nut until approximately 1-inch of the threaded adjuster rod is exposed beyond the nut **(see illustration)**.
6   Release the lever and rotate the rear wheels. The wheels should turn freely, but a slight drag is acceptable.
7   If the brake lever travels too far or the parking brake fails to hold the vehicle on a hill, tighten the adjusting nut a little more and recheck the operation of the parking brake.

---

12   Parking brake cables – removal and installation

Refer to illustrations 12.4 and 12.7

Removal

1   Remove the console trim that surrounds the parking brake lever. Partially apply the parking brake lever to gain access to the adjusting nut.

11.5   The center console trim panel must be removed to reveal the parking brake adjusting nut (arrow)

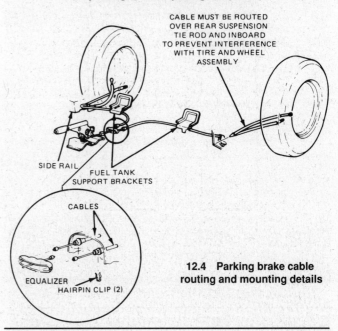

CABLE MUST BE ROUTED OVER REAR SUSPENSION TIE ROD AND INBOARD TO PREVENT INTERFERENCE WITH TIRE AND WHEEL ASSEMBLY

SIDE RAIL

FUEL TANK SUPPORT BRACKETS

CABLES

EQUALIZER

HAIRPIN CLIP (2)

12.4   Parking brake cable routing and mounting details

Loosen but do not remove the nut, then return the lever to the released position.
2   Loosen the wheel lug nuts on the side of the vehicle that the cable is to be removed from, raise the rear of the vehicle and support it on jackstands. Block the front wheels.
3   Remove the wheel and the brake drum (see Section 5 in this Chapter).
4   Disengage the parking brake cable from the equalizer, located above the exhaust pipe and heat shield in the floor pan tunnel **(see illustration)**. It may be necessary to remove the exhaust pipe and heat shield to gain access to the equalizer (see Chapter 4).
5   Remove the cable retaining clips from the fuel tank support bracket and the screw from the rear tie-rod mounting bracket.
6   Unhook the other cable end from the brake shoe lever. Refer to Section 6 in this Chapter if necessary.
7   Depress the cable housing retention tangs and pull the cable from the backing plate **(see illustration)**.

Installation

8   Push the cable and housing through the backing plate until the retention tangs pop into place. Attach the cable end to the parking brake lever.
9   Attach the cable housing retaining clip to the rear tie-rod mounting bracket.
10   Route the cable around the fuel tank and install the retaining clips.
11   Slip the cable end into the equalizer.
12   Reinstall the brake drum and wheel.

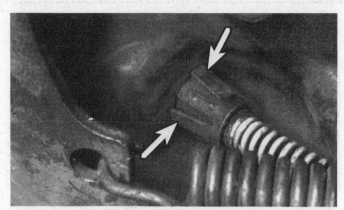

12.7   Depress the retention tangs (arrows) to free the cable and housing from the brake backing plate

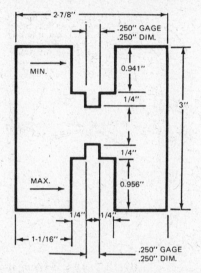

13.11a   Power brake booster pushrod gauge template (1981 through 1983 models)

13   Install the heat shield and exhaust pipe if previously removed.
14   Lower the vehicle and adjust the parking brake as outlined in Section 11.

13   Power brake booster – removal, installation and adjustment

Refer to illustrations 13.5, 13.11a, 13.11b and 13.15
1   The power brake booster unit requires no special maintenance apart from periodic inspection of the vacuum hose and the case.
2   Dismantling of the brake booster requires special tools and is not ordinarily done by the home mechanic. If a problem develops, install a new or factory rebuilt unit.

Removal

3   Remove the master cylinder (see Section 8).
4   Disconnect the vacuum hose where it attaches to the power brake booster.
5   Working in the passenger compartment under the steering column, unplug the wiring connector from the brake light switch, then remove the pushrod retaining clip and nylon washer from the brake pedal pin. Slide the pushrod off the pin **(see illustration)**.
6   Also remove the nuts attaching the brake booster to the firewall **(see illustration 13.5)**.
7   Carefully detach the booster from the firewall and lift it out of the engine compartment.

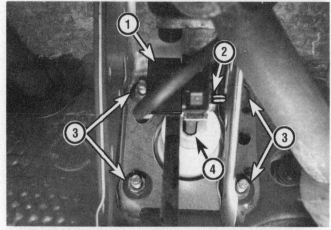

13.5   The following under-dash components must be removed/disconnected to allow power brake booster removal:

1 Brake light switch wire connector	3 Booster mounting nuts
2 Pushrod retaining clip	4 Pushrod

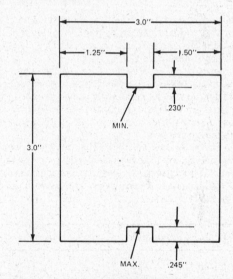

13.11b   Power brake booster pushrod gauge template (1984 and later models)

Installation

8   Place the booster into position on the firewall and tighten the mounting nuts. Connect the pushrod and brake light switch to the brake pedal. Install the retaining clip in the brake pedal pin.
9   Install the master cylinder and vacuum hose. Refer to Section 8 for the master cylinder bleeding procedure.
10   Carefully check the operation of the brakes before driving the vehicle in traffic.

Adjustment

11   Some boosters feature an adjustable pushrod. They are matched to the booster at the factory and most likely will not require adjustment, but if a misadjusted pushrod is suspected, a gauge can be fabricated out of heavy gauge sheet metal using the accompanying template **(see illustrations)**.
12   Some common symptoms caused by a misadjusted pushrod include dragging brakes (if the pushrod is too long) or excessive brake pedal travel accompanied by a groaning sound from the brake booster (if the pushrod is too short).

9

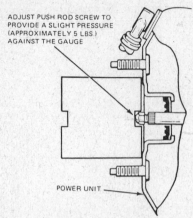

ADJUST PUSH ROD SCREW TO
PROVIDE A SLIGHT PRESSURE
(APPROXIMATELY 5 LBS.)
AGAINST THE GAUGE

POWER UNIT

**13.15   Checking the pushrod length (the pushrod is
factory preset and most likely will never need adjusting)**

13   To check the pushrod length, unbolt the master cylinder from the booster and position it to one side. It isn't necessary to disconnect the hydraulic lines, but be careful not to bend them.
14   Block the front wheels, apply the parking brake and place the transaxle in Park or Neutral.
15   Start the engine and place the pushrod gauge against the end of the pushrod, exerting a force of approximately 5-pounds to seat the pushrod in the power unit **(see illustration)**. The rod measurement should fall somewhere between the minimum and maximum cutouts on the gauge. If it doesn't, adjust it by holding the knurled portion of the pushrod with a pair of pliers and turning the end with a wrench.
16   When the adjustment is complete, reinstall the master cylinder and check for proper brake operation before driving the vehicle in traffic.

14   Brake light switch – removal and installation

Refer to illustration 14.2

Removal

1   Remove the under dash panel.
2   Locate the switch near the top of the brake pedal and disconnect the electrical connector **(see illustration)**.
3   Remove the pushrod retaining clip and nylon washer from the brake pedal pin and slide the pushrod off far enough for the outer hole of the switch to clear the pin. Now pull up on the switch to remove it.

Installation

4   Position the switch so it straddles the pushrod and the slot on the inner side of the switch rests on the pedal pin. Slide the pushrod and switch back onto the pin, then install the nylon washer and retaining clip.
5   Plug in the electrical connector.
6   Install the under dash panel.
7   Check the brake lights for proper operation.

15   Brake pedal – removal and installation

Refer to illustration 15.7

Removal

1   Disconnect the cable from the negative terminal of the battery.
2   Remove the under dash panel and unplug the electrical connector at the brake light switch.

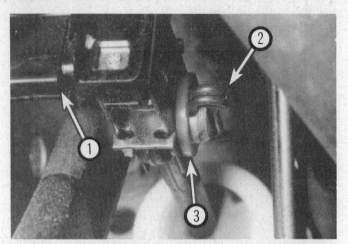

**14.2   Unplug the brake light switch electrical connector (1),
remove the retaining clip (2) and nylon washer (3), then slide the
pushrod off the pedal pin just enough to allow switch removal**

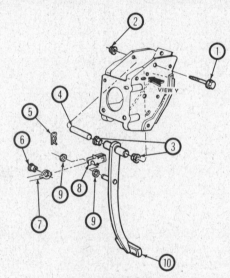

**15.7   Installation details of the brake pedal and
associated hardware**

1	Pivot bolt	5	Pushrod retaining clip	8	Brake light switch
2	Nut	6	Pushrod bushing	9	Nylon washers
3	Bushings	7	Pushrod	10	Brake pedal
4	Spacer				

3   Disconnect the brake pedal from the power brake booster pushrod by removing the retaining clip and washer and sliding the pushrod off the pedal pin (see Section 13).
4   Remove the nut and pivot bolt from the top of the pedal.
5   The brake pedal, spacer and bushings can now be removed from the bracket.

Installation

6   Use new bushings and lubricate the bushings, spacer, bolt and all friction parts with a light coat of engine oil.
7   Place the pedal, bushings and spacer in position and slide the pivot bolt into place. Note that it should be installed with the head on the left side of the bracket.
8   Tighten the nut and attach the booster pushrod and brake light switch to the pedal.
9   Operate the brake pedal several times to ensure proper operation.
10   Plug in the electrical connector to the brake light switch and install the under dash cover. Connect the battery.

Chapter 10
Suspension and steering systems

Contents

Specifications

Torque specifications   Ft-lbs

Front suspension

	Ft-lbs
Control arm pivot bolt/nut	44 to 55
Control arm-to-steering knuckle pinch bolt	
1981 through 1989	37 to 44
1990	40 to 54
Strut upper mounting nut	23 to 30
Strut-to-steering knuckle pinch bolt	66 to 81
Strut damper shaft-to-upper mount nut	48 to 70
Stabilizer bar bracket-to-body bolts	50 to 60
Stabilizer bar-to-control arm nuts	80 to 115
Stabilizer bar U-bracket bolts	60 to 70

Rear suspension

	Ft-lbs
Control arm-to-body bolts	65 to 75
Control arm-to-spindle nuts/bolts	90 to 100
Strut upper mounting nut	35 to 55
Strut-to-spindle nuts/bolts	90 to 100
Tie-rod end-to-body nut/bolt	
1981 through 1985	90 to 100
1986 through 1990	52 to 74
Tie-rod end-to-spindle nut	
1981 through 1985	65 to 75
1986 through 1990	70 to 95

Steering

	Ft-lbs
Tie-rod end-to-steering knuckle arm nut*	23 to 35
Steering gear lower shaft pinch bolt	20 to 37
Steering wheel nut	30 to 40
Steering gear mounting bolts	48 to 55

*Tighten to the minimum specified torque, then align the next castellation in the nut with the cotter pin hole

1.1   Details of the front suspension

1   Stabilizer bar
2   Stabilizer bar bracket
3   Strut assembly
4   Steering knuckle
5   Control arm
6   Steering gear

1.2   Details of the rear suspension

1   Coil spring   3   Control arm   5   Rear tie-rod
2   Strut   4   Spindle

10

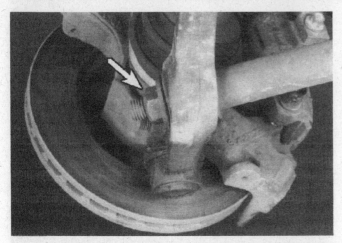

2.2   The stabilizer bar-to-control arm nuts and washers must be removed to separate the bar from the control arms (note how the washer is dished away from the control arm bushing)

2.3a   Remove one of the control arm-to-body pivot bolts to relieve tension on the stabilizer bar

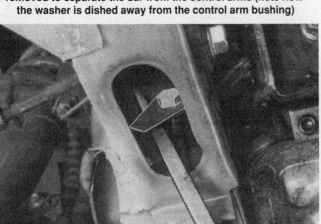

2.3b   Pry the control arm pivot bolt from the control arm and body bracket

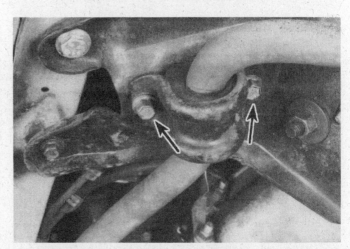

2.4   Remove the stabilizer bar U-bracket bolts – the nuts on the other side of the mounting bracket are pressed into the bracket and don't require a wrench unless they strip out (in which case a 17 mm wrench must be used)

1   General information

Refer to illustrations 1.1 and 1.2

The front suspension is a MacPherson strut design. The steering knuckle is located by a lower control arm and both front control arms are connected by a stabilizer bar, which also controls fore-and-aft movement of the control arms **(see illustrations)**.

The rear suspension also utilizes MacPherson struts and consists of a shock absorber strut attached to the spindle that is mounted on the end of the control arm. The spring is mounted between the control arm and the chassis crossmember. Longitudinal movement is controlled by tie-rods mounted between the body and the rear spindles **(see illustration)**.

The rack-and-pinion steering gear is located behind the engine/transaxle assembly and actuates the steering arms which are integral with the steering knuckles. Some vehicles are equipped with power steering. The steering column is connected to the steering gear through an articulated intermediate shaft. The steering column is designed to collapse in the event of an accident.

Note: *These vehicles use a combination of standard and metric fasteners on the various suspension and steering components, so it would be a good idea to have both types of tools available when beginning work.*

Warning: *Ford recommends that whenever any of the suspension or steering fasteners are loosened or removed they should be replaced with new ones – the original fasteners should be discarded, not reused. They must be replaced with new ones of the same part number or of original*

equipment quality and design. Torque specifications must be followed for proper reassembly and component retention.

2   Stabilizer bar and bushings – removal and installation

Refer to illustrations 2.2, 2.3a, 2.3b, 2.4 and 2.6
Note: *The stabilizer bar used on these vehicles is unique in that it also serves to prevent longitudinal movement of the control arms.*

Removal

1   Raise the vehicle and support it securely on jackstands. If only the stabilizer bar bushings are being replaced, proceed to Step 6, as it isn't necessary to unbolt the stabilizer bar from the control arms for bushing replacement.

2   Remove both large stabilizer-to-control arm nuts and concave washers **(see illustration)**.

3   Remove the control arm-to-body pivot bolt from one side of the vehicle **(see illustrations)**.

4   Remove the four stabilizer bar U-bracket bolts. Support the bar while removing the last two bolts to prevent the stabilizer bar from falling **(see illustration)**.

5   Separate the stabilizer bar from the control arms (be careful not to lose the stabilizer bar-to-control arm spacers).

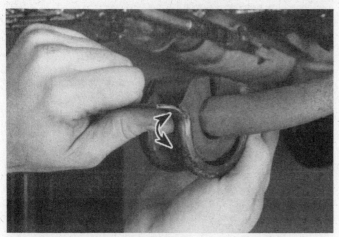

2.6   Use a rocking motion to detach the U-brackets from the bushings

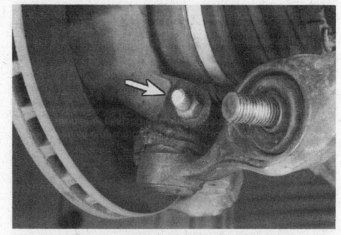

4.4   Remove the balljoint pinch bolt from the steering knuckle – a punch may be used to drive the bolt out

Bushing replacement

6   Pull the U-bracket off the stabilizer bar rubber bushing using a rocking motion **(see illustration)**.

7   Remove the bushing from the bar and clean the bushing area with a stiff wire brush to remove any rust, dirt or rubber deposits.

8   Lubricate the inside and outside of the new bushing with vegetable oil (used in cooking) to simplify reassembly. **Caution:** *Don't use petroleum or mineral-based lubricant or brake fluid – they will lead to deterioration of the bushing.*

9   Place the new bushing on the stabilizer bar and install the U-bracket, use the same rocking motion used during removal if resistance is encountered.

Installation

10   Push the stabilizer bar-to-control arm spacers into the rubber insulators in the control arm, with the washer end facing the front of the vehicle.

11   Insert the stabilizer bar ends into the control arms, install the concave washers (with the dished portion facing away from the bushing) and new nuts. Start the nuts on the threads by hand, but don't tighten them yet.

12   Using a new pivot bolt and nut, attach the control arm to the body. It may be necessary to pry between the body and the stabilizer bar to push the control arm in far enough to insert the pivot bolt through the body and the control arm.

13   Install the stabilizer bar U-bracket bolts, starting all four by hand before tightening any of them.

14   Tighten the U-bracket bolts to the torque listed in this Chapter's Specifications.

15   Tighten the two large stabilizer bar-to-control arm nuts to the torque listed in this Chapter's Specifications. Recheck your work, then lower the vehicle.

3   Balljoints – check and replacement

The balljoints on this vehicle are not replaceable separately. The entire control arm must be replaced if the balljoints are worn out. Refer to the Steering and suspension check in Chapter 1 for the checking procedure. Refer to Section 4 in this Chapter for control arm removal and installation.

4   Control arm (front) – removal, inspection and installation

Refer to illustrations 4.4 and 4.6

Removal

1   Loosen the wheel lug nuts on the side to be disassembled, raise the

4.6   After the balljoint stud has been detached from the knuckle, pull the lower control arm off the stabilizer bar

front of the vehicle and support it securely on jackstands. Apply the parking brake. Remove the wheel.

2   Remove the stabilizer bar-to-control arm nut and dished washer **(see illustration 2.2)**.

3   Remove the bolt and nut from the inner control arm pivot **(see illustrations 2.3a and 2.3b)**.

4   Remove the balljoint pinch bolt and nut from the steering knuckle **(see illustration)**. Spread the joint slightly with a screwdriver or pry bar.

5   Pry the control arm down to separate it from the steering knuckle.

6   Pull the control arm off the stabilizer bar and remove it from the vehicle (be careful not to lose the stabilizer bar spacer) **(see illustration)**.

Inspection

7   Check the control arm for distortion and the bushings for wear, damage and deterioration. Replace a damaged or bent control arm with a new one. If the inner pivot or stabilizer bar bushings are worn, take the control arm to a dealer service department or other repair shop, as special tools are required to replace them. If the balljoint is worn or damaged, the control arm must be replaced.

Installation

8   Place the control arm balljoint stud into the steering knuckle. Note that the notch in the balljoint stud must be aligned with the hole in the knuckle before the pinch bolt is inserted. Using a new pinch bolt and nut, insert the bolt from the front of the steering knuckle and tighten the new nut to the torque listed in this Chapter's Specifications.

10

5.2   Remove the brake hose bracket bolts, . . .

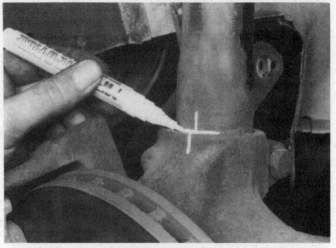

5.3   . . . then mark the relationship of the strut to the steering knuckle

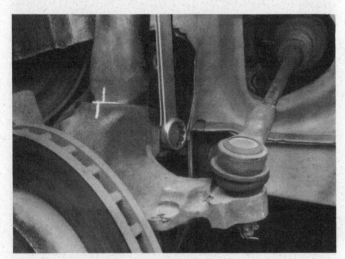

5.4   Remove the strut-to-steering knuckle pinch bolt, . . .

5.6   . . . then apply penetrating oil to the strut/knuckle joint and wedge a screwdriver in the joint to spread it apart

9   Push the stabilizer bar spacer into the rubber insulator in the control arm from the front side. Swing the control arm into position over the stabilizer bar end.

10   Install the control arm pivot bolt and tighten the nut to the torque listed in this Chapter's Specifications. It may be necessary to pry between the body and stabilizer bar to push the control arm in far enough to insert the pivot bolt through the body and control arm.

11   Install the stabilizer bar-to-control arm washer and nut (with the dished portion of the washer facing away from the rubber insulator). Tighten the nut to the torque listed in this Chapter's Specifications.

12   Install the wheel and lug nuts, lower the vehicle and tighten the lug nuts to the torque listed in the Chapter 1 Specifications.

5   Front strut/shock absorber and coil spring assembly – removal, inspection and installation

Refer to illustrations 5.2, 5.3, 5.4, 5.6, 5.7a, 5.7b, 5.8 and 5.12

Removal

1   Loosen the wheel lug nuts on the side to be disassembled, raise the front of the vehicle and support it securely on jackstands. Apply the parking brake. Remove the wheel.

2   Disconnect the brake hose support bracket from the strut **(see illustration)**.

3   Using white paint, a marker or a scribe, mark the strut-to-steering knuckle joint **(see illustration)**. This will help position the strut during reassembly and simplify pinch bolt installation.

4   Remove the strut-to-steering knuckle pinch bolt **(see illustration)**.

5   Apply penetrating oil to the strut where it joins the steering knuckle and allow it to soak in for a few minutes.

6   Using a screwdriver or pry bar, spread the pinch bolt joint slightly to relieve the pressure on the strut **(see illustration)**.

7   Using a large pry bar positioned between the body and steering knuckle, pry down until the end of the strut nears the top of the knuckle, then pull out on the strut to disengage it from the knuckle **(see illustrations)**.

8   Remove the two upper strut mounting nuts from the strut tower while supporting the strut/spring assembly so it doesn't fall **(see illustration)**.

9   Carefully guide the strut and spring assembly out of the wheel well.

Inspection

10   Check the strut body for leaking fluid, dents, cracks and other obvious damage which would warrant repair or replacement. Check the coil spring for cracks or chips in the spring coating (this may cause spring failure due to corrosion). Inspect the spring seat for cuts, hardness and general deterioration. If any undesirable conditions exist, proceed to Section 6 for the strut disassembly procedure.

5.7a   Pry down on the knuckle until the strut nears the top, . . .

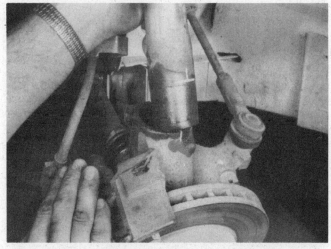

5.7b   . . . then pull the strut out of the knuckle

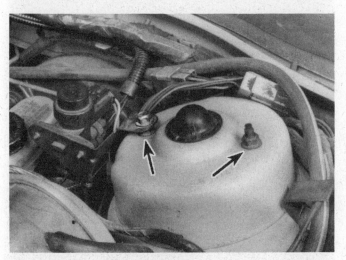

5.8   Remove the upper mounting nuts and detach the strut from the vehicle

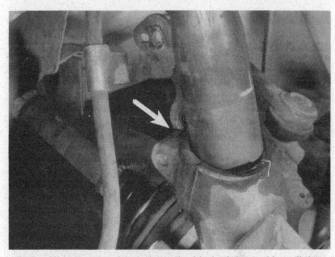

5.12   Align the strut blade (arrow) with the joint and install the strut in the knuckle

Installation

11   To install the strut, place it in position with the studs extending up through holes in the shock tower. Install the nuts and tighten them finger tight.

12   Prying down on the stabilizer bar, insert the strut into the steering knuckle with the blade on the strut positioned in the joint opening **(see illustration)**. Align the marks that were previously applied to the strut and knuckle.

13   Install a new pinch bolt and tighten it to the torque listed in this Chapter's Specifications.

14   Attach the brake hose support bracket to the strut.

15   Tighten the two strut upper mounting nuts to the torque listed in this Chapter's Specifications.

16   Install the wheel and lug nuts, lower the vehicle and tighten the lug nuts to the torque listed in the Chapter 1 Specifications.

---

6   Front strut/shock absorber and coil spring assembly – replacement

Refer to illustrations 6.3, and 6.4

1   If the struts exhibit the telltale signs of wear (leaking fluid, loss of dampening capability) explore all options before beginning any work. The strut/shock absorber assemblies are not serviceable and must be replaced if a problem develops. However, strut assemblies complete with

springs may be available on an exchange basis, which eliminates much time and work. Whichever route you choose to take, check on the cost and availability of parts before disassembling the vehicle. **Warning:** *Disassembling a strut is dangerous – be very careful and follow all instructions or serious injury could result. Use only a high quality spring compressor and carefully follow the manufacturer's instructions furnished with the tool. After removing the coil spring from the strut assembly, set it aside in a safe, isolated area.*

2   Remove the strut and spring assembly following the procedure described in Section 5. Mount the strut assembly in a vise, with the jaws of the vise clamping onto the steering knuckle bracket. Line the jaws of the vise with rags to avoid damaging the strut tube.

3   Following the tool manufacturer's instructions, install the spring compressor (which can be obtained at most auto parts stores or equipment yards on a daily rental basis) on the spring and compress it sufficiently to relieve all pressure from the spring seat **(see illustration)**. This can be verified by wiggling the spring.

4   Loosen the damper shaft nut while using a socket wrench on the shaft hex to prevent it from turning. Remove the nut and upper concave washer **(see illustration)**.

5   Lift the upper mount, thrust plate, bearing and spring seat from the damper shaft. Inspect the bearing in the spring seat for smooth operation and replace it if necessary.

6   Carefully remove the compressed spring assembly and set it in a safe place. **Warning:** *Never place your head near the end of the spring!*

7   Slide the dust boot and rubber jounce bumper off the damper shaft.

10

6.3   Install a spring compressor and compress the spring until there is no pressure being exerted on the bearing and seat assembly

8   Assemble the strut beginning with the jounce bumper and dust boot, washer and spring, then the spring seat, bearing, thrust plate and upper mount.
9   Install the damper shaft nut and tighten it to the torque listed in this Chapter's Specifications.
10   Install the strut and spring assembly on the vehicle as outlined in Section 5.

---

7   Steering knuckle and hub – removal and installation

Refer to illustrations 7.5 and 7.10

Warning: *Dust created by the brake system may contain asbestos, which is harmful to your health. Never blow it out with compressed air and don't inhale any of it. Do not, under any circumstances, use petroleum-based solvents to clean brake parts. Use brake cleaner or denatured alcohol only.*

Note: *This procedure requires a special puller and adapters to install the driveaxle in the hub. Refer to Chapter 8 and read the driveaxle removal and installation procedure carefully before beginning this operation, to decide whether or not to undertake a job of this nature.*

Removal

1   Loosen the wheel lug nuts on the side to be disassembled, raise the front of the vehicle and support it securely on jackstands. Apply the parking brake. Remove the wheel.
2   Remove the brake caliper and support it with a piece of wire as described in Chapter 9. Separate the brake disc from the hub.
3   Loosen but do not remove the strut-to-steering knuckle pinch bolt **(see illustration 5.4)**.
4   Separate the tie-rod from the steering knuckle arm as outlined in Section 16 of this chapter.
5   Remove the balljoint pinch bolt and nut from the steering knuckle **(see illustration 4.4)**. Using a large pry bar between the lower control arm pivot and the stabilizer bar, pry the balljoint stud from the steering knuckle arm **(see illustration)**.
6   Loosen but do not remove the strut upper mounting nuts.
7   Push the driveaxle from the hub as described in Chapter 8.
8   Using white paint, a marker or a scribe, mark the strut-to-steering knuckle joint **(see illustration 5.3)**. This will help position the strut during reassembly and simplify pinch bolt installation.
9   Remove the strut-to-steering knuckle pinch bolt. Apply penetrating oil to the strut-to-knuckle joint. Spread the pinch bolt joint slightly with a screwdriver or pry bar **(see illustration 5.6)**.

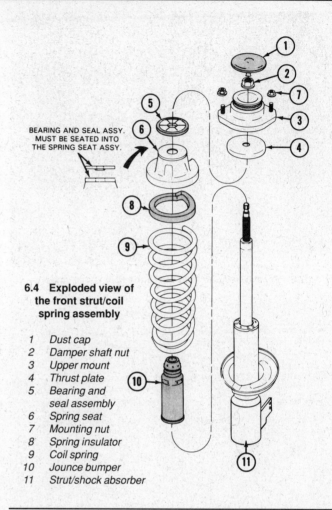

6.4   Exploded view of the front strut/coil spring assembly

BEARING AND SEAL ASSY. MUST BE SEATED INTO THE SPRING SEAT ASSY.

1   Dust cap
2   Damper shaft nut
3   Upper mount
4   Thrust plate
5   Bearing and seal assembly
6   Spring seat
7   Mounting nut
8   Spring insulator
9   Coil spring
10   Jounce bumper
11   Strut/shock absorber

10   Gently tap the steering knuckle and hub assembly off the strut with a brass, lead or shot-filled hammer. Support the steering knuckle with your other hand to prevent it from falling when it comes off the strut **(see illustration)**.

Installation

11   Position the knuckle and hub assembly on the end of the strut, aligning the blade on the strut with the joint. Align the marks that were previously applied to the strut and knuckle.
12   Install the strut-to-steering knuckle pinch bolt. Don't tighten it at this time.
13   Install the driveaxle in the hub (see Chapter 8).
14   Pry down on the stabilizer bar and insert the balljoint stud into the steering knuckle. Note that the notch in the balljoint stud must be aligned with the hole in the knuckle before the pinch bolt is inserted. Install the pinch bolt and tighten the nut to the torque listed in this Chapter's Specifications.
15   Tighten the strut-to-knuckle pinch bolt to the torque listed in this Chapter's Specifications.
16   Tighten the strut upper mounting nuts to the torque listed in this Chapter's Specifications.
17   Attach the tie-rod to the steering knuckle arm as described in Section 16.
18   Install the brake disc onto the hub and install the caliper as described in Chapter 9.
19   Install the wheel and lug nuts, lower the vehicle and tighten the lug nuts to the torque listed in the Chapter 1 Specifications.

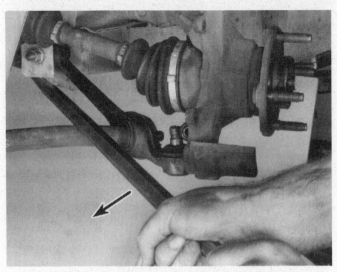

7.5   Pry the balljoint stud out of the steering knuckle

7.10   Using a brass, lead, or shot-filled hammer, tap the steering knuckle out of the strut

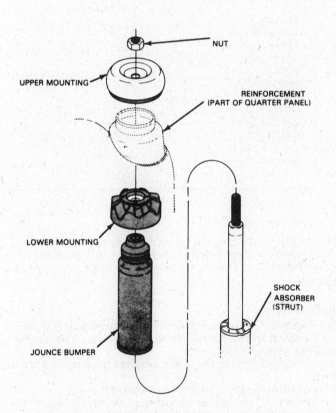

9.3   Top mount components of the rear strut/shock absorber

(Diagram labels: NUT, UPPER MOUNTING, REINFORCEMENT (PART OF QUARTER PANEL), LOWER MOUNTING, JOUNCE BUMPER, SHOCK ABSORBER (STRUT))

9.7   While supporting the control arm with a jack, remove the strut-to-spindle bolts (arrows) – it's a good idea to support the spindle with wire so it doesn't swing outward and place stress on the brake hose

9   Rear strut/shock absorber – removal, inspection and installation

Refer to illustrations 9.3 and 9.7

Removal

1   Remove any interior panel necessary to gain access to the top of the strut/shock absorber tower.

2   Remove the cap and covering the top of the strut.

3   Hold onto the strut rod with a 6 mm Allen wrench, or 8 mm deep socket (depending on model year). Loosen, but do not remove, the strut top nut **(see illustration)**. **Note:** *If the same strut is going to be used again, do not grip the shaft with pliers as this will cause damage.*

4   Loosen the rear wheel lug nuts, raise the rear of the vehicle and support it securely on jackstands. Block the front wheels. Remove the rear wheel.

5   Support the lower control arm of the side being worked on with a floor jack.

6   Remove the clip securing the flexible brake hose to the shock absorber and move the hose out of the way.

7   Loosen but do not remove the strut-to-spindle bolts **(see illustration)**.

8   Front hub and bearing – removal and installation

Due to the special tools and expertise required to press the hub and bearings from the steering knuckle, this job should be left to a professional mechanic. However, the steering knuckle and hub may be removed and the assembly taken to a dealer service department or repair shop. Refer to Section 7 of this Chapter for steering knuckle and hub removal.

10

10.3a   Location of the control arm-to-spindle bolt/nut (arrow) (brake assembly removed for clarity)

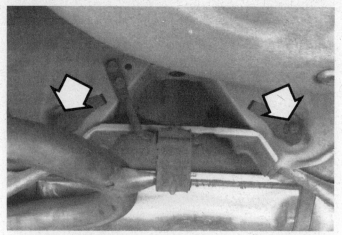

10.3b   Location of the control arm-to-body bolt (arrow)

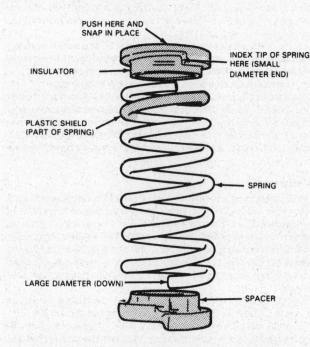

10.7   Installation details of the coil spring insulators

8   Remove the strut top mounting nut, washer and upper mounting insulator.
9   Remove the strut-to-spindle bolts.
10   Remove the strut assembly from the vehicle.
11   Remove the lower mount.

Inspection

12   Check the strut/shock absorber assembly for leaking fluid, dents, damage and corrosion. A thin film of fluid is permissible but the assembly should be replaced if leakage is excessive.
13   Place the shock absorber in a vise and compress and extend it fully several times. If there is a lag or skip in the action or a clicking noise, replace the assembly.

Installation

14   Prior to installing the strut, turn it upside down and extend and compress it fully several times to expel any trapped air.

15   Extend the strut to its full length and install a new lower mount. Apply rubber lubricant (do not use soapy water as it may damage the mount) to ease installation into the strut tower.
16   Position the upper part of the shock absorber shaft into the strut tower opening in the body. Slowly push it upward and align the mounting holes of the strut with those in the spindle.
17   Position the new lower mounting bolts with their heads facing toward the rear of the vehicle and install them. Don't tighten them at this time.
18   Install a new upper mount, washer and nut onto the top of the strut. Use the same tool set-up used during removal and tighten the nut to the torque listed in this Chapter's Specifications.
19   Tighten the strut-to-spindle pinch bolt to the torque listed in this Chapter's Specifications.
20   Install the flexible brake hose onto the shock absorber and install the clip.
21   Install the rear wheel and lug nuts. Lower the car and tighten the lug nuts to the torque listed in the Chapter 1 Specifications.
22   Install the cap and covering the top of the shock absorber.
23   Install any interior panels that were removed.

10   Control arm (rear) and coil spring – removal and installation

Refer to illustrations 10.3a, 10.3b, 10.7 and 10.8

Removal

1   Loosen the wheel lug nuts on both rear wheels. Raise the rear of the vehicle and support it securely on jackstands. Block the front wheels and remove both rear wheels.
2   With the rear suspension fully extended, place a jack under the control arm to support it. Raise the jack slightly to take the spring pressure off the control arm-to-spindle bolt.
3   Remove the nuts securing the control arm to the spindle and the body **(see illustrations)**. Leave the bolts in place. It is not necessary to remove the control arm-to-body bolt and nut if only the spring is going to be removed.
4   Remove the control arm-to-spindle bolt, then slowly lower the jack and the control arm until the spring and insulator can be removed. Remove the spring and insulator from the vehicle.
5   To remove the control arm, remove the control arm-to-body bolt. Remove the control arm from the vehicle.

Installation

6   Install the control arm into position on the body mount and install a new bolt and nut. Do not tighten the bolt and nut at this time.
7   Install the upper insulator onto the top of the spring, making sure to properly index the spring end **(see illustration)**.

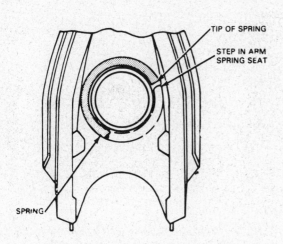

10.8   Proper indexing of the spring to the control arm

11.2   Use a backup wrench on the flats of the tie-rod when removing the nuts

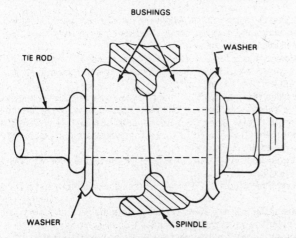

11.6   When installing the tie-rod-to-spindle bushings, make sure the washers and bushings are positioned as shown

8   Install the spring into the lower control arm pocket and correctly index the spring's pigtail with the lower insulator in place **(see illustration)**.
9   Raise the jack and control arm until the control arm and spindle bolt holes align.
10   Position the bolt with the head toward the front of the vehicle and install the nut. Do not tighten the bolt and nut at this time.
11   Raise the jack and control arm to simulate normal ride height. Tighten the control arm-to-spindle and the control arm-to-body bolts and nuts to the torque listed in this Chapter's Specifications.
12   Install the rear wheels and lug nuts. Lower the car and tighten the lug nuts to the torque listed in the Chapter 1 Specifications.

11   Rear tie-rod assembly – removal and installation

Refer to illustrations 11.2 and 11.6

Removal

1   Loosen the wheel lug nuts, raise the rear of the vehicle and support it securely on jackstands. Block the front wheels and remove the rear wheel. Place a floor jack under the control arm to support it.
2   Remove the tie-rod-to-spindle nut, washers and insulators **(see illustration)**.
3   On 1986 and later models, loosen, but do not remove, the strut upper mounting nut.
4   On 1985 and earlier models, mark the tie-rod front bracket bolt lo-

cation for ease of installation, then remove the bolt. On 1986 and later models, remove the tie-rod-to-body nut and remove the washers and insulators.
5   Lift the tie-rod away from the vehicle. On 1985 and earlier models, it may be necessary to pry the front bracket sheet metal apart to remove the tie-rod from the body. **Note:** *If the bushing at the front of the tie-rod is in need of replacement, take the tie-rod to a dealer service department or other repair shop, as special tools are required. On 1986 and later models, pull the spindle out and to the rear far enough to allow removal of the rod. If difficulty is encountered, remove the spindle-to-control arm bolt, first making sure that the control arm is properly supported with a floor jack.* **Caution:** *Be careful not to stretch the flexible brake hose or bend the brake tube.*

Installation

6   Assemble the dished washer, marked FRONT (with the flanged portion facing the center of the rod) and bushing on the the rear end of the rod **(see illustration)**. Insert the rear end of the rod into the spindle, then slip the other bushing and dished washer, marked REAR (with the flanged portion of the washer facing away from the spindle) over the end of the rod. Install the nut, but don't tighten it completely yet. If the spindle-to-control arm nut and bolt were removed, reinstall them (but don't tighten them completely yet).
7   On 1985 and earlier models, insert the forward end of the rod into the body bracket. Install the bolt and nut, but don't tighten the nut yet.
8   On 1986 and later models, position a new dished washer (with the flange toward the middle of the rod) over the forward end of the rod then install the bushing. Place the rod into the body bracket. Install the other bushing and dished washer (with the flanged portion of the washer facing the front of the vehicle) over the end of the rod, but don't tighten the nut yet.
9   Raise the jack and control arm to simulate normal ride height. If you're working on a 1985 or earlier model, align the mark made on the tie-rod front bracket in Step 4, and tighten the bolt to the torque listed in this Chapter's Specifications.
10   Tighten the remaining fasteners to the torque values listed in this Chapter's Specifications.
11   Install the rear wheel and lug nuts. Lower the car and tighten the lug nuts to the torque listed in the Chapter 1 Specifications.

12   Rear hub and wheel bearings – inspection and lubrication

Refer to illustrations 12.3, 12.5, 12.7, 12.9, 12.11a and 12.11b
Warning: *Dust created by the brake system may contain asbestos, which is harmful to your health. Never blow it out with compressed air and don't inhale any of it. Do not, under any circumstances, use petroleum-based solvents to clean brake parts. Use brake cleaner or denatured alcohol only.*

10

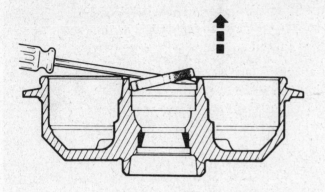

12.3   Pry the inner grease seal out of the hub

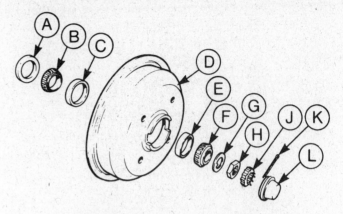

12.5   Exploded view of the rear hub components

A	Inner grease seal	G	Washer
B	Bearing	H	Nut
C	Bearing race	J	Nut retainer
D	Drum/hub	K	Cotter pin
E	Bearing race	L	Cap
F	Bearing		

12.7   The bearing race can be driven out with a hammer and punch (work carefully and don't damage the hub)

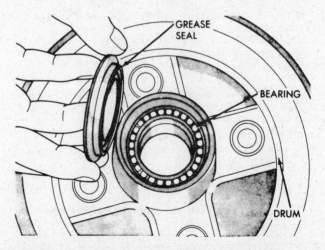

12.9   Work grease completely into the rollers

1   Remove the rear brake drum/hub assembly (see Chapter 9).
2   Check the bearings for proper lubrication and signs that the grease has been contaminated by dirt or water (it will have a gritty feel or a milky-white appearance).
3   Use a screwdriver and carefully pry the grease seal out of the hub (discard the grease seal) **(see illustration)**.
4   Clean the bearings with solvent and dry them with compressed air. **Note:** *Do not allow the bearings to spin while using the compressed air.*
5   Check the bearings for wear, pitting and scoring of the rollers and cage **(see illustration)**. Light discoloration of the bearing surface is normal, but if the surfaces are badly worn or damaged, install new bearings. **Note:** *If new bearings are installed, new bearing races must also be installed.*
6   Remove the old grease from the hub cavity and clean the hub in solvent. Dry the hub with compressed air. Try not to get solvent on the brake shoe contact area of the drum, but if you do, clean the drum with brake system cleaner.
7   Inspect the bearing races for wear, signs of overheating, pitting and corrosion. If the races are worn or damaged, drive them out with a hammer and punch **(see illustration)**.
8   Drive the new races in with a bearing driver (or a section of pipe of the appropriate size) and hammer, but be careful not to damage them or get them cocked in the hub bore.
9   Pack the bearings with high-temperature, multi-purpose EP grease prior to installation. Work generous amounts of grease in from the back of the cage so the grease is forced up through the rollers **(see illustration)**.
10   Add a small amount of grease to the hub cavity and to the spindle.
11   Lubricate the outer edge of the new grease seal, insert the bearing and press the seal into position with the lip facing in **(see illustration)**.

12.11a   Make sure the bearing is in place in the hub, . . .

12.11b . . . then tap the seal into place with a hammer and block of wood

13.3 Remove the rear brake brake backing plate bolts (arrows)

Make sure the grease seal is seated completely in the hub by tapping it evenly into place using a hammer and block of wood **(see illustration)**. Apply grease to the seal cavity and lip and the polished sections of the spindle.

12   Install the rear brake drum/hub assembly and adjust the wheel bearings following the procedures in Chapter 9.

13   Rear wheel spindle – removal and installation

Refer to illustrations 13.3 and 13.6
Warning: *Dust created by the brake system may contain asbestos, which is harmful to your health. Never blow it out with compressed air and don't inhale any of it. Do not, under any circumstances, use petroleum-based solvents to clean brake parts. Use brake cleaner or denatured alcohol only.*

Removal

1   Loosen the wheel lug nuts, raise the rear of the vehicle and support it securely on jackstands. Block the front wheels and remove the rear wheel.
2   Remove the rear brake drum/hub assembly (see Chapter 9).
3   Remove the four bolts that secure the brake backing plate to the spindle **(see illustration)**. Detach the backing plate and rear brake assembly from the spindle and suspend it with a piece of wire. It isn't necessary to remove the parking brake cable from the backing plate.
4   Support the control arm with a floor jack. Raise the jack slightly to take the spring pressure off the strut-to-spindle bolts and the spindle-to-control arm bolt.
5   Loosen the rear tie-rod nut. Use a wrench on the flats of the rod to prevent it from turning **(see illustration 11.2)**. Remove the nut and dished washer.
6   Remove the bolts and nuts securing the strut to the spindle **(see illustration)**.

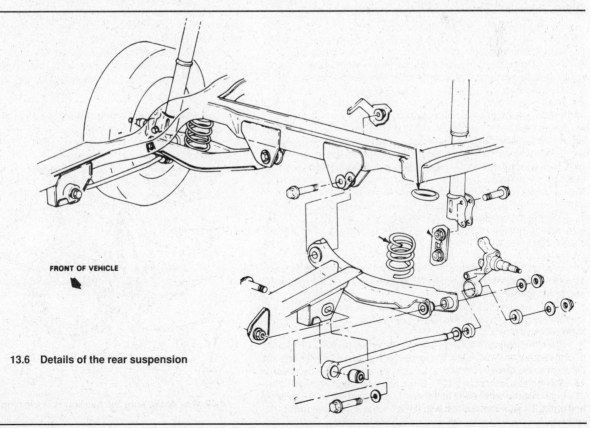

FRONT OF VEHICLE

13.6 Details of the rear suspension

10

**15.4   Remove the steering wheel from the shaft with a puller –
DON'T beat on the shaft!**

7   Remove the control arm-to-spindle bolt and nut. Be sure to support
the spindle so it doesn't fall.
8   Detach the spindle from the strut bracket and control arm.

Installation

9   Inspect the tie-rod bushings for cracks, deformation and signs of
wear. Replace them if necessary.
10   With the tie-rod bushing and washer in place on the tie-rod, install the
spindle onto the tie-rod.
11   Install the spindle onto the strut, aligning the two bolt holes. Position
the bolts with the heads toward the rear of the vehicle and install new
spindle-to-shock bolts and nuts. Tighten them finger tight.
12   Attach the lower control arm-to-spindle and install a new bolt, washers and nut. Tighten the nut only finger tight.
13   Install the dished washer (with REAR stamped on it), with the dished
side facing out, onto the tie-rod. Install a new nut.
14   Place a jack under the spindle and raise it to simulate normal ride
height.
15   Tighten the strut-to-spindle bolts to the torque listed in this Chapter's
Specifications.
16   Tighten the tie-rod nut to the torque listed in this Chapter's Specifications.
17   Tighten the control arm bolt/nut to the torque listed in this Chapter's
Specifications.
18   Install the brake backing plate to the spindle, then install the four bolts
and tighten them to the torque listed in the Chapter 9 Specifications.
19   Install the rear brake drum/hub assembly and adjust the rear wheel
bearings (see Chapter 9).
20   Install the rear wheels and lug nuts.
21   Lower the vehicle and tighten the lug nuts to the torque listed in the
Chapter 1 Specifications.

14   Steering system – general information

All models are equipped with rack-and-pinion steering. Some are power assisted. The steering gear is bolted to the firewall and operates the
steering arms via tie-rods. The inner ends of the tie-rods are protected by
rubber boots which should be inspected periodically for secure attachment, tears and leaking lubricant.
The power assist system consists of a belt-driven pump and associated lines and hoses. The power steering pump reservoir fluid level
should be checked periodically (see Chapter 1).

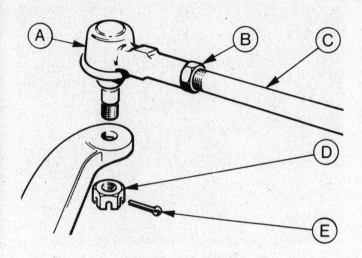

16.2   Tie-rod components

A	Balljoint	D	Nut
B	Jam nut	E	Cotter pin
C	Tie-rod		

The steering wheel operates the steering shaft, which actuates the
steering gear through universal joints and the intermediate shaft. Looseness in the steering can be caused by wear in the steering shaft universal
joints, the steering gear, the tie-rod ends and loose retaining bolts.

15   Steering wheel – removal and installation

Refer to illustration 15.4
Warning: *Some later models are equipped with airbags. If the vehicle you
are working on is equipped with an airbag, have this procedure performed
at a dealer service department or other qualified repair shop.*
1   Disconnect the cable from the negative terminal of the battery.
2   Detach the horn pad from the steering wheel and disconnect the wire
to the horn switch. On some models the horn pad is retained by two or
more screws. On other models, it can simply be pulled straight off the
steering wheel.
3   Remove the steering wheel retaining nut then mark the relationship of
the steering shaft to the hub (if marks don't already exist or don't line up) to
simplify installation and ensure steering wheel alignment.
4   Use a puller to detach the steering wheel from the shaft **(see illustration)**. Don't hammer on the shaft to dislodge the steering wheel.
5   To install the wheel, align the mark on the steering wheel hub with the
mark on the shaft and slip the wheel onto the shaft. Install the nut and tight-
en it to the torque listed in this Chapter's Specifications.
6   Connect the horn wire and install the horn pad.
7   Connect the negative battery cable.

16   Steering tie-rod ends – removal and installation

Refer to illustrations 16.2, 16.3, 16.4a, 16.4b and 16.4c

Removal

1   Loosen the front wheel lug nuts. Raise the front of the vehicle, support
it securely, block the rear wheels and set the parking brake. Remove the
front wheel.
2   Remove the cotter pin and loosen the nut on the tie-rod end stud **(see
illustration)**. Discard the cotter pin.

16.3   Use a two-jaw puller to detach the tie-rod end from the steering knuckle arm

16.4a   Loosen the jam nut while holding the tie-rod end with a wrench to prevent it from turning

3   Disconnect the tie-rod from the steering knuckle arm with a puller **(see illustration)**. Remove the nut and separate the tie-rod.
4   Hold the tie-rod end with a wrench and loosen the jam nut enough to mark the position of the tie-rod end in relation to the threads **(see illustrations)**. Remove the tie-rod end **(see illustration)**.

Installation

5   Thread the tie-rod end on to the marked position and insert the tie-rod stud into the steering knuckle arm. Tighten the jam nut securely.
6   Install a new nut on the stud and tighten it to the torque listed in this Chapter's Specifications. Install a new cotter pin and bend the ends over completely.
7   Install the wheel and lug nuts. Lower the vehicle and tighten the lug nuts to torque listed in the Chapter 1 Specifications.
8   Have the alignment checked by a dealer service department or an alignment shop.

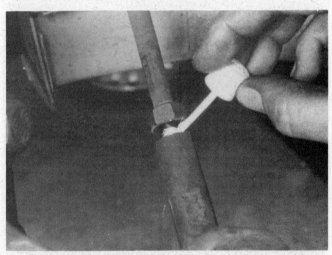

16.4b   Mark the relationship of the tie-rod end to the tie-rod

---

17   Steering gear boots – replacement

1   Loosen the front wheel lug nuts, raise the front of the vehicle, support it securely on jackstands, block the rear wheels and set the parking brake. Remove the front wheel.
2   Refer to Section 16 and remove the tie-rod end and jam nut.
3   Remove the steering gear boot clamps and slide the boot off.
4   Before installing the new boot, wrap the threads and serrations on the end of the steering rod with a layer of tape so the small end of the new boot isn't damaged.
5   Slide the new boot into position on the steering gear until it seats in the groove in the steering rod and install new clamps.
6   Remove the tape and install the tie-rod end (see Section 16).
7   Install the wheel and lug nuts. Lower the vehicle and tighten the lug nuts to torque listed in the Chapter 1 Specifications.

---

18   Steering gear – removal and installation

Refer to illustration 18.8

Removal

1   Set the front wheels to the straight-ahead position.
2   Disconnect the cable from the negative battery terminal.

16.4c   Remove the tie-rod end from the tie-rod (if necessary, prevent the tie-rod from turning by holding it with a pair of pliers positioned directly behind the threads)

10

18.8   Typical rack and pinion steering gear installation

3   Turn the ignition key to the Run position to unlock the steering wheel.

4   Loosen the lug nuts of both front wheels, raise the front of the vehicle and support it securely on jackstands. Block the rear wheels and set the parking brake. Remove the front wheels.

5   Place a pan under the steering gear (power steering only). Detach the hoses/lines and cap the ends to prevent excessive fluid loss and contamination.

6   Mark the relationship of the lower shaft universal joint to the steering gear input shaft so they can be reassembled in the same relative positions. Remove the lower shaft pinch bolt and spread the clamp joints slightly with a screwdriver.

7   Separate the tie-rod ends from the steering knuckle arms (see Section 16).

8   Flatten the locking tabs on the steering gear mounting bolts, then remove the bolts **(see illustration)**.

9   Gently pull the steering gear assembly forward and down, away from the firewall. Have an assistant pull up on the lower shaft from inside the vehicle to dislocate it from the steering gear input shaft.

10   Carefully lower the entire assembly down and out while guiding the power steering hoses (if so equipped) out from behind the transaxle.

Installation

11   If a new steering gear assembly is being installed, the tie-rod ends must be removed from the original assembly and installed on the new unit at approximately the same setting. The most important thing is that the tie-rod ends are screwed on an equal amount at this stage.

12   Make sure the steering gear is centered. Turn the pinion shaft to full lock in one direction, then count and record the number of turns required to rotate it to the opposite full lock position. Turn the pinion shaft back through one-half the number of turns just counted, this will center the assembly.

13   Check that the front wheels are in the straight ahead position.

14   Move the rack and pinion assembly into position on the firewall. Push the steering gear input shaft through the opening in the firewall. Have an assistant guide the lower shaft onto the input shaft, aligning the previously applied marks. Install the mounting bolts and lockwashers and tighten them to the torque listed in this Chapter's Specifications. Bend up the locking tabs to lock the bolts in place.

15   Install a new lower shaft pinch bolt and tighten it to the torque listed in this Chapter's Specifications

16   On models so equipped, route the power steering hoses into the proper position.

17   Connect the tie-rod ends in the steering knuckle arms (see Section 16).

18   Install the wheels and lug nuts. Lower the vehicle and tighten the lug nuts to the torque listed in the Chapter 1 Specifications.

19   On power steering-equipped vehicles, connect the pressure and return lines and install them in the support bracket.

20   Turn the ignition key Off and connect the negative battery cable.

21   On power steering equipped vehicles, fill the fluid reservoir with the specified fluid and refer to Section 21 for the power steering bleeding procedure.

22   Have the front end alignment checked by a dealer service department or an alignment shop.

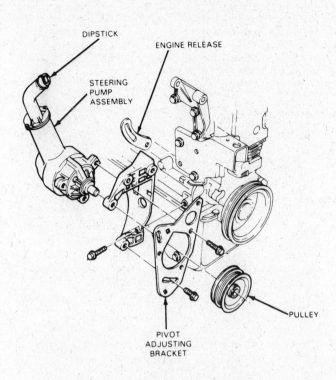

19.4   Power steering pump installation

19   Power steering pump – removal and installation

Refer to illustrations 19.4

Removal

1   Disconnect the cable from the negative battery terminal.
2   Remove the air cleaner assembly, the Thermactor air pump and drivebelt and the power steering pump reservoir filler extension. Plug the dipstick opening to prevent the entry of dirt or foreign matter.
3   On models equipped with a remote reservoir, disconnect the reservoir supply hose from the pump and drain the fluid. Plug or cap the pump opening to prevent the entry of dirt or foreign matter.
4   Working under the vehicle, loosen the pump adjusting bolt. Remove one pump mounting bracket bolt **(see illustration)**.
5   Disconnect the return hose from the pump. The 1986 through 1990 models are equipped with quick disconnect fittings (see Section 20).
6   Working in the engine compartment, loosen one adjusting bolt and the pivot bolt.
7   Remove the drivebelt.
8   Remove the two remaining mounting bolts.
9   Remove the pump and pulley through the mounting bracket.
10   Disconnect the pressure line from the pump and allow the fluid to drain into a container.

Installation

11   Place the pump in the bracket and install the mounting bolts. Tighten the bolts securely.
12   Working under the vehicle, connect the pressure hose.
13   Install the drivebelt and adjust the tension (see Chapter 3).
14   Connect the return hose to the pump.
15   Install the filler extension for the pump reservoir.
16   Install the Thermactor air pump and drivebelt and the air cleaner assembly.

17   On models equipped with a remote reservoir, connect the reservoir supply hose onto the pump.
18   Fill the pump reservoir with the specified fluid (see Chapter 1), then bleed the system (see Section 21).

20   Power steering line quick-disconnect fittings (1986 through 1990 models) – general information

The power steering pump return line connection, pressure line connection and both steering gear connections are equipped with new-design fittings that can result in line separation when the line is under pressure. If the line separates from the fitting, or if a leak occurs between the line and the fitting, a new line or hose assembly must be installed. Service kits are available for the steering gear connections.

If a leak occurs between the threaded part of the fitting (tube end) and the component it threads into, the plastic seal on the tube nut can be replaced with a new one. Use a tapered tool, such as a large centerpunch, the stretch the seal until it fits over the tube nut threads. It will slowly return to its original size.

21   Power steering system – bleeding

1   The power steering system must be bled whenever a line is disconnected. Bubbles can be seen in power steering fluid which has air in it and the fluid will often have a tan or milky appearance. On later models, low fluid level can cause air to mix with the fluid, resulting in a noisy pump as well as foaming of the fluid.
2   Open the hood and check the fluid level in the reservoir, adding the specified fluid necessary to bring it up to the proper level (see Chapter 1).
3   Start the engine and slowly turn the steering wheel several times from left-to-right and back again. **Caution:** *Do not turn the wheel completely from lock-to-lock. Check the fluid level, topping it up as necessary until it remains steady and no more bubbles appear in the reservoir.*

22   Steering angles and wheel alignment – general information

Proper wheel alignment is essential for safe steering and even tire wear. Symptoms of alignment problems are pulling of the steering to one side or the other and uneven tire wear.

If these symptoms are present, check for the following before having the alignment adjusted:

Loose steering gear mounting bolts
Damaged or worn steering gear mounts
Worn or damaged wheel bearings
Bent tie-rods
Worn balljoints
Improper tire pressures
Mixing tires of different construction

Rear suspension alignment problems are indicated by uneven tire wear or uneven tracking of the rear wheels. This can be easily checked by driving the vehicle straight across a puddle of water onto a dry patch of pavement. If the rear wheels don't follow the front wheels exactly, the alignment should be adjusted.

Front or rear wheel alignment should be left to a dealer service department or an alignment shop.

23   Wheels and tires – general information

1   Check the tire pressures (cold) weekly (see Chapter 1).
2   Inspect the sidewalls and treads periodically for damage and signs of abnormal or uneven wear.
3   Make sure the wheel lug nuts are tightened to the proper torque specification (see Chapter 1).

10

4   Don't mix radial and bias ply tires or tires with different tread patterns on the same axle.

5   Never include the temporary spare in the tire rotation pattern as it's designed for use only until a damaged tire is repaired or replaced.

6   Periodically inspect the wheels for elongated or damaged lug holes, distortion and nicks in the rim. Replace damaged wheels.

7   Clean the wheels inside and out and check for rust and corrosion, which could lead to wheel failure.

8   If the wheel and tire are balanced on the vehicle, one wheel stud and lug hole should be marked whenever the wheel is removed so it can be reinstalled in the original position. If balanced on the vehicle, the wheel should not be moved to a different axle position.

Chapter 11   Body

Contents

Specifications

Torque specifications

	Ft-lbs (unless otherwise indicated)
Bumper-to-isolator bolts	
1981 through 1985 (front and rear)	26 to 40
1986 through 1988	
Front	15 to 22
Rear	13 to 19
1989 on (front and rear)	17 to 25
Bumper extension screw	18 to 24 in-lbs
Door latch-to-door screws	36 to 72 in-lbs
Door hinge bolts	14 to 21
Front seat track bolts and nuts	9 to 17
Hood-to-hinge bolts	84 to 132 in-lbs
Hood latch nuts/bolts	84 to 132 in-lbs
Liftgate-to-hinge bolts	60 to 96 in-lbs
Liftgate-to-body screws	12 to 20
Rear folding seat-to-body bolts	13 to 20
Seat back articulating arm bolts	13 to 20
Seat back and cushion hinge bolts	13 to 20
Seat belt retractor bolts	22 to 32
Steering column bolts	15 to 25
Window glass-to-regulator nuts	36 to 60 in-lbs

11

1   General information

These models feature a "unibody" layout, using a floor pan with front and rear side frame rails which support the body components, front and rear suspension systems and other mechanical components.

Certain components are particularly vulnerable to accident damage and can be unbolted and repaired or replaced. Among these parts are the body moldings, bumpers, the hood, the hatchback or the liftgate and all glass.

Only general body maintenance procedures and body panel repair procedures within the scope of the do-it-yourselfer are included in this Chapter.

2   Body – maintenance

1   The condition of your vehicle's body is very important, because the resale value depends a great deal on it. It's much more difficult to repair a damaged body than it is to repair mechanical components. The hidden areas of the body, such as the wheel wells, the frame and the engine compartment, are equally important, although they don't require as frequent attention as the rest of the body.

2   Once a year, or every 12,000 miles, it's a good idea to have the underside of the body steam cleaned. All traces of dirt and oil will be removed and the area can then be inspected carefully for rust, damaged brake lines, frayed electrical wires, damaged cables and other problems. The front suspension components should be greased after completion of this job.

3   At the same time, clean the engine and the engine compartment with a steam cleaner or water soluble degreaser.

4   The wheel wells should be given close attention, since undercoating can peel away and stones and dirt thrown up by the tires can cause the paint to chip and flake, allowing rust to set in. If rust is found, clean down to the bare metal and apply an anti-rust paint.

5   The body should be washed about once a week. Wet the vehicle thoroughly to soften the dirt, then wash it down with a soft sponge and plenty of clean soapy water. If the surplus dirt is not washed off very carefully, it can wear down the paint.

6   Spots of tar or asphalt thrown up from the road should be removed with a cloth soaked in solvent.

7   Once every six months, wax the body and chrome trim. If a chrome cleaner is used to remove rust from any of the vehicle's plated parts, remember that the cleaner also removes part of the chrome, so use it sparingly.

3   Vinyl trim – maintenance

Don't clean vinyl trim with detergents, caustic soap or petroleum-based cleaners. Plain soap and water works just fine, with a soft brush to clean dirt that may be ingrained. Wash the vinyl as frequently as the rest of the vehicle. After cleaning, application of a high quality rubber and vinyl protectant will help prevent oxidation and cracks. The protectant can also be applied to weatherstripping, vacuum lines and rubber hoses, which often fail as a result of chemical degradation, and to the tires.

4   Upholstery and carpets – maintenance

1   Every three months remove the carpets or mats and clean the interior of the vehicle (more frequently if necessary). Vacuum the upholstery and carpets to remove loose dirt and dust.

2   Leather upholstery requires special care. Stains should be removed with warm water and a very mild soap solution. Use a clean, damp cloth to remove the soap, the wipe again with a dry cloth. Never use alcohol, gasoline, nail polish remover or thinner to clean leather upholstery.

3   After cleaning, regularly treat leather upholstery with a leather wax. Never use car wax on leather upholstery.

4   In areas where the interior of the vehicle is subject to bright sunlight, cover leather seats with a sheet if the vehicle is to be left out for any length of time.

5   Body repair – minor damage

See photo sequence

Repair of minor scratches

1   If the scratch is superficial and does not penetrate to the metal of the body, repair is very simple. Lightly rub the scratched area with a fine rubbing compound to remove loose paint and built-up wax. Rinse the area with clean water.

2   Apply touch-up paint to the scratch, using a small brush. Continue to apply thin layers of paint until the surface of the paint in the scratch is level with the surrounding paint. Allow the new paint at least two weeks to harden, then blend it into the surrounding paint by rubbing with a very fine rubbing compound. Finally, apply a coat of wax to the scratch area.

3   If the scratch has penetrated the paint and exposed the metal of the body, causing the metal to rust, a different repair technique is required. Remove all loose rust from the bottom of the scratch with a pocket knife, then apply rust inhibiting paint to prevent the formation of rust in the future. Using a rubber or nylon applicator, coat the scratched area with glaze-type filler. If required, the filler can be mixed with thinner to provide a very thin paste, which is ideal for filling narrow scratches. Before the glaze filler in the scratch hardens, wrap a piece of smooth cotton cloth around the tip of a finger. Dip the cloth in thinner and then quickly wipe it along the surface of the scratch. This will ensure that the surface of the filler is slightly hollow. The scratch can now be painted over as described earlier in this section.

Repair of dents

4   When repairing dents, the first job is to pull the dent out until the affected area is as close as possible to its original shape. There is no point in trying to restore the original shape completely as the metal in the damaged area will have stretched on impact and cannot be restored to its original contours. It is better to bring the level of the dent up to a point about 1/8-inch below the level of the surrounding metal. In cases where the dent is very shallow, it is not worth trying to pull it back out at all.

5   If the back side of the dent is accessible, it can be hammered out gently from behind using a soft-face hammer. While doing this, hold a block of wood firmly against the opposite side of the metal to absorb the hammer blows and prevent the metal from being stretched.

6   If the dent is in a section of the body which has double layers, or some other factor makes it inaccessible from behind, a different technique is required. Drill several small holes through the metal inside the damaged area, particularly in the deeper sections. Screw long, self tapping screws into the holes just enough for them to get a good grip in the metal. Now the dent can be pulled out by pulling on the protruding heads of the screws with locking pliers.

7   The next stage of repair is the removal of the paint from the damaged area and from an inch or so of the surrounding metal. This is easily done with a wire brush or sanding disk in a drill motor, although it can be done just as effectively by hand with sandpaper. To complete the preparation for filling, score the surface of the bare metal with a screwdriver or the tang of a file or drill small holes in the affected area. This will provide a good grip for the filler material. To complete the repair, see the Section on filling and painting.

Repair of rust holes or gashes

8   Remove all paint from the affected area and from an inch or so of the surrounding metal using a sanding disk or wire brush mounted in a drill motor. If these are not available, a few sheets of sandpaper will do the job just as effectively.

9   With the paint removed, you will be able to determine the severity of the corrosion and decide whether to replace the whole panel, if possible, or repair the affected area. New body panels are not as expensive as most people think and it is often quicker to install a new panel than to repair large areas of rust.

10   Remove all trim pieces from the affected area except those which will act as a guide to the original shape of the damaged body, such as headlight shells, etc. Using metal snips or a hacksaw blade, remove all loose metal and any other metal that is badly affected by rust. Hammer the edges of the hole inward to create a slight depression for the filler material.

11   Wire brush the affected area to remove the powdery rust from the surface of the metal. If the back of the rusted area is accessible, treat it with rust inhibiting paint.

12   Before filling is done, block the hole in some way. This can be done with sheet metal riveted or screwed into place, or by stuffing the hole with wire mesh.

13   Once the hole is blocked off, the affected area can be filled and painted. See the following subsection on filling and painting.

Filling and painting

14   Many types of body fillers are available, but generally speaking, body repair kits which contain filler paste and a tube of resin hardener are best for this type of repair work. A wide, flexible plastic or nylon applicator will be necessary for imparting a smooth and contoured finish to the surface of the filler material. Mix up a small amount of filler on a clean piece of wood or cardboard (use the hardener sparingly). Follow the manufacturer's instructions on the package, otherwise the filler will set incorrectly.

15   Using the applicator, apply the filler paste to the prepared area. Draw the applicator across the surface of the filler to achieve the desired contour and to level the filler surface. As soon as a contour that approximates the original one is achieved, stop working the paste. If you continue, the paste will begin to stick to the applicator. Continue to add thin layers of paste at 20-minute intervals until the level of the filler is just above the surrounding metal.

16   Once the filler has hardened, the excess can be removed with a body file. From then on, progressively finer grades of sandpaper should be used, starting with a 180-grit paper and finishing with 600-grit wet-or-dry paper. Always wrap the sandpaper around a flat rubber or wooden block, otherwise the surface of the filler will not be completely flat. During the sanding of the filler surface, the wet-or-dry paper should be periodically rinsed in water. This will ensure that a very smooth finish is produced in the final stage.

17   At this point, the repair area should be surrounded by a ring of bare metal, which in turn should be encircled by the finely feathered edge of good paint. Rinse the repair area with clean water until all of the dust produced by the sanding operation is gone.

18   Spray the entire area with a light coat of primer. This will reveal any imperfections in the surface of the filler. Repair the imperfections with fresh filler paste or glaze filler and once more smooth the surface with sandpaper. Repeat this spray-and-repair procedure until you are satisfied that the surface of the filler and the feathered edge of the paint are perfect. Rinse the area with clean water and allow it to dry completely.

19   The repair area is now ready for painting. Spray painting must be carried out in a warm, dry, windless and dust free atmosphere. These conditions can be created if you have access to a large indoor work area, but if you are forced to work in the open, you will have to pick the day very carefully. If you are working indoors, dousing the floor in the work area with water will help settle the dust which would otherwise be in the air. If the repair area is confined to one body panel, mask off the surrounding panels. This will help minimize the effects of a slight mismatch in paint color. Trim pieces such as chrome strips, door handles, etc. will also need to be masked off or removed. Use masking tape and several thicknesses of newspaper for the masking operations.

20   Before spraying, shake the paint can thoroughly, then spray a test area until the spray painting technique is mastered. Cover the repair area with a thick coat of primer. The thickness should be built up using several thin layers of primer rather than one thick one. Using 600-grit wet-or-dry sandpaper, rub down the surface of the primer until it is very smooth. While doing this, the work area should be thoroughly rinsed with water and the wet-or-dry sandpaper periodically rinsed as well. Allow the primer to dry before spraying additional coats.

21   Spray on the top coat, again building up the thickness by using several layers of paint. Begin spraying in the center of the repair area and then, using a circular motion, work outward until the whole repair area and about

two inches of the surrounding original paint is covered. Remove all masking material 10 to 15 minutes after spraying on the final coat. Allow the new paint at least two weeks to harden, then use a very fine rubbing compound to blend the edges of the new paint into the existing paint. Finally, apply a coat of wax.

6   Body repair – major damage

1   Major damage must be repaired by an auto body shop specifically equipped to perform unibody repairs. These shops have the specialized equipment required to do the job properly.

2   If the damage is extensive, the body must be checked for proper alignment or the vehicle's handling characteristics may be adversely affected and other components may wear at an accelerated rate.

3   Due to the fact that all of the major body components (hood, fenders, etc.) are separate and replaceable units, any seriously damaged components should be replaced rather than repaired. Sometimes the components can be found in a wrecking yard that specializes is used vehicle components, often at a considerable savings over the cost of new parts.

7   Hinges and locks – maintenance

Once every 3,000 miles, or every three months, the hinges and latch assemblies on the doors, hood and the hatchback or the liftgate should be given a few drops of light oil or lock lubricant. The door latch strikers should also be lubricated with a thin coat of grease to reduce wear and ensure free movement. Lubricate the door and the hatchback or the liftgate locks with spray-on graphite lubricant.

8   Hood – removal, installation and adjustment

Refer to illustrations 8.4 and 8.10

Note: *The hood is heavy and somewhat awkward to remove and install – at least two people should perform this procedure.*

Removal and installation

1   Open the hood and support it in the open position with a long piece of wood.

2   Cover the fenders and cowl with blankets or heavy cloths to protect the paint.

3   Scribe or paint alignment marks around the bolt heads to ensure proper alignment on reinstallation.

4   Have an assistant hold onto the hood and remove the hood-to-hinge assembly bolts **(see illustration)**.

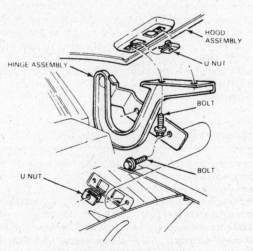

8.4   Hood hinge components

11

These photos illustrate a method of repairing simple dents. They are intended to supplement *Body repair - minor damage* in this Chapter and should not be used as the sole instructions for body repair on these vehicles.

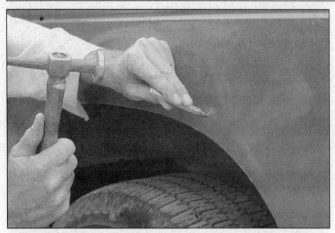

1   If you can't access the backside of the body panel to hammer out the dent, pull it out with a slide-hammer-type dent puller. In the deepest portion of the dent or along the crease line, drill or punch hole(s) at least one inch apart . . .

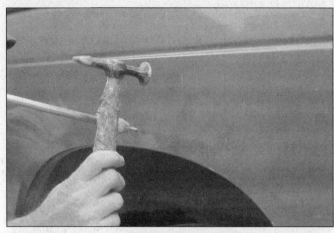

2   . . . then screw the slide-hammer into the hole and operate it. Tap with a hammer near the edge of the dent to help 'pop' the metal back to its original shape. When you're finished, the dent area should be close to its original contour and about 1/8-inch below the surface of the surrounding metal

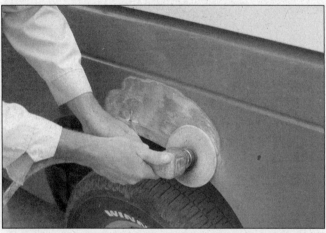

3   Using coarse-grit sandpaper, remove the paint down to the bare metal. Hand sanding works fine, but the disc sander shown here makes the job faster. Use finer (about 320-grit) sandpaper to feather-edge the paint at least one inch around the dent area

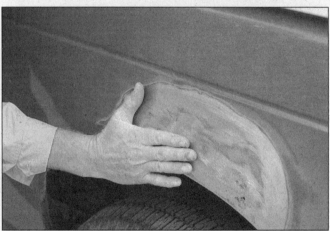

4   When the paint is removed, touch will probably be more helpful than sight for telling if the metal is straight. Hammer down the high spots or raise the low spots as necessary. Clean the repair area with wax/silicone remover

5   Following label instructions, mix up a batch of plastic filler and hardener. The ratio of filler to hardener is critical, and, if you mix it incorrectly, it will either not cure properly or cure too quickly (you won't have time to file and sand it into shape)

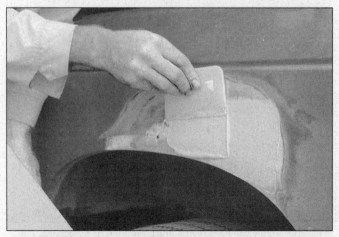

6   Working quickly so the filler doesn't harden, use a plastic applicator to press the body filler firmly into the metal, assuring it bonds completely. Work the filler until it matches the original contour and is slightly above the surrounding metal

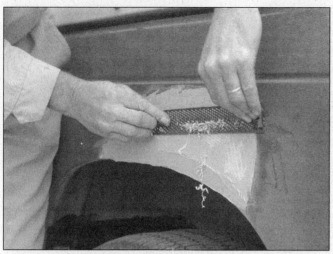

7   Let the filler harden until you can just dent it with your fingernail. Use a body file or Surform tool (shown here) to rough-shape the filler

8   Use coarse-grit sandpaper and a sanding board or block to work the filler down until it's smooth and even. Work down to finer grits of sandpaper - always using a board or block - ending up with 360 or 400 grit

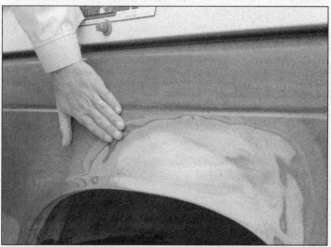

9   You shouldn't be able to feel any ridge at the transition from the filler to the bare metal or from the bare metal to the old paint. As soon as the repair is flat and uniform, remove the dust and mask off the adjacent panels or trim pieces

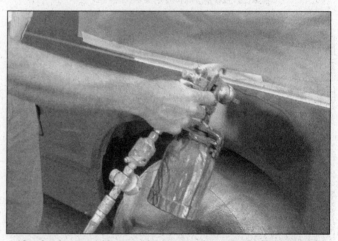

10   Apply several layers of primer to the area. Don't spray the primer on too heavy, so it sags or runs, and make sure each coat is dry before you spray on the next one. A professional-type spray gun is being used here, but aerosol spray primer is available inexpensively from auto parts stores

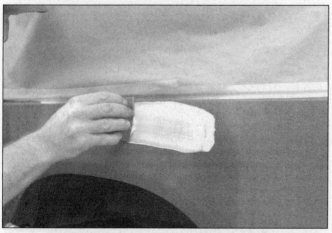

11   The primer will help reveal imperfections or scratches. Fill these with glazing compound. Follow the label instructions and sand it with 360 or 400-grit sandpaper until it's smooth. Repeat the glazing, sanding and respraying until the primer reveals a perfectly smooth surface

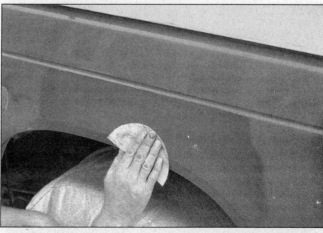

12   Finish sand the primer with very fine sandpaper (400 or 600-grit) to remove the primer overspray. Clean the area with water and allow it to dry. Use a tack rag to remove any dust, then apply the finish coat. Don't attempt to rub out or wax the repair area until the paint has dried completely (at least two weeks)

5   Remove the hood.
6   Installation is the reverse of the removal procedure, with the following additions:
7   Align the hood-to-hinges using the alignment marks made in Step 3.
8   Tighten the bolts to the torque listed in this Chapter's Specifications.

Adjustment

9   The hood latch (striker) can be adjusted to obtain a flush fit between the hood and fenders.
10   Loosen the latch retaining bolt **(see illustration)**.
11   Move the latch from side-to-side until the hood is properly aligned with the fenders at the front. Tighten the bolt securely.
12   Loosen the hood bumper locknuts and lower the bumpers.
13   Move the latch up and down until alignment is correct when the hood is pulled up. Tighten the latch bolt securely.
14   Adjust the hood bumpers upward to eliminate any hood looseness. Tighten the locknuts.

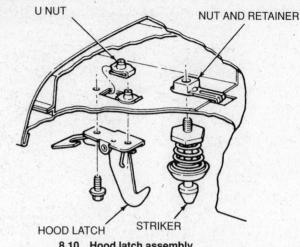

U NUT   NUT AND RETAINER

HOOD LATCH   STRIKER

8.10   Hood latch assembly

---

9   Hood latch control cable – removal and installation

Refer to illustration 9.2
1   Open the hood and support it in the open position with a long piece of wood.
2   Remove the screws securing the latch cable and remove the plate and cable clip **(see illustration)**.
3   Disengage the cable and the ferrule from the latch assembly.
4   Remove the cable retaining clips from the engine compartment.
5   Working in the passenger compartment, remove the bracket retaining screws and remove the bracket.
6   Carefully withdraw the cable through the rubber grommet in the fire-wall opening.
7   To install, insert the cable through the grommet in the firewall and make sure the grommet is properly seated within the firewall hole.
8   Install the cable mounting bracket and screws.
9   Correctly route the cable within the engine compartment and attach it to the retaining clips.
10   Engage the cable and the ferrule onto the latch assembly.
11   Install the cable clip and hood latch retaining plate and tighten the screws securely.
12   Prior to closing the hood, operate the control cable and make sure it operates correctly.

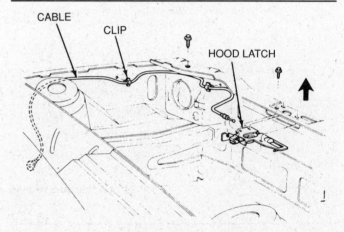

CABLE   CLIP   HOOD LATCH

9.2   Hood latch control cable layout

---

10   Hood support rod – removal and installation

1   Open the hood and support it in the open position with a long piece of wood.
2   Disconnect the support rod from its stowed position on the radiator support.
3   Remove the retaining bolt securing the support rod mounting bracket on the left side of the radiator support.
4   Remove the support rod and bracket.
5   Installation is the reverse of the removal procedures.

---

11   Hatchback and liftgate – removal, installation and adjustment

Refer to illustrations 11.5a, 11.5b and 11.6
Note 1: *The hatchback and the liftgate are heavy and somewhat awkward to remove and install – at least two people should perform this procedure.*
Note 2: *The procedure is basically identical for both types of doors.*
1   Open the hatchback, or liftgate, to the fully open position.
2   On models so equipped, disconnect the electrical connectors from the rear window heater or wiper mechanism.
3   At the top edge of the hatchback or liftgate opening, carefully remove the weatherstrip, then peel back the headlining.

4   Have an assistant hold onto the hatchback or liftgate in the open position.
5   Remove the bolt securing the support cylinder on each side **(see illustrations)**.
6   To maintain correct adjustment, mark around the screws and washers securing the hinges to the body, then remove them **(see illustration)**.
7   If necessary, rotate the inner trim panel retainers 90-degrees and remove the panel to gain access to the lock and wiper motor (if so equipped).
8   Installation is the reverse of the removal procedures.
9   Tighten the hinge bolts after an equal gap is achieved all around the opening.

---

12   Front and rear bumper – removal and installation

Warning: *If the vehicle you are working on is equipped with an airbag, disconnect the cable from the negative terminal of the battery and unplug the auxiliary battery for the airbag (located near the steering column under the dash) before beginning this procedure.*

1981 through 1985 models
Refer to illustrations 12.2a and 12.2b
Note: *The bumpers are heavy and somewhat awkward to remove and install – at least two people should perform this procedure.*
1   Scribe an alignment line around the bumper isolator attachment bolts to ensure proper alignment on reinstallation.

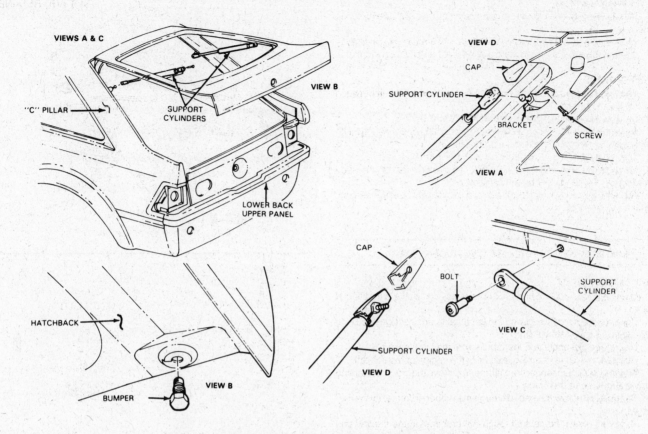

11.5a Liftgate strut cylinder installation (two-door models)

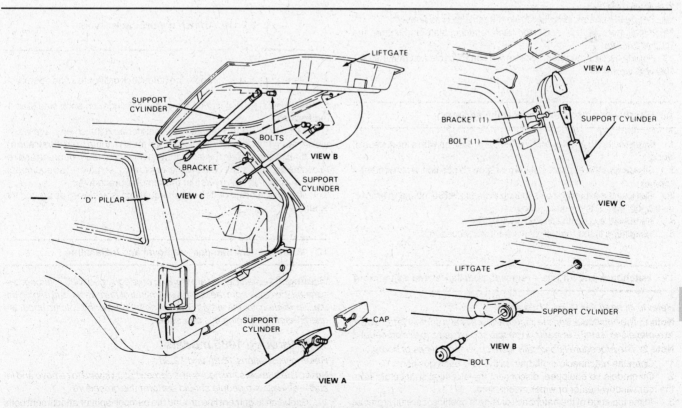

11.5b Liftgate strut cylinder installation (wagon models)

11

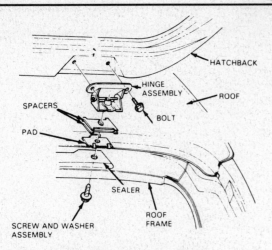

11.6   Liftgate hinge installation

2   Have an assistant hold onto the bumper assembly and remove the bumper-to-isolator assembly bolts and washers **(see illustrations)**.

3   Remove the bumper and take note of the sequence and number of spacers. The spacer must be reinstalled in the same order and number.

4   Installation is the reverse of the removal procedures with the following additions:

5   If installing a new bumper, transfer the bumper guards, pads, extensions and any additional items to the new bumper.

6   Tighten the bolts to the torque listed in this Chapter's Specifications.

1986 through 1988 standard models

Refer to illustrations 12.8a, 12.8b, 12.9a and 12.9b

Note: *The bumpers are heavy and somewhat awkward to remove and install – at least two people should perform this procedure.*

7   Scribe an alignment line around the bumper isolator attachment bolts to ensure proper alignment on reinstallation.

8   Remove the nuts securing the bumper end caps to each end of the main portion of the bumper **(see illustrations)**. It is not necessary to remove the end caps, just disconnect them.

9   Have an assistant hold onto the bumper assembly and remove the bumper-to-isolator assembly bolts and washers **(see illustrations)**.

10   Remove the bumper and take note of the sequence and number of spacers. The spacers must be reinstalled in the same order and number.

11   Installation is the reverse of the removal procedures with the following additions:

12   If installing a new bumper, transfer the bumper guards, pads, extensions and any additional items to the new bumper.

13   Tighten the bolts to the torque listed in this Chapter's Specifications.

1986 through 1988 GT and XR-3 models

Refer to illustrations 12.14a and 12.14b

Note: *The bumpers are heavy and somewhat awkward to remove and install – at least two people should perform this procedure.*

14   Remove the screws (three for the front bumper and two for the rear bumper) and washers securing the bumper cover to the wheel wells on each side **(see illustrations)**.

15   Working inside the wheel well, remove the nuts and washers securing the bumper cover to the fender on each side.

16   On front bumpers, perform the following:
   a) Remove the three screws and washers securing the bumper cover lower mounting reinforcement to the grille opening panel.
   b) Remove the two nut and washer assemblies securing the front bumper cover upper mounting reinforcement-to-grille opening on each end.

17   On rear bumpers, perform the following:
   a) Drill out the two push-pin rivets securing the rear bumper cover to the outer mounting reinforcement on each end.
   b) Remove the seven nut and sealer washer assemblies securing the front bumper cover to the lower back panel.

18   Remove the bumper cover.

19   To remove the structural portion of the bumper, perform Steps 7 and 9 through 11 of this Section.

20   Installation is the reverse of the removal procedure with the following addition:

21   Tighten the bolts to the torque listed in this Chapter's Specifications.

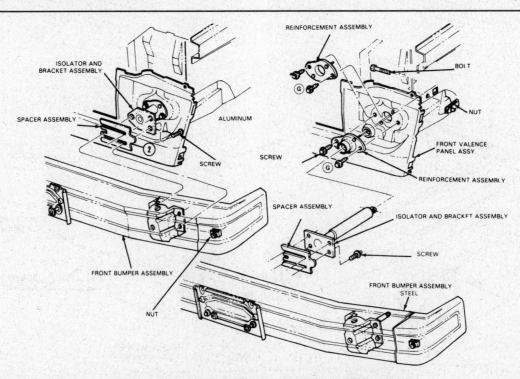

12.2a   Front bumper installation (1981 through 1985 models)

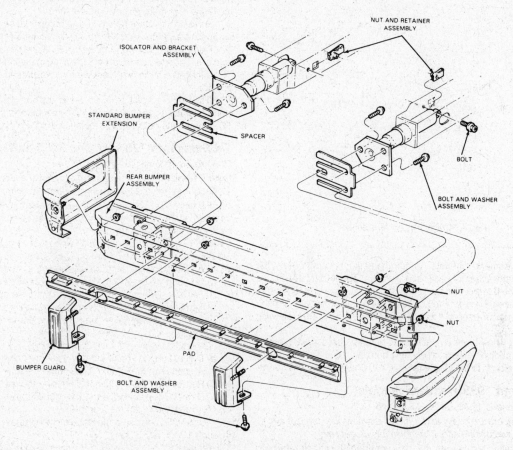

12.2b   Rear bumper installation (1981 through 1985 models)

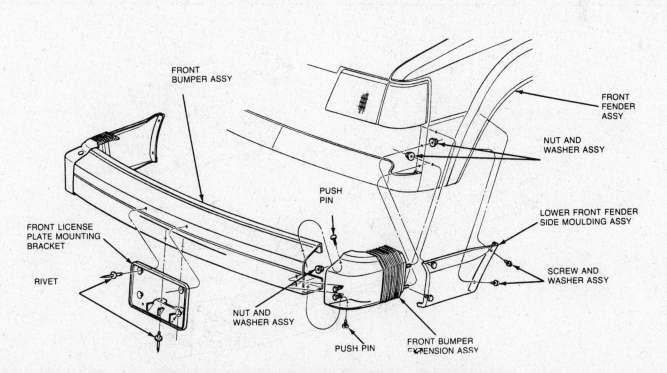

12.8a   Front bumper end cap installation (1986 through 1988 models)

11

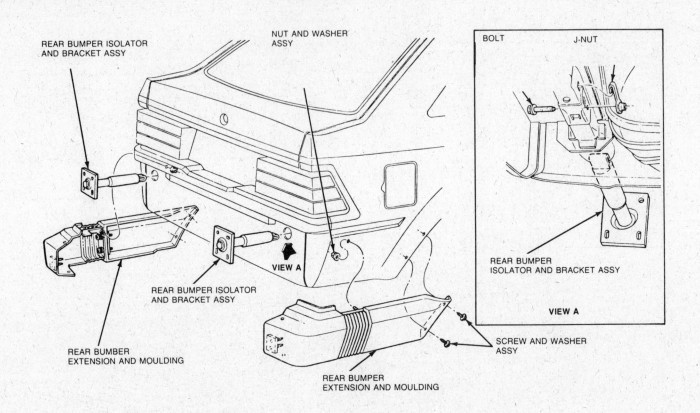

12.8b   Rear bumper end cap installation (1986 through 1988 models)

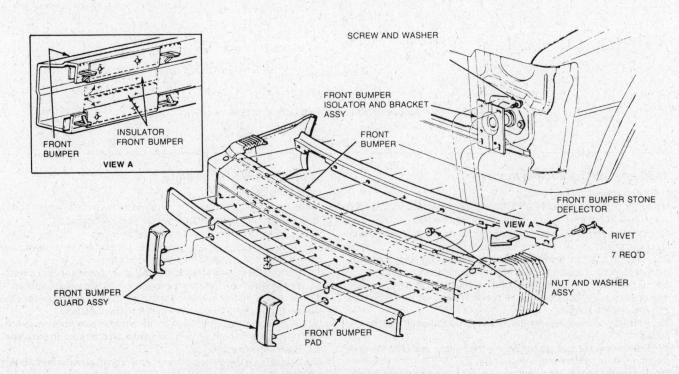

12.9a   Front bumper installation (1986 through 1988 models)

REAR BUMPER
STONE DEFLECTOR

PUSH PIN

EXTENSION
AND MOULDING ASSY

REAR BUMPER ASSY

NUT AND WASHER
ASSY

REAR BUMPER PAD

VIEW A

REAR BUMPER
ASSY

VIEW B

ISOLATOR AND BRACKET ASSY

EXTENSION AND MOULDING
ASSY

SCREW AND WASHER ASSY

REAR BUMPER STONE DEFLECTOR

NUT AND
WASHER ASSY

VIEW A

VIEW B

RIVET

SCREW AND WASHER ASSY

REAR BUMPER
GUARD ASSY

REAR BUMPER
PAD

REAR BUMPER ASSY

ISOLATOR AND BRACKET ASSY

EXTENSION AND MOULDING ASSY

12.9b   Rear bumper installation (1986 through 1988 models)

1989 and 1990 standard models

Refer to illustrations 12.23a and 12.23b

Note: *The bumpers are heavy and somewhat awkward to remove and install – at least two people should perform this procedure.*

22   Scribe an alignment line around the bumper isolator attachment bolts to ensure proper alignment on reinstallation.

23   Have an assistant hold onto the bumper assembly and remove the bumper-to-isolator assembly bolts and washers **(see illustrations)**.

24   Slightly lower the bumper and pull the bumper away from the vehicle, then disengage the bumper from the special attachments on each side.

25   Remove the bumper.

26   Installation is the reverse of the removal procedure with the following additions:

27   Position the bumper assembly onto the vehicle and slide the ends onto the special attachments on each side.

28   Tighten the bolts to the torque listed in this Chapter's Specifications.

1989 and 1990 GT models

Refer to illustrations 12.31

Note: *The bumpers are heavy and somewhat awkward to remove and install – at least two people should perform this procedure.*

29   Support the fog lamp and bracket assemblies.

30   Scribe an alignment line around the bumper isolators attachment bolts to ensure proper alignment on reinstallation.

31   Remove the four lower bumper-to-isolator assembly bolts and washers **(see illustration)**. Remove the fog lamp and bracket assemblies.

32   Have an assistant hold onto the bumper assembly and remove the four upper bumper-to-isolator assembly bolts and washers.

33   Slightly lower the bumper and pull the bumper away from the vehicle, then disengage the bumper from the special attachments on each side.

34   Remove the bumper.

35   Installation is the reverse of the removal procedures with the following additions:

36   Tighten the bolts to the torque listed in this Chapter's Specifications.

11

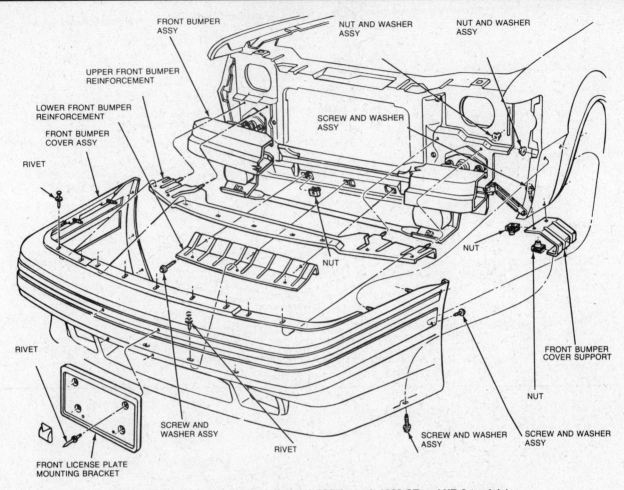

FRONT BUMPER
ASSY

UPPER FRONT BUMPER
REINFORCEMENT

LOWER FRONT BUMPER
REINFORCEMENT

FRONT BUMPER
COVER ASSY

RIVET

NUT AND WASHER
ASSY

NUT AND WASHER
ASSY

SCREW AND WASHER
ASSY

NUT

RIVET

FRONT BUMPER
COVER SUPPORT

NUT

FRONT LICENSE PLATE
MOUNTING BRACKET

SCREW AND
WASHER ASSY

RIVET

SCREW AND WASHER
ASSY

SCREW AND WASHER
ASSY

12.14a   Front bumper cover installation (1986 through 1988 GT and XR-3 models)

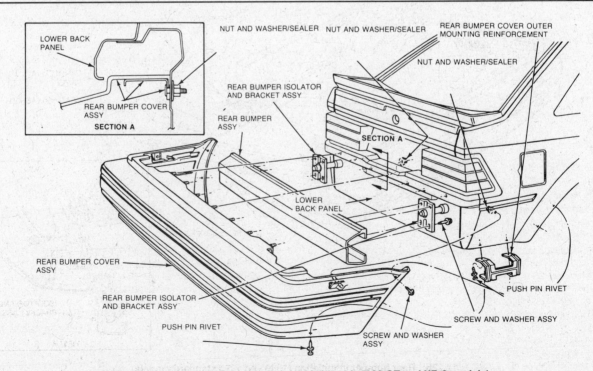

LOWER BACK
PANEL

REAR BUMPER COVER
ASSY

SECTION A

NUT AND WASHER/SEALER

NUT AND WASHER/SEALER

REAR BUMPER COVER OUTER
MOUNTING REINFORCEMENT

NUT AND WASHER/SEALER

REAR BUMPER ISOLATOR
AND BRACKET ASSY

REAR BUMPER
ASSY

SECTION A

LOWER
BACK PANEL

REAR BUMPER COVER
ASSY

REAR BUMPER ISOLATOR
AND BRACKET ASSY

PUSH PIN RIVET

PUSH PIN RIVET

SCREW AND WASHER ASSY

SCREW AND WASHER
ASSY

12.14b   Rear bumper cover installation (1986 through 1988 GT and XR-3 models)

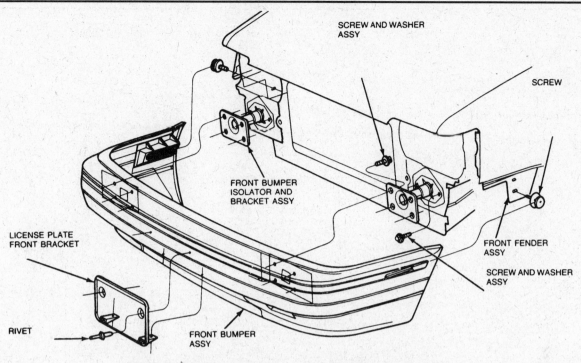

12.23a   Front bumper installation (1989 and 1990 standard models)

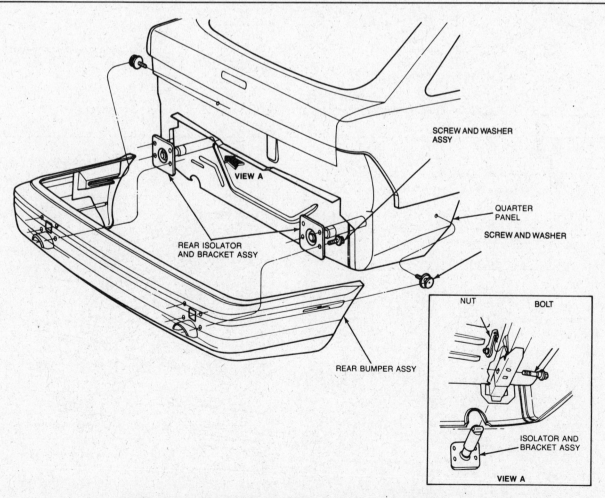

12.23b   Rear bumper installation (1989 and 1990 standard models)

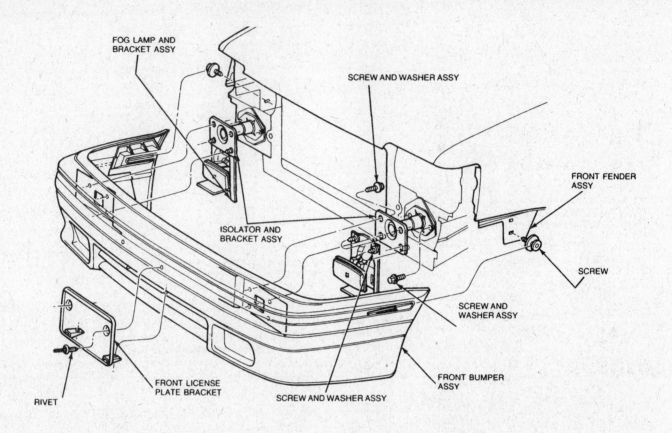

12.31   Front bumper installation (1989 and 1990 GT models)

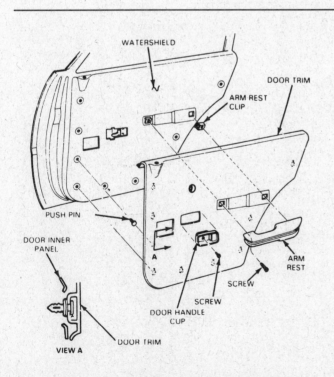

13.1a   An exploded view of the door trim panel

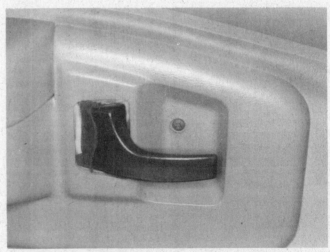

13.1b   Remove the Phillips screw behind the door handle

---

13   Door trim panel – removal and installation

Refer to illustrations 13.1a, 13.1b, 13.2, 13.3, 13.4, 13.5, 13.6, 13.7 and 13.8

1   Remove the inner door handle and cup **(see illustrations)**.
2   Remove the window crank **(see illustration)**. This may be secured by a Torx screw; if it is, be sure to use the proper Torx driver to remove it.

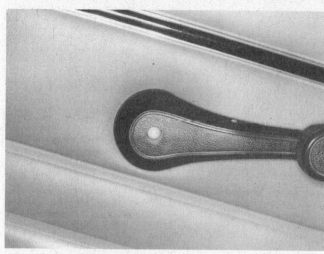

13.2   **The window crank may be secured by a Torx screw – if it is, use the proper Torx driver to remove it**

13.3   **On some models, one of the arm rest retaining screws is accessible from the top**

13.4   **If the vehicle has an internal mirror control handle, remove it with a small Allen wrench**

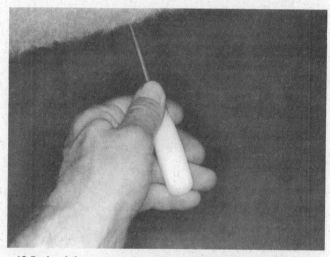

13.5   **Look for screws along the bottom edge of the door trim panel – if they are there, be sure to remove them before trying to pry the panel off**

3   Remove the arm rest. On some models, one retaining screw is accessible from the top **(see illustration)**.

4   Remove the mirror control knob with a small Allen wrench **(see illustration)**.

5   Remove the trim screws (if equipped) along the bottom edge of the door trim panel **(see illustration)**

6   Insert a putty knife or door trim removal tool between the door trim panel and the door and disengage the retaining clips **(see illustration)**. Pry around both sides and bottom perimeter of the door trim panel until the panel is free from the door.

7   Once all of the clips are disengaged, detach the door trim panel and remove the trim panel from the vehicle **(see illustration)**.

8   For access to the inner door, carefully peel back the plastic watershield **(see illustration)**.

9   Installation is the reverse of the removal procedure with the following additions:

10   Be sure to install any clips in the door trim panel which may have come out during the removal procedure.

11   Position the watershield against the inner door panel, aligning the watershield adhesive with the door panel adhesive and press it into place.

12   Make sure all pins are pressed into place correctly.

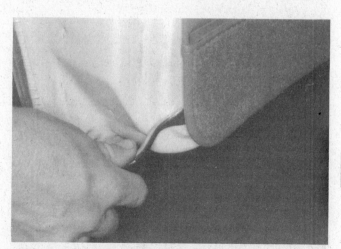

13.6   **Once all the door panel retaining screws are removed, the panel can be pried off – the special tool shown here works well, but a putty knife can also be used**

11

13.7   Be careful not to damage the plastic retaining pins when removing the trim panel.

13.8   Do not damage the watershield adhesive surface during removal

14   Door latch striker – removal, installation and adjustment

1   Use vise grip pliers to unscrew the door latch striker stud from the door jamb.
2   Installation is the reverse of the removal procedure with the following additions:
3   The door latch striker can be adjusted vertically and laterally as well as fore-and-aft.
4   The door latch striker is not to be used to compensate for door misalignment (see Section 19).
5   The door latch striker can be shimmed to obtain the correct clearance between the latch and the striker.
6   To check the clearance between the latch jamb and the striker area, spread a layer of dark grease on to the striker.
7   Open and close the door several times and note the pattern of the grease.
8   Move the door striker assembly laterally to provide a flush fit at the door and pillar or at the quarter panel.
9   Tighten the door latch striker after adjustment is complete.

15   Door lock – removal and installation

1   Remove the door trim panel and watershield (see Section 13).
2   Disconnect the lock cylinder rod.
3   Pry the retaining clip from the lock cylinder and door.
4   Remove the lock cylinder from the door.
5   Install the lock cylinder into the door opening from the outside and push the retaining clip into place. Make sure it's seated correctly.
6   Reconnect the lock cylinder rod.
7   Check for proper lock operation, then install the watershield and the door trim panel.

16   Door latch assembly – removal and installation

Front door

Refer to illustration 16.2

1   Remove the door trim panel and watershield (see Section 13).
2   Disconnect the clip securing the remote control assembly and remove the assembly **(see illustration)**.

3   Disconnect the lock cylinder rod from the cylinder and push the rod button from the latch.
4   Remove the clip securing the outside door handle rod to the latch assembly. Remove the three screws securing the latch assembly and remove the latch assembly, control link and lock cylinder rod from the door.
5   Attach the remote control link and the lock cylinder rods to the latch assembly levers.
6   Install the latch assembly and three screws. Attach the push button, lock cylinder and remote control links.
7   Install the watershield and door trim panel.

Rear door

Refer to illustration 16.9

8   Remove the door trim panel and watershield (see Section 13).
9   Disconnect the remote control assembly **(see illustration)**.
10   Remove the nut securing the bellcrank to the door panel and remove the bellcrank from the door.
11   Disconnect the door latch bracket assembly from the latch assembly and remove the assembly.
12   Prior to installing the latch assembly, connect the remote control and bellcrank links to the latch assembly.
13   Install the latch and link assembly onto the door and install the screws.
14   Connect the bellcrank links and push-button rod to the bellcrank.
15   Install the bellcranks to the door inner panel and tighten the nut until it is snug.
16   Check for proper operation, then install the watershield and the door trim panel.

Remote control

17   Remove the door trim panel and watershield (see Section 13).
18   Disconnect the clip securing the remote control link, squeeze it and then disengage it from the hole in the inner door panel.
19   Remove the screw securing the remote control, squeeze the tabs inward to disengage them and push the assembly forward and remove it from the inner door panel.
20   Disconnect the remote control link from the assembly.
21   Install the control link onto the remote control assembly and position the assembly in the inner door. Install the screw and tighten securely.
22   Connect the clip securing the remote control link and engage it in the hole in the inner door panel.
23   Check for proper operation, then install the watershield and the door trim panel.

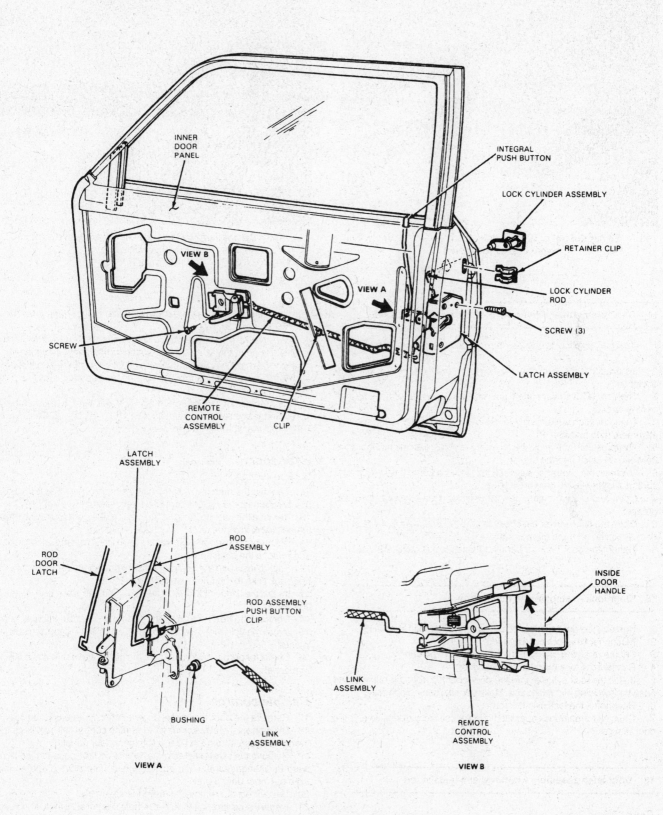

INNER
DOOR
PANEL

INTEGRAL
PUSH BUTTON

LOCK CYLINDER ASSEMBLY

RETAINER CLIP

VIEW B

VIEW A

LOCK CYLINDER
ROD

SCREW

SCREW (3)

LATCH ASSEMBLY

REMOTE
CONTROL
ASSEMBLY

CLIP

LATCH
ASSEMBLY

ROD
ASSEMBLY

ROD
DOOR
LATCH

INSIDE
DOOR
HANDLE

ROD ASSEMBLY
PUSH BUTTON
CLIP

LINK
ASSEMBLY

BUSHING

LINK
ASSEMBLY

REMOTE
CONTROL
ASSEMBLY

VIEW A

VIEW B

16.2   Front door component layout

11

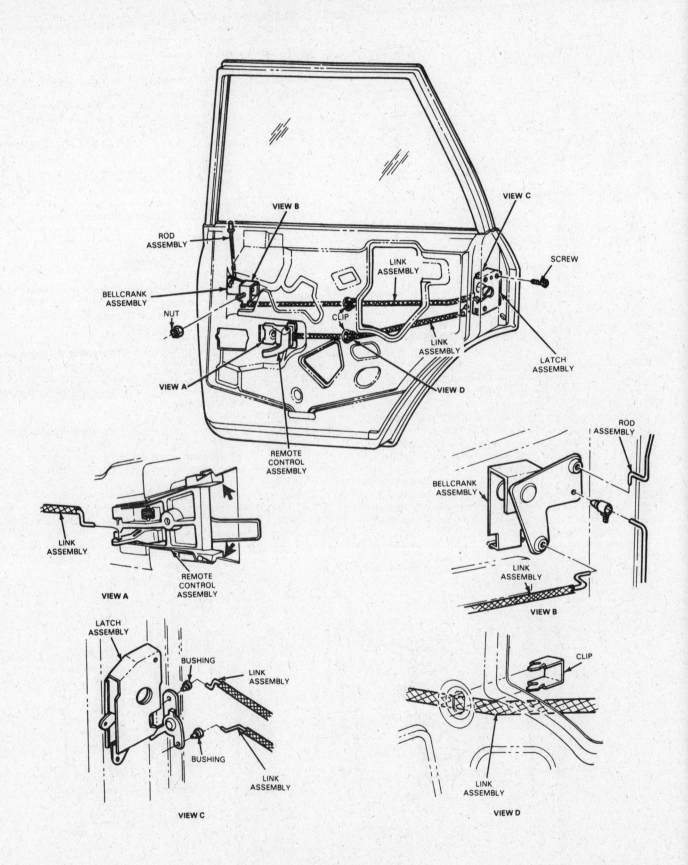

16.9   Rear door component layout

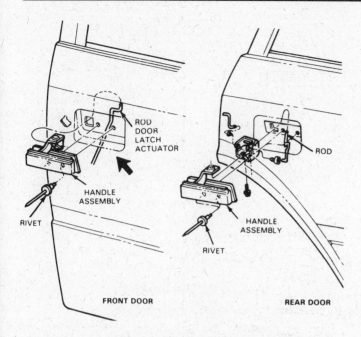

17.4   Outside door handle installation

17   Door outside handles – removal and installation

Refer to illustration 17.4

1   Remove the door trim panel and watershield (see Section 13).
2   On two-door models, remove the retaining clip and disconnect the control rod from the latch assembly. On four-door and station wagon models, remove the clip retaining the outside handle control rod to the latch bracket assembly and remove the rod.
3   Apply tape or padding around the door handle opening to protect the paint. Prop the handle in the open position with a piece of wood.
4   Drive out the center of the pop-rivet with a suitable size drift. Use a suitable size drill and drill out the remainder of the rivet **(see illustration)**. Repeat for the other rivet.

5   Remove the piece of wood installed in Step 3 and remove the door handle from the door.
6   On two-door models, install the door handle and control rod assembly into the hole in the door. On four-door and station wagon models, install the door handle without the control rod attached.
7   Prop the handle in the open position with a piece of wood. Install the two pop-rivets, then remove the piece of wood.
8   On two-door models, attach the control rod to the latch lever. On four-door and station wagon models, install the control rod into the hole in the latch, the clip the other end to the latch bracket assembly.
9   Check for proper operation, then remove the tape or padding from the door.
10   Install the watershield and door trim panel.

18   Door – removal, installation and alignment

Refer to illustration 18.3

Removal and installation

1   With the door in the open position, place a jack or jackstand under the door or have an assistant hold the door while the door hinge bolts are removed. **Note:** *If a jack or jackstand is used, place thick padding on top of the jack to protect the door's painted finish.*
2   Scribe around the door hinges.
3   Remove the hinge-to-door bolts and carefully lift off the door **(see illustration).**
4   Installation is the reverse of the removal procedure. Align the hinges with the scribe marks to restore the same alignment as before removal.

Alignment

5   Following installation of the door, check the alignment and adjust, if necessary, as follows:
  a) Up-and-down and forward-and-backwards adjustments are made by loosening the hinge-to-body bolts and moving the door as necessary.
  b) The door lock striker can also be adjusted both up-and-down and sideways to provide positive engagement with the lock mechanism. This is done by loosening the mounting bolts and moving the striker as necessary.

11

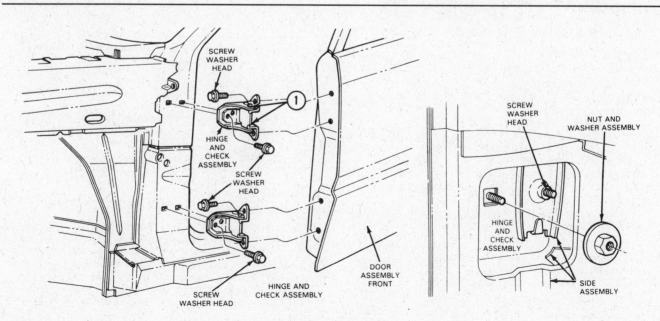

18.3   Door hinge layout

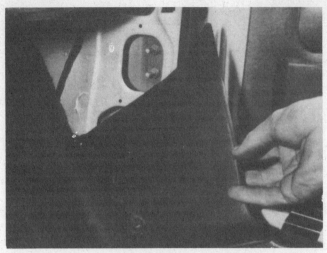

**19.2   The front door hinge bolts are accessible behind
the cowl trim panel**

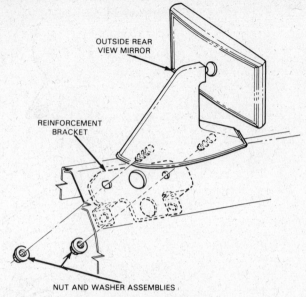

21.2   Outside mirror (manual)

---

19   Door hinge and check – removal and installation

Refer to illustration 19.2

Door hinge

Note: *If both hinges are to be replaced, it is easier to leave the door in place and replace one hinge at a time.*

1   With the door in the open position, place a jack or jackstand under the door or have an assistant hold the door while the door hinge bolts are removed. **Note:** *If a jack or jackstand is used, place thick padding on top of the jack to protect the door's painted finish.*

2   On front doors, remove the cowl side trim panel **(see illustration)**. On some models, it is also necessary to remove the air conditioning ducts, body shake braces or glove box.

3   Scribe around the door hinge(s), then remove the hinge-to-door bolts **(see illustration 18.3)**. Carefully remove the hinge(s) or lift off the door.

4   Installation is the reverse of the removal procedure with the following addition:

5   Adjust the door if necessary (see Section 18).

Door hinge check

Note: *The door hinge check is located either on the upper or lower hinge, depending on model and year.*

6   The door hinge check can be replaced without removing the door or door hinge.

7   Remove the exposed bolt securing the hinge to the body.

8   Insert a suitable length cold chisel with a 3/4-inch cutting blade between the hinge half on the body and the backside of the hinge check. Using a hammer, chisel the rivet securing the hinge check and the reinforcement. Remove the hinge check and the reinforcement.

9   Install a new reinforcement and hinge check onto the hinge, then install the bolt.

10   Tighten the bolt to the torque listed in this Chapter's Specifications.

11   Lubricate the hinge check with multi-purpose grease.

---

20   Door weatherstripping – replacement

---

1   Remove interior garnish that covers the weatherstripping.

2   Prior to removing the weatherstripping note its direction. It is not symmetrical and must be reinstalled in the correct direction with the larger soft section facing out toward the door to form the seal.

3   Pull the old weatherstripping away from the door and remove it.

4   Adhesive is not used to hold the weatherstripping in place but a prior owner may have applied some to hold a damaged section in place. If any adhesive is present on the raised lip, remove it.

5   If necessary, straighten the raised lip that the weatherstripping is attached to.

6   The new weatherstripping will have a paint mark at one spot. This paint mark indicates the installation start point. On two-door models, position the paint mark at the top rear corner of the door jamb, on four-door and station wagon models position the paint mark at the top front corner of the jamb.

7   Starting at the indicated corner, install the weatherstripping onto the raised lip of the doorjamb. **Note:** *Do not stretch the weatherstripping during installation.*

8   Where the two ends of the weatherstripping meet, trim the length about 1/4 to 1/2-inch longer than needed.

---

21   Outside mirror – removal and installation

Manual

Refer to illustration 21.2

1   Remove the door trim panel and watershield (see Section 13).

2   Remove the nuts and washers securing the mirror to the door **(see illustration)**.

3   Remove the mirror and gasket from the door.

4   Installation is the reverse of the removal procedure.

Remote control

Refer to illustration 21.5

5   Remove the set screw securing the control lever end of the cable assembly to the trim bezel. Remove the bezel and gasket **(see illustration)**.

6   Remove the door trim panel and watershield (see Section 13).

7   Disengage the control cable from the retaining clips on the door panel.

8   Remove the nuts and washers securing the mirror to the door.

9   Remove the mirror and control cable assembly from the door.

10   Installation is the reverse of the removal procedure with the following addition:

11   Prior to installing the door panel, operate the window up and down several times to ensure the cable does not interfere with the window operation.

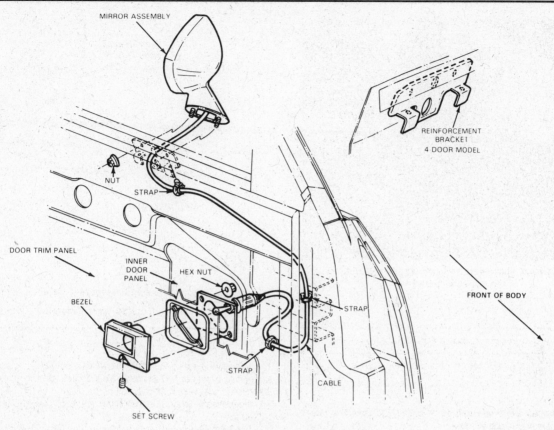

21.5   Outside mirror (remote control)

22   Front door window glass – replacement and adjustment

Refer to illustration 22.2

Replacement

1   Remove the door trim panel and watershield (see Section 13).
2   Remove the rivets securing the glass to the regulator as follows:
  a) Place a block of wood behind the glass at the regulator.
  b) Drive out the center of the pop-rivet with a punch.
  c) Drill out the remainder of the rivet **(see illustration)**. Repeat for the other rivet.
3   Remove the window glass from the door. Clean any drilling or rivet remnants or any broken glass from the bottom of the door.
4   Install the plastic retainer and spacer into the holes in the glass. Install the metal retainer on the outside surface of the window glass.
5   Carefully insert the window glass into the door, place the glass bracket on the regulator and install two 1 X 1/4-inch bolts, washers and nuts to secure the glass to the regulator. Tighten the nuts finger-tight at this time.

Adjustment

6   Move the glass fore and aft or in and out in the guide runs in the door until smooth glass operation is achieved.
7   Tighten the nuts installed in Step 5 to the torque listed in this Chapter's Specifications.
8   Install the watershield and door trim panel.

23   Front door window regulator – replacement

1   Remove the door trim panel and watershield (see Section 13).
2   Remove the pop-rivets securing the glass to the regulator as described in Section 22, Step 2. Secure the glass in the full up position – a rubber doorstop between the glass and door works well.

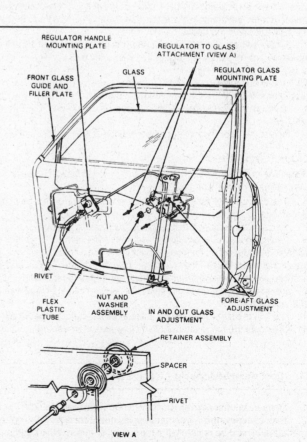

22.2   Front door window glass and regulator layout

11

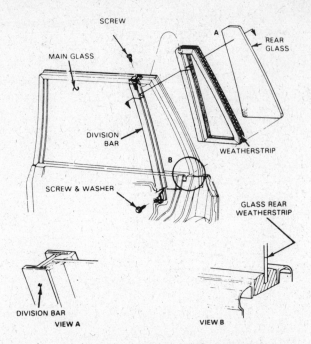

24.9   Rear door window glass installation

3   Remove the pop-rivets securing the window regulator to the door panel as described in Section 22, Step 2.
4   Remove the two nuts and washers securing the regulator tube to the base of the door panel and door sill **(see illustration 22.2)**. Remove the regulator assembly through the door access hole.
5   Clean any drilling remnants from the bottom of the door.
6   To install, insert the regulator assembly into the door panel and install the two nuts and washers. Do not tighten the nuts at this time.
7   Install two 1/2 X 1-inch bolts, nuts and washers to secure the regulator to the door.
8   Route the drain tube to the bottom of the door.
9   Install the window glass into the regulator as described in Section 22, Steps 4 and 5.
10   Move the glass into the full up position and tighten the nuts installed in Step 6 of this Section.
11   Check for proper window glass operation, then install the watershield and door trim panel.

24   Rear door window glass – replacement and adjustment

Replacement

Refer to illustration 24.9

1   Remove the door trim panel and watershield (see Section 13).
2   Remove the pop-rivets securing the glass to the regulator as described in Section 22, Step 2. Lower the glass to the bottom of the door.
3   Remove the glass guide run from the front of the division bar and the top of the door frame.
4   Remove the screws securing the division bar, tilt the bar forward and remove it along with the quarter glass and weatherstripping.
5   Lift the window glass up and remove it from the door.
6   Clean any drilling or rivet remnants or any broken glass from the bottom of the door.
7   Install the plastic retainer and spacer into the holes in the glass. Install the metal retainer on the outside surface of the window glass **(see illustration 22.2)**.
8   Carefully insert the window glass into the door and lower the glass to the bottom of the door.

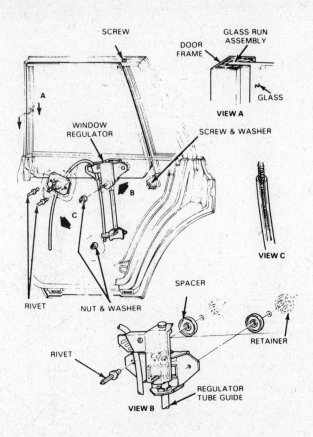

25.4   Rear door window regulator installation

9   Install the quarter window glass and weatherstripping into the rear of the door **(see illustration)**. Use soapy water to ease the installation. Seat the weatherstripping firmly into the door frame.
10   Install the division bar, then firmly seat the weatherstripping. Install and tighten the top retaining screw while leaving the lower screw only finger-tight at this time.
11   Install the glass guide into the door frame and division bar.
12   Raise the window glass and install two 1 X 1/2-inch bolts, washers and nuts to secure the glass to the regulator mounting bracket. Tighten the nuts to the torque listed in this Chapter's Specifications.

Adjustment

13   Move the glass fore and aft or in and out in the guide runs in the door until smooth glass operation is achieved.
14   Install the watershield and door trim panel.
15   Tighten the lower screw installed in Step 10 of this Section.
16   Check for proper window glass operation, then install the watershield and door trim panel.

25   Rear door window regulator – replacement

Refer to illustration 25.4

1   Remove the door trim panel and watershield (see Section 13).
2   Remove the pop-rivets securing the glass to the regulator as described in Section 22, Step 2. Secure the glass in the full up position – a rubber doorstop between the window and the door will usually secure the window.
3   Remove the pop-rivets securing the window regulator to the door panel as described in Section 22, Step 2.
4   Remove the two nuts and washers securing the regulator tube to the door panel **(see illustration)**.

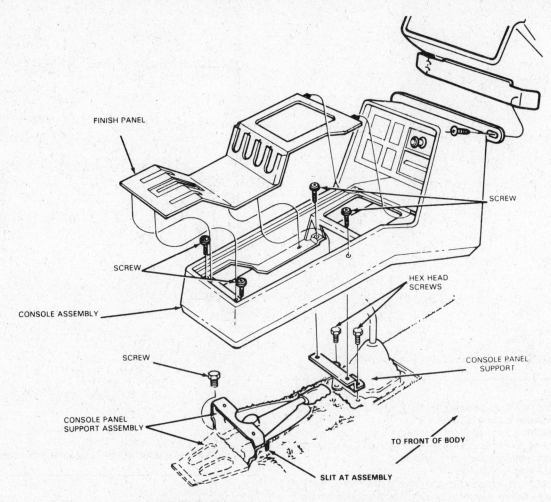

FINISH PANEL

SCREW

SCREW

CONSOLE ASSEMBLY

SCREW

CONSOLE PANEL
SUPPORT ASSEMBLY

HEX HEAD
SCREWS

CONSOLE PANEL
SUPPORT

TO FRONT OF BODY

SLIT AT ASSEMBLY

28.3   Center console installation (1981 through 1984 models)

5   Disconnect the door latch remote rods at the latch and remove the regulator assembly through the door access hole.
6   Clean any drilling or rivet remnants from the bottom of the door.
7   To install, insert the regulator assembly into the door panel and install the two nuts and washers. Do not tighten the nuts at this time.
8   Install two 1/2 X 1-inch bolts, nuts and washers to secure the regulator to the door.
9   Install the window glass into the regulator as described in Section 22, Steps 4 and 5.
10   Move the glass into the full up position and tighten the nuts installed in Step 7 of this Section.
11   Connect the remote rods to the door latch.
12   Check for proper window glass operation, then install the watershield and door trim panel.

26   Rear quarter flipper window – replacement

1   Remove the screws securing the glass hinge and disconnect the cable retainer from the glass.
2   Remove the glass from the vehicle, noting the number and locations of spacers.
3   To remove the hinge plastic cover, use a screwdriver and carefully pry on one side only.
4   Drill out the pop-rivet securing the hinge(s) to the glass. Remove the screw securing the hinge(s) to the body pillar and remove the hinge(s).
5   Installation is the reverse of the removal procedure with the following addition:

6   Be sure to install all spacers in the correct location.

27   Windshield, stationary quarter window and rear glass – replacement

Replacement of the windshield and fixed glass requires the use of special fast-setting adhesive/caulk materials and some specialized tools and techniques. These operations should be left to a dealer service department or a shop specializing in automotive glass work.

28   Center console – removal and installation (1981 through 1987 models)

1981 through 1984 models
Refer to illustration 28.3
1   Move the parking brake lever forward until you can insert a finger into the lever slot finish panel. Pull the rear of the panel upward, pull the parking brake lever all the way up.
2   Pull the finish panel toward the rear to disengage the locking tabs at the from and remove the panel.
3   Remove the screws securing the console base to the floor pan and the screws securing it to the instrument panel **(see illustration)**.
4   Block the wheels so the vehicle will not roll in either direction. Release the parking brake lever.

11

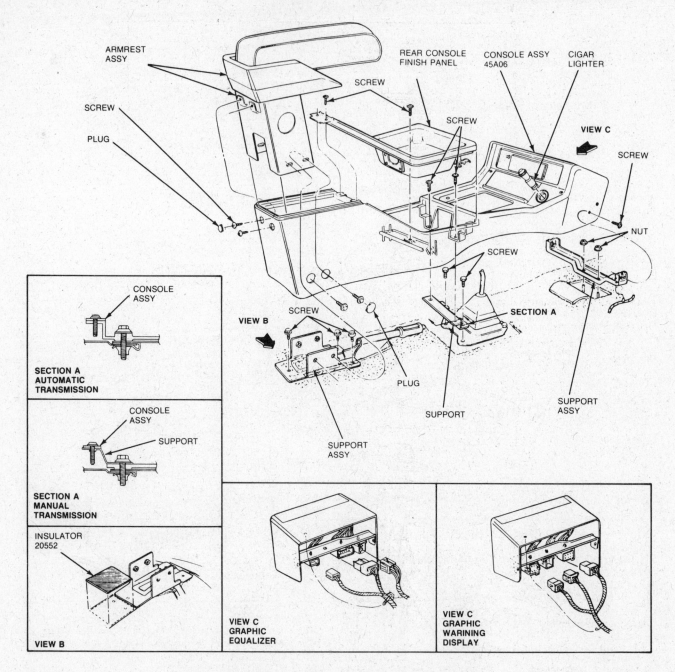

28.10 Center console installation (1985 through 1987 models)

5   Move the gearshift lever into Low (automatic) or Fourth (manual).
6   Pull the console upward and to the rear to gain access to any electrical connectors and disconnect them.
7   Remove the console.
8   Installation is the reverse of the removal procedure.

1985 through 1987 models

Refer to illustration 28.10

9   Remove the plastic trim screw covers, two at back and two on each side at the rear. **Note:** *The seats may have to be moved to gain access to the covers and screws.*

10   Remove the two screw securing the arm rest at the rear and the four bolts securing the console to the floor bracket **(see illustration)**. Lift the arm rest straight up and out of the console.
11   Remove the three screws securing the rear finish panel to the console. Carefully slide the finish panel off of the parking brake lever through the hole in the end of the finish panel.
12   Remove the two screws securing the console to the front support bracket.
13   Remove the two screws securing the console to the rear mounting bracket.
14   Unsnap the main wiring harness locators from the front of the console.

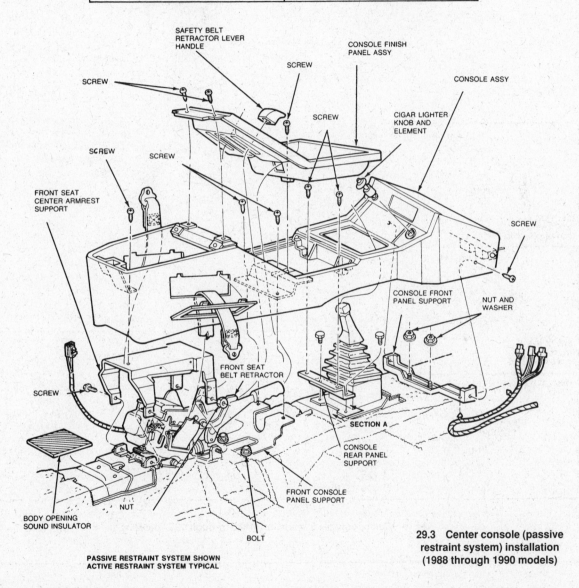

29.3 Center console (passive restraint system) installation (1988 through 1990 models)

PASSIVE RESTRAINT SYSTEM SHOWN
ACTIVE RESTRAINT SYSTEM TYPICAL

15 Disconnect the electrical connectors at the front of the console and remove the console assembly.

16 Installation is the reverse of the removal procedure.

29 Center console (with passive restraint system) – removal and installation (1988 through 1990 models)

Refer to illustration 29.3

1 Cycle the shoulder belts to the A-pillar position.

2 Remove the seat belt anchor plug buttons, then remove the two bolts securing the seat belts. Allow the belts to retract into the console.

3 On models so equipped, remove the plug buttons at the rear of the console. Remove the two screws securing the armrest to the console at the rear **(see illustration)**.

4 Carefully snap out and remove the seat belt trim bezels from each side of the console.

5 Remove the four screws securing the rear of the arm rest. Gain access to the screws through the seat belt openings in the console. Remove the arm rest.

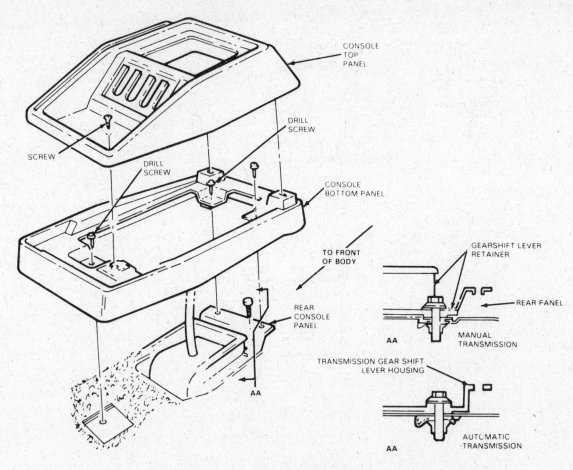

30.1   Center consolette installation (1981 through 1987 models)

6   Relieve pressure of the emergency release lever handle retaining clips on the underside of the handle while pulling on the handle. Carefully remove the emergency release lever handles.
7   Remove the three screws securing the finish plate to the console. Lift the panel out of the console and disconnect all electrical connectors. Remove the finish plate.
8   Remove the seven screws securing the console to the floor pan (two in front, four in the center and one at the rear).
9   Lift the console up and toward the rear. Disconnect the electrical connectors at the front, then remove the console assembly.
10   Installation is the reverse of the removal procedure with the following addition:
11   Tighten the seat belt retractor attachment bolts to the torque listed in this Chapter's Specifications.

30   Center consolette – removal and installation

1981 through 1987 models

Refer to illustration 30.1

1   Remove the screw securing the top panel **(see illustration)**.
2   Insert a putty knife and pry up the top panel from the bottom panel and remove it.
3   Remove the three drill screws and remove the bottom panel.
4   Installation is the reverse of the removal procedure.

1988 through 1990 models

Refer to illustration 30.6

5   Cycle the shoulder belts to the A-pillar position.
6   Remove the seat belt anchor plug buttons, then remove the two bolts securing the seat belts **(see illustration)**. Allow the belts to retract into the console.
7   On models so equipped, at the rear of the console, remove the plug buttons. Remove the two screws securing the armrest to the console at the rear.
8   Carefully snap out and remove the seat belt trim bezels from each side of the console.
9   Remove the four screws securing the rear of the arm rest (two on each side). Gain access to the screws through the seat belt openings in the console. Remove the arm rest.
10   Relieve pressure of the emergency release lever handle retaining clips on the underside of the handle while pulling on the handle. Carefully remove the emergency release lever handles.
11   Remove the two screws securing the finish plate to the console. Push the panel forward and up.
12   Disconnect all electrical connectors and remove the finish plate.
13   Remove the two screws securing the console to the floor pan and remove the console
14   If necessary, remove the bolts and nuts securing the armrest support at the rear and the two nuts securing it at the front, then remove the support.
15   If necessary, remove the two bolts securing the retractor assembly to the floor brace. Disconnect the electrical connector and remove the retractor assembly.
16   Installation is the reverse of the removal procedure with the following addition:
17   Tighten the seat belt retractor attachment bolts to the torque listed in this Chapter's Specifications.

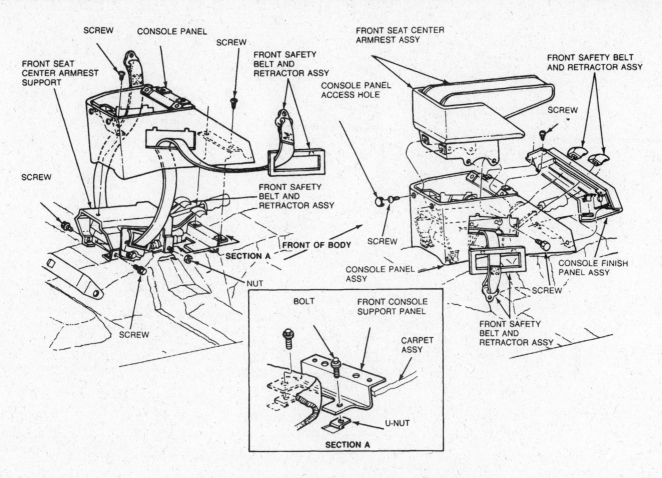

30.6 Center consolette installation (1988 through 1990 models)

31   Seats – removal and installation

Front seats

Refer to illustration 31.1

1   Remove the seat track retaining bolts and nuts, disconnect any electrical or other connectors and lift the seat and track assembly from the vehicle **(see illustration)**.

2   Installation is the reverse of removal. Tighten the retaining nuts and bolts securely.

Conventional rear seats (1981 through 1983 models)

Refer to illustration 31.3

3   Kneel on the seat cushion to push it downward, then push it rearward to unhook it from its supports **(see illustration)**. Lift the cushion out.

4   Remove one of the quarter armrests (if equipped).

5   Remove the seatback lower retaining screws, then lift the seatback up and out.

6   Installation is the reverse of removal procedure with the following addition:

7   Make sure the seat cushion is secured into its floor retainers.

Fold-down full rear seat back (1984 through 1990 models)

Refer to illustration 31.10

8   Remove the luggage compartment cover from the seat back.

9   Remove the carpeting from the seat back.

10   Disengage the inboard seat belts from the guides and the outboard

seat belts from the strap retainers. Pull the strap retainers through the holes in the seat back from the rear **(see illustration)**.

11   Fold the seat cushion and seat back forward.

12   Remove the bolts securing the seat back hinge to the floor pan.

13   Remove the seat back from the vehicle.

14   Installation is the reverse of removal procedure with the following addition:

15   Tighten the seat back hinge bolts to the torque listed in this Chapter's Specifications.

Fold-down full rear seat cushion (1984 through 1990 models)

Refer to illustration 31.17

16   Pull the seat cushion into the raised position.

17   Remove the bolt securing the retaining strap **(see illustration)**.

18   Remove the bolts securing the seat cushion hinge to the floor pan.

19   Remove the seat cushion from the vehicle.

20   Installation is the reverse of removal procedure with the following addition:

21   Tighten the seat back hinge bolts to the torque listed in this Chapter's Specifications.

Fold-down split rear seat back (1984 through 1990 models)

Refer to illustration 31.24

22   Remove the luggage compartment cover from the seat back.

23   Remove the carpeting from the seat back.

11

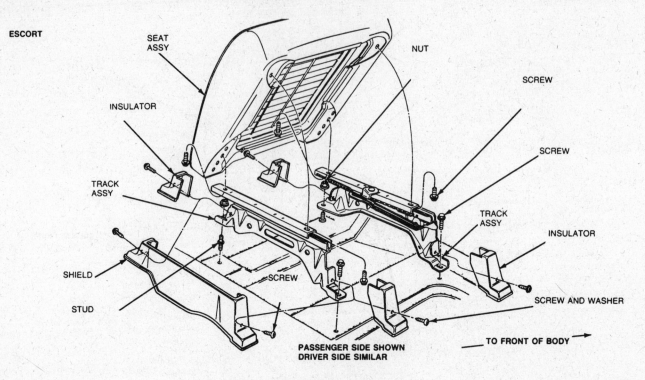

31.1   Front seat and track installation

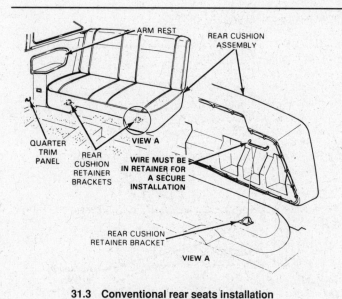

31.3   Conventional rear seats installation
(1981 through 1983 models)

24   Disengage the inboard seat belts from the guides and the outboard seat belts from the strap retainers. Pull the strap retainers through the holes in the seat back from the rear **(see illustration)**.
25   Fold the seat cushion and seat back forward.
26   Remove the bolts securing the seat back articulating arm to the seat. Don't lose the bushing and spacer on either side of the arm.
27   Remove the bolts securing the seat cushion hinge to the floor pan.
28   Pull the seat cushion outboard and away from the center pivot bushing.
29   Remove the seat back from the vehicle.

30   Installation is the reverse of removal procedure with the following addition:
31   Tighten the articulating arms and hinge bolts to the torque listed in this Chapter's Specifications.

Fold-down split rear seat cushion (1984 through 1990 models)

Refer to illustration 31.32

32   Remove the bolts securing the seat back articulating arms to the cushion **(see illustration)**. Don't lose the bushing, spacer and washer on either side of the arms.
33   Remove the bolts securing the seat cushion hinge to the floor pan.
34   Fold the seat cushion up and forward.
35   Pull the seat cushion outboard and away from the center pivot bushing.
36   Remove the seat cushion from the vehicle.
37   Installation is the reverse of removal procedure with the following addition:
38   Tighten the articulating arms and hinge bolts to the torque listed in this Chapter's Specifications.

32   Seat belt check

1   Check the seat belts, buckles, latchplates and guide loops for obvious damage and signs of wear.
2   Check that the seat belt reminder light comes on when the ignition key is turned to the Run or Start positions.
3   The seat belts are designed to lock up during a sudden stop or impact, yet allow free movement during normal driving. Check that the retractors return the belt against your chest while driving and rewind the belt fully when the buckle is unlatched.
4   If any of the above checks reveal problems with the seat belt system, replace parts as necessary.

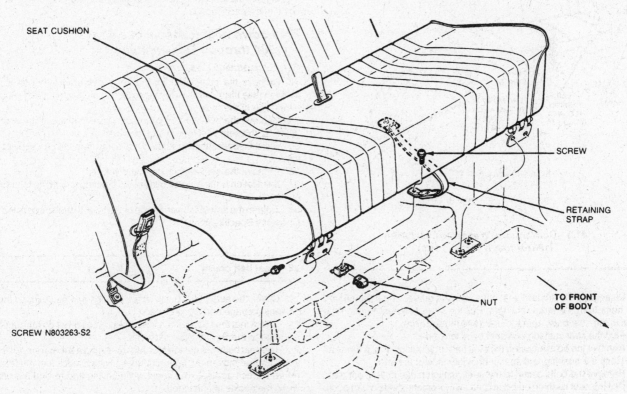

SEAT BACK
60032

SEAT BELT
GUIDES

SCREW
N803263-S2
4 REQ'D
17-27 N·m
(13-20 LB-FT)

STRAP
RETAINER

SEAT BELTS

TO FRONT OF BODY

31.10   Fold-down full rear seat back installation (1984 through 1990 models)

SEAT CUSHION

SCREW

RETAINING
STRAP

SCREW N803263-S2

NUT

TO FRONT
OF BODY

11

31.17   Fold-down full rear seat cushion installation (1984 through 1990 models)

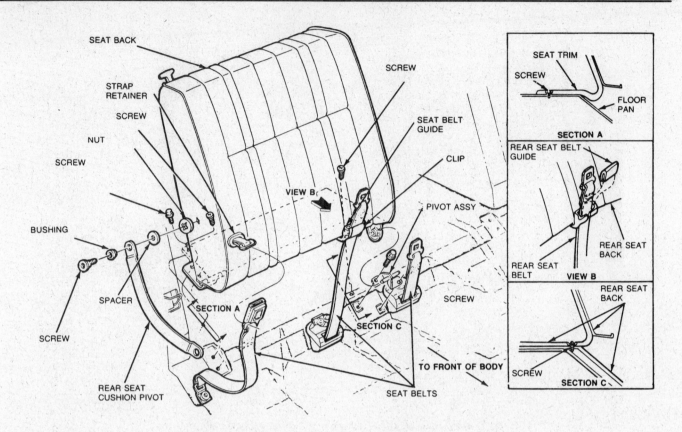

31.24   Fold-down split rear seat back installation (1984 through 1990 models)

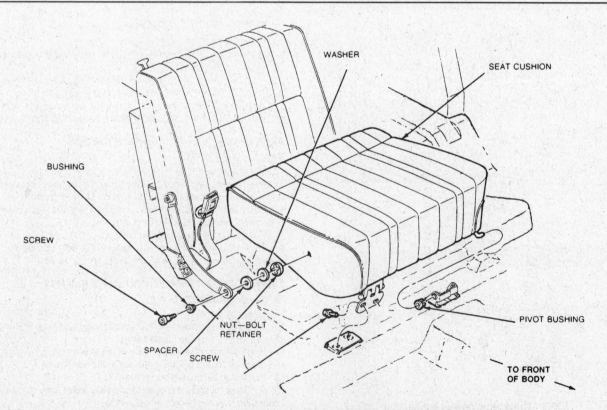

31.32   Fold-down split rear seat cushion installation (1984 through 1990 models)

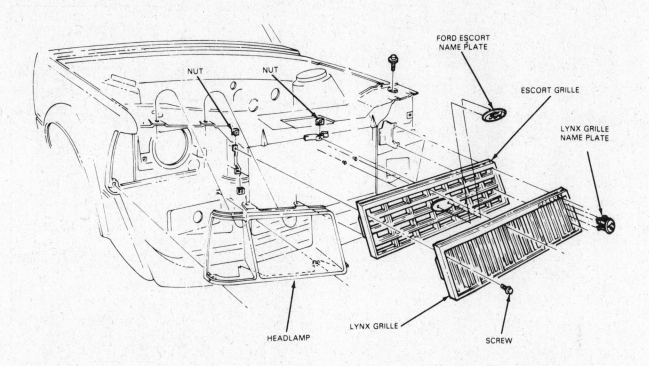

33.1 Grille removal and installation (1981 through 1985 models)

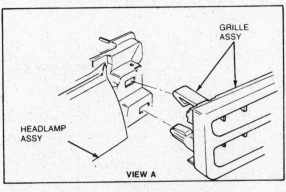

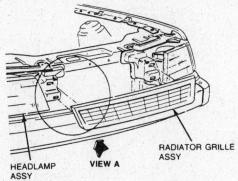

**33.5 Grille removal and installation
(1986 through 1988 standard models)**

33   Radiator grille – removal and installation

1981 through 1985 models

Refer to illustration 33.1

1   Remove the screws securing the grille to the body. Remove the grille assembly **(see illustration)**.

2   To install, position the grille on the locating tabs extending from the headlamp doors and loosely install the five mounting screws.

3   Adjust the grille so that there is an even gap between the grille sides and the headlight openings and tighten the retaining screws securely.

1986 through 1988 standard models

Refer to illustration 33.5

4   Open the hood.

5   Push down on the top side of the lower snap-in retainer at each end of the grille **(see illustration)**. Pull the grille out at the bottom.

6   Push up on the bottom of the upper snap-in retainer at each end of the grille and pull the grille out at the top.

7   Pull the grille forward and remove it.

8   To install, align the snap-in retainers with the appropriate slots and push the grille in until the retainers are correctly seated.

1986 through 1988 GT and XR-3 models

Refer to illustration 33.10

9   Open the hood.

10   Remove the screw on the top side of the grille at each end and pull the grille out at the top **(see illustration)**.

11   Push down on the bottom side of the lower snap-in retainer at each end of the grille and pull the grille out at the bottom.

12   Pull the grille forward and remove it.

13   To install, position the grille to align the lower snap-in retainers and upper tabs over the U-nuts on each side.

14   Push the grille into place to seat the lower retainers.

15   Install the screw on the top side of the grille at each end.

11

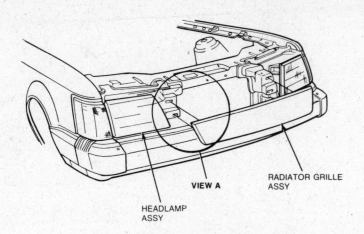

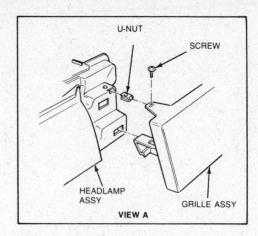

33.10   Grille removal and installation (1986 through 1988 GT and XR-3 models)

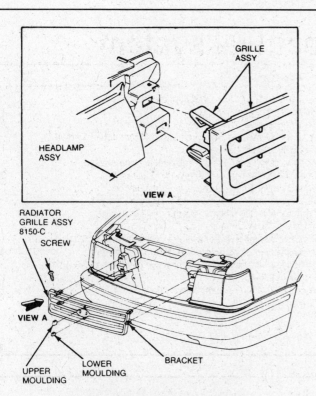

**33.17   Grille removal and installation
(1989 and 1990 standard models)**

1989 and 1990 standard models

Refer to illustration 33.17

16   Open the hood.

17   Push down on the top side of the lower snap-in retainer at each end of the grille **(see illustration)**. Pull the grille out at the bottom.

18   Push up on the bottom of the upper snap-in retainer at each end of the grille and pull the grille out at the top.

19   Pull the grille forward and remove it from the lamp housing.

20   To install, align the snap-in retainers with the appropriate slots and push the grille in until the retainers are correctly seated.

1989 and 1990 GT models

21   Open the hood.

22   Push up on the three retaining tabs located on the back of the grille and remove the grille bar.

23   Remove the two screws securing the grille top ends to the mounting brackets at each side.

24   Pull the grille forward and remove it.

25   To install, position the grille to align the upper and lower snap-in retainers on each side.

26   Push the grille into place to seat the retainers.

27   Align the bar retainers with the holes in the grille and push it until it seats correctly.

Chapter 12   Chassis electrical system

Contents

Specifications

Lights

	Bulb number
Air conditioner control	1982
Back-up	1168
Cargo and dome	906
Dome/map	906/1816
Engine compartment	906
Front parking and turn signal	1157
Headlamp	
Sealed beam	H6054
Aero headlamps	9004
Heater	161
PRNDL shift selector	1445
Rear license plate	168
Rear parking, stop and side marker	1157

Torque specifications

Ignition switch mounting bolts (1987 and later models only)	50 to 60 in-lbs
Steering column attachment bolts and nuts	15 to 25 ft-lbs

12

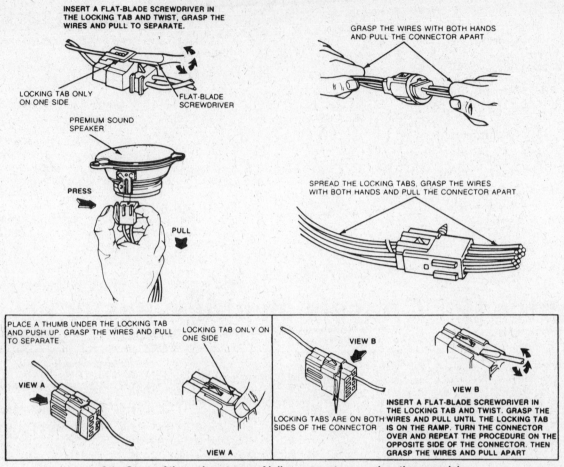

3.1   Some of the various types of inline connectors used on these models

1   General information

Warning: *To prevent electrical shorts, fires and injury, always disconnect the cable from the negative terminal of the battery before checking, repairing or replacing electrical components.*

The chassis electrical system of this vehicle is a 12-volt, negative ground type. Power for the lights and all electrical accessories is supplied by a lead/acid-type battery which is charged by the alternator.

This chapter covers repair and service procedures for various chassis (non-engine related) electrical components. For information regarding the engine electrical system components (battery, alternator, distributor and starter motor), see Chapter 5.

2   Electrical troubleshooting – general information

A typical electrical circuit consists of an electrical component, any switches, relays, motors, fuses, fusible links or circuit breakers, etc. related to that component and the wiring and connectors that link the components to both the battery and the chassis. To help you pinpoint an electrical circuit problem, wiring diagrams are included at the end of this book.

Before tackling any troublesome electrical circuit, first study the appropriate wiring diagrams to get a complete understanding of what makes up that individual circuit. Trouble spots, for instance, can often be isolated by noting if other components related to that circuit are often routed through the same fuse and ground connections.

Electrical problems usually stem from simple causes such as loose or corroded connectors, a blown fuse, a melted fusible link or a bad relay. Vi-sually inspect the condition of all fuses, wires and connectors in a problem circuit before troubleshooting it.

The basic tools needed for electrical troubleshooting include a circuit tester, a high impedance (10 K-ohm) digital voltmeter, a continuity tester and a jumper wire with an inline circuit breaker for bypassing electrical components. Before attempting to locate or define a problem with electrical test instruments, use the wiring diagrams to decide where to make the necessary connections.

Voltage checks

Perform a voltage check first when a circuit is not functioning properly. Connect one lead of a circuit tester to either the negative battery terminal or a known good ground.

Connect the other lead to a connector in the circuit being tested, preferably nearest to the battery or fuse. If the bulb of the tester lights up, voltage is present, which means that the part of the circuit between the connector and the battery is problem free. Continue checking the rest of the circuit in the same fashion.

When you reach a point at which no voltage is present, the problem lies between that point and the last test point with voltage. Most of the time the problem can be traced to a loose connection. **Note:** *Keep in mind that some circuits receive voltage only when the ignition key is in the Accessory or Run position.*

Finding a short circuit

One method of finding shorts in a circuit is to remove the fuse and connect a test light or voltmeter in its place. There should be no voltage present in the circuit. Move the wiring harness from side-to-side while watching the test light. If the bulb goes on, there is a short to ground somewhere in that area, probably where the insulation has been rubbed through. The same test can be performed on each component in a circuit, even a switch.

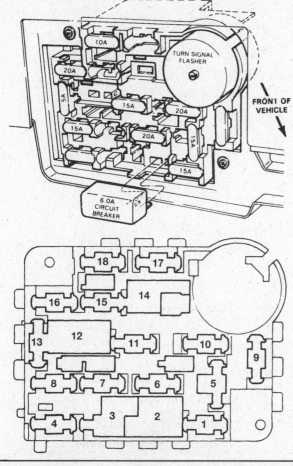

4.3 A typical fuse and circuit breaker panel

1   Stop lamps, hazard warning lamps, air conditioner fan 15-amp fuse
2   Windshield wiper, washer pump interval wiper six-amp circuit breaker
3   Not used
4   Tail, parking, side marker lamps, instrument cluster illumination lamp, license plate lamp ten- or 15-amp fuse standard
5   Turn signal, back-up lamps, air conditioner fan controller relay, heated rear window relay 15-amp fuse
6   Heated rear window relay, graphic display module, liftgate release, speed control module, rear wiper/washer, digital clock display module 20-amp fuse
7   Fog lamps 15-amp fuse
8   Courtesy lamps, key warning buzzer, clock, glove compartment lamp, engine compartment lamp, power mirror 15-amp fuse
9   Blower motor 30-amp fuse
10 Flash-to-pass 20-amp fuse
11 Radio, tape player, premium sound with one amplifier 15-amp fuse
12 Not used
13 Instrument cluster illumination, radio, climate control, clock, ash tray, diagnostic module five-amp fuse
14 Radiator cooling fan (without air conditioning) circuit breaker
15 Not used
16 Horn, front cigar lighter 25-amp fuse
17 Air conditioner clutch, engine cooling fan controller ten-amp fuse
18 Warning indicator lamps, low fuel module, dual timer buzzer, anti-diesel solenoid, upshift indicator lamp, WOT cutout relay, carburetor bowl vent solenoid, tachometer, low washer fluid LED ten-amp fuse

Ground check

Perform a ground test to check whether a component is properly grounded. Disconnect the battery and connect one lead of a self-powered test light, known as a continuity tester, to a known good ground. Connect the other lead to the wire or ground connection being tested. If the bulb goes on, the ground is good.

If the bulb does not go on, the ground is not good.

Continuity check

A continuity check determines if there are any breaks in a circuit – if it is conducting electricity properly. With the circuit off (no power in the circuit), a self-powered continuity tester can be used to check the circuit. Connect the test leads to both ends of the circuit, and if the test light comes on the circuit is passing current properly. If the light doesn't come on, there is a break somewhere in the circuit. The same procedure can be used to test a switch, by connecting the continuity tester to the power in and power out sides of the switch. With the switch turned on, the test light should come on.

Finding an open circuit

When diagnosing for possible open circuits it is often difficult to locate them by sight because oxidation or terminal misalignment are hidden by the connectors. Merely wiggling a connector on a sensor or in the wiring harness may correct the open circuit condition. Remember this if an open circuit is indicated when troubleshooting a circuit. Intermittent problems may also be caused by oxidized or loose connections.

Electrical troubleshooting is simple if you keep in mind that all electrical circuits are basically electricity running from the battery, through the wires, switches, relays, fuses and fusible links to each electrical component (light bulb, motor, etc.) and then to ground, from which it is passed back to the battery. Any electrical problem is an interruption in the flow of electricity to and from the battery.

3   Electrical connectors – general information

Refer to illustration 3.1

Always release the lock lever(s) before attempting to unplug inline type connectors. There are a variety of lock lever configurations **(see illustration)**. Although nothing more than a finger is usually necessary to pry lock levers open, a small pocket screwdriver is effective for hard-to-release levers. Once the lock levers are released, try to pull on the connectors themselves, not the wires, when unplugging two connector halves (there are times, however, when this is not possible – use good judgment).

It is usually necessary to know which side, male or female, of the connector you're checking. Male connectors are easily distinguished from females by the shape of their terminals.

When checking continuity or voltage with a circuit tester, insertion of the test probe into the receptacle may open the fitting to the connector and result in poor contact. Instead, insert the test probe from the wire harness side of the connector (known as "backprobing").

4   Fuses – general information

Refer to illustrations 4.3, 4.4 and 4.6

The electrical circuits are protected by a combination of fuses, fusible links and circuit breakers. The fuse panel is located in the left end of the dashboard, behind a panel.

The fuse block is equipped with miniaturized fuses because their compact dimensions and convenient blade-type terminal design allow fingertip removal and installation.

Each fuse protects one or more circuits. The protected circuit is identified on the face of the fuse panel cover above each fuse. A fuse guide is included here **(see illustration)** but consult your owner's manual – it will have the most accurate guide for your vehicle.

12

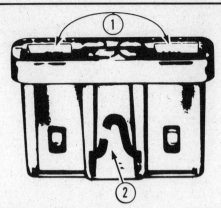

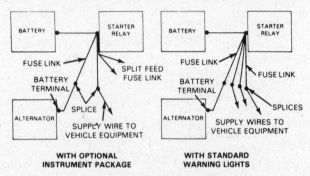

4.4   To test for a blown miniature fuse, turn the ignition to the On position and probe each of the terminal ends (1) with a test light – to visually check the fuse, pull it out and inspect it for an open (2)

5.1a   Fusible link locations

If an electrical component fails, always check the fuse first. A blown fuse, which is nothing more than a broken element, is easily identified through the clear plastic body. Before removing the fuses to check them, however, turn the ignition switch to the On position and probe each terminal at the top of each fuse with a test light connected to a good ground. If the fuse is good, there will be power available to both terminals. If a fuse is blown, one side will have power to it but the other side will not. Visually inspect the element for evidence of damage **(see illustration)**.

Remove and insert fuses straight in and out without twisting. Twisting could force the terminal open too far, resulting in a bad connection.

Be sure to replace blown fuses with the correct type and amp rating. Fuses of different ratings are physically interchangeable, but replacing a fuse with one of a higher or lower value than specified is not recommended. Each electrical circuit needs a specific amount of protection. The amperage value of each fuse is usually molded into the fuse body. Different colors are also used to denote fuses of different amperage types. The accompanying color code **(see illustration)** shows common amperage values and their corresponding colors. **Caution:** *Always turn off all electrical components and the ignition switch before replacing a fuse. Never bypass a fuse with pieces of metal or foil. Serious damage to the electrical system could result.*

If the replacement fuse immediately fails, do not replace it again until the cause of the problem is isolated and corrected. In most cases, this will be a short circuit in the wiring caused by a pinched, broken or deteriorated wire.

5   Fusible links – general information

Refer to illustrations 5.1a, 5.1b and 5.1c

Some circuits are protected by fusible links. These links are used in circuits which are not ordinarily fused, such as the ignition circuit **(see illustrations)**.

Although fusible links appear to be of heavier gauge that the wire they

Fuse Value Amps	Color Code
4	Pink
5	Tan
10	Red
15	Light Blue
20	Yellow
25	Natural
30	Light Green

4.6   Each fuse amp value has a corresponding color code

**WIRING ASSEMBLY — FUSE LINK
(WITH INSULATION STRIPPED BOTH ENDS)**

D3AZ—14A526-H   #14 GA. WIRE — 9.00" ± .50 LENGTH
(GREEN INSULATION)

D3AZ—14A526-J   #16 GA. WIRE — 9.00" ± .50 LENGTH
(ORANGE INSULATION) AS REQ'D.

D3AZ—14A526-K   #17 GA. WIRE — 9.00" ± .50 LENGTH
(YELLOW INSULATION) AS REQ'D.
(SPECIAL USED WITH AIR CONDITIONING SYSTEM)

D3AZ—14A526-L   #18 GA. WIRE — 9.00" ± .50 LENGTH
(RED INSULATION) AS REQ'D.

D3AZ—14A526-M   #20 GA. WIRE — 9.00" ± .50 LENGTH
(BLUE INSULATION) AS REQ'D.

**WIRING ASSEMBLY — FUSE LINK
(WITH EYELET TERMINAL AND ONE END STRIPPED)**

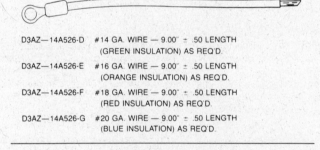

D3AZ—14A526-D   #14 GA. WIRE — 9.00" ± .50 LENGTH
(GREEN INSULATION) AS REQ'D.

D3AZ—14A526-E   #16 GA. WIRE — 9.00" ± .50 LENGTH
(ORANGE INSULATION) AS REQ'D.

D3AZ—14A526-F   #18 GA. WIRE — 9.00" ± .50 LENGTH
(RED INSULATION) AS REQ'D.

D3AZ—14A526-G   #20 GA. WIRE — 9.00" ± .50 LENGTH
(BLUE INSULATION) AS REQ'D.

BUTT CONNECTOR — WIRING SPLICE

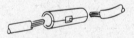

D3AZ—14488-Y   FOR #10 AND 12 GA. WIRE (LOAD CIRCUIT) AS REQ'D.

D3AZ—14488-Z   FOR #14 AND 16 GA. WIRE (LOAD CIRCUIT) AS REQ'D.

5.1b   Fusible link and connector types

are protecting, their appearance is due to thicker insulation. All fusible links are several wire gauges smaller than the wire they are designed to protect.

Fusible links cannot be repaired, but a new link of the same size wire can be put in its place. The procedure is as follows:

a) Disconnect the negative cable at the battery.
b) Disconnect the fusible link from the wiring harness.
c) Cut the damaged fusible link out of the wiring just behind the connector.
d) Strip the insulation back approximately 1/2-inch.
e) Position the connector on the new fusible link and crimp it into place.

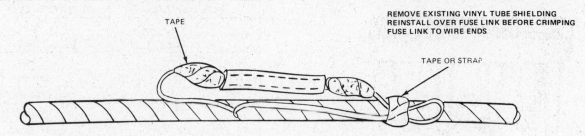

REMOVE EXISTING VINYL TUBE SHIELDING
REINSTALL OVER FUSE LINK BEFORE CRIMPING
FUSE LINK TO WIRE ENDS

TAPE

TAPE OR STRAP

TYPICAL REPAIR USING THE SPECIAL #17 GA. (9.00'' LONG-YELLOW) FUSE LINK REQUIRED FOR THE AIR/COND.
CIRCUITS (2) # 687E AND #261A LOCATED IN THE ENGINE COMPARTMENT

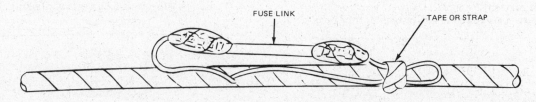

FUSE LINK

TAPE OR STRAP

TYPICAL REPAIR FOR ANY IN-LINE FUSE LINK USING THE SPECIFIED GAUGE FUSE LINK FOR THE SPECIFIED CIRCUIT

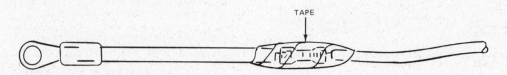

TAPE

TYPICAL REPAIR USING THE EYELET TERMINAL FUSE LINK OF THE SPECIFIED GAUGE FOR ATTACHMENT TO A CIRCUIT WIRE END

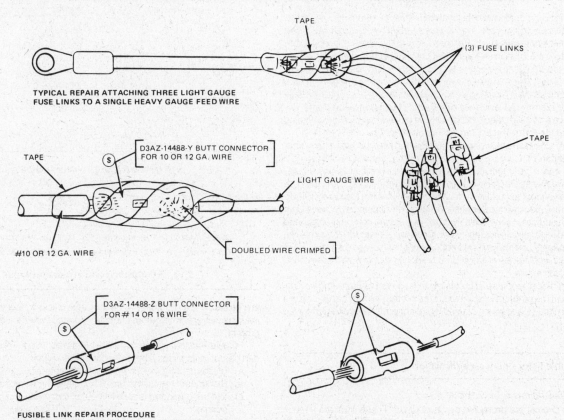

TAPE

(3) FUSE LINKS

TYPICAL REPAIR ATTACHING THREE LIGHT GAUGE
FUSE LINKS TO A SINGLE HEAVY GAUGE FEED WIRE

TAPE

D3AZ-14488-Y BUTT CONNECTOR
FOR 10 OR 12 GA. WIRE

$

LIGHT GAUGE WIRE

#10 OR 12 GA. WIRE

DOUBLED WIRE CRIMPED

D3AZ-14488-Z BUTT CONNECTOR
FOR # 14 OR 16 WIRE

$

$

FUSIBLE LINK REPAIR PROCEDURE

5.1c   Fusible link service procedures

12

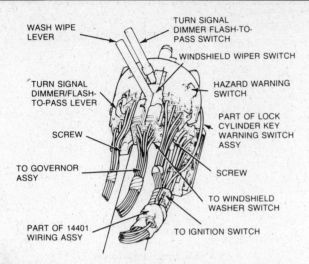

WASH WIPE LEVER

TURN SIGNAL DIMMER FLASH-TO-PASS SWITCH

WINDSHIELD WIPER SWITCH

TURN SIGNAL DIMMER/FLASH-TO-PASS LEVER

HAZARD WARNING SWITCH

PART OF LOCK CYLINDER KEY WARNING SWITCH ASSY

SCREW

SCREW

TO GOVERNOR ASSY

TO WINDSHIELD WASHER SWITCH

PART OF 14401 WIRING ASSY

TO IGNITION SWITCH

7.6   Turn signal/hazard flasher/dimmer (multi-function) switch details

f) Splice and solder the new fusible link to the wires from which the old link was cut. Use rosin core solder at each end of the new link to obtain a good solder joint.
g) Wrap the splices completely with vinyl electrical tape around the soldered joint. No wires should be exposed.
h) Install the repaired wiring as before, using existing clips, if provided.
i) Connect the battery ground cable.
j) Test the circuit for proper operation.

6   Circuit breakers – general information

Circuit breakers protect accessories such as power windows, power door locks, the windshield wipers, windshield washer pump, interval wiper, low washer fluid, etc. Circuit breakers are located in the fuse box. Refer to the fuse panel guide in your owner's manual for the location of the circuit breakers used in your vehicle.

Because a circuit breaker resets itself automatically, an electrical overload in a circuit breaker protected system will cause the circuit to fail momentarily, then come back on. If the circuit does not come back on, check it immediately.

a) Remove the circuit breaker from the fuse panel **(see illustration 4.3)**.
b) Using an ohmmeter, verify that there is continuity between both terminals of the circuit breaker. If there is no continuity, replace the circuit breaker.
c) Install the old or new circuit breaker. If it continues to cut out, a short circuit is indicated. Troubleshoot the appropriate circuit (see the wiring diagrams at the back of this book) or have the system checked by a professional mechanic.

7   Turn signal/hazard flasher/dimmer (multi-function) switch – replacement

Refer to illustration 7.6

1   Disconnect the negative cable from the battery.
2   Remove the five screws securing the steering column lower shroud and remove the shroud.
3   Loosen the two bolts and nuts securing the steering column to the support bracket enough to allow removal of the steering column upper shroud. Remove the upper shroud.
4   To remove the turn signal lever, carefully move the outer end of the lever around in a circular motion, then pull it straight out of the switch assembly.

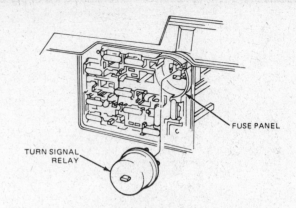

FUSE PANEL

TURN SIGNAL RELAY

8.2   The turn signal flasher is located on the front of the fuse panel

5   Peel back the foam sight shield from the turn signal switch.
6   Disconnect the switch electrical connectors **(see illustration)**.
7   Remove the switch mounting screws and remove the switch from the lock cylinder housing. Disengage and remove the switch from the housing.
8   Installation is the reverse of the removal procedure with the following additions.
9   Align the turn signal switch mounting holes with the corresponding holes in the lock cylinder housing. Install and tighten the two screws securely.
10 Tighten the steering column attachment nuts to the torque listed in this Chapter's Specifications.
11 Check the steering column and switch for proper operation.

8   Turn signal/hazard flashers – replacement

Refer to illustrations 8.2 and 8.3
Note: *No functional or operation check of the hazard/turn signal flashers is necessary. If they stop working, replace them.*

1   Disconnect the negative cable from the battery.
2   The turn signal flasher is located on the front of the fuse panel **(see illustration)**. Remove the flasher by turning it 90-degrees counterclockwise then pull straight out.
3   The hazard flasher is located on the back of the fuse panel **(see illustration)**. Remove the flasher by turning it 90-degrees counterclockwise then pull straight out.
4   Install the new flasher unit. Be sure to line up the metal contacts with the slots in the fuse panel. Press the flasher firmly into place and turn it 90-degrees clockwise to lock it.

9   Ignition switch – replacement

Refer to illustration 9.4

1   Disconnect the negative cable from the battery.
2   Remove the five screws securing the steering column lower shroud and remove the shroud.
3   Remove the two bolts and nuts securing the steering column to the support bracket and lower the column.
4   Disconnect the ignition switch electrical connector **(see illustration)**.
5   Turn the ignition key lock cylinder to the On (Run) position.
6   On 1981 through 1986 models, perform the following:
   a) Use a 1/8-inch drill bit to drill out the shear-head bolts that connect the switch to the lock cylinder housing.
   b) Remove both bolts with an EX-3 easy-out tool or equivalent.
7   On 1987 through 1990 models, remove the two screws securing the ignition switch.
8   Disengage the ignition switch from the actuator pin.

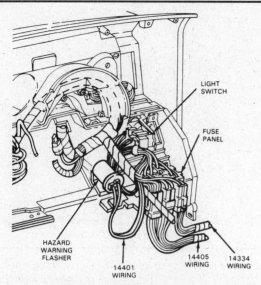

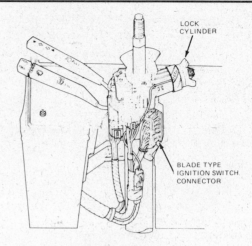

9.4 Ignition switch details

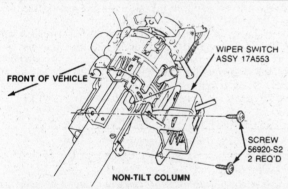

8.3 The hazard flasher is located on the rear of the fuse panel

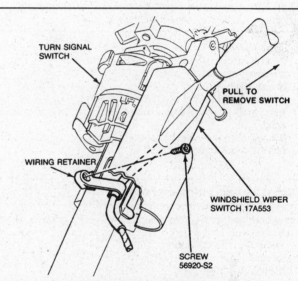

10.6 Windshield wiper/washer switch attachment details (standard column)

10.11 Windshield wiper/washer switch attachment details (tilt column)

9   Make sure the actuator pin slot in the new ignition switch is in the Run position. **Note:** *A new replacement switch assembly will be set in the On (Run) position.*
10   Make sure the ignition key lock cylinder is in approximately the RUN position. The RUN position is achieved by rotating the key lock cylinder approximately 90-degrees from the LOCK position.
11   Install the ignition switch onto the actuator pin. It may be necessary to slightly move the switch back and forth to align the switch mounting holes.
12   On 1981 through 1986 models, install the shear head bolts. Tighten the bolts until the heads break off.
13   On 1987 through 1990 models, install the bolts and tighten to the torque listed in this Chapter's Specifications.
14   Connect the electrical connector into the switch.
15   Connect the negative battery cable.
16   Insert the ignition key and check the ignition switch for proper function including the START and ACC positions. Also make sure the steering column is locked in the LOCK position.
17   Raise the steering column into position and install the two bolts and nuts securing the steering column to the support bracket. Tighten the bolt and nuts to the torque listed in this Chapter's Specifications.
18   Install the steering column lower shroud and screws.

10   Windshield wiper/washer switch – removal and installation

Refer to illustrations 10.6 and 10.11
Note: *The switch handle is an integral part of the switch assembly and*

cannot be replaced separately.

Standard (non-tilt) steering column models

1   Disconnect the negative cable from the battery.
2   Remove the five screws securing the steering column lower shroud and remove the shroud.
3   Loosen the two bolts and nuts securing the steering column to the support bracket enough to allow removal of the steering column upper shroud. Remove the upper shroud.
4   Unplug the switch electrical connector. **Note:** *On some models, it may be easier to remove the switch from the steering column first, then unplug the electrical connector.*
5   Peel back the foam sight shield from the switch.
6   Remove the two screws securing the switch assembly to the steering column **(see illustration)** and remove the switch assembly.
7   Installation is the reverse of the removal procedure.

Tilt steering column models

8   Disconnect the negative cable from the battery.
9   Remove the five screws securing the steering column lower shroud and remove the shroud.
10   Loosen the two bolts and nuts securing the steering column to the support bracket enough to allow removal of the steering column upper shroud. Remove the upper shroud.
11   Pull back the side shield **(see illustration)**.

12

11.2a   To gain access to the windshield wiper motor, peel away the weatherstrip from the passenger side of the cowl . . .

11.2b   . . . then pop the watershield clips loose from the cowl and set the shield aside

12   Unplug the switch electrical connector.
13   Remove the screw securing the wiring retainer to the steering column.
14   Grasp the switch handle and pull straight out and disengage the switch from the turn signal switch.
15   Installation is the reverse of removal.

11.3   To detach the wiper motor electrical connector, first remove the tape or tie wrap that secures the motor harness to the main harness, then unplug the connector and push the grommet and connector through the hole (arrow)

11   Windshield wiper motor – removal and installation

Refer to illustration 11.2a, 11.2b, 11.3, 11.4, 11.6, 11.7 and 11.9
1   Disconnect the negative cable from the battery.
2   Remove the rubber weatherstrip and watershield cover from the cowl on the passenger side **(see illustrations)**.
3   Remove the tie wrap or tape that secures the wiper motor harness to the main wiring harness. Disconnect the electrical connector, then push the grommet and connector through the grommet hole into the cowl area **(see illustration)**.
4   Remove the link retaining clip and detach the wiper linkage from the motor **(see illustration)**.

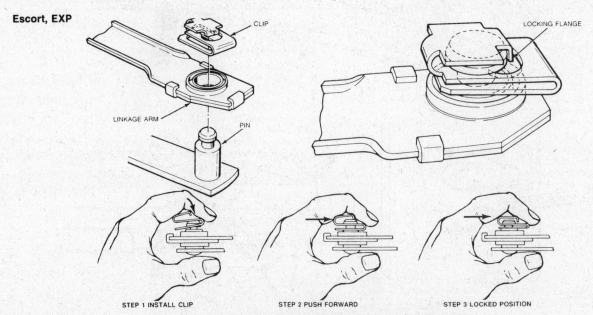

Escort, EXP

CLIP

LOCKING FLANGE

LINKAGE ARM

PIN

STEP 1 INSTALL CLIP   STEP 2 PUSH FORWARD   STEP 3 LOCKED POSITION

11.4   The wiper motor is secured to the linkage by a clip

11.6 To remove the windshield wiper arm assembly from the pivot shaft, raise the arm off the windshield and pry the latching lever away from the arm with a screwdriver

5   Remove the screws securing the motor (**see illustration 11.3**). Lift the motor out.
6   To remove the wiper arms, first note their position on the windshield so they can be reinstalled in exactly the same position. Then raise the blade end of the arm off the windshield and use a screwdriver to move the latching lever away from the pivot shaft (**see illustration**). This unlocks the wiper arm from the pivot shaft and holds the blade end of the arm off the

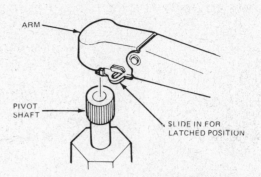

11.9 To install the windshield wiper arm assembly onto the pivot shaft, press the arm head onto the shaft, slide the latching lever all the way in until it locks underneath the shaft, then lower the arm onto the windshield

glass at the same time. The wiper arm can now be pulled off the pivot shaft without any tools.
7   To remove the wiper linkage, remove the pivot retainers and guide the assembly out from the cowl (**see illustration**).
8   Installation is the reverse of removal with the following additions.
9   To reinstall the wiper arm, push it onto the shaft, slide the latching lever in and lower the blade onto the windshield (**see illustration**).

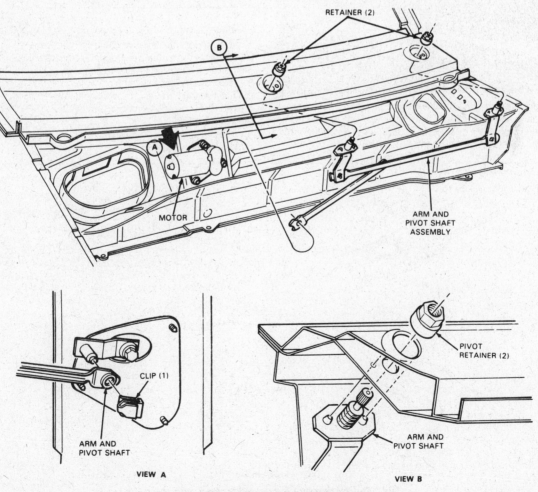

11.7 Wiper motor and linkage layout

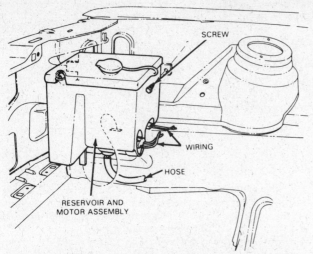

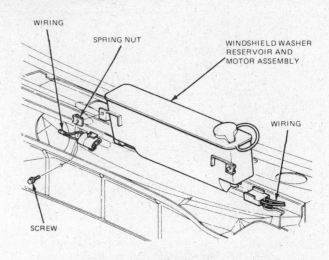

12.2 Windshield washer reservoir and pump assembly layout (early models)

12.3 Windshield washer reservoir and pump assembly layout (later models)

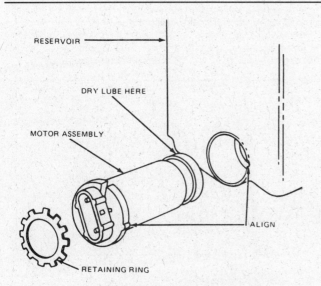

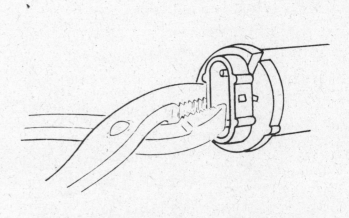

12.6 Windshield washer motor details

12.7 Grasp one wall surrounding the electrical terminal with a pair of pliers, then pull the motor, seal and impeller assembly out

10   Make sure the wiper blades are in the parked position before attaching the linkage to the motor.

12   Windshield washer and pump assembly – removal and installation

Refer to illustrations 12.2, 12.3, 12.6 and 12.7

1   Use a small screwdriver and unlock the electrical connector tabs, then unplug the electrical connector from the washer pump.
2   On early models, remove the screw securing the washer reservoir and pump motor assembly to the wheel well **(see illustration)**.
3   On later models, remove the two screws or nuts securing the washer reservoir and pump motor assembly to the firewall **(see illustration)**.
4   Lift the washer reservoir up and disconnect the small hose from the base of the reservoir. Place your finger over the end of the small hose fitting on the reservoir to prevent spilling the washer fluid in the engine compartment. Remove the reservoir.
5   Drain the washer fluid from the reservoir into a clean container. If the fluid is kept clean it can be reused.

6   Use a small screwdriver and carefully pry out the retaining ring securing the pump motor in the reservoir receptacle **(see illustration)**.
7   Grasp one wall surrounding the electrical terminal with a pair of pliers, then pull the motor, seal and impeller assembly out of the reservoir **(see illustration)**. **Note:** *If the impeller and seal separate from the motor they can be reassembled after removal.*
8   Flush out the reservoir with clean water to remove any residue. Inspect it for any foreign matter.
9   Inspect the reservoir pump chamber prior to installing an old motor into a new reservoir. Clean if necessary.
10   Lubricate the outer surface of the seal with powdered graphite to make installation easier **(see illustration 12.6)**.
11   Align the small projection on the motor end cap with the slot in the reservoir and push it in until the seal seats against the bottom of the motor receptacle in the reservoir.
12   Use a 1 inch 12-point socket and hand press the retaining ring securely against the motor and plate.
13   Connect the hose to the fitting on the base of the reservoir.
14   Install the reservoir in the engine compartment or fire wall and secure with the screw(s) or nuts.
15   Connect the electrical connector.

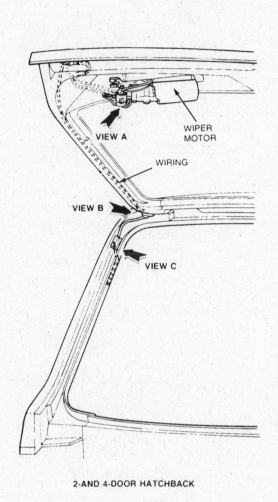

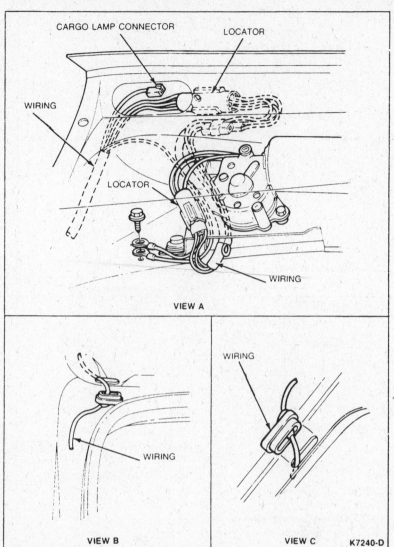

13.5   Rear window wiper motor layout (two- and four-door models)

16 **Caution:** *Do not operate the pump without fluid in the reservoir as it could be damaged. Fill the reservoir with fluid, operate the pump and check for leaks.*

13   Rear window wiper motor – removal and installation

Refer to illustration 13.5 and 13.13

Two- and four-door models

1   Raise the wiper arm off the rear window. Pull the slide latch and remove the wiper arm from the shaft.
2   Remove the pivot shaft nuts and spacers.
3   Remove the liftgate trim screws and remove the inner trim panel.
4   Disconnect the motor electrical connectors.
5   Remove the three screws securing the retaining bracket to the door inner panel **(see illustration)**.
6   Remove the motor and linkage as an assembly.
7   Installation is the reverse of removal with the following additions.
8   Operate the wiper prior to installing the inner trim panel.

Station wagon models

9   Raise the wiper arm off the rear window. Pull the slide latch and remove the wiper arm from the shaft.
10   Remove the pivot shaft nuts and spacers.
11   Remove the screws securing the license plate housing.
12   Disconnect the license plate electrical connector and remove the license plate housing.
13   Remove the screws that secure the motor and linkage to the door **(see illustration)**.
14   Remove the motor and linkage as an assembly.
15   Installation is the reverse of removal.
16   Operate the wiper prior to installing the license plate housing.

14   Rear window washer reservoir and pump motor – removal and installation

Refer to illustrations 14.2 and 14.3

1   On two- and four-door models, remove the left hand quarter trim panel. On station wagon models, remove the right hand quarter trim panel.

12

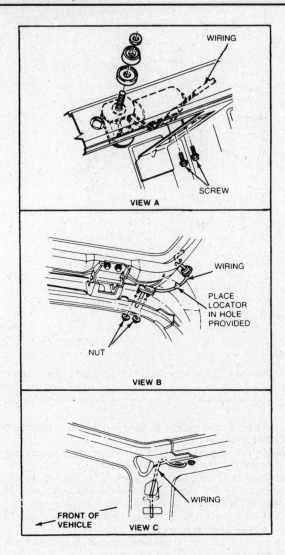

VIEW A

WIRING
SCREW

VIEW B

WIRING
PLACE
LOCATOR
IN HOLE
PROVIDED
NUT

VIEW C

FRONT OF
VEHICLE
WIRING

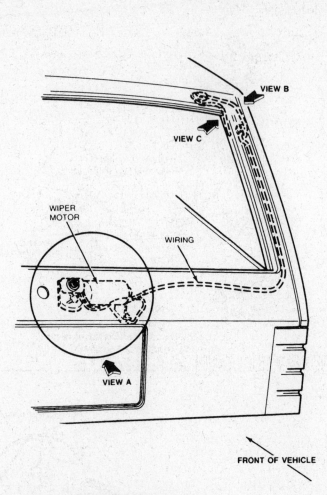

VIEW B

VIEW C

WIPER MOTOR

WIRING

VIEW A

FRONT OF VEHICLE

**13.13   Rear window wiper motor layout
(station wagon models)**

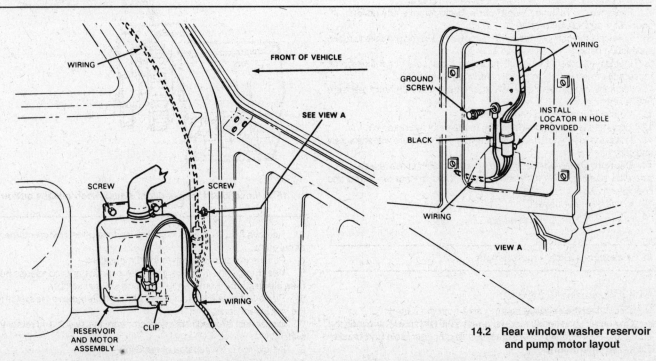

WIRING

FRONT OF VEHICLE

SEE VIEW A

SCREW

SCREW

WIRING

RESERVOIR
AND MOTOR
ASSEMBLY

CLIP

GROUND
SCREW

WIRING

BLACK

INSTALL
LOCATOR IN HOLE
PROVIDED

WIRING

VIEW A

**14.2   Rear window washer reservoir
and pump motor layout**

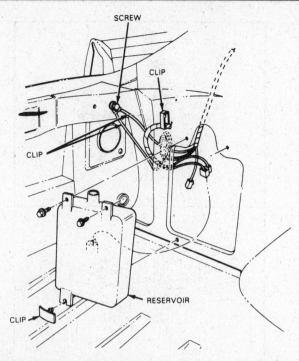

14.3   Rear window washer reservoir and pump motor removal

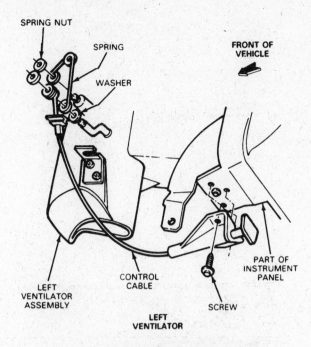

15.2   Left ventilator cable and bracket removal (non-air-conditioned models)

2   Remove the screws and clip securing the reservoir to the inner body panel **(see illustration)**.
3   Partially withdraw the reservoir from the inner body panel and disconnect the electrical connectors **(see illustration)**.
4   Disconnect the small hose from the base of the reservoir. Place your finger over the end of the small hose fitting on the reservoir to prevent spilling the washer fluid in the interior area. Remove the reservoir.
5   Drain the washer fluid from the reservoir into a clean container. If the fluid is kept clean it can be reused.
6   Use a small screwdriver and carefully pry out the pump motor out of the reservoir receptacle. Remove the screen and seal.
7   Flush out the reservoir with clean water to remove any residue. Inspect it for any foreign matter.
8   Lubricate the outer surface of the seal with powered graphite to make installation easier.
9   Install the screen and install the pump motor seal into the reservoir receptacle. Push in until they are completely seated.
10   Align the motor with the reservoir and push it in with hand pressure until it seats.
11   Connect the electrical connectors.
12   Connect the hose to the fitting on the base of the reservoir.
13   Install the reservoir in the inner body panel and secure with the screw and clip.
14   **Caution:** *Do not operate the pump without fluid in the reservoir as it would be damaged. Fill the reservoir with fluid, operate the pump and check for leaks.*
15   Install the inner panel.

15   Headlight switch – replacement

Refer to illustrations 15.2 and 15.5

1   Disconnect the negative battery cable from the battery.
2   On non-air conditioned models, remove the two screws securing the left-hand air vent control cable bracket and drop the cable and bracket down **(see illustration)**.

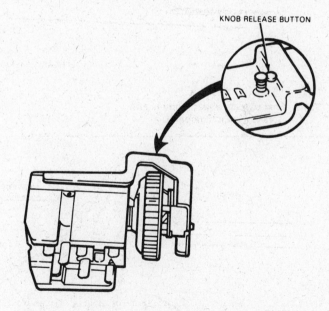

15.5   Location of the headlight switch knob release button

3   Remove the two screws securing the fuse panel and move the fuse panel aside.
4   Pull the headlamp switch to the On position.
5   Reach under the instrument panel and press the knob release button **(see illustration)**. Remove the knob and shaft assembly.
6   Remove the switch retaining nut and partially remove the switch from the instrument panel.
7   Disconnect the electrical connector from the switch and remove the switch.
8   Installation is the reverse of removal.

12

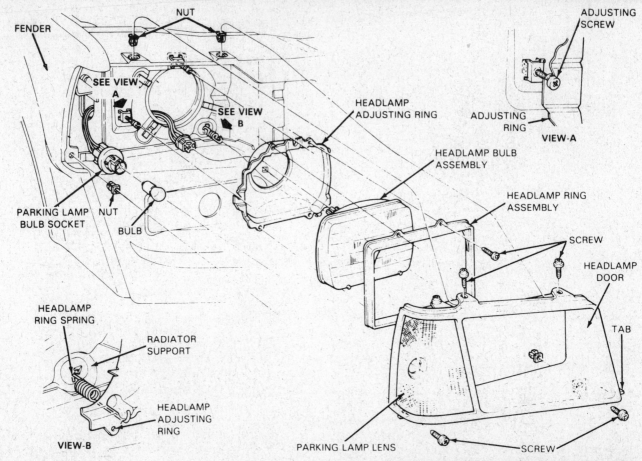

16.2   Sealed beam headlight and parking light details

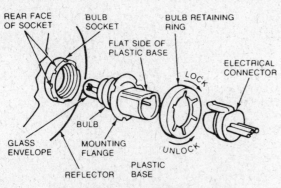

16.11   Halogen headlight bulb details

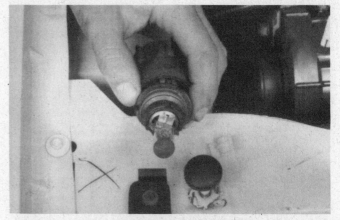

16.12   Carefully pull the halogen bulb straight out of the socket

16   Headlights – removal and installation

1   Disconnect the negative battery cable from the battery.

Sealed beam headlights

Refer to illustration 16.2

2   Remove the headlight bezel screws and remove the bezel **(see illustration)**.

3   Remove the headlight retaining screws, taking care not to disturb the adjustment screws.

4   Remove the retainer and pull the headlight out enough to disconnect the electrical connector.

5   Remove the headlight.

6   To install the headlight, plug in the electrical connector, place the headlight in position and install the retainer and screws.

7   Place the headlight bezel in position and install the retaining screws.

8   Have the headlights adjusted by a dealer service department or service station at the earliest opportunity.

Halogen bulb type

Refer to illustrations 16.11 and 16.12

Warning: *Halogen gas filled bulbs are under pressure and may shatter if the surface is scratched or the bulb is dropped. Wear eye protection and handle the bulbs carefully, grasping only the base whenever possible. Do not touch the surface of the bulb with your fingers because the oil from your skin could cause the bulb to overheat and fail prematurely. If you do touch the bulb surface, clean it with rubbing alcohol.*

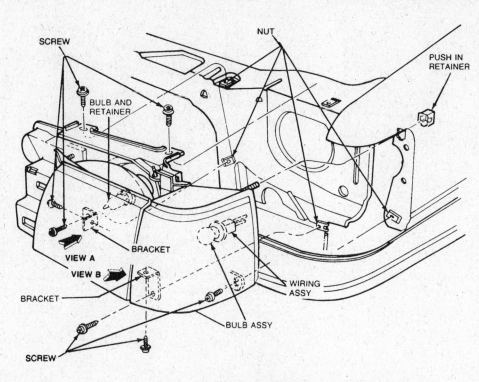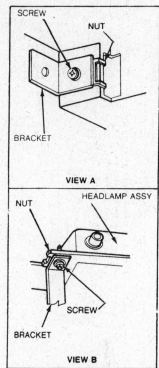

18.5 Parking/turn signal light (1989 and 1990 models)

9 Open the hood.
10 Disconnect the electrical connector from the back of the bulb.
11 Rotate the retaining ring about 1/8-turn counterclockwise (viewed from the rear) and slide it off the base **(see illustration)**.
12 Carefully pull the bulb straight out of the socket **(see illustration)**.
13 Insert the bulb into the socket. Position the flat on the plastic base upward.
14 Align the socket locating tabs with the grooves in the forward part of the plastic base, then push the socket firmly into the base. Make sure the base mounting flange contacts the socket.
15 Slide the retaining ring on. Turn it clockwise until it hits the stop.
16 Plug in the electrical connector. Test headlight operation, then close the hood.
17 Have the headlights adjusted by a dealer service department or service station at the earliest opportunity.

17 Headlights – adjusting

Note: *The headlights must be aimed correctly. If adjusted incorrectly they could blind the driver of an oncoming vehicle and cause a serious accident or seriously reduce your ability to see the road. The headlights should be checked for proper aim every 12 months and any time a new headlight is installed or front end body work is performed. It should be emphasized that the following procedure is only an interim step which will provide temporary adjustment until the headlights can be adjusted by a properly equipped shop.*

1 Headlights have two spring loaded adjusting screws, one on the top controlling up-and-down movement and one on the side controlling left-and-right movement.
2 There are several methods of adjusting the headlights. The simplest method requires a blank wall 25 feet in front of the vehicle and a level floor.
3 Position masking tape vertically on the wall in reference to the vehicle centerline and the centerline of both headlights.
4 Position a horizontal line in reference to the centerline of all headlights. **Note:** *It may be easier to position the tape on the wall with the vehicle parked only a few inches away.*

5 Adjustment should be made with the vehicle sitting level, the gas tank half-full and no unusually heavy load in the vehicle.
6 Starting with the low beam adjustment, position the high intensity zone so it is two inches below the horizontal line and two inches to the right of the headlight vertical line. Adjustment is made by turning the top adjusting screw clockwise to raise the beam and counterclockwise to lower the beam. The adjusting screw on the side should be used in the same manner to move the beam left or right.
7 With the high beams on, the high intensity zone should be vertically centered with the exact center just below the horizontal line. **Note:** *It may not be possible to position the headlight aim exactly for both high and low beams. If a compromise must be made, keep in mind that the low beams are the most used and have the greatest effect on safety.*
8 Have the headlights adjusted by a dealer service department or service station at the earliest opportunity.

18 Bulb replacement

Parking/turn signal light

1981 through 1988 models
1 Remove the headlight door and parking lamp lens assembly **(see illustration 16.2)**.
2 Turn the parking lamp bulb socket counterclockwise and remove from the headlight door.
3 Push the bulb inward, turn it counterclockwise and remove it.
4 Installation is the reverse of removal.

1989 and later models
Refer to illustration 18.5
5 Remove the two lower and one upper screws securing the parking light to the headlight **(see illustration)**.
6 Hold the parking lamp housing with both hands and pull the assembly forward to release the assembly from the hidden retainer.
7 Turn the parking lamp bulb socket counterclockwise and remove from the parking lamp assembly.

12

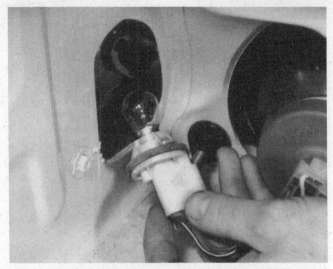

18.10   The front side marker socket is accessible through the fender from the engine compartment

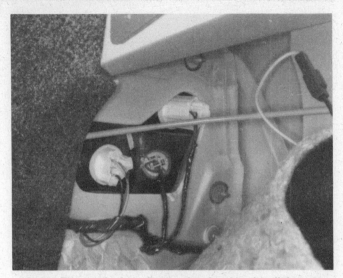

18.13   The rear brake, tail, turn signal and backup lights are accessible through the opening in the rear storage area (two- and four-door models)

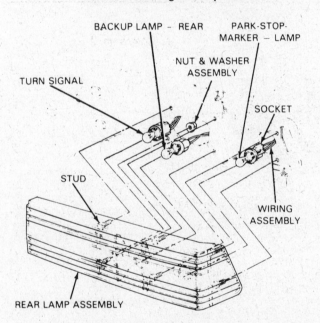

18.14a   Rear combination lights (brake, tail and turn signal) bulb locations – two- and four-door models (1981 through 1988 models)

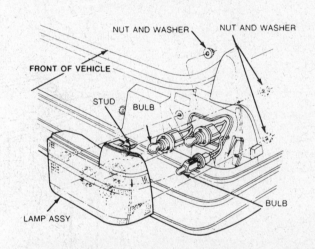

18.14b   Rear combination lights (brake, tail and turn signal) bulb locations – two- and 4-door models (1989 and later models)

8   Push the bulb inward, turn it counterclockwise and remove it.
9   Installation is the reverse of removal.

Front side marker light

Refer to illustration 18.10

10   From inside the engine compartment, twist the bulb socket and remove it from the fender **(see illustration)**.
11   Push in on the bulb and turn counterclockwise and then pull the bulb out of the socket, then reverse the procedure to install a new bulb.
12   Install the socket in the fender.

Rear combination lights (brake, tail and turn signal)

Two- and four-door models

Refer to illustrations 18.13, 18.14a, 18.14b and 18.15

13   The various lamps are all accessible from inside the rear compartment. Remove any necessary interior trim panels to gain access to the backside of the combination light assembly **(see illustration)**.

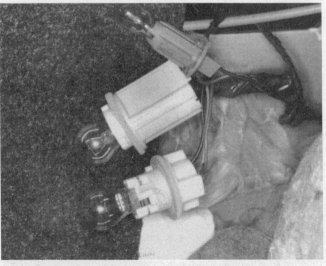

18.15   Rear combination lights (brake, tail and turn signal) bulb removal details

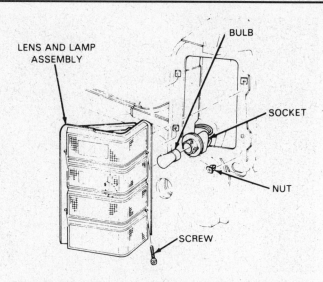

18.18   Rear combination light details – station wagon models

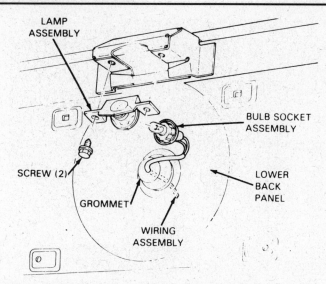

18.22   Rear license plate light details (Two and four-door models)

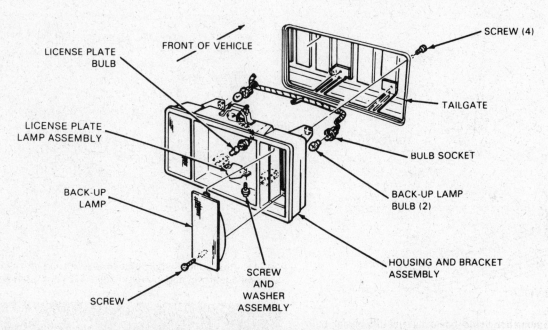

18.24   Rear license plate light and back-up light details (station wagon models)

14   Twist the bulb socket and remove it from the combination light assembly **(see illustrations)**.

15   To remove a bulb, either push in on the bulb and turn counterclockwise and then pull the bulb out of the socket, or pull it straight out (depending on bulb type). Reverse the procedure to install a new bulb **(see illustration)**.

16   Install the socket in the combination light assembly.

Station wagon models

Refer to illustration 18.18

17   The various lamps are all accessible from inside the rear compartment. Remove any necessary interior trim panels to gain access to the backside of the combination light assembly.

18   Twist the bulb socket and remove it from the combination light assembly **(see illustration)**.

19   Push in on the bulb, turn it counterclockwise and pull it out of the socket, then reverse the procedure to install a new bulb.

20   Install the socket in the combination light assembly.

License plate light

Refer to illustration 18.22

21   Remove the screws securing the licence plate bulb socket assembly and pull the assembly away from the body.

22   Push in on the bulb and turn counterclockwise and then pull the bulb out of the socket, then reverse the procedure to install a new bulb **(see illustration)**.

Back-up light

Refer to illustration 18.24

23   On two- and four-door models, perform Steps 17 through 20 of this Section.

24   On station wagon models, perform the following:

  a)   Remove the screw securing the lens assembly and remove it from the housing **(see illustration)**.

  b)   Pull the bulb and socket from the lens assembly, remove the bulb and install the bulb/socket assembly.

  c)   Install the lens assembly and screw.

12

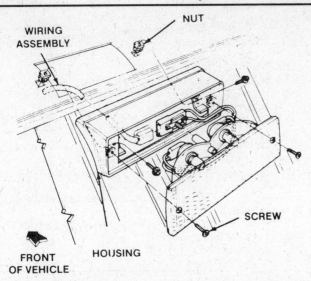

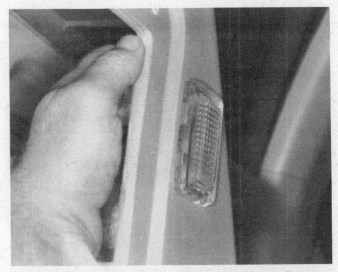

18.25a   High-mount brake light details (two- and four-door models)   **18.25b   High-mount brake light details (station wagon models)**

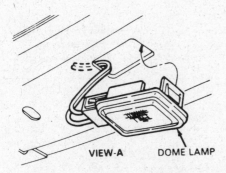

18.28a   Dome light removal details

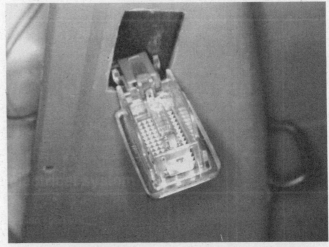

18.28b   Push the cargo light assembly out with your fingers from the backside

High-mount brake light

Refer to illustrations 18.25a and 18.25b

25   Remove the two retaining screws and remove the lens assembly **(see illustrations)**.

26   Grasp the bulb and pull it from the socket. Install a new bulb.

27   Install the lens assembly and screws.

Dome light and/or cargo light

Refer to illustrations 18.28a, 18.28b and 18.29

28   Grasp the right-hand side of the dome light lens and pull the assembly downward **(see illustration)** or push it out from the backside **(see illustration)**.

29   **Caution:** *Wear eye protection during bulb removal. Use needle-nose pliers and carefully pull the bulb from the lens assembly. Do not break the bulb during removal* **(see illustration)**.

30   Install a new bulb and press it in all the way, then install the dome light lens assembly.

Transaxle shift indicator light

Refer to illustration 18.33

31   On floor-mounted control, remove the screw securing the console cover and remove the cover.

32   Remove the selector cover and dial indicator.

33   Lift the cover assembly off and turn the bulb socket counterclockwise and remove it **(see illustration)**.

34   Install a new bulb, install the socket and parts removed.

35   On console mounted control, remove the finish panel and quadrant bezel. Move the selector lever to its first position.

18.29   Carefully pull the bulb from the lens assembly (do not break the bulb during removal)

36 Remove the bulb/socket assembly and remove the bulb.
37 Install a new bulb, then install the socket and parts removed.

Glove-box light
38 Open the glove box door.
39 Grasp the bulb with your thumb and forefinger and pull it out of the lock striker assembly.
40 Install a new bulb.

Instrument cluster lights
Refer to illustration 18.43
41 Remove the instrument cluster to gain access to the bulbs (see Section 20).
42 On some models it is necessary to remove the printed circuit board (see Section 21).
43 Carefully pull the bulb/socket assembly from the backside of the instrument cluster **(see illustration)**.

19   Radio – removal and installation

Refer to illustrations 19.4 and 19.10
1981 through 1983 models
1 Disconnect the negative battery cable from the battery.
2 Remove the air conditioner floor duct (if equipped).
3 Disconnect the power, speaker and antenna wires from the radio.

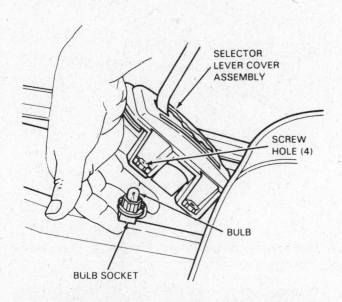

18.33   Transaxle shift indicator bulb removal

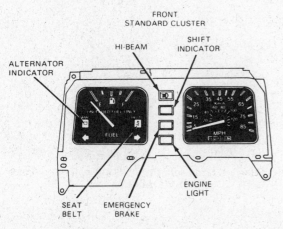

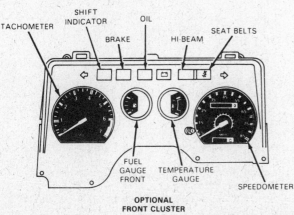

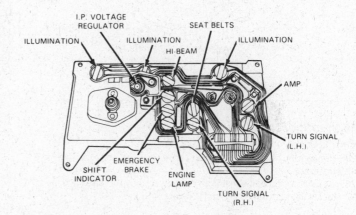

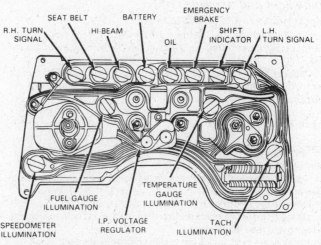

18.43   Locations of the instrument cluster illumination bulbs

12

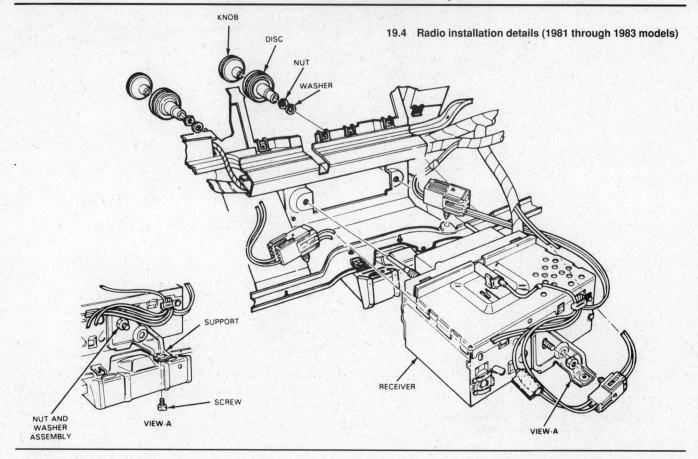

19.4   Radio installation details (1981 through 1983 models)

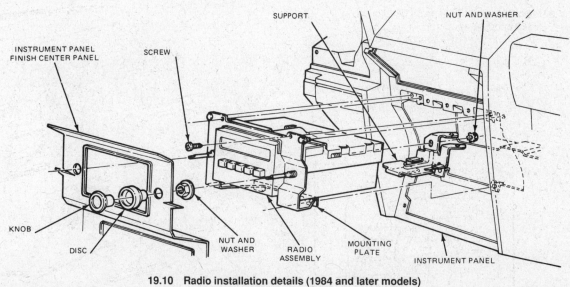

19.10   Radio installation details (1984 and later models)

4   Remove the control knobs, discs, radio retaining nuts and washers **(see illustration)**.
5   Remove the ash tray and bracket.
6   Remove the screw securing the radio to the support bracket.
7   Carefully slide the radio assembly forward in the vehicle. Tip the rear of the radio assembly down and remove it from the instrument panel.
8   Installation is the reverse of removal.

1984 and later models

9   Disconnect the negative battery cable from the battery.

10   Remove the control knobs and discs **(see illustration)**.
11   Remove the instrument panel center finish panel.
12   Remove the screws securing the radio mounting plate to the instrument panel.
13   Partially pull the radio assembly out of the instrument panel disengaging it from the lower support.
14   Disconnect the power, speaker and antenna wires from the radio, then remove the radio assembly.
15   If necessary, remove the control shaft nuts securing the mounting plate to the radio and remove the plate.
16   Installation is the reverse of the removal procedure.

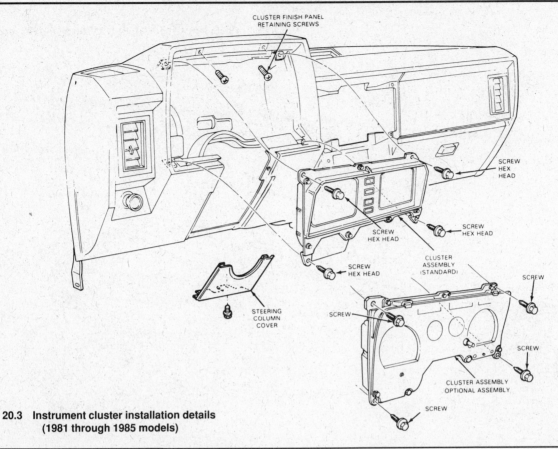

**20.3 Instrument cluster installation details
(1981 through 1985 models)**

**20.10 Instrument cluster finish panel details
(1986 and later models)**

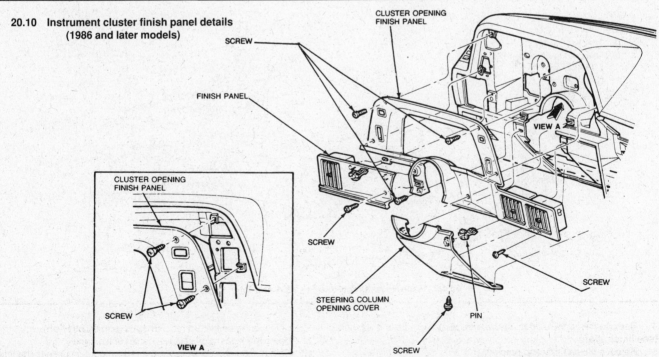

20 Instrument cluster – removal and installation

Refer to illustrations 20.3, 20.10 and 20.11

1981 through 1985 models

1 Disconnect the negative battery cable from the battery.

2 Remove the two retaining screws the bottom of the steering column opening and snap the steering column cover out and remove it.

3 Remove the four screws securing the cluster opening finish panel and remove the panel (**see illustration**).

4 Remove the two upper and two lower screws securing the cluster to the instrument panel.

5 Reach under the instrument panel, press on the flat portion of the

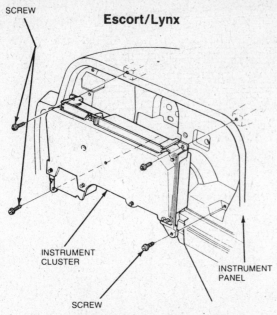

Escort/Lynx

SCREW

SCREW

INSTRUMENT
CLUSTER

INSTRUMENT
PANEL

SCREW

**20.11   Instrument cluster mounting details
(1986 and later models)**

quick-disconnect plastic connector and detach the speedometer cable
from the instrument cluster.
6   Pull the instrument cluster partially out and disconnect its electrical
connectors. Remove the cluster.
7   Installation is the reverse of the removal procedure.

1986 and later models

8   Disconnect the negative battery cable from the battery.
9   Remove the two retaining screws at the bottom of the steering column
opening and snap the steering column cover out and remove it.
10   Remove the ten screws securing the cluster opening finish panels
and remove the panels **(see illustration)**.
11   Remove the two upper and two lower screws securing the cluster to
the instrument panel **(see illustration)**.
12   Reach under the instrument panel, press on the flat portion of the
quick-disconnect plastic connector and detach the speedometer cable
from the instrument cluster.
13   Pull the instrument cluster partially out and disconnect its electrical
connectors. Remove the cluster.
14   Installation is the reverse of the removal procedure.

---

21   Instrument cluster printed circuit board – removal and installation

Caution: *The printed circuit board contains the "electrical wiring" of the
instrument panel and is very fragile. Do not handle the panel any more
than necessary to avoid any possible damage that could lead to premature
component replacement.*

1   Remove the instrument cluster (see Section 20).
2   Carefully unsnap the printed circuit board from the Instrument Voltage
Regulator (IVR). Remove the screw securing the IVR and remove it.
3   Remove the illumination and indicator bulb and socket assemblies
(see illustration 18.43).
4   On models so equipped, remove the screws securing the instrument
cluster resistor and remove the resistor.
5   Remove the nuts securing the fuel gauge, temperature gauge, am-
meter/or tachometer.
6   Remove the printed circuit board from the locating pins.
7   Installation is the reverse of the removal procedure.

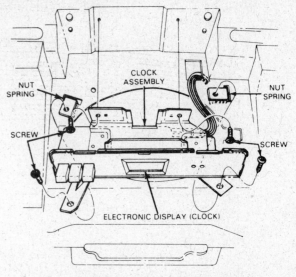

22.3   Digital clock removal and installation

22   Digital clock – removal and installation

Refer to illustration 22.3
1   Disconnect the negative battery cable from the battery.
2   Remove the radio speaker and grille.
3   Remove the four mounting screws, partially remove the clock and disconnect the electrical connector **(see illustration)**. Remove the clock.
4   To install, position the clock, attach the electrical connector and install
the four screws.
5   Connect the negative battery cable.
6   Reset the clock.

---

23   Speedometer cable – removal and installation

1   Disconnect the negative battery cable from the battery.
2   Reach under the instrument panel, press on the flat portion of the
quick-disconnect plastic connector and detach the speedometer cable
from the speedometer head.
3   From the upper end of the cable casing, pull out the speedometer
cable core. Models equipped with a speed sensor have an upper and lower cable.
4   If the speedometer core is broken, it is necessary to disconnect the
lower end of the cable casing from the transaxle and remove the broken
piece of core from the casing.
5   To install, insert the core into the speedometer casing from the speedometer head end.
6   Connect the speedometer casing to the head and (if removed) install
the hex nut securing the casing to the transaxle.
7   Connect the negative battery cable.

---

24   Speedometer head – removal and installation

1   Disconnect the negative battery cable from the battery.
2   Disconnect the speedometer cable and remove the instrument cluster (see Section 20).
3   Remove the lens assembly from the instrument cluster.
4   Remove the gauge assembly followed by the speedometer head assembly, from the instrument cluster backplate.
5   Install the speedometer head assembly into the instrument cluster
backplate followed by the gauge assembly.
6   Install the lens assembly into the instrument cluster.
7   Reinstall the instrument cluster assembly (see Section 20).

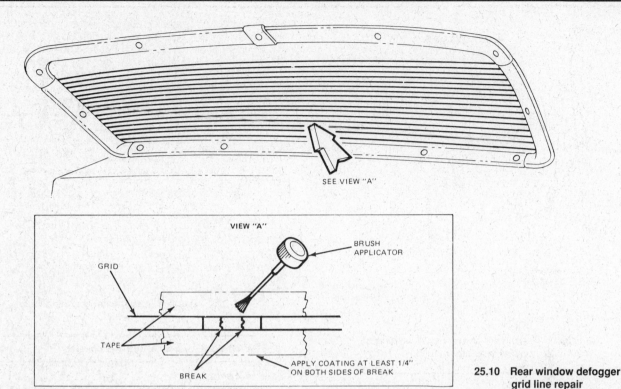

SEE VIEW "A"

VIEW "A"

BRUSH APPLICATOR

GRID

TAPE

BREAK

APPLY COATING AT LEAST 1/4"
ON BOTH SIDES OF BREAK

25.10   Rear window defogger
grid line repair

8   Connect the speedometer cable.
9   Connect the battery negative cable.

25   Rear window defogger – check and repair

Refer to illustration 25.10 and 25.20

The rear window defogger consists of a rear window with a number of horizontal elements that are baked onto the inner glass surface. Small breaks in the element can be repaired without removing the rear window.

Defogger grid repair

1   Place a strong inspection light in the interior and direct it against the rear window.
2   Visually inspect the wire grid from outside the vehicle. A broken grid wire will appear as a brown spot.
3   Start the engine and allow it to idle. Turn the defogger switch on. The indicator light should come on, indicating the system is operating.
4   Mark the broken area(s) on the outer surface of the glass with a grease pencil or piece of masking tape. Turn the inspection light off.
5   Working inside the vehicle with a voltmeter, contact the broad red-brown strips (buss bars) on each side of the rear window. The meter should read 10-to-13 volts. A lower reading indicates a loose ground wire (pigtail) connection at the ground side of the glass.
6   Contact a good ground point with the negative lead of the test meter. The voltage should not change.
7   With the negative lead of the meter grounded, touch each grid line of the heated rear window at its midpoint with the positive test lead:
  a) A reading of approximately six-volts indicates that the grid line is good.
  b) A reading of 0-volts indicates that the grid line is broken between the mid-point and the positive side of the grid line.
  c) A reading of 12-volts indicates that the circuit is broken between the mid-point of the grid wire and ground.

Grid line repair

Note: *Any break in the grid wire longer than one inch cannot be repaired. The rear window must be replaced. For breaks less than one inch in length, use the following procedure. You will need to obtain grid repair compound and brown touch-up paint from a Ford dealer.*

8   Place the vehicle in a garage or out of direct sunlight. Allow the vehicle to reach ambient temperature, which should be 60-degrees or above.
9   Clean the entire grid line repair area with glass cleaner or a suitable non-petroleum based cleaning solvent. Remove all dirt, wax, grease, oil or other foreign matter. The repair area must be clean, grease-free and dry.
10   Using cellulose tape, mask off the area directly above and below the grid break. The break area should be at the center of the mask and the tape gap must no wider than the existing grid line **(see illustration)**.
11   If both the brown and silver layers of the grid are broken or missing, apply a coating of the brown touch-up paint across the break area first. Two coats may be necessary to obtain the proper color. Allow the touch-up paint to thoroughly dry.
12   Apply three coats of the silver grid repair compound. Allow three to five minutes drying time between coats. The coating of the silver grid repair compound should extend at least 1/4-inch on both sides of the break. **Note:** *If the brown layer of the grid is not broken or missing, apply only the silver grid compound to the break. Allow the compound to dry for five minutes, then remove the mask.*
13   After removing the mask, check the outside appearance of the grid repair. If the silver repair compound is visible above or below the grid, the excess should be removed. Use a single edge razor blade on the glass parallel to the grid and scrape gently toward the grid. **Caution:** *Be careful not to damage the grid line with the razor blade.*
14   The repair coating will air dry in about one minute and can be energized within three to five minutes. Optimum hardness and adhesion occurs after approximately 24 hours. At that time, the repair area may be cleaned with a mild window cleaner and a soft cloth.

Lead wire terminal service

15   Allow the rear window to warm up to room temperature for a half hour to an hour.
16   Clean the glass bar in the area to be repaired using fine steel wool (3/0 to 4/0 grade).
17   Restore the area where the bus bar terminal was originally attached by applying three coats of repair compound. Allow approximately ten minutes drying time between coats.

12

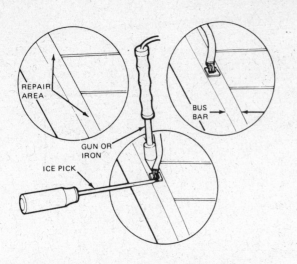

25.20   Position the terminal on the bus bar in the area that was tinned and hold it in place with an ice pick or screwdriver

18 Working as fast as possible to avoid overheating the glass, tin the bus bar with solder in the area where the terminal will be reattached.
19 Using a heat gun or heat lamp, pre-heat the glass in the solder area to between 120 and 150-degrees F just prior to soldering the terminal on.
20 Position the terminal on the bus bar in the area that was tinned and hold it in place with an ice pick or screwdriver **(see illustration)**.
21 Apply soldering heat to the pad on the terminal until the solder flows. **Note:** *To avoid damaging the bus bar, remove the soldering gun or iron as soon as the solder flows.*
22 Start the vehicle, turn the rear window defogger on and leave it on for five minutes. Then shut if off

---

26   Heater electrical components – check and replacement

Refer to illustrations 26.1a and 26.1b

Blower switch continuity check

1 Referring to the accompanying heater system electrical wiring diagrams **(see illustrations)**, check terminal continuity at every lever position:
 a) The test light should go on for each connected pair of terminals.
 b) There should be no continuity between any terminal and the switch case.

26.1a   Heater electrical components wiring diagram (1981 through 1983 models)

HEATER BLOWER SWITCH — 18578 —			
BLOWER SPEED	TERMINAL CONNECTIONS	CURRENT IN CAR (AMPS)	BLOWER VOLTAGE
LOW	L·B	2.2	5.6
MEDIUM	L·M·B	3.5	8.0
HIGH	M·H·B	6.5	12.8

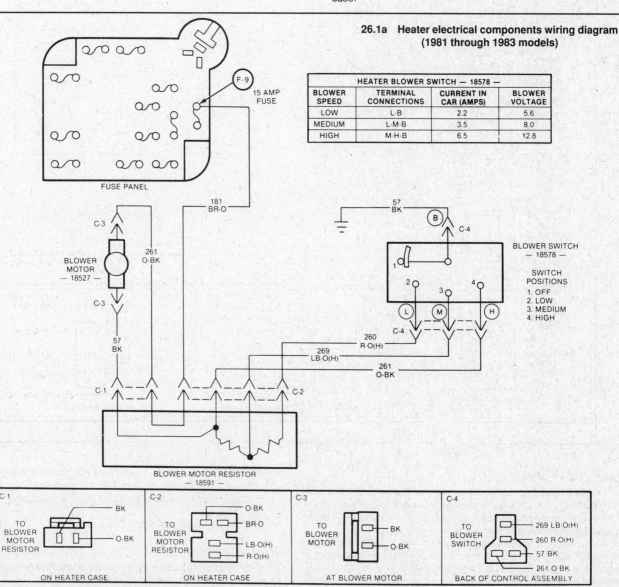

26.1b   Heater electrical components wiring diagram
(1984 and later models)

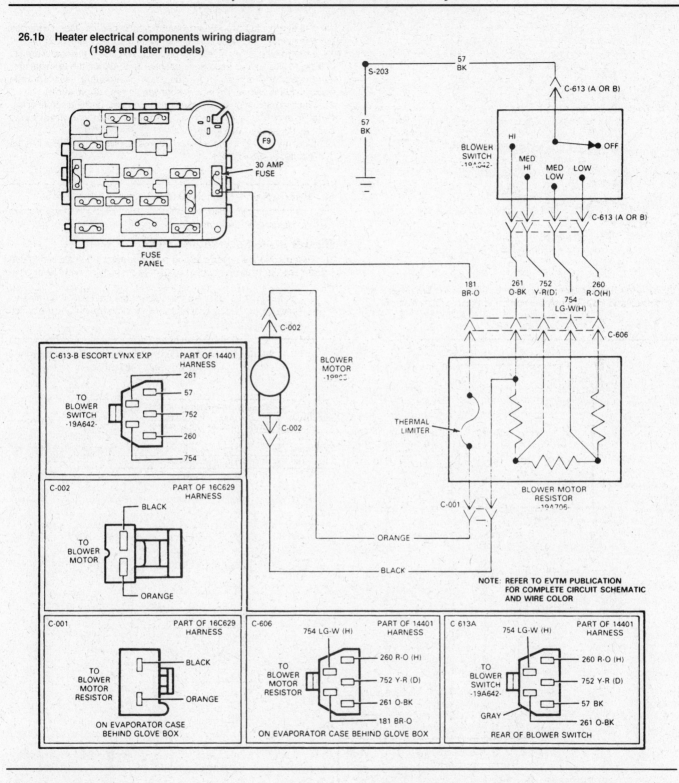

Open circuit check

2   On all electrical circuits, continuity must exist from the source of power (the battery) to the unit where the power is used, and back to ground. A check at each connection in a circuit, beginning at the battery, will locate an open circuit or will show that the circuit is complete.

3   An ohmmeter or self-powered test light connected at any two points of a circuit with the power removed from the circuit will show if the circuit between the two connections is open or complete:

a) If the meter does not move or has a light movement (high resis-

tance), the circuit may have a poor connection or broken wire.
b) If the test light does not light, the circuit is open
c) If the meter movement is great or full (low resistance), the circuit is complete.
d) If the test light lights, the circuit is complete.

Replacement

4   If the heater/air conditioning control assembly, blower motor or resistor require replacement, refer to Chapter 3.

12

27   Horn – testing, removal and installation

Refer to illustration 27.2

Testing

1   If the horn does not work, first check the fuse in the horn circuit.
2   If the fuse is in good condition, disconnect the electrical connectors from the horn. Connect jumpers wires from the battery positive and negative terminals to the horn **(see illustration)**.
3   If the horn does not work and there is no evidence of spark at the battery terminal, turn the adjustment screw 1/4 to 3/8 of a turn counterclockwise. After adjustment, secure the adjustment screw by clinching the housing extension against the screw with pliers.
4   If the horn does not sound after adjusting, replace with a new unit.

Removal and installation

5   Disconnect the battery negative cable from the battery.
6   Raise the front of the vehicle and place is securely on jackstands. Block the rear wheels so the vehicle will not roll in either direction.
7   The horn is either located on the right-hand shock absorber tower or in the front right-hand wheel well.
8   Disconnect the electrical connectors from the horn(s).
9   Remove the nut(s) securing the horn strap to the body panel and remove the horn(s).
10   Installation is the reverse of the removal procedure.

28   Power window system – description and check

The power window system operates the electric motors mounted in the doors which lower and raise the windows. The system consists of the control switches, the motors, glass mechanisms (regulators) and the associated wiring.
Because of the complexity of the power window system and the special tools and techniques required for diagnosis, repair should be left to a dealer service department or repair shop. However, it is possible for the home mechanic to make simple checks of the wiring connections and motors for minor faults which can be easily repaired. These are:
a) Inspect the power window actuating switches for broken wires and loose connections.
b) Check the power window fuse/and or circuit breaker.
c) Remove the door panel(s) and check the power window motor wires to see if they're loose or damaged. Inspect the glass mechanisms for damage which could cause binding.

29   Cruise control system – description and check

The cruise control system maintains vehicle speed with a vacuum actuated motor located in the engine compartment, which is connected to the throttle linkage by a cable. The system consists of the servo motor, clutch switch, brake switch, control switches, a relay and associated vacuum hoses.
Because of the complexity of the cruise control system and the special tools and techniques required for diagnosis, repair should be left to a dealer service department or repair shop. However, it is possible for the home

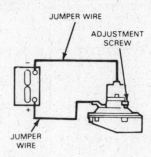

27.2   Using jumper wires, connect battery voltage to the horn – if it doesn't work, try turning the adjustment screw

mechanic to make simple checks of the wiring and vacuum connections for minor faults which can be easily repaired. These are:
a) Inspect the cruise control actuating switches for broken wires and loose connections.
b) Check the cruise control fuse.
c) The cruise control system is operated by vacuum so it's critical that all vacuum switches, hoses and connections are secure. Check the hoses in the engine compartment for tight connections, cracks and obvious vacuum leaks.

30   Wiring diagrams – general information

Since it isn't possible to include all wiring diagrams for every year and model covered in this manual, the following diagrams are those that are typical and most commonly needed.
Prior to troubleshooting any circuits, check the fuse and circuit breakers (if equipped) to make sure they're in good condition. Make sure the battery is properly charged and check the cable connections (see Chapter 1).
When checking a circuit, make sure that all connectors are clean, with no broken or loose terminals. When unplugging a connector, do not pull on the wires. Pull only on the connector housings themselves.
Refer to the accompanying table for the wire color codes applicable to your vehicle.

B	Black	P	Purple
BR	Brown	PK	Pink
DB	Dark blue	R	Red
DG	Dark green	T	Tan
GY	Gray	W	White
LB	Light blue	Y	Yellow
LG	Light green	(H)	Hash*
N	Natural	(D)	Dot*
O	Orange		

Note: *The presence of a tracer on the wire is indicated by a secondary color or followed by an "H" for hash or "D" for dot. A stripe is understood if no letter follows.*

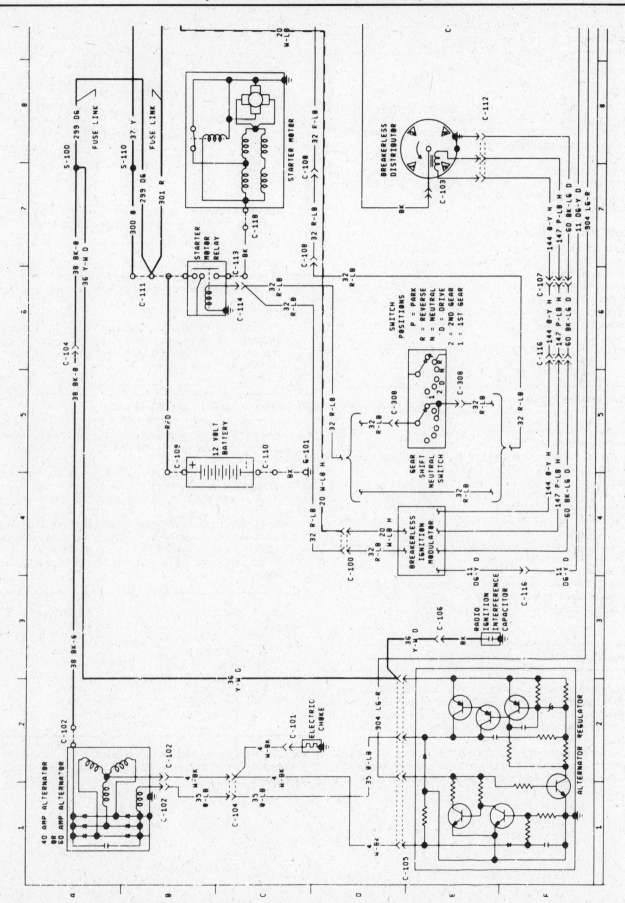

Wiring diagram, engine compartment, 1981 models (1982 similar)

12

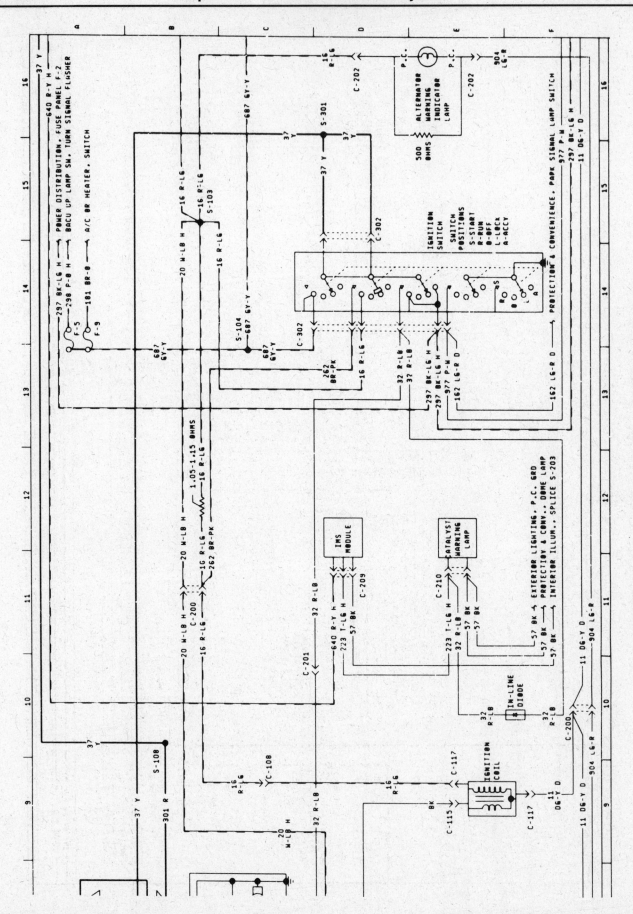

Wiring diagram, engine compartment (cont.), 1981 models (1982 similar)

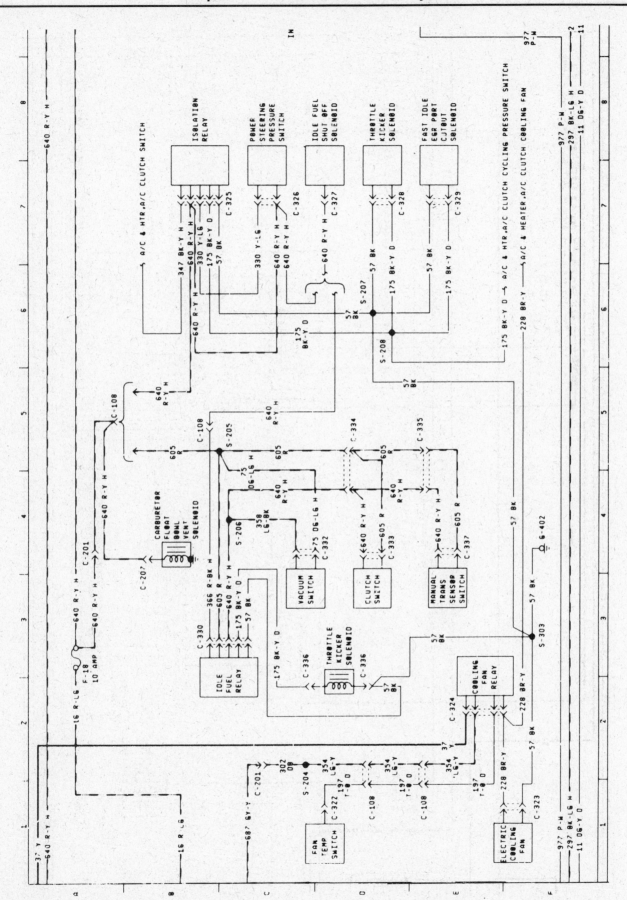

Wiring diagram, engine compartment (cont.), 1981 models (1982 similar)

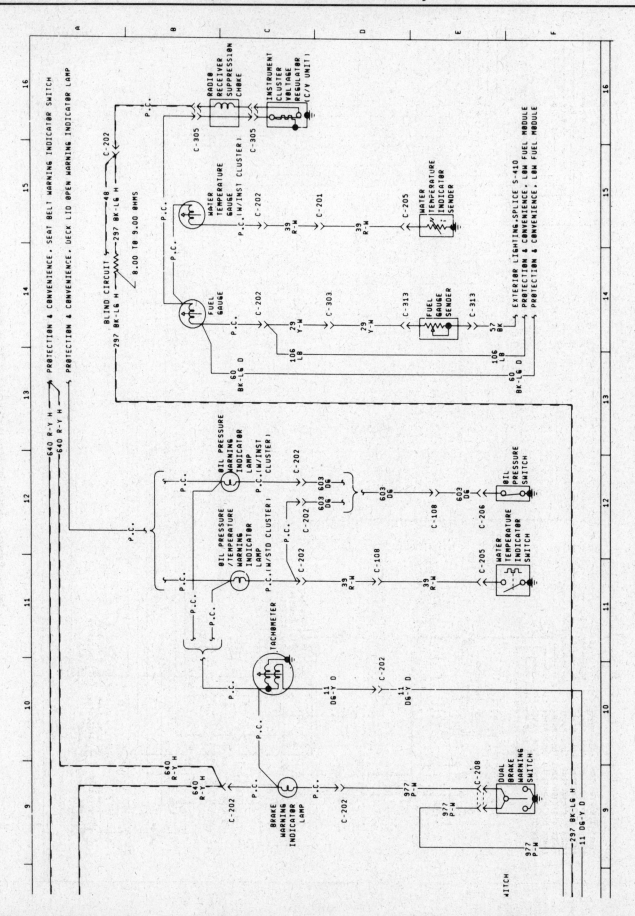

Wiring diagram, engine compartment (cont.), 1981 models (1982 similar)

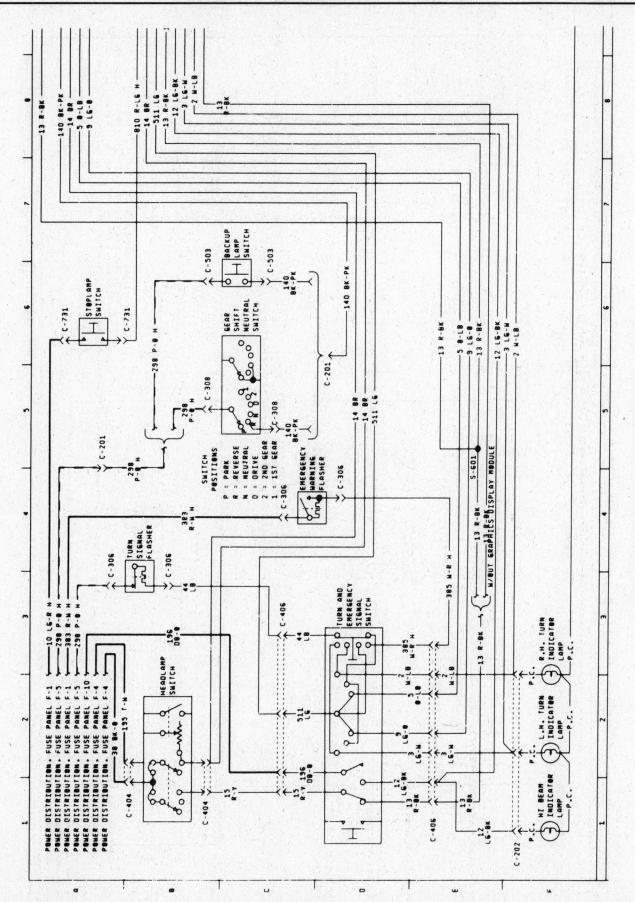

Wiring diagram, exterior lighting, 1981 models (1982 similar)

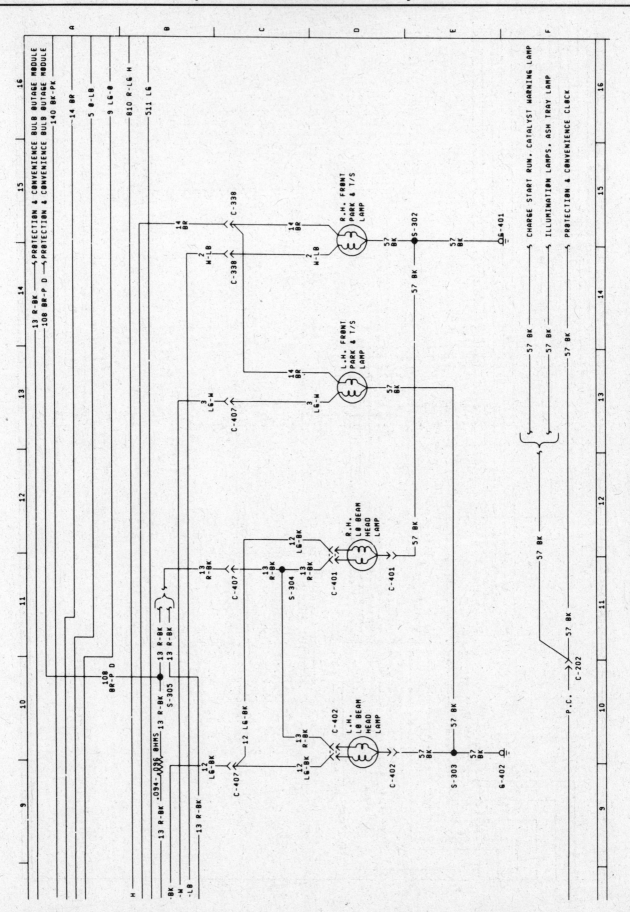

Wiring diagram, exterior lighting (cont.), 1981 models (1982 similar)

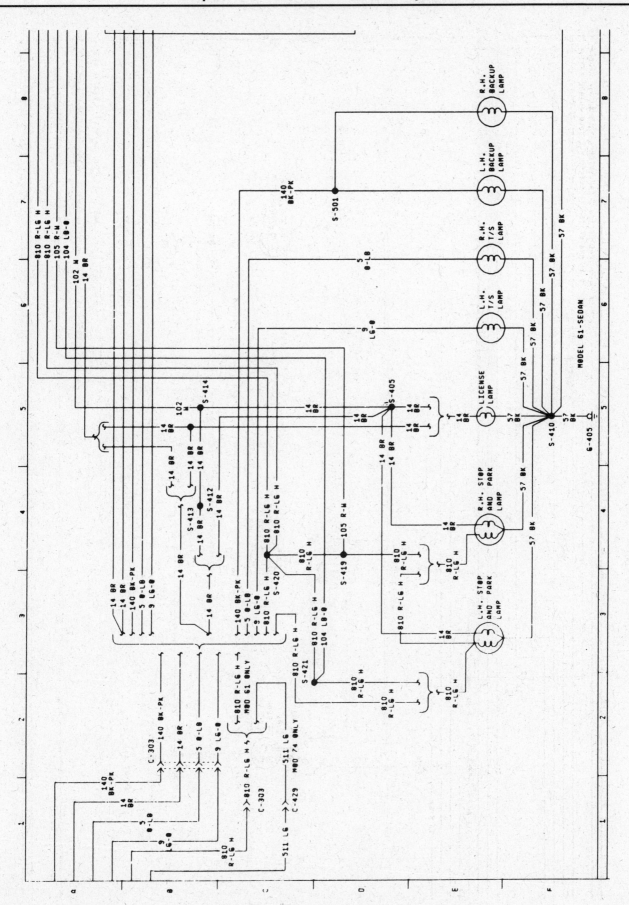

Wiring diagram, exterior lighting (cont.), 1981 models (1982 similar)

12

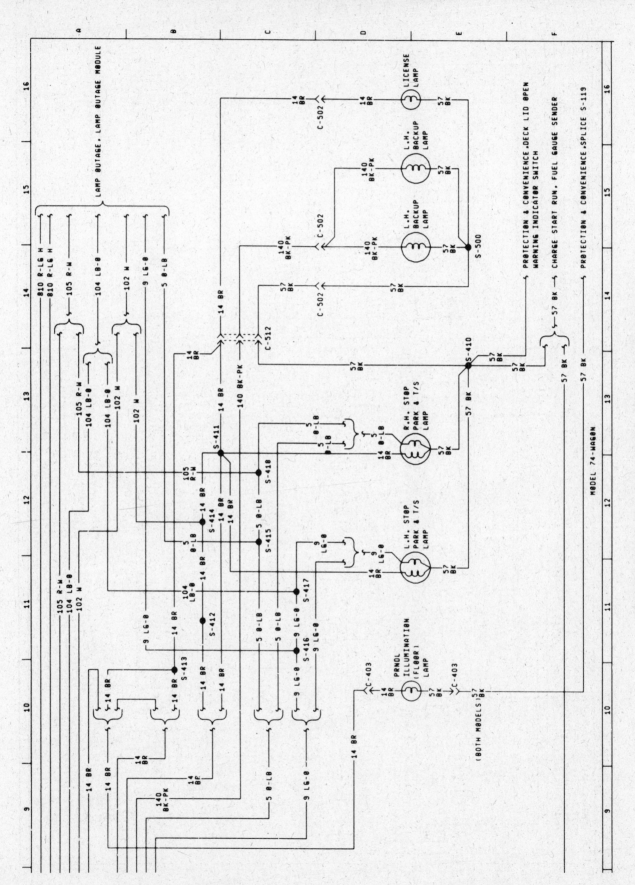

Wiring diagram, exterior lighting (cont.), 1981 models (1982 similar)

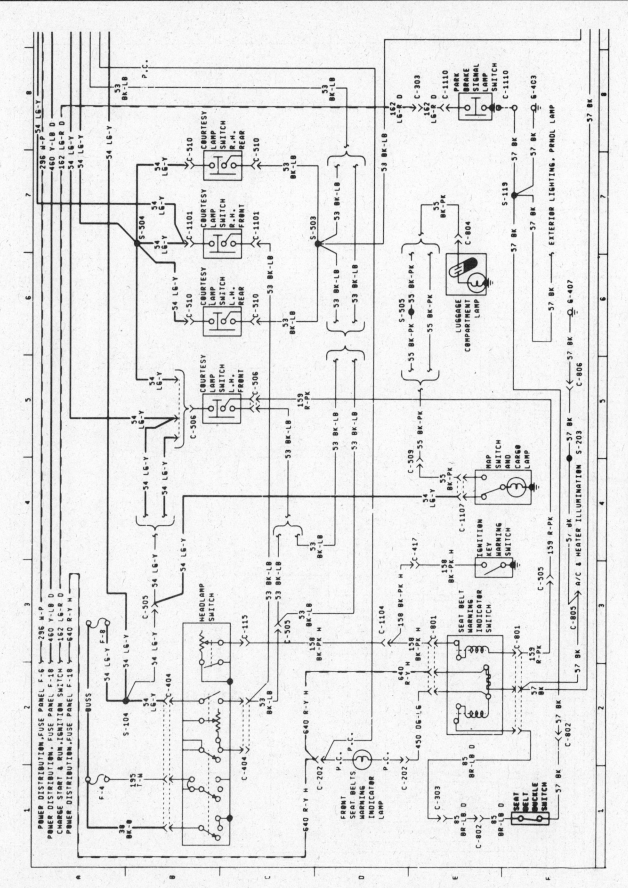

Wiring diagram, interior lighting, 1981 models (1982 similar)

12

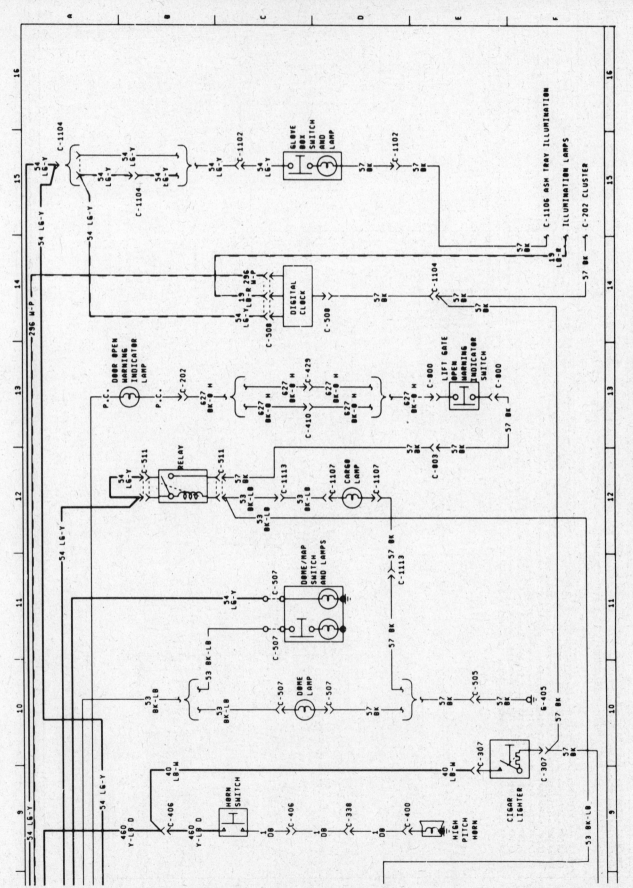

Wiring diagram, interior lighting (cont.), 1981 models (1982 similar)

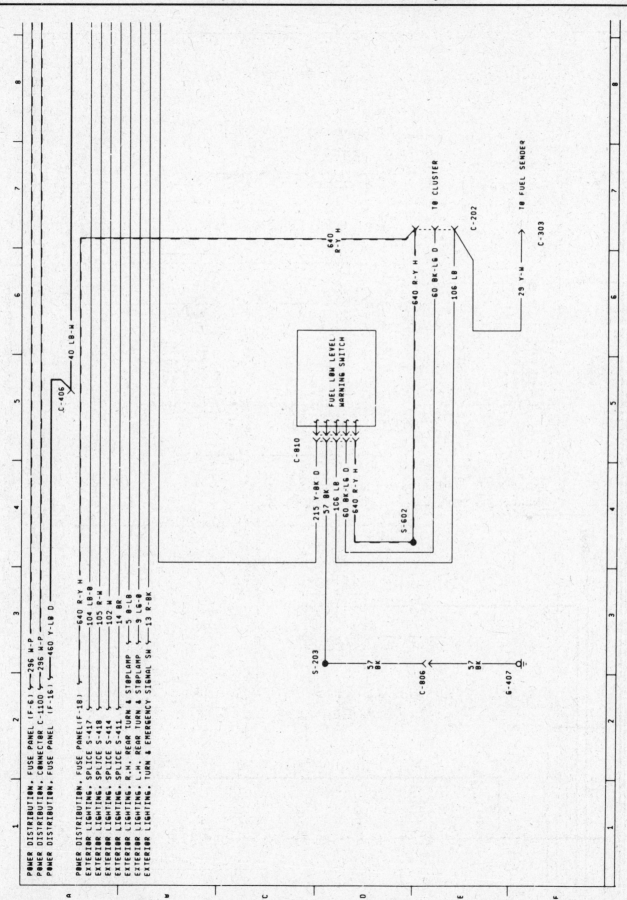

Wiring diagram, fuel level indicator, 1981 models (1982 similar)

12

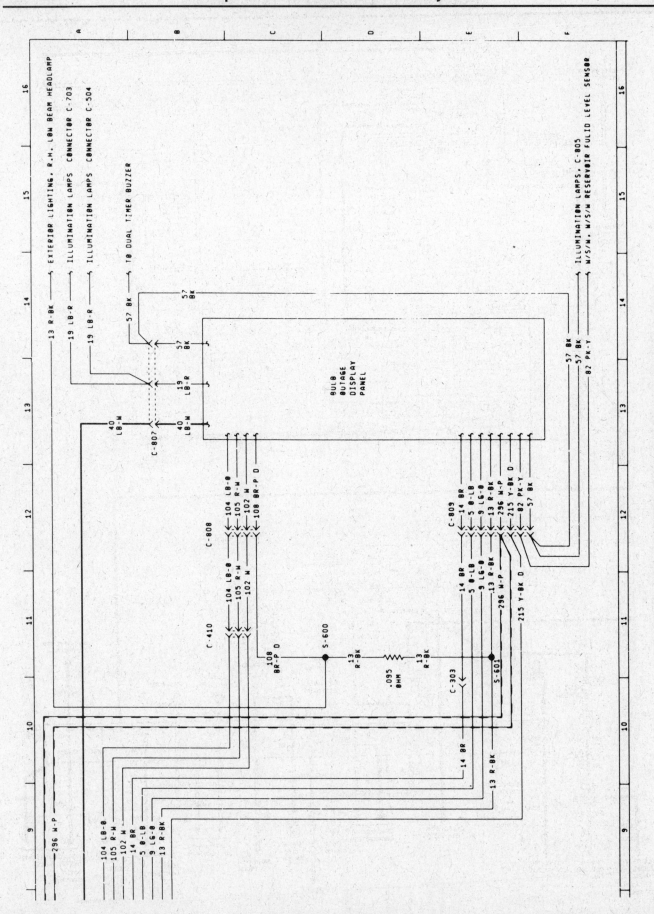

Wiring diagram, interior lighting (cont.), 1981 models (1982 similar)

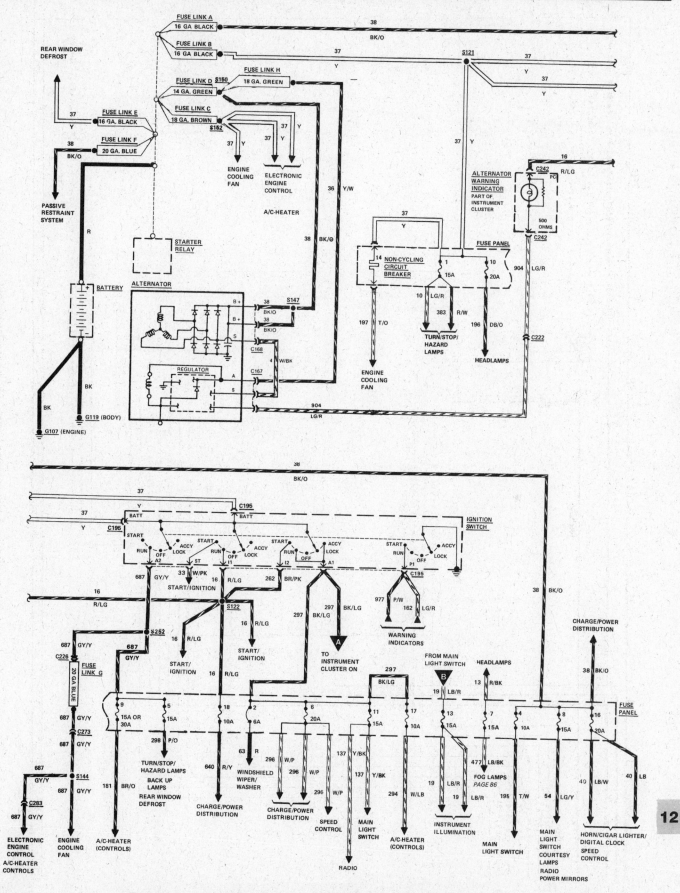

Typical charging system and power distribution wiring diagram (later models)

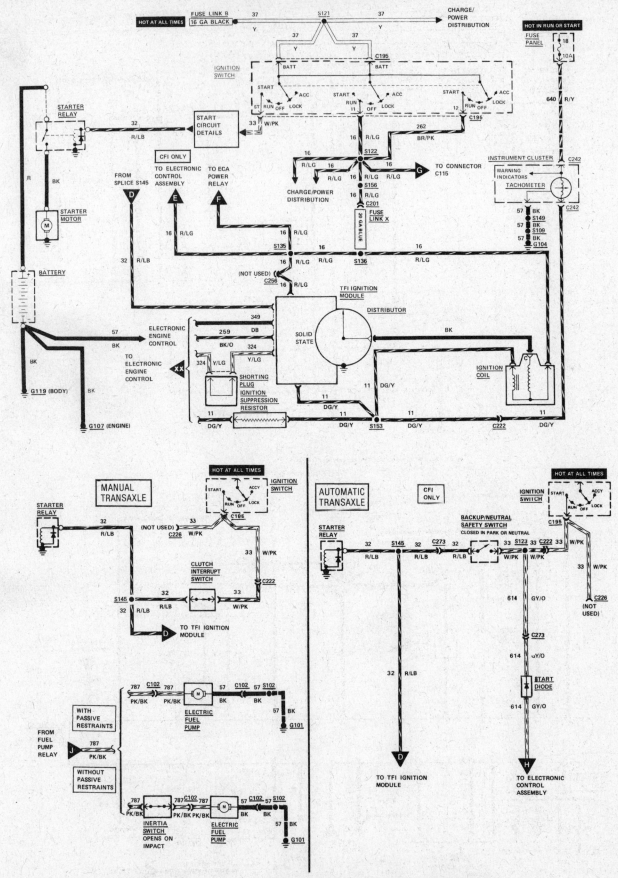

Typical starting system and ignition system wiring diagram (later models)

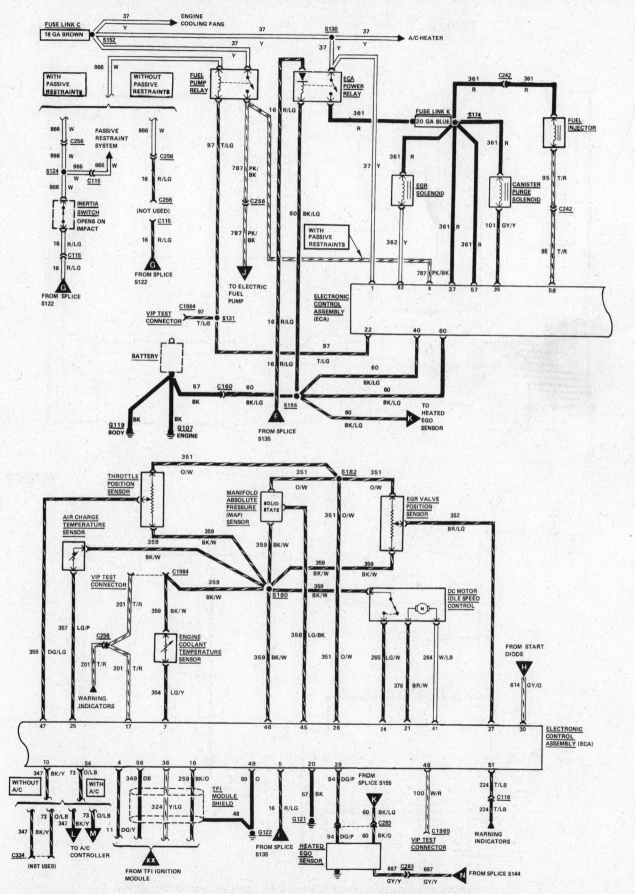

Typical Electronic Engine Control (EEC) system with Central Fuel Injection (CFI) wiring diagram (later models)

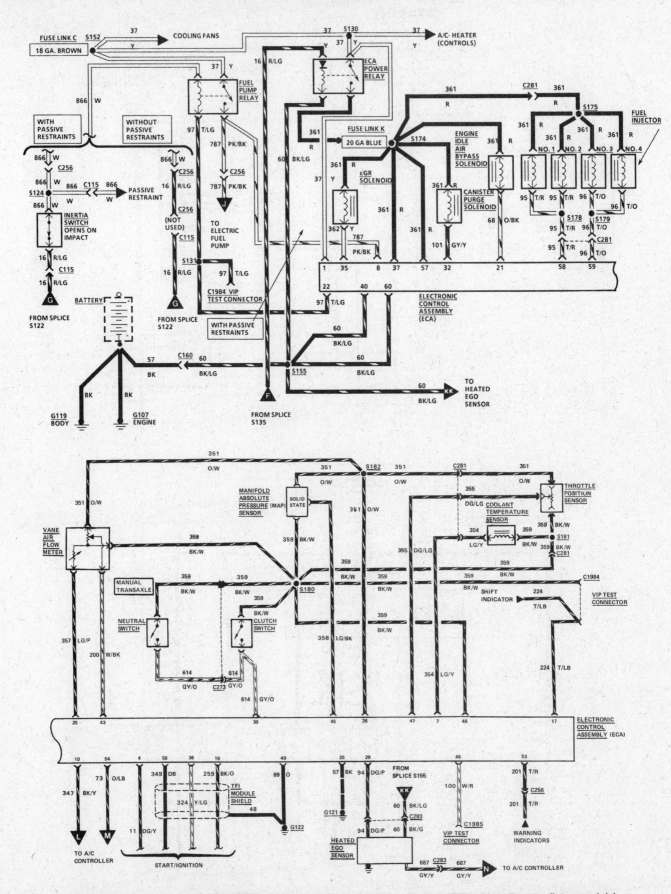

Typical Electronic Engine Control (EEC) system with Electronic Fuel Injection (EFI) wiring diagram (later models)

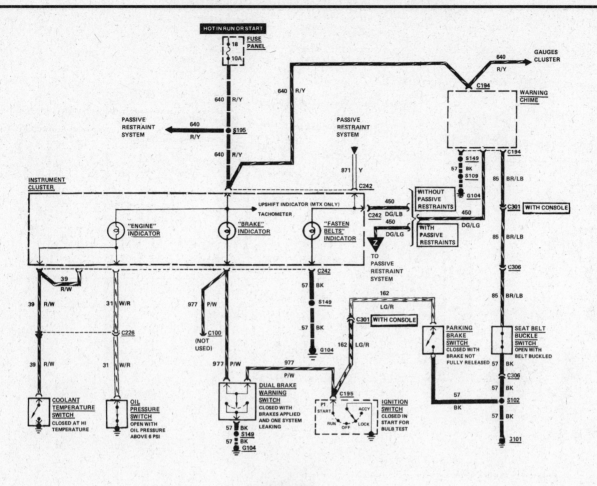

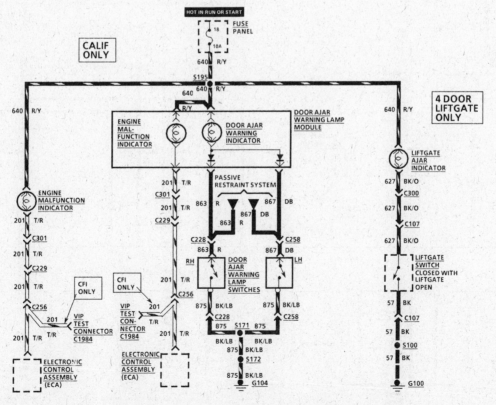

Typical warning indicators wiring diagram (later models)

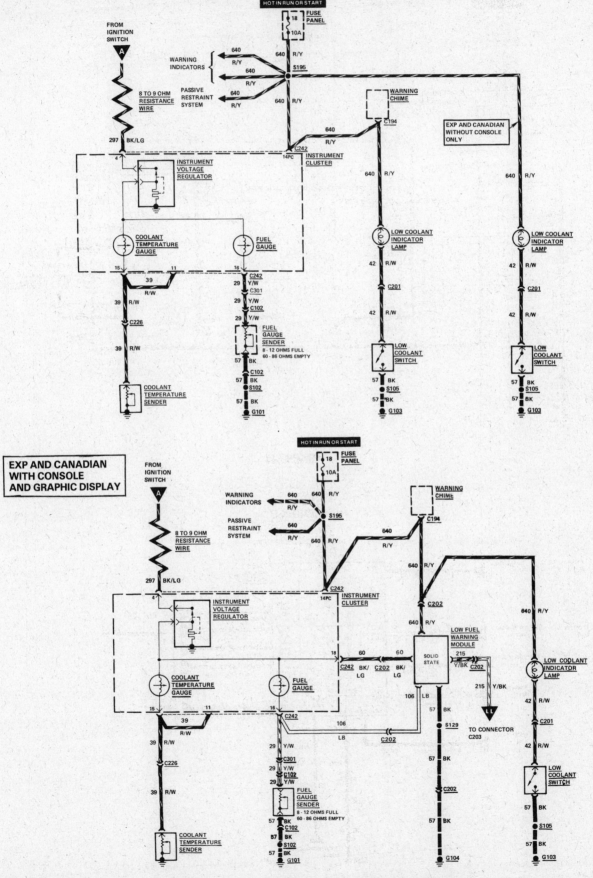

Typical instrument cluster gauges wiring diagram (later models)

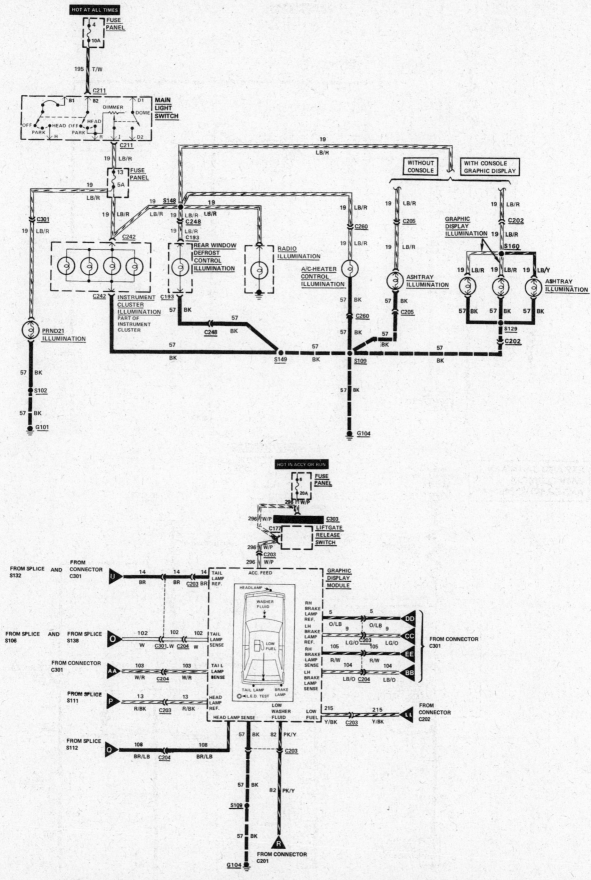

Typical instrument panel illumination and graphic display wiring diagram (later models)

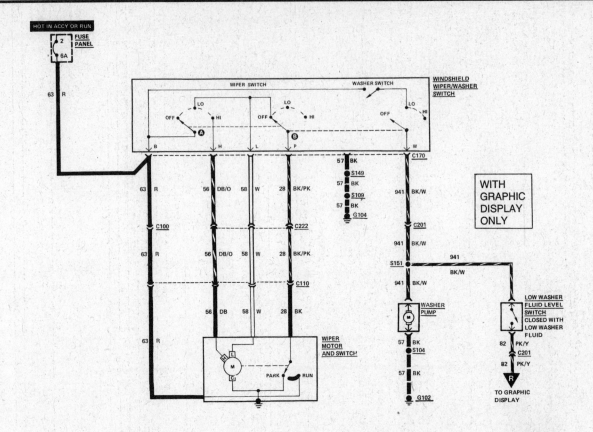

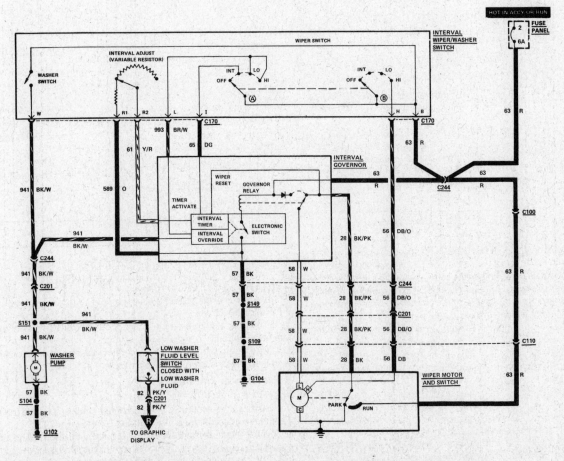

Typical windshield wiper and interval wiper wiring diagram (later models)

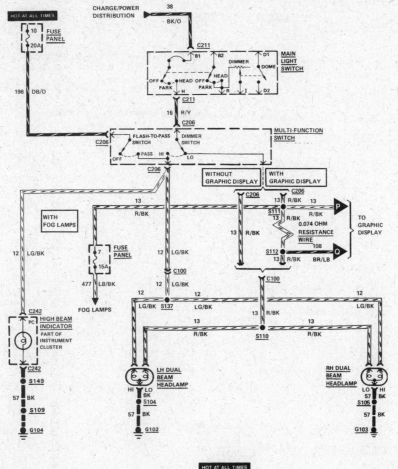

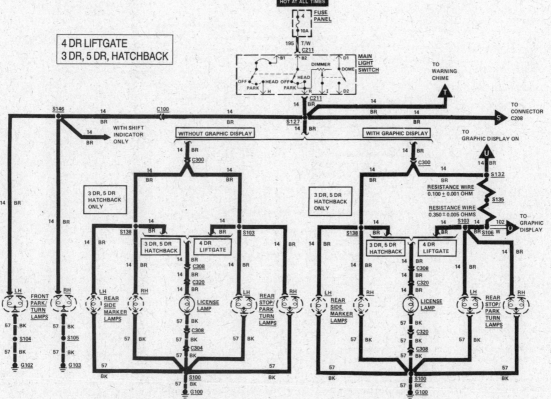

Typical headlamps and exterior lamps wiring diagram (later models)

12

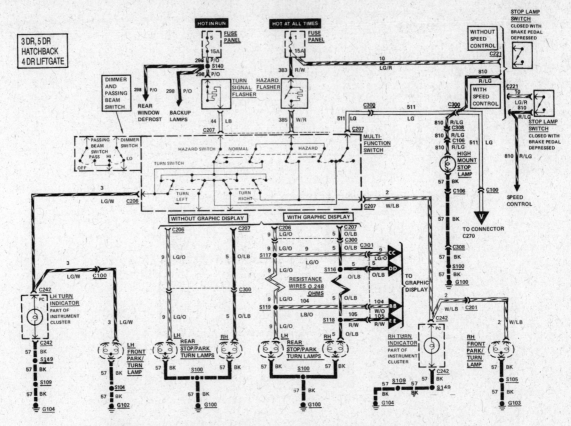

Typical turn, stop, and hazard lamps wiring diagram (later models)

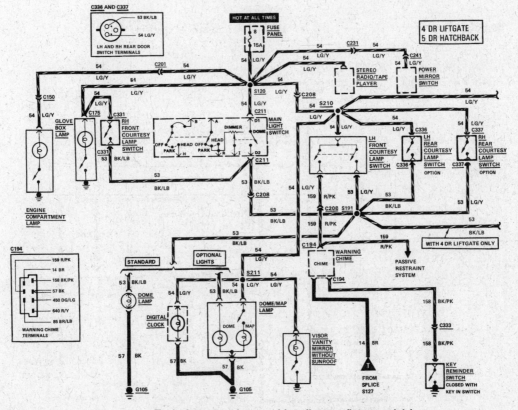

Typical courtesy lamps wiring diagram (later models)

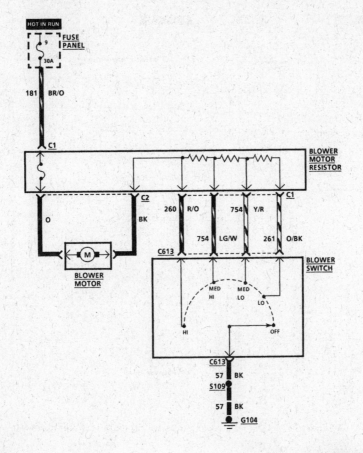

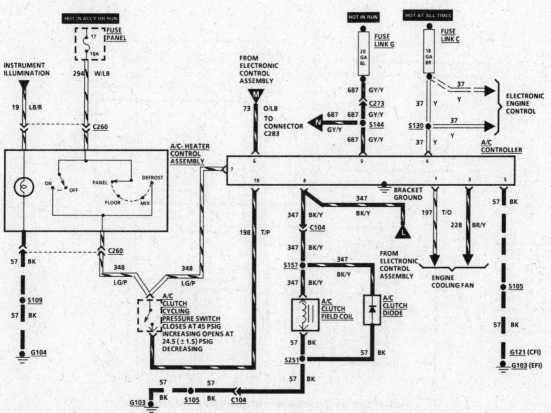

Typical air-conditioning and heater controls wiring diagram (later models)

12

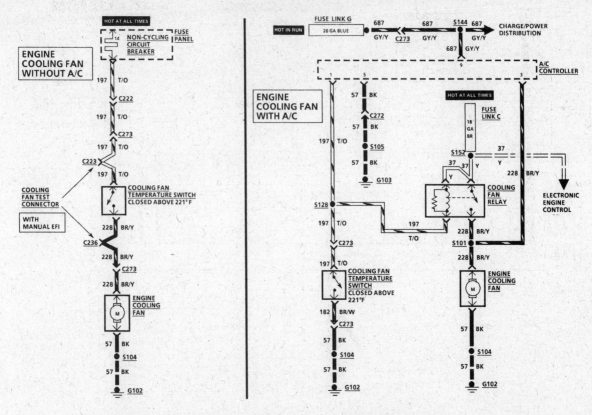

Typical engine cooling fan wiring diagram (later models)

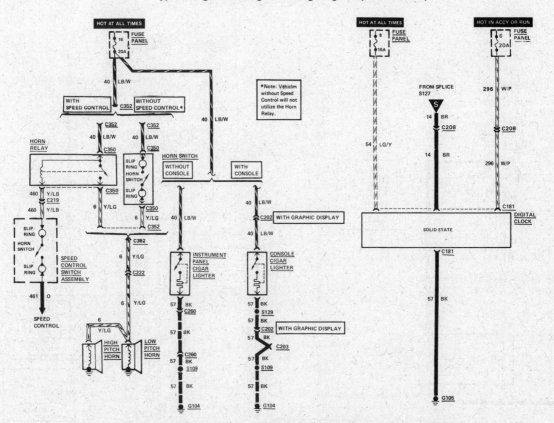

Typical horn, cigar lighter, and clock wiring diagram (later models)

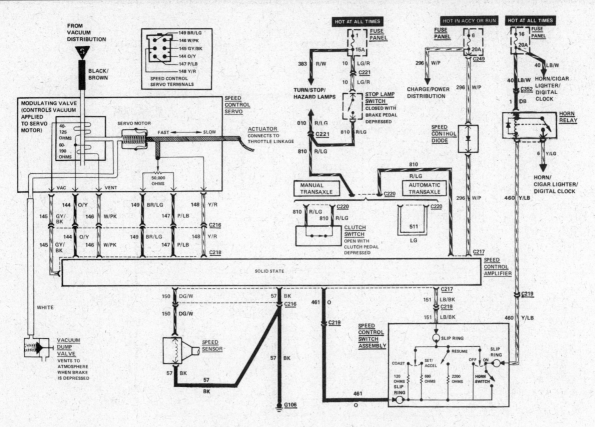

Typical speed control wiring diagram (later models)

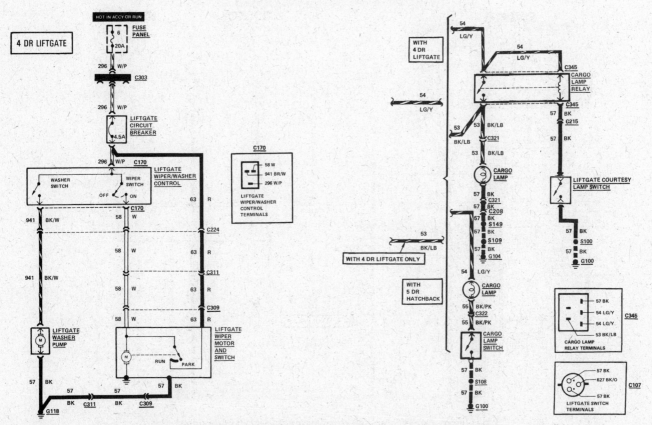

Typical liftgate/hatchback wiper and courtesy lamps wiring diagram (later models)

12

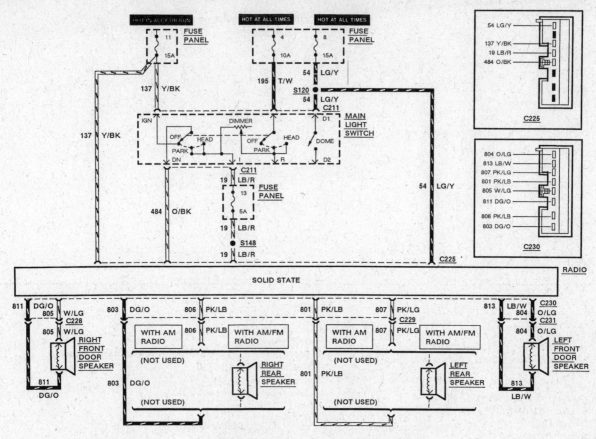

Typical radio wiring diagram (later models)

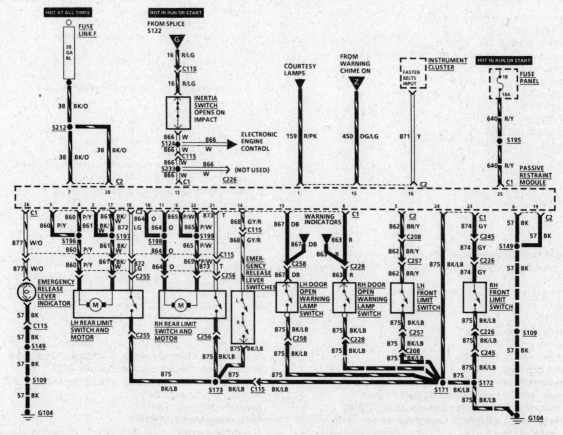

Typical passive restraint system wiring diagram (later models)

Index

IND

Haynes Automotive Manuals

ACURA
*1776 Integra & Legend all models '86 thru '90

AMC
Jeep CJ - see JEEP (412)
694 Mid-size models, Concord, Hornet, Gremlin & Spirit '70 '83
934 (Renault) Alliance & Encore all models '83 thru '87

AUDI
615 4000 all models '80 thru '87
428 5000 all models '77 thru '83
1117 5000 all models '84 thru '88

AUSTIN
Healey Sprite - see MG Midget Roadster (265)

BMW
*2020 3/5 Series not including diesel or all-wheel drive models '82 thru '92
276 320i all 4 cyl models '75 thru '83
632 528i & 530i all models '75 thru '80
240 1500 thru 2002 all models except Turbo '59 thru '77
348 2500, 2800, 3.0 & Bavaria all models '69 thru '76

BUICK
Century (front wheel drive) - see GENERAL MOTORS (829)
*1627 Buick, Oldsmobile & Pontiac Full-size (Front wheel drive) all models '85 thru '95
Buick Electra, LeSabre and Park Avenue; Oldsmobile Delta 88 Royale, Ninety Eight and Regency; Pontiac Bonneville
1551 Buick Oldsmobile & Pontiac Full-size (Rear wheel drive)
Buick Estate '70 thru '90, Electra'70 thru '84, LeSabre '70 thru '85, Limited '74 thru '79
Oldsmobile Custom Cruiser '70 thru '90, Delta 88 '70 thru '85,Ninety-eight '70 thru '84
Pontiac Bonneville '70 thru '81, Catalina '70 thru '81, Grandville '70 thru '75, Parisienne '83 thru '86
627 Mid-size Regal & Century all rear-drive models with V6, V8 and Turbo '74 thru '87
Regal - see GENERAL MOTORS (1671)
Skyhawk - see GENERAL MOTORS (766)
Skylark '80 thru '85 - see GENERAL MOTORS (38020)
Skylark '86 on - see GENERAL MOTORS (1420)
Somerset - see GENERAL MOTORS (1420)

CADILLAC
*751 Cadillac Rear Wheel Drive all gasoline models '70 thru '93
Cimarron - see GENERAL MOTORS (766)

CHEVROLET
*1477 Astro & GMC Safari Mini-vans '85 thru '93
554 Camaro V8 all models '70 thru '81
866 Camaro all models '82 thru '92
Cavalier - see GENERAL MOTORS (766)
Celebrity - see GENERAL MOTORS (829)
625 Chevelle, Malibu & El Camino all V6 & V8 models '69 thru '87
449 Chevette & Pontiac T1000 '76 thru '87
550 Citation all models '80 thru '85
*1628 Corsica/Beretta all models '87 thru '95
274 Corvette all V8 models '68 thru '82
*1336 Corvette all models '84 thru '91
1762 Chevrolet Engine Overhaul Manual
704 Full-size Sedans Caprice, Impala, Biscayne, Bel Air & Wagons '69 thru '90

Lumina - see GENERAL MOTORS (1671)
Lumina APV - see GENERAL MOTORS (2035)
319 Luv Pick-up all 2WD & 4WD '72 thru '82
626 Monte Carlo all models '70 thru '88
241 Nova all V8 models '69 thru '79
*1642 Nova and Geo Prizm all front wheel drive models, '85 thru '92
420 Pick-ups '67 thru '87 - Chevrolet & GMC, all V8 & in-line 6 cyl, 2WD & 4WD '67 thru '87; Suburbans, Blazers & Jimmys '67 thru '91
*1664 Pick-ups '88 thru '95 - Chevrolet & GMC, all full-size pick-ups, '88 thru '95; Blazer & Jimmy '92 thru '94; Suburban '92 thru '95; Tahoe & Yukon '95
*831 S-10 & GMC S-15 Pick-ups all models '82 thru '93
*1727 Sprint & Geo Metro '85 thru '94
*345 Vans - Chevrolet & GMC, V8 & in-line 6 cylinder models '68 thru '95

CHRYSLER
2114 Chrysler Engine Overhaul Manual
*2058 Full-size Front-Wheel Drive '88 thru '93
K-Cars - see DODGE Aries (723)
Laser - see DODGE Daytona (1140)
*1337 Chrysler & Plymouth Mid-size front wheel drive '82 thru '93
Rear-wheel Drive - see Dodge Rear-wheel Drive (2098)

DATSUN
402 200SX all models '77 thru '79
647 200SX all models '80 thru '83
228 B - 210 all models '73 thru '78
525 210 all models '78 thru '82
206 240Z, 260Z & 280Z Coupe '70 thru '78
563 280ZX Coupe & 2+2 '79 thru '83
300ZX - see NISSAN (1137)
679 310 all models '78 thru '82
123 510 & PL521 Pick-up '68 thru '73
430 510 all models '78 thru '81
372 610 all models '72 thru '76
277 620 Series Pick-up all models '73 thru '79
720 Series Pick-up - see NISSAN (771)
376 810/Maxima all gasoline models, '77 thru '84
Pulsar - see NISSAN (876)
Sentra - see NISSAN (982)
Stanza - see NISSAN (981)

DODGE
400 & 600 - see CHRYSLER Mid-size (1337)
*723 Aries & Plymouth Reliant '81 thru '89
1231 Caravan & Plymouth Voyager Mini-Vans all models '84 thru '95
699 Challenger & Plymouth Saporro all models '78 thru '83
Challenger '67-'76 - see DODGE Dart (234)
236 Colt all models '71 thru '77
610 Colt & Plymouth Champ (front wheel drive) all models '78 thru '87
*1668 Dakota Pick-ups all models '87 thru '93
234 Dart, Challenger/Plymouth Barracuda & Valiant 6 cyl models '67 thru '76
*1140 Daytona & Chrysler Laser '84 thru '89
*545 Omni & Plymouth Horizon '78 thru '90
*912 Pick-ups all full-size models '74 thru '91
*556 Ram 50/D50 Pick-ups & Raider and Plymouth Arrow Pick-ups '79 thru '93
2098 Dodge/Plymouth/Chrysler rear wheel drive '71 thru '89
*1726 Shadow & Plymouth Sundance '87 thru '94
*1779 Spirit & Plymouth Acclaim '89 thru '95
*349 Vans - Dodge & Plymouth V8 & 6 cyl models '71 thru '91

EAGLE
Talon - see Mitsubishi Eclipse (2097)

FIAT
094 124 Sport Coupe & Spider '68 thru '78
273 X1/9 all models '74 thru '80

FORD
*1476 Aerostar Mini-vans all models '86 thru '94
788 Bronco and Pick-ups '73 thru '79
*880 Bronco and Pick-ups '80 thru '95
268 Courier Pick-up all models '72 thru '82
2105 Crown Victoria & Mercury Grand Marquis '88 thru '94
1763 Ford Engine Overhaul Manual
789 Escort/Mercury Lynx all models '81 thru '90
*2046 Escort/Mercury Tracer '91 thru '95
*2021 Explorer & Mazda Navajo '91 thru '95
560 Fairmont & Mercury Zephyr '78 thru '83
334 Fiesta all models '77 thru '80
754 Ford & Mercury Full-size, Ford LTD & Mercury Marquis ('75 thru '82); Ford Custom 500,Country Squire, Crown Victoria & Mercury Colony Park ('75 thru '87); Ford LTD Crown Victoria & Mercury Gran Marquis ('83 thru '87)
359 Granada & Mercury Monarch all in-line, 6 cyl & V8 models '75 thru '80
773 Ford & Mercury Mid-size, Ford Thunderbird & Mercury Cougar ('75 thru '82); Ford LTD & Mercury Marquis ('83 thru '86); Ford Torino,Gran Torino, Elite, Ranchero pick-up, LTD II, Mercury Montego, Comet, XR-7 & Lincoln Versailles ('75 thru '86)
*654 Mustang & Mercury Capri all models including Turbo. Mustang, '79 thru '93; Capri, '79 thru '86
357 Mustang V8 all models '64-1/2 thru '73
231 Mustang II 4 cyl, V6 & V8 models '74 thru '78
649 Pinto & Mercury Bobcat '75 thru '80
1670 Probe all models '89 thru '92
*1026 Ranger/Bronco II gasoline models '83 thru '93
*1421 Taurus & Mercury Sable '86 thru '94
*1418 Tempo & Mercury Topaz all gasoline models '84 thru '94
1338 Thunderbird/Mercury Cougar '83 thru '88
*1725 Thunderbird/Mercury Cougar '89 and '93
344 Vans all V8 Econoline models '69 thru '91
*2119 Vans full size '92-'95

GENERAL MOTORS
*829 Buick Century, Chevrolet Celebrity, Oldsmobile Cutlass Ciera & Pontiac 6000 all models '82 thru '93
*1671 Buick Regal, Chevrolet Lumina, Oldsmobile Cutlass Supreme & Pontiac Grand Prix all front wheel drive models '88 thru '95
*766 Buick Skyhawk, Cadillac Cimarron, Chevrolet Cavalier, Oldsmobile Firenza & Pontiac J-2000 & Sunbird all models '82 thru '94
38020 Buick Skylark, Chevrolet Citation, Olds Omega, Pontiac Phoenix '80 thru '85
1420 Buick Skylark & Somerset, Oldsmobile Achieva & Calais and Pontiac Grand Am all models '85 thru '95
*2035 Chevrolet Lumina APV, Oldsmobile Silhouette & Pontiac Trans Sport all models '90 thru '94
General Motors Full-size Rear-wheel Drive - see BUICK (1551)

GEO
Metro - see CHEVROLET Sprint (1727)
Prizm - see CHEVROLET Nova (1642)
*2039 Storm all models '90 thru '93
Tracker - see SUZUKI Samurai (1626)

GMC
Safari - see CHEVROLET ASTRO (1477)
Vans & Pick-ups - see CHEVROLET (420, 831, 345, 1664)

(Continued on other side)

Haynes North America, Inc., 861 Lawrence Drive, Newbury Park, CA 91320 • (805) 498-6703

Haynes Automotive Manuals (continued)

NOTE: New manuals are added to this list on a periodic basis. If you do not see a listing for your vehicle, consult your local Haynes dealer for the latest product information.

HONDA

351	**Accord CVCC** all models '76 thru '83
1221	**Accord** all models '84 thru '89
2067	**Accord** all models '90 thru '93
42013	**Accord** all models '94 thru '95
160	**Civic 1200** all models '73 thru '79
633	**Civic 1300 & 1500 CVCC** '80 thru '83
297	**Civic 1500 CVCC** all models '75 thru '79
1227	**Civic** all models '84 thru '91
*2118	**Civic & del Sol** '92 thru '95
*601	**Prelude CVCC** all models '79 thru '89

HYUNDAI

*1552	**Excel** all models '86 thru '94

ISUZU

*1641	**Trooper & Pick-up**, all gasoline models Pick-up, '81 thru '93; Trooper, '84 thru '91

JAGUAR

*242	**XJ6** all 6 cyl models '68 thru '86
*478	**XJ12 & XJS** all 12 cyl models '72 thru '85

JEEP

*1553	**Cherokee, Comanche & Wagoneer Limited** all models '84 thru '93
412	**CJ** all models '49 thru '86
50025	**Grand Cherokee** all models '93 thru '95
*1777	**Wrangler** all models '87 thru '94

LINCOLN

2117	**Rear Wheel Drive** all models '70 thru '95

MAZDA

648	**626** Sedan & Coupe (rear wheel drive) all models '79 thru '82
*1082	**626 & MX-6** (front wheel drive) all models '83 thru '91
267	**B Series Pick-ups** '72 thru '93
370	**GLC Hatchback** (rear wheel drive) all models '77 thru '83
757	**GLC** (front wheel drive) '81 thru '85
*2047	**MPV** all models '89 thru '94
	Navajo-see Ford Explorer (2021)
460	**RX-7** all models '79 thru '85
*1419	**RX-7** all models '86 thru '91

MERCEDES-BENZ

*1643	**190 Series** all four-cylinder gasoline models, '84 thru '88
346	**230, 250 & 280** Sedan, Coupe & Roadster all 6 cyl sohc models '68 thru '72
983	**280 123 Series** gasoline models '77 thru '81
698	**350 & 450** Sedan, Coupe & Roadster all models '71 thru '80
697	**Diesel 123 Series** 200D, 220D, 240D, 240TD, 300D, 300CD, 300TD, 4- & 5-cyl incl. Turbo '76 thru '85

MERCURY

See FORD Listing

MG

111	**MGB** Roadster & GT Coupe all models '62 thru '80
265	**MG Midget & Austin Healey Sprite** Roadster '58 thru '80

MITSUBISHI

*1669	**Cordia, Tredia, Galant, Precis & Mirage** '83 thru '93
*2097	**Eclipse, Eagle Talon & Plymouth Laser** '90 thru '94
*2022	**Pick-up & Montero** '83 thru '95

NISSAN

1137	**300ZX** all models including Turbo '84 thru '89
*1341	**Maxima** all models '85 thru '91
*771	**Pick-ups/Pathfinder** gas models '80 thru '95
876	**Pulsar** all models '83 thru '86

*982	**Sentra** all models '82 thru '94
*981	**Stanza** all models '82 thru '90

OLDSMOBILE

	Bravada - see CHEVROLET S-10 (831)
	Calais - see GENERAL MOTORS (1420)
	Custom Cruiser - see BUICK Full-size RWD (1551)
*658	**Cutlass** all standard gasoline V6 & V8 models '74 thru '88
	Cutlass Ciera - see GENERAL MOTORS (829)
	Cutlass Supreme - see GM (1671)
	Delta 88 - see BUICK Full-size RWD (1551)
	Delta 88 Brougham - see BUICK Full-size FWD (1551), RWD (1627)
	Delta 88 Royale - see BUICK Full-size RWD (1551)
	Firenza - see GENERAL MOTORS (766)
	Ninety-eight Regency - see BUICK Full-size RWD (1551), FWD (1627)
	Ninety-eight Regency Brougham - see BUICK Full-size RWD (1551)
	Omega - see GENERAL MOTORS (38020)
	Silhouette - see GENERAL MOTORS (2035)

PEUGEOT

663	**504** all diesel models '74 thru '83

PLYMOUTH

Laser - see MITSUBISHI Eclipse (2097)
For other PLYMOUTH titles, see DODGE listing.

PONTIAC

	T1000 - see CHEVROLET Chevette (449)
	J-2000 - see GENERAL MOTORS (766)
	6000 - see GENERAL MOTORS (829)
	Bonneville - see Buick Full-size FWD (1627), RWD (1551)
	Bonneville Brougham - see Buick (1551)
	Catalina - see Buick Full-size (1551)
1232	**Fiero** all models '84 thru '88
555	**Firebird** V8 models except Turbo '70 thru '81
867	**Firebird** all models '82 thru '92
	Full-size Front Wheel Drive - see BUICK Oldsmobile, Pontiac Full-size FWD (1627)
	Full-size Rear Wheel Drive - see BUICK Oldsmobile, Pontiac Full-size RWD (1551)
	Grand Am - see GENERAL MOTORS (1420)
	Grand Prix - see GENERAL MOTORS (1671)
	Grandville - see BUICK Full-size (1551)
	Parisienne - see BUICK Full-size (1551)
	Phoenix - see GENERAL MOTORS (38020)
	Sunbird - see GENERAL MOTORS (766)
	Trans Sport - see GENERAL MOTORS (2035)

PORSCHE

*264	**911** all Coupe & Targa models except Turbo & Carrera 4 '65 thru '89
239	**914** all 4 cyl models '69 thru '76
397	**924** all models including Turbo '76 thru '82
*1027	**944** all models including Turbo '83 thru '89

RENAULT

141	**5 Le Car** all models '76 thru '83
	Alliance & Encore - see AMC (934)

SAAB

247	**99** all models including Turbo '69 thru '80
*980	**900** all models including Turbo '79 thru '88

SATURN

2083	**Saturn** all models '91 thru '94

SUBARU

237	**1100, 1300, 1400 & 1600** '71 thru '79
*681	**1600 & 1800** 2WD & 4WD '80 thru '89

SUZUKI

*1626	**Samurai/Sidekick and Geo Tracker** all models '86 thru '95

TOYOTA

1023	**Camry** all models '83 thru '91
92006	**Camry** all models '92 thru '95
935	**Celica Rear Wheel Drive** '71 thru '85
*2038	**Celica Front Wheel Drive** '86 thru '92
1139	**Celica Supra** all models '79 thru '92
361	**Corolla** all models '75 thru '79
961	**Corolla** all rear wheel drive models '80 thru '87
*1025	**Corolla** all front wheel drive models '84 thru '92
636	**Corolla Tercel** all models '80 thru '82
360	**Corona** all models '74 thru '82
532	**Cressida** all models '78 thru '82
313	**Land Cruiser** all models '68 thru '82
*1339	**MR2** all models '85 thru '87
304	**Pick-up** all models '69 thru '78
*656	**Pick-up** all models '79 thru '95
*2048	**Previa** all models '91 thru '93
2106	**Tercel** all models '87 thru '94

TRIUMPH

113	**Spitfire** all models '62 thru '81
322	**TR7** all models '75 thru '81

VW

159	**Beetle & Karmann Ghia** all models '54 thru '79
238	**Dasher** all gasoline models '74 thru '81
*884	**Rabbit, Jetta, Scirocco, & Pick-up** gas models '74 thru '91 & Convertible '80 thru '92
451	**Rabbit, Jetta & Pick-up** all diesel models '77 thru '84
082	**Transporter 1600** all models '68 thru '79
226	**Transporter 1700, 1800 & 2000** all models '72 thru '79
084	**Type 3 1500 & 1600** all models '63 thru '73
1029	**Vanagon** all air-cooled models '80 thru '83

VOLVO

203	**120, 130 Series & 1800 Sports** '61 thru '73
129	**140 Series** all models '66 thru '74
*270	**240 Series** all models '76 thru '93
400	**260 Series** all models '75 thru '82
*1550	**740 & 760 Series** all models '82 thru '88

TECHBOOK MANUALS

2108	**Automotive Computer Codes**
1667	**Automotive Emissions Control Manual**
482	**Fuel Injection Manual, 1978 thru 1985**
2111	**Fuel Injection Manual, 1986 thru 1994**
2069	**Holley Carburetor Manual**
2068	**Rochester Carburetor Manual**
10240	**Weber/Zenith/Stromberg/SU Carburetors**
1762	**Chevrolet Engine Overhaul Manual**
2114	**Chrysler Engine Overhaul Manual**
1763	**Ford Engine Overhaul Manual**
1736	**GM and Ford Diesel Engine Repair Manual**
1666	**Small Engine Repair Manual**
10355	**Ford Automatic Transmission Overhaul**
10360	**GM Automatic Transmission Overhaul**
1479	**Automotive Body Repair & Painting**
2112	**Automotive Brake Manual**
2113	**Automotive Detailing Manual**
1654	**Automotive Eelectrical Manual**
1480	**Automotive Heating & Air Conditioning**
2109	**Automotive Reference Manual & Illustrated Dictionary**
2107	**Automotive Tools Manual**
10440	**Used Car Buying Guide**
2110	**Welding Manual**

SPANISH MANUALS

98905	**Códigos Automotrices de la Computadora**
98915	**Inyección de Combustible 1986 al 1994**
99040	**Chevrolet & GMC Camionetas** '67 al '87 Incluye Suburban, Blazer & Jimmy '67 al '91
99041	**Chevrolet & GMC Camionetas** '88 al '95 Incluye Suburban '92 al '95, Blazer & Jimmy '92 al '94, Tahoe & Yukon '95
99075	**Ford Camionetas y Bronco** '80 al '94
99125	**Toyota Camionetas y 4-Runner** '79 al '95

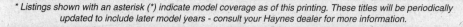

Haynes North America, Inc., 861 Lawrence Drive, Newbury Park, CA 91320 • (805) 498-6703